John B. Alden

The World's Cyclopedia of History

Volume III

John B. Alden

The World's Cyclopedia of History
Volume III

ISBN/EAN: 9783743401402

Manufactured in Europe, USA, Canada, Australia, Japa

Cover: Foto ©Andreas Hilbeck / pixelio.de

Manufactured and distributed by brebook publishing software (www.brebook.com)

John B. Alden

The World's Cyclopedia of History

THE WORLD'S

CYCLOPEDIA OF HISTORY.

VOLUME III.

CONTAINING:

CARLYLE'S HISTORY OF THE FRENCH REVOLUTION.

NEW YORK:
JOHN B. ALDEN, PUBLISHER.
1883.

CONTENTS.

FRENCH REVOLUTION..

THE BASTILLE.

BOOK FIRST.

DEATH OF LOUIS XV.

CHAPTER I.
LOUIS THE WELL-BELOVED.

1. President Hénault, remarking on royal surnames of honor how difficult it often is to ascertain not only why, but even when, they were conferred, takes occasion, in his sleek official way, to make a philosophical reflection. "The surname of Bien-aimé (Well-beloved)," says he, "which Louis XV. bears, will not leave posterity in the same doubt. This prince, in the year 1744, while hastening from one end of his kingdom to the other, and suspending his conquests in Flanders that he might fly to the assistance of Alsace, was arrested at Metz by a malady which threatened to cut short his days. At the news of this, Paris, all in terror, seemed a city taken by storm; the churches resounded with supplications and groans; the prayers of priests and people were every moment interrupted by their sobs; and it was from an interest so dear and tender that this surname of Bien-aimé fashioned itself—a title higher still than all the rest which this great prince has earned." *

2. So stands it written, in lasting memorial of that year 1744. Thirty other years have come and gone, and "this great prince" again lies sick; but in how altered circumstances now! Churches resound not with excessive groanings; Paris is stoically calm; sobs interrupt no prayers, for indeed none are offered, except priests' litanies, read or chanted at fixed money-rate per hour, which are not liable to interruption. The shepherd of the people has been carried home from Little Trianon, heavy of heart, and been put to bed in his own château of Versailles: the flock knows it, and heeds it not. At most, in the immeasurable tide of French speech (which ceases not day after day, and only ebbs toward the sh ǫ t hours of night), may this of the royal sickness emerge from time to time as an article of news. Bets are doubtless depending; nay, some people "express themselves loudly in the streets."† But for the rest, on green field and steepled city, the May sun shines out, the May evening fades, and men ply their useful or useless business as if no Louis lay in danger.

3. Dame Dubarry, indeed, might pray, if she had a talent for it; Duke d'Aiguillon too, Maupeou and the Parlement Maupeou; these, as they sit in their high places, with France harnessed under their feet, know well on what basis they continue there. Look to it, D'Aiguillon, sharply, as thou didst, from the mill of St. Cast, on Quiberon and the invading English; thou, "covered, if not with glory, yet with

meal!" Fortune was ever accounted inconstant, and each dog has but his day.

4. Forlorn enough languished Duke d'Aiguillon some years ago, covered, as we said, with meal; nay, with worse. For La Chalotais, the Breton parlementeer, accused him not only of poltroonery and tyranny, but even of *concussion* (official plunder of money); which accusations it was easier to get "quashed" by back-stairs influences than to get answered; neither could the thoughts or even the tongues of men be tied. Thus, under disastrous eclipse, had this grandnephew of the great Richelieu to glide about, unworshipped by the world, resolute Choiseul, the abrupt proud man, disdaining him, or even forgetting him. Little prospect but to glide into Gascony, to rebuild châteaus there,* and die ingloriously killing game! However, in the year 1770, a certain young soldier, Dumouriez by name, returning from Corsica, could see "with sorrow, at Compiègne, the old king of France, on foot, with doffed hat, in sight of his army, at the side of a magnificent phaeton, doing homage to the—Dubarry."†

5. Much lay therein! Thereby, for one thing, could D'Aiguillon postpone the rebuilding of his château, and rebuild his fortunes first. For stout Choiseul would discern in the Dubarry nothing but a wonderfully dizened scarlet-woman, and go on his way as if she were not. Intolerable; the source of sighs, tears, of pettings and poutings, which would not end till "France" (La France, as she named her royal valet) finally mustered heart to see Choiseul; and with that "quivering in the chin (tremblement du menton)" natural in such case,‡ faltered out a dismissal—dismissal of his last substantial man, but pacification of his scarlet-woman. Thus D'Aiguillon rose again and culminated. And with him there rose Maupeou, the banisher of parlements, who plants you a refractory president "at Croe in Combrailles, on the top of steep rocks, inaccessible except by litters," there to consider himself. Likewise there rose Abbé Terray, dissolute financier, paying eightpence in the shilling, so that wits exclaim in some press at the play-house, "Where is Abbé Terray, that he might reduce us to two-thirds?" And so have these individuals (verily by black-art) built them a Domdaniel, or enchanted Dubarrydom—call it an Armida-palace—where they dwell pleasantly; Chancellor Maupeou "playing blind-man's-buff" with the scarlet enchantress, or gallantly presenting her with dwarf negroes; and a most Christian king has unspeakable peace within doors, whatever he may have without. "My chan-

---

* "Abrege Chronologique de l'Histoire de France" (Paris, 1775), p. 701.
† "Memoires de M. le Baron Besenval" (Paris, 1805), ii. 59-90.

* Arthur Young. "Travels during the Years 1787-88-89" (Bury St. Edmunds, 1792), i. 44.
† "La Vie et les Memoires du General Dumouriez" (Paris, 1822), i. 141.
‡ "Besenval." "Memoires," ii. 21

cellor is a scoundrel; but I cannot do without him."*

6. Beautiful Armida-palace, where the inmates live enchanted lives, lapped in soft music of adulation, waited on by the splendors of the world, which, nevertheless, hangs wondrously as by a single hair. Should the most Christian king die, or even get seriously afraid of dying? For, alas! had not the fair, haughty Chateauroux to fly, with wet cheeks and flaming heart, from that fever scene at Metz, long since, driven forth by sour shavelings? She hardly returned, when fever and shavelings were both swept into the background. Pompadour, too, when Damiens wounded royalty "slightly, under the fifth rib," and our drive to trianon went off futile, in shrieks and madly shaken torches, had to pack and be in readiness, yet did not go, the wound not proving poisoned. For his majesty has religious faith; believes, at least, in a devil. And now a third peril; and who knows what may be in it? For the doctors look grave, ask privily if his majesty had not the small-pox long ago, and doubt it may have been a false kind. Yes, Maupeou, pucker those sinister brows of thine, and peer out on it with thy malign rat-eyes; it is a questionable case. Sure only that man is mortal; that with the life of one mortal snaps irrevocably the wonderfulest talisman, and all Dubarrydom rushes off, with tumult, into infinite space; and ye, as subterranean apparitions are wont, vanish utterly, leaving only a smell of sulphur!

7. These, and what holds of these, may pray—to Beelzebub, or whoever will hear them. But from the rest of France there comes, as was said, no prayer, or one of an *opposite* character, "expressed openly in the streets." Château or hotel, where an enlightened philosophism scrutinizes many things, is not given to prayer; neither are Rossbach victories, Terray finances, nor, say only "sixty thousand lettres de cachet" (which is Maupeou's share), persuasives toward that. O Hénault! prayers? From a France smitten (by black-art) with plague after plague, and lying now, in shame and pain, with a harlot's foot on its neck, what prayer can come? Those lank scarecrows that prowl hunger-stricken through all highways and byways of French existence, will they pray? The dull millions that, in the workshop or throw-field, grind foredone at the wheel of labor, like haltered gin-horses, if blind so much the quieter? Or they that in the Bicétre hospital, "eight to a bed," lie waiting their manumission? Dim are those heads of theirs, dull stagnant those hearts; to them the great sovereign is known mainly as the great regrater of bread. If they hear of his sickness, they will answer with a dull, Tant pis pour lui, or with the question, Will he die?

Yes, will he die? that is now, for all France, the grand question and hope whereby alone the king's sickness has still some interest.

CHAPTER II.

REALIZED IDEALS.

8. Such a changed France have we, and a changed Louis! Changed, truly, and further than thou yet seest! To the eye of history many things in that sick-room of Louis are now visible which to the courtiers there present were invisible. For, indeed, it is well said, "In every object there is inexhaustible meaning; the eye sees in it what the eye brings means of seeing." To Newton and to Newton's dog Diamond, what a different pair of universes; while the painting on the optical retina of both was, most

likely, the same! Let the reader here, in this sick-room of Louis, endeavor to look with the mind too.

9. Time was when men could (so to speak) of a given man, by nourishing and decorating him with fit appliances, to the dear pitch *make* themselves a king, almost as the bees do; and, what was still more to the purpose, loyally obey him when made. The man so nourished and decorated, thenceforth named royal, does verily bear rule; and is said, and even thought, to be, for example, "prosecuting conquests in Flanders," when he lets himself, like luggage, be carried thither—and no light luggage—covering miles of road. For he has his unblushing Chateauroux, with her band-boxes and rouge-pots, at his side, so that at every new station a wooden gallery must be run up between their lodgings. He has not only his maison bouche, and valetaille without end, but his very troop of players, with their pasteboard coulisses, thunder-barrels, their kettles, fiddles, stage wardrobes, portable larders (and chaffering and quarreling enough)—all mounted in wagons, tumbrils, second-hand chaises—sufficient, not to conquer Flanders, but the patience of the world. With such a flood of loud-jingling appurtenances does he lumber along, prosecuting his conquests in Flanders, wonderful to behold. So, nevertheless, it was and had been. To some solitary thinker it might seem strange; but even to him inevitable, not unnatural.

10. For ours is a most fictile world; and man is the most fingent, plastic of creatures. A world not fixable, not fathomable! An unfathomable somewhat, which is *not we*; which we can work with, and live amidst, and model miraculously in our miraculous being, and name world. But if the very rocks and rivers (as metaphysic teaches) are, in strict language, *made* by those outward senses of ours, how much more, by the inward sense, are all phenomena of the spiritual kind; dignities, authorities, holies, unholies! Which inward sense, moreover, is not permanent, like the outward ones, but forever growing and changing. Does not the black African take of sticks and old clothes (say, exported Monmouth street cast clothes) what will suffice, and of these, cunningly combining them, fabricate for himself an eidolon (idol, or thing seen), and name it Mumbo Jumbo! which he can thenceforth pray to, with upturned, awe-struck eye, not without hope? The white European mocks, but ought rather to consider, and see whether he, at home, could not do the like a little more wisely.

11. So it *was*, we say, in those conquests of Flanders, thirty years ago; but so it no longer is. Alas! much more lies sick than poor Louis; not the French king only, but the French kingship; this, too, after long, rough tear and wear, is breaking down. The world is all so changed; so much that seemed vigorous has sunk decrepit, so much that was not is beginning to be! Borne over the Atlantic, to the closing ear of Louis, king by the grace of God, what sounds are these, muffled, ominous, new in our centuries? Boston harbor is black with unexpected tea. Behold a Pennsylvanian congress gather; and ere long, on Bunker Hill, democracy announcing, in rifle volleys death-winged, under her star banner, to the tune of Yankee-doodle-doo, that she is born, and, whirlwind-like, will envelop the whole world!

12. Sovereigns die, and sovereignties; how all dies, and is for a time only—is a "time-phantasm, yet reckons itself real!" The Merovingian kings, slowly wending on their bullock-carts through the streets of Paris, with their long hair flowing, have all wended slowly on—into eternity. Charlemagne sleeps at Salzburg, with truncheon grounded, only fable expecting that he will awaken. Charles the Hammer, Pepin Bow-legged, where now is their eye of menace,

---

* Dulaure, "Histoire de Paris" (Paris, 1824), vii. 328.

their voice of command? Rollo and his shaggy Northmen cover not tho Seine with ships, but have sailed off on a longer voyage. The hair of Tow-head (Tête d'étoupes) now needs no combing; Iron-cutter (Taillefer) cannot cut a cobweb; shrill Fredegonda, shrill Brunhilda, have had out their hot life-scold, and lie silent, their hot life-frenzy cooled. Neither from that black Tower de Nesle descends now darkling the doomed gallant, in his sack, to the Seine waters, plunging into night; for Dame de Nesle now cares not for this world's gallantry, heeds not this world's scandal; Dame de Nesle is herself gone into night. They are all gone; sunk—down, down, with the tumult they made; and the rolling and the trampling of ever new generations passes over them; and they hear it not any more forever.

13. And yet, withal, has there not been realized somewhat? Consider (to go no further) these strong stone edifices, and what they hold! Mud-town of the borderers (Lutetia, Parisiorum or Barisiorum) has paved itself, has spread over all the Seine islands, and far and wide on each bank, and become city of Paris, sometimes boasting to be "Athens of Europe," and even "Capital of the universe." Stone towers frown aloft, long-lasting, grim with a thousand years. Cathedrals are there, and a creed (or memory of a creed) in them; palaces, and a state and law. Thou seest the smoke-vapor, unextinguished breath as of a thing living. Labor's thousand hammers ring on her anvils; also a more miraculous labor works noiselessly, not with the hand but with the thought. How have cunning workmen in all crafts, with their cunning head and right hand, tamed the four elements to be their ministers; yoking the winds to their sea-chariot, making the very stars their nautical timepiece; and written and collected a Bibliothèque du Roi, among whose books is the Hebrew book! A wondrous race of creatures! *These* have been realized, and what of skill is in these. Call not the past time, with all its confused wretchedness, a lost one.

14. Observe, however, that of man's whole terrestrial possessions and attainments, unspeakably the noblest are his symbols, divine or divine-seeming, under which he marches and fights, with victorious assurance, in this life-battle—what we can call his realized ideals. Of which realized ideals, omitting the rest, consider only these two—his church, or spiritual guidance; his kingship, or temporal one. The church—what a word was there, richer than Golconda and the treasures of the world! In the heart of the remotest mountains rises the little kirk, the dead all slumbering round it, under their white memorial-stones, "in hope of a happy resurrection." Dull wert thou, O reader, if never in any hour (say of moaning midnight, when such kirk hung spectral in the sky, and being was as if swallowed up of darkness) it spoke to thee—things unspeakable, that went into thy soul's soul. Strong was he that had a church, what we can call a church; he stood thereby, though "in the center of immensities, in the conflux of eternities," yet man-like toward God and man; the vague, shoreless universe had become for him a firm city and dwelling which he knew. Such virtue was in belief, in these words, well spoken—*I believe.* Well might men prize their credo, and raise stateliest temples for it, and reverend hierarchies, and give it the tithe of their substance; it was worth living for and dying for.

15. Neither was that an inconsiderable moment when wild armed men first raised their strongest aloft on the buckler-throne, and, with clanging armor and hearts, said solemnly, Be thou our acknowledged strongest! In such acknowledged strongest (well named king, könning, can-ning, or man that was able) what a symbol shone now for them, significant

with the destinies of the world! A symbol of true guidance in return for loving obedience; properly, if he knew it, the prime want of man. A symbol which might be called sacred, for is there not in reverence for what is better than we an indestructible sacredness? On which ground, too, it was well said there lay in the acknowledged strongest a divine right; as surely there might in the strongest, whether acknowledged or not, considering who it was that made him strong. And so, in the midst of confusions and unutterable incongruities (as all growth is confused), did this of royalty, with loyalty environing it, spring up, and grow mysteriously, subduing and assimilating (for a principle of life was in it), till it also had grown world-great, and was among the main facts of our modern existence. Such a fact that Louis XIV., for example, could answer the expostulatory magistrate with his "L'etat c'est moi (The state? I am the state)," and he replied to by silence and abashed looks. So far had accident and forethought—had your Louis Elevenths, with the leaden Virgin in their hat-band, and torture-wheels and conical oubliettes (man-eating!) under their feet; your Henri Fourths, with their prophesied social millennium, "when every peasant should have his fowl in the pot;" and, on the whole, the fertility of this most fertile existence (named of good and evil)—brought it in the matter of the kingship. Wondrous! Concerning which may we not again say that in the huge mass of evil, as it rolls and swells, there is ever some good working imprisoned—working toward deliverance and triumph?

16. How such ideals do realize themselves, and grow wondrously from amid the incongruous, ever fluctuating chaos of the actual! this is what world-history, if it teach anything, has to teach us. How they grow, and, after long, stormy growth, bloom out mature, supreme; then quickly (for the blossom is brief) fall into decay, sorrowfully dwindle, and crumble down, or rush down, noisily or noiselessly disappearing! The blossom is so brief, as of some centennial cactus-flower, which, after a century of waiting, shines out for hours! Thus, from the day when rough Clovis, in the Champ de Mars, in sight of his whole army, had to cleave retributively the head of that rough Frank, with sudden battle axe, and the fierce words, "It was thus thou clavest the vase"(St. Remi's and mine) "at Soissons," forward to Louis the Grand and his L'etat c'est moi, we count some twelve hundred years; and now this the very next Louis is dying, and so much dying with him! Nay, thus too, if Catholicism, with and against feudalism (but *not* against nature and her bounty), gave us English a Shakespeare and era of Shakespeare, and so produced a blossom of Catholicism, it was not till Catholicism itself, so far as law could abolish it, had been abolished here.

17. But of those decadent ages in which no ideal either grows or blossoms? When belief and loyalty have passed away, and only the cant and false echo of them remains; and all solemnity has become pageantry, and the creed of persons in authority has become one of two things, an imbecility or a Machiavelism? Alas! of these ages, world-history can take no notice; they have to become compressed more and more, and finally suppressed in the annals of mankind: blotted out as spurious, which indeed they are. Hapless ages, wherein, if ever in any, it is an unhappiness to be born! To be born, and to learn only, by every tradition and example, that God's universe is Belial's and a lie; and "the Supreme Quack" the hierarch of men! In which mournfulest faith, nevertheless, do we not see whole generations (two, and sometimes even three successively) live—what they call living—and vanish, without chance of reappearance?

18. In such a decadent age, or one fast verging that way, had our poor Louis been born. Grant, also, that if the French kingship had not, by course of nature, long to live, he of all men was the man to accelerate nature. The blossom of French royalty, cactus-like, has accordingly made an astonishing progress. In those Metz days, it was still standing with all its petals, though bedimmed by Orleans regents and roué ministers of cardinals; but now, in 1774, we behold it bald, and the virtue nigh gone out of it.

19. Disastrous, indeed, does it look with those same "realized ideals," one and all! The church, which in its palmy season, seven hundred years ago, could make an emperor wait barefoot, in penance shirt, three days in the snow, has for centuries seen itself decaying; reduced even to forget all purposes and enmities, and join interest with the kingship. On this younger strength it would fain stay its decrepitude, and these two will henceforth stand and fall together. Alas! the Sorbonne still sits there, in its old mansion; but mumbles only jargon of dotage, and no longer leads the consciences of men. Not the Sorbonne; it is encyclopédies, philosophie, and who knows what nameless innumerable multitude of ready writers, profane singers, romancers, players, disputators, and pamphleteers, that now form the spiritual guidance of the world. The world's practical guidance, too, is lost, or has glided into the same miscellaneous hands. Who is it that the king (able-man, named also roi, rex, or director) now guides? His own huntsmen and prickers. When there is to be no hunt, it is well said, "Le roi ne fera rien (To-day his majesty will do *nothing*.)"* He lives and lingers there, because he is living there and none has yet laid hands on him.

20. The nobles, in like manner, have nearly ceased either to guide or misguide; and are now, as their master is, little more than ornamental figures. It is long since they have done with butchering one another or their king. The workers, protected, encouraged by majesty, have ages ago built walled towns, and there ply their craft; will permit no robber baron to "live by the saddle," but maintain a gallows to prevent it. Ever since that period of the "fronde," the noble has changed his fighting sword into a court rapier; and now loyally attends his king as ministering satellite; divides the spoil, not now by violence and murder, but by soliciting and finesse. These men call themselves supports of the throne; singular gilt-pasteboard caryatides in that singular edifice! For the rest, their privileges every way are now much curtailed. That law authorizing a seigneur, as he returned from hunting, to kill not more than two serfs, and refresh his feet in their warm blood and bowels, has fallen into perfect desuetude, and even into incredibility; for if Deputy Lapoule can believe in it, and call for the abrogation of it, so cannot we. † No Charolois, for these last fifty years, though never so fond of shooting, has been in use to bring down slaters and plumbers, and see them roll from their roofs;‡ but contents himself with partridges and grouse. Close viewed, their industry and function is that of dressing gracefully and eating sumptuously. As for their debauchery and depravity, it is, perhaps, unexampled since the era of Tiberius and Commodus. Nevertheless, one has still partly a feeling with the lady Maréchale: "Depend upon it, sir, God thinks twice before damning a man of that quality."§ These people, of old, surely had

* "Mémoires sur la Vie Privée de Marie Antoinette." par Madame Campan (Paris, 1826), i. 12.
† "Histoire de la Revolution Francaise," par Deux Amis de la Liberté (Paris, 1792), ii. 212.
‡ Lacretelle, "Histoire de France," pendant le 18me Siècle" (Paris, 1819), i. 271.
§ Dulaure, vii. 261.

virtues, uses, or they could not have been there' Nay, one virtue they are still required to have (for mortal man cannot live without a conscience), the virtue of perfect readiness to fight duels.

21. Such are the shepherds of the people, and now how fares it with the flock? With the flock, as is inevitable, it fares ill, and ever worse. They are not tended, they are only regularly shorn. They are sent for to do statute labor, to pay statute taxes, to fatten battle-fields ("named bed of honor") with their bodies, in quarrels which are not theirs; their hand and toil is in every possession of man, but for themselves they have little or no possession. Untaught, uncomforted, unfed, to pine stagnantly in thick obscuration, in squalid destitution and obstruction, this is the lot of the millions—people taillable et corvéable a merci et miséricorde. In Brittany they once rose in revolt at the first introduction of pendulum clocks, thinking it had something to do with the gabelle. Paris requires to be cleared out periodically by the police, and the horde of hunger-stricken vagabonds to be sent wandering again over space—for a time. "During one such periodical clearance," says Lacretelle, "in May, 1750, the police had presumed, withal, to carry off some reputable people's children, in the hope of extorting ransoms for them. The mothers fill the public places with cries of despair; crowds gather, get excited; so many women in distraction run about exaggerating the alarm; an absurd and horrid fable rises among the people; it is said that the doctors have ordered a great person to take baths of young human blood for the restoration of his own, all spoiled by debaucheries. Some of the rioters," adds Lacretelle, quite coolly, "were hanged on the following days." The police went on.* O ye poor naked wretches! and this, then, is your inarticulate cry to heaven, as of a dumb tortured animal, crying from uttermost depths of pain and debasement? Do these azure skies, like a dead crystalline vault, only reverberate the echo of it on you? Respond to it only by "hanging on the following days"? Not so; not forever! Ye are heard in heaven. And the answer, too, will come, in a horror of great darkness, and shakings of the world, and a cup of trembling which all the nations shall drink;

22. Remark, meanwhile, how from amid the wrecks and dust of this universal decay, new powers are fashioning themselves, adapted to the new time and its destinies. Besides the old noblesse, originally of fighters, there is a new recognized noblesse of lawyers, whose gala-day and proud battle-day even now is. An unrecognized noblesse of commerce, powerful enough, with money in its pocket. Lastly, powerfulest of all, least recognized of all, a noblesse of literature, without steel on their thigh, without gold in their purse, but with the "grand thaumaturgic faculty of thought" in their head. French philosophism has arisen, in which little word how much do we include! Here, indeed, lies properly the cardinal symptom of the whole widespread malady. Faith is gone out, skepticism is come in. Evil abounds and accumulates; no man has faith to withstand it, to amend it, to begin by amending himself: it must even go on accumulating. While hollow languor and vacuity is the lot of the upper, and want and stagnation of the lower, and universal misery is very certain, what other thing is certain? That a lie cannot be believed! Philosophism knows only this; her other belief is mainly, that in spiritual, supersensual matters no belief is possible. Unhappy! Nay, as yet the contradiction of a lie is some kind of belief; but the lie with its contradiction once swept

* Lacretelle, iii. 175.

away, what will remain? The five unsatiated senses will remain; the sixth insatiable sense (of vanity)—the whole demonic nature of man—will remain, hurled forth to rage blindly without rule or rein; savage itself, yet with all the tools and weapons of civilization—a spectacle new in history.

23. In such a France, as in a powder-tower, where fire unquenched and now unquenchable is smoking and smoldering all round, has Louis XV. lain down to die. With Pompadourism and Dubarryism, his fleur-de-lis has been shamefully struck down in all lands and on all seas; poverty invades even the royal exchequer, and tax-farming cau squeeze out no more; there is a quarrel of twenty-five years' standing with the parlement; everywhere want, dishonesty, unbelief, and hot-brained sciolists for state-physicians: it is a portentious hour.

24. Such things can the eye of history see in this sick-room of King Louis, which were invisible to the courtiers there. It is twenty years, gone Christmas day, since Lord Chesterfield, summing up what he had noted of this same France, wrote and sent off by post the following words, that have become memorable: "In short, all the symptoms which I have ever met with in history, previous to great changes and revolutions in government, now exist and daily increase in France."[*]

CHAPTER III.

VIATICUM.

25. For the present, however, the grand question with the governors of France is, shall extreme unction, or other ghostly viaticum (to Louis, not to France), be administered?

It is a deep question. For, if administered, if so much as spoken of, must not, on the very threshold of the business, witch Dubarry vanish, hardly to return should Louis even recover? With her vanishes Duke d'Aiguillon and company, and all their Armida-palace, as was said; chaos swallows the whole again, and there is left nothing but a smell of brimstone. But then, on the other hand, what will the dauphinists and choiseulists say? Nay, what may the royal martyr himself say, should he happen to get deadly worse, without getting delirious? For the present, he still kisses the Dubarry hand; so we, from the anteroom, can note; but afterward? Doctors' bulletins may run as they are ordered, but it is "confluent small-pox"—of which, as is whispered, too, the gate-keeper's once so buxom daughter lies ill—and Louis XV. is not a man to be trifled with in his viaticum. Was he not wont to catechise his very girls in the parc-aux-cerfs, and pray with and for them, that they might preserve their—orthodoxy?[†] A strange fact, not an unexampled one; for there is no animal so strange as man.

26. For the moment, indeed, it were all well, could Archbishop Beaumont but be prevailed upon—to wink with one eye! Alas, Beaumont would himself so fain do it; for, singular to tell, the church, too, and whole posthumous hope of Jesuitism, now hangs by the apron of this same unmentionable woman. But then, "the force of public opinion?" Rigorous Christophe de Beaumont, who has spent his life in persecuting hysterical Jansenists and incredulous non-confessors, or even their dead bodies, if no better might be—how shall he now open heaven's gate, and give absolution with the corpus delicti still under his nose? Our grand-almoner, Roche-Aymon, for his part, will not higgle with a royal sinner about

* "Chesterfield's Letters," December 25, 1753.

† Dulaure (viii. 217), Besenval, etc.

turning of the key; but there are other churchmen; there is a king's confessor, foolish Abbé Moudon; and fanaticism and decency are not yet extinct. On the whole, what is to be done? The doors can be well watched, the medical bulletin adjusted, and much, as usual, be hoped for from time and chance.

27. The doors are well watched, no improper figure can enter. Indeed, few wish to enter, for the putrid infection reaches even to the Œil-de-Bœuf, so that "more than fifty fall sick, and ten die." Mesdames the princesses alone wait at the loathsome sick-bed, impelled by filial piety. The three princesses, Graille, Chiffe, Coche (Rag, Snip, Pig, as he was wont to name them), are assiduous there when all have fled. The fourth princess, Loque (Dud), as we guess, is already in the nunnery, and can only give her orisons. Poor Graille and sisterhood, they have never known a father; such is the hard bargain grandeur must make. Scarcely at the débotter (when royalty took off its boots) could they snatch up their "enormous hoops, gird the long train round their waists, huddle on their black cloaks of taffeta up to the very chin;" and so, in fit appearance of full dress, "every evening at six," walk majestically in, receive their royal kiss on the brow, and then walk majestically out again, to embroidery, small scandal, prayers and vacancy. If majesty came some morning, with coffee of its own making, and swallowed it with them hastily while the dogs were uncoupling for the hunt, it was received as a grace of heaven.[*] Poor, withered, ancient women! in the wild tossings that yet await your fragile existence, before it be crushed and broken; as ye fly through hostile countries, over tempestuous seas, are almost taken by the Turks; and wholly, in the sansculottic earthquake, know not your right hand from your left, be this always an assured place in your remembrance, for the act was good and loving! To us, also, it is a little sunny spot in that dismal howling waste, where we hardly find another.

28. Meanwhile, what shall an impartial, prudent courtier do? In these delicate circumstances, while not only death or life, but even sacrament or no sacrament, is a question, the skilfulest may falter. Few are so happy as the Duke d'Orléans and the Prince de Condé, who can themselves, with violatile salts, attend the king's antechamber; and at the same time send their brave sons (Duke de Chartres, Egalité that is to be; Duke de Bourbon, one day Condé too, and famous among dotards) to wait upon the dauphin. With another few, it is a resolution taken—jacta est alea. Old Richelieu—when archbishop Beaumont, driven by public opinion, is at last for entering the sick-room—will twitch him by the rochet, into a recess; and there, with his old dissipated mastiff-face, and the oiliest vehemence, be seen pleading (and even, as we judge by Beaumont's change of color, prevailing) "that the king be not killed by a proposition in divinity." Duke de Fronsac, son of Richelieu, can follow his father, when the curé of Versailles whimpers something about sacraments, he will threaten to "throw him out of the window if he mention such a thing."

29. Happy these, we may say; but to the rest that hover between two opinions, is it not trying? He who would understand to what a pass Catholicism, and much else, had now got—and how the symbols of the holiest have become gambling-dice of the basest—must read the narrative of those things by Besenval and Soulavie, and the other court newsmen of the time. He will see the Versailles galaxy all scattered asunder, grouped into new ever-shifting constellations. There are nods and sagacious glances;

* Campan, i. 11-36.

go-betweens, silk dowagers mysteriously gliding, with smiles for this constellation, sighs for that; there is tremor, of hope or desperation, in several hearts. There is the pale, grinning shadow of death, ceremoniously ushered along by another grinning shadow, of etiquette: at intervals the growl of chapel organs, like prayer by machinery, proclaiming, as in a kind of horrid, diabolic horse-laughter, *Vanity of vanities, all is vanity!*

CHAPTER IV.

LOUIS THE UNFORGOTTEN.

30. Poor Louis! With these it is a hollow phantasmagory, where like mimes they mope and mowl, and utter false sounds for hire; but with thee it is frightful earnest.

Frightful to all men is death, from of old named King of Terrors. Our little compact home of an existence, where we dwelt complaining, yet as in a home, is passing, in dark agonies, into an unknown of separation, foreignness, unconditioned possibility. The heathen emperor asks of his soul, Into what places art thou now departing? The Catholic king must answer, To the judgment-bar of the most high God! Yes, it is a summing-up of life; a final settling and giving-in the "account of the deeds done in the body;" they are done now, and lie there unalterable, and do bear their fruits, long as eternity shall last.

31. Louis XV. had always the kingliest abhorrence of death. Unlike that praying Duke of Orleans, Egalité's grandfather—for, indeed, several of them had a touch of madness—who honestly believed that there was no death! He, if the court newsmen can be believed, started up, once on a time, glowing with sulphurous contempt and indignation on his poor secretary, who had stumbled on the words, feu roi d'Espagne (the late king of Spain): "Feu roi, mousieur?" "Monseigneur," hastily answered the trembling but adroit man of business, "c'est une titre qu'ils prennent ('tis a title they take)."[*] Louis, we say, was not so happy; but he did what he could. He would not suffer death to be spoken of; avoided the sight of churchyards, funereal monuments, and whatsoever could bring it to mind. It is the resource of the ostrich, who, hard hunted, sticks his foolish head in the ground, and would fain forget that his foolish unseeing body is not unseen too. Or, sometimes, with a spasmodic antagonism, significant of the same thing, and of more, he *would* go—or stopping his court carriages, would send—into churchyards, and ask "how many new graves there were to-day," though it gave his poor Pompadour the disagreeablest qualms. We can figure the thought of Louis that day, when, all royally caparisoned for hunting, he met, at some sudden turning in the wood of Senart, a ragged peasant with a coffin: "For whom?" It was for a poor brother slave, whom majesty had sometimes noticed slaving in those quarters. "What did he die of?" "Of hunger." The king gave his steed the spur.[†]

32. But figure his thought when death is now clutching at his own heart-strings, unlooked for, inexorable! Yes, poor Louis, death has found thee. No palace-walls or life-guards, gorgeous tapestries or gilt buckram of stiffest ceremonial, could keep him out; but he is here, here at thy very life-breath, and will extinguish it. Thou, whose whole existence hitherto was a chimera and scenic show, at length becometh a reality; sumptuous Versailles bursts asunder, like a dream, into void immensity; time is

* Besenval, i. 199.
† Campan, iii. 39.

done, and all the scaffolding of time falls wrecked with hideous clangor round thy soul; the pale kingdoms yawn open; there must thou enter naked, all unking'd, and await what is appointed thee! Unhappy man, there as thou turnest, in dull agony, on thy bed of weariness, what a thought is thine! Purgatory and hell-fire, now all too possible, in the prospect: in the retrospect, alas! what thing didst thou do that were not better undone? what mortal didst thou generously help? what sorrow hadst thou mercy on? Do the "five hundred thousand" ghosts, who sank shamefully on so many battlefields from Rossbach to Quebec that thy harlot might take revenge for an epigram, crowd round thee in this hour? Thy foul harem, the curses of mothers, the tears and infamy of daughters? Miserable man! thou "hast done evil as thou couldst;" thy whole existence seems one hideous abortion and mistake of nature, the use and meaning of thee not yet known. Wert thou a fabulous griffin, devouring the works of men, daily dragging virgins to thy cave; clad also in scales that no spear would pierce, no spear but Death's? A griffin not fabulous but real! Frightful, O Louis, seem these moments for thee. We will pry no further into the horrors of a sinner's death-bed.

33. And yet let no meanest man lay flattering unction to his soul. Louis was a ruler, but art thou not also one? His wide France, look at it from the fixed stars (themselves not yet infinitude), is no wider than thy narrow brickfield, where thou, too, didst faithfully or didst unfaithfully. Man, "symbol of eternity imprisoned into time!" it is not thy works, which are all mortal, infinitely little, and the greatest no greater than the least, but only the spirit thou workest in, that can have worth or continuance.

34. But reflect, in any case, what a life-problem this of poor Louis, when he rose as Bien-aimé from that Metz sick-bed, really was! What son of Adam could have swayed such incoherences into coherence? Could he? Blindest fortune alone has cast *him* on the top of it; he swims there; can as little sway it as the drift-log sways the wind-tossed, moon-stirred Atlantic. "What have I done to be so loved?" he said then. He may say now, "What have I done to be so hated? Thou hast done nothing, poor Louis! Thy fault is properly even this, that thou didst *nothing.* What could poor Louis do? Abdicate and wash his hands of it, in favor of the first that would accept. Other clear wisdom there was none for him. As it was, he stood gazing dubiously, the absurdest mortal extant, a very solecism incarnate, into the absurdest confused world; wherein at last nothing seemed so certain as this, that he, the incarnate solecism, had five senses; that there were flying tables (tables volantes, which vanish through the floor to come back reloaded), anda parc-aux-cerfs.

35. Whereby, at least, we have again this historical curiosity, a human being in an original position, swimming passively, as on some boundless "mother of dead dogs," toward issues which he partly saw. For Louis had, withal a kind of insight in him. So when a new minister of marine, or what else it might be, came announcing his new era, the scarlet-woman would hear from[1] the lips of majesty at supper: "Yes, he spread out his ware like another, promised the beautifulest things in the world, not a thing of which will come; he does not know this region; he will see." Or again: "'Tis the twentieth time I have heard all that; France will never get a navy, I believe." How touching, also, was this: "If *I* were lieutenant of police, I would prohibit those Paris cabriolets."[*]

36. Doomed mortal—for is it not a doom to be solecism incarnate? A new roi fainéant, king do-

* "Journal de Madame de Hausset," p. 285, etc.

nothing; but with [the strangest new mayor of the palace. No bow-legged Pepin now for mayor, but that same cloud-capt, fire-breathing speeter of democracy incalculable which is enveloping the world! Was Louis, then, no wickederthan this or the other private do-nothing and eat-all, such as we often see, under the name of man of pleasure, cumbering God's diligent creation for a time? Say wretcheder! His life-soleeism was seen and felt of a whole scandalized world; him endless oblivion cannot engulf and swallow to endless depths—not yet for a generation or two.

37. However, be this as it will, we remark, not without interest, that "on the evening of the 4th," Dame Dubarry issued from the sick-room, with perceptible "trouble in her visage." It is the fourth evening of May, year of grace 1774. Such a whispering in the Œil de Bœuf! Is he dying, then? What can be said is that Dubarry seems making up her packages; she sails, weeping, through her gilt boudoirs, as if taking leave. D'Aiguillon and company are near their last card; nevertheless, they will not yet throw up the game. But as for the sacramental controversy, it is as good as settled without being mentioned; Louis sends for his Abbé Moudon in the course of next night, is confessed by him, some say for the space of "seventeen minutes," and demands the sacraments of his own accord.

38. Nay, already, in the afternoon, behold, is not this your sorceress Dubarry with the handkerchief at her eyes, mounting D'Aiguillon's chariot, rolling off in his duchess's consolatory arms? She is gone and her place knows her no more. Vanish, false sorceress, into space! Needless to hover at neighboring Ruel, for thy day is done. Shut are the royal palace gates for evermore; hardly in coming years shalt thou, under cloud of night, descend once, in black domino, like a black night-bird, and disturb the fair Antoinette's music-party in the park; all birds of paradise flying from thee, and musical wind-pipes growing mute.* Thou nuclean, yet unmalignant, not unpitiable thing! What a course was thine, from that first truckle-bed (in Joan of Arc's country), where thy mother bore thee, with tears, to an unnamed father, forward, through lowest subterranean depths and over highest sunlight heights of harlotdom and rascaldom, to the guillotine axe, which shears away thy vainly whimpering head! Rest there uncursed, only buried and abolished; what else befitted thee?

39. Louis, meanwhile, is in considerable impatience for his sacraments; sends more than once to the window to see whether they are not coming. Be of comfort, Louis, what comfort thou canst; they are under way, those sacraments. Toward six in the morning they arrive. Cardinal Grand-Almoner Roche-Aymon is here in pontificals with his pyxes and his tools; he approaches the royal pillow, elevates his wafer, mutters or seems to mutter somewhat; and so (as the Abbé Georgel, in words that stick to one, expresses it) has Louis "made the amende honorable to God:" so does your Jesuit construe it. "Wa, wa," as the wild Clotaire groaned out when life was departing, "what great God is this that pulls down the strength of the strongest kings!"†

40. The amende honorable, what "legal apology" you will, to God, but not, if D'Aiguillon can help it, to man. Dubarry still hovers in his mansion at Ruel; and while there is life, there is hope. Grand-Almoner Roche-Aymon, accordingly (for he seems to be in the secret), has no sooner seen his pyxes and gear repacked than he is stepping majestically forth again,

as if the work were done! But king's confessor Abbé Moudon starts forward, with anxious, acidulent face, twitches him by the sleeve, whispers in his ear. Whereupon the poor cardinal has to turn around and declare audibly "that his majesty repents of any subjects of scandal he may have given (a pudonner), and purposes, by the strength of heaven assisting him, to avoid the like—for the future!" Words listened to by Richelieu, with mastiff-face growing blacker; and answered to, aloud, "with an epithet," —which Besenval will not repeat. Old Richelieu, conqueror of Minorca, companion of flying-table orgies, perforator of bed-room walls,* is thy day also done?

41. Alas, the chapel organs may keep going, the shrine of Sainte Geneviève be let down, and pulled up again, without effect. In the evening the whole court, with dauphin and dauphiness, assist at the chapel; priests are hoarse with chanting their "prayers of forty hours," and the heaving bellows blow. Almost frightful! for the very heaven blackens, battering rain torrents dash, with thunder, almost drowning the organ's voice, and electric fire-flashes make the very flambeaux on the altar pale. So that the most, as we are told, retired when it was over, with hurried steps, "in a state of meditation, (recueillement)," and said little or nothing.†

42. So it has lasted for the better half of a fortnight, the Dubarry gone almost a week. Besenval says all the world was getting impatient que cela finit; that poor Louis would have done with it. It is now the 10th of May, 1774. He will soon have done now.

43. This tenth of May day falls into the loathsome sick-bed, but dull, unnoticed there; for they that look out of the windows are quite darkened; the cistern-wheel moves discordant on its axis; life, like a spent steed, is panting toward the goal. In their remote apartments, dauphin and dauphiness stand road-ready, all grooms and equerries booted and spurred, waiting for some signal to escape the house of pestilence.‡ And, hark! across the Œil-de-Bœuf, what sound is that—sound "terrible and absolutely like thunder?" It is the rush of the whole court, rushing as in wager, to salute the new sovereigns: Hail to your majesties! The dauphin and dauphiness are king and queen! Overpowered with many emotions, they two fall on their knees together, and, with streaming tears, exclaim, "O God, guide us, protect us; we are too young to reign!" Too young indeed.

44. But thus, in any case, "with a sound absolutely like thunder," has the horologe of time struck, and an old era passed away. The Louis that was, lies forsaken, a mass of abhorred clay; abandoned "to some poor persons, and priests of the Chapelle Ardente," who make haste to put him "in two lead coffins, pouring in abundant spirits of wine." The new Louis, with his court, is rolling toward Choisy through the summer-afternoon: the royal tears still flow; but a word mispronounced by Monseigneur d'Artois sets them all laughing, and they weep no more. Light mortals, how ye walk your light life-

* Campan, i. 197.
† Gregorius Turonensis, "Histor." lib. iv. cap. 21.

* Besenval, i. 159-172. Genlis; Duc de Levis, etc.
† Weber "Memoires concernant Marie Antoinette" (London, 1809), i. 22.
‡ One grudges to interfere with the beautiful theatrical "candle," which Madame Campan (i. 79) has lit on this occasion, and 'blown out at the moment of death. What candles might be lit or blown out, in so large an establishment as that of Versailles, no man at such distance would like to affirm: at the same time, as it was two o'clock in a May afternoon, and these royal stables must have been some five or six hundred yards from the royal sick-room, the "candle" does threaten to go out in spite of us. It remains burning, indeed—in her fantasy; throwing light on much in these "Memoires" of hers.

minuet over bottomless abysses, divided from you by a film!

45. For the rest, the proper authorities felt that no funeral could be too unceremonious. Besenval himself thinks it was unceremonious enough. Two carriages containing two noblemen of the usher species and a Versailles clerical person; some score of mounted pages, some fifty palfreniers, these, with torches, but not so much as in black, start from Versailles on the second evening, with their leaden bier. At a high trot, they start, and keep up that pace. For the jibes (brocards) of those Parisians who stand planted in two rows all the way to St. Denis, and 'give vent to their pleasantry, the characteristic of the nation," do not tempt one to slacken. Toward midnight the vaults of St. Denis receive their own, unwept by any eye of all these, if not by poor Loque, his neglected daughter's, whose nunnery is hard by.

Him they crush down, and huddle under ground, in this impatient way; him and his era of sin and tyranny and shame, for behold, a new era is come; the future all the brighter that the past was base.

BOOK SECOND.

THE PAPER AGE.

CHAPTER I.

ASTRÆA REDUX.

46. A paradoxical philosopher, carrying to the uttermost length that aphorism of Montesquieu's, "Happy the people whose annals are tiresome," has said, "Happy the people whose annals are vacant." In which saying, mad as it looks, may there not still be found some grain of reason? For truly, as it has been written, "Silence is divine," and of heaven; so in all earthly things, too, there is a silence which is better than any speech. Consider it well, the event, the thing which can be spoken of and recorded, is it not, in all cases, some disruption, some solution of continuity? Were it even a glad event, it involves change, involves loss (of active force); and so far, either in the past or the present, is an irregularity, a disease. Stillest perseverance were our blessedness; not dislocation and alteration—could they be avoided.

47. The oak grows silently in the forest a thousand years; only in the thousandth year, when the woodman arrives with his axe, is there heard an echoing through the solitudes, and the oak announces itself when, with far-sounding crash, it *falls*. How silent, too, was the planting of the acorn, scattered from the lap of some wandering wind! Nay, when our oak flowered, or put on its leaves (its glad events), what shout of proclamation could there be? Hardly from the most observant a word of recognition. These things *befell* not, they were slowly *done*; not in an hour, but through the flight of days. What was to be said of it? This hour seemed altogether as the last was, as the next would be.

48. It is thus everywhere that foolish rumor babbles, not of what was done, but of what was misdone or undone; and foolish history (ever, more or less, the written epitomized synopsis of rumor) knows so little that was not as well unknown—Attila invasions, Walter-the-Penniless crusades, Sicilian vespers, Thirty Years' wars; mere sin and misery; not work, but hindrance of work! For the earth, all this while, was yearly green and yellow with her kind harvests; the hand of the craftsman, the mind of the thinker, rested not; and so, after all, and in spite of all, we have this so glorious, high-domed, blossom-

ing world, concerning which poor history may well ask, with wonder, whence *it* came. She knows so little of it, knows so much of what obstructed it, what would have rendered it impossible. Such, nevertheless, by necessity or foolish choice, in her rule and practice; whereby that paradox, "Happy the people whose annals are vacant," is not without its true side.

49. And yet, what seems more pertinent to note here, there is a stillness, not of unobstructed growth, but of passive inertness, the symptom of imminent downfall. As victory is silent, so is defeat. Of the opposing forces the weaker has resigned itself; the stronger marches on, noiseless now, but rapid, inevitable: the fall and overturn will not be noiseless. How all grows, and has its period, even as the herbs of the fields, be it annual, centennial, millennial! All grows and dies, each by its own wondrous laws, in wondrous fashion of its own; spiritual things most wondrously of all. Inscrutable to the wisest, are these latter; not to be prophesied of or understood. If, when the oak stands proudliest flourishing to the eye, you know that its heart is sound, it is not so with the man; how much less with the society, with the nation of men! Of such it may be affirmed even that the superficial aspect, that the inward feeling of full health, is generally ominous. For, indeed, it is of apoplexy, so to speak, and a plethoric, lazy 'habit of body, that churches, kingships, social institutions, oftenest die. Sad, when such institution plethorically says to itself, Take thy ease, thou hast goods laid up; like the fool of the gospel, to whom it was answered, Fool, *this night* thy life shall be required of thee!

50. Is it the healthy peace, or the ominous unhealthy, that rests on France for these next ten years? Over which the historian can pass lightly, without call to linger; for as yet events are not, much less performances. Time of sunniest stillness; shall we call it, what all men thought it, the new age of gold? Call it, at least, of paper; which in many ways is the succedaneum of gold. Bank-paper, wherewith you can still buy where there is no gold left; book-paper, splendid with theories, philosophies, sensibilities—beautiful art, not only of revealing thought, but also of so beautifully hiding from us the want of thought! Paper is made from the *rags* of things that did once exist; there are endless excellences in paper. What wisest philosopher, in this halcyon, uneventful period, could prophesy that there was approaching, big with darkness and confusion, the event of events? Hope ushers in a revolution, as earthquakes are preceded by bright weather. On the 5th of May, fifteen years hence, old Louis will not be sending for the sacraments; but a new Louis, his grandson, with the whole pomp of astonished, intoxicated France, will be opening the states-general.

51. Dubarrydom and its D'Aiguillons are gone forever. There is a young, still docile, well-intentioned king; a young, beautiful, and bountiful, well-intentioned queen; and with them all France, as it were, become young. Maupeou and his parlement have to vanish into thick night; respectable magistrates, not indifferent to the nation, were it only for having been opponents of the court, descend now unchained from their "steep rocks at Croe in Combrailles" and elsewhere, and return singing praises: the old parlement of Paris resumes its functions. Instead of a profligate, bankrupt Abbé Terray, we have now, for controller-general, a virtuous, philosophic Turgot, with a whole reformed France in his head. By whom whatsoever is wrong, in finance or otherwise, will be righted—as far as possible. Is it not as if Wisdom herself were henceforth to have seat and voice in the council of kings? Turgot has taken

office, with the noblest plainness of speech to that effect; been listened to with the noblest royal trustfulness.* It is true, as King Louis objects, "They say he never goes to mass;" but liberal France likes him little worse for that; liberal France answers, "The Abbé Terray always went." Philosophism sees, for the first time, a philosophe (or even a philosopher) in office; she in all things will applausively second him; neither will light old Maurepas obstruct, if he can easily help it.

52. Then how "sweet" are the manners; vice "losing all its deformity;" becoming *decent* (as established things, making regulations for themselves, do); becoming almost a kind of "sweet" virtue! Intelligence so abounds, irradiated by wit and the art of conversation. Philosophism sits joyful in her glittering saloons, the dinner-guest of opulence grown ingenuous—the very nobles proud to sit by her—and preaches, lifted up over all Bastilles, a coming millennium. From far Ferney, patriarch Voltaire gives sign; veterans Diderot, D'Alembert, have lived to see this day; these, with their younger Marmontels, Morellets, Chamforts, Raynals, make glad the spicy board of rich ministering dowager, of philosophic farmer-general. O nights and suppers of the gods! Of a truth, the long-demonstrated will now be done; "the age of revolutions approaches" (as Jean Jacques wrote), but then of happy blessed ones. Man awakens from his long somnambulism, chases the phantasms that beleaguered and bewitched him. Behold the new morning glittering down the eastern steeps! Fly, false phantasms, from its shafts of light; let the absurd fly utterly, forsaking this lower earth forever. It is truth and astræa redux that (in the shape of philosophism) henceforth reign. For what imaginable purpose was man made if not to be "happy?" By victorious analysis, and progress of the species, happiness enough now awaits him. Kings can become philosophers, or else philosophers kings. Let but society be once rightly constituted, by victorious analysis. The stomach that is empty shall be filled; the throat that is dry shall be wetted with wine. Labor itself shall be all one as rest, not grievous, but joyous. Wheat-fields, one would think, cannot come to grow untilled; no man made clayey or made weary thereby—unless, indeed, machinery will do it? Gratuitous tailors and restaurateurs may start up at fit intervals, one as yet sees not how. But if each will, according to rule of benevolence, have a care for all, then surely no one will be mourned for. Nay, who knows but, by sufficiently victorious analysis, "human life may be indefinitely lengthened," and men get rid of death, as they have already done of the devil? We shall then be happy in spite of death and the devil. So preaches magniloquent philosophism her Redeunt Saturnia regna.

53. The prophetic song of Paris and its philosophes is audible enough in the Versailles Œil-de-Bœuf; and the Œil-de-Bœuf, intent chiefly on nearer blessedness, can answer, at worst, with a polite "Why not?" Good old cheery Maurepas is too joyful a prime minister to dash the world's joy. Sufficient for the day be its own evil. Cheery old man; he cuts his jokes, and hovers careless along, his cloak well adjusted to the wind, if so be he may please all persons. The simple young king, whom a Maurepas cannot think of troubling with business, has retired into the interior apartments, taciturn, irresolute, though with a sharpness of temper at times: he, at length, determines on a little smith-work; and so, in apprenticeship with a

Sieur Gamain (whom one day he shall have little cause to bless), is learning to make locks.* It appears, further, he understood geography, and could read English. Unhappy young king; his childlike trust in that foolish old Maurepas deserved another return. But friend and foe, destiny and himself. have combined to do him hurt.

54. Meanwhile the fair young queen, in her halls of state, walks liks a goddess of beauty, the cynosure of all eyes; as yet mingles not with affairs, heeds not the future, least of all, dreads it. Weber and Campan† have pictured her, there within the royal tapestries, in bright boudoirs, baths, peignoirs, and the grand and little toilette; with a whole brilliant world waiting obsequious on her glance; fair young daughter of time, what things has time in store for thee? Like earth's brightest appearance, she moves gracefully, environed with the grandeur of earth; a reality, and yet a magic vision; for, behold, shall not .utter darkness swallow it? The soft young heart adopts orphaus, portions meritorious maids, delights to succor the poor, such poor as come picturesqnely in her way; and sets the fashion of doing it; for, as was said, benevolence has now begun reigning. In her Duchess de Polignac, in her Princess de Lamballe, she enjoys something almost like friendship; now, too, after seven long years, she has a child, and soon even a dauphin, of her own; can reckon herself, as queens go, happy in a husband.

55. Events? The grand events are but charitable feasts of morals (fêtes des mœurs), with their prizes and speeches; poissarde processions to the dauphin's cradle; above all, flirtations, their rise, progress, decline, and fall. There are snow statues raised by the poor in hard winter to a queen who has given them fuel. There are masquerades, theatricals, beautifyings of Little Trianon, purchase and repair of St. Cloud; journeyings from the summer court-elysium to the winter one. There are poutings and grudgings from the Sardinian sisters-in-law (for the princes, too, are wedded); little jealousies, which court-etiquette can moderate. Wholly the lightest-hearted, frivolous foam of existence, yet au artfully refined foam; pleasant were it not so costly, like that which mantles on the wine of Champagne!

56. Monsieur, the king's elder brother, has set up for a kind of wit, and leans toward the philosophe side. Monseigneur d'Artois pulls the mask from a fair impertinent, fights a duel in consequence, almost drawing blood.‡ He has breeches of a kind new in this world, a fabulous kind. "Four tall lackeys," says Mercier, as if he had seen it, "hold him up in the air, that he may fall into the garment without vestige of wrinkle; from which rigorous incasement the same four, in the same way, and with more effort, have to deliver him at night."§ This last is he who now, as a gray, time-worn man, sits desolate at Grätz; ‖ having winded up his destiny with the three days. In such sort are poor mortals swept and shoveled to and fro.

CHAPTER II.

PETITION IN HIEROGLYPHS.

57. With the working people, again, it is not so well. Unlucky! For there are from twenty to twenty-five millions of them. Whom, however, we lump together into a kind of dim, compendious unity, monstrous but dim, far off, as the canaille, or more humanely, as "the masses." Masses, indeed! and

* Turgot's letter; Condorcet, "Vie de Turgot" ("Œuvres de Condorcet," t. v.), p. 67. The date is 24th August, 1774.

* Campan, i. 125.
† ib. i. 100 151. Weber, i 11-60.
‡ Besenval, ii 282-330.
§ Mercier, "Nouveau Paris," iii. 147.
‖ A. D. 1834.

yet, singular to say, if, with an effort of imagination, thou follow them, over broad France, into their clay hovels, into their garrets and hutches, the masses consist all of units. Every unit of whom has his own heart and sorrows, stands covered there with his own skin, and if you prick him he will bleed. O purple sovereignty, holiness, reverence; thou, for example, cardinal grand-almoner, with thy plush-covering of honor, who hast thy hands strengthened with dignities and moneys, and art set on thy world watch-tower solemnly, in sight of God, for such ends; what a thought, that every unit of these masses is a miraculous man, even as thou thyself art; struggling, with vision or with blindness, for *his* infinite kingdom (this life which he has got, once only, in the middle of eternities); with a spark of the divinity, what thou callest an immortal soul, in him!

58. Dreary, languid, do these struggle in their obscure remoteness; their hearth cheerless, their diet thin. For them, in this world, rises no era of hope; hardly now in the other—if it be not hope in the gloomy rest of death, for their faith, too, is failing. Untaught, uncomforted, unfed! A dumb generation; their voice only an inarticulate cry; spokesman, in the king's council, in the world's forum, they have none that finds credence. At rare intervals (as now, in 1775) they will fling down their hoes and hammers, and, to the astonishment of thinking mankind,* flock hither and thither, dangerous, aimless; get the length even of Versailles. Turgot is altering the corn-trade, abrogating the absurdest corn-laws; there is dearth, real, or were it even "factitious;" an indubitable scarcity of bread. And so, on the second day of May, 1775, these waste multitudes do here, at Versailles château, in wide-spread wretchedness, in sallow faces, squalor, winged raggedness, present, as in legible hieroglyphic writing, their petition of grievances. The château gates have to be shut, but the king will appear on the balcony and speak to them. They have seen the king's face; their petition of grievances has been, if not read, looked at. For answer, two of them are hanged, on a "new gallows forty feet high," and the rest driven back to their dens—for a time.

59. Clearly a difficult "point" for government, that of dealing with these masses—if, indeed, it be not rather the sole point and problem of government, and all other points mere accidental crochets, superficialities, and beatings of the wind? For, let charter-chests, use and wont, law common and special, say what they will, the masses count to so many millions of units; made, to all appearance, by God, whose earth this is declared to be. Besides, these people are not without ferocity; they have sinews and indignation. Do but look what holiday old Marquis Mirabeau, the crabbed old friend of men, looked on, in these same years, from his lodging, at the baths of Mont d'Or: "The savages descending in torrents from the mountains; our people ordered not to go out. The curate in surplice and stole, justice in its peruke, Marechaussée, saber in hand, guarding the place, till the bagpipes can begin. The dance interrupted, in a quarter of an hour, by battle; the cries, the squealings of children, of infirm persons, and other assistants, tarring them on, as the rabble does when dogs fight; frightful men, or rather frightful wild animals, clad in jupes of coarse woolen, with large girdles of leather studded with copper nails; of gigantic stature, heightened by high wooden-clogs (sabots); rising on tiptoe to see the fight; trampling time to it; rubbing their sides with their elbows, their faces hagard (figures hâves), and covered with their long greasy hair; the upper part of the visage

waxing pale, the lower distorting itself into the attempt at a cruel laugh, and a sort of ferocious impatience. And these people pay the 'taille!' And you want, further, to take their salt from them! And you know not what it is you are stripping barer, or, as you call it, governing; what, by the spurt of your pen, in its cold, dastard indifference, you will fancy you can starve always with impunity; always till the catastrophe come! Ah, madame, such government by blind-man's-buff, stumbling along too far, will end in the general overturn ('culbute generale')."*

60. Undoubtedly a dark feature this in an age of gold—age, at least, of paper and hope! Meanwhile, trouble us not with the prophecies, O croaking friend of men, 'tis long that we have heard such, and still the old world keeps wagging in its old way.

CHAPTER III.

QUESTIONABLE.

61. Or is this same age of hope itself but a simulacrum, as hope too often is? Cloud-vapor with rainbows painted on it, beautiful to see, to sail toward—which hovers over Niagara Falls? In that case, victorious Analysis will have enough to do.

Alas, yes! a whole world to remake, if she could see it; work for another than she! For all is wrong, and gone out of joint; the inward spiritual and the outward economical; head or heart, there is no soundness in it. As, indeed, evils of all sorts are more or less of kin, and do usually go together; especially it is an old truth that wherever huge physical evil is, there, as the parent and origin of it, has moral evil to a proportionate extent been. Before those five-and-twenty laboring millions, for instance, could get that haggardness of face, which old Mirabeau now looks on, in a nation calling itself Christian, and calling man the brother of man—what unspeakable, nigh infinite dishonesty (of *seeming* and not *being*) in all manner of rulers and appointed watchers, spiritual and temporal, must there not, through long ages, have gone on accumulating! It will accumulate; moreover, it will reach a head for the first of all gospels is this, that a lie cannot endure forever.

62. In fact, if we pierce through that rose-pink vapor of sentimentalism, philanthropy, and feast of morals, there lies behind it one of the sorriest spectacles. You might ask, What bonds that ever held a human society happily together, or held it together at all, are in force here? It is an unbelieving people; which has suppositions, hypotheses, and froth-systems of victorious analysis; and for *belief*, this mainly, that pleasure is pleasant. Hunger they have for all sweet things, and the law of hunger, but what other law? Within them, or over them, properly none!

63. Their king has become a king popinjay, with his Maurepas government, gyrating as the weather-cock does, blown about by every wind. Above them they see no God; or they even do not look above, except with astronomical glasses. The church, indeed, still is; but in the most submissive state; quite tamed by philosophism, in a singularly short time: for the hour was come. Some twenty years ago, your Archbishop Beaumont would not even let the poor Jansenists get buried: your Loménie Brienne (a rising man, whom we shall meet with yet) could, in the name of the clergy, insist on having the anti-Protestant laws, which condemn to death for preaching,

* Lacretelle. "France pendant le 18me Siècle," ii. 455. Biographie Universelle," § Turgot (by Durozoir).

* "Memoires de Mirabeau." ecrits par lui-meme, par son pere, son oncle, et son fils adoptif (Paris, 1834-51), ii. 186.

"put in execution."* And, alas, now not so much as Baron Holbach's atheism can be burnt—except as pipe-matches by the private speculative individual. Our church stands haltered, dumb, like a dumb ox ; lowing only for provender (of tithes) ; content if it can have that; or, with dumb stupor, expecting its further doom. And the twenty millions of "haggard faces;" and, as finger-post and guidance to them in their dark struggle, "a gallows forty feet high!" Certainly a singular golden age; with its feasts of morals, its "sweet manners," its sweet institutions (institutions douces) ; betokening nothing but peace among men!—Peace? O philosophe-sentimentalism, what hast thou to do with peace, when thy mother's name is Jezebel? Foul product of still fouler corruption, thou with the corruption art doomed!

64. Meanwhile it is singular how long the rotten will hold together, provided you do not handle it roughly. For whole generations it continues standing, "with a ghastly affectation of life," after all life and truth has fled out of it; so loth are men to quit their old ways, and, conquering indolence and inertia, venture on new. Great, truly, is the actual; is the thing that has rescued itself from bottomless deeps of theory and possibility, and stands there as a definite, indisputable fact, whereby men do work and live, or once did so. Wisely shall men cleave to that, while it will endure; and quit it with regret, when it gives way under them. Rash enthusiast of change' beware! Hast thou well considered all that habit does in this life of ours; how all knowledge and all practice hang wondrous over infinite abysses of the unknown, impracticable ; and our whole being is an infinite abyss, *overarched* by habit, as by a thin earth-rind, laboriously built together?

65. But if "every man," as it has been written, "holds confined within him a *mad*-man," what must every society do—society, which in its commonest state is called "the standing miracle of this world?" "Without such earth-rind of habit," continues our author, "call it system of habits, in a word, *fixed ways* of acting and believing, society would not exist at all. With such it exists, better or worse. Herein, too, in this its* system of habits acquired, retained how you will, lies the true law-code and constitution of a society; the only code, though an unwritten one, which it can in nowise *disobey.* The thing we call written code, constitution, form of government, and the like, what is it but some miniature image, and solemnly expressed summary of this unwritten code? *Is*, or rather, alas! is *not;* but only should be, and always tends to be! In which latter discrepancy lies struggle without end." And now, we add in the same dialect, let but, by ill chance, in such ever-enduring struggle, your "thin earth-rind" be once *broken!* The fountains of the great deep boil forth—fire-fountains, enveloping, engulfing. Your "earth-rind" is shattered, swallowed up: instead of a green, flowery world, there is a waste wild-weltering chaos; which has again, with tumult and struggle, to *make* itself into a world.

66. On the other hand, be this conceded : Where thou findest a lie that is oppressing thee, extinguish it. Lies exist there only to be extinguished; they wait and cry earnestly for extinction. Think well, meanwhile, in what spirit thou wilt do it. Not with hatred, with headlong, selfish violence, but in clearness of heart, with holy zeal, gently, almost with pity. Thou wouldst not *replace* such extinct lie by a new lie, which a new injustice of thy own were; the parent of still other lies? Whereby the latter end of that business were worse than the beginning.

67. So, however, in this world of ours, which has both an indestructible hope in the future and an in-

destructible tendency to persevere as in the past, must innovation and conservation wage their perpetual conflict as they may and can. Wherein the "demonic element" that lurks in all human things *may*, doubtless, some once in the thousand years, get vent! But, indeed, may we not regret that such conflict, which, after all, is but like that classical one of "hate-filled Amazons with heroic youths," and will end in *embraces*, should usually be so spasmodic! For conservation, strengthened by that mightiest quality in us, our indolence, sits for long ages, not victorious only, which she should be, but tyrannical, incommunicative. She holds her adversary as if annihilated; such adversary lying all the while like some buried Enceladus, who, to gain the smallest freedom, has to stir a whole Trinacria with its Ætnas.

68. Wherefore, on the whole, we will honor a paper age too; an era of hope! For in this same frightful process of Enceladus revolt, when the task, on which no mortal would willingly enter, has become imperitive, inevitable, is it not even a kindness of nature that she lures us forward by cheerful promises, fallacious or not, and a whole generation plunges into the Erebus blackness, lighted on by an era of hope? It has been well said: "Man is based on hope; he has properly no other possession but hope; this habitation of his is named the place o hope."

CHAPTER IV.

MAUREPAS.

69. But now, among French hopes, is not that of old M. de Maurepas one of the best-grounded, who hopes that he, by dexterity, shall contrive to continue minister? Nimble old man, who, for all emergencies, has his light jest; and ever, in the worst confusion, will emerge, cork-like, unsunk! Small care to him is perfectibility, progress of the species, and astræa redux; good only that a man of light wit, verging toward fourscore, can in the seat of authority feel himself important among men. Shall we call him, as haughty Châteauroux was wont of old, "M. Faquinet" (diminutive of scoundrel)? In courtier dialect, he is now named "the Nestor of France ;" such governing Nestor as France has.

70. At bottom, nevertheless, it might puzzle one to say where the government of France, in these days, specially is. In that château of Versailles we have Nestor, king, queen, ministers, and clerks, with paper bundles tied in tape. But the government? For government is a thing that *governs*, that guides, and, if need be, compels. Visible in France there is not such a thing. Invisible, inorganic, on the other hand, there is; in philosophe saloons, in œil-de-bœuf galleries, in the tongue of the babbler, in the pen of the pamphleteer. Her majesty appearing at the opera is applauded; she returns all radiant with joy. Anon the applauses wax fainter, or threaten to cease; she is heavy of heart; the light of her face has fled. Is sovereignty some poor montgolfier, which, blown into by the popular wind, grows great and mounts, or sinks flaccid if the wind be withdrawn? France was long a "despotism tempered by epigrams," and now, it would seem, the epigrams have got the upper hand.

71. Happy were a young "Louis the Desired" to make France happy, if it did not prove too troublesome, and he only knew the way. But there is endless discrepancy round him; so many claims and clamors ; a mere confusion of tongues. Not reconcilable by man, not manageable, suppressible, save by some strongest and wisest man; which only a

* Dor*ey d'Anglas. "Vie de Malesherbes," i. 15-22.

lightly-jesting, lightly-gyrating M. de Maurepas can so much as subsist amidst. Philosophism claims her new era, meaning thereby innumerable things; and claims it in no faint voice; for France at large, hitherto mute, is now beginning to speak also, and speaks in that same sense. A huge, many-toned sound; distant, yet not unimpressive. On the other hand, the Œil-de-Bœuf, which, as nearest, one can hear best, claims with shrill vehemence that the monarchy be as heretofore a horn of plenty, wherefrom loyal courtiers may draw, to the just support of the throne. Let liberalism and a new era, if such is the wish, be introduced—only no curtailment of the royal moneys! Which latter condition, alas! is precisely the impossible one.

72. Philosophism, as we saw, has got her Turgot made controller-general, and there shall be endless reformation. Unhappily, this Turgot could continue only twenty months. With a miraculous *Fortunatus's purse* in his treasury, it might have lasted longer; with such purse, indeed, every French controller-general that would prosper in these days ought first to provide himself. But here, again, may we not remark the bounty of nature in regard to hope? Man after man advances confident to the Augean stable, as if *he* could clean it; expends his little fraction of an ability on it, with such cheerfulness, does, in so far as he was honest, accomplished something. Turgot has faculties, honesty, insight, heroic volition, but the Fortunatus's purse he has not. Sanguine controller-general! a whole pacific French revolution may stand schemed in the head of the thinker, but who shall pay the unspeakable "indemnities" that will be needed? Alas! far from that; on the very threshold of the business, he proposes that the clergy, the noblesse, the very parlements, be subjected to taxes like the people! One shriek of indignation and astonishment reverberates though all the château galleries; M. de Maurepas has to gyrate, the poor king, who had written few weeks ago, "Il n'y a que vous et moi qui aimions le peuple (There is none but you and I that has the people's interest at heart)," must write now a dismissal,* and let the French revolution accomplish itself, pacifically or not, as it can.

73. Hope, then, is deferred? Deferred—not destroyed or abated. Is not this for example, our Patriarch Voltaire, after long years of absence, revisiting Paris? With face shriveled to nothing, with "huge peruke à la Louis Quatorze, which leaves only two eyes visible, glittering like carbuncles," the old man is here.† What an outburst! Sneering Paris has suddenly grown reverent, devotional with hero-worship. Nobles have disguised themselves as tavern-waiters to obtain sight of him; the loveliest of France would lay their hair beneath his feet. "His chariot is the nucleus of a comet, whose train fills whole streets;" they crown him in the theater, with immortal vivats; finally "stifle him under roses"—for old Richelieu recommended opium in such state of the nerves; and the excessive patriarch took too much. Her majesty herself had some thought of sending for him, but was dissuaded. Let majesty consider it, nevertheless. The purport of this man's existence has been to wither up and annihilate all whereon majesty and worship for the present rests; and is it *so* that the world recognizes him? With apotheosis; as its prophet and speaker, who has spoken wisely the thing it so longed to say? Add only that the body of this same rose-stifled, beautified patriarch cannot get buried except by stealth. It is wholly a notable business, and France, without doubt, is *big* (what the Germans call "of good hope"):

we shall wish her a happy birth-hour and blessed fruit.

74. Beaumarchais, too, has now winded up his law-pleadings ("Mémoires"),* not without result to himself and to the world. Caron Beaumarchais (or de Beaumarchais, for he got enobled) had been born poor, but aspiring, esurient; with talents, audacity, adroitness; above all, with the talent for intrigue—a lean, but also a tough, indomitable man. Fortune and dexterity brought him to the harpsichord of Mesdames our good Princesses Loque, Graille, and sisterhood. Still better, Páris Duvernier, the court banker, honored him with some confidence, to the length even of transactions in cash. Which confidence, however, Duvernier's heir, a person of quality, would not continue. Quite otherwise; there springs a lawsuit from it, wherein tough Beaumarchais, losing both money and repute, is, in the opinion of Judge-Reporter Goezman, of the Parlement Maupeou, and of a whole indifferent, acquiescing world, miserably beaten. In all men's opinion, only not in his own! Inspired by the indignation which makes, if not verses, satirical law-papers, the withered music-master, with a desperate heroism, takes up his lost cause in spite of the world; fights for it against reporters, parlements, and principalities, with light banter, with clear logic; adroitly, with an inexhaustible toughness and resource, like the skillfulest foucer; on whom, so skillful is he, the world now looks. Three long years it lasts, with wavering fortune. In fine, after labors comparable the twelve of Hercules, our unconquerable Caron triumphs—regains his lawsuit and lawsuits, strips Reporter Goezman of the judicial ermine, covering him with a perpetual garment of obloquy instead . and in regard to the Parlement Maupeou (which he has helped to extinguish), to parlements of all kinds,and to French justice generally given rise to endless reflections in the minds of men. Thus has Beaumarchais, like a lean French Hercules, ventured down, driven by distiny, into the nether king doms, and victoriously tamed hell-dogs there. He also is henceforth among the notabilities of his generation.

CHAPTER V

ASTRÆA REDUX WITHOUT CASH.

75. Observe, however, beyond the Atlantic, has not the new day verily dawned? Democracy, as we said, is born; storm-girt, is struggling for life and victory. A sympathetic France rejoices over the rights of man: in all saloons it is said, What a spectacle! Now, too, behold our Deane, our Franklin, American plenipotentiaries, here in person soliciting † the sons of the Saxon Puritans, with their old-Saxon temper, old-Hebrew culture, sleek Silas, sleek Benjamin. here on such errand among the light children of heathen-ism, monarchy, sentimentalism, and the scarlet-woman. A spectacle, indeed, over which saloons may cackle joyous, though Kaiser Joseph, questioned on it, gave this answer, most unexpected from a philosophe: "Madame, the trade I live by is that of royalist (Mon metier à moi c'est d'être royaliste)."

76. So thinks light Maurepas too; but the wind of philosophism and the force of public opinion will blow him round. Best wishes, meanwhile, are sent; clandestine privateers armed. Paul Jones shall equip his *Bon Homme Richard*; weapons, military stores, can be smuggled over (if the English do not seize them); wherein once more Beaumarchais, dimly, as the giant smuggler, becomes visible, filling his own

---

* In May, 1776.
† February, 1778.

* 1773-6. See "Œuvres de Beaumarchais," where they and the history of them are given.
† 1777; Deane somewhat earlier. Franklin remained till 1785.

lank pocket withal. But surely in any case France should have a navy. For which great object were not now the time—now when that proud termagant of the seas has her hands full? It is true, an impoverished treasury cannot build ships; but the hint once given (which Beaumarchais says *he* gave), this and the other loyal seaport, chamber of commerce, will build and offer them. Goodly vessels bound into the waters—a *Ville de Paris*, leviathan of ships.

77. And now when gratuitous three-deckers dance there at anchor, with streamers flying, and the eleutheromaniac philosophedom grows even more clamorous, what can a Maurepas do—but gyrate? Squadrons cross the ocean; Gateses, Lees, rough Yankee generals, " with woolen night-caps under their hats," present arms to the far-glancing chivalry of France; and newborn democracy sees, not without amazement, " despotism tempered by epigrams" light at her side. So, however, it is. King's forces and heroic volunteers, Rochambeaus, Bouillés, Lameths, Lafayettes, have drawn their swords in this sacred quarrel of mankind—shall draw them again elsewhere, in the strangest way.

78. Off Ushant some naval thunder is heard. In the course of which did our young prince, Duke de Chartres, " hide in the hold," or did he materially, by *active* heroism, contribute to the victory? Alas! by a second edition we learn that there was no victory, or that English Keppel had it.* Our poor young prince gets his opera plaudits changed into mocking te-hees, and cannot become grand admiral—the source to him of woes which one may call endless.

79. Woe, also, for *Ville de Paris*, the leviathan of ships! English Rodney has clutched it and led it home with the rest, so successful was his new"maneuver of breaking the enemy's line."† It seems as if, according to Louis XV., " France were never to have a navy." Brave Suffren must return from Hyder Ally and the Indian waters with small result, yet with great glory for " six" *non-defeats*, which, indeed, with such seconding as he had, one may reckon heroic. Let the old sea-hero rest now, honored of France, in his native Cevennes mountains; send smoke, not of gunpowder, but mere culinary smoke, through the old chimneys of the castle of Jalès, which one day, in other hands, shall have other fame. Brave Lapérouse shall by and by lift anchor on philanthropic voyage of discovery, for the king knows geography.‡ But, alas! this also will not prosper: the brave navigator goes, and returns not; the seekers search far seas for him in vain. He has vanished trackless into blue immensity, and only some mournful, mysterious shadow of him hovers long in all heads and hearts.

80. Neither, while the war yet lasts, will Gibraltar surrender. Not though Crillon, Nassau-Siegen, with the ablest projectors extant, are there, and Prince Condé and Prince d'Artois have hastened to help. Wondrous leather-roofed floating batteries, set afloat by French-Spanish pacte de famille, give gallant summons, to which, nevertheless, Gibraltar answers Plutonically with mere torrents of red-hot iron, as if stone Calpe had become a throat or the pit, and utters such a doom's-blast of a *No* as all men must credit.§

81. And so, with this loud explosion, the noise of war has ceased; an age of benevolence may hope, forever. Our noble volunteers of freedom have returned to be her missionaries. Lafayette, as the matchless of his time, glitters in the Versailles Œil-de-Bœuf;

* 27th July, 1778.
† 9th and 12th April, 1782.
‡ August 1, 1785.
§ "Annual Register" (Dodsley's), xxv. 258-267 September, October, 1782.

has his bust set up in the Paris Hotel-de-Ville. Democracy stands inexpugnable, immensurable, in her New World; has even a foot lifted toward the Old; and our French finances, little strengthened by such work, are in no healthy way.

82. What to do with the finances? This, indeed, is the great question; a small but most black weathersympton, which no radiance of universal hope can cover. We saw Turgot cast forth from the controllership, with shrieks, for want of a Fortunatus's purse. As little could M. de Clugny manage the duty; or, indeed, do anything but consume his wages; attain "a place in history," where as an ineffectual shadow thou beholdest him still lingering, and let the duty manage itself. Did Genevese Necker *possess* such a purse, then? He possessed banker's skill, banker's honesty; *credit* of all kinds, for he had written academic prize essays, struggled for India companies, given dinners to philosophes, and " realized a fortune in twenty years." He possessed, further, a taciturnity and solemnity, of depth, or else of dullness. How singular for Celadon Gibbon, false swain as he had proved—whose father, keeping most probably his own gig, " would not hear of such a union "—to find now his forsaken Demoiselle Curchod sitting in the high places of the world, as minister's madame, and " Necker not jealous!"*

83. A new young demoiselle, one day to be famed as a madame and a De Staël, was romping about the knees of the Decline and Fall; the Lady Necker founds hospitals, gives solemn philosophe dinner-parties, to cheer her exhausted controller-general. Strange things have happened—by clamor of philosophism, management of Marquis de l'ezay, and poverty constraining even kings. And so Necker, Atlaslike, sustains the burden of the finances for five years long.† Without wages, for he refused such; cheered only by public opinion, and the ministering of his noble wife. With many thoughts in him, it is hoped, which, however, he is shy of uttering. His "Compte Rendu," published by the royal permission—fresh sign of a new era—shows wonders, which what but the genius of some Atlas-Necker can prevent from becoming portents? In Necker's head, too, there is a whole pacific French revolution, of its kind; and in that taciturn dull depth, or deep dullness, ambition enough.

84. Meanwhile, alas, his Fortunatus's purse turns out to be little other than the old " vectigal of parsimony." Nay, he too has to produce his scheme of taxing; clergy, noblesse, to be taxed; provincial assemblies, and the rest, like a mere Turgot! The expiring M. de Maurepas must gyrate one other time. Let Necker also depart, not unlamented.

85. Great in a private station, Necker looks on from the distance, abiding his time. " Eighty thousand copies" of his new book, which he calls "Administration des Finances," will be sold in a few days. He is gone, but shall return, and that more than once, borne by a whole shouting nation. Singular controller-general of the finances, once clerk in Thelusson's bank!

CHAPTER VI.

WINDBAGS.

86. So marches the world, in this its paper age, or era of hope. Not without obstructions, war-explosions; which, however, heard from such distance, are little other than a cheerful marching music. If, indeed, that dark, living chaos of ignorance and hun-

* Gibbon's "Letters," date, 16th June, 1777, etc.
† Till May, 1781.

ger, five-and-twenty million strong, under your feet, were to begin playing!

87. For the present, however, consider Longchamp now when Lent is ending, and the glory of Paris and France has gone forth, as in annual wont. Not to assist at tenebris masses, but to sun itself and show itself, and salute the young spring.* Manifold, bright-tinted, glittering with gold; all through the Bois de Boulogne, in long-drawn variegated rows, like long-drawn living flower-borders, tulips, dahlias, lilies of the valley; all in their moving flower-pots (of new-gilt carriages); pleasure of the eye, and pride of life! So rolls and dances the procession, steady, of firm assurance, as if it rolled on adamant and the foundations of the world; not on mere heraldic parchment, under which smolders a lake of fire. Dance on, ye foolish ones; ye sought not wisdom, neither have ye found it. Ye and your fathers have sown the wind, ye shall reap the whirlwind. Was it not, from of old, written : *The wages of sin is death ?*

88. But at Longchamp, as elsewhere, we remark for one thing, that dame and cavalier are waited on each by a kind of human familiar, named *jokei.* Little elf, or imp; though young, already withered, with its withered air of premature vice, of knowingness, of completed elf-hood; useful in various emergencies. The name jokei (jockey) comes from the English, as the thing also fancies that it does. Our Anglomania, in fact, is grown considerable; prophetic of much. If France is to be free, why shall she not, now when mad-war is hushed, love neigboring freedom? Cultivated men, your Dukes de Liancourt, de la Rochefoucault, admire the English constitution, the English national character; would import what of it they can.

89. Of what is lighter, especially if it be light as wind, how much easier the freightage? Non-Admiral Duke de Chartres (not yet d'Orleans or Egalite) flies to and fro across the strait, importing English fashions; this he—as hand-and-glove with an English Prince of Wales—is surely qualified to do. Carriages and saddles, top-boots and redingotes, as we call riding-coats. Nay, the very mode of riding; for now no man on a level with his age but will trot à l'Anglaise, rising in the stirrups; scornful of the old sitfast method, in which, according to Shakespeare, "butter and eggs" go to market. Also, he can urge the fervid wheels, this brave Chartres of ours; no whip in Paris is rasher and surer than the unprofessional one of monseigneur.

90. Elf jokeis we have seen, but see now real Yorkshire jockeys, and what they ride on and train—English racers for French races. These, likewise, we owe first (under the providence of the devil) to monseigneur. Prince d'Artois has, withal, the strangest horse-leech, a moon-struck, much-enduring individual of Neufchâtel in Switzerland, named *Jean Paul Marat.* A problematic Chevalier d'Eon, now in petticoats, now in breeches, is no less problematic in London than in Paris, and causes bets and lawsuits. Beautiful days of international communion! Swindlery and blackguardism have stretched hands across the channel and saluted mutually; on the race-course of Vincennes or Sablons, behold, in English curricle-and-four, wafted glorious among the principalities and rascalities, an English Dr. Dodd,† for whom, also, too early gallows gapes.

91. Duke de Chartres was a young prince of great promise, as young princes often are; which promise, unfortunately, has belied itself. With the huge Orléans property, with Duke de Penthièvre for

father-in-law (and now the young brother-in-law Lamballe killed by excesses), he will one day be the richest man in France. Meanwhile, "his hair is all falling out, his blood is quite spoiled," by early transcendentalism of debauchery. Carbuncles stud his face—dark studs on a ground of burnished copper. A most signal failure, this young prince! The stuff prematurely burnt out of him, little left but foul smoke and ashes of expiring sensualities; what might have been thought, insight, and even conduct, gone now, or fast going, to confused darkness, broken by bewildering dazzlements; to obstreperous crotchets, to activities which you may call semi-delirious, or even semi-galvanic! Paris affects to laugh at his charioteering, but he heeds not such laughter.

92. On the other hand, what a day, not of laughter, was that when he threatened, for lucre's sake, to lay sacrilegious hands on the Palais Royal garden!* The flower-parterres shall be riven up, the chestnut avenues shall fall—time-honored boscages, under which the opera hamadryads were wont to wander, not inexorable to men. Paris moans aloud. Philidor, from his Café de la Régence, shall no longer look on greenness; the loungers and losels of the world, where now shall they haunt? In vain is moaning. The axe glitters, the sacred groves fall crashing, for indeed monseigneur was short of money; the opera hamadryads fly with shrieks. Shriek not, ye opera hamadryads, or not as those that have no comfort. He will surround your garden with new edifices and piazzas; though narrowed, it shall be replanted, dizened with hydraulic jets, cannon which the sun fires at noon; things bodily, things spiritual, such as man has not imagined—and in the Palais Royal shall again, and more than ever, be the *sorcerer's Sabbath* and *Satan-at-home* of our planet.

93. What will not mortals attempt? From remote Annonay in the Vivarais, the brothers Montgolfier send up their paper-dome, filled with the smoke of burnt wool.† The Vivarais provincial assembly is to be prorogued this same day; Vivarais assembly-members applaud, and the shouts of congregated men. Will victorious analysis scale the very heavens, then?

94. Paris hears with eager wonder; Paris shall ere long see. From Réveillon's paper-warehouse there, in the Rue St. Antoine (a noted warehouse), the new Montgolfier air-ship launches itself. Ducks and poultry have been borne skyward, but now shall men be borne.‡ Nay, Chemist Charles thinks of hydrogen and glazed silk. Chemist Charles will himself ascend, from the Tuileries garden, Montgolfier solemnly cutting the cord. By heaven, this Charles does also mount, he and another! Ten times ten thousand hearts go palpitating, all tongues are mute with wonder and fear—till a shout, like the voice of seas, rolls after him, on his wild way. He soars, he dwindles upward; has become a mere gleaming circlet—like some Turgotine snuff-box, what we call "Turgotine-platitude;" like some new daylight moon! Finally he descends, welcomed by the universe. Duchess Polignac, with a party, is in the Bois de Boulogne, waiting, though it is drizzly winter, the 1st of December, 1873. The whole chivalry of France, Duke de Chartres foremost, gallops to receive him.‡

95. Beautiful invention, mounting heavenward, so beautifully—so unguidably! Emblem of much, and of our age of hope itself; which shall mount, specifically-light, majestically in this same manner; and hover—tumbling whither fate will. Well if it do not, Pilâtre-like, explode, and demount all the more tragically! So, riding on windbags, will men scale the empyrean.

---

* Mercier, "Tableau de Paris," ii. 51. Louvet, "Roman de Faublas," etc.
† Adelung. " Geschichte der Menschlichen Narrheit."
‡ Dood.

* 1781-82. (Dulaure, viii. 423).
† 5th June, 1783.
‡ October and November, 1783.
§ Lacretelle, " 18me Siècle,' iii. 258.

96. Or observe Herr Doctor Mesmer, in his spacious magnetic halls. Long-stoled he walks, reverend, glancing upward, as in rapt-commerce—an antique Egyptian hierophant in this new age. Soft music flits, breaking fitfully the sacred stillness. Round their magnetic mystery—which to the eye is mere tubs with water—sit breathless, rod in hand, the circles of beauty and fashion, each circle a living circular *passion-flower*, expecting the magnetic afflatus and new-manufactured heaven-on-earth. O women, O men, great is your infidel faith? A parliamentary Duport, a Bergasse, D'Esprémènil we notice there; Chemist Berthollet too—on the part of Monseigneur de Chartres.

97. Had not the Academy of Sciences, with its Baillys, Franklins, Lavoisiers, interfered! But it did interfere.* Mesmer may pocket his hard money, and withdraw. Let him walk silent by the shore of the Bodensee, by the ancient town of Constance, meditating on much. For so, under the strangest new vesture, the old great truth (since no vesture can hide it) begins again to be revealed, that man is what we call a miraculous creature, with miraculous power over men; and, on the whole, with such a life in him, and such a world round him, as victorious analysis, with her physiologies, nervous-systems, physic and metaphysic, will never completely *name*, to say nothing of explaining. Wherein also the quack shall, in all ages, come in for his share.

CHAPTER VII.

CONTRAT SOCIAL.

98. In such succession of singular prismatic tints, flush after flush suffusing our horizon, does the era of hope dawn on toward fulfillment. Questionable! As indeed, with an era of hope that rests on mere universal benevolence, victorious analysis, vice cured of its deformity, and, in the long run, on twenty-five dark, savage millions, looking up, in hunger and weariness, to that ecce-signum of theirs " forty feet high "—how could it but be questionable?

99. Through all time, if we read aright, sin was, is, will be, the parent of misery. This land calls itself most Christian, and has crosses and cathedrals, but its high-priest is some Roche-Aymon, some Necklace-Cardinal Louis de Rohan. The voice of the poor, through long years, ascends inarticulate, in jacqueries, meal-mobs; low-whimpering of infinite moan, unheeded of the earth, not unheeded of heaven. Always, moreover, where the millions are wretched, there are the thousands straitened, unhappy; only the units can flourish, or say rather, be ruined the last. Industry, all noosed and haltered, as if it, too, were some beast of chase for the mighty hunters of this world to bait, and cut slices from, cries passionately to these its well-paid guides and watchers, not *Guide me*, but, Laissez faire; leave me alone of *your* guidance! What market has industry in this France? For two things there may be market and demand—for the coarser kind of field-fruits, since the millions will live; for the finer kinds of luxury and spicery, of multiform taste, from opera-melodies down to racers and courtesans, since the units will be amused. It is at bottom but a mad state of things.

100. To mend and remake all which we have, indeed, victorious analysis! Honor to victorious analysis! nevertheless, out of the workshop and laboratory, what thing was victorious analysis yet known to make? Detection of incoherences, mainly; destruction of the incoherent. From of old, doubt was but half a magician; she evokes the specters which she cannot quell. We shall have " endless vortices of

* August, 1784.

froth-logic," whereon first words, and then things, are whirled and swallowed. Remark, accordingly, as acknowledged grounds of hope, at bottom mere precursors of despair, this perpetual theorizing about man, the'mind of man, philosophy of government, progress of the species and such-like—the main thinking furniture of every head. Time, and so many Montesquieus, Mablys, spokesmen of time, have discovered innumerable things; and now has not Jean Jacques promulgated his new evangel of a " Contrat Social," explaining the whole mystery of government, and how it is *contracted* and bargained for, to universal satisfaction? Theories of government? Such have been, and will be, in ages of decadence. Acknowledge them in their degree, as processes of Nature, who does nothing in vain, as steps in her great process. Meanwhile, what theory is so certain as this, that all theories, were they never so earnest, painfully elaborated, are, and, by the very conditions of them must be, incomplete, questionable, and even false? Thou shalt know that this universe is what it professes to be, an *infinite* one. Attempt not to swallow *it*, for thy logical digestion; be thankful if, skillfully planting down this and the other fixed pillar in the chaos, thou prevent its swallowing *thee*. That a new young generation has exchanged the skeptic creed, *What shall I believe?* for passionate faith in this gospel according to Jean Jacques, is a further step in the business, and betokens much.

101. Blessed, also, is hope; and always from the beginning there was some millennium prophesied—millennium of holiness—but (what is notable) never, till this new era, any millennium of mere ease and plentiful supply. In such prophesied lubberland of happiness, benevolence, and vice cured of its deformity, trust not, my friends! Man is not what one calls a happy animal, his appetite for sweet victual is so enormous. How, in this wild universe, which storms in on him, infinite, vague-menacing, shall poor man find, say not happiness, but existence, and footing to stand on, if it be not by girding himself together for continual endeavor and endurance? Woe, if in his heart there dwelt no devout faith, if the word duty had lost its meaning for him! For as to this of sentimentalism, so useful for weeping with over romances and on pathetic occasions, it otherwise verily will avail nothing; nay, less. The healthy heart that said to itself, " How healthy am I!" was already fallen into the fatalest sort of disease. Is not sentimentalism twin sister to cant, if not one and the same with it? Is not cant the materia prima of the devil, from which all falsehoods, imbecilities, abominations, body themselves, from which no true thing can come? For cant is itself properly a double-distilled lie, the second-power of a lie.

102. And now if a whole nation fell into that? In such case, I answer, infallibly they will return out of it! For life is no cunningly-devised deception or self-deception: it is a great truth that thou art alive, that thou hast desires, necessities; neither can these subsist and satisfy themselves on delusions, but on fact. To fact, depend on it, we shall come back—to such fact, blessed or cursed, as we have wisdom for. The lowest, least blessed fact one knows of, on which necessitous mortals have ever based themselves, seems to be the primitive one of cannibalism—that *I* can devour *thee*. What if such primitive fact were precisely the one we had (with our improved methods) to revert to, and begin anew from!

CHAPTER VIII.

PRINTED PAPER.

103. In such a practical France, let the theory of perfectibility say what it will, discontents cannot be

wanting; your promised reformation is so indispensable; yet it comes not; who will begin it—with himself? Discontent with what is around us, still more with what is above us, goes on increasing; seeking ever new events.

104. Of street ballads, of epigrams that from of old tempered despotism, we need not speak. Nor of manuscript newspapers (nouvelles à la main) do we speak. Bachaumont and his journeymen and followers may close those "thirty volumes of scurrilous eaves-dropping," and quit that trade; for at length, if not liberty of the press, there is license. Pamphlets can be surreptitiously vened and read in Paris, did they even bear to be "printed at Pekin." We have a Courrier de l'Europe in those years, regularly published, at London, by a De Morande, whom the guillotine has not yet devoured. There, too, an unruly Linguet, still unguillotined, when his own country has become too hot for him, and his brother advocates have cast him out can emit his hoarse wailing and "Bastille Dévoilée" (Bastille Unveiled.) Loquacious Abbé Raynal at length has his wish; sees the "Histoire Philosophique," with its "lubricity," unveracity, loose, loud, eleutheromaniac rant (contributed they say, by philosophedom at large, though in the abbé's name and to his glory), burnt by the common hangman—and sets out on his travels as a martyr. It was the edition of 1871; perhaps the last notable book that had such fire-beatitude—the hangman discovering now that it did not serve.

105. Again, in courts of law, with their money-quarrels, divorce-cases, wheresover a glimpse into the household-existence can be had, what indications! The parlements of Besançon and Aix ring, audible to all France, with the amours and destinies of a young Mirabeau. He, under the nurture of a "friend of men," has, in state prisons, in marching regiments, Dutch author's-garrets, and quite other scenes, "been for twenty years learning to resist despotism" —despotism of men, and, alas! also of gods. How, beneath this rose-colored veil of universal benevolence and astræa redux, is the sanctuary of home so often a dreary void, or a dark, contentious hell-on-earth! The old friend of men has his own divorce-case, too, and at times, "his whole family but one" under lock and key. He writes much about reforming and enfranchising the world; and for his own private behoof he has needed sixty lettres-de-cachet. A man of insight, too; with resolution, even with manful principle; but in such an element, inward and outward; which he could not rule, but only madden. Edacity, rapacity—quite contrary to the finer sensibilities of the heart! Fools, that expect your verdant millennium, and nothing but love and abundance, brooks running wine, winds whispering music—with the whole ground and basis of your existence champed into a mud of sensuality which, daily growing deeper, will soon have no bottom but the abyss!

106. Or consider that unutterable business of the diamond necklace. Red-hatted Cardinal Louis de Rohan; Sicilian jail-bird Balsamo Cagliostro; milliner Dame de Lamotte, "with a face of some piquancy:" the highest church dignitaries waltzing, in Walpurgis dance, with quack-prophets, pickpurses and public women—a whole Satan's invisible world displayed; working there continually under the daylight visible one; the smoke of its torment going up forever! The throne has been brought into scandalous collision with the treadmill. Astonished Europe rings with the mystery for nine months; sees only lie unfold itself from lie; corruption among the lofty and the low, gulosity, credulity, imbecility—strength nowhere but in the hunger. Weep, fair queen, thy first tear of unmixed wretchedness! Thy

fair name has been tarnished by foul breath; irremediably while life lasts. No more shalt thou be loved and pitied by living hearts, till a new generation has been born, and thy own heart lies cold, cured of all its sorrows. The epigrams henceforth become, not sharp and bitter, but cruel, atrocious, unmentionable. On that 31st of May, 1786, a miserable Cardinal Grand-Almoner Rohan, on issuing from his Bastille, is escorted by hurrahing crowds; unloved he, and worthy of no love; but important since the court and queen are his enemies.*

107. How is our bright era of hope dimmed, and the whole sky growing bleak with signs of hurricane and earthquake! It is a doomed world: gone all "obedience that made men free:" fast going the obedience that made men slaves—at least to one another. Slaves only of their own lusts they now are, and will be. Slaves of sin; inevitable also of sorrow. Behold the moldering mass of sensuality and falsehood; round which plays foolishly, itself a corrupt phosphorescence, some glimmer of sentimentalism; and over all, rising, as ark of their covenant, the grim patibulary fork "forty feet high;" which also is now nigh rotted. Add only that the French nation distinguishes itself among nations by the characteristic of excitability; with the good, but also with the perilous evil, which belongs to that. Rebellion, explosion, of unknown extent is to be calculated on. There are, as Chesterfield wrote, "all the symptoms I have ever met with in history!"

108. Shall we say, then, woe to philosophism, that it destroyed religion, what it called "extinguishing the abomination (écraser l'infâme)?" Woe rather to those that made the holy an abomination, and extinguishable; woe to all men that live in such a time of world-abomination and world-destruction! Nay, answer the courtiers, it was Turgot, it was Necker, with their mad innovating; it was the queen's want of etiquette; it was he, it was she, it was that. Friends! it was every scoundrel that had lived, and quack-like pretended to be doing, and been only eating and misdoing, in all provinces of life, as shoe-black or as sovereign lord, each in his degree, from the time of Charlemagne and earlier. All this (for be sure no falsehood perishes, but is as seed sown out to grow) has been storing itself for thousands of years; and now the account-day has come. And rude will the settlement be: of wrath laid up against the day of wrath. O my brother, be not thou a quack! die rather, if thou wilt take counsel; 'tis but dying once, and thou art quit of it forever. Cursed is that trade; and bears curses, thou knowest not how, long ages after thou art departed, and the wages thou hast are all consumed; nay, as the ancient wise have written—through eternity itself, and is verily marked in the doom-book of a god!

109. Hope deferred maketh the heart sick. And yet, as we said, hope is but deferred; not abolished, not abolishable. It is very notable, and touching, how this same hope does still light onward the French nation through all its wild destinies. For we shall still find hope shining, be it for fond invitation, be it for anger and menace; as a mild heavenly light it shone; as a red conflagration it shines: burning sulphurous-blue, through darkest regions of terror, it still shines; and goes out not at all, since desperation itself is a kind of hope. Thus is our era still to be named of hope, though in the saddest sense—when there is nothing left but hope.

110. But if any one would know summarily what a Pandora's box is there for the opening, he may see it in what by its nature is the symptom of all

* Fils Adoptif, "Mémoires de Mirabeau," iv. 325. See Carlyle's "Biographical Essays," § Diamond Necklace. § Count Cagliostro.

symptoms, the surviving literature of the period. Abbé Raynal, with his lubricity and loud, loose rant, has spoken *his* word ; and already the fast-hasteuing generation responds to another. Glance at Beaumar chais's "Mariage de Figaro;" which now (in 1784), after difficulty enough, has issued on the stage; and "runs its hundred nights," to the admiration of all men. By what virtue or internal vigor it so ran, the reader of our day will rather wonder—and indeed will know so much the better that it flattered some pruriency of the time, that it spoke what all were feeling, and longing to speak. Small substance in that "Figaro:" thin, wire-drawn intrigues, thin, wire-drawn sentiments and sarcasms; a thing lean, barren, yet which winds and whisks itself, as through a wholly mad universe, adroitly, with a high-sniffing air : wherein each, as was hinted, which is the grand secret, may see some image of himself, and of his own state and ways. So it runs its hundred nights, and all France runs with it; laughing applause. If the soliloquizing barber ask, "What has your lordship done to earn all this?" and can only answer, "You took the trouble to be born (Vous vous êtes donné la peine de nâtre)," all men must laugh ; and a gay, horse-racing, Anglomaniac noblesse loudest of all. For how can small books have a great danger in them ? asks the Sieur Caron, and fancies his thin epigram may be a kind of reason. Conqueror of a golden fleece, by giant smuggling; tamer of hell-dogs, in the Parlement Maupeon; and finally crowned Orpheus in the Théâtre Français, Beaumarchais has now culminated, and unites the attributes of several demi-gods. We shall meet him once again, in the course of his decline.

111. Still more significant are two books produced on the eve of the ever memorable explosion itself, and read eagerly by all the world, Saint Pierre's "Paul et Virginie," and Louvet's "Chevalier de Faublas." Noteworthy books, which may be considered as the last speech of old feudal France. In the first, there rises melodiously, as it were, the wail of a moribund world ; everywhere wholesome nature in unequal conflict with diseased, perfidious art; cannot escape from it in the lowest hut, in the remotest island of the sea. Ruin and death must strike down the loved one; and, what is most significant of all, death even here not by necessity but by etiquette. What a world of prurient corruption lies visible in that super-sublime of modesty! Yet, on the whole, our good Saint Pierre is musical, poetical, though most morbid : we will call his book the swan-song of old dying France.

112. Louvet's, again, let no man account musical. Truly, if this wretched "Faublas" is a death-speech, it is one under the gallows, and by a felon that does not repent. Wretched cloaca of a book, without depth even as a cloaca! What "picture of French society" is here? Picture properly of nothing, if not of the mind that gave it out as some sort of picture. Yet symptom of much ; above all, of the world that could nourish itself thereon.

BOOK THIRD.

THE PARLEMENT OF PARIS.

CHAPTER I.

DISHONORED BILLS.

113. While the unspeakable confusion is everywhere weltering within, and through so many cracks in the surface sulphur-smoke is issuing, the question arises. Through what crevice will the main explosion carry itself? Through which of the old craters or

chimneys; or must it at once form a new crater for itself? In every society are such chimneys, are institutions serving as such ; even Constantinople is not without its safety-valves ; there, too, discontent can vent itself—in material fire ; by the number of nocturnal conflagrations, or of hanged bakers, the reigning power can read the signs of the times, and change course according to these.

114. We may say that this French explosion will doubtless first try all the old institutions of escape; for by each of these there is, or at least there used to be, some communication with the interior deep ; they are national institutions in virtue of that. Had they even become personal institutions, and what we can call choked up from their original uses, there, nevertheless, must the impediment be weaker than elsewhere. Through which of them, then ? An observer might have guessed, Through the law parlements ; above all, through the parlement of Paris.

115. Men, though never so thickly clad in dignities, sit not inaccessible to the influences of their time ; especially men whose life is business; who at all turns, were it even iron behind judgment-seats, have come in contact with the actual workings of the world. The counselor of parlement, the president himself, who has bought his place with hard money that he might be looked up to by his fellow-creatures, how shall he, in all philosophic soirées, and saloons of elegant culture, become notable as a friend of darkness ? Among the Paris long-robes there may be more than one patriotic Malesherbes, whose rule is conscience and the public good; there are clearly more than one hot-headed D'Esprémenil, to whose confused thought any loud reputation of the Brutus sort may seem glorious. The Lepelletiers, Lamoignons, have titles and wealth; yet, at court, are only styled "noblesse of the robe." There are Duports of deep scheme; Fréteaus, Sabatiers, of incontinent tongue—all nursed more or less on the milk of the contrat social. Nay, for the whole body, is not this patriotic opposition also a-fighting for oneself? Awake, parlement of Paris, renew thy long warfare! Was not the Parlement Maupeon abolished with ignominy ? Not now hast thou to dread a Louis XIV., with the crack of his whip, and his Olympian looks; not now a Richelieu and bastilles: no, the whole nation is behind thee. Thou, too (O heavens !), mayest become a political power; and with the shakings of thy horse-hair wig shake principalities and dynasties, like a very Jove with his ambrosial curls!

116. Light old M. de Maurepas, since the end of 1781, has been fixed in the frost of death. "Never more," said the good Louis, "shall I hear his step in the room there overhead ;" his light jestings and gyratings are at an end. No more can the importunate reality be hidden by pleasant wit, and to-day's evil be deftly rolled over upon to-morrow. The morrow itself has arrived ; and now nothing but a solid, phlegmatic M. de Vergennes sits there, in dull matter of fact, like some dull, punctual clerk (which be originally was); admits what cannot be denied, let the remedy come whence it will. In him is no remedy, only clerk-like "dispatch of business" according to routine. The poor king, grown older, yet hardly more experienced, must himself, with such no-faculty as he has, begin governing, wherein also his queen will give help. Bright queen, with her quick, clear glances and impulses; clear, and even noble; but all to superficial, vehement-shallow, for that work! To govern France were such a problem ! and now it has grown well-nigh too hard to govern even the Œil-de-Bœuf. For if a distressed people has its cry, so likewise, and more audibly, has a bereaved court. To the Œil-de-Bœuf it remains inconceivable how, in a France of such resources, the horn of plenty should

run dry; did it not *use* to flow? Nevertheless, Necker, with his revenue of parsimony, has "suppressed above six hundred places," before the courtiers could oust him, parsimonious finance-pedant as he was. Again, a military pedant, Saint-Germain, with his Prussian manœuvers, with his Prussian notions, as if merit and not coat of arms should be the rule of promotion, has disaffected military men, the mousquetaires, with much else, are suppressed · for he, too, was one of your suppressors; and unsettling and oversetting did mere mischief—to the Œil-de-Bœuf. Complaints abound; scarcity, anxiety · it is a changed Œil-de-lœuf. Besenval says, already in these years (1781) there was such a melancholy (such a tristesse) about court, compared with former days, as made it quite dispiriting to look upon.

117. No wonder that the Œil-de-Bœuf feels melancholy, when you are suppressing its places! Not a place can be suppressed but some purse is the lighter for it, and more than one heart the heavier; for did it not employ the working-classes too—manufacturers, male and female, of laces, essences; of pleasure generally—whosoever could manufacture pleasure? Miserable economies, never felt over twenty-five millions! So, however, it goes on, and is not yet ended. Few years more and the wolf-hounds shall fall suppressed, the bear-hounds, the falconry; places shall fall, thick as autumnal leaves. Duke de Polignac demonstrates, to the complete silencing of ministerial logic, that his place cannot be abolished; then gallantly, turning to the queen, surrenders it, since her majesty so wishes. Less chivalrous was Duke de Coigny, and yet not luckier. "We got into a real quarrel, Coigny and I," said King Louis; "but if he had even struck me, I could not have blamed him."* In regard to such matters there can be but one opinion. Baron Besenval, with that frankness or speech which stamps the independent man, plainly assures her majesty that it is frightful (affreux); "you go to bed, and are not sure but you shall rise impoverished on the morrow: one might as well be in Turkey." It is, indeed, a dog's life.

118. How singular this perpetual distress of the royal treasury! And yet it is a thing not more incredible than undeniable. A thing mournfully true the stumbling-block on which all ministers successively stumble, and fall. Be it "want of fiscal genius," or some far other want, there is the palpablest discrepancy between revenue and expenditure; a *deficit* of the revenue: you must "choke (combler) the deficit," or else it will swallow you! This is the stern problem; hopeless, seemingly, as squaring of the circle. Controller Joly de Fleury, who succeeded Necker, could do nothing with it; nothing but propose loans, which were tardily filled up; impose new taxes, unproductive of money, productive of clamor and discontent. As little could Controller d'Ormesson do, or even less; for if Joly maintained himself beyond year and day, D'Ormesson reckons only by months: till "the king purchased Rambouillet without consulting him," which he took as a hint to withdraw. And so, toward the end of 1783, matters threatened to come to a stand-still. Vain seems human ingenuity. In vain has our newly-devised "council of finances" struggled; our intendants of finance, controller-general of finances; there are so unhappily no finances to control. Fatal paralysis invades the social movement; clouds, of blindness or of blackness, envelop us: are we breaking down, then, into the black horrors of *national bankruptcy?*

119. Great is bankruptcy—the great bottomless gulf into which all falsehoods, public and private, do sink, disappearing; whither from the first origin of them, they were all doomed. For nature is true and

*Besenval, III. 255-58.

not a lie. No lie you can speak or act but it will come, after longer or shorter circulation, like a bill drawn on nature's reality, and be presented there for payment—with the answer, *No effects.* Pity only that it often had so long a circulation; that the original forger were so seldom he who bore the final smart of it! Lies, and the burden of evil they bring, are passed on; shifted from back to back, and from rank to rank; and so land ultimately on the dumb lowest rank, who with spade and mattock, with sore heart and empty wallet, daily come in *contact* with reality, and can pass the cheat no further.

120. Observe, nevertheless, how, by a just compensating law, if the lie with his burden (in this confused whirlpool of society) sinks and is shifted ever downward, then in return the distress of it rises ever upward and upward. Whereby, after the long pining and demi-starvation of those twenty millions, a Duke de Coigny and his majesty come also to have their "real quarrel." Such is the law of just nature; bringing—though at long intervals, and were it only by bankruptcy—matters round again to the mark.

121. But with a Fortunatus's purse in his pocket, through what length of time might not almost any falsehood last! Your society, your household, practical or spiritual arrangement, is untrue, unjust, offensive to the eye of God and man. Nevertheless, its hearth is warm, its larder well replenished: the innumerable Swiss of heaven, with a kind of natural loyalty, gather round it; will prove, by pamphleteering, musketeering, that it is a truth; or if not an unmixed (unearthly, impossible) truth, then better, a wholesomely attempered one (as wind is to the shorn lamb), and works well. Changed outlook, however, when purse and larder grow empty! Was your arrangement so true, so accordant to nature's ways, then, how, in the name of wonder, has nature, with her infinite bounty, come to leave it famishing there? To all men, to all women, and all children, it is now indubitable that your arrangement was *false.* Honor to bankruptcy; ever righteous on the great scale, though in detail it is so cruel! Under all falsehoods it works, unweariedly mining. No falsehood, did it rise heaven-high and cover the world, but bankruptcy, one day, will sweep it down, and make us free of it.

CHAPTER II.

CONTROLLER CALONNE.

122. Under such circumstances [of 'tristesse,' obstruction, and sick languor, when to an exasperated court it seems as if fiscal genius had departed from among men, what apparition could be welcomer than that of M. de Calonne? Calonne, a man of indisputable genius, even fiscal genius, more 'or less; of experience both in managing finance and parlements, for he has been intendant at Metz, at Lille; king's procureur at Douai. A man of weight, connected with the moneyed classes; of unstained name—if it were not some peccadillo (of showing a client's letter) in that old D'Aiguillou-Lachalotais business, as good as forgotten now. He has kinsmen of heavy purse, felt on the stock exchange. Our Foulons, Berthiers, intrigue for him—old Foulon, who has now nothing to do but intrigue; who is known and even seen to be what they call a scoundrel; but of unmeasured wealth; who, from commissariat clerk which he once was, may hope, some think, if the game go right, to be minister himself one day.

123. Such propping and backing has M. de Calonne; and then intrinsically such qualities! Hope radiates from his face; persuasion hangs on his tongue. For all straits he has present remedy, and will make the world roll on wheels before him. On the 3d of No-

vember, 1783, the Œil-de-Bœuf rejoices in its new controller-general. Calonne also shall have trial; Calonne, also in his way, as Turgot and Necker had done in theirs, shall forward the consummation; suffuse, with one other flush of brilliancy, our now too leaden colored era of hope, and wind it up—into fulfillment.

124. Great, in any case, is the felicity of the Œil-de-Bœuf. Stinginess has fled from these royal abodes: suppression ceases; your Besenval may go peaceably to sleep, sure that he shall awake unplundered. Smiling plenty, as if conjured by some enchanter, has returned; scatters contentment from her new flowing horn. And mark what suavity of manners! A bland smile distinguishes our controller: to all men he listens with an air of interest, nay, of anticipation; makes their own wish clear to themselves, and grants it; or, at least, grants conditional promise of it. "I fear this is a matter of difficulty," said her majesty. "Madame," answered the controller, "if it is but difficult, it is done; if it is impossible, it shall be done (se fera)." A man of such "facility," withal. To observe him in the pleasure-vortex of society, which none partakes of with more gusto, you might ask, When does he work? And yet his work, as we see, is never behind-hand; above all, the fruit of his work—ready money. Truly a man of incredible facility; facile action, facile elocution, facile thought; how, in mild suasion, philosophic depth sparkles up from him, as mere wit and lambent sprightliness; and in her majesty's soirées, with the weight of a world lying on him, he is the delight of men and women! By what magic does he accomplish miracles? By the only true magic, that of genius. Men name him "*the* minister;" as, indeed, when was there another such? Crooked things are become straight by him, rough places plain; and over the Œil-de-Bœuf there rest an unspeakable sunshine.

125. Nay, in seriousness, let no man say that Calonne had not genius—genius for persuading; before all things, for borrowing. With the skillfulest judicious appliances of underhand money, he keeps the stock exchanges flourishing; so that loan after loan is filled up as soon as opened. "Calculators likely to know"* have calculated that he spent, in extraordinaries, "at the rate of one million daily;" which, indeed, is some 50,000 pounds sterling; but did he not procure something with it; namely, peace and prosperity, for the time being? Philosophedom grumbles and croaks; buys, as we said, 80,000 copies of Necker's new book: but Nonpareil Calonne, in her majesty's apartment, with the glittering retinue of dukes, duchesses, and more happy admiring faces, can let Necker and philosophedom croak.

126. The misery is, such a time cannot last! Squandering and payment by loan is no way to choke a deficit. Neither is oil the substance for quenching conflagrations—alas, no, only for assuaging them, *not* permanently! To the Nonpareil himself, who wanted not insight, it is clear at intervals, and dimly certain at all times, that his trade is by nature temporary, growing daily more difficult; that changes incalculable lie at no great distance. Apart from financial deficit,'the world is wholly in such a new-fangled humor; all things working loose from their old fastenings toward new issues and combinations. There is not a dwarf jokei, a cropt Brutus's head, or Anglomaniac horseman rising on his stirrups, that does not betoken change. But what then? The day, in any case, passes pleasantly; for the morrow, if the morrow come, there shall be counsel too. Once mounted (by munificence, suasion, magic of genius) high enough in favor with the Œil-de-Bœuf, with the

king, queen, stock exchange, and so far as possible with all men, a nonpareil controller may hope to go careering through the inevitable, in some unimagined way, as handsomely as another.

127. At all events, for these three miraculous years, it has been expedient heaped on expedient; till now, with such cumulation and height, the pile topples perilous. And here has this world's-wonder of a diamond necklace brought it at last to the clear verge of tumbling. Genius in that direction can no more: mounted high enough, or not mounted, we must fare forth. Hardly is poor Rohan, the necklace-cardinal, safely bestowed in the Auvergne mountains, Dame de Lamotte (unsafely) in the Salpêtrière, and that mournful business hushed-up, when our sanguine controller once more astonishes the world. An expedient, unheard of for these 160 years, has been propounded; and by dint of suasion (for his light audacity, his hope and eloquence, are matchless) has been got adopted—*convocation of the notables.*

128. Let notable persons, the actual or virtual rulers of their districts, be summoned from all sides of France; let a true tale, of his majesty's patriotic purposes and wretched pecuniary impossibilities, be sunsively told them; and then the question put, What are we to do? Surely to adopt healing measures, such as the magic of genius will unfold; such as, once sanctioned by notables, all parlements and all men must, with more or less reluctance, submit to.

CHAPTER III.

THE NOTABLES.

129. Here, then, is verily a sign and wonder; visible to the whole world: bodeful of much. The Œil-de-Bœuf dolorously grumbles; were we not well as we stood—quenching conflagrations by oil? Constitutional philosophedom starts with joyful surprise; stares eagerly what the result will be. The public creditor, the public debtor, the whole thinking and thoughtless public, have their several surprises, joyful or sorrowful. Count Mirabeau, who has got his matrimonial and other lawsuits huddled up, better or worse, and works now in the dimmest element at Berlin, compiling "Prussian Monarchies," pamphlets "On Cagliostro," writing, with pay, but not with honorable recognition, innumerable dispatches for his government—scents or descries richer quarry from afar. He, like an eagle or vulture, or mixture of both, preens his wings for flight homeward.*

130. M. de Calonne has stretched out an Aaron's rod over France; miraculous; and is summoning quite unexpected things. Audacity and hope alternate in him with misgivings, though the sanguine-valiant side carries it. Anon he writes to an intimate friend, "Je me fais pitié à moi-même (I am an object of pity to myself);" anon, invites some dedicating poet or poetaster to sing "this assembly of the notables, and the revolution that is preparing."† Preparing, indeed; and a matter to be sung, only not till we have *seen* it, and what the issue of it is. In deep, obscure unrest, all things have so long gone rocking and swaying, will M. de Calonne, with this, his alchemy of the notables, fasten altogether again, and get new revenues? Or wrench all asunder, so that it go no longer rocking and swaying, but clashing and colliding?

131. Be this as it may, in the bleak, short days, we behold men of weight and influence threading the great vortex of French locomotion, each on his several line, from all sides of France, toward the château

* Fils Adoptif, "Memoires de Mirabeau," t. iv. llvy. 4, et 5.

† "Biographie Universelle," i Calonne (by Guizot).

* Besenval, iii. 216.

of Versailles, summoned thither de par le roi. There, on the 22d day of February, 1787, they have met and got installed: notables to the number of 137 as we count them name by name;[*] add seven princes of the blood, it makes the round gross of notables. Men of the sword, men of the robe, peers, dignified clergy, parlementary presidents: divided into seven boards (bureaux), under our seven princes of the blood, Monsieur D'Artois, Penthièvre, and the rest, among whom let not our new Duke d'Orleans (for, since 1785 he is Chartres no longer) be forgotten. Never yet made admiral, and now turning the corner of his fortieth year, with spoiled blood and prospects, half weary of a world which is more than half weary of him, monseigneur's future is most questionable. Not in illumination and insight, not even in conflagration, but, as was said, "in dull smoke and ashes of outburnt sensualities," does he live and digest. Sumptuosity and sordidness, revenge, life-weariness, ambition, darkness, putrescence; and, say, in sterling money, 300,000 a year, were this poor prince once to burst loose from his court-moorings, to what regions, with what phenomena, might he not sail and drift? Happily, as yet, he "affects to hunt daily;" sits there, since he must sit, presiding that bureau of his, with dull moon-visage, dull, glassy eyes, as if it were a mere tedium to him.

132. We observe, finally, that Count Mirabeau has actually arrived. He descends from Berlin on the scene of action, glares into it with flashing sun-glance, discerns that it will do nothing for him. He had hoped these notables might need a secretary. They do need one, but have fixed on Dupont de Nemours, a man of smaller fame, but then of better, who, indeed, as his friends often hear, labors under this complaint, surely not a universal one, of having "five kings to correspond with."[†] The pen of a Mirabeau cannot become an official one, nevertheless it remains a pen. In defect of secretaryship, he sets to denouncing stock-brokerage (dénonciation de l'agiotage), testifying, as his wont is, by loud bruit, that he is present and busy; till, warned by friend Talleyrand, and even by Calonne himself underhand, that a "seventeenth lettre-de-cachet may be launched against him," he timefully flits over the marches.

133. And now, in stately royal apartments, as pictures of that time still represent them, our hundred and forty-four notables sit organized, ready to hear and consider. Controller Calonne is dreadfully behind hand with his speeches, his preparatives; however, the man's "facility of work" is known to us. For freshness of style, lucidity, ingenuity, largeness of view, that opening harangue of his was unsurpassable—had not the subject-matter been so appalling. A deficit, concerning which accounts vary—and the controller's own account is not unquestioned—but which all accounts agree in representing as "enormous." This is the epitome of our controller's difficulties; and then his means? Mere Turgotism, for thither, it seems, we must come at last: provincial assemblies, new taxation; nay, strangest of all, new land-tax, what he calls subvention territoriale, from which neither privileged nor unprivileged, noblemen, clergy, nor parlementeers, shall be exempt.

134. Foolish enough! These privileged classes have been used to tax; levying toll, tribute, and custom, at all hands, while a penny was left—but to be themselves taxed? Of such privileged persons, meanwhile, do these notables, all but the merest fraction, consist. Headlong Calonne had given no heed to the "composition," or judicious packing of

them; but chosen such notables as were really notable, trusting for the issue to off-hand ingenuity, good-fortune, and eloquence that never yet failed. Headlong controller-general! Eloquence can do much, but not all. Orpheus, with eloquence grown rhythmic, musical (what we call poetry), drew iron tears from the cheek of Pluto; but by what witchery of rhime or prose wilt thou from the pocket of Plutus draw gold?

135. Accordingly, the storm that now rose and began to whistle round Calonne, first in these seven bureaus, and then on the outside of them, awakened by them, spreading wider and wider over all France, threatens to become unappeasable. A deficit so enormous! Mismanagement, profusion, is too clear. Peculation itself is hinted at; nay, Lafayette and others go so far as to speak it out, with attempts at proof. The blame of his deficit our brave Calonne, as was natural, had endeavored to shift from himself on his predecessors; not excepting even Necker. But now Necker vehemently denies; whereupon an "angry correspondence," which also finds its way into print.

136. In the Œil-de-Bœuf and her majesty's private apartments, an eloquent controller, with his "madame, if it is but difficult, "had been persuasive; but, alas, the cause is now carried elsewhither. Behold him, one of these sad days, in monsieur's bureau; to which all the other bureaus have sent deputies. He is standing at bay; alone; exposed to an incessant fire of questions, interpellations, objurgations, from those "hundred and thirty-seven" pieces of logic-ordnance—what we may call bouches à feu, fire-mouths literally! Never, according to Besenval, or hardly ever, had such display of intellect, dexterity, coolness, suasive eloquence, been made by man. To the raging play of so many fire-mouths he opposes nothing angrier than light-beams, self-possession, and fatherly smiles. With the imperturbablest bland clearness, he, for five hours long, keeps answering the incessant volley of fiery, captious questions, reproachful interpellations in words prompt as lightning, quiet as light. Nay, the cross-fire, too; such side-questions and incidental interpellations as, in the heat of the main battle, he (having only one tongue) could not get answered; these, also, he takes up, at the first slake; answers even these.[*] Could blandest suasive eloquence have saved France, she were saved.

137. Heavy-laden controller! In the seven bureaus seems nothing but hindrance: in monsieur's bureau, a Loménie de Brinne, Archbishop of Toulouse, with an eye himself to the controllership, stirs up the clergy; there are meetings, underground intrigues. Neither from without anywhere comes sign of help or hope. For the nation (where Mirabeau is now, with stentor-lungs, "denouncing agio") the controller has hitherto done nothing, or less. For philosophedom he has done as good as nothing—sent out some scientific Lapérouse, or the like: and he is not in "angry correspondence" with its Necker? The very Œil-de-Bœuf looks questionable; a falling controller has no friends. Solid M. de Vergennes, who with his phlegmatic, judicious punctuality might have kept down many things, died the very week before these sorrowful notables met. And now a seal-keeper, Garde-des-Sceaux, Miroménil, is thought to be playing the traitor—spinning plots for Loménie-Brienne! Queen's-Reader Abbé de Vermond, unloved individual, was Brienne's creature, the work of his hands from the first: it may be feared the back-stairs passage is open, the ground getting mined under our feet. Treacherous Garde-des-Sceaux Miroménil, at least, should be dismissed; Lamoignon, the eloquent notable, a stanch man, with connections, and even ideas,

* Lacretelle, iii. 236. Montgaillard, i, 347.
† Dumont, "Souvenirs sur Mirabeau" (Paris, 1832), p. 30.
* Besenval, iii. 196.

parlement-president yet intent on reforming parle-ments, were not he the right keeper? So, for one, thinks busy Besenval; and, at dinner-table, rounds the same into the controller's ear—who always, in the intervals of landlord-duties, listens to him as with charmed look, but answers nothing positive.*

138. Alas, what to answer? The force of private intrigue, and then also the force of public opinion, grows so dangerous, confused! Philosophedom sneers aloud, as if its Necker already triumphed. The gaping populace gapes over wood-cuts or copper cuts; where for example, a rustic is represented convoking the poultry of his barnyard, with this opening ad-dress: "Dear animals, I have assembled you to ad-vise me what sauce I shall dress you with:" to which a cock responded, "We don't want to be eaten;" is checked by, "You wander from the point. (Vous vous écartez de la question),"† Laughter and logic; ballad-singer, pamphleteer; epigram and caricature: what wind of public opinion is this—as if the cave of the winds were bursting loose! At nightfall Pre-sident Lamoignon steals over to the controller's, finds him "walking with large strides in his chamber; like one out of himself."‡ With rapid confused speech the controller begs M. de Lamoignon to give him "an advice." Lamoignon candidly answers that, except in regard to his own anticipated keepership, unless that would prove remedial, he really cannot take upon him to advise.

139. "On the Monday after Easter," the 9th of April, 1787, a date one rejoices to verify, for nothing can excel the indolent falsehood of these "Histoires" and "Mémoires"—"on the Monday after Easter, as I, Besenval, was riding towards Romainville to the Maréchal de Ségur's, I met a friend on the boulevard, who told me that M. de Calonne was out. A little further on came M. the duke d'Orléans, dashing toward me, head to the wind"(trotting à l'Anglaise), "and confirmed the news."§ It is true news. Treach-erous Garde-des-Sceaux Biroménil is gone, and Lamoignon is appointed in his room; but appointed for his own profit only, not for the controller's: "next day" the controller, also, has had to move. A little longer he may linger near; be seen among the money-changers, and even "working in the control-ler's office," where much lies unfinished; but neither will that hold. Too strong blows and beats this tempest of public opinion, of private intrigue, as from the cave of all the winds; and blows him (higher authority giving sign) out of Paris and France—over the horizon, into invisibility, or outer darkness.

140. Such destiny the magic of genius could not forever avert Ungrateful Œil-de-Bœuf! did he not miraculously rain gold manna on you; so that, as a courtier said, "All the world held out its hand, and I held out my hat"—for a time? Himself is poor; penniless, had not a "financier's widow in Lorraine" offered him, though he was turned of fifty, her hand and the rich purse it held. Dim, henceforth, shall be his activity, though unwearied; letters to the king, appeals, prognostications, pamphlets (from Lon-don), written with the old suasive facility, which, however, do not persuade. Luckily his widow's purse fails not. Once, in a year or two, some shadow of him shall be seen hovering on the northern border, seeking election as national deputy; but be sternly beckoned away. Dimmer, then, far-borne over ut-most European lands, in uncertain twilight of diplo-macy, he shall hover, intriguing for "exiled princes,"

and have adventures; be overset into the Rhine-stream and half-drowned, nevertheless save his papers dry. Unwearied, but in vain! In France he works miracles no more, shall hardly return thither to find a grave. Farewell, thou facile, sanguine controller-general, with thy light rash hand, thy suasive mouth of gold: worse men there have been, and better; but to thee, also, was allotted a task—of raising the wind, and the winds; and thou has done it.

141. But now, while Ex-Controller Calonne flies storm-driven over the horizon, in this singular way, what has become of the controllership? It hangs vacant, one may say extinct, like the moon in her vacant interlunar cave. Two preliminary shadows, poor M. Fourqueux, poor M. Villedeuil, do hold, in quick succession, some simulacrum of it*—as the new moon will sometimes shine out with a dim, prelimi-nary old one in her arms. Be patient, ye notables! An actual new controller is certain, and even ready; were the indispensable manœuvres but gone through. Long-headed Lamoignon, with Home-Secretary Bre-teuil, and Foreign Secretary Montmorin have ex-changed looks; let these three once meet and speak. Who is it that is strong in the queen's favor, and the Abbé de Vermond's? That is a man of great capa-city? Or, at least, that has struggled, these fifty years, to have it thought great; now, in the clergy's name, demanding to have Protestant death-penalties " put in execution ;" now flaunting it in the Œil-de-Bœuf, as the gayest man-pleaser and woman-pleaser; gleaning even a good word from philosophedom and your Voltaires and D'Alemberts? That has a party, ready-made for him in the notables? Loménie de Brienne, Archbishop of Toulouse! answer all the three, with the clearest instantaneous concord; and rush off to propose him to the king, "in such haste," says Besenval, " that M. de Lamoignon had to bor-row a simarre," seemingly some kind of cloth appara-tus necessary for that.†

142. Loménie-Brienne, who had all his life "felt a kind of predestination for the highest offices," has now, therefore, obtained them. He presides over the finances; he shall have the title of prime minister itself, and the effort of his long life be realized. Un-happy only that it took such talent and industry to *gain* the place, that to *qualify* for it hardly any talent or industry was left disposable! Looking now into his inner man, what qualification he may have, Lom-énie beholds, not without astonishment, next to nothing but vacuity and possibility. Principles or methods, acquirement outward or inward (for his very body is wasted, by hard tear and wear) he finds none; not so much as a plan, even an unwise one. Lucky, in these circumstances, that Calonne has had a plan! Calonne's plan was gathered from Turgot's and Necker's by compilation, shall become Loménie's by adoption. Not in vain has Loménie studied the working of the British constitution; for he professes to have some Anglomania, of a sort. Why in that free country, does one minister, driven out by parlia-ment, vanish from his king's presence, and another enter, borne in by parliament?‡ Surely not for mere change (which is ever wasteful), but that all men may have share of what is going; and so the strife of freedom indefinitely prolong itself, and no harm be done.

143. The notables, mollified by Easter festivities, by the sacrifice of Calonne, are not in the worst humor. Already his majesty, while the "interlunar shadows" were in office, had held session of notables; and from his throne delivered promissory conciliatory eloquence : " the queen stood waiting at a window,

---

* Besenval, iii 203
† "Republished in the Musee de la Caricature" (Paris, 1840).
‡ Besenval III 209.
§ Besenval, III. 211.

* Ib. iii. 225.
† Besenval, III. 224.
‡ Montgaillard, "Histoire de France," i. 410-17.

till his carriage came back, and monsieur from afar clapped hands to her," in sign that all was well.* It has had the best effect, if such do but last. Leading notables, meanwhile, can be "caressed;" Brienne's new gloss, Lamoignon's long head, will profit somewhat; conciliatory eloquence shall not be wanting. On the whole, however, it is not undeniable that this of ousting Calonne and adopting the plans of Calonne is a measure which, to produce its best effect, should be looked at from a certain distance, cursorily; not dwelt on with minute near scrutiny? In a word, that no service the notables could now do were so obliging as, in some handsome manner, to—take themselves away? Their "six propositions" about provisional assemblies, suppression of corvées and suchlike, can be accepted without criticism. The *subvention* or land-tax, and much else, one must glide hastily over; safe nowhere but in flourishes of conciliatory eloquence. Till at length, on this 25th of May, year 1787, in solemn final session, there bursts forth what we can call an explosion of eloquence; king, Loménie, Lamoignon and retinue taking up the successive strain, in harangues to the number of ten, besides his majesty's, which last the livelong day—whereby, as in a kind of choral anthem, or bravura peal, of thanks, praises, promises, the notables are, so to speak, organed out, and dismissed to their respective places of abode. They had sat, and talked, some nine weeks; they were the first notables since Richelieu's, in the year 1626.

144. By some historians, sitting much at their ease in the safe distance, Loménie has been blamed for this dismissal of his notables; nevertheless, it was clearly time. There are things, as we said, which should not be dwelt on with minute close scrutiny. Over hot coals you cannot glide too fast. In these seven bureaus, where no work could be done, unless talk were work, the questionablest matters were coming up. Lafayette, for example, in Monseigneur d'Artois's bureau, took upon him to set forth more than one deprecatory oration about lettres-de-cachet, liberty of the subject, agio, and such like, which monseigneur, endeavoring to repress, was answered that a notable being summoned to speak his opinion must speak it.†

145. Thus, to, his grace the Archbishop of Aix, perorating once, with a plaintive pulpit tone, in these words, "Tithe, that free-will offering of the piety of Christians"—"Tithe," interrupted Duke la Rochefoucault, with the cold business manner he has learned from the English, "that free-will offering of the piety of Christians, on which there are now 40,000 lawsuits in this realm."‡ Nay, Lafayette, bound to speak his opinion, went the length, one day, of proposing to convoke a "national assembly." "You demand states-general?" asked monseigneur, with an air of minutory surprise. "Yes, monseigneur; and even better than that," "Write it," said monseigneur to the clerks.§ Written accordingly it is; and, what is more, will be acted by and by.

CHAPTER IV.

LOMÉNIE'S EDICTS.

146. Thus, then, have the notables returned home, carrying to all quarters of France such notions of deficit, decrepitude, distraction, and that states-general will cure it, or will not cure it but kill it.

* Bescnval, iii. 220.
† Montgaillard, i. 360.
‡ Dumont. "Souvenirs sur Mirabeau," p. 21.
§ Toulongeon, "Histoire de France depuis de Revolution de 1789" (Paris, 1803), i. or p. 4.

Each notable, we may fancy, is as a funereal torch-disclosing hideous abysses, better left hid! The unquietest humor possesses all men, ferments, seeks issue in pamphleteering, caricaturing, projecting, declaiming—vain jangling of thought, word, and deed.

147. It is spiritual bankruptcy, long tolerated, verging now toward economical bankruptcy, and become intolerable; for, from the lowest dumb rant, the inevitable misery, as was predicted, has spread upward. In every man is some obscure feeling that his position, oppressive or else oppressed, is a false one; all men, in one or the other acrid dialect, as assaulters or as defenders, must give vent to the unrest that is in them. Of such stuff, national well-being, and the glory of rulers is not made. O Loménie, what a wild-heaving, waste-looking, hungry, and angry world hast thou, after life-long effort, got promoted to take charge of!

148. Loménie's first edits are mere soothing ones; creation of provincial assemblies "for apportioning the imposts," when we get any, suppression of corvées or statute labor, alleviation of gabelle, soothing measures recommended by the notables, long clamored for by all liberal men. Oil cast upon the waters has been known to produce a good effect. Before venturing with great essential measures, Loménie will see this singular "swell of the public mind" abate somewhat.

149. Most proper, surely. But what if it were not a swell of the abating kind? There are swells that come of upper tempest and wind-gust. But, again, there are swells that come of subterranean pent wind, some say, and even of inward decomposition, of decay that has become self-combustion—as when, according to Neptuno-Plutonic geology, the world is all decayed down into due attritus of this sort, and shall now be *exploded* and new made! These latter abate not by oil. The fool says in his heart, How shall not to-morrow be as yesterday, as all days, which were once to-morrows? The wise man, looking on this France, moral, intellectual, economical, sees, "in short, all the symptoms he has ever met with in history," unabatable by soothing edicts.

150. Meanwhile, abate or not, cash must be had; and for that, quite another sort of edicts, namely, "bursal" or fiscal ones. How easy were fiscal edicts, did you know for certain that the parlement of Paris would what they call "register" them! Such right of registering, properly of mere *writing down*, the parlement has got by old want, and, though but a law court, can remonstrate, and higgle considerably about the same. Hence many quarrels, desperate Maupeou devices, and victory and defeat, a quarrel now near forty years long. Hence fiscal edicts, which otherwise were easy enough, become such problems. For example, is there not Calonne's subvention territoriale, universal, unexempting land-tax, the sheet-anchor of finance. Or, to show, so far as possible, that one is not without original finance talent, Loménie himself can devise an edit du timbre, or stamp-tax, borrowed also, it is true, but then from America. May it prove luckier in France than there!

151. France has her resources; nevertheless, it cannot be denied, the aspect of that parlement is questionable. Already among the notables, in that final symphony of dismissal, the Paris president had an ominous tone. Adrien Duport, quitting magnetic sleep, in this agitation of the world, threatens to rouse himself into preternatural wakefulness. Shallower, but also louder, there is magnetic D'Espréménil, with his tropical heat (he was born at Madras), with his dusky, confused violence, holding of illumination, animal magnetism, public opinion, Adam Weisshaupt, Harmodius, and Aristogiton, and all manner of confused, violent things, of whom can

come no good. The very peerage is infected with the leaven. Our peers have, in too many cases, laid aside their frogs, laces, bag-wigs, and go about in English costume, or ride rising in their stirrups, in the most headlong manner; nothing but insubordination, eleutheromania, confused, unlimited opposition in their heads. Questionable; not to be ventured upon, if we had a Fortunatus's purse! But Loménie has waited all June, casting on the waters what oil he had; and now, betide as it may, the two finance edicts must out. On the 6th of July he forwards his proposed stamp-tax and land-tax to the parlement of Paris, and, as if putting his own leg foremost, not his borrowed Calonne's-leg, places the stamp-tax first in order.

152. Alas! the parlement will *not* register; the parlement demands instead a "state of the expenditure," a "state of the contemplated reductions;" "states" enough, which his majesty must decline to furnish. Discussions arise, patriotic eloquence, the peers are summoned. Does the Nemean lion begin to bristle? Here, surely, is a duel, which France and the universe may look upon, with prayers, at lowest, with curiosity and bets. Paris stirs with new animation. The outer courts of the Palais de Justice roll with unusual crowds, coming and going; their huge outer hum mingles with the clang of patriotic eloquence within, and gives vigor to it. Poor Loménie gazes from the distance, little comforted; has his invisible emissaries flying to and fro, assiduous, without result.

153. So pass the sultry dog-days, in the most electric manner, and the whole month of July. And still, in the sanctuary of justice, sounds nothing but Harmodius-Aristogiton eloquence, environed with the hum of crowding Paris, and no registering accomplished, and no "states" furnished. "States?" said a lively parlementeer; "messieurs, the states that should. he furnished us, in my opinion, are the *states-general*." On which timely joke there follow cachinnatory buzzes of approval. What a word to be spoken in the Palais de Justice! Old D'Ormesson (the ex-controller's uncle) shakes his judicious head, far enough from laughing. But the outer courts, and Paris and France, catch the glad sound, and repeat it; shall repeat it, and re-echo and reverberate it, till it grow a deafening peal. Clearly enough—here is no registering to be thought of.

154. The pious proverb says, "There are remedies for all things but death." When a parlement refuses registering, the remedy, by long practice, has become familiar to the simplest—a bed of justice. One complete month this parlement has spent in mere idle jargoning, and sound and fury; the timbre edict not registered, or like to be; the subvention not yet so much as spoken of. On the 6th of August let the whole refractory body roll out, in wheeled vehicles, as far as the king's château of Versailles; there shall the king, holding his bed of justice, *order* them, by his own royal lips, to register. They may remonstrate in an undertone, but they must obey, lest a worse, unknown thing befall them.

155. It is done: the parlement has rolled out on royal summons; has heard the express royal order to register. Whereupon it has rolled back again, amid the hushed expectancy of men. And now, behold, on the morrow this parlement, seated once more in its own palais, with "crowds inundating the outer courts," not only does not register, but (O, portent!) declares all that was done on the prior day to be *null*, and the bed of justice as good as a futility. In the history of France here verily is a new feature. Nay, better still, our heroic parlement, getting suddenly enlightened on several things, declares that for its part it is incompetent to register tax-edicts at all, having done it by mistake during these late centuries; that for such act one authority only is competent—the assembled three estates of the realm.

156. To such length can the universal spirit of a nation penetrate the most isolated body-corporate: say rather with such weapons, homicidal and suicidal, in exasperated political duel, will bodies-corporate fight! But in any case, is not this the real death-grapple of war and internecine duel, Greek meeting Greek; whereon men, had they even no interest in it, might look with interest unspeakable? Crowds, as was said, inundate the outer courts: inundation of young eleutheromaniac noblemen in English costume, uttering audacious speeches; of procureurs, basoche-clerks, who are idle in these days; of loungers, news-mongers, and other nondescript classes, rolls tumultuous there. "From three to four thousand persons," waiting eagerly to hear the arrêtés (resolutions) you arrive at within; applauding with bravos, with the clapping of from six to eight thousand hands. Sweet, also, is the meed of patriotic eloquence, when your D'Esprémenil, your Fréteau, or Sabatier, issuing from his Demosthenic Olympus; the thunder being hushed for the day, is welcomed in the outer courts with a shout from 4,000 throats, is borne home shoulder-high "with benedictions,"and strikes the stars with his sublime head.

CHAPTER V.

LOMÉNIE'S THUNDERBOLTS.

157. Arise, Loménie-Brienne, here is no case for "letters of jussion;" for faltering or compromise. Thou seest the whole loose *fluent* population of Paris (whatsoever is not solid, and fixed to work) inundating these outer courts like a loud destructive deluge; the very basoche of lawyers, clerks talks sedition. The lower classes, in this duel of authority with authority, Greek throttling Greek, have ceased to respect the city-watch; police-satellites are marked on the back with chalk (the M signifies mouchard, spy); they are hustled, hunted like feræ naturæ. Subordinate rural tribunals send messengers of congratulation, of adherence. Their fountain of justice is becoming a fountain of revolt. The provincial parlements look on with intent eye, with breathless wishes, while their elder sister of Paris does battle; the whole twelve are of one blood and temper, the victory of one is that of all.

158. Ever worse it grows; on the 10th of August, there is "plainte" emitted touching the "prodigalities of Calonne," and permission to "proceed" against him. No registering, but instead of it, denouncing—of delapidation, peculation; and ever the burden of the song, States-general! Have the royal armories no thunderbolt, that thou couldst, O Loménie, with red right hand launch it among these Demosthenic, theatrical thunder-barrels—mere resin and noise for most part—and shatter and smite them silent? On the night of the 14th of August, Loménie launches his thunderbolt, or handful of them. Letters named of the seal (de-cachet), as many as needful, some six-score and odd, are delivered over night. And so, next day betimes, the whole parlement, once more set on wheels, is rolling incessantly toward Troyes in Champagne, "escorted," says history, "with the blessings of all people," the very innkeepers and postillions looking gratuitously reverent.[*] This is the 15th of August, 1787.

159. What will not people bless, in their extreme need? Seldom had the parlement of Paris deserved much blessing, or received much. An isolated body-

[*] A Lameth, "Histoire de l'Assemblee Constituante" (Int. 73),

corporate, which, out of old confusions (while the scepter of the sword was confusedly struggling to become a scepter of the pen), had got itself together better and worse, as bodies-corporate do, to satisfy some dim desire of the world, and many clear desires of individuals; and so had grown in the course of centuries, on concession, on acquirement, and usurpation, to be what we see it, a prosperous social anomaly, deciding lawsuits, sanctioning or rejecting laws, and withal, disposing of its places and offices by sale for ready money—which method sleek President Hénault, after meditation, will demonstrate to be the indifferent-best.*

160. In such a body, existing by purchase for ready money, there could not be excess of public spirit; there might well be excess of eagerness to divide the public spoil. Men in helmets have divided that with swords; men in wigs with quill and ink-horn do divide it; and even more hatefully these latter, if more peaceably, for the wig-method is at once irresistibler and baser. By long experience says Besenval, it has been found useless to sue a parlementeer at law; no officer of justice will serve a writ on one; his wig and gown are his Vulcan's-panoply, his enchanted cloak-of-darkness.

161. The parlement of Paris may count itself an unloved body; mean, not magnanimous on the political side. Were the king weak, always, (as now) has his parlement barked, cur-like, at his heels, with what popular cry there might be. Were he strong, it barked before his face, hunting for him as his alert beagle. An unjust body, where foul influences have more than once worked shameful perversion of judgment. Does not, in these very days, the blood of murdered Lally cry aloud for vengeance? Baited, circumvented, driven mad like the snared lion, valor had to sink extinguished under vindictive chicane. Behold him, that hapless Lally, his wild dark soul looking through his wild dark face; trailed on the ignominious death-hurdle, the voice of his despair choked by a wooden gag! The wild fire-soul that has known only peril and toil, and for three-score years has buffeted against fate's obstruction and men's perfidy, like genius and courage amid poltroonery, dishonesty, and commonplace, faithfully enduring and endeavoring—O parlement of Paris, dost thou reward it with a gibbet and a gag?.† The dying Lally bequeathed his memory to his boy: a young Lally has arisen, demanding redress in the name of God and man. The parlement of Paris does its utmost to defend the indefensible, abominable; nay, what is singular, dusky-glowing Aristogiton d'Esprémenil is the man chosen to be its spokesman in that.

162. Such social anomaly is it that France now blesses. An unclean social anomaly; but in duel against another worse, the exiled parlement is felt to have "covered itself with glory." There are quarrels in which even Satan, bringing help, were not unwelcome; even Satan, fighting stiffly, might cover himself with glory—of a temporary sort.

163. But what a stir in the outer courts of the palais, when Paris finds its parlement trundled off to Troyes in Champagne; and nothing left but a few mute keepers of records; the Demosthenic thunder become extinct, the martyrs of liberty clean gone! Confused wail and menace rises from the four thousand throats of procureurs, basoche-clerks, nondescripts, and Anglomaniac noblesse; ever new idlers crowd to see and hear; rascality, with increasing numbers and vigor, hunts mouchards. Loud whirl-

pool rolls through these spaces; the rest of the city, fixed to its work, cannot yet go rolling. Audacious placards are legible; in and about the palais, the speeches are as good as seditious. Surely the temper of Paris is much changed. On the third day of this business (18th of August) Monsieur and Monseigneur d'Artois, coming in state carriages, according to use and wont, to have these late obnoxious arrêtés and protests "expunged" from the records, are received in the most marked manner. Monsieur, who is thought to be in opposition, is met with vivats and captain of the guards has to give order, "Haut les armes (Handle arms)!" at which thunder-word, indeed, and the flash of the clear iron, the rascal-flood recoils, through all avenues, fast enough.* New features these. Indeed, as good M. de Malesherbes pertinently remarks, "it is a quite new kind of contest this with the parlement;" no transitory splutter, as from collision of hard bodies more like "the first strewed flowers; monseigneur, on the other hand, with silence, with murmurs, which rise to hisses and groans; nay an irreverent rascality presses toward him in floods, with such hissing vehemence that the sparks of what, if not quenched, may become a great conflagration.†

164. This good Malesherbes sees himself now again in the king's council, after an absence of ten years. Loménie would profit if not by the faculties of the man, yet by the name he has. As for the man's opinion, it is not listened to; wherefore he will soon withdraw, a second time, back to his books and his trees. In such king's council what can a good man profit? Turgot tries it not a second time. Turgot has quitted France and this earth some years ago; and now cares for none of these things. Singular enough, Turgot, this same Loménie, and the Abbé Morellet were once a trio of young friends, fellow-scholars in the Sorbonne. Forty new years have carried them severally thus far.

165. Meanwhile the parlement sits daily at Troyes, calling cases, and daily adjourns, no procureur making his appearance to plead. Troyes is as hospitable as could be looked for, nevertheless, one has comparatively a dull life. No crowds now to carry you, shoulder high, to the immortal [gods; scarcely a patriot or two will drive out so far, and bid you be of firm courage. You are in furnished lodgings, far from home and domestic comfort, little to do but wander over the unlovely Champagne fields, seeing the grapes ripen, taking counsel about the thousand times consulted, a prey to tedium, in danger even that Paris may forget you. Messengers come and go; Pacific Loménie is not slack in negotiating, promising; D'Ormesson and the prudent elder members see no good in strife.

166. After a dull month, the parlement, yielding and retaining, makes truce, as all parlements must. The stamp-tax is withdrawn, the subvention land-tax is also withdrawn; but in its stead there is granted what is called a "prorogation of the second twentieth," itself a kind of land-tax, but not so oppressive to the influential classes; which lies mainly on the dumb class. Moreover, secret promises exist (on the part of the elders) that finances may be raised by loan. Of the ugly word states-general there shall be no mention.

167. And so, on the 20th of September, our exiled parlement returns. D'Esprémenil said, "It went out covered with glory, but had come back covered with mud (de boue)." Not so, Aristogiton, or if so, thou surely art the man to clean it.

* "Abrege Chronologique," p. 975.
† 9th May, 1766: 'Biographie Universelle." § Lally.

* Montgaillard, i. 369.   Besenval, etc.
† Montgaillard, i. 373.

CHAPTER VI.

LOMÉNIE'S PLOTS.

168. Was ever unfortunate chief minister so bested as Loménie-Brienne? The reins of the state fairly in his hand these six months, and not the smallest motive-power (of finance) to stir from the spot with, this way or that! He flourishes his whip, but advances not. Instead of ready money, there is nothing but rebellious debating and recalcitrating.

169. Far is the public mind from being calmed; it goes chafing and fuming ever worse; and in the royal coffers, with such yearly deficit running on, there is hardly the color of coin. Ominous prognostics! Malesherbes, seeing an exhausted, exasperated France grow hotter and hotter, talks of "conflagration;" Mirabeau, without talk, has, as we perceive, descended on Paris again, close on the rear of the parlement*—not to quit his native soil any more.

170. Over the frontiers, behold Holland invaded by Prussia,† the French party oppressed, England and the stadtholder triumphing, to the sorrow of War-Secretary Montmorin and all men. But without money, sinews of war, as of work, and of existence itself, what can a chief minister do? Taxes profit little; this of the second twentieth falls not due till next year, and will then, with its "strict valuation," produce more controversy than cash. Taxes on the privileged classes cannot be got registered, are intolerable to our supporters themselves; taxes on the unprivileged yield nothing—as from a thing drained dry more cannot be drawn. Hope is nowhere if not in the old refuge of loans.

171. To Loménie, aided by the long head of Lamoignon, deeply pondering this sea of troubles, the thought suggested itself, Why not have a successive loan (emprunt successif), or loan that went on lending, year after year, as much as needful, say till 1792? The trouble of registering such loan were the same; we had then breathing time, money to work with, at least to subsist on. Edict of a successive loan must be proposed. To conciliate the philosophies, let a liberal edict walk in front of it, for emancipation of Protestants: let a liberal promise guard the rear of it, that when our loan ends, in that final 1792, the states-general shall be convoked.

172. Such liberal edict of Protestant emancipation, the time having come for it, shall cost a Loménie as little as the "death-penalties to be put in execution" did. As for the liberal promise of states-general, it can be fulfilled or not: the fulfillment is five good years off, in five years much intervenes. But the registering? Ah, truly, there is the difficulty! However, we have that promise of the elders, given secretly at Troyes. Judicious gratuities, cajoleries, underground intrigues, with old Foulon, named " Âme damnée—Familiar-demon—of the parlement," may, perhaps, do the rest. At worst and lowest, the royal authority has resources—which ought it not to put forth? If it cannot realize money, the royal authority is as good as dead—dead of that surest and miserablest death, inanition. Risk and win; without risk, all is already lost! For the rest—as in enterprises of pith a touch of stratagem often proves furthersome—his majesty announces a royal hunt, for the 19th of November next, and all whom it concerns are joyfully getting their gear ready.

173. Royal hunt, indeed, but of two-legged unfeathered game! At eleven in the morning of that royal hunt day, 19th of November, 1787, unexpected blare of trumpeting, tumult of charioteering and cavalcading, disturbs the seat of justice: his majesty is come, with Garde-des-Sceaux Lamoignon, and peers and retinue, to hold royal session and have edicts registered. What a change since Louis XIV. entered here in boots; and, whip in hand, ordered his registering to be done—with an Olympian look, which none durst gainsay; and did, without stratagem, in such unceremonious fashion, hunt as well as register!* For Louis XVI., on this day, the registering will be enough, if, indeed, he and the day suffice for it.

174. Meanwhile, with fit ceremonial words, the purpose of the royal breast is signified—two edicts, for Protestant emancipation, for successive loan, of both which edicts our trusty Garde-des-Sceaux Lamoignon will explain the purport; on both which a trusty parlement is requested to deliver its opinion, each member having free privilege of speech. And so, Lamoignon, too, having perorated not amiss, and wound up with that promise of states-general—the sphere-music of parlementary eloquence begins. Explosive, responsive, sphere answering sphere, it waxes louder and louder. The peers sit attentive, of diverse sentiment, unfriendly to states-general, unfriendly to despotism, which cannot reward merit, and is suppressing places. But what agitates his highness D'Orléans? The rubicund moon-head goes wagging; darker beams the copper visage, like unscoured copper; in the glazed eye is disquietude; he rolls uneasy in his seat, as if he meant something. Amid unutterable satiety, has suddenly new appetite, for new forbidden fruit, been vouchsafed him? Disgust and edacity, laziness that cannot rest; futile ambition, revenge, non-admiralship—O, within that carbuncled skin what a confusion of confusions sits bottled!

175. " Eight couriers," in the course of the day, gallop from Versailles, where Loménie waits palpitating, and gallop back again, not with the best news. In the outer courts of the palais, huge buzz of expectation reigns; it is whispered the chief minister has lost six votes over night. And from within resounds nothing but forensic eloquence, pathetic and even indignant heartrending appeals to the royal clemency, that his majesty would please to summon states-general forthwith, and be the savior of France —wherein dusky-glowing D'Espréménil, but still more Sabatier de Cabre, and Fréteau, since named Commère Fréteau (Goody Fréteau), are among the loudest. For six mortal hours it lasts, in this manner, the infinite hubbub unslackened.

176. And so now, when brown dusk is falling through the windows, and no end visible, his majesty, on hint of Garde-des-Sceaux Lamoignon, opens his royal lips once more to say, in brief, that he must have his loan-edicts registered. Momentary deep pause! See! Monseigneur d'Orléans rises; with moon-visage turned toward the royal platform, he asks, with a delicate graciosity of manner covering unutterable things, " whether it is a bed of justice, then, or a royal session." Fire flashes on him from the throne and neighborhood; surly answer that " it is a session." In that case, monseigneur will crave leave to remark that edicts cannot be registered by order in a session; and, indeed to enter against such registry, his individual humble protest. " Vous êtes bien le maître (You will do your pleasure)," answers the king; and thereupon, in high state, marches out, escorted by his court retinue; D'Orléans himself, as in duty bound, escorting him, but only to the gate. Which duty done, D'Orléans returns in from the gate, redacts his protest, in the face of an applauding parlement, an applauding France; and so—has cut his court-moorings. shall wo

* Fils Adoptif, "Mirabeau," iv. i. 5.
† October, 1787. Montgaillard, i. 374. Besenval, iii. 283.

* Dulaure, vi. 306.

say? And will now sail and drift, fast enough, toward chaos?

177. Thou foolish D'Orléans; equality that art to be! Is royalty grown a mere wooden scarecrow, whereon thou, pert, scald-headed crow, mayest alight at pleasure and peck? Not yet wholly.

178. Next day a lettre-de-cachet sends D'Orléans to bethink himself in his château of Villers-Cotterets, where, alas, is no Paris, with its joyous necessaries of life; no facinating, indispensable Madame de Buffon—light wife of a great naturalist much too old for her. Monseigneur, it is said, does nothing but walk distractedly at Villers-Cotterets, cursing his stars. Versailles itself shall hear penitent wail from him, so hard is his doom. By a second, simultaneous lettre-de-cachet, Goody Fréteau is hurled into the stronghold of Ham, amid the Norman marshes; by a third, Sabatier de Cabre into Mont St. Michel, amid the Norman-quicksands. As for the parlement, it must, on summons, travel out to Versailles, with its register-book under its arm, to have the protest biffé (expunged); not without admonition, and even rebuke. A stroke of authority which, one might have hoped, would quiet matters.

179. Unhappily, no; it is a mere taste of the whip to rearing coursers, which make them rear worse! When a team of twenty-five millions begins rearing, what is Loménie's whip? The parlement will nowise acquiesce meekly, and set to register the Protestant edict, and do its other work, in salutary fear of these three lettres-de-cachet. Far from that, it begins questioning lettres-de-cachet generally, their legality, endurability; emits dolorous objurgation, petition on petition to have its three martyrs delivered; cannot, till that be complied with, so much as think of examining the Protestant edict, but puts it off always " till this day week."*

180. In which objurgatory strain Paris and France joins it, or rather has preceded it, making fearful chorus. And now, also, the other parlements, at length opening their mouths, begin to join; some of them, as at Grenoble and at Rennes, with portentous emphasis, threatening, by way of reprisal, to interdict the very tax-gatherer.† " In all former contests," as Malesherbes remarks, " it was the parlement that excited the public; but here it is the public that excites the parlement."

CHAPTER VII.

INTERNECINE.

181. What a France, through these winter months of the year 1787! The very Œil-de-Bœuf is doleful, uncertain with a general feeling among the suppressed that it were better to be in Turkey. The wolf-hounds are suppressed, the bear-hounds, Duke de Coigny, Duke de Polignac; in the Trianon little-heaven, her majesty, one evening, takes Besenval's arm; asks his candid opinion. The intrepid Besenval, having, as he hopes, nothing of the sycophant in *him*, plainly signifies that, with a parlement in rebellion, and an Œil-de-Bœuf in suppression, the king's crown is in danger; whereupon, singular to say, her majesty, as if hurt, changed the subject, Et ne me parla plus de rien !‡

182. To whom, indeed, can this poor queen speak? In need of wise counsel, if ever mortal was, yet beset here only by the hubbub of chaos! Her dwelling place is so bright to the eye, and confusion and black care darkens it all. Sorrows of the sovereign, sor-

rows of the woman, thick-coming sorrows environ her more and more. Lamotte, the necklace-countess, has in these late months escaped, perhaps been suffered to escape, from the Salpêtrière. Vain was the hope that Paris might thereby forget her, and this ever-widening lie, and heap of lies, subside. The Lamotte, with a V. (for voleuse—thief) branded on both shoulders has got to England, and will therefrom emit lie on lie, defiling the highest queenly name; mere distracted lies,* which, in its present humor, France will greedily believe.

183. For the rest, it is too clear our successive loan is not filling, as, indeed, in such circumstances, a loan registered by expunging of protests was not the likeliest to fill. Denunciation of lettres-de-cachet, of despotism generally, abates not; the twelve parlements are busy; the twelve hundred placarders, ballad-singers, pamphleteers. Paris is what, in figurative speech, they call " flooded with pamphlets (regorge de brochures);" flooded and eddying again Hot deluge, from so many patriot ready-writers, all at the *fervid* or boiling point; each ready-writer, now in the hour of eruption, going like an Iceland geyser! Against which what can a judicious friend Morellet do, a Rivarol, an unruly Linguet (well paid for it), spouting *cold*?

184. Now also, at length, does come discussion of the Protestant edict : but only for new embroilment, in pamphlet and counter-pamphlet, increasing the madness of men. Not even orthodoxy, bed-rid as she seemed, but will have a hand in this confusion. She once again, in the shape of Abbé Lenfant, "whom prelates drive to visit and congratulate," raises audible sound from her pulpit-drum.† Or mark how D'Espréménil, who has his own confused way in all things, produces at the right moment in parlementary harangue, a pocket crucifix, with the apostrophe, " Will ye crucify him afresh ? " *Him,* O D'Espréménil, without scruple—considering what poor stuff, of ivory and filigree, *he* is made of!

185. To all which add only that poor Brienne has fallen sick, so hard was the tear and wear of his sinful youth; so violent, incessant, is this agitation of his foolish old age. Baited, bayed at through so many throats, his grace, growing consumptive, inflammatory (with humeur de dartre), lies reduced to milk diet; in exasperation, almost in desperation, with "repose," precisely the impossible recipe, prescribed as the indispensable.‡

186. On the whole, what can a poor government do but once more recoil ineffectual ? The king's treasury is running toward the lees, and Paris "eddies with a flood of pamphlets." At all rates, let the *latter* subside a little! D'Orléans gets back to Raincy, which is nearer Paris and the fair frail Buffon; finally to Paris itself; neither does Fréteau and Sabatier banished forever. The Protestant edict is registered, to the joy of Boissy d'Anglas and good Malesherbes; successive loan, all protests expunged or else withdrawn, remains open—the rather as few or none come to fill it. States-general, for which the parlement has clamored, and now the whole nation clamors, will follow "in five years," if, indeed, not sooner. O parlement of Paris, what a clamor was that! " Messieurs," said old D'Ormesson, " you will get states-general, and you will repent it." Like the horse in the fable, who, to be avenged of his enemy, applied to the man. The man mounted, did swift execution on the enemy, but, unhappily, would not dismount! Instead of five years, let three years pass, and this

---

* Besenval, iii. 309.

† Weber, i. 266.

‡ Besenval, iii. 284.

* " Mémoires Justificatifs de la Comtesse de Lamotte," (London, 1788). " Vie de Jeanne de St. Remi, Comtesse de Lamotte," etc., etc. See " Diamond Necklace " (ut supra)

† Lacretelle, iii. 343. Montgaillard, etc.

‡ Besenval, iii. 317.

clamorous parlement shall have both seen its enemy hurled prostrate, and been itself ridden to foundering (say, rather, jugulated for hide and shoes), and lie dead in the ditch.

187. Under such omens, however, we have reached the spring of 1788. By no path can the king's government find passage for itself, but is everywhere shamefully flung back. Beleaguered by twelve rebellious parlements, which are grown to be the organs of an angry nation, it can advance nowhither; can accomplish nothing, obtain nothing, not so much as money to subsist on; but must sit there, seemingly, to be eaten up of deficit.

188. The measure of the iniquity, then, of the falsehood which has been gathering through long centuries, is nearly full. At least that of the misery is! From the hovels of the twenty-five millions the misery, permeating upward and forward, as its law is, has got so far—to the very Œil-de-Bœuf of Versailles. Man's hand, in this blind pain, is set against man; not only the low against the higher, but the higher against each other; provincial noblesse is bitter against court noblesse, robe against sword, rochet against pen. But against the king's government, who is *not* bitter? Not even Besenval in these days. To it, all men and bodies of men are become as enemies; it is the center whereon infinite contentions unite and clash. What new universal vertiginous movement is this of institutions, social arrangements, individual minds, which once worked co-operative, now rolling and grinding in distracted collision? Inevitable; it is the breaking up of a world-solecism, worn out at last, down even to bankruptcy of money! And so this poor Versailles court, as the chief or central solecism, finds all the other solecisms arrayed against it. Most natural! For your human solecisms, be it person or combination of persons, is ever, by law of nature, uneasy; if verging toward bankruptcy, it is even miserable; and when would the meanest solecism consent to blame or amend *itself* while there remained another to amend?

189. These threatening signs do not terrify Loménie, much less teach him. Loménie, though of light nature, is not without courage, of a sort. Nay, have we not read of lightest creatures, trained canary-birds, that could fly cheerfully with lighted matches, and fire cannon—fire whole powder magazines? To sit and die of deficit is no part of Loménie's plan. The evil is considerable; but can he not remove it; can be not attack it? At lowest, he can attack the *symptom* of it; these rebellious parlements he can attack, and, perhaps, remove. Much is dim to Loménie, but two things are clear—that such parlementary duel with royalty is growing perilous, nay, internecine; above all, that money must be had. Take thought, brave Loménie, thou Garde-des-Sceaux Lamoignon, who hast ideas! So often defeated, balked cruelly, when the golden fruit seemed within clutch, rally for one other struggle. To tame the parlement, to fill the king's coffers—these are now life-and-death questions.

190. Parlements have been tamed more than once. Set to perch "on the peaks of rocks inaccessable except by litters," a parlement grows reasonable. O Maupeou, thou bold, bad man, had we left thy work where it was! But apart from exile, or other violent methods, is there not one method whereby all things are tamed, even lions? The method of hunger! What if the parlement's supplies were cut off, namely, its lawsuits!

191. Minor courts, for the trying of innumerable minor causes, might be instituted; these we could call grand bailliages. Whereon the parlement, shortened of its prey, would look with yellow despair; but the public, fond of cheap justice, with favor and hope. Then for finance, for registering of edicts, why not from our own Œil-de-Bœuf dignitaries, our princes, dukes, marshals, make a thing we could call *plenary court;* and there, so to speak, do our registering ourselves. St. Louis had his plenary court, of great barons,* most useful to him, our great barons are still here (at least the name of them is still here), our necessity is greater than his.

192. Such is the Loménie-Lamoignon device, welcome to the king's council as a light-beam in great darkness. The device seems feasible; it is eminently needful: be it once well executed, great deliverance is wrought. Silent, then, and steady; now or never —the world shall see one other historical scene, and so singular a man as Loménie de Brienne still the stage-manager there.

193. Behold, accordingly, a Home-Secretary Bréteuil "beautifying Paris," in the peaceablest manner, in this hopeful spring weather of 1788; the old hovels and hutches disappearing from our bridges, as if for the state, too, there were halcyon weather, and nothing to do but beautify. Parlement seems to sit acknowledged victor. Brienne says nothing of finance, or even says and prints that it is all well. How is this, such halcyon quiet, though the successive loan did not fill? In a victorious parlement, Counselor Goeslard de Monsabert even denounces that "levying of the second twentieth on strict valuation;" and gets decree that the valuation shall not be strict—not on the privileged classes. Nevertheless, Brienne endures it, launches no lettre-de-cachet against it. How is this?

194. Smiling is such vernal weather, but treacherous, sudden! For one thing, we hear it whispered, "the intendants of provinces have all got order to be at their posts on a certain day." Still mo.· singular, what incessant printing is this that goes on at the king's château under lock and key? Sentries occupy all gates and windows; the printers come not out; they sleep in their work rooms; their very food is handed in to them!† A victorious parlement smells new danger. D'Espréménil has ordered horses to Versailles, prowls round that guarded printing-office; prying, snuffing, if so be the sagacity and ingenuity of man may penetrate it.

195. To a shower of gold most things are penetrable. D'Espréménil descends on the lap of a printer's Danae, in the shape of "five hundred louis d'or;" the Danae's husband smuggles a ball of clay to her, which she delivers to the golden counselor of parlement. Kneaded within it there stick printed proof-sheets—by heaven! the royal edict of that same self-registering *plenary court,* of those grand bailliages that shall cut short our lawsuits! It is to be promulgated over all France on one and the same day.

196. This, then, is what the intendants were bid wait for at their posts; this is what the court sat hatching, as its accursed cockatrice-egg, and would not stir, though provoked, till the brood were out! Hie with it, D'Espréménil, home to Paris; convoke instantaneous sessions; let the parlement, and the earth, and the heavens know it.

CHAPTER VIII.

LOMÉNIE'S DEATH-THROES.

197. On the morrow, which is the 3d of May, 1788, an astonished parlement sits convoked, listens speech-less to the speech of D'Espréménil, unfolding the infinite misdeed. Denounce it, O parlement of Paris; awaken France and the universe;

* Montgaillard, i. 405.
† Weber, i. 276.

roll what thunder-barrels of forensic eloquence thou hast; with thee, too, it is verily now or never!

198. The parlement is not wanting at such juncture. In the hour of his extreme jeopardy, the lion first incites himself by roaring, by lashing his sides. So here the parlement of Paris. On the motion of D'Espréménil, a most patriotic oath, of the one-and-all sort, is sworn, with united throat—an excellent new idea, which, in these coming years, shall not remain unimitated. Next comes indomitable declaration, almost of the rights of man, at least of the rights of parlement; invocation to the friends of French freedom, in this and in subsequent time. All which, or the essence of all which, is brought to paper; in a tone wherein something of plaintiveness blends with and tempers heroic valor. And thus, having sounded the storm-bell, which Paris hears, which all France will hear; and hurled such defiance in the teeth of Loménie and despotism, the parlement retires as from a tolerable first day's work.

199. But how Loménie felt to see his cockatrice-egg (so essential to the salvation of France) broken in this premature manner, let readers fancy! Indignant, he clutches at his thunderbolts (de-cachet, of the seal), and launches two of them—a bolt for D'Espréménil; a bolt for that busy Goeslard, whose service in the second twentieth and "strict valuation" is not forgotten. Such bolts clutched promptly overnight, and launched with the early new morning, shall strike agitated Paris, if not into requiescence, yet into wholesome astonishment.

200. Ministerial thunderbolts may be launched; but if they do not *hit?* D'Espréménil and Goeslard, warned both of them, as is thought, by the singing of some friendly bird, elude the Loménie tipstaves; escape disguised through sky windows, over roofs, to their own Palais de Justice; the thunderbolts have *missed*, Paris (for the buzz flies abroad) is struck into astonishment *not* wholesome. The two martyrs of liberty doff their disguises, don their long gowns: behold, in the space of an hour, by aid of ushers and swift runners, the parlement, with its counselors, presidents, even peers, sits anew assembled. The assembled parlement declares that these its two martyrs cannot be given up to any sublunary authority; moreover, that the " session is permanent," admitting of no adjournment till pursuit of them has been relinquished.

201. And so, with forensic eloquence, denunciation and protest, with couriers going and returning, the parlement, in this state of continual explosion that shall cease neither night nor day, waits the issue. Awakened Paris once more inundates those outer courts; boils, in floods wilder than ever, through all avenues. Dissonant hubbub there is; jargon as of Babel in the hour when they were first smitten (as here) with mutual unintelligibility, and the people had not yet dispersed!

202. Paris city goes through its diurnal epochs of working and slumbering; and now, for the second time, most European and African mortals are asleep. But here in this whirlpool of words, sleep falls not; the night spreads her coverlid of darkness over it in vain. Within is the sound of mere martyr invincibility; tempered with the due tone of plaintiveness. Without is the infinite expectant hum—growing drowsier a little. So has it lasted for six-and-thirty hours.

203. But hark, through the dead of midnight, what tramp is this? Tramp as of armed men, foot and horse; gardes Françaises, gardes Suisses; marching hither, in silent regularity, in the flare of torch-light! There are sappers, too, with axes and crowbars: apparently, if the doors open not, they will be forced! It is Captain d'Agoust, missioned from Ver-

sailles. D'Agoust, a man of known firmness, who once forced Prince Condé himself, by mere incessant looking at him, to give satisfaction and fight;[*] he now, with axes and torches, is advancing on the very sanctuary of justice. Sacrilegious, yet what help? The man is a soldier; looks merely at his orders; impassive, moves forward like an inanimate engine.

204. The doors open on summons, there need no axes—door after door. And now the innermost door opens, discloses the long-gowned senators of France, a hundred and sixty-seven by tale, seventeen of them peers, sitting there, majestic, " in permanent session." Were not the man military, and of cast-iron, this sight, this silence re-echoing the clank of his own boots, might stagger him! For the hundred and sixty-seven receive him in perfect silence, which some liken to that of the Roman senate overfallen by Brennus; some to that of a nest of coiners surprised by officers of the police.[†] Messieurs, said D'Agoust, de par le roi! Express order has charged D'Agoust with the sad duty of arresting two individuals, M. Duval d'Espréménil and M. Goeslard de Monsabert. Which respectable individuals, as he has not the honor of knowing them, are hereby invited, in the king's name, to surrender themselves. Profound silence! buzz, which grows a murmur: " We are all D'Espréménils !" ventures a voice, which other voices repeat. The president inquires whether he will employ violence? Captain d'Agoust, honored with his majesty's commission, has to execute his majesty's order; would so gladly do it without violence, will in any case do it; grants an august senate space to deliberate which method *they* prefer. And thereupon D'Agoust, with grave military courtesy, has withdrawn for the moment.

205. What boots it, august senators? All avenues are closed with fixed bayonets. Your courier gallops to Versailles, through the dewy night; but also gallops back again, with tidings that the order is authentic, that it is irrevocable. The outer courts simmer with idle population; but D'Agoust's grenadier-ranks stand there as immovable flood-gates; there will be no revolting to deliver you. " Messieurs!" thus spoke D'Espréménil, " when the victorious Gauls entered Rome, which they had carried by assault, the Roman senators, clothed in their purple, sat there, in their curule chairs, with a proud and tranquil countenance, awaiting slavery or death. Such, too, is the lofty spectacle which you, in this hour, offer to the universe (à l'univers), after having generously"—with much more of the like, as can still be read.[‡]

206. In vain, O D'Espréménil! Here is this cast-iron Captain d'Agoust, with his cast-iron military air, come back. Despotism, constraint, destruction, sit waving in his plumes. D'Espréménil must fall silent; heroically give himself up, lest worst befall. Him Goeslard heroically imitates. With spoken and speechless emotion, they fling themselves into the arms of their parlementary brethren, for a last embrace; and so, amid plaudits and plaints, from a hundred and sixty-five throats, amid wavings, sobbings, a whole forest-sigh of parlementary pathos,—they are led through winding passages to the rear-gate, where, in the grey of the morning, two conches with exempts stand waiting. There must the victims mount, bayonets menacing behind. D'Espréménil's stern question to the populace, " Whether they have courage?" is answered by silence. They mount and roll, and neither the rising of the May

---

* Weber, i. 283

† Besenval, iii. 365.

‡ Toulongeon, t. App. 20.

sun (it is the 6th morning) nor its setting shall lighten their heart; but they fare forward continually; D'Espréménil toward the utmost Isles of Sainte Marguerite, or Hières (supposed by some, if that is any comfort, to be Calypso's island); Goeslard toward the land-fortress of Pierre-en-Cize, extant then near the city of Lyons.

207. Captain D'Agoust may now, therefore, look forward to majorship, to commandantship of the Tuileries*—and, withal, vanish from history, where, nevertheless, he has been fated to do a notable thing. For not only are D'Espréménil and Goeslard safe whirling southward, but the parlement itself has straightway to march out—to that also his inexorable order reaches. Gathering up their long skirts, they file out, the whole hundred and sixty-five of them, through two rows of unsympathetic grenadiers, a spectacle to gods and men. The people revolt not, they only wonder and grumble; also, we remark, these unsympathetic grenadiers are grades Françaises —who, one day, will sympathize! In a word, the Palais de Justice is swept clear, the doors of it are locked; and D'Agoust returns to Versailles with the key in his pocket, having, as was said, merited preferment.

208. As for this parlement of Paris, now turned out to the street, we will without reluctance leave it there. The beds of justice it had to undergo, in the coming fortnight at Versailles, in registering, or rather refusing to register, those new-hatched edicts; and how it assembled in taverns and tap-rooms there, for the purpose of protesting;† or hovered disconsolate, with outspread skirts, not knowing where to assemble; and was reduced to lodge protest "with a notary;" and in the end, to sit still (in a state of forced "vacation") and do nothing; all this, natural now as the burying of the dead after battle, shall not concern us. The parlement of Paris has as good as performed its part; doing and misdoing, so far, but hardly further, could it stir the world.

209. Loménie has removed the evil, then? Not at all, not so much as the symptom of the evil; scarcely the *twelfth* part of the symptom, and exasperated the other eleven! The intendant of provinces, the military commandants, are at their posts on the appointed 8th of May, but in no parlement, if not in the single one of Douai, can these new edicts get registered. Not peaceable signing with ink, but browbeating, bloodshedding, appeal to primary club-law! Against these bailliages, against this plenary court, exasperated Themis everywhere shows face of battle; the provincial noblesse are of her party, and whoever hates Loménie and the evil time, with her attorneys and tipstaves, she enlists and operates down even to the populace. At Rennes in Brittany, where the historical Bertrand de Moleville is intendant, it has passed from fatal continual duelling, between the military and gentry, to street fighting, to stonevolleys and musket-shot; and still the edicts remain unregistered. The afflicted Bretons send remonstrance to Loménie, by a deputation of twelve, whom, however, Loménie having heard them, shuts up in the Bastille. A second, larger, deputation he meets, by his scouts, on the road, and persuades or frightens back. But now a third, largest, deputation is indignantly sent by *many* people; refused audience on arriving, it meets to take council; invites Lafayette and all patriot Bretons in Paris to assist, agitates itself—becomes the *Breton Club*, first germ of the *Jacobin's society.*‡

210. So many as eight parlements get exiled;§

* Montgaillard, i. 404.
† Weber, i. 290-303.
‡ A. F. de Bertrand-Moleville, "Mémoires Particuliers" (Paris, 1816), i. ch. i. Marmontel, "Mémoires," iv. 27.
§ Montgaillard, i. 306.

others might need that remedy, but it is one not always easy of appliance. At Grenoble, for instance, where a Mounier, a Barnave, have not been idle, the parlement had due order (by lettres-de-cachet) to depart, and exile itself, but on the morrow, instead of coaches getting yoked, the alarm-bell bursts forth, ominous, and peals and booms all day—crowds of mountaineers rush down, with axes, even with firelocks—whom (most ominous of all!) the soldiery shows no eagerness to deal with. "Axe over head," the poor general has to sign capitulation, to engage that the lettres-de-cachet shall remain unexecuted, and a beloved parlement stay where it is. Besançon, Dijon, Rouen, Bourdeaux, are not what they should be! At Pau in Bearn, where the old commandant had failed, a new one (a Grammont, native to them) is met by a procession of townsmen with the cradle of Henri Quatre, the palladium of their town; is conjured as he venerates this old tortoise-shell, in which the great Henri was rocked, not to trample on Bearnese liberty; is informed, withal, that his majesty's cannon are all safe, in the keeping of his majesty's faithful burghers of Pau, and do now lie pointed on the walls there, ready for action.*

211. At this rate, your grand bailliages are like to have a stormy infancy. As for the plenary court, it has literally expired in the birth. The very courtiers looked shy at it; old Marshal Broglie declined the honor of sitting therein. Assaulted by a universal storm of mingled ridicule and execration,† this poor plenary court met once, and never any second time. Distracted country! Contention hisses up, with forked hydra-tongue, wheresoever poor Loménie sets his foot. "Let a commandant, a commissioner of the king," says Weber, "enter one of these parlements to have an edict registered, the whole tribunal will disappear, and leave the commandant alone with the clerk and first president. The edict registered and the commandant gone, the whole tribunal hastens back, to declare such registration null. The highways are covered with *grand deputations* of parlements, proceeding to Versailles, to have their registers expunged by the king's hand; or returning home, to cover a new page with a new resolution still more audacious."‡

212. Such is the France of this year 1788. Not now a golden or paper age of hope, with its horse-racings, balloon-flyings, and finer sensibilities of the heart. Ah! gone is that; its golden effulgence paled, bedarkened in *this* singular manner, brewing toward preternatural weather! For, as in that wreck-storm, of Paul et Virginie and Saint Pierre, "One huge motionless cloud" (say, of sorrow and indignation) "girdles our whole horizon, streams up, hairy, copper-edged, over a sky of the color of lead." Motionless itself, but "small clouds," as exiled parlements and such-like, "parting from it, fly over the zenith with the velocity of birds," till, at last, with one loud howl, the whole four winds be dashed together, and all the world exclaim, There is the tornado! Tout le monde s'écria, voilà l'ouragan!

213. For the rest, in such circumstances, the successive loan, very naturally, remains unfilled; neither, indeed, can that impost of the second twentieth, at least not on "strict valuation," be levied to good purpose. "Lenders," says Weber, in his hyster-

* Besenval, iii. 348.
† "LaCour Plénière," heroï-tragi-comédie en trois actes et en prose; jouée le 1 Juillet, 1788, par une société d'amateurs dans un château aux environs de Versailles; par M. l'Abbé de Vermond, Lecteur de la Reine: A Baville (Lamoignon's country-house), et se trouve à Paris, chez la Veuve Liberté, à l'enseigne de la Révolution, 1788. "La Passion, la Mort et la Résurrection du Peuple;" Imprimé à Jerusalem, etc. etc. See Montgaillard, i. 407.

ical, vehement manner, "are afraid of ruin; tax-gatherers of hanging." The very clergy turn away their face; convoked in extraordinary assembly, they afford no gratuitons gift (don gratuit), if it be not that of advice. Here, too, instead of cash, is clamor for states-general.[*]

214. O Loménie-Brienne, with thy poor flimsy mind all bewildered, and now "three actual cauteries" on thy worn-out body, who art like to die of inflammation, provocation, milk-diet, dartres vives, and maladie (best untranslated),[†] and presidest over, a France with innumerable *actual cauteries*, which, also is dying of inflammation and the rest! Was it wise to quit the hosky verdures of Brienne, and thy new ashlar château there, and what is held for *this?* Soft were those shades and lawns; sweet the hymns of poetasters, the banishments of high-ronged graces,[‡] and always this and the other philosopher Morellet (nothing deeming himself or thee a questionable sham priest) could be so happy in making happy; and, also (hadst thou known it), in the military school hard by, there sat, studying mathematics, a dusky-complexioned, taciturn boy, under the name of *Napoleon Bonaparte!* With fifty years of effort, and one final dead-lift struggle, thou hast made an exchange! Thou hast got thy robe of office, as Hercules had his Nessus's shirt.

215. On the 13th of July of this 1788, there fell, on the very edge of harvest, the most frightful hailstorm, scattering into wild waste the fruits of the year, which had otherwise suffered grievously by drought. For sixty leagues round Paris, especially, the ruin was almost total.[§] To so many other evils, then, there is to be added that of dearth, perhaps of famine.

216. Some days before this hailstorm, on the 5th of July, and still more decisively some days after it, on the 8th of August, Loménie announces that the states-general are actually to meet in the following month of May. Till after which period, this of the plenary court, and the rest, shall remain *postponed.* Further, as in Loménie there is no plan of forming or holding these most desirable states-general, "thinkers are invited" to furnish him with one, through the medium of discussion by the public press!

217. What could a poor minister do? There are still ten months of respite reserved. A sinking pilot will fling out all things, his very biscuit-bags, lead, log, compass, and quadrant, before flinging out *himself.* It is on this principle of sinking, and the incipient delirium of despair, that we explain, likewise, the almost miraculous "invitation to thinkers." Invitation to chaos to be so kind as build, out of its tumultuous drift-wood, an ark of escape for him? In these cases, not invitation, but command, has usually proved serviceable. The queen stood that evening, pensive, in a window, with her face turned toward the garden. The chef de gobelet had followed her with an obsequious cup of coffee, and then retired till it were sipped. Her majesty beckoned Dame Campan to approach. "Grand Dieu!" murmured she, with the cup in her hand, "what a piece of news will be made public to-day! The King grants states-general." Then raising her eyes to heaven (if Campan were not mistaken), she added, "'Tis a first beat of the drum of ill-omen for France. This noblesse will ruin us."[‖]

218. During all that hatching of the plenary court, while Lamoignon looked so mysterious, Besenval had kept asking him one question: Whether they had cash? To which, as Lamoignon always answered (on

the faith of Loménie), that the cash was safe, judicious Besenval rejoined then that all was safe. Nevertheless, the melancholy fact is, that the royal coffers are almost getting literally void of coin. Indeed, apart from all other things, this "invitation to thinkers," and the great change now at hand, are enough to "arrest the circulation of capital," and forward only that of pamphlets. A few thousand gold louis are now all of money or money's worth that remains in the king's treasury. With another movement, as of desperation, Loménie invites Necker to come and be controller of finances! Necker has other work in view than controlling finances for Loménie; with a dry refusal, he stands taciturn, awaiting his time.

219. What shall a desperate prime minister do? He has grasped at the strong-box of the King's Theater. Some lottery had been set on foot for those sufferers by the hailstorm; in his extreme necessity, Loménie lays hands even on this.[*] To make provision for the passing day, on any terms, will soon be impossible. On the 16th of August, poor Weber heard at Paris and Versailles, hawkers, "with a hoarse, stifled tone of voice (voix étouffée, sourde)," drawling and snuffling through the streets an *edict concerning payments* (such was the soft title Rivarol had contrived for it). All payments at the royal treasury shall be made henceforth three-fifths in cash, and the remaining two-fifths—in paper bearing interest! Poor Weber almost swooned at the sound of these cracked voices, with their doleful raven-note, and will never forget the effect it had on him.[†]

220. But the effect on Paris, on the world generally? From the dens of stock brokerage, from the heights of political economy, of Neckerism and philosophism, from all articulate and inarticulate throats, rise hootings and howlings, such as ear had not yet heard. Sedition itself may be imminent! Monseigneur d'Artois, moved by Duchess Polignac, feels called to wait upon her majesty, and explain frankly what crisis matters stand in. "The queen wept," Brienne himself wept, for it is now visible and palpable that he must go.

221. Remains only that the court, to whom his manners and garrulities were always agreeable, shall make his fall soft. The grasping old man has already got his archbishopship of Toulouse exchanged for the richer one of Sens; and now, in this hour of pity, he shall have the co-adjutorship for his nephew (hardly yet of due age); a dameship of the palace for his niece, a regiment for her husband, for himself a red cardinal's hat, a coupe de bois (cutting from the royal forests) and, on the whole, "from five to six hundred thousand livres of revenue."[‡] Finally, his brother, the Comte de Brienne, shall still continue war-minister. Buckled round with such bolsters and huge featherbeds of promotion, 'let him now fall as soft as he can!

222. And so Loménie departs; rich, if court-tiles and money-bonds can enrich him, but, if these cannot, perhaps the poorest of all extant men. "Hissed at by the people of Versailles," he drives forth to Jardi, southward to Brienne, for recovery of health, Then to Nice, to Italy, but shall return; shall glide to and fro, tremulous, faint-twinkling, fallen on awful times, till the guillotine snuff out his weak existence? Alas! worse; for it is *blown* out, or choked out, foully, pitiably, on the way to the guillotine! In his palace of Sens, rude Jacobin bailiffs made him drink with them from his own wine-cel-

* Lameth, "Assemb. Const." (Introd.) p. 87.
† Montgaillard, i. 424.
‡ See "Mémoires de Morellet."
§ Marmontel, iv. 30.
‖ Campan, iii. 104, 111.

* Besenval, iii. 300.
† Weber, i. 339.
‡ Weber, i. 341.

lars, feast with them from his own larder, and on the morrow morning the miserable old man lies dead. This is the *end* of Prime Minister Cardinal Archbishop Loménie de Brienne. Flimsier mortal was never fated to do as weighty a mischief, to have a life as despicable-envied, an exit as frightful. *Fired* as the phrase is, with ambition; blown, like a kindled rag, the sport of winds, not this way, not that way, but of all ways, straight toward *such* a powder-mine—which he kindled! Let us pity the hapless Loménie, and forgive him; and as soon as possible, forget him.

CHAPTER IX.

BURIAL WITH BONFIRE.

223. Besenval, during these extraordinary operations of payment two-fifths in paper, and change of prime minister, had been out on a tour through his district of command, and, indeed, for the last months peacefully drink'; the waters of Contrexéville. Returning now in the end of August toward Moulins, and "knowing nothing," he arrives one evening at Langres, finds the whole town in a state of uproar (grande rumeur). Doubtless some sedition, a thing too common in these days. He alights, nevertheless, inquires of a "man tolerably dressed," what the matter is. "How," answers the man; "you have not heard the news? The archbishop is thrown out, and M. Necker is recalled; and all is going to go well."[*]

224. Such rumour and vociferous acclaim has arisen round M. Necker, ever from "that day when he issued from the queen's apartments," a nominated minister. It was on the 24th of August, "the galleries of the château, the courts, the streets of Versailles, in few hours the capital, and as the news flew, all France, resounded with the cry of Vive le Roi! Vive M. Necker!"[†] In Paris, indeed, it unfortunately got the length of "turbulence." Petards, rockets go off in the Place Dauphine, more than enough. A "wicker figure (mannequin d'osier)," in archbishop's stole made emblematically, three-fifths of it satin, two-fifths of it paper, is promenaded, not in silence, to the popular judgment-bar; is doomed, shriven by a mock Abbé de Vermond, then solemnly consumed by fire at the foot of Henri's statue on the Pont Neuf—with such petarding and huzzaing that Chevalier Dubois and his city-watch see good finally to make a charge (more or less ineffectual); and there wanted not burning of sentry-boxes, forcing of guard-houses, and also "dead bodies thrown into the Seine overnight," to avoid new effervescence.[‡]

225. Parlements, therefore,'shall return from exile; plenary court, payment two-fifths in paper, have vanished, gone off in smoke, at the foot of Henri's statue. States-general (with a political millennium) are now certain, nay, it shall be announced, in our fond haste, for January next; and all, as the Langres man said, is "going to go."

226. To the prophetic glance of Besenval, one other thing is too apparent, that friend Lamoignon cannot keep his keepership. Neither he nor war-minister Comte de Brienne! Already old Foulon, with an eye to be war-minister himself, is making underground movements. This is that same Foulon named Ame damnée du parlement, a man grown gray in treachery, in griping, projecting, intriguing, and iniquity; who, once when it was objected to some finance scheme of his, "What will the people do?" made

answer in the fire of discussion, "The people may eat grass;" hasty words, which fly abroad irrevocable, and will send back tidings.

227. Foulon, to the relief of the world, fails on this occasion; and will always fail. Nevertheless, it stands not M. de Lamoignon. It stands not the doomed man that he have interviews with the king, and be "seen to return radieux," emitting *rays*. Lamoignon is the hated of parlements; Comte de Brienne is brother to the cardinal archbishop. The 24th of August has been, and the 14th September is not yet, when they two, as their great principal had done, descend—made to fall *soft*, like him.

228. And now, as if the last burden had been rolled from its heart, and assurance were at length perfect, Paris bursts forth anew into extreme jubilee. The hasoche rejoices aloud that the foe of parlements is fallen; nobility, gentry, commonalty have rejoiced, and rejoice. Nay, now, with emphasis, rascality itself, starting suddenly from its dim depths, will arise and do it; for down even thither the new political evangel, in some rude version or other, has penetrated. It is Monday, the 14th of September, 1788: rascality assembles anew in great force, in the Place Dauphine; lets off petards, fires blunderbusses, to an incredible extent, without interval, for eighteen hours. There is again a wicker figure, "mannequin of osier" the center of endless howlings. Also Necker's portrait snatched or purchased from a print-shop, is borne processionally, aloft on a.perch, with huzzas—an example to be remembered.

229. But chiefly on the Pont Neuf, where the great Henri, in bronze, rides sublime, there do the crowds gather. All passengers must stop till they have bowed to the people's king, and said audibly, Vive Henri Quatre; au diable Lamoignon! No carriage but must stop, not even that of his highness d'Orléans. Your coach-doors are opened; monsieur will please to put forth his head and bow, or even if refractory, to alight altogether and kneel; from madame a wave of her plumes, a smile of her fair face where she sits shall suffice; and surely a coin or two (to buy fusées) were not unreasonable from the upper classes, friends of liberty? In this manner it proceeds for days, in such rude horse-play—not without kicks. The city-watch can do nothing—hardly save its own skin. For the last twelvemonths, as we have sometimes seen, it has been a kind of pastime to *hunt* the watch. Besenval, indeed, is at hand with soldiers; but they have orders to avoid firing, and are not prompt to stir.

230. On Monday morning, the explosion of petards began, and now it is near midnight of Wednesday; and the "wicker mannequin" is to be buried—apparently in the antique fashion. Long rows of torches following it, move toward the Hotel Lamoignon; but "a servant of mine" (Besenval's) has run to give warning, and there are soldiers come. Gloomy Lamoignon is not to die by conflagration; or this night—not yet for a year, and then by gunshot (suicidal or accidental is unknown).[*] Foiled rascality burns its "mannikin of osier," under his windows, "tears up the sentry-box," and rolls off to try Brienne; to try Dubois, captain of the watch. Now, however, all is bestirring itself, gardes Françaises, invalides, horse-patrol: the torch procession is met with sharp shot, with the thrusting of bayonets, the slashing of sabers. Even Dubois makes a charge with that cavalry of his, and the cruelest charge of all: "there are a great many killed and wounded." Not without clangor, complaint, subsequent criminal trials, and official persons dying of heart-break.[†] So, however, with

* Besenval, iii. 306.
† Weber i. 342.
‡ "Histoire Parlementaire de la Révolution Française, ou Journal des Assemblées Nationales depuis 1789" (Paris 1833 et seqq.), i. 253. Lameth, "Assemblées Constituante," i. (Introd.) p. 89.

* "Histoire de la Révolution," par Deux Amis de la Liberté, i. 50.
† "Histoire de la Révolution," par Deux Amis de la Liberté, i. 58.

steel-besom, rascality is brushed back into its dim depths, and streets are swept clear.

231. Not for a century and a half had rascality ventured to step forth in this fashion; not for so long showed its huge rude lineaments in the light of day, A wonder and new thing, as yet gamboling merely. in awkward Brobdignag sport, not without quaintness, hardly in anger: yet in its huge, half-vacant laugh lurks a shade of grimness—which could unfold itself.

232. However, the thinkers invited by Loménie are now far on with their pamphlets; states-general on one plan or another, will infallibly meet; if not in January, as was once hoped, yet at latest in May. Old Duke de Richelieu, moribund in these autumn days, opens his eyes once more, murmuring, "What would Louis Fourteenth" (whom he remembers) "have said?"—then closes them again, forever, before the evil time.

BOOK FOURTH.

STATES-GENERAL.

CHAPTER I.

THE NOTABLES AGAIN.

233. The universal prayer, therefore, is to be fulfilled! Always in days of national perplexity, when wrong abounded and help was not, this remedy of states-general was called for, by a Malesherbes, nay, by a Féuelon;[*] even parlements calling for it were "escorted with blessings." And now, behold, it is vouchsafed us; states-general shall verily be!

234. To say, let states-general be, was easy; to say in what manner they shall be, is not so easy. Since the year 1614, there have no states-general met in France, all trace of them has vanished from the living habits of men. Their structure, powers, methods of procedure, which were never in any measure fixed, have now become wholly a vague possibility. Clay which the potter may shape, this way or that—say, rather, the twenty-five millions of potters; for so many have now, more or less, a vote in it! How to shape the states-general? There is a problem. Each body-corporate, each privileged, each organized class, has secret hopes of its own in that matter; and also secret misgivings of its own—for, behold, this monstrous twenty-million class, hitherto the dumb sheep which these others had to agree about the manner of shearing, is now also arising with hopes! It has ceased or is ceasing to be dumb; it speaks through pamphlets, or at least brays and growls behind them, in unison—increasing wonderfully their volume of sound.

235. As for the parlement of Paris, it has at once declared for the "old form of 1614." Which form had this advantage, that the tiers etat, third estate, or commons, figured there as a show mainly; whereby the noblesse and clergy had but to avoid quarrel between themselves, and decide unobstructed what *they* thought best. Such was the clearly declared opinion of the Paris parlement. But, being met by a storm of mere hooting and howling from all men, such opinion was blown straightway to the winds, and the popularity of the parlement along with it—never to return. The parlement's part, we said above, was as good as played. Concerning which, however, there is this further to be noted, the proximity of dates. It was on the 22d of September that the parlement returned from "vacation" or "exile in its estates," to be reinstalled amid boundless jubilee from all Paris. Precisely next day it was that the same

* Montgaillard, i. 461.

parlement came to its "clearly declared opinion;" and then, on the morrow after that, you behold it "covered with outrages;" its outer court one vast sibilation, and the glory departed from it for evermore.[*] A popularity of twenty-four hours was, in those times, no uncommon allowance.

236. On the other hand, how superfluous was that invitation of Loménie's, the invitation to thinkers! Thinkers and unthinkers, by the million, are spontaneously at their post, doing what is in them. Clubs labor; Société Publicole, Breton Club, Enraged Club (Club des Enragés). Likewise dinner-parties in the Palais Royal; your Mirabeaus, Talleyrands dining there, in company with Chamforts, Morellets, with Duponts and hot parlementeers, not without object! For a certain *Neckerean* lion's provider, whom one could name, assembles them there†—or even their own private determination to have dinner does it. And then as to pamphlets—in figurative language, "It is a sheer snowing of pamphlets; like to snow-up the government thoroughfares!" Now is the time for friends of freedom: sane, and even insane.

237. Count, or self-styled Count, d'Aintrigues, "the young Languedocian gentleman," with perhaps, Chamfort the cynic to help him, rises into furor almost Pythic; highest where many are high.‡ Foolish young Languedocian gentleman, who himself so soon, "emigrating among the foremost," has to fly indignant over the marches, with the "contrat social" in his pocket, toward outer darkness, thankless intriguings, ignis-fatuus hoverings, and death by the stiletto! Abbé Sieyes has left Chartres Cathedral, and canonry and book-shelves there; has let his tonsure grow, and come to Paris with a secular head, of the most irrefragable sort, to ask three questions, and answer them: *What is the third estate? All. What has it hitherto been in our form of government? Nothing. What does it want? To become something.*

238. D'Orléans—for be sure he, on his way to chaos, is in the thick of this—promulgates his "Deliberations,"§ fathered by him, written by Laclos of the "Liaisons Dangereuses." The result of which comes out simply, "The third estate is the nation." On the other hand, Monseigneur d'Artois, with other princes of the blood, publishes, in solemn "memorial" to the king, that if such things be listened to, privilege, nobility, monarchy, church, state, and strongbox are in danger.|| In danger truly; and yet if you do not listen, are they out of danger? It is the voice of all France, this sound that rises. Immeasurable, manifold, as the sound of outbreaking waters; wise were he who knew what to do in it—if not to fly to the mountains, and hide himself?

239. How an ideal, all-seeing Versailles government, sitting there on such principles, in such an envionment, would have determined to demean itself at this new juncture, may even yet be a question. Such a government would have felt too well that its long task was now drawing to a close; that, under the guise of these states-general, at length inevitable, a new omnipotent unknown of democracy was coming into being; in presence of which no Versailles government either could or should. except in a provisory character, continue extant. To enact which provisory character, so unspeakably important, might its whole faculties but have sufficed; and so a peacea-

* Weber, i. 347.
† Ibid. i. 360
‡ "Mémoires, sur les Etats-Généraux." See Montgaillard i 457-9.
§ "Délibérations à prendre pour les Assemblées de Bailliages."
|| "Mémoire présenté au Roi" par Monseigneur Comte d'Artois, M. le Prince de Condé, M. le Duc Bourbon, d'Enghien. et M. le Prince de Conti. (Given in "Hist. -Parl." i. 250).

ble, gradual, well-conducted abdication and Domine-dimittas have been the issue!

240. This for our ideal, all-seeing Versailles government. But for the actual, irrational Versailles government? Alas, that is a government existing there only for its own behoof; without right, except possession; and now also without might. It foresees nothing, sees nothing; has not so much as a purpose, but has only purposes—and the instinct whereby all that exists will struggle to keep existing. Wholly a vortex, in which vain counsels, hallucinations, false-hoods, intrigues, and imbecilities whirl, like withered rubbish in the meeting of winds! The Œil-de-Bœuf has its irrational hopes, if also its fears. Since hitherto all states-general have done as good as nothing, why should these do more? The commons, indeed, look dangerous; but, on the whole, is not revolt, unknown now for five generations, an impossibility? The three estates can, by management, be set against each other; the third will, as heretofore, join with the king; will, out of mere spite and self-interest, be eager to tax and vex the other two. The other two are thus delivered bound into our hands, that we may fleece them likewise. Whereupon, money being got, and the three estates all in quarrel, dismiss them, and let the future go as it can! As good Archbishop Loménie was wont to say, "There are so many accidents; and it needs but one to save us." Yes; and how many to destroy us·

241. Poor Necker in the midst of such an anarchy does what is possible for him. He looks into it with obstinately hopeful face; lauds the known rectitude of the kingly mind; listens indulgent-like to the known perverseness of the queenly and courtly—emits, if any proclamation or regulation, one favoring the tiers c'st; but settling nothing; hovering afar off, rather, 'd advising all things to settle themselves. The grand questions, for the present, have got reduced to two—the double representation, and the vote by head. Shall the commonshave a "double representation," that is to say, have as many members as the noblesse and clergy united? Shall the states-general, when once assembled, vote and deliberate, in one body, or in three separate bodies; "vote by head, or vote by class"—ordre, as they call it? These are the moot-points now filling all French with jargon, logic, and eleutheromania. To terminate which, Necker bethinks him, might not a second convocation of the notables be fittest? Such second convocation is resolved on.

242. On the 6th of November of this year 1788, these notables accordingly have reassembled, after an interval of some eighteen months. They are Calonne's old notables, the same hundred and forty-four—to show one's impartiality; likewise to save time. They sit there once again, in their seven bureaus, in the hard winter weather: it is the hardest winter since 1709; thermometer below zero of Fahrenheit, Seine river frozen over.* Cold, scarcity, and eleutheromaniac clamor; a changed world since these notables were "organed out," in May gone a year! They shall see now whether, under their seven princes of the blood, in their seven bureaus, they can settle the moot-points.

243. To the surprise of patriotism, these notables, once so patriotic, seem to incline the wrong way, toward the anti-patriotic side. They stagger at the double representation, at the vote by head: there is not affirmative decision; there is mere debating, and that not with the best aspects. For, indeed, were not these notables themselves mostly of the privileged classes? They clamored once; now they have their misgivings, make their dolorous representations. Let

them vanish, ineffectual, and return no more! They vanish, after a month's session, on this 12th of December, year 1788—the *last* terrestrial notables—not to reappear any other time in the history of the world.

244. And so, the clamor still continuing, and the pamphlets, and nothing but patriotic addresses, louder and louder, pouring in on us from all corners of France—Necker himself, some fortnight after, before the year is yet done, has to present his "Report,"* recommending at his own risk that same double representations; nay, almost enjoining it, so loud is jargon and eleutheromania. What dubitating, what circumambulating! These whole six noisy months, (for it began with Brienne in July), has not "report" followed "report," and one proclamation flown in the teeth of the other?"†

245. However, that first moot-point, as we see, is now settled. As for the second, that of voting by head or by order, it unfortunately is still left hanging. It hangs there, we may say, between the privileged orders and the unprivileged, as a ready-made battle-prize, and necessity of war, from the very first, which battle-prize, whosoever seizes it may thenceforth bear as battle-flag, with the best omens!

246. But so, at least, by royal edict of the 24th of January,‡ does it finally, to impatient, expectant France, become not only indubitable that national deputies *are* to meet, but possible (so far and hardly farther has the royal regulation gone) to begin electing them.

CHAPTER II.

THE ELECTION.

247. Up, then, and be doing! The royal signal-word flies through France, as through vast forests the rushing of a mighty wind. At parish churches, in town-halls, and every house of convocation; by bailliages, by seneschalsies, in whatsoever form men convene; there, with confusion enough, are primary assemblies forming. To elect your electors, such is the form prescribed; then to draw up your "writ of plaints and grievances (cahier de plaintes et doléances!," of which latter there is no lack.

248. With such virtue works this royal January edict, as it rolls rapidly, in its lanthern mails, along these frost-bound high ways, toward all the four winds. Like some *fiat,* or magic spell-word—which such things do resemble! For always, as it sounds out "at the market-cross," accompanied with trumpet-blast, presided by bailli, seneschal, or other minor functionaries, with beef-eaters, or, in country churches, is droned forth after sermon, "au prone des messes paroissales," and is registered, posted, and let fly over all the world—you behold how this multitudinous French people, so long simmering and buzzing in eager expectancy, begins heaping and shaping itself into organic groups. Which organic groups, again, hold smaller organic grouplets; the inarticulate buzzing becomes articulate speaking and acting. By primary assembly, and then by secondary; by "successive elections," and infinite elaboration and scrutiny, according to prescribed process—shall the genuine "plaints and grievances" be at length got to paper, shall the fit national representative be at length laid hold of. ·

249. How the whole people shakes itself, as if it

---

* Marmontel, "Mémoires" (London, 1905), iv. 30. "Hist. Parl." etc.

* "Rapport fait an Roi dans son Conseil, le 27 Décembre, 1788."

† 5th July; 8th August; 23d September, etc., etc.

‡ "Réglement du Roi pour la Convocation des Etats-Généraux à Versailles." (Reprinted, wrong dated, in 'Histoire Parlementaire,' i. 202).

had one life, and, in thousand-voiced rumor, announces that it is awake, suddenly out of long death-sleep, and will thenceforth sleep no more! The long-looked-for has come at last; wondrous news, of victory, deliverance, enfranchisement, sounds magical through every heart. To the proud, strong man it has come, whose strong hands shall no more be gyved, to whom boundless unconquered continents lie disclosed. The weary day-drudge has heard of it; the beggar with his crust moistened in tears. What! to us also has hope reached, down even to us? Hunger and hardship are not to be eternal? The bread we extorted from the rugged glebe, and, with the toil of our sinews, reaped and ground, and kneaded into loaves, was not wholly for another, then, but we, also, shall eat of it, and be filled? Glorious news (answer the prudent elders), but all too unlikely! Thus, at any rate, may the lower people, who pay no money taxes, and have no right to vote,* assiduously crowd round those that do, and most halls of assembly, within doors and without, seem animated enough.

250. Paris alone, of towns, is to have representatives; the number of them, twenty. Paris is divided into sixty districts, each of which (assembled in some church, or the like) is choosing two electors. Official deputations pass from district to district, for all is inexperience as yet, and there is endless consulting. The streets swarm strangely with busy crowds, pacific, yet restless and loquacious; at intervals is seen the gleam of military muskets, especially about the palais, where the parlement, once more on duty, sits querulous, almost tremulous.

251. Busy is the French world! In those great days, what poorest speculative craftsman but will leave his workshop, if not to vote, yet to assist in voting? On all highways is a rustling and bustling. Over the wide surface of France, ever and anon, through the spring months, as the sower casts his corn abroad upon the furrows, sounds of congregating and dispersing, of crowds in deliberation, acclamation, voting by ballot and by voice, rise discrepant toward the ear of heaven. To which political phenomena add this economical one, that trade is stagnant, and also bread getting dear; for before the rigorous winter there was, as we said, a rigorous summer, with drought, and on the 13th of July with destructive hail. What a fearful day! all cried while that tempest fell. Alas, the next anniversary of it will be a worse.† Under such aspects is France electing national representatives.

252. The incidents and specialties of these elections belong not to universal, but to local or parish history, for which reason let not the new troubles of Grenoble or Besançon, the bloodshed on the streets of Rennes, and consequent march thither of the Breton " young men," with manifesto by their " mothers, sisters, and sweethearts,"‡ nor such-like, detain us here. It is the same sad history everywhere, with superficial variations. A reinstated parlement (as at Besançon), which stands astonished at this behemoth of a states-general it had itself evoked, starts forward, with more or less audacity, to fix a thorn in its nose, and, alas, is instantaneously struck down, and hurled quite out, for the new popular force can use not only arguments but brickbats! Or else, and perhaps combined with this, it is an order of noblesse (as in

* "Règlement du Roi," (in "Histoire Parlementaire," as above, i. 267–307).

† Bailly, " Mémoires," i. 336.

* " Protestation and Arrêté des Jeunes Gens de la Ville de Nantes, du 28 Janvier, 1789, avant leur départ pour Rennes. Arrêté des Jeunes Gens de la Ville d'Angers, du 4 Février, 1789. Arrêté des Mères, Sœurs, Epouses, et Amantes des Jeunes Citoyens d'Angers, du 6 Février, 1789." (Reprinted in "Histoire Parlementaire," i. 290–3).

Brittany), which will beforehand tie up the third estate, that it harm not the old privileges. In which act of tying up, never so skilfully set about, there is likewise no possibility of prospering; but the behemoth-Briareus snaps your cords like green rushes. Tie up? Alas, messieurs! And then, as for your chivalry rapiers, valor, and wager-of-battle, think one moment, how can that answer? The plebeian heart, too, has red life in it, which changes not to palenesss at glance even of you, and " the six hundred Breton gentlemen assembled in arms, for seventy-two hours, in the Cordeliers' cloister, at Rennes," have to come out again, wiser than they entered. For the Nantes youth, the Angers youth, all Brittany, was astir, " mothers, sisters, and sweethearts " shrieking after them, March! The Breton noblesse must even let the mad world have its way.*

253. In other provinces, the noblesse, with equal good-will, finds it better to stick to protests, to well-redacted " cahiers of grievances," and satirical writings and speeches. Such is partially their course in Provence, whither, indeed, Gabriel Honoré Riquetti, Comte de Mirabeau, has rushed down from Paris to speak a word in season. In Provence, the privileged, backed by their Aix parlement, discover that such novelties, enjoined though they be by royal edict, tend to national detriment, and, what is still more indisputable, " to impair the dignity of the noblesse." Whereupon, Mirabeau protesting aloud, this same noblesse, amid huge tumult within doors and without, flatly determines to expel him from their assembly. No other method, not even that of successive-duels, would answer with him, the obstreperous,e fierce-glaring man. Expelled he accordingly is.

254. " In all countries, in all times," exclaims he, departing, " the aristocrats have implacably pursued every friend of the people, and with tenfold implacability if such a one were himself born of the aristocracy. It was thus that the last of the Gracchi perished, by the hands of the patricians. But he, being struck with the mortal stab, flung dust toward heaven, and called on the avenging deities; and from this dust there was born Marius—Marius not so illustrious for exterminating the Cimbri as for overturning in Rome the tyranny of the nobles."† Casting up which new curious handful of dust (through the printing-press) to breed what it can and may, Mirabeau stalks forth into the third estate.

255. That he now, to ingratiate himself with this third estate, " opened a cloth-shop in Marseilles," and, for moments, became a furnishing tailor, or even the fable that he did so, is to us always among the pleasant memorabilities of this era. Stranger clothier never wielded the ell-wand and rent webs for men, or fractional parts of men. The fils adoptif is indignant at such disparaging fable,‡ which, nevertheless, was widely believed in those days.§ But, indeed, if Achilles, in the heroic ages, killed mutton, why should not Mirabeau, in the unheroic ones, measure broadcloth?

256. More authentic are his triumph-progresses through that disturbed district, with mob-jubilee, flaming torches, " windows hired for two louis," and voluntary guard of a hundred men. He is deputy elect, both of Aix and of Marseilles, but will prefer Aix. He has opened his far-sounding voice, the depths of his far-sounding soul; he can quell (such virtue is in a spoken word) the pride-tumults of the rich, the hunger-tumults of the poor; and wild mul-

* "Hist. Parl." i. 287. "Deux Amis de la Liberté," i. 105–123.

† "Fils Adoptif," v. 256.

‡ "Mémoires de Mirabeau," v. 307.

§ Marat. Ami-du-Peuple newspaper in "Histoire Parlementaire," ii. 163, etc.

titudes move under him, as under the moon do billows of the sea; he has become a world-compeller, and ruler over men.

257. One other incident and specialty we note, with how different an interest! It is of the parlement of Paris, which starts forward like the others (only with less audacity, seeing better how it lay), to nose-ring that behemoth of a states-general. Worthy Doctor Guillotin, respectable practitioner in Paris, has drawn up his little "plan of a cahier of doléances"—as he had not, having the wish and gift, the clearest liberty to do? He is getting the people to sign it, whereupon the surly parlement summons him to give account of himself. He goes, but with all Paris at his heels, which floods the outer courts, and copiously signs the cahier even there, while the doctor is giving account of himself within! The parlement cannot too soon dismiss Guillotin, with compliments, to be borne home shoulder-high.* This respectable Guillotin we hope to behold once more, and perhaps only once; the parlement not even once, but let it be ingulfed unseen by us.

258. Meanwhile, such things, cheering as they are, tend little to cheer the national creditor, or indeed, the creditor of any kind. In the midst of universal portentous doubt, what certainty can seem so certain as money in the purse, and the wisdom of keeping it there? Trading speculation, commerce of all kinds, has, as far as possible, come to a dead pause, and the hand of the industrious lies idle in his bosom. Frightful enough, when now the rigor of the season has also done its part, and to scarcity of work is added scarcity of food! In the opening spring, there come rumors of forestallment; there come king's edicts, petitions of bakers against millers; and, at length, in the month of April, troops of ragged lack-alls, and fierce cries of starvation! These are the thrice-famed *brigands;* an actual existing quotity of persons, who, long reflected and reverberated through so many millions of heads, as in concave multiplying mirrors, become a whole brigand world, and, like a kind of supernatural machinery, wondrously move the epos of the revolution. The brigands are here, the brigands are there, the brigands are coming! Not otherwise sounded the clang of Phœbus Apollo's silver bow, scattering pestilence and pale terror; for this clang, too, was of the imagination, preternatural, and it, too, walked in formless immensurability, *having made itself like to the night.*

259. But remark, at least, for the first time, the singular sense of suspicion in those lands in those days. If poor famishing men shall, prior to death, gather in groups and crowds, as the poor fieldfares and plovers do in bitter weather, were it but that they may chirp mournfully together, and misery look in the eyes of misery; if famishing men (what famishing fieldfares cannot do) should discover, once congregated, that they need not die while food is in the land, since they are many, and with empty wallets have right hands—in all this what need were there of preternatural machinery? To most people none, but not to French people in a time of revolution. These brigands (as Turgot's also were, fourteen years ago) have all been set on; enlisted though without tap of drum, by aristocrats, by democrats, by D'Orléans, D'Artois, and enemies of the public weal. Nay, historians, to this day, will prove it by one argument: these brigands, pretending to have no victual, nevertheless contrive to drink, nay, have been seen drunk.‡ An unexampled fact! But, on the whole, may we not predict that a people,

with such a width of credulity and of incredulity (the proper union of which makes suspicion, and, indeed, unreason generally), will see shapes enough of immortals fighting in its battle-ranks, and never want for epical machinery?

260. Be this as it may, the brigands are clearly got to Paris in considerable multitudes,† with sallow faces, lank hair (the true enthusiast complexion), with sooty rags, and, also, with large clubs, which they smite angrily against the pavement! These mingle in the election tumult; would fain sign Guillotin's cahier, or any cahier or petition whatsoever, could they but write. Their enthusiast complexion, the smiting of their sticks, bodes little good to any one, least of all to rich master-manufacturers of the suburb Saint-Antoine, with whose workmen they consort.

CHAPTER III.

GROWN ELECTRIC.

261. But, now also, national deputies from all ends of France are in Paris, with their commissions, what they call pouvoirs, or powers, in their pockets, inquiring, consulting, looking out for lodgings at Versailles. The states-general shall open there, if not on the 1st, then, surely, on the 4th of May, in grand procession and gala. The Salle des Menus is all new carpentered, bedizened for them; their very costume has been fixed; a grand controversy which there was as to "slouch-hats or slouched-hâts" for the commons deputies, has got as good as adjusted. Ever new strangers arrive; loungers, miscellaneous persons, officers on furlough—as the worthy Captain Dampmartin, whom we hope to be acquainted with—these, also, from all regions, have repaired hither to see what is toward. Our Paris committees, of the sixty districts, are busier than ever: it is now too clear, the Paris elections will be late.

262. On Monday, the 27th day of April, astronomer Bailly notices that the Sieur Réveillon is not at his post. The Sieur Réveillon—"extensive paper manufacturer of the Rue Saint-Antoine"—he, commonly so punctual, is absent from electoral committee, and even will never reappear there. In those "immense magazines of velvet paper" has aught befallen? Alas, yes! Alas! it is no montgolfier rising there to-day, but drudgery, rascality, and the suburb that is rising! Was the Sieur Réveillon, himself once a journeyman, heard to say that "a journeyman might live handsomely on fifteen sous a day?" Some sevenpence half-penny. 'Tis a slender sum! Or was he only thought and believed to be heard saying it? By this long chafing and friction, it would appear, the national temper has got *electric.*

263. Down in those dark dens, in those dark heads and hungry hearts, who knows in what strange figure the new political evangel may have shaped itself; what miraculous "communion of drudges" may be getting formed! Enough grim individuals—soon waxing to grim multitudes, and other multitudes crowding to see—beset that paper-warehouse; demonstrate in loud ungrammatical language (addressed to the passions too), the insufficiency of sevenpence half-penny a day. The city watch cannot dissipate them, broils arise, and bellowings. Réveillon, at his wits' end, entreats the populace, entreats the authorities. Besenval, now in active command, commandant of Paris, does, toward evening, to Réveillon's earnest prayer, send some thirty Gardes Françaises. These clear the street, happily without firing, and take post there for the night, in hope that it may be all over.*

---

* "Deux Amis de la Liberté," i. 141.
† Lacretelle, "18me Siècle," ii. 155.
‡ Besenval, iii. 385, etc.

* Besenval, iii. 385-88.

264. Not so; on the morrow it is far worse. Saint-Antoine has arisen anew, grimmer than ever—reinforced by the unknown tatterdemalion figures, with their enthuiast complexion and large sticks. The city, through all streets, is flowing thitherward to see; "two cartloads of paving-stones, that happened to pass that way, "have been seized as a visible godsend. Another detachment of Gardes Françaises must be sent—Besenval and the colonel taking earnest counsel. Then still another; they hardly, with bayonets and menace of bullets, penetrate to the spot. What a sight! A street choked up with lumber, tumult, and the endless press of men. A paper warehouse eviscerated by axe and fire; mad din of revolt; musket-volleys responded to by yells, by miscellaneous missiles, by tiles raining from roof and window—tiles, execrations, and slain men!

265. The Gardes Françaises like it not, but have to persevere. All day it continues, slackening and rallying; the sun is sinking, and Saint-Antoine has not yielded. The city flies hither and thither; alas! the sound of that musket-volleying booms into the far dining-rooms of the Chaussée d'Antin, alters the dinner-gossip there. Captain Dampmartin leaves his wine; goes out with a friend or two to see the fighting. Unwashed men growl on him, with murmurs of "A bas les aristocrats (Down with the aristocrats);" and insult the cross of St. Louis! They elbow him, and hustle him, but do not pick his pocket—as indeed at Réveillon's, too, there was not the slightest stealing.*

266. At fall of night, as the thing will not end, Besenval takes his resolution; orders out the Gardes Suisses with two pieces of artillery. The Swiss guards shall proceed thither, summon that rabble to depart, in the king's name. If disobeyed, they shall load their artillery with grape-shot, visibly to the general eye; shall again summon; if again disobeyed, fire—and keep firing "till thy last man" be in this manner blasted off, and the street clear. With which spirited resolution, as might have been hoped, the business is got ended. At sight of the lit matches, of the foreign red-coated Switzers, Saint-Antoine dissipates, hastily, in the shades of dusk. There is an encumbered street; there are "from four to five hundred" dead men. Unfortunate, Réveillon has found shelter in the Bastille; does therefrom, safe behind stone bulwarks, issue plaint protestation, explanation, for the next month. Bold Besenval has thanks from all the respectable Parisian classes, but finds no special notice taken of him at Versailles—a thing the man of true worth is used to.†

267. But how it originated, this fierce electric sputter and explosion? From D'Orléans! cries the courtparty; he, with his gold, enlisted these brigands—surely in some surprising manner, without sound of drum; he raked them hither, from all corners, to ferment and take fire; evil is his good. From the court! cries enlightened patriotism; it is the cursed gold and wiles of aristocrats that enlisted them, set them upon ruining an innocent Sieur Réveillon; to frighten the faint, and disgust men with the career of freedom.

268. Besenval, with reluctance, concludes that it came from "the English, our natural enemies." Or, alas, might not one rather attribute it to Diana in the shape of hunger? To some twin Dioscuri, oppression and revenge so often seen in the battles of men? Poor lackalls, all betoiled, besoiled, incrusted into dim defacement—into whom, nevertheless, the breath of the Almighty has breathed a living soul! To them it is clear only that eleutheromaniac philosophism has yet baked no bread; that patriot committee-men will level down to their own level, and no lower. Brigands, or whatever they might be, it was bitter earnest with them. They bury their dead with the title of défenseurs de la patrie, martyrs of the good cause.

269. Or shall we say, insurrection has now served its apprenticeship, and this was its proof-stroke, and no inconclusive one? Its next will be a master-stroke, announcing indisputable mastership to a whole astonished world. Let that rock-fortress, tyranny's stronghold, which they name Bastille, or building—as if there were no other building—look to its guns!

270. But in such wise, with primary and secondary assemblies, and cahiers of grievances; with motions, congregations of all kinds, with much thunder of froth-eloquence, and at last with thunder of platoon-musketry—does agitated France accomplish its elections. With confused winnowing and sifting, in this rather tumultuous manner, it has now (all except some remnants of Paris) sifted out the true wheatgrains of national deputies, twelve hundred and fourteen in number, and will forthwith open its statesgeneral.

CHAPTER IV.

THE PROCESSION.

271. On the first Saturday of May, it is gala at Versailles, and Monday, fourth of the month, is to be a still greater day. The deputies have mostly got thither, and sought out lodgings; and are now successively, in long, well-ushered files, kissing the hand of majesty in the château. Supreme Usher de Brézé does not give the highest satisfaction; we cannot but observe that in ushering noblesse or clergy into the anointed presence, he liberally opens both its folding-doors, and, on the other hand, for members of the third estate opens only one! However, there is room to enter; majesty has smiles for all.

272. The good Louis welcomes his honorable members with smiles of hope. He has prepared for them the Hall of Menus, the largest near him; and often surveyed the workmen as they went on. A spacious hall; with raised platform for throne, court, and blood-royal; space for 600 commons deputies in front, for half as many clergy on this hand, and half as many noblesse on that. It has lofty galleries, wherefrom dames of honor, splendid in gaze d'or; foreign diplomacies, and other gilt-edged, white-frilled individuals, to the number of 2,000—may sit and look Broad passages flow through it, and, outside the inner wall, all round it. There are committee-rooms, guard-rooms, robing-rooms; really a noble hall, where upholstery, aided by the subject fine-arts, has done its best, and crimson-tasseled cloths and emblematic fleurs-de-lis are not wanting.

273. The hall is ready; the very costume, as we said, has been settled; what means are not to wear that hated slouch-hat (chapeau clabaud), but one not quite so slouched (chapeau rabattu). As for their manner of working when all dressed, for their "voting by head or by order" and the rest—this which it were perhaps still time to settle, and in few hours will be no longer time—remains unsettled. hangs dubious in the breast of twelve hundred men.

274. But now, finally, the sun, on Monday the 4th of May, has risen—unconcerned as if it were no special day. And yet, as his first rays could strike music from the Memnon's statue on the Nile, what tones were these, so thrilling, tremulous of preparation and foreboding, which he awoke in every bosom at Versailles? Huge Paris, in all conceivable and

* "Evénemens qui se sont passés sous mes yeux pendant la Révolution Française," par A. H. Dampmartin (Berlin, 1790), i. 25-27.

† Besenval, iii, 359.

inconceivable vehicles, is pouring itself forth; from each town and village come subsidiary rills; Versailles is a very sea of men. But above all, from the church of St. Louis to the church of Notre Dame, one vast suspended-billow of life—with *spray* scattered even to the chimney-tops! For on chimney-tops, too, as over the roofs, and up thitherward on every lamp-iron, sign-post, break-neck coign of vantage, sits patriotic courage; and every window bursts with patriotic beauty; for the deputies are gathering at St. Louis church, to march in procession to Notre Dame and hear sermon.

275. Yes, friends, ye may sit and look, bodily or in thought, all France, and all Europe, may sit and look; for it is a day like few others. Oh, one might weep like Xerxes, so many serried rows sit perched there, like winged creatures, alighted out of heaven; all these, and so many more that follow them, shall have wholly fled aloft again, vanishing into the blue deep, and the memory of this day still be fresh. It is the baptism-day of democracy; sick Time has given it birth, the numbered months being run. The extreme-unction day of feudalism! A superannuated system of society, decrepit with toils (for has it not done much; produced *you*, and what ye have and know!—and with thefts and brawls, named glorious victories; and with profligacies, sensualities, and, on the whole, with dotage and senility—is now to die; and so, with death-throes and birth-throes, a new one is to be born. What a work, O earth! and heavens, what a work? Battles and bloodshed, September massacres, bridges of Lodi, retreats of Moscow, Waterloos, Peterloos, ten-pound franchises, tar-barrels and guillotines—and from this present date, if one might prophesy, some two centuries of it still to fight! Two centuries, hardly less, before democracy go through its due, most baleful, stages of *quackocracy*; and a pestilential world be burnt up, and have begun to grow green and young again.

276. Rejoice, nevertheless, ye Versailles multitudes; to you, from whom all this is hid, the glorious end of it is visible. This day, sentence of death is pronounced on shams; judgment of resuscitation, were it but afar off, is pronounced on realities. This day it is declared aloud, as with a doom-trumpet, that *a lie is unbelievable*. Believe that, stand by that, if more there be not; and let what thing or things soever will follow it, follow. "Ye can no other, God be your help!" So spake a greater than any of you, opening *his* chapter of world-history.

277. Behold, however! The doors of St. Louis church flung wide; and the procession of processions advancing toward Notre-Dame! Shouts rend the air, one shout, at which Grecian birds might drop dead. It is, indeed, a stately, solemn sight. The elected of France, and then the court of France; they are marshaled and marched there, all in prescribed place and costume. Our commons "in plain black mantle and white cravat;" noblesse, in gold-worked, bright-dyed cloaks of velvet, resplendent, rustling with laces, waving with plumes; the clergy in rocket, alb, or other best pontificalibus; lastly comes the king himself, and king's household, also in their brightest blaze of pomp—their brightest and final one. Some fourteen hundred men blown together from all winds, on the deepest errand.

278. Yes, in that silent marching mass there lies futurity enough. No symbolic ark, like the old Hebrews, do these men bear, yet with them, too, is a covenant; they, too, preside at a new era in the history of men. The whole future is there, and destiny dim-brooding over it; in the hearts and unshaped thoughts of these men it lies, illegible, inevitable. Singular to think, *they* have it in them, yet not they, not mortal, only the Eye above can read it—as it

shall unfold itself in fire and thunder of siege and field-artillery; in the rustling of battle-banners, the tramp of hosts, in the glow of burning cities, the shriek of strangled nations! Such things lie hidden, safe-wrapt in this fourth day of May—say rather, had lain in some other unknown day, of which this latter is the public fruit and outcome. As, indeed, what wonders lie in every day—had we the sight, as happily we have not, to decipher it; for is not every meanest day "the conflux of two eternities!"

279. Meanwhile, suppose we, too, good reader should, as now without miracle Muse Clio enables us —take *our* station also on some coign of vantage, and glance momentarily over this procession and this life-sea, with far other eyes than the rest do, namely, with prophetic? We can mount, and stand there, without fear of falling.

280. As for the life-sea, or onlooking unnumbered multitude, it is unfortunately all too dim. Yet as we gaze fixedly, do not nameless figures not a few, which shall not always be nameless, disclose themselves, visible or presumable there! Young Baroness de Staël—she evidently looks from a window, among older honorable women.* Her father is minister, and one of the gala personages; to his own eyes the chief one. Young spiritual amazon, thy rest is not there, nor thy loved father's: "as Malebranche saw all things in God, so M. Necker sees all things in Necker" —a theorem that will not hold.

281. But where is the brown-locked, light-behaved, fire-hearted Demoiselle Théroigne? Brown, eloquent beauty, who with thy winged words and glances shalt thrill rough bosoms, whole steel battalions, and persuade an Austrian kaiser—pike and helm lie provided for thee in due season; and, alas, also, strait-waistcoat and long lodging in the Salpêtrière. Better hadst thou staid in native Luxemburg, and been the mother of some brave man's children, but it was not thy task, it was not thy lot.

282. Of the rougher sex, how, without tongue, or hundred tongues, of iron, enumerate the notabilities! Has not Marquis Valadi hastily quitted his Quaker broad-brim, his Pythagorean Greek in Wapping, and the city of Glasgow?† De Morande from his Courrier de l'Europe; Linguet from his Annales, they looked eager through the London fog, and became ex-editors—that they might feed the guillotine, and have their due. Does Louvet (of Faublas) stand a-tiptoe? And Brissot, hight De Warville, friend of the blacks? He, with Marquis Condorcet and Clavière the Genevese," have created the Moniteur newspaper," or are about creating it. Able editors must give account of a day.

283. Or seest thou with any distinctness, low down probably, not in places of honor, a Stanislas Maillard, riding-tipstaff (huissier à cheval) of the châtelet, one of the shiftiest of men? A Captain Hulin of Geneva, Captain Elie of the Queen's Regiment; both with an air of half-pay? Jourdan, with tile-colored whiskers, not yet with tile-beard, an unjust dealer in mules? He shall be, in few months, Jourdan the Headsman, and have other work.

284. Surely, also, in some place not of honor, stands or sprawls up querulous, that he, too, though short, may see—one squalidest bleared mortal, redolent of soot and horse-drugs—Jean Paul Marat of Neuchâtel! O Marat, renovator of human science, lecturer on optics; O thou remarkablest horse-leech, once in D'Artois's stables—as thy bleared soul looks forth, through thy bleared, dull-acrid, woe-stricken face, what sees it in all this? Any faintest light of hope,

---

* Madame de Staël, "Considérations sur la Révolution Française" (London, 1818), i. 114-191.
† "Founders of the French Republic" (London, 1798)
§ Valadi.

like dayspring after Nova-Zembla night? Or is it but *blue* sulphur-light, and spectres; woe, suspicion, revenge without end?

285. Of draper Lecointre, how he shut his cloth-shop hard by, and stepped forth, one need hardly speak. Nor of Santerre, the sonorous brewer from the Faubourg St. Antoine. Two other figures, and only two, we signalize there. The huge, brawny figure, through whose black brows and rude flattened face (figure écrasée) there looks a waste energy as of Hercules not yet furibund—he is an esurient, unprovided advocate, Danton by name, him mark. Then that other, his slight-built comrade and craft-brother; he with the long curling locks, with the face of dingy blackguardism, wondrously irradiated with genius, as if a naphtha-lamp burnt within it; that figure is Camille Desmoulins. A fellow of infinite shrewdness' wit, nay, humor; one of the sprightliest, clearest souls in all these millions. Thou poor Camille, say of thee what they may, it were but falsehood to pretend one did not almost love thee, thou headlong, lightly-sparkling man! But the brawny, not yet furibund figure, we say is Jacques Danton, a name that shall be "tolerably known in the revolution." He is president of the electoral Cordeliers district at Paris, or about to be it, and shall open his lungs of brass.

We dwell no longer on the mixed shouting multitude, for now, behold, the commons deputies are at hand!

286. Which of these 600 individuals, in plain white cravat, that have come up to regenerate France, might one guess would become their *king*? For a king or leader they, as all bodies of men, must have, be their work what it may; there is one man there who, by character, faculty, position, is fittest of all to do it: that man, as future, not-yet-elected king, walks there among the rest. He with the thick black locks, will it be? With the bure, as himself calls it, or black *boar's-head*, fit to be "shaken" as a senatorial portent? Through whose shaggy beetle-brows and rough-hewn, seamed, carbuncled face there look natural ugliness, small-pox, incontinence, bankruptcy, and burning fire of genius, like comet-fire glaring fuliginous through murkiest confusions? It is Gabriel Honoré Riquetti de Mirabeau, the world-compeller; man-ruling Deputy of Aix! According to the Baroness de Staël, he steps proudly along, though looked at askance here, and shakes his black chevelure, or lion's mane, as if prophetic of great deeds.

287. Yes, reader, that is the Type-Frenchman of this epoch, as Voltaire was of the last. He is French in his aspirations, acquisitions, in his virtues, in his vices; perhaps more French than any other man—and intrinsically such a mass of manhood too. Mark him well. The national assembly were all-different without that one; nay, he might say, with the old despot: "The national assembly? I am that."

288. Of a Southern climate, of wild southern blood—for the Riquettis, or Arrighettis, had to fly from Florence and the Guelfs, long centuries ago, and settled in Provence, where from generation to generation they have ever approved themselves a peculiar kindred, irascible, indomitable sharp-cutting, true, like the steel they wore; of an intensity and activity that sometimes verged toward madness, yet did not reach it. One ancient Riquetti, in mad fulfillment of a mad vow, chains two mountains together, and the chain, with its "iron star of five rays," is still to be seen. May not a modern Riquetti unchain so much, and set it drifting—which also shall be seen?

289. Destiny has work for that swart, hurly-headed Mirabeau; destiny has watched over him,

prepared him from afar. Did not his grandfather, stout Col-d'Argent (Silver-Stock, so they named him), shattered and slashed by seven-and-twenty wounds in one fell day, lie sunk together on the bridge at Casano, while Prince Eugène's cavalry galloped and regalloped over him—only the flying sergeant had thrown a camp-kettle over that loved head; and Vendome, dropping his spy-glass moaned out, "Mirabeau is *dead*, then!" Nevertheless, he was not dead: he awoke to breath and miraculous surgery—for Gabriel was yet to be. With his *silver stock* he kept his scarred head erect, through long years, and wedded, and produced tough Marquis Victor, the *friend of men*. Whereby at last in the appointed year, 1749, this long-expected, rough-hewn Gabriel Honoré did likewise see the light; roughest lion's-whelp ever littered of that rough breed. How the old lion (for our old marquis, too, was lion-like, most unconquerable, kingly genial, most perverse) gazed wondering on his offspring, and determined to train him as no lion had yet been! It is in vain, O marquis! This cub, though thou slay him and flay him, will not learn to draw in dog-cart of political economy and be a *friend of men*; he will not be thou, but must and will be himself, another than thou. Divorce, lawsuits, "whole family save one in prison, and three-score lettres-de-cachet" for thy own sole use, do but astonish the world.

290. Our luckless Gabriel, sinned against and sinning, has been in the isle of Rhé, and heard the Atlantic from his tower; in the castle of If, and heard the Mediterranean at Marseilles. He has been in the fortress of Joux, and forty-two months, with hardly clothing to his back, in the dungeon of Vincennes—all by lettre-de-cachet, from his lion father. He has been in Pontarlier jail (self-constituted prisoner); was noticed fording estuaries of the sea (at low water), in flight from the face of men. He has pleaded before Aix parlements (to get back his wife), the public gathering on roofs, to see, since they could not hear: "The clatter-teeth (claque dents)!" snarls singular old Mirabeau; discerning in such admired forensic eloquence nothing but two clattering jawbones, and a head vacant, sonorous, of the drum species.

291. But as for Gabriel Honoré, in these strange wayfarings, what has he not seen and tried! From drill-sergeants, to prime-ministers, to foreign and domestic booksellers, all manner of men he has seen. All manner of men he has gained; for at bottom it is a social, loving heart, that wild, unconquerable one—more especially all manner of women. From the archer's daughter at Saintes to that fair young Sophie Madame Monnier, whom he could not but "steal," and be beheaded for—in effigy! For, indeed, hardly since the Arabian prophet lay dead, to Ali's admiration, was there seen such a love-hero, with the strength of thirty men. In war again he has helped to conquer Corsica; fought duels, irregular brawls; horsewhipped calumnious barons. In literature, he has written on "Despotism," on "Lettres-de-Cachet;" erotics Sapphic-Werterean, obscenities, profanities; books on the "Prussian Monarchy," on "Cagliostro," on "Calonne," on "The Water Companies of Paris"—each book comparable, we will say, to a bituminous alarm-fire, huge, smoky, sudden! The fire-pan, the kindling, the bitumen, were his own; but the lumber, of rags, old wood, and nameless combustible rubbish (for all is fuel to him), was gathered from hucksters, and ass-panniers, of every description under heaven. Whereby, indeed, hucksters enough have been heard to exclaim, Out upon it, the fire is *mine*.

292. Nay, consider it more generally, seldom had man such a talent for borrowing. The idea, the

faculty of another man he can make his; the man himself he can make his. "All reflex and echo (tout de reflet et de réverbère)!" snarls old Mirabeau, who can see, but will not. Crabbed old friend of men! it is his sociality, his aggregative nature; and, will now be the quality of qualities for him! In that forty-years' "struggle against despotism," he has gained the glorious faculty of *self-help*, and yet not lost the glorious natural gift of *fellowship*, of being helped. Rare union: this man can live self-sufficing—yet lives also in the life of other men; can make men love him, work with him; a born king of men!

293. But consider further how, as the old marquis still snarls, he has "made away with (*humé*, swallowed, snuffed up) all *formulas*"—a fact which, if we meditate it, will in these days mean much. This is no man of system, then; he is only a man of instincts and insights. A man, nevertheless, who will glare fiercely on any object, and see through it, and conquer it; for he has intellect, he has will, force beyond other men. A man not with *logic-spectacles*, but with an *eye!* Unhappily without decalogue, moral code or theorem of any fixed sort, yet not without a strong living soul in him, and sincerity there; a reality, not an artificiality, not a sham! And so he, having struggled "forty years against despotism," and "made away with all formulas," shall now become the spokesman of a nation bent to do the same. For is it not precisely the struggle of France, also, to cast off despotism, to make away with *her* old formulas—having found them naught, worn out, far from the reality? She will make away with *such* formulas, and even go *bare*, if need be, till she have found new ones.

294. Toward such work, in such manner, marches he, this singular Riquetti Mirabeau. In fiery rough figure, with black Samson-locks under the slouch hat, he steps along there. A fiery, fuliginous mass, which could be choked and smothered, but would fill all France with smoke! And now it has got *air;* it will burn its whole substance, its whole smoke-atmosphere, too, and fill all France with flame. Strange lot! Forty years of that smoldering, with foul firedamp and vapor enough; then victory over that, and like a burning mountain he blazes heaven-high, and, for twenty-three resplendent months, pours out, in flame and molten fire-torrents, all that is in him, the Pharos and wonder-signs of an amazed Europe—and then lies hollow, cold forever! Pass on, thou questionable Gabriel Honoré, the greatest of them all: in the whole national deputies, in the whole nation, there is none like and none second to thee.

295. But now, if Mirabeau is the greatest, who of these 600 may be the meanest? Shall we say, that anxious, slight, ineffectual-looking man, under thirty, in spectacles; his eyes (were the glasses off) troubled, careful; with upturned face, snuffing dimly the uncertain future time; complexion of a multiplex atrabiliar color, the final shade of which may be the pale sea-green.[*] That greenish-colored (verdâtre) individual is an advocate of Arras; his name is Maximilien Robespierre. The son of an advocate; his father founded mason-lodges under Charles Edward, the English prince or pretender. Maximilien, the first-born, was thriftily educated; he had brisk Camille Desmoulins for school-mate in the college of Louis le Graud, at Paris. But he begged our famed necklace-cardinal, Rohan, the patron, to let him depart thence, and resign in favor of a younger brother. The strict-minded Max departed, home to paternal Arras; and even had a law-case there, and pleaded, not unsuccessfully, "in favor of the first Franklin thunder-rod." With a strict, painful mind, an understanding small but clear and ready, he grew in favor with official persons, who could foresee in him an excellent man of business, happily quite free from genius. The bishop, therefore, taking counsel, appoints him judge of his diocese, and he faithfully does justice to the people, till behold, one day, a culprit comes whose crime merits hanging, and the strict-minded Max must abdicate, for his conscience will not permit the dooming of any son of Adam to die. A strict-minded, strait-laced man! A man unfit for revolutions, whose small soul, transparent, wholesome-looking as small ale, could by no chance ferment into virulent *alegar*—the mother of ever-new alegar—till all France were grown acetous virulent? We shall see.

296. Between which two extremes of grandest and meanest, so many grand and mean roll on, toward their several destinies, in that procession! There is Cazalès, the learned young soldier, who shall become the eloquent orator of royalism, and earn the shadow of a name. Experienced Mounier, experienced Malouet, whose presidential parliamentary experience the stream of things shall soon leave stranded. A Pétion has left his gown and briefs at Chartres for a stormier sort of pleading; has not forgotten his violin, being fond of music. His hair is grizzled, though he is still young; convictions, beliefs placid-unalterable, are in that man: not hindmost of them, belief in himself. A Protestant-clerical Rabaut-St.-Etienne, a slender, young, eloquent, and vehement Barnave, will help to regenerate France. There are so many of them young. Till thirty the Spartans did not suffer a man to marry; let how many men here, under thirty, coming to produce not one sufficient citizen, but a nation and a world of such! The old to heal up rents, the young to remove rubbish—which latter is it not, indeed, the task here?

297. Dim, formless from this distance, yet authentically there, thou noticest the deputies from Nantes? To us mere clothes-screens, with slouch-hat and cloak, but bearing in their pocket a cahier of doléances with this singular clause, and more such, in it: "That the master wig-makers of Nantes be not troubled with new guild-brethren, the actually existing number of ninety-two being more than sufficient!"[*] The Rennes people have elected farmer Gérard, "a man of natural sense and rectitude without any learning." He walks there with solid step; unique, "in his rustic farmer-clothes," which he will wear always, careless of short cloaks and costumes. The name Gérard, or "Père Gérard, Father Gérard," as they please to call him, will fly far borne about in endless banter, in royalist satires, in republican didactic almanacs.[†] As for the man Gérard, being asked once what he did, after trial of it, candidly think of this parlementary work, "I think," answered he, "that there are a good many scoundrels among us." So walks father Gérard, solid in his thick shoes, whithersoever bound.

298. And worthy Doctor Guillotin, whom we hoped to behold one other time? If not here, the doctor should be here, and we see him with the eye of prophecy; for indeed the Parisian deputies are all a little late. Singular Guillotin, respectable practitioner; doomed by a satiric destiny to the strangest immortal glory that ever kept obscure mortal from his resting-place, the bosom of oblivion! Guillotin can improve the ventilation of the hall, in all cases of medical police and hygiène be a present aid; but, greater far, he can produce his "Report on the Penal Code," and reveal therein a cunningly devised beheading machine, which shall become famous and

* See De Staël, "Considerations" (ii. 142); Barbaroux, "Mémoires," etc.

* "Histoire Parlementaire," i. 335.

† "Actes des Apôtres" (by Peltier and others): "Almanach du Père Gérard," (by Collot d'Herbois), etc., etc.

world-famous. This is the product of Guillotin's endeavors, gained not without meditation and reading; which product popular gratitude or levity christens by a feminine derivative name, as if it were his daughter—La Guillotine! "With my machine, messieurs, I whisk off your head (vous fais sauter la tête) in a twinkling, and you have no pain"—whereat they all laugh.* Unfortunate doctor! For two-and-twenty years he, unguillotined, shall hear nothing but guillotine, see nothing but guillotine; then dying, shall through long centuries wander, as it were, a disconsolate ghost, on the wrong side of Styx and Lethe his name like to outlive Cæsar's.

299. See Bailly, likewise of Paris, time-honored historian of astronomy ancient and modern. Poor Bailly, how thy serenely beautiful philosophizing, with its soft moonshiny clearness and thinness, ends in foul thick confusion—of presidency, mayorship, diplomatic officiality, rabid triviality, and the throat of everlasting darkness! Far was it to descend from the heavenly galaxy to the drapeau rouge; beside that fatal dung-heap, on that last holl-day, thou must "tremble," though only with cold—"de froid." Speculation is not practice: to be weak is not so miserable, but to be weaker than our task. Woe the day when they mounted thee, a peaceable pedestrian on that wild hippogriff of a democracy, which, spurning the firm earth, nay, lashing at the very stars, no yet known Astolpho could have ridden!

300. In the commons deputies there are merchants, artists, men of letters, 374 lawyers,† and at least one clergyman, the Abbé Sieyes. Him also Paris sends among its twenty. Behold him, the light, thin man; cold, but elastic, wiry; instinct with the pride of logic; passionless, or with but one passion, that of self-conceit. If, indeed, that can be called a passion, which, in its independent concentrated greatness, seems to have soared into transcendentalism; and to sit there with a kind of godlike indifference, and look down on passion! He is the man, and wisdom shall die with him. This is the Sieyes who shall be system-builder, constitution-builder general, and build constitutions (as many as wanted) sky-high—which shall all unfortunately fall before he get the scaffolding away. "La politique," said he to Dumont, "polity is a science I think I have completed (achevée)."‡ What things, O Sieyes, with thy clear assiduous eyes, art thou to see! But were it not curious to know how Sieyes, now in these days (for he is said to be still alive)§ looks out on all that constitution masonry, through the rheumy soberness of extreme age? Might we hope, still with the old irrefragable transcendentalism? The victorious cause pleased the gods, the vanquished one pleased Sieyes (victa Catoni).

Thus, however, amid sky-rending vivats, and blessings from every heart, has the procession of the commons deputies rolled by.

301. Next follow the noblesse, and next the clergy; concerning both of whom it might be asked what they specially have come for. Specially, little as they dream of it, to answer this question, put in a voice of thunder: What are you doing in God's fair earth and task-garden, where whosoever is not working is begging or stealing? Woe, woe to themselves and to all, if they can only answer, Collecting tithes, preserving game. Remark, meanwhile, how D'Orléans affects to step before his own order and mingle with the commons. For him are vivats; few for the rest, though all wave in plumed "hats of a feudal

cut," and have sword on thigh; though among them is D'Antraigues, the young Languedocian gentleman —and, indeed, many a peer more or less noteworthy.

302. There are Liancourt and La Rochefoucalt, the liberal Anglomaniac dukes. There is a filially pious Lally; a couple of liberal Lameths. Above all, there is a Lafayette, whose name shall be Cromwell-Grandison, and fill the world. Many a "formula" has this Lafayette, too, made away with, yet not all formulas. He sticks by the Washington formula; and by that he will stick—and hang by it, as by sure bower-anchor hangs and swings the tight war-ship, which, after all changes of wildest weather and water, is found still hanging. Happy for him, be it glorious or not! Alone of all Frenchmen he has a theory of the world, and right mind to conform thereto; he can become a hero and perfect character, were it but the hero of one idea. Note, further, our old parlementary friend, Crispin-Catiline d'Espréménil. He is returned from the Mediterranean islands, a red-hot royalist, repentant to the finger-ends, unsettled-looking; whose light, dusky-glowing at best, now flickers foul in the socket; whom the national assembly will by and by, to save time, "regard as in a state of distraction." Note lastly that globular younger Mirabeau, indignant that his elder brother is among the commons; it is Viscomte Mirabeau; named oftener Mirabeau Tonneau (Barrel Mirabeau), on account of his rotundity, and the quantities of strong liquor he contains.

303. There, then, walks our French noblesse. All in the old pomp of chivalry: and yet, alas, how changed from the old position, drifted far down from their native latitude, like Arctic icebergs got into the equatorial sea, and fast thawing there! Once these chivalry duces (dukes, as they are still named) did actually lead the world—were it only toward battle-spoil, where lay the world's best wages then; moreover, being the ablest leaders going, they had their lion's share, those duces, which none could grudge them. But now, when so many looms, improved plow-shares, steam-engines, and bills of exchange have been invented; and, for battle-brawling itself, men hire drill-sergeants at eighteen pence a day—what mean these gold-mantled chivalry figures, walking there "in black-velvet cloaks," in high-plumed "hats of a feudal cut?" Reeds shaken in the wind!

304. The clergy have got up, with cahiers for abolishing pluralities, enforcing residence of bishops, better payment of tithes.* The dignitaries, we can observe, walk stately, apart from the numerous undignified—who, indeed, are properly little other than commons disguised in curate-frocks. Here, however, though by strange ways, shall the precept be fulfilled, and they that are greatest (much to their astonishment) become least. For one example out of many, mark that plausible Grégoire: one day Curé Grégoire shall be a bishop, when the now stately are wandering distracted, as bishops in partibus. With other thought, mark also the Abbé Maury, his broad bold face, mouth accurately primmed, full eyes, that ray out intelligence, falsehood—the sort of sophistry which is astonished you should find it sophistical. Skillfulest vamper-up of old rotten leather, to make it look like new; always a rising man; he used to tell Mercier, "You will see, I shall be in the Academy before you."† Likely, indeed, thou skillfulest Maury; nay, thou shalt have a cardinal's hat, and plush and glory; but alas, also, in the long-run—mere oblivion, like the rest of us, and six feet of earth! What boots it, vamping rotten leather on these terms? Glorious in comparison is the livelihood thy good

* Moniteur newspaper, of December 1st, 1789 (in "Histoire Parlementaire").
† Bouille, "Mémoires sur la Révolution Française" (London, 1797), i. 68.
‡ Dumont, "Souvenirs sur Mirabeau," p. 64.
§ A. D. 1834.

"Hist. Parl." i. 322–327.
Mercier, "Nouveau Paris."

old father earns by making shoes—one may hope, in a sufficient manner. Maury does not want for audacity. He shall wear pistols by and by; and, at death-cries ot"La lanterne, The lamp-iron!" answer coolly, " Friends, will you see better there ?"

305. But yonder, halting lamely along, thou noticeest next Bishop Talleyrand-Perigord, his reverence of Autun. A sardonic grimness lies in that irreverend reverence of Autun. He will do and suffer strange things; and will *become* surely one of the strangest things ever seen, or like to be seen. A man living in falsehood and on falsehood, yet not what you call a false man—there is the specialty ! It will be an enigma for future ages, one may hope: hitherto such a product of nature and art was possible only for this age of ours—age of paper, and of the burning of paper. Consider Bishop Talleyrand and Marquis Lafayette as the topmost of their two kinds, and say once more, looking at what they did and what they were, O tempus ferax rerum !

306. On the whole, however, has not this unfortunate clergy also drifted in the time-stream, far from its native latitude? An anomalous mass of men ; of whom the whole world has already a dim understanding that it can understand nothing. They were once a priesthood, interpreters of wisdom, revealers of the holy that is in man ; a true clerus (of inheritance of God on earth); but now? They pass silently, with such cahiers as they have been able to redact; and none cries, God bless them.

307. King Louis with his court brings up the rear ; he cheerful, in this day of hope, is saluted with plaudits; still more Necker his minister. Not so the queen, on whom hope shines not steadily any more. Ill-fated queen ! Her hair is already gray with many cares and crosses ; her first-born son is dying in these weeks ; black falsehood has ineffaceably soiled her fair name—ineffaceably while this generation lasts. Instead of Vive le reine, voices insult her with Vive d'Orléans. Of her queenly beauty little remains except its stateliness; not now gracious, but haughty, rigid, silently enduring. With a most mixed feeling, wherein joy has no part, she resigns herself to a day she hoped never to have seen. Poor Marie Antoinette; with thy quick, noble instincts, vehement glancings, vision all too fitful narrow for the work thou hast to do ! Oh! there are. tears in store for thee; bitterest wailings, soft womanly meltings, though thou hast the heart of an imperial Theresa's daughter. Thou doomed one, shut thy eyes on the future!

308. And so, in stately procession, have passed the elected of France. Some toward honor and quick fire-consummation ; most toward dishonor ; not a few toward massacre, confusion, emigration, desperation ; all toward eternity ! · So many heterogeneities cast together into the fermenting-vat ; there, with incalculable action, counteraction, elective affinities, explosive developments, to work out healing for a sick, moribund system of society ! Probably the strangest body of men, if we consider well, that ever met together on our planet on such an errand. So thousandfold complex a society, ready to burst up from its infinite depths; and these men, its rulers and healers, without life-rule for themselves—other life-rule than a gospel according to Jean Jacques ! To the wisest of them, what we must call the wisest, man is properly an accident under the sky. Man is without duty round him ; except it be "to make the constitution." He is without heaven above him, or hell beneath him ; he has no God in the world.

309. What further or better belief can be said to exist in these twelve hundred ? Belief in high plumed hats of a feudal cut; in heraldic scutcheons ; in the divine right of kings, in the divine right of game destroyers.

Belief, or what is still worse, canting half-belief; or worst of all, mere Machiavelic pretense-of belief—in consecrated dough-wafers, and the Godhood of a poor old Italian man ! Nevertheless, in that immeasurable confusion and corruption, which struggles there so blindly to become less confused and corrupt, there is, as we said, this one salient point of a new life discernible—the deep fixed determination to have done with shams. A determination which, consciously or unconsciously, is *fixed;* which waxes ever more fixed, into very madness and fixed-idea; which in such embodiment as lies provided there, shall now unfold itself rapidly; monstrous, stupendous, unspeakable; new for long thousands of years! How has the heaven's *light,* oftentimes in this earth, to clothe itself in thunder and electric murkiness, and descend as molten *lightning,* blasting, if purifying! Nay, is it not rather the very murkiness, and atmospheric suffocation, that *brings* the lightning and the light ? The new evangel, as the old had been, was it to be born in the destruction of a world?

310. But how the deputies assisted at high mass, and heard sermon, and applauded the preacher, church as it was, when he preached politics ; how, next day, with sustained pomp, there are, for the first time, installed in their Salle des Menus (hall no longer of *amusements*), and become a states-general—readers can fancy for themselves. The king from his estrade, gorgeous as Solomon in all his glory, runs his eye over that majestic hall ; many-plumed, many-glancing ; bright-tinted as rainbow, in the galleries and near side-spaces, where beauty sets raining bright influence. Satisfaction as of one that after long voyaging had got to port, plays over his broad simple face—the innocent king! He rises and speaks, with sonorous tone, a conceivable speech. With which—still more with the succeeding one-hour and two hours' speeches of Garde-des-Sceaux and M. Necker, full of nothing but patriotism, hope, faith, and deficiency of the revenue—no reader of these pages shall be tried.

311. We remarked only that, as his majesty, on finishing the speech, put on his plumed hat, and the noblesse according to custom imitated him, our tiers-état deputies did mostly, not without a shade of fierceness, in like manner clap on, and even crush on their slouched hats, and stand there awaiting the issue.[†] Thick buzz among them, between majority and minority, of Couvrez-vous, Découvrez-vous (Hats off, Hats on)! To which his majesty puts an end by taking *off* his own royal hat again.

The session terminates without further accident or omen than this ; with which, significantly enough, France has opened her states-general.

BOOK FIFTH.

THE THIRD ESTATE.

CHAPTER I.

INERTIA.

312. That exasperated France, in this same national assembly of hers, has got something, nay, something great, momentous, indispensable, cannot be doubted ; yet still the question were, Specially *what ?* A question hard to solve, even for calm onlookers at this distance ; wholly insoluble to actors in the middle of it. The states-general, created and conflated by the passionate effort of the whole nation, is there as a thing high and lifted up. Hope, jubilating, cries

* Moniteur (in " Histoire Parlementaire." i. 405).
† " Histoire Parlementaire" (i. 356). Mercier, "Nouveau Paris,"etc.

aloud that it will prove a miraculous brazen erpents in the wilderness, whereon whosoever looks, with faith and obedience, shall be healed of all woes and serpent-bites.

313. We may answer, it will at least prove a symbolic banner; round which the exasperated complaining twenty-five millions, otherwise isolated and without power, may rally, and work—what it is in them to work. If battle must be the work, as one cannot help expecting, then shall it be a battle-banner (say, an Italian gonfalon, in its old republican carroccio); and shall tower up, car-borne, shining in the wind; and with iron tongue peal forth many a signal. A thing of prime necessity; which, whether in the van or in the center, whether leading or led and driven, must do the fighting multitude incalculable services. For a season, while it floats in the very front, nay, as it were, stands solitary there, waiting whether force will gather round it, this same national carroccio, and the signal-peals it rings, are a main object with us.

314. The omen of the "slouch-hats clapt on" shows the common deputies to have made up their minds on one thing, that neither noblesse nor clergy shall have precedence of them, hardly even majesty itself. To such length has the "Contrat Social" and force of public opinion carried us. For what is majesty but the delegate of the nation, delegated and bargained with (even rather tightly)—in some very singular posture of affairs, which Jean Jacques has not fixed the date of?

315. Coming therefore into their hall on the morrow, an inorganic mass of 600 individuals, these commons deputies perceive, without terror, that they have it all to themselves. Their hall is also the grand or general hall for all three orders. But the noblesse and clergy, it would seem, have retired to their two separate apartments or halls, and are there "verifying their powers," not in a conjoint, but in a separate capacity. They are to constitute two separate, perhaps separately-voting orders, then? It is as if both noblesse and clergy had silently taken for granted that they already were such! Two orders against one, and so the third order to be left in a perpetual minority?

316. Much may remain unfixed; but the negative of that is a thing fixed in the slouch-hatted heads, in the French nation's head. Double representation, and all else hitherto gained, were otherwise futile, null. Doubtless the "powers must be verified"—doubtless the commission, the electoral documents of your deputy must be inspected by his brother deputies, and found valid; it is the preliminary of all. Neither is this question, of doing it separately or doing it conjointly, a vital one; but if it lead to such? It must be resisted; wise was that maxim, resist the beginnings! Nay, were resistance unadvisable, even dangerous, yet surely pause is very natural—pause, with twenty-five millions behind you, may become resistance enough. The inorganic mass of commons deputies will restrict itself to a "system of inertia," and for the present remain inorganic.

317. Such method, recommendable alike to sagacity and to timidity, do the commons deputies adopt; and, not without adroitness, and with evermore tenacity, they persist in it day after day, week after week. For six weeks their history is of the kind named barren, which indeed, as philosophy knows, is often the fruitfullest of all. These were their still creation-days, wherein they sat incubating! In fact, what they did was to do nothing in a judicious manner. Daily the inorganic body reassembles; regrets that they cannot get organization, "verification of powers in common," and begin regenerating France. Headlong motions may be made, but let such be re-

pressed; inertia alone is at once unpunishable and unconquerable.

318. Cunning must be met by cunning, proud pretension by inertia, by a low tone of patriotic sorrow; low, but incurable, unalterable. Wise as serpents, harmless as doves, what a spectacle for France! Six hundred inorganic individuals, essential for its regeneration and salvation, sit there on their elliptic benches, longing passionately toward life, in painful durance, like souls waiting to be born. Speeches are spoken, eloquent, audible within doors and without. Mind agitates itself against mind, the nation looks on with ever deeper interest. Thus do the commons deputies sit incubating.

319. There are private conclaves, supper-parties, consultations, Breton club, club of Viroflay, germs of many clubs. Wholly an element of confused noise, dimness, angry heat—wherein, however, the Eros-egg, kept at the fit temperature, may hover safe, unbroken till it be hatched. In your Mouniers, Malouets, Lechapeliers, is science sufficient for that; fervor in your Barnaves, Rabauts. At times shall come an inspiration from royal Mirabeau: he is nowise yet recognized as royal; nay, he was "groaned at" when his name was first mentioned, but he is struggling toward recognition.

320. In the course of the week, the commons having called their eldest to the chair, and furnished him with young, stronger-lunged assistants, can speak articulately; and in audible lamentable words declare, as we said, that they are an inorganic body longing to become organic. Letters arrive; but an inorganic body cannot open letters, they lie on the table unopened. The eldest may at most procure for himself some kind of list or muster-roll, to take the votes by, and wait what will betide. Noblesse and clergy are all elsewhere; however, an eager public crowds all galleries and vacancies, which is some comfort. With effort it is determined, not that a deputation shall be sent—for how can an inorganic body send deputations?—but that certain individual commons members shall, in an accidental way, stroll into the clergy chamber and then into the noblesse one, and mention there as a thing they have happened to observe, that the commons seem to be sitting waiting for them, in order to verify their powers. That is the wiser method!

321. The clergy, among whom are such a multitude of undignified, of mere commons in curates' frocks, depute instant respectful answer that they are, and will now more than ever be, in deepest study as to that very matter. Contrariwise the noblesse, in cavalier attitude, reply after four days, that they, for their part, are all verified and constituted, which, they had trusted, the commons also were; such separate verification being clearly the proper constitutional wisdom-of-ancestors method—as they the noblesse will have much pleasure in demonstrating by a commission of their number, if the commons will meet them, commission against commission! Directly in the rear of which comes a deputation of clergy, reiterating, in their insidious conciliatory way, the same proposal. Here, then, is a complexity; what will wise commons say to this?

322. Warily, inertly, the wise commons, considering that they are, if not a French third estate, at least an aggregate of individuals pretending to some title of that kind, determine, after talking on it five days, to name such a commission—though, as it were, with proviso not to be convinced; a sixth day is taken up in naming it; a seventh and an eighth day in getting the forms of meeting, place, hour, and the like, settled: so that it is not till the evening of the 23d of May that noblesse commission first meets commons commission, clergy acting as conciliators; and

begins the impossible task of convincing it. One other meeting, on the 25th, will suffice; the commons are inconvincible, the noblesse and clergy irrefragably convincing; the commissions retire, each order persisting in its first pretensions.*

323. Thus have three weeks passed. For three weeks, the third-estate carroccio, with far-seen gonfalon, has stood stock-still, flouting the wind, waiting what force would gather round it.

Fancy can conceive the feeling of the court, and how counsel met counsel, and loud-sounding inanity whirled in that distracted vortex, where wisdom could not dwell. Your cunningly devised taxing-machine has been got together, set up with incredible labor, and stands there, its three pieces in contact, its two fly-wheels of noblesse and clergy, its huge working-wheel of tiers-état. The two fly-wheels whirl in the softest manner, but, prodigious to look upon, the huge working-wheel hangs motionless, refuses to stir! The cunningest engineers are at fault. How *will* it work when it does begin? Fearfully, my friends, and to many purposes; but to gather taxes or grind court-meal, one may apprehend, never. Could we but have continued gathering taxes *by hand!* Messeigneurs d'Artois, Conti, Condé (named court triumvirate), they of the anti-democratic " Mémoire au Roi," has not their foreboding proved true? They may wave reproachfully their high heads, they may beat their poor brains, but the cunningest engineers can do nothing. Necker himself, were he even listened to, begins to look blue. The only thing one sees advisable is to bring up soldiers. New regiments, two, and a battalion of a third, have already reached Paris; others shall get in march. Good were it in all circumstances to have troops within reach; good that the command were in sure hands. Let Broglie be appointed; old Marshal Duke de Broglie, veteran disciplinarian, of a firm drill-sergeant morality, such as may be depended on.

324. For, alas! neither are the clergy nor the very noblesse what they should be, and might be, when so menaced from without; entire, undivided within. The noblesse, indeed, have their Catiline or Crispin d'Esprémenil, dusky-glowing, all in renegade heat; their boisterous Barrel Mirabeau : but also they have their Lafayettes, Liancourts, Lameths; above all, their D'Orléans, now cut forever from his court-moorings, and musing drowsily of high and highest sea-prizes (for is not he too a son of Henri Quatre, and partial potential heir-apparent?) on his voyage towards chaos. From the clergy again, so numerous are the curés, actual deserters have run over : two small parties, in the second party Cure Grégoire. Nay, there is talk of a whole hundred and forty-nine of them about to desert-in mass, and only restrained by an archbishop of Paris. It seems a losing game.

325. But judge if France, so idle all this while! Addresses from far and near flow in; for our commons have now grown organic enough to open letters. Or indeed to cavil at them! Thus poor Marquis de Brézé, supreme usher, master of ceremonies, or whatever his title was, writing about this time on some ceremonial matter, sees no harm in winding up with a "Monsieur, yours with sincere attachment." "To whom does it address itself, this sincere attachment?" inquires Mirabeau. "To the dean of the tiers-état." " There is no man in France entitled to write that," rejoins he, whereat the galleries and the world will not be kept from applauding.* Poor De Brézé! These commons have a still older grudge at him, nor has he yet done with them.

326. In another way Mirabeau has had to protest

against the quick suppression of his newspaper, Journal of the States-General, and to continue it under a new name. In which act of valor the Paris electors, still busy redacting their cahier, could not but support him by address to his majesty; they claim utmost "provisory freedom of the press;" they have spoken even about demolishing the Bastille, and erecting a bronze patriot king on the site! These are the rich burghers; but now consider how it went, for example, with such loose miscellany—now all grown eleutheromaniac—of loungers, prowlers, social non-descripts (and the distilled rascality of our planet), as whirls forever in the Palais Royal; or what low infinite groan, fast changing into a growl, comes from Saint Antoine and the twenty-five millions in danger of starvation!

327. There is the indisputablest scarcity of corn—be it aristocrat-plot, D'Orléans-plot of this year, or drought and hail of last year; in city and province the poor man looks desolately toward a nameless lot. And this states-general, that could make us an age of gold, is forced to stand motionless, cannot get its powers verified! All industry necessarily languishes, if it be not that of making motions.

328. In the Palais Royal there has been erected, apparently by subscription, a kind of wooden tent (en planches de bois)*, most convenient, where select patriotism can now redact resolutions, deliver harangues, with comfort, let the weather be as it will. Lively is that Satan-at-home. On his table, on his chair, in every café, stands a patriotic orator, a crowd round him within, a crowd listening from without, open-mouthed, through open door and window, with "thunders of applause for every sentiment of more than common hardiness." In Monsieur Dessein's pamphlet-shop, close by, you cannot without strong elbowing get to the counter; every hour produces its pamphlets, or litter of pamphlets; "there were thirteen to-day, sixteen yesterday, ninety-two last week."† Think of tyranny and scarcity, fervid eloquence, rumor, pamphleteering, Société Publicole, Breton Club, Enraged Club—and whether every tap-room, coffee-room, social reunion, accidental street-group, over wide France, was not an enraged club!

329. To all which the commons deputies can only listen with a sublime inertia of sorrow, reduced to busy themselves "with their internal police." Surer position no deputies ever occupied, if they keep it with skill. Let not the temperature rise too high; break not the Eros-egg till it be hatched, till it break itself! An eager public crowds all galleries and vacancies—"cannot be restrained from applauding." The two privileged orders, the noblesse, all verified and constituted, may look on with what face they will, not without a secret tremor of heart. The clergy, always acting the part of conciliators, make a clutch at the galleries, and the popularity there, and miss it. Deputation of them arrives, with dolorous message about the " dearth of grains," and the necessity there is of casting aside vain formalities, and deliberating on this. An insidious proposal, which, however, the commons (moved thereto by sea-green Robespierre) dexterously accept as a sort of hint, or even pledge, that the clergy will forthwith come over to them, constitute the states-general, and *so* cheapen grains!‡ Finally, on the 27th day of May, Mirabeau, judging the time now nearly come, proposes that "the inertia cease;" that, leaving the noblesse to their own stiff ways, the clergy be summoned, "in the name of the God of peace," to join the commons, and begin.§ To which summons, if

---

* Reported debates, 6th May to 1st June, 1789 (in " Histoire Parlementaire," l. 379-422).

* "Histoire Parlementaire." l. 429.
† Arthur Young, "Travels," 1. 104.
‡ Bailly, "Mémoires," 1. 114.
§ "Histoire Parlementaire," l. 413.

they turn a deaf ear—we shall see! Are not 149 of them ready to desert?

330. O triumvirate of princes, new Garde-des-Sceaux Barentin, thou Home Secretary Breteuil, Duchess Poliguac, and queen eager to listen, what is now to be done? This third estate will get in motion, with the force of all France in it, clergy machinery with noblesse machinery, which were to serve as beautiful counter-balances and drags, will be shamefully dragged after it, and take fire along with it. What is to be done? The Œil-de-Bœuf waxes more confused than ever. Whisper and counter-whisper; a very tempest of whispers! Leading men from all the three orders are nightly spirited thither; conjurors, many of them, but can they conjure this? Necker himself were now welcome, could he interfere to purpose.

331. Let Necker interfere, then, and in the king's name! Happily that incendiary "God-of-peace" message is not yet *answered*. The three orders shall again have conferences; under this patriot minister of theirs, somewhat may be healed, clouted up, we meanwhile getting forward Swiss regiments and a "hundred pieces of field artillery." This is what the Œil-de-Bœuf, for its part, resolves on.

332. But as for Necker—alas, poor Necker, thy obstinate third estate has one first-last word, *verification in common*, as the pledge of voting and deliberating in common! Half-way proposals, from such a tried friend, they answer with a stare. The tardy conferences speedily break up; the third estate, now ready and resolute, the whole world backing it, returns to its hall of the three orders, and Necker to the Œil-de-Bœuf, with the character of a disconjurer there—fit only for dismissal.*

333. And so the commons deputies are at last on their own strength getting under way? Instead of chairman, or dean, they have now got a president—astronomer Bailly. Under way, with a vengeance! With endless, vociferous, and temperate eloquence, borne on newspaper wings to all lands, they have now, on this 17th day of June, determined that their name 'is not *third estate*, but *national assembly!* They, then, are the nation? Triumvirate of princes, queen, refractory noblesse, and clergy, what, then, are *you?* A most deep question—scarcely answerable in living political dialects.

334. All regardless of which, our new national assembly proceeds to appoint a "committee of subsistences," dear to France, though it can find little or no grain. Next, as if our national assembly stood quite firm on its legs, to appoint "four other standing committees;" then to settle the security of the national debt, then that of the annual taxation, all within eight-and-forty hours. At such rate of velocity it is going, the conjurers of the Œil-de-Bœuf may well ask themselves, whither?

CHAPTER II.

MERCURY DE BREZE.

335. Now surely were the time for a "god from the machine;" there is a nodus worthy of one. The only question is, which god? Shall it be Mars de Broglie, with his hundred pieces of cannon? Not yet, answers prudence, so soft, irresolute, is King Louis. Let it be messenger *Mercury*, our Supreme Usher de Brézé!

336. On the morrow, which is the 20th of June, these hundred and forty-nine false curates, no longer restrainable by his grace of Paris, will desert in a body; let De Brézé intervene, and produce—closed

* Debates, 1st to 17th June, 1789 (in "Histoire Parlementaire," i. 422-478).

doors! Not only shall there be royal session in that Salle des Menus, but no meeting, nor working (except by carpenters), till then. Your third estate, self-styled "national assembly," shall suddenly see itself extruded from its hall, by carpenters, in this dexterous way, and reduced to do nothing, not even to meet, or articulately lament, till majesty, with séance royale and new miracles, be ready! In this manner shall De Brézé, as Mercury ex machinâ, intervene, and, if the Œil-de-Bœuf mistake not, work deliverance from the nodus.

337. Of poor De Brezé we can remark that he has yet prospered in none of his dealings with these commons. Five weeks ago, when they kissed the hand of majesty, the mode he took got nothing but censure; and then his "sincere attachment," how was it scornfully whiffed aside! Before supper this night he writes to President Bailly a new letter, to be delivered shortly after dawn to-morrow, in the king's name. Which letter, however, Bailly, in the pride of office, will merely crush together into his pocket, like a bill he does not mean to pay.

338. Accordingly on Saturday morning the 20th of June, shrill-sounding heralds proclaim, through the streets of Versailles, that there is to be séance royale next Monday, and no meeting of the states-general till then. And yet, we observe, President Bailly, in sound of this, and with De Brézé's letter in his pocket, is proceeding, with national assembly at his heels, to the accustomed Salle des Menus, as if De Brézé and heralds were mere wind. It is shut, this salle, occupied by gardes Françaises. "Where is your captain?" The captain shows his royal order: workmen, he is grieved to say, are all busy setting up the platform for his majesty's séance; most unfortunately no admission; admission, at furthest, for president and secretaries to bring away papers, which the joiners might destroy! President Bailly enters with secretaries and returns bearing papers; alas, within doors, instead of patriotic eloquence, there is now no noise but hammering, sawing, and operative screeching and rumbling! A profanation without parallel.

339. The deputies stand grouped on the Paris road, on this umbrageous Avenue de Versailles; complaining aloud of the indignity done them. Courtiers, it is supposed, look from their windows and giggle. The morning is none of the comfortablest; raw, it is even drizzling a little.* But all the travelers pause; patriot gallery-men, miscellaneous spectators increase the groups. Wild counsels alternate. Some desperate deputies propose to go and hold session on the great outer staircase at Marly, under the king's windows; for his majesty, it seems, has driven over thither. Others talk of making the Château Forécourt, what they call Place d'Armes, a Runnymede and new Champ de Mai of free Frenchmen; nay, of awakening to sounds of indiguant patriotism the echoes of the Œil-de-Bœuf itself. Notice is given that President Bailly, aided by judicious Guillotin and others, has found place in the tennis-court of the Rue St. François. Thither, in long-drawn files, hoarse-jingling, like cranes on wing, the common deputies angrily wend.

340. Strange sight was this in the Rue St. François, Vieux Versailles! A naked tennis-court, as the pictures of that time still give it; four walls, naked, except aloft some poor wooden penthouse, or roofed spectators'-gallery hanging round them—on the floor not now an idle tee-heeing, a snapping of balls and rackets; but the bellowing din of an indignant national representation, scandalously exiled hither! However, a cloud of witnesses looks down on them from wooden penthouse, from wall-top, from adjoin-

* Bailly, "Mémoires," i. 185-206.

ing roof and chimney, rolls toward them from all quarters, with passionate spoken blessings. Some table can be procured to write on; some chair, if not to sit on, then to stand on. The secretaries undo their tapes; Bailly has constituted the assembly.

341. Experienced Mounier, not wholly new to such things, in parlementary revolts, which he has seen or heard of, thinks that it were well, in these lamentable threatening circumstances, to unite themselves by an oath. Universal acclamation, as from smoldering bosoms getting vent. The oath is redacted, pronounced aloud by President Bailly—and, indeed, in such a sonorous tone that the cloud of witnesses, even out-doors, hear it, and bellow response to it. Six hundred right-hands rise with President Bailly's, to take God above to witness that they will not separate for man below, but will meet in all places, under all circumstances, wheresoever two or three can get together, till they have made the constitution. Made the constitution, friends! That is a long task. Six hundred hands, meanwhile, will sign as they have sworn; six hundred save *one*, one loyalist Abdiel, still visible by this sole light-point, and namable, poor "M. Martin d'Auch, from Castelnaudary, in Languedoc." Him they permit to sign or signify refusal; they even save him from the cloud of witnesses, by declaring "his head deranged." At four o'clock, the signatures are all appended; new meeting is fixed for Monday morning, earlier than the hour of the royal session, that our hundred and forty-nine clerical deserters be not balked; we will meet "at the Recollets church or elsewhere," in hope that our hundred and forty-nine will join us—and now it is time to go to dinner.

342. This, then, is the Session of the Tennis-Court, famed Séance du Jeu de Paume; the fame of which has gone forth to all lauds. This is Mercurius de Brézé's appearance as Deus ex machina; this is the fruit it brings! The giggle of courtiers in the Versailles avenue has already died into gaunt silence. Did the distracted court, with Garde-des-Sceaux Barentin, Triumvirate and Company, imagine that they could scatter 600 national deputies, big with national constitution, like as much barn-door poultry, big with next to nothing—by the white or black rod of a supreme usher? Barn-door poultry fly cackling, but national deputies turn round, lion-faced, and, with uplifted right-hand, swear an oath that makes the four corners of France tremble.

343. President Bailly has covered himself with honor, which shall become rewards. The national assembly is now doubly and trebly the nation's assembly; not militant, martyred only, but triumphant, insulted, and which could not *be* insulted. Paris disembogues itself once more, to witness, "with grim looks," the *séance royale;*" which, by a new felicity, is postponed till Tuesday. The hundred and forty-nine, and even with bishops among them, all in processional mass, have had free leisure to march off and solemnly join the commons sitting waiting in their church. The commons welcomed them with shouts, with embracings, nay, with tears,† for it is growing a life-and-death matter now.

344. As for the séance itself, the carpenters seem to have accomplished their platform, but all else remains unaccomplished. Futile, we may say fatal, was the whole matter. King Louis enters, through seas of people, all grim-silent, angry with many things—for it is a bitter rain too. Enters, to a third estate, likewise grim-silent, which has been wetted waiting under mean porches, at back-doors, while court and privilege were entering by the front. King

and Garde-des-Sceaux (there is no Necker visible) make known, not without long-windedness, the determinations of the royal breast. The three orders *shall* vote separately. On the other hand, France may look for considerable constitutional blessings, as specified in these five-and-thirty articles,* which Garde-des-Sceaux is waxing hoarse with reading. Which five-and-thirty articles, adds his majesty, again rising, if the three orders most unfortunately, cannot agree together to effect them, I myself will effect: "Soul je ferai le bien de mes peuples "—which being interpreted may signify, You, contentious deputies of the states-general, have probably not long to be here! But, in fine, all shall now withdraw for this day, and meet again, each order in its separate place, to-morrow morning, for dispatch of business. *This* is the determination of the royal breast, pithy and clear. And herewith king, retinue, noblesse, majority of clergy, file out, as if the whole matter were satisfactorily completed.

345. These file out through grim-silent seas of people. Only the commons deputies file not out, but stand there in gloomy silence, uncertain what they shall do. One man of them is certain, one man of them discerns and dares! It is now that King Mirabeau starts to the tribune, and lifts up his lion-voice. Verily a word in season, for, in such scenes, the moment is the mother of ages! Had not Gabriel Honoré been there—one can well fancy, how the commons deputies, affrighted at the perils which now yawned dim all round them, and waxing ever paler in each other's paleness, might very naturally, one after one, have *glided off;* and the whole course of European history have been different!

346. But he is there. List to the *brool* of that royal forest-voice; sorrowful, low, fast swelling to a roar! Eyes kindle at the glance of his eye: National deputies were missioned by a nation, they have sworn an oath, they—But lo! while the lion's voice roars loudest, what apparition is this? Apparition of Mercurius de Brézé, muttering somewhat! "Speak out," cry several. "Messieurs," shrills De Brézé, repeating himself, "you have heard the king's orders!" Mirabeau glares on him with fire-flashing face, shakes the black lion's mane: "Yes, monsieur, we have heard what the king was advised to say, and you, who cannot be the interpreter of his orders to the states-general; you, who have neither place nor right of speech here; *you* are not the man, to remind us of it. Go, monsieur, tell those who sent you that we are here by the will of the people, and that nothing but the force of bayonets shall send us hence!"† And poor De Brézé shivers forth from the national assembly—and also (if it be not in one faintest glimmer, months later) finally from the page of history!

347. Hapless De Brézé; doomed to survive long ages in men's memory, in this faint way, with tremulant white roof! He was true to etiquette, which was his faith here below, a martyr to respect of persons. Short woolen cloaks could not kiss majesty's hand as long velvet ones did. Nay, lately, when the poor little dauphin lay dead, and some ceremonial visitation came, he not punctual to announce it even to the dauphin's *dead body*—"Monseigneur, a deputation of the states-general?"‡ Sunt lachrymæ rerum.

348. But what does the Œil-de-Bœuf, now when De Brézé shivers back thither? *Dispatch* that same force of bayonets? Not so, the seas of people still hang multitudinous, intent on what is passing; nay, rush and roll, loud-billowing, into the courts of the château itself, for a report has risen that Necker is to

* See Arthur Young ("Travels," i. 115-118); A. Lameth, etc.
† Dumont, "Souvenirs sur Mirabeau," c. 4.

* "Histoire Parlementaire," i. 13.
† Moniteur ("Histoire Parlementaire," ii. 22).
‡ Montgaillard, ii. 38.

be dismissed. Worst of all, the Gardes Françaises seem indisposed to act; "two companies of them *do not fire* when ordered!"* Necker, for not being at the séance, shall be shouted for, carried home in triumph, and must not be dismissed. His grace of Paris, on the other hand, has to fly, with broken conch-panels, and owe his life to furious driving. The gardes-du-corps (body-guards), which you were drawing out, had better be drawn in again.† There is no sending of bayonets to be thought of.

349. Instead of soldiers, the Œil-de-Bœuf sends—carpenters, to take down the platform. Ineffectual shift! In few instants the very carpenters cease wrenching and knocking at their platform, standing on it hammer in hand, and listen open-mouthed.‡ The third estate is decreeing that it is, was, and will be nothing but a national assembly; and now, moreover, an inviolable one, all members of it inviolable: "infamous, traitorous toward the nation, and guilty of capital crime, is any person, body-corporate, or Tribunal, court or commission, that now or henceforth, during the present session or after it, shall dare to pursue, interrogate, arrest, or cause to be arrested, detain or cause to be detained, any" etc., etc., "on *whose part soever* the same be commanded,"§ Which done, one can wind up with this comfortable reflection from Abbé Sieyes, "Messieurs, you are to-day what you were yesterday."

350. Courtiers may shriek; but it is, and remains, even so. Their well-charged explosion has exploded *through the touch-hole;* covering themselves with scorches, confusion, and unseemly soot! Poor triumvirate, poor queen; and, above all, poor queen's husband, who means well, had he any fixed meaning! Folly is that wisdom which is wise only behindhand. Few months ago these thirty-five concessions had filled France with a rejoicing which might have lasted for several years. Now it is unavailing, the very mention of it slighted: majesty's express orders set at naught.

351. All France is in a roar; a sea of persons, estimated at 10,000, whirls "all this day in the Palais Royal."¶ The remaining clergy, and likewise some forty-eight noblesse, D'Orléans among them, have now forthwith gone over to the victorious commons —by whom, as is natural, they are received "with acclamation."

352. The third estate triumphs; Versailles town shouting round it; 10,000 whirling all day in the Palais Royal; and all France standing a-tiptoe, not unlike whirling! Let the Œil-de-Bœuf look to it. As for King Louis, he will swallow his injuries; will temporize, keep silence; will at all costs have present peace. It was Tuesday, the 23d of June, when he spoke that peremptory royal mandate, and the week is not done till he has written to the remaining obstinate noblesse, that they also must oblige him, and give in. D'Esprémenil rages his last; Barrel Mirabeau breaks his sword, making a vow—which he might as well have kept. The "triple family" is now, therefore, complete; the third erring brother, the noblesse, having joined it—erring, but pardonable; soothed, so far as possible, by sweet eloquence from President Bailly.

353. So triumphs the third estate; and states-general are becoming national assembly; and all France may sing Te Deum. By wise inertia, and wise cessation of inertia, great victory has been gained. It is the last night of June; all night you meet nothing on the streets of Versailles but "men running with

torches," with shouts and jubilation. From the 2d of May when they kissed the hand of majesty, to this 30th of June when men run with torches, we count eight weeks and three days. For eight weeks the national carroccio has stood far-seen, ringing many a signal; and so much having now gathered round it, may hope to stand.

CHAPTER III.
BROGLIE THE WAR-GOD.

354. The court feels indignant that it is conquered; but what then? Another time it will do better. Mercury descended in vain; now has the time come for Mars. The gods of the Œil-de-Bœuf have withdrawn into the darkness of their cloudy Ida; and sit there, shaping and forging what may be needful, be it "billets of a new national bank," munitions of war, or things forever inscrutable to men.

355. Accordingly, what means this "apparatus of troops?" The national assembly can get no furtherance for its committee of subsistences; can bear only that at Paris the bakers' shops are besieged; that in the provinces people are "living on meal-husks and boiled grass." But on all highways there hover dust-clouds, with the march of regiments, with the trailing of cannon: foreign Pandours, of fierce aspect; Salis-Samande, Esterhazy, Royal-Allemand; so many of them foreign; to the number of 30,000—which fear can magnify to fifty; all wending toward Paris and Versailles! Already on the heights of Montmartre is a digging and delving, too like a scarping and trenching. The effluence of Paris is arrested Versailles-ward by a barrier of cannon at Sèvres bridge. From the queen's mews cannon stand pointed on the national assembly hall itself. The national assembly has its very slumbers broken by the tramp of soldiery, swarming and defiling, endless, or seemingly endless, all round those spaces at dead of night, "without drum-music, without audible word of command."* What means it?

356. Shall eight, or even shall twelve deputies, our Mirabeaus, Barnaves at the head of them, be whirled suddenly to the castle of Ham; the rest ignominiously dispersed to the winds? No national assembly can make the constitution with cannon leveled on it from the queen's mews! What means this reticence of the Œil-de-Bœuf, broken only by nods and shrugs? In the mystery of that cloudy Ida, what is it that they forge and shape? Such questions must distracted patriotism keep asking and receive no answer but an echo.

357. Questions and echo bad enough in themselves —and now, above all, while the hungry food-year, which runs from August to August, is getting older; becoming more and more a famine-year! With "meal-husks and boiled grass," brigands may actually collect, and in crowds at farm and mansion, howl angrily, *Food!* It is vain to send soldiers against them: at sight of soldiers they disperse, they vanish as under ground; then directly reassemble elsewhere for new tumult and plunder. Frightful enough to look upon, but what to *hear* of, reverberated through 25,000,000 of suspicious minds! Brigands and Broglie, open conflagration, preternatural rumor, are driving mad most hearts in France. What will the issue of these things be?

358. At Marseilles, many weeks ago, the townsmen have taken arms for "suppressing of brigands" and other purposes: the military commandant may make of it what he will. Elsewhere, everywhere, could not the like be done? Dubious, on the distracted patriot imagination, wavers, as a last deliver-

---

* "Histoire Parlementaire," ii. 26.
† Bailly, i. 217.
‡ "Histoire Parlementaire," ii. 23.
§ Montgaillard, ii 47.
¶ Arthur Young, i. 119.

* A. Lameth, "Assemblée Constituante," i. 41.

ance, some foreshadow of a *national guard.* But conceive, above all, the wooden tent in the Palais Royal! A universal hubbub there, as of dissolving worlds: there loudest bellows the mad, mad-making voice of rumor; there sharpest gazes suspicion into the pale, dim world-whirlpool, discerning shapes and phantasms; imminent, bloodthirsty regiments camped on the Champ de Mars; dispersed national assembly; red-hot cannon-balls (to burn Paris); the mad wargod and Bellona's sounding thongs. To the calmest man it is becoming too plain that battle is inevitable.

359. Inevitable, silently not messeigneurs and Broglie; inevitable and brief! Your national assembly, stopped short in its constitutional labors, may fatigue the royal ear with addresses and remonstrances, those cannon of ours stand duly leveled; those troops are here. The king's declaration, with its thirty-five too generous articles, was spoken, was not listened to, but remains yet unrevoked: he himself shall effect it, seul il fera!

360. As for Broglie, he has his headquarters at Versailles, all as in a seat of war; clerks writing; significant staff officers, inclined to taciturnity; plumed aids-de-camp, scouts, orderlies flying or hovering. He himself looks forth, important, impenetrable; listens to Besenval, commandant of Paris, and his warning and earnest counsels (for he has come out repeatedly on purpose), with a silent smile.* The Parisians resist? scornfully cry messeigneurs. As a meal-mob may! They have sat quiet, these five generations, submitting to all. Their Mercier declared in these very years that a Parisian revolt was, henceforth, "impossible."† Stand by the royal declaration of the 23d of June. The nobles of France, valorous, chivalrous as of old, will rally round us with one heart; and as for this which you call third estate, and which we call canaille of unwashed sans-culott, of patelins, scribblers, factious spouters—brave Broglie, "with a whiff of grapeshot (salve de canons)," if need be, he will give quick account of it. Thus reason they on their cloudy Ida; hidden from men—men also hidden from them.

361. Good is grapeshot, messeigneurs, on one condition: that the shooter also were made of metal! But unfortunately he is made of flesh; under his buffs and bandoleers your hired shooter has instincts, feelings, even a kind of thought. It is his kindred, bone of his bone, this same canaille that shall be whiffed; he has brothers in it, a father and a mother—living on meal-husks and boiled grass. His very doxy, not yet "dead i' the spital," drives him into military heterodoxy; declares that if he shed patriot blood he shall be accursed among men. The soldier, who has seen his pay stolen by rapacious Foulons, his blood wasted by Soubises, Pompadours, and the gates of promotion shut inexorably on him if he were not born noble—is himself not without griefs against you. Your cause is not the soldier's cause, but, as would seem, your own only, and no other god's nor man's.

362. For example, the world may have heard how, at Béthune lately, when there rose some "riot about grains," of which sort there are so many, and the soldiers stood drawn out, and the word "Fire!" was given—not a trigger stirred; only the butts of all muskets rattled angrily against the ground; and the soldiers stood glooming, with a mixed expression of countenance—till clutched "each under the arm of a patriot householder," they were all hurried off, in this manner, to be treated and caressed, and have their pay increased by subscription!‡

363. Neither have the Gardes Françaises, the best

regiment of the line, shown any promptitude for street-firing lately. They returned grumbling from Réveillon's, and have not burnt a single cartridge since; nay, as we saw, not even when bid. A dangerous humor dwells in these gardes. Notable men, too, in their way! Valadi the Pythagorean was at one time an officer of theirs. Nay, in the ranks, under the three-cornered felt and cockade, what hard heads may there not be, and reflections going on—unknown to the public! One head of the hardest we do now discern there: on the shoulders of a certain Sergeant Hoche. Lazare Hoche, that is the name of him; he used to be about the Versailles royal stables, nephew of a poor herbwoman; a handy lad, exceedingly addicted to reading. He is now Sergeant Hoche, and can rise no farther; he lays out his pay in rushlights and cheap editions of books.*

364. On the whole, the best seems to be: Consign these Gardes Françaises to their barracks. So Besenval thinks and orders. Consigned to their barracks, the Gardes Françaises do but form a "secret association," an engagement not to act against the national assembly. Debauched by Valadi the Pythagorean; debauched by money and women! cry Besenval and innumerable others. Debauched by what you will, or in need of no debauching, behold them, long files of them, their consignment broken, arrive, headed by their sergeants, on the 26th day of June, at the Palais Royal! Welcomed with vivats, with presents, and a pledge of patriot liquor, embracing and embraced, declaring in words that the cause of France is their cause! Next day and the following days the like. What is singular, too, except this patriot humor, and breaking of their consignment, they behave otherwise with "the most rigorous accuracy."†

365. They are growing questionable, these gardes! Eleven ringleaders of them are put in the Abbaye prison. It boots not in the least. The imprisoned eleven have only, "by the hand of an individual," to drop, toward nightfall, a line in the Café de Foy, where patriotism harangues loudest on its table. "Two hundred young persons, soon waxing to four thousand," with fit crowbars, roll toward the Abbaye, smite asunder the needful doors, and bear out their eleven, with other military victims—to supper in the Palais Royal garden, to board, and lodging "in campbeds" in the Théâtre des Variétés; other national Prytaneum as yet not being in readiness. Most deliberate! Nay, so punctual were these young persons, that finding one military victim to have been imprisoned for real civil crime, they returned him to his cell with protest.

366. Why new military force was not called out? New military force was called out. New military force did arrive, full gallop, with drawn saber; but the people gently "laid hold of their bridles," the dragoons sheathed their swords, lifted their caps by way of salute, and sat like mere statues of dragoons—except, indeed, that a drop of liquor being brought them, they "drank to the king and nation with the greatest cordiality."‡

367. And now ask in return why Messeigneurs and Broglie, the great god of war, on seeing these things, did not pause and take some other course, any other course. Unhappily, as we said, we could see nothing. Pride, which goes before a fall; wrath, if not reasonable, yet pardonable, most natural, had hardened their hearts and heated their heads; so, with imbecility and violence (ill-matched pair), they rush to seek their hour. All regiments are not Gardes Françaises, or debauched by Valadi the Pythagorean:

---

* Besenval, iii. 398.
† Mercier. "Tableau de Paris," vi. 22.
‡ "Histoire Parlementaire."

* "Dictionnaire des Hommes Marquans," Londres (Paris), 1800, ii. 198.
† Besenval, iii. 394-396.
‡ "Histoire Parlementaire," ii 32.

let fresh, undebauched regiments come up; let Royal-Allemand, Salis-Samade, Swiss Château-Vieux come up—which can fight, but can hardly speak except in German gutterals—let soldiers march and highways thunder with artillery-wagons: majesty has a *new* royal session to hold—and miracles to work there! The whiff of grapeshot can, if needful, become a blast and tempest!

368. In which circumstances, before the red-hot balls begin raining, may not the hundred-and-twenty Paris electors, though their cahier is long since finished, see good to meet again daily, as an "electoral club?" They meet first "in a tavern," where "a large wedding-party" cheerfully gives place to them.* But latterly they meet in the Hotel-de-Ville, in the town-hall itself. Flesselles, provost of merchants, with his four echevins (scabins, assessors), could not prevent it; such was the force of public opinion. He, with his echevins and the six-and-twenty town-councilors, all appointed from above, may well sit silent there, in their long gowns, and consider, with awed eye, what prelude this is of convulsion coming from below, and how they themselves shall fare in that!

CHAPTER IV.

TO ARMS!

369. So hangs it, dubious, fateful, in the sultry days of July. It is the passionate printed *advice* of M. Marat to abstain, of all things, from violence.† Nevertheless the hungry poor are already burning town barriers, where tribute on eatables is levied, getting clamorous for food.

370. The twelfth July morning is Sunday; the streets are all placarded with an enormous-sized De par le roi, "inviting peaceable citizens to remain within doors," to feel no alarm, to gather in no crowd. Why so? What means these "placards of enormous size?" Above all, what means this clatter of military; dragoons; hussars, rattling in from all points of the compass toward the Place Louis Quinze, with a staid gravity of face, though saluted with mere nicknames, hootings, and even missiles?‡ Besenval is with them. Swiss guards of his are already in the Champs Elysées, with four pieces of artillery.

371. Have the destroyers descended on us, then? From the bridge of Sévres to utmost Vincennes, from Saint-Denis to the Champ-de-Mars, we are there! Alarm, of the vague unknown, is in every heart. The Palais Royal has become a place of awestruck interjections. silent shakings of the head; one can fancy with what dolorous stound the noontide cannon (which the sun fires at crossing of his meridian) went off there—bodeful. like an inarticulate voice of doom.§ Are these troops verily come out "against brigands? Where are the brigands? What mystery is in the wind? Hark! a human voice reporting articulately the Joh's-news: *Necker, people's minister, saviour of France, is dismissed!* Impossible; incredible! Treasonous to the public peace! Such a voice ought to be choked in the water-works,¶ had not the news-bringer quickly fled. Nevertheless, friends make of it what you will, the news is true. Necker is gone. Necker hies northward incessantly, in obedient secrecy, since yesternight. We have a new ministry—Broglie. the war-

* Dusaulx, "Prise de la Bastille" (Collection des Mémoires," par Berville et Barrière, Paris, 1821), p. 269.
† "Avis au Peuple, ou les Ministres dévoilés," 1st July, 1789 (in "Histoire Parlementaire," ii. 37).
‡ Besenval, iii. 411.
§ "Histoire Parlementaire," ii. 81.
¶ Ibid.

god; aristocrat Breteuil; Foulon, who said the people might eat grass!

372. Rumor, therefore, shall arise in the Palais Royal, and in broad France. Paleness sits on every face; confused tremor and fremescence, waxing into thunder-peals, of fury stirred on by fear.

373. But see Camille Desmoulins, from the Café de Foy, rushing out, sibylline in face; his hair streaming, in each hand a pistol! He springs to a table; the police satellites are eyeing him; alive they shall not take him, not they alive him alive. This time he speaks without stammering, Friends! shall we die like hunted hares? Like sheep hounded into their pinfold, bleating for mercy, where is no mercy, but only a whetted knife? The hour is come, the supreme hour of Frenchman and man; when oppressors are to try conclusions with oppressed, and the word is, Swift death or deliverance forever. Let such hour be *well*-come! Us, messeems, one cry only befits: To arms! Let universal Paris, universal France, as with the throat of the whirlwind, sound only, To arms! "To arms!" yell responsive the innumerable voices, like one great voice, as of a demon yelling from the air; for all faces wax fire-eyed, all hearts burn up into madness. In such, or fitter words,* does Camille evoke the elemental powers, in this great moment. Friends, continues Camille, some rallying sign! Cockades, green ones—the color of hope! As with the flight of locusts, these green tree-leaves, green ribbons from the neighboring shops, all green things are snatched and made cockades of. Camille descends from his table, "stifled with embraces, wetted with tears;" has a bit of green ribbon handed him, sticks it in his hat. And now to Curtius's image-shop there, to the boulevards, to the four winds, and rest not till France be on fire.

374. France, so long shaken and wind-parched, is probably at the right inflammable point. As for poor Curtius, who, one grieves to think, might be but imperfectly paid—he cannot make two words about his images. The wax bust of Necker, the wax bust of D'Orléans, helpers of France, these, covered with crape, as in funeral procession, or after the manner of suppliants appealing to heaven, to earth, and Tartarus itself, a mixed multitude bears off. For a sign! As indeed man, with his singular imaginative faculties, can do little or nothing without signs. Thus Turks look to their prophet's banner, also osier *manikins* have been burnt, and Necker's portrait has erewhile figured aloft on its perch.

375. In this manner march they, a mixed, continually increasing multitude, armed with axes, staves, and miscellanea; grim, many-sounding, through the streets. Be all theaters shut; let all dancing on planked floor, or on the natural green-sward, cease! Instead of a Christian Sabbath, and feast of guinguette tabernacles, it shall be a sorcerer's Sabbath, and Paris gone rabid, dance—with the fiend for piper!

376. However, Besenval, with horse and foot, is in the Place Louis Quinze. Mortals promenading homeward in the fall of the day, saunter by, from Chaillot or Passy, from flirtation and a little thin wine, with sadder step than usual. Will the bust procession pass that way? Behold it, behold also Prince Lambesc dash forth on it, with his Royal-Allemands! Shots fall, and saber-strokes; busts are hewed asunder, and, alas! also heads of men. A sabered procession has nothing for it but to *explode*, along what streets, alleys, Tuileries avenues it finds, and disappear. One unarmed man lies hewed down, a Garde Française by his uniform: bear him (or bear

* "Vieux Cordelier," par Camille Desmoulins, No. 5 (reprinted in "Collection des Mémoires." par Baudouin Freres, Paris, 1825), p. 81.

even the report of him) dead and gory to his barracks—where he has comrades still alive!

377. But why not now, victorious Lambesc, charge through that Tuileries garden itself, where the fugitives are vanishing? Not show the Sunday promenaders, too, how steel glitters, besprent with blood; that it be told of, and men's ears tingle? Tingle, alas! they did, but the wrong way. Victorious Lambesc, in this his second or Tuileries charge, succeeds but in overturning (call it not slashing, for he struck with the flat of his sword) one man, a poor old school-master, most pacifically tottering there; and is driven out, by barricade of chairs, by flights of "bottles and glasses," by execrations in bass voice and treble. Most delicate is the mob-queller's vocation, wherein too-much may be as bad as not-enough. For each of these bass voices, and more each treble voice, borne to all parts of the city, rings now nothing but distracted indignation—will ring all night. The cry, *To arms!* roars tenfold; steeples with their metal storm-voice boom out, as the sun sinks; armorers' shops are broken open, plundered; the streets are a living foam-sea, chafed by all the winds.

378. Such issue came of Lambesc's charge on the Tuileries garden, no striking of salutary terror into Chaillot promenaders; a striking into broad wakefulness of frenzy and the three furies—which otherwise were not asleep! For they lie always, those subterranean Eumenides (fabulous and yet so true), in the dullest existence of man—and can dance, brandishing their dusky torches, shaking their serpent-hair. Lambesc with Royal-Allemand may ride to his barracks, with curses for his marching-music, then ride back again, like one troubled in mind; vengeful Gardes Française, *sacreing*, with knit brows start out on him, from their barracks in the Chaussé d'Antin, pour a volley into him (killing and wounding), which he must not answer, but ride on.*

379. Counsel dwells not under the plumed hat. If the Eumenides awaken, and Broglie has given no orders, what can a Besenval do? When the Gardes Françaises, with Palais-Royal volunteers, roll down, greedy of more vengeance, to the Place Louis Quinze itself, they find neither Besenval, Lambesc, Royal-Allemand, nor any soldier now there. Gone is military order. On the far eastern boulevard, of Saint-Antoine, the Chasseurs Normandie arrive, dusty, thirsty, after a hard day's ride; but can find no billet-master, see no course in this city of confusions; cannot get to Besenval, cannot so much as discover where he is. Normandie must even bivouac there, in its dust and thirst—unless some patriot will treat it to a cup of liquor, with advices.

380. Raging multitudes surround the Hotel-de-Ville, crying, Arms! Orders! The six-and-twenty town-councillors, with their long gowns have ducked under (into the raging chaos)—shall never emerge more. Besenval is painfully wriggling himself out, to the Champ-de-Mars; he must sit there "in the cruelest uncertainty;" courier after courier may dash off for Versailles, but will bring back no answer, can hardly bring himself back. For the roads are all blocked with batteries and pickets, with floods of carriages arrested for examination; such was Broglie's one sole order; the Œil-de-Bœuf, hearing in the distance such mad din, which sounded almost like invasion, will before all things keep its own head whole. A new ministry, with as it were, but one foot in the stirrup, cannot take leaps. Mad Paris is abandoned altogether to itself.

381. What a Paris when the darkness fell! A European metropolitan city hurled suddenly forth from its old combinations and arrangements, to crash tumultuously together, seeking new. Use and wont

will now no longer direct any man; each man, with what of originality he has, must begin thinking, or following those that think. Seven hundred thousand individuals, on the sudden, find all their old paths, old ways of acting and deciding, vanish from under their feet. And so there go they, with clangor and terror—they know not as yet whether running, swimming, or flying—headlong into the new era. With clangor and terror from above, Broglie the war-god impends, preternatural, with his red-hot cannon-balls; and from below a preternatural brigand world menaces with dirk and firebrand; madness rules the hour.

382. Happily, in place of the submerged twenty-six, the electoral club is gathering; has declared itself a "provisional municipality." On the morrow it will get Provost Flesselles, with an echevin or two, to give help in many things. For the present it decrees one most essential thing, that forthwith a Parisian militia shall be enrolled. Depart, ye heads of districts, to labor in this great work, while we here, in permanent committee, sit alert. Let fencible men, each party in its own range of streets, keep watch and ward all night. Let Paris court a little fever-sleep: confused by such fever-dreams; of "violent motions at the Palais Royal;"—or from time to time start awake, and look out, palpitating, in its night-cap, at the clash of discordant mutually-unintelligible patrols, on the gleam of distant barriers, going up all too ruddy toward the vault of night.*

CHAPTER V.
GIVE US ARMS.

383. On Monday the huge city has awoke, not to its week-day industry, to what a different one? The working man has become a fighting man: has one want only, that of arms. The industry of all crafts has paused—except it be the smith's, fiercely hammering pikes; and, in a faint degree, the kitchener's cooking off-hand victuals; for bouche va toujours. Women, too, are sewing cockades—not now of *green*, which being D'Artois color, the Hotel-de-Ville has had to interfere in it; but of *red* and *blue*, our old Paris colors: these, once based on a ground of constitutional *white*, are the famed *tricolor*—which (if prophecy err not) "will go round the world."

384. All shops, unless it be the bakers' and vintners', are shut. Paris is in the streets—rushing, foaming like some Venice wine-glass into which you had dropped poison. The tocsin, by order, is pealing madly from all steeples. Arms, ye elector municipals; thou Flesselles with thy echevins, give us arms! Flesselles gives what he can: fallacious, perhaps insidious promises of arms from Charleville; order to seek arms here, order to seek them there. The new municipals give what they can: some three-hundred and sixty indifferent firelocks, the equipment of the city-watch. "A man in wooden shoes and without coat, directly clutches one of them, and mounts guard." Also, as hinted, an order to all smiths to make pikes with their whole soul.

385. Heads of districts are in fervent consultation, subordinate patriotism roams distracted, ravenous for arms. Hitherto at the Hotel-de-Ville was only such modicum of indifferent firelocks as we have seen. At the so-called arsenal, there lies nothing but rust, rubbish, and saltpetre—overlooked, too, by the guns of the Bastille. His majesty's repository, what they call garde meuble, is forced and ransacked; tapestries enough, and gauderies; but of serviceable fighting-gear small stock! Two silver-mounted cannons there are, an ancient gift from his majesty of Siam to Louis Fourteenth: gilt sword of the Good

---

* Weber, ii. 75-91.

* "Deux Amis," i. 267-302.

Henri; antique chivalry arms and armor. These and such as these, a necessitous patriotism snatches greedily, for want of better. The Siamese cannons go trundling on an errand they were not meant for. Among the indifferent firelocks are seen tourney-lances; the princely helm and hauberk glittering amid ill-hatted heads—as in a time when all times and their possessions are suddenly sent jumbling!

386. At the Maison de Saint-Lazare, lazar-house once, now a correction house with priests, there was no trace of arms; but, on the other hand, corn plainly to a culpable extent. Out with it, to market, in this scarcity of grains! Heavens, will "fifty-two carts," in long row, hardly carry it to the halle aux bleds? Well, truly, ye reverend fathers, was your pantry filled; fat are your larders, overgenerous your wine-bins, ye plotting exasperators of the poor, traitorous forestallers of bread?

387. Vain is protesting, entreaty on bare knees, the house of Saint-Lazarus has that in it which comes not out by protesting. Behold, how, from every window, it *vomits* mere torrents of furniture, of bellowing and hurly-burly—the cellars also leaking wine. Till, as was natural, smoke rose, kindled, some say, by the desperate Saint-Lazaristes themselves, desperate of other riddance; and the establishment vanished from this world in flame. Remark nevertheless that "a thief" (set on or not by aristocrats), being detected there, is "instantly hanged."

388. Look also at the Châtelet prison. The debtors' prison of La Force is broken from without; and they that sat in bondage to aristocrats go free; hearing of which the felons at the Châtelet do likewise " dig up their pavements," and stand on the offensive, with the best prospects—had not patriotism, passing that way, "fired a volley" into the felon world; and crushed it down again under hatches. Patriotism consorts not with thieving and felony; surely also punishment, this day, hitches, (if she still bitch), after crime, with frightful shoes-of-swiftness! "Some score or two" of wretched persons, found prostrate with drink in the cellars of that Saint-Lazare, are indignantly haled to prison; the jailor has no room; whereupon, other place of security not suggesting itself, it is written, " on les pendit, (they hanged them)"[*] Brief is the word, not without significance, be it true or untrue!

389. In such circumstances, the aristocrat, the unpatriotic rich man, is packing-up for departure. But he shall not get departed. A wooden-shod force has seized all barriers, burnt or not; all that enters, all that seeks to issue, is stopped there and dragged to the Hotel-de-Ville; coaches, trumbrils, plate, furniture, "many meal-sacks," in time even "flocks and herds," encumber the Place de Grève.[†]

390. And so it roars, and rages, and brays: drums beating, steeples pealing, criers rushing with handbells: " Oyez, oyez. All men to their districts to be enrolled !" The districts have met in gardens, open squares, are getting marshaled into volunteer troops No red-hot ball has yet fallen from Besenval's camp; on the contrary, deserters with their arms are continually dropping in, nay, now, joy of joys, at two in the afternoon, the Gardes Françaises, being ordered to Saint-Denis, and flatly declining, have come over in a body! It is a fact worth many. Three thousand six hundred of the best fighting men, with complete accoutrement; with cannoneers even, and cannon. Their officers are left standing alone—could not so much as succeed in "spiking the guns." The very Swiss, it may now he hoped, Château-Vieux and the others, will have doubts about fighting.

391. Our Parisian militia—which some think it

* "Histoire Parlementaire." ii. 96.
† Dusaulx, " Prise de la Bastille," p. 290.

were better to name national guard—is prospering as heart could wish. It promised to be 48,000, but will in few hours double and quadruple that number, invincible if we had only arms!

392. But see the promised Charleville boxes, marked artillerie! Here, then, are arms enough? Conceive the blank face of patriotism when it found them filled with rags, foul linen, candle-ends, and bits of wood. Provost of the merchants, how is this? Neither at the Chartreux convent, whither we were sent with signed order, is there or ever was there any weapon of war. Nay, here in this Seine boat, safe under tarpaulins (had not the nose of patriotism been of the finest), are "five thousand-weight of gunpowder," not coming *in*, but surreptitiously going out! What meanest thou, Flesselles? 'Tis a ticklish game, that of "amusing" us. Cat plays with captive mouse; but mouse, with enraged cat, with enraged national tiger?

393. Meanwhile, the faster, O ye black-aproned smiths, smite, with strong arm and willing heart. This man and that, all stroke from head to heel, shall thunder alternating, and ply the great forge-hammer, till stithy reel and ring again, while ever and anon, overhead booms the alarm cannon—for the city has now got gunpowder. Pikes are fabricated, fifty thousand of them, in six-and-thirty hours; judge whether the black-aproned have been idle, Dig trenches, unpave the streets, ye others, assiduous. man and maid; cram the earth in barrel-barricades, at each of them a volunteer sentry; pile the whinstones in window sills and upper rooms. Have scalding pitch, at least boiling water, ready, ye weak old women, to pour it and dash it on Royal-Allemand, with your old skinny arms; your shrill curses along with it will not be wanting. Patrols of the newborn national guard, bearing torches, scour the streets all that night, which otherwise are vacant, yet illuminated in every window by order. Strange looking, like some naptha-lighted city of the dead, with here and there a flight of perturbed ghosts.

O poor mortals, how ye make this earth bitter for each other; this fearful and wonderful life fearful and horrible, and Satan has his place in all hearts! Such agonies and ragings and wailing ye have, and have had, in all times—to be hurled all in so deep silence; and the salt sea is not swollen with your tears.

394. Great, meanwhile, is the moment when tidings of freedom reach us; when the long-inthralled soul, from amid its chains and squalid stagnancy, arises, were it still only in blindness and bewilderment, and swears by Him that made it that it will be *free !* Free ? Understand that well; it is the deep commandment, dimmer or clearer, of our whole being to be *free*. Freedom is the one purport, wisely aimed at, or unwisely, of all man's struggles, toilings and sufferings in this earth. Yes, supreme is such a moment (if thou have known it), first vision as of a flame-girt Sinai, in this our waste pilgrimage —which thenceforth wants not its pillar of cloud by day and pillar of fire by night. Something it is even —nay, something considerable, when the chains have grown *corrosive*, poisonous—to be free "from oppression by our fellow-man." Forward, ye maddened sons of France; be it toward this destiny or toward that! Around you is but starvation, falsehood, corruption and the clam of death. Where ye are is no abiding.

395. Imagination may, imperfectly, figure how Commandant Besenval, in the Champ-de-Mars, has worn out these sorrowful hours. Insurrection raging all round, his men melting away! From Versailles, to the most pressing messages, comes no answer, or once only some vague word of answer which is worse

than none. A council of officers can decide merely that there is no decision, colonels inform him, "weeping," that they do not think their men will fight. Cruel uncertainty is here, war-god Broglie sits yonder, inaccessible in his Olympus; does not descend terror-clad, does not produce his whiff of grape-shot, sends no orders.

396. Truly, in the Château of Versailles all seems mystery; in the town of Versailles, were we there, all is rumor, alarm, and indignation. An august national assembly sits, to appearance, menaced with death, endeavoring to defy death. It has resolved "that Necker carries with him the regrets of the nation." It has sent solemn deputation over to the château, with entreaty to have these troops withdrawn. In vain; his majesty, with a singular composure, invites us to be busy rather with our own duty, making the constitution! Foreign pandours, and such-like, go pricking and prancing, with a swashbuckler air, with an eye, too, probably to the Salle des Menus—were it not for the "grim-looking countenances" that crowd all avenues there.* Be firm, ye national senators, the cynosure of a firm grim-looking people!

397. The august national senators determine that there shall, at least, be permanent session till this thing end. Wherein, however, consider that worthy Lafranc de Pompignan, our new president, whom we have named Bailly's successor, is an old man, wearied with many things. He is the brother of that Pompignan who meditated lamentably on the book of Lamentations:

Savez vous pourquoi Jeremie
Se lamentait toute sa vie?
C'est qu'il prevoyait
Que Pompignan le traduirait!

Poor Bishop Pompignan withdraws, having got Lafayette for helper or substitute; this letter, as nocturnal vice-president, with a thin house in disconsolate humor, sits sleepless, with lights unsnuffed, waiting, what the hours will bring.

398. So at Versailles. But at Paris, agitated Besenval, before retiring for the night, has stept over to old M. de Sombreuil, of the Hotel des Invalides hard by. M. de Sombreuil has, what is a great secret, some eight-and-twenty thousand stand of muskets deposited in his cellars there, but no trust in the temper of his invalides. This day, for example, he sent twenty of the fellows down to unscrew those muskets, lest sedition might snatch at them; but scarcely, in six hours, had the twenty unscrewed twenty gun-locks, or dogs-heads (chiens) of locks, each invalide his dogs-head! If ordered to fire, they would, he imagines, turn their cannon against himself.

399. Unfortunate old military gentlemen, it is your hour, not of glory! Old Marquis de Launay, too, of the Bastille, has pulled up his drawbridges long since, "and retired into his interior," with sentries walking on his battlements, under the midnight sky, aloft over the glare of illuminated Paris—whom a national patrol, passing that way, takes the liberty of firing at, "seven shots toward twelve at night," which do not take effect.† This was the 13th day of July, 1789, a worse day, many said, than the last 13th was, when only hail fell out of heaven, not madness rose out of Tophet, ruining worse than crops!

400. In these same days, as chronology will teach us, hot old Marquis Mirabeau lies stricken down at Argenteuil—not within sound of these alarm-guns; for he properly is not there, and only the body of him now lies, deaf and cold forever. It was on Saturday night that he, drawing his last life-breaths, gave up

the ghost there—leaving a world which would never go to his mind, now broken out, seemingly, into deliration and the culbute générale. What is it to him, departing elsewhither, on his long journey? The old Château Mirabeau stands silent, far off, on its scarped rock, in that "gorge of two windy valleys;" the pale-fading specter now of château; this huge world-riot, and France, and the world itself, fades also, like a shadow on the great still mirror-sea; and all shall be as God wills.

401. Young Mirabeau, sad of heart, for he loved this crabbed, brave old father—sad of heart, and occupied with sad cares, is withdrawn from public history. The great crisis transacts itself without him.*

CHAPTER VI.

STORM AND VICTORY.

402. But, to the living and the struggling, a new fourteenth morning dawns. Under all roofs of this distracted city is the nodus of a drama, not untragical, crowding toward solution. The bustlings and preparings, the tremors and menaces, the tears that fell from old eyes! This day, my sons, ye shall quit you like men. By the memory of your fathers wrongs; by the hope of your children's rights! Tyranny impends in red wrath: help for you is none, if not in your own right hands. This day ye must do or die.

403. From earliest light, a sleepless permanent committee has heard the old cry, now waxing almost frantic, mutinous, Arms! Arms! Provost Flesselles, or what traitors there are among you, may think of those Charleville boxes. A hundred and fifty thousand of us, and but the third man furnished with so much as a pike! Arms are the one thing needful, with arms we are an unconquerable man-defying national guard; without arms, a rabble to be whiffed with grape-shot.

404. Happily the word has arisen, for no secret can be kept, that there lie muskets at the Hotel des Invalides. Thither will we, King's Procureur M. Ethys de Corny, and whatsoever of authority a permanent committee can lend, shall go with us. Besenval's camp is there; perhaps he will not fire on us; if he kill us, we shall but die.

405. Alas! poor Besenval, with his troops melting away in that manner, has not the smallest humor to fire! At five o'clock this morning, as he lay dreaming, oblivious in the Ecole Militaire, a "figure" stood suddenly at his bedside; "with face rather handsome, eyes inflamed, speech rapid and curt, air audacious:" such a figure drew Priam's curtains! The message and monition of the figure was that resistance would be hopeless; that if blood flowed, woe to him who shed it. Thus spoke the figure, and vanished: "Withal there was a kind of eloquence that struck one." Besenval admits that he should have arrested him, but did not.† Who this figure with inflamed eyes, with speech rapid and curt, might be, Besenval knows, but mentions not. Camille Desmoulins? Pythagorean Marquis Valadi, inflamed with "violent notions all night at the Palais Royal?" Fame names him "Young M. Moillar;"‡ then shuts her lips about him forever.

406. In any case, behold, about nine in the morning, our national volunteers rolling in long wide flood south-westward to the Hotel des Invalides, in search of the one thing needful. King's Procureur M.

---

* See Lamoth: Ferrieres, etc.
† "Deux Amis de la Liberté," i. 312.

* Fils Adoptif, "Mirabeau," v. l. 1.
† Besenval, iii. 414.
‡ "Tableaux de la Révolution, Prise de la Bastille" (a folio collection of pictures and portraits, with letter-press, not always uninstructive—part of it is said to be by Chamfort).

Éthys de Corny and officials are there; the curé of Saint-Etienne du Mont marches unpacific at the head of his militant parish; the clerks of the basoche in red coats we see marching, now volunteers of the basoche, the volunteers of the Palais Royal, national volunteers, numerable by tens of thousands, of one heart and mind. The king's muskets are the nation's; think, old M. de Sombreuil, how, in this extremity, thou wilt refuse them! Old M. de Sombreuil would fain hold parley, send couriers, but it skills not; the walls are scaled, no invalide firing a shot; the gates must be flung open. Patriotism rushes in tumultuous, from grunsel up to ridge-tile, through all rooms and passages, rummaging distractedly for arms. What cellar or what cranny can escape it? The arms are found, all safe there, lying packed in straw, apparently with a view to being burnt! More ravenous than famishing lions over dead prey, the multitude, with clangor and vociferation, pounces on them, struggling, dashing, clutching, to the jamming up, to the pressure, fracture, and probable extinction of the weaker patriot.[*] And so, with such protracted crash of deafening, most discordant orchestra-music, the scene is changed; and eight-and-twenty thousand sufficient fire-locks are on the shoulders of as many national guards, lifted thereby out of darkness into fiery light.

407. Let Besenval look at the glitter of these muskets as they flash by! Gardes Françaises, it is said, have cannon leveled on him, ready to open, if need were, from the other side of the river.[†] Motionless sits he; "astonished," one may flatter one's self, "at the proud bearing (fière contenance) of the Parisians." And now to the Bastille, ye intrepid Parisians! There grape-shot still threatens: thither all men's thoughts and steps are now tending.

408. Old De Launay, as we hinted, withdrew "into his interior" soon after midnight of Sunday. He remains there ever since, hampered, as all military gentlemen now are, in the saddest conflict of uncertainties. The Hotel-de-Ville "invites" him to admit national soldiers, which is a soft name for surrendering. On the other hand his majesty's orders were precise. His garrison is but eighty-two old invalides, reinforced by thirty-two young Swiss; his walls, indeed, are nine feet thick; he has cannon and powder, but, alas! only one day's provision of victuals. The city, too, is French, the poor garrison mostly French. Rigorous old De Launay, think what thou wilt do!

409. All morning, since nine, there has been a cry everywhere, To the Bastille! Repeated "deputations of citizens" have been here, passionate for arms, whom De Launay has got dismissed by soft speeches through port-holes. Toward noon, Elector Thuriot de la Rosière gains admittance, finds De Launay indisposed for surrender, nay, disposed for blowing up the place rather. Thuriot mounts with him to the battlements; heaps of paving-stones, old iron, and missiles lie piled; cannon all duly leveled; in every embrasure a cannon—only drawn back a little! But outwards, behold, O Thuriot, bow the multitude flows on, welling through every street; tocsin furiously pealing, all drums beating the générale; the suburb Saint-Antoine rolling hitherward wholly, as one man! Such vision (spectral, yet real) thou, O Thuriot, as from thy mount of visions, beholdest in this moment, prophetic of what other phantasmagories and loud-gibbering spectral realities which thou yet beholdest not, but shalt! "Que voulez-vous?" said De Launay, turning pale at the sight, with an air of reproach, almost of menace. "Monsieur," said Thuriot, rising into the moral sublime, "what mean

* "Deux Amis," i. 302.
† Besenval, iii. 416.

you? Consider if I could not precipitate *both* of us from this height," say only a hundred feet, exclusive of the walled ditch! Whereupon De Launay fell silent. Thuriot shows himself from some pinnacle, to comfort the multitude becoming suspicious, fremescent, then descends, departs with protests, with warning addressed also to the invalides, on whom, however, it produces but a mixed, indistinct impression. The old heads are none of the clearest; besides, it is said, De Launay has been profuse of beverages (prodigue des buissons). They think they will not fire—if not fired on—if they can help it; but must, on the whole, be ruled considerably by circumstances.

410. Woe to thee, De Launay, in such an hour, if thou canst not, taking some one firm decision, *rule* circumstances! Soft speeches will not serve hard, grape-shot is questionable, but hovering between the two is *unquestionable*. Ever wilder swells the tide of men, their infinite hum waxing ever louder, into imprecations, perhaps into crackle of stray musketry —which latter, on walls nine feet thick, cannot do execution. The outer drawbridge has been lowered for Thuriot; new *deputation of citizens* (it is the third and noisest of all) penetrates that way into the outer court; soft speeches producing no clearance of these, De Launay gives fire, pulls up his drawbridge. A slight sputter, which has *kindled* the too combustible chaos, made it a roaring fire-chaos! Bursts forth insurrection, at sight of its own blood (for there were deaths by that sputter of fire), into endless, rolling explosion of musketry, distraction, execration, and over head, from the fortress, let one great gun, with its grape-shot, go booming, to show what we *could* do. The Bastille is besieged!

411. On, then, all Frenchmen that have hearts in your bodies! Roar with all your throats of cartilage and metal, ye sons of liberty; stir spasmodically whatsoever of utmost faculty is in you, soul, body, or spirit, for it is the hour! Smite thou, Louis Tournay, cartwright of the Marais, old soldier of the Regiment Dauphiné; smite at that outer drawbridge chain, though the fiery hail whistles round thee! Never, over nave or felloc, did thy axe strike such a stroke. Down with it, man; down with it to Orcus; let the whole accursed edifice sink thither, and tyranny be swallowed up forever! Mounted, some say, on the roof of the guard-room, some "on bayonets stuck into joints of the wall," Louis Tournay smites, brave Aubin Bonnemère (also an old soldier) seconding him. The chain yields, breaks; the huge drawbridge slams down, thundering (avec fracas). Glorious! and yet, alas! it is still but the outworks. The eight grim towers, with their invalide musketry, their paving-stones and cannon-mouths, still soar aloft intact; ditch yawning impassable, stone-faced; the inner drawbridge with its *back* toward us; the Bastille is still to take!

412. To describe this siege of the Bastille (thought to be one of the most important in history) perhaps transcends the talent of mortals. Could one but, after infinite reading, get to understand so much as the plan of the building! But there is open esplanade at the end of the Rue Saint-Antoine; there are such forecourts, (cour avancé), cour de l'orme, arched gateway (where Louis Tournay now fights); then new drawbridges, dormant-bridges, rampart-bastions and the grim eight towers, a labyrinthic mass, high-frowning there, of all ages from twenty years to four hundred and twenty, beleaguered in this its last hour, as we said, by mere chaos come again! Ordnance of all calibers, throats of all capacities, men of all plans, every man his own engineer; seldom since the war of pygmies and cranes was there seen so anomalous a thing. Half-pay Elie is home for a suit of regimentals, no one would heed him in colored clothes;

half-pay Hulin is haranguing Gardes Françaises in the Place de Grève. Frantic patriots pick up the grape-shots, bear them, still hot (or seemingly so), to the Hotel-de-Ville. Paris, you perceive, is to be burnt! Flesselles is "pale to the very lips," for the roar of the multitude grows deep. Paris, wholly, has got to the acme of its frenzy, whirled all ways by panic madness. At every street-barricade there whirls, simmering, a minor whirlpool, strengthening the barricade, since God knows what is coming; and all minor whirlpools play distractedly into that grand fire-mahlstrom which is lashing round the Bastille.

413 And so it lashes and it roars. Cholat, the wine-merchant, has become an impromptu cannoneer. See Georget, of the marine service, fresh from Brest, ply the King of Siam's cannon. Singular (if we were not used to the like). Georget lay, last night, taking his ease at his inn; the King of Siam's cannon also lay, knowing nothing of *him* for a hundred years; yet now, at the right instant, they have got together, and discourse eloquent music; for, hearing what was toward, Georget sprang from the Brest diligence, and ran. Gardes Françaises, also, will be here, with real artillery. Were not the walls so thick! Upward from the esplanade, horizontally from all neighboring roofs and windows, flashes one irregular deluge of musketry, without effect. The invalides lie flat, firing comparatively at their ease from behind stone; hardly through port-holes show the tip of a nose. We fall, shot, and make no impression!

414. Let conflagration rage of whatsoever is combustible! Guard-rooms are burnt, invalides mess-rooms. A distracted "peruke-maker with two fiery torches" is for burning "the saltpeters of the arsenal," had not a woman run screaming, had not a patriot, with some tincture of natural philosophy, instantly struck the wind out of him (butt of musket on pit of stomach), overturned barrels, and stayed the devouring element. A young beautiful lady, seized, escaping, in these outer courts, and thought, falsely, to be De Launay's daughter, shall be burnt in De Launay's sight: she lies, swooned, on a paillasse; but, again, a patriot—it is brave Aubin Bonnemère, the old soldier—dashes in, and rescues her. Straw is burnt; three cartloads of it, hauled hither, go up in white smoke, almost to the choking of patriotism itself; so that Elie had, with singed brows, to drag back one cart, and Réole, the "gigantic haberdasher," another. Smoke as of Tophet, confusion as of Babel, noise as of the crack of doom!

415. Blood flows, the aliment of new madness. The wounded are carried into houses of the Rue Cerisaie; the dying leave their last mandate not to yield till the accursed stronghold fall. And yet, alas! how fall? The walls are so thick! Deputations, three in number, arrive from the Hotel-de-Ville, Abbé Fauchet (who was of one) can say with what almost superhuman courage of benevolence.* These wave their town-flag in the arched gateway, and stand, rolling their drum, but to no purpose. In such crack of doom, De Launay cannot hear them, dare not believe them; they return, with justified rage, the whew of lead still singing in their ears. What to do? The firemen are here, squirting with their fire-pumps on the Invalides cannon, to wet the touch-holes; they unfortunately cannot squirt so high, but produce only clouds of spray. Individuals of classical knowledge propose *catapults*. Santerre, the sonorous brewer of the suburb Saint-Antoine, advises rather that the place be fired by a "mixture of phosphorous and oil of turpentine spouted up

through forcing-pumps." O Spinola-Santerre, hast thou the mixture ready? Every man his own engineer! And still the fire-deluge abates not; even women are firing, and Turks—at least one woman (with her sweetheart), and one Turk.* Gardes Françaises have come; real cannon, real cannoneers. Usher Maillard is busy; half-pay Elie, half-pay Hulin, rage in the midst of thousands.

416. How the great Bastille clock ticks (inaudible) in its inner court, there, at its ease, hour after hour; as if nothing special, for it or the world, were passing! It tolled one when the firing began, and is now pointing toward five, and still the firing slakes not. Far down, in their vaults, the seven prisoners hear muffled din as of earthquakes; their turnkeys answer vaguely.

417. Woe to thee, De Launay, with thy poor hundred invalides! Broglie is distant, and his ears heavy; Besenval hears, but can send no help. One poor troop of hussars has crept, reconnoitering, cautiously along the quais, as far as Pont Neuf. "We are come to join you," said the captain, for the crowd seems shoreless. A large-headed dwarfish individual, of smoke-bleared aspect, shambles forward, opening his blue lips, for there is sense in him, and croaks, "Alight then, and give up your arms!" The hussar-captain is too happy to be escorted to the barriers and dismissed on parole. Who the squat individual was? Men answer It is M. Marat, author of the excellent pacific "Avis au Peuple!" Great, truly, O thou remarkable dog-leech, is this thy day of emergence and new-birth; and yet this same day come four years—but let the curtains of the future hang.

418. What shall De Launay do? One thing only De Launay could have done—what he said he would do. Fancy him sitting, from the first, with lighted taper, within arm's-length of the powder-magazine; motionless, like old Roman senator, or bronze lamp-holder; coldly apprising Thuriot, and all men, by a slight motion of his eye, what his resolution was. Harmless he sat there, while unharmed; but the king's fortress, meanwhile, could, might, would or should in nowise be surrendered save to the king's messenger; one old man's life is worthless, so it be lost with honor; but think, ye brawling canaille, how will it be when a whole Bastille springs skyward? In such statuesque, taper-holding attitude, one fancies De Launay might have left Thuriot, the red clerks of the basoche, curé of Saint-Stephen, and all the tag-rag and bobtail of the world, to work their will.

419. And yet, withal, he could not do it. Hast thou considered how each man's heart is so tremulously responsive to the hearts of all men? hast thou noted how omnipotent is the very sound of many men? How their shriek of indignation palsies the strong soul? their howl of contumely withers with unfelt pangs? The Ritter Gluck confessed that the ground-tone of the noblest passage in one of his noblest operas was the voice of the populace he had heard at Vienna, crying to their kaiser, Bread! Bread! Great is the combined voice of men, the utterance of their *instincts*, which are truer than their *thoughts;* it is the greatest a man encounters, among the sounds and shadows which make up this world of time! He who can resist that, has his footing somewhere *beyond* time. De Launay could not do it. Distracted, he hovers between two—hopes in the middle of despair; surrenders not his fortress; declares that he will blow it up, seizes torches to blow it up, and does not blow it. Unhappy old De Launay, it is the

---

* Fauchet's "Narrative" ("Deux Amis," i. 324).

* "Deux Amis," i. 319, Dusaulx, etc.

death-agony of thy Bastille and thee! Jail, jailoring, and jailor, all three, such as they may have been, must finish.

420. For four hours now has the world-bedlam roared; call it the world-chimera, blowing fire! The poor invalides have sunk under their battlements, or rise only with reversed muskets; they have made a white flag of napkins, go beating the chamade, or seeming to beat, for one can hear nothing. The very Swiss at the portcullis look weary of firing, disheartened in the fire-deluge; a port-hole at the drawbridge is opened, as by one that would speak. See Huissier Maillard, the shifty man! On his plank, swinging over the abyss of that stone ditch, plank resting on parapet, balanced by weight of patriots, he hovers perilous—such a dove toward such an ark! Deftly, thou shifty usher; one man already fell, and lies smashed, far down there, against the masonry! Usher Maillard falls not; deftly, unerring, he walks, with outspread palm. The Swiss holds a paper through his port-hole; the shifty usher snatches it and returns. Terms of surrender, Pardon, immunity to all! Are they accepted? "Foi d'officier (On the word of an officer)," answer shall half-pay Hulin, or half-pay Elie—for men do not agree on it—"they are!" Sinks the drawbridge, Usher Maillard bolting it when down; rushes—in the living deluge; the Bastille is fallen! Victoire! La Bastille est prise!*

CHAPTER VII.

NOT A REVOLT.

421. Why dwell on what follows? Hulin's foi d'officier should have been kept, but could not. The Swiss stand drawn up, disguised in white canvas smocks; the invalides without disguise, their arms all piled against the wall. The first rush of victors, in ecstasy that the death-peril is passed, "leaps joyfully on their necks;" but new victors rush, and ever new, also in ecstasy not wholly of joy. As we said, it was a living deluge, plunging headlong; had not the Gardes Françaises, in their cool military way, "wheeled round with arms leveled," it would have plunged suicidally, by the hundred or the thousand, into the Bastille-ditch.

422. And so it goes plunging through court and corridor; billowing uncontrollable, firing from windows—on itself; in hot frenzy of triumph, of grief; and vengeance for its slain. The poor invalides will fare ill; one Swiss, running off in his white smock, is driven back, with a death-thrust. Let all prisoners be marched to the town-hall to be judged! Alas, already one poor invalide has his right hand slashed off him, his maimed body dragged to the Place de Grève, and hanged there. This same right hand, it is said, turned back De Launay from the powder-magazine, and saved Paris.

423. De Launay, "discovered in gray frock with poppy-colored ribbon," is for killing himself with the sword of his cane. He shall to the Hotel-de-Ville, Hulin, Maillard, and others escorting him, Elie marching foremost, "with the capitulation-paper on his sword's point." Through roarings and cursings, through hustlings, clutchings, and at last through strokes! Your escort is hustled aside, fell down; Hulin sinks exhausted on a heap of stones. Miserable De Launay! He shall never enter the Hotel-de-

Ville; only his "bloody hair-queue, held up in a bloody hand," that shall enter, for a sign. The bleeding trunk lies on the steps there; the head is off through the streets, ghastly, aloft on a pike.

424. Rigorous De Launay has died, crying out, "O friends, kill me fast!" Merciful De Losme must die; though gratitude embraces him, in this fearful hour, and will die for him, it avails not. Brothers, your wrath is cruel! Your Place de Grève is become a throat of the tiger, full of mere fierce bellowings, and thirst of blood. One other officer is massacred; one other invalide is hanged on the lamp-iron; with difficulty, with generous perseverance, the Gardes Françaises will save the rest. Provost Flesselles, stricken long since with the paleness of death, must descend from his seat, "to be judged at the Palais Royal;"—alas, to be shot dead by an unknown hand at the turning of the first street!

425. O evening sun of July, how, at this hour, thy beams fall slant on reapers amid peaceful woody fields, on old women spinning in cottages, on ships far out in the silent main; on balls of the orangerie of Versailles, where high-rouged dames of the palace are even now dancing with double-jacketed hussar-officers; and also on this roaring hell-porch of a Hotel-de-Ville! Babel tower, with the confusion of tongues, were not bedlam added with the conflagration of thoughts, was no new type of it. One forest of distracted steel bristles, endless, in front of an electoral committee; points itself, in horrid radii, against this and the other accused breast. It was the Titans warring with Olympus; and they, scarcely crediting it, have *conquered;* prodigy of prodigies; delirious—as it could not but be. Denunciation, vengeance, blaze of triumph on a dark ground of terror; all outward, all inward things fallen into one general wreck of madness!

426. Electoral committee? Had it a thousand throats of brass, it would not suffice. Abbé Lefevre, in the vaults down below, is black as Vulcan, distributing that "five thousand-weight of powder," with what perils, these eight-and-forty hours! Last night, a patriot, in liquor, insisted on sitting to smoke on the edge of one of the powder-barrels; there smoked he, independent of the world—till the Abbé "purchased his pipe for three francs," and pitched it far.

427. Elie, in the grand hall, electoral committee looking on, sits "with drawn sword bent in three places;" with battered helm, for he was of the Queen's Regiment, cavalry; with torn regimentals, face singed and soiled; comparable, some think, to "an antique warrior"—judging the people, forming a list of Bastille heroes. O friends, stain not with blood the greenest laurels ever gained in this world, such is the burden of Elie's song, could it but be listened to. Courage, Elie! Courage, ye municipal electors! A declining sun, the need of victuals and of telling news, will bring assuagement, dispersion—all earthly things must end.

428. Along the streets of Paris circulate seven Bastille prisoners, borne shoulder-high, seven heads on pikes, the keys of the Bastille, and much else. See, also, the Gardes Françaises, in their steadfast military way, marching home to their barracks, with the invalides and Swiss kindly inclosed in hollow square. It is one year and two months since these same men stood unparticipating, with Brennus d'Agoust at the Palais de Justice, when fate overtook D'Esprémenil; and now they have participated, and will participate. Not Gardes Françaises henceforth, but *Center Grenadiers of the National Guard*—men of iron discipline and humor, not without a kind of thought in them!

429. Likewise, ashlar stones of the Bastille con-

* "Histoire de la Révolution," par Deux Amis de la Liberté, i. 267-306; Besenval, iii. 410-434; Dusaulx, "Prise de la Bastille," 301-303; Bailly, "Mémoires (Collection de Berriére"), i. 322 et seqq.

tinue thundering through the dusk; its paper archives shall fly white. Old secrets come to view, and long-buried despair finds voice. Read this portion of an old letter:* "If for my consolation monseigneur would grant me, for the sake of God and the most blessed Trinity, that I could have news of my dear wife, were it only her name on a card, to show that she is alive! It were the greatest consolation I could receive, and I should forever bless the greatness of monseigneur." Poor prisoner, who namest thyself Quéret-Démery, and has no other history—she is *dead*, that dear wife of thine, and thou art dead! 'Tis fifty years since thy breaking heart put this question, to be heard now first, and long heard, in the hearts of men.

430. But so does the July twilight thicken; so must Paris, as sick children and all distracted creatures do, brawl itself finally into a kind of sleep. Municipal electors, astonished to find their heads still uppermost, are home; only Moreau de Saint-Méry, of tropical birth and heart, of coolest judgment, he, with two others, shall sit permanent at the town-hall. Paris sleeps; gleams upward the illuminated city; patrols go clashing, without common watchword; there go rumors, alarms of war, to the extent of "15,000men marching through the suburb Saint-Antoine"—who never got it marched through. Of the day's distraction judge by this of the night—Moreau de Saint-Méry, "before rising from his seat, gave upward of 3,000 orders."† What a head, comparable to Friar Bacon's brass head! Within it lies all Paris. Prompt must the answer be, right or wrong; in Paris is no other authority extant. Seriously, a most cool, clear head—for which also thou, O brave Saint-Méry, in many capacities, from august senator to merchant's clerk, book dealer, vice-king in many places, from Virginia to Sardinia, shalt, ever as a brave man, find employment.‡

431. Besenval has decamped under cloud of dusk, "amid a great affluence of people," who did not harm him; he marches with faint-growing tread, down the left bank of the Seine, all night—toward infinite space. Re-summoned shall Besenval himself be, for trial, for difficult acquittal. His king-troops, his Royal-Allemand, are gone hence forever.

432. The Versailles ball and lemonade is done; the orangerie is silent except for night-birds. Over in the Salle des Menus Vice-President Lafayette, with unsnuffed lights, "with some hundred or so of members stretched on tables ronnd him," sits erect, outwatching the bear. This day a second solemn deputation went to his majesty, a second, and then a third—with no effect. What will the end of these things be?

433. In the court all is mystery, not without whisperings of terror, though ye dream of lemonade and epaulettes, ye foolish women! His majesty, kept in happy ignorance, perhaps dreams of double-barrels and the woods of Meudon. Late at night, the Duke de Liancourt, having official right of entrance, gains access to the royal apartments, unfolds, with earnest clearness, in his constitutional way, the Job's news. "Mais," said poor Louis, "c'est une révolte (Why, that is a revolt)!" "Sire," answered Liancourt, "it is not a revolt—it is a revolution."

CHAPTER VIII.
CONQUERING YOUR KING.

434. On the morrow a fourth deputation to the château is on foot, of a more solemn, not to say awful

* Dated à la Bastille, 7 Octobre, 1752; signed Quéret-Demery. "Bastille Dévoilée;" in Linguet. "Mémoires sur la Bastille" (Paris, 1821), p. 199.
† Dusaulx.
‡ "Biographie Universelle." § Moreau Saint-Mery (by Fournier-Pescay).

character; for, besides "orgies in the orangery," it seems "the grain-convoys are all stopped," nor has Mirabeau's thunder been silent. Such deputation is on the point of setting out—when lo, his majesty himself, attended only by his two brothers, steps in, quite in the paternal manner, announces that the troops, and all causes of offense, are gone; and henceforth there shall be nothing but trust, reconcilement, good-will; whereof he "permits, and even requests," a national assembly to assure Paris in his name! Acclamation, as of men suddenly delivered from death, gives answer. The whole assembly spontaneously rises to escort his majesty back, "interlacing their arms to keep off the excessive pressure from him," for all Versailles is crowding and shouting. The château musicians, with a felicitous promptitude, strike up the Sein de sa Famille (Bosom of One's Family); the queen appears at the balcony with her little boy and girl, "kissing them several times," infinite vivats spread far and wide—and suddenly there has come, as it were, a new heaven-on-earth.

435. Eighty-eight august senators, Bailly, Lafayette, and our repentant archbishop among them, take coach for Paris, with the great intelligence; benedictions without end on their heads. From the Place Louis Quinze, where they alight, all the way to the Hotel-de-Ville, it is one sea of tricolor cockades, of clear national muskets, one tempest of huzzaings, hand-clappings, aided by "occasional rollings" of drum music. Harangues of due fervor are delivered, especially by Lally Tollendal, pious son of the ill-fated murdered Lally, on whose head, in consequence, a civic crown (of oak or parsley) is forced—which he forcibly transfers to Bailly's.

436. But surely, for one thing, the national guard should have a general! Moreau de Saint-Méry, he of the "three thousand orders," casts one of his significant glances on the bust of Lafayette, which has stood there ever since the American war of liberty. Whereupon, by acclamation, Lafayette is nominated. Again, in room of the slain traitor or quasi-traitor Flesselles, President Bailly shall be—provost of the merchants? No; mayor of Paris! So be it. Maire de Paris! Mayor Bailly, General Lafayette; vive Bailly, vive Lafayette! the universal out-of-doors multitude rends the welkin in confirmation. And now, finally, let us to Notre-Dame for a Te Deum.

437. Toward Notre-Dame cathedral, in glad procession, these regenerators of the country walk, through a jubilant people, in fraternal manner, Abbé Lefevre, still black with his gunpowder services, walking arm in arm with the white-stoled archbishop. Poor Bailly comes upon the foundling children, sent to kneel to him, and "weeps." Te Deum, our archbishop officiating, is not only sung, but *shot*—with blank cartridges. Our joy is boundless, as our woe threatened to be. Paris, by her own pike and musket, and the valor of her own heart, has conquered the very war-gods—to the satisfaction now of majesty itself. A courier is, this night, getting under way for Necker; the people's minister, invited back by king, by national assembly, and nation, shall traverse France amid shoutings, and the sound of trumpet and timbrel.

438. Seeing which course of things, messeigneurs of the court triumvirate, messieurs of the dead-born Broglie ministry, and others such, consider that their part also is clear—to mount and ride. Off, ye too-royal Broglies, Polignacs, and princes of the blood; off while it is yet time! Did not the Palais Royal, in its late nocturnal "violent motions," set a specific price (place of payment not mentioned) on each of your heads? With precautions, with the aid of pieces of cannon and regiments that can be depended on, messeigneurs, between the sixteenth night and

seventeenth morning, get to their several roads. Not without risk! Prince Condé has (or seems to have) "men galloping at full speed," with a view, it is thought, to fling him into the river Oise, at Pont-Sainte-Maycnce.* The l'oliguacs travel disguised, friends, not servants on their coach-box. Broglie has his own difficulties at Versailles, runs his own risks at Metz and Verdun, does, nevertheless, get safe to Luxemburg, and there rests.

439. This is what they call the first emigration, determined on, as appears, in full court-conclave, his majesty assisting—prompt he, for his share of it, to follow any counsel whatsoever. "Three sons of France and four princes of the blood of Saint Louis," says Weber, "could not more effectually humble the burghers of Paris than by appearing to withdraw in rear of their life." Alas, the burghers of Paris bear it with unexpected stoicism! The man D'Artois, indeed, is gone, but has he carried, for example, the land D'Artois, with him? Not even Bagatelle, the country-house (which shall be useful as a tavern); hardly the four-valet breeches, leaving the breeches-maker! As for old Foulon, one learns that he is dead; at least "a sumptuous funeral" is going on; the undertakers honoring him, if no other will. Intendant Berthier, his son-in-law, is still living, lurking; he joined Besenval on that Eumenides Sunday, appearing to treat it with levity, and is now fled, no man knows whither.

440. The emigration is not gone many miles, Prince Condé hardly across the Oise, when his majesty, according to arrangement—for the emigration also thought it might do good—undertakes a rather daring enterprise, that of visiting Paris in person. With a hundred members of assembly, with small or no military escort, which, indeed, he dismissed at the bridge of Sèvres, poor Louis sets out, leaving a desolate palace, a queen weeping, the present, the past, and the future all so unfriendly for her.

441. At the barrier of Passy, Mayor Bailly, in grand gala, presents him with the keys, harangues him, in academic style, mentions that it is a great day; that in Henri Quatre's case, the king had to make conquest of his people, but in this happier case, the people makes conquest of its king (a conquis son Roi). The king, so happily conquered, drives forward slowly, through a steel people, all silent, or shouting only Vive la nation; is harangued at the town-hall by Moreau of the three thousand orders, by King's Procureur M. Ethys de Corny, by Lally Tollendal and others; knows not what to think of it or say of it; learns that he is "restorer of French liberty"—as a statue of him, to be raised on the site of the Bastille, shall testify to all men. Finally, he is shown at the balcony, with a tricolor cockade in his hat; is greeted now with vehement acclamation, from square and street, from all windows and roofs—and so drives home again amid glad mingled and, as it were, intermarried shouts of Vive le roi and Vive la nation, wearied but safe.

442. It was Sunday when the red-hot balls hung over us, in mid air; it is now but Friday and "the revolution is sanctioned." An august national assembly shall make the constitution; and neither foreign pandour, domestic triumvirate, with leveled cannon, Guy-Faux powder plots (for that, too, was spoken of), nor any tyrannic power on the earth or under the earth, shall say to it, What dost thou? So jubilates the people, sure now of a constitution. Cracked Marquis Saint-Huruge is heard under the windows of the Château, murmuring sheer speculative-treason.†

* Weber, ii. 126.
† Campan, ii. 46–64.

CHAPTER IX.

THE LANTERNE.

443. The fall of the Bastille may be said to have shaken all France to the deepest foundations of its existence. The rumors of these wonders flies everywhere, with the natural speed of rumor, with an effect thought to be preternatural, produced by plots. Did D'Orléans or Laclos, nay, did Mirabeau (not overburdened with money at this time) send riding couriers out from Paris, to gallop "on all radii," or highways toward all points of France? It is a miracle which no penetrating man will call in question.*

444. Already in most towns electoral committees were met, to regret Necker, in harangue and resolution. In many a town, as Rennes, Caen, Lyons, an ebullient people was already regretting him in brickbats and musketry. But now at every town's-end in France there do arrive, in these days of terror, "men," as men will arrive; nay, "men on horseback," since rumor oftenest travels riding. These men declare, with alarmed countenance, *the brigands* to be coming, to be just at hand; and do then—ride on about their further business, be what it might! Whereupon the whole population of such town defensively flies to arms. Petition is soon thereafter forwarded to national assembly; in such peril and terror of peril, leave to organize yourself cannot be withheld; the armed population becomes everywhere an enrolled national guard. Thus rides rumor, careering along all radii, from Paris outward to such purpose; in few days, some say, in not many hours, all France to the utmost borders bristles with bayonets. Singular, but undeniable—miraculous, or not! But thus may any chemical liquid, though cooled to the freezing-point, or far lower, still continue liquid; and then, on the slightest stroke or shake, it at once rushes wholly into ice. Thus, has France, for long months and even years, been chemically dealt with; brought below zero; and now shaken by the fall of a Bastille, it instantaneously congeals into one crystallized mass of sharp-cutting steel! Guai a chi la tocca,—'Ware who touches it!

445. In Paris an electoral committee, with a new mayor and general, is urgent with belligerent workmen to resume their handicrafts. Strong dames of the market (dames de la halle) deliver congratulatory harangues, present "bouquets to the shrine of Sainte Geneviève." Unenrolled men deposit their arms—not so readily as could be wished—and receive "nine francs." With Te Deums, royal visits, and sanctioned revolution, there is halcyon weather, weather even of preternatural brightness· the hurricane being overblown.

446. Nevertheless, as is natural, the waves still run high, hollow rocks retaining their murmur. We are but at the 22d of the month, hardly above a week since the Bastille fell, when it suddenly appears that old Foulon is alive; nay, that he is here, in early morning, in the streets of Paris—the extortioner, the plotter, who would make the people eat grass, and was a liar from the beginning! It is even so. The deceptive "sumptuous funeral" (of some domestic that died); the hiding-place at Vitry toward Fontainebleau, have not availed that wretched old man. Some living domestic or dependent, for none loves Foulon, has betrayed him to the village. Merciless boors of Vitry unearth him, pounce on him, like hell-hounds; westward, old infamy, to Paris, to be judged at the Hotel-de-Ville! His old head, which seventy-four years have bleached, is bare; they have tied an emblematic bundle of grass on his back, a garland of nettles and thistles is round his neck; in

* Toulongeon, i. 95: Weber, etc., etc.

this manner, led with ropes, goaded on with curses and menaces, must he, with his old limbs, sprawl forward—the pitiablest, most unpitied of all old men.

447. Sooty Saint-Antoine, and every street, musters its crowds as he passes—the hall of the Hotel-de-Ville, the Place de Grève itself will scarcely hold his escort and him. Foulon must not only be judged righteously, but judged there where he stands, without any delay. Appoint seven judges, ye municipals, or seventy-and-seven; name them yourselves, or we will name them—but judge him!* Electoral rhetoric, eloquence of Mayor Bailly, is wasted, for hours, explaining the beauty of the law's delay. Delay, and still delay! Behold, O mayor of the people, the morning has worn itself into noon, and he is still unjudged! Lafayette, pressingly sent for, arrives, gives voice. This Foulon, a known man, is guilty almost beyond doubt; but may he not have accomplices? Ought not the truth to be cunningly pumped out of him—in the Abbaye prison? It is a new light! Sansculottism claps hands—at which hand-clapping, Foulon (in his fainness, as his destiny would have it) also claps. "See! they understand one another!" cries dark sansculottism, blazing into fury of suspicion. "Friends," said "a person in good clothes," stepping foward, "what is the use of judging this man? Has not he been judged these thirty years?" With wild yells, sansculottism clutches him in its hundred hands: he is whirled across the Place de Grève, to the "lanterne" (lamp-iron), which there is at the corner of the Rue de la Vannerie; pleading bitterly for life—to the deaf winds. Only with the third rope—for two ropes broke, and the quavering voice still pleaded—can he be so much as got hanged! His body is dragged through the streets; his head goes aloft on a pike, the mouth filled with grass · amid sounds as of Tophet, from a grass-eating people.†

448. Surely if revenge is a "kind of justice," it is a "wild" kind! O mad sansculottism, hast thou risen, in thy mad darkness, in thy soot and rags; unexpectedly, like an Enceladus, living buried, from under his Trinacria? They that would make grass be eaten do now eat grass in *this* manner? After long dumb-groaning generations, has the turn suddenly become thine? To such abysmal overturns, and frightful instantaneous inversions of the center-of-gravity, are human solecism all liable, if they but knew it; the more liable, the falser (and topheavier) they are!

449. To add to the horror of Mayor Bailly and his municipals, word come that Berthier has also been arrested; that he is on his way hither from Compiègne. Berthier, intendant (say tax-levier) of Paris, sycophant and tyrant, forestaller of corn, contriver of camps against the people, accused of many things; is he not Foulon's son-in-law, and, in that one point, guilty of all? In these hours, too, when sansculottism has its blood up! The shuddering municipals send one of their number to escort him with mounted national guards.

450. At the fall of day the wretched Berthier, still wearing a face of courage, arrives at the · barrier, in an open carriage, with the municipal beside him; 500 horsemen with drawn sabres; unarmed footmen enough, not without noise! Placards go brandished round him, bearing legibly his indictment, as sansculottism, with unlegal brevity, "in huge letters," draws it up.‡ Paris is come forth to meet him; with

* "Histoire Parlementaire," ii. 146–49.
† "Deux Amis de la Liberté," ii. 60–66.
‡ "Il a volé le Roi et la France." (He robbed the King and France). "He devoured the substance of the people." "He was the slave of the rich, and the tyrant of the poor." "He drunk the blood of the widow and orphan." "He betrayed his country." See "Deux Amis," ii. 67–75.

hand-clappings, with windows flung up, with dances, triumph songs, as of the furies. Lastly, the head of Foulon; this also meets him on a pike. Well might his "look become glazed" and sense fail him at such sight! Nevertheless, be the man's conscience what it may, his nerves are of iron. At the Hotel-de-Ville he will answer nothing. He says he obeyed superior orders; they have his papers; they may judge and determine; as for himself, not having closed an eye these two nights, he demands before all things to have sleep. Leaden sleep, thou miserable Berthier! Guards rise with him in motion toward the Abbaye. At the very door of the Hotel-de-Ville they are clutched, flung asunder as by a vortex of mad arms; Berthier whirls toward the lanterne. He snatches a musket, fells and strikes, defending himself like a mad lion; he is borne down, trampled, hanged, mangled; his head, too, and even his heart, flies over the city on a pike.

451. Horrible in lands that had known equal justice! Not so unnatural in lands that had never known it. "Le sang qui coule, est-il donc si pur?" asks Barnave, intimating that the gallows, though by irregular methods, has its own. Thou, thyself, O reader, when thou turnest that corner of the Rue de la Vannerie, and discernest still that same grim bracket of old iron, wilt not want for reflections. "Over a grocer's shop," or otherwise, with "a bust of Louis XIV. in the niche under it," now no longer in the niche—*it* still sticks there; still holding out an ineffectual light of fish-oil, and has seen worlds wrecked, and says nothing.

452. But to the eye of enlightened patriotism what a thunder-cloud was this, suddenly shaping itself in the radiance of the halcyon weather! Cloud of Erebus blackness, betokened latent electricity without limit. Mayor Bailly, General Lafayette throw up their commissions in an indignant manner; need to be flattered back again. The cloud disappears, as thunder-clouds do. The halcyon weather returns, though of a grayer complexion, of a character more and more evidently *not* supernatural.

453. Thus, in any case, with what rubs soever, shall the Bastille be abolished from our earth, and with it feudalism, despotism, and one hopes, scoundrelism generally, and all hard usage of man by his brother man. Alas, the scoundrelism and hard usage are not so easy of abolition! But, as for the Bastille, it sinks day after day, and month after month, its ashlars and boulders tumbling down continually by express order of our municipals. Crowd of the curious roam through its caverns; gaze on the skeletons found walled-up, on the oubliettes iron-cages, monstrous stone blocks, with padlock chains. One day we discern Mirabeau there, along with the Genevese Dumont.* Workers and onlookers make reverent way for him, fling verses, flowers, on his path, Bastille-papers and curiosities into his carriage, with vivats.

454. Able editors compile books from the Bastille archives, from what of them remain unburnt. The key of that robber-den shall cross the Atlantic, shall lie on Washington's hall-table. The great clock ticks now in a private patriotic clock-maker's apartment, no longer measuring hours of mere heaviness. Vanished is the Bastille, what we call vanished; the *body*, or sandstones, of it hanging in benign metamorphosis, for centuries to come, over the Seine waters as Pont Louis Seize; † the soul of it living, perhaps, still longer in the memories of men.

455. So far, ye august senators, with your tennis-court oaths, your inertia and impetus, your sagacity and pertinacity, have ye brought us. "And yet think, messieurs," as the petitioners justly urged, "you who

* Dumont, "Souvenirs sur Mirabeau," p. 305.
† Dulaure, "Histoire de Paris," viii. 434.

were our saviors did themselves need saviors "—the brave Bastillers, namely, workmen of Paris, many of them in straitened pecuniary circumstances !* Subscriptions are opened, lists are formed, more accurate than Elie's; harangues are delivered. A body of Bastille heroes, tolerably complete, did get together—comparable to the Argonauts, hoping to endure like them. But in little more than a year the whirlpool of things threw them asunder again, and they sank. So many highest superlatives achieved by man are followed by new higher, and dwindled into comparatives and positives! The siege of the Bastille, weighed with which, in the historical balance, most other sieges, including that of Troy town, are gossamer, cost, as we find, in killed and mortally wounded, on the part of the besiegers, some eighty-three persons ; on the part of the besieged, after all that straw-burning, fire-pumping, and deluge of musketry, one poor solitary invalide shot stone-dead (roide-mort) on the battlements !† The Bastille fortress, like the city of Jericho, was overthrown by miraculous *sound*.

BOOK SIXTH.

CONSOLIDATION.

CHAPTER I.

MAKE THE CONSTITUTION.

456. Here, perhaps, is the place to fix a little more precisely what these two words, *French revolution*, shall mean ; for, strictly considered, they may have as many meanings as there are speakers of them. All things are in revolution, in change from moment to moment, which becomes sensible from epoch to epoch ; in this time-world of ours there is properly nothing else but revolution and mutation, and even nothing else conceivable. Revolution, you answer, means *speedier* change. Whereupon one has still to ask, How speedy ? At what degree of speed, in what particular points of this variable course, which varies in velocity, but can never stop till time itself stops, does revolution begin and end, cease to be ordinary mutation, and again become such ? It is a thing that will depend on definition more or less arbitrary.

457. For ourselves, we answer that French revolution means here the open violent rebellion, and victory of disimprisoned anarchy against corrupt, worn-out authority; how anarchy breaks prison, bursts up from the infinite deep, and rages uncontrollable, immeasurable, enveloping a world, in phasis after phasis of fever-frenzy, till the frenzy burning itself out, and what elements of new order it held (since all force holds such) developing themselves, the uncontrollable be got, if not reimprisoned, yet harnessed, and its mad forces made to work toward their object as sane regulated ones. For as hierarchies and dynasties of all kinds, theocracies, aristocracies, autocracies, strumpetocracies, have ruled over the world, so it was appointed in the decrees of providence, that this same victorious anarchy, Jacobinism, sansculottism, French revolution, horrors of French revolution, or what else mortals name it, should have its turn. The "destructive wrath" of sansculottism—this is what we speak, having unhappily no voice for singing.

458. Surely a great phenomenon, nay, it is a *transcendental* one, over-stepping all rules and experience, the crowning phenomenon of our modern time. For here, again, most unexpectedly, comes antique fanaticism in new and newest vesture, miraculous, as all

* Moniteur, "Séance du Samedi, 18 Juillet 1879" (in "Histoire Parlementaire," ii. 137).
† Dusaulx, "Prise de la Bastille," p. 447, etc.

fanaticism is. Call it the fanaticism of "making away with formulas (de humer les formules)." The world of formulas, the *formed*, regulated world, which all habitable world is, must needs hate such fanaticism like death, and be at deadly variance with it. The world of formulas must conquer it; or failing that, must die execrating it, anathematizing it—can, nevertheless, in nowise prevent its being and its having been. The anathemas are there, and the miraculous thing is there.

459. Whence it cometh ? Whither it goeth? These are questions ! When the age of miracles lay faded into the distance as an incredible tradition, and even the age of conventionalities was now old, and man's existence had for long generations rested on mere formulas which were grown hollow by course of time, and it seemed as if no reality any longer existed, but only phantasms of realities, and God's universe were the work of the tailor and upholsterer mainly, and men were buckram masks that went about becking and grimacing there—on a sudden, the earth yawns asunder, and amid Tartarean smoke and glare of fierce brightness, rises *sansculottism*, many-headed, fire-breathing, and asks, What think ye of me? Well may the buckram masks start together, terror-struck, "into expressive well-concerted groups!" It is, indeed, friends, a most singular, most fatal thing. Let whosoever is but buckram and a phantasm look to it; ill verily may it fare with him ; here methinks he cannot much longer be. Woe also to many a one who is not wholly buckram, but partly real and human! The age of miracles has come back! "Behold the world-phœnix, in fire-consummation and fire-creation ; wide are her fanning wings ; loud is her death-melody of battle-thunders and falling towns; skyward lashes the funeral flame, enveloping all things—it is the death-birth of a world!"

460. Whereby, however, as we often say, shall one unspeakable blessing seem attainable. This, namely, that man and his life rest no more on hollowness and a lie, but on solidity and some kind of truth. Welcome the beggarliest truth, so it *be* one, in exchange for the royalest sham! Truth of any kind breeds ever new and better truth ; thus hard granite rock will crumble down into soil, under the blessed skyey influences, and cover itself with verdure, with fruitage and umbrage. But as for falsehood, which in like contrary manner grows ever falser, what can it, or what should it do but decease, being ripe, decompose itself gently or even violently, and return to the father of it—too probably in flames of fire?

461. Sansculottism will burn much, but what is incombustible it will not burn. Fear not sansculottism; recognize it for what it is, the portentous, inevitable end of much, the miraculous beginning of much. One other thing thou mayest understand of it, that it, too, came from God, for has it not *been*? From of old, as it is written, are his goings forth in the great deep of things, fearful and wonderful now as in the beginning; in the whirlwind, also, he speaks, and the wrath of men is made to praise him. But to guage and measure this immeasurable thing, and what is called *account for it*, and reduce it to a dead logic-formula, attempt not! Much less shalt thou shriek thyself hoarse cursing it, for that, to all needful lengths, has been already done. As an actually existing son of time, *look* with unspeakable manifold interest, oftenest in silence, at what the time did bring, therewith edify, instruct, nourish thyself, or were it but amuse and gratify thyself, as it is given thee.

462. Another question which at every new turn will rise on us, requiring ever new reply, is this, Where the French revolution specially *is?* In the king's palace, in his majesty's or her majesty's man-

agements and maltreatments, cabals, imbecilities and woes answer some few—whom we do not answer. In the national assembly, answer a large mixed multitude, who accordingly seat themselves in the reporter's chair, and therefrom noting what proclamations, acts, reports, passages of logic-fence, bursts of parliamentary eloquence seem notable within doors, and what tumults and rumor of tumult become audible from without, produce volume on volume, and naming it History of the French Revolution, contentedly publish the same. To do the like, to almost any extent, with so many filed newspapers, choix des rapports, histoires parlementaires, as there are, amounting to many horse-loads, were easy for us. Easy, but unprofitable. The national assembly, named now constituent assembly, goes its course, making the constitution, but the French revolution also goes *its* course.

463. In general, may we not say that the French revolution lies in the heart and head of every violent-speaking, of every violent-thinking French man? How the 25,000,000 of such, in their perplexed combination, acting and counter-acting, may give birth to events, which event successively is the cardinal one, and from what point of vision it may best he surveyed, this is a problem. Which problem the best insight, seeking light from all possible sources, shifting its point of vision whithersoever vision or glimpse of vision can be had, may employ itself in solving, and be well content to solve in some tolerably approximate way.

464. As to the national assembly, in so far as it still towers eminent over France, after the manner of a car-borne carroccio, though now no longer in the van, and rings signals for retreat or for advance—it is and continues a reality among other realities. But in so far as it sits making the constitution, on the other hand, it is a fatuity and chimera mainly. Alas! in the never so heroic building of Montesquieu-Mably card-castles, though shouted over by the world, what interest is there? Occupied in that way, an august national assembly becomes for us little other than a sanhedrim of pedants, not of the gerund-grinding, yet of no fruitfuller sort; and its loud debatings and recriminations about rights of man, right of peace and war, veto suspensif, veto absolu, what are they but so many pedant's-curses, "May God confound you for your *theory of irregular verbs!*"

465. A constitution can be built, constitutions enough à Sieyes; but the frightful difficulty is that of getting men to come and live, in them. Could Sieyes have drawn thunder and lightning out of heaven to sanction his constitution, it had been well, but without any thunder? Nay, strictly considered, is it not still true that without some such celestial sanction, given visibly in thunder or invisibly otherwise, no constitution can in the long-run be worth much more than the waste-paper that is written on? The constitution, the set of laws or prescribed habits of acting, that men will live under, is the one which images their convictions, their faith as to this wondrous universe, and what rights, duties, capabilities they have there; which stands sanctioned, therefore, by necessity itself, if not by a seen deity, then by an unseen one. Other laws, whereof there are always enough *ready*-made, are usurpations, which men do not obey but rebel against, and abolish at their earliest convenience.

466. The question of questions accordingly were, Who is that, especially for rebellers and abolishers, can make a constitution? He that can image forth the general belief when there is one, that can impart one when, as here, there is none. A most rare man, ever, as of old, a god-missioned man! Here, how-

ever, in defect of such transcendent supreme man, time with its infinite succession of merely superior men, each yielding his little contribution, does much. Force, likewise (for, as antiquarian philosophers teach, the royal scepter was from the first something of a hammer, to *crack* such heads as could not be convinced), will all along find somewhat to do. And thus, in perpetual abolition and reparation, rending and mending, with struggle and strife, with present evil and the hope and effort toward future good, must the constitution, as all human things do, build itself forward, or unbuild itself and sink, as it can and may. O Sieyes, and ye other committee-men, and twelve hundred miscellaneous individuals from all parts of France! what is the belief of France, and yours, if ye knew it? Properly, that there shall be no belief, that all formulas be swallowed. The constitution which will suit that? Alas! too clearly a no-constitution, an anarchy—which also, in due season, shall be vouchsafed you.

467. But, after all, what can an unfortunate national assembly do? Consider only this, that there are twelve hundred miscellaneous individuals, not a unit of whom but has his own thinking-apparatus, his own speaking-apparatus! In every unit of them is some belief and wish, different for each, both that France should be regenerated, and also that he individually should do it. Twelve hundred separate forces, yoked miscellaneously to any object, miscellaneously to all sides of it, and hidden pull for life!

468. Or is it the nature of national assemblies generally to do, with endless labor and clamor, nothing? Are representative governments mostly at bottom tyrannies too? Shall we say the *tyrants*, the ambitious, contentious persons, from all corners of the country do, in this manner, get gathered into one place, and there, with motion and counter motion, with jargon and hubbub, *cancel* one another, like the fabulous Kilkenny cats, and produce, for net-result, *zero*—the country meanwhile *governing* or guiding *itself* by such wisdom, recognized, or for most part unrecognized, as may exist in individual heads here and there? Nay, even that were a great improvement; for of old, with their Guelf factions and Ghibelline factions, with their red roses and white roses, they were wont to cancel the whole country as well. Besides, they do it now in a much narrower cockpit, within the four walls of their assembly house, and here and there an outpost of hustings and barrel-heads; do it with tongues, too, not with swords—all which improvements in the art of producing zero, are they not great? Nay, best of all, some happy continents (as the western one, with its savannahs, where whosoever has four willing limbs finds food under his feet and an infinite sky over his head) can do without governing. What spinx-questions, which the distracted world, in these very generations, must answer or die!

CHAPTER II.

THE CONSTITUENT ASSEMBLY.

469. One thing an elected assembly of twelve hundred is fit for—destroying. Which, indeed, is but a more decided exercise of its natural talents for doing nothing. Do nothing, only keep agitating, debating, and things will destroy themselves.

470. So and not otherwise proved it with an august national assembly. It took the name "constituent," as if its mission and function had been to construct or build; which also, with its whole soul, it endeavored to do; yet, in the fates, in the nature of things, there lay for it precisely of all functions the most opposite to that. Singular what gospel men will be-

lieve, even gospels according to Jean Jacques! It was the fixed faith of these national deputies, as of thinking Frenchmen, that the constitution could be *made;* that they, there and then, were called to make it. How, with the toughness of old Hebrews or Ishmaelite Moslem, did the otherwise light unbelieving people persist in this their credo quia impossible, and front the armed world with it, and grow fanatic and even heroic, and do exploits by it! The constituent assembly's constitution, and several others, will, being printed and not manuscript, survive to future generations as an instructive, well-nigh incredible, document of the time; the most significant picture of the then existing France, or at lowest, picture of these men's picture of it.

471. But in truth and seriousness, what could the national assembly have done? The thing to *be* done was, actually as they said, to regenerate France, to abolish the old France and make a new one, quietly or forcibly, by concession or by violence; this by the law of nature has become inevitable. With what degree of violence depends on the wisdom of those that preside over it. With perfect wisdom on the part of the national assembly, it had all been otherwise; but whether, in any wise, it could have been pacific, nay, other than bloody and convulsive, may still be a question.

472. Grant, meanwhile, that this constituent assembly does to the last continue to be something. With a sigh, it sees itself incessantly forced away from its infinite divine task of perfecting "the theory of irregular verbs"—to finite terrestrial tasks, which latter have still a significance for us. It is the cynosure of revolutionary France, this national assembly. All work of government has fallen into its hands, or under its control; all men look to it for guidance. In the middle of that huge revolt of twenty-five millions, it hovers always aloft as carroccio or battle-standard, impelling and impelled, in the most confused way; if it cannot give much guidance, it will still seem to give some. It emits pacificatory proclamations not a few, with more or with less result. It authorizes the enrollment of national guards, lest brigands come to devour us, and reap the unripe crops. It sends missions to quell "effervescences," to deliver men from the lanterne. It can listen to congratulatory addresses, which arrive daily by the sackful, mostly in King Cambyses's vein; also to petitions and complaints from all mortals, so that every mortal's complaint, if it cannot get redressed, may at least hear itself complain. For the rest, an august national assembly can produce parliamentary eloquence, and appoint committees. Committees of the constitution, of reports, of researches, and of much else, which again yield mountains of printed paper, the theme of new parliamentary eloquence, in bursts or in plenteous smooth-flowing floods. And so, from the waste vortex whereon all things go whirling and grinding, organic laws, or the similitude of such, slowly emerge.

473. With endless debating, we get the *rights of man* written down and promulgated—true paper basis of all paper constitutions. Neglecting, cry the opponents, to declare the duties of man! Forgetting, answer we, to ascertain the *mights* of man—one of the fatalest omissions! Nay sometimes, as on the 4th of August, our national assembly, fired suddenly by an almost preternatural enthusiasm, will get through whole masses of work in one night. A memorable night, this 4th of August; dignitaries temporal and spiritual, peers, archbishops, parliament-presidents, each outdoing the other in patriotic devotedness, come successively to throw their now untenable possessions on the "altar of the fatherland." With louder and louder vivats—for, indeed, it is

"after dinner" too—they abolish tithes, seignorial dues, gabelle, excessive preservation of game; nay, privilege, immunity, feudalism root and branch; then appoint a Te Deum for it, and so finally disperse about three in the morning, striking the stars with their sublime heads. Such night, unforeseen but forever memorable, was this of the 4th of August, 1789. Miraculous, or semi-miraculous, some seem to think it. A new night of Pentecost, shall we say, shaped according to the new time and new church of Jean Jacques Rousseau? It had its causes, also its effects.

474. In such manner labor the national deputies; perfecting their theory of irregular verbs, governing France and being governed by it, with toil and noise —cutting asunder ancient and intolerable bonds, and, for new ones, assiduously spinning ropes of sand. Were their labors a nothing or a something, yet the eyes of all France being reverently fixed on them history can never very long leave them altogether out of sight.

475. For the present, if we glance into that assembly-hall of theirs, it will be found, as is natural, "most irregular." As many as "a hundred members are on their feet at once;" no rule in making motions, or only commencements of a rule; spectators' gallery allowed to applaud, and even to hiss;[*] president appointed once a fortnight, raising many times no serene head above the waves. Nevertheless, as in all human assemblages, like does begin arranging itself to like; the perennial rule, Ubi homines sunt modi sunt, proves valid. Rudiments of methods disclose themselves, rudiments of parties. There is a right side (coté droit), a left side (coté gauche), sitting on M. le President's right hand, or on his left; the coté droit conservative, the coté gauche destructive. Intermediate in Anglomaniac constitutionalism, or two-chamber royalism, with its Mouniers, its Lallys, fast verging toward nonentity. Pre-eminent, on the right side, pleads and perorates Cazalès the dragoon-captain, eloquent, mildly fervent, earning for himself the shadow of a name. There also blusters Barrel Mirabeau, the younger Mirabeau, not without wit; dusky D'Esprémenil does nothing but sniff and ejaculate, *might*, it is fondly thought, lay prostrate the elder Mirabeau himself would be but try,[†] which he does not. Last and greatest, see, for one moment, the Abbé Maury, with his jesuitic eyes, his impassive brass face, "image of all the cardinal sins." Indomitable, unquenchable, he fights jesuitico-rhetorically, with toughest lungs and heart—for throne, especially for altar and tithes. So that a shrill voice exclaims once, from the gallery, "Messieurs of the clergy, you *have* to be shaved; if you wriggle too much, you will get cut."[‡]

476. The left side is also called the D'Orléans side, and sometimes, derisively, the Palais Royal. And yet, so confused, real-imaginary seems everything, "it is doubtful as Mirabeau said, whether D'Orléans himself belonged to that same D'Orléans party." What can be known and seen is that his moon-visage does beam forth from that point of space. There, likewise, sits sea-green Robespierre, throwing in his light weight with decision, not yet with effect. A thin, lean puritan and precisian, he would make away with formulas, yet lives, moves, and has his being wholly in formulas of another sort. "Peuple," such, according to Robespierre, ought to be the royal method of promulgating laws. "Peuple, this is the law I have framed for thee;· dost thou accept it?" —answered, from right side, from centre and left, by

* Arthur Young, i. 111.
† "Biographic Universelle." ‡ D'Esprémenil (by Beaulieu).
‡ "Dictionnaire des Hommes Marquans," ii. 519.

inextinguishable laughter.* Yet men of insight discern that Sea-green may by chance go far. "This man," observes Mirabeau, "will do somewhat; he believes every word he says."

Abbé Sieyes is busy with mere constitutional work, wherein, unluckily, fellow-workmen are less pliable than, with one who has completed the science of polity, they ought to be. Courage, Sieyes, nevertheless! Some twenty months of heroic travail, of contradiction from the stupid, and the constitution shall be built; the top-stone of it brought out with shouting —say, rather, the top-paper, for it is all paper; and *thou* hast done it in it what the earth or the heaven could require, thy utmost. Note likewise this trio, memorable for several things, memorable were it only that history is written in an epigram : "Whatsoever these three have in hand," it is said "Duport thinks it, Barnave speaks it, and Lameth does it."[+]

477. But royal Mirabeau? Conspicuous among all parties, raised above and beyond them all, this man rises more and more. As we often say, he has an *eye*, he is a reality, while others are formulas and *eye-glasses*. In the transient he will detect the perennial,find some firm footing even among paper vortexes. His fame is gone forth to all lands ; it gladdened the heart of the crabbed old friend of man himself before he died. The very postilions of inns have heard of Mirabeau ; when an impatient traveler complains that the team is insufficient, his postilion answers, "Yes, Monsieur, the wheelers are weak but my mirabeau (main horse), you see, is a right one (Mais mon mirabeau est excellent)."[‡]

478. And now, reader, thou shalt quit this noisy discrepancy of a national assembly, not (if thou be of human mind) without pity. Twelve hundred brother-men are there, in the center of 25,000,000, fighting so fiercely with fate and with one another ; struggling their lives out, as most sons of Adam do, for that which profiteth not. Nay, on the whole, it is admitted further to be very *dull*. "Dull as this day's assembly," said some one. "Why date (Pourquoi dater)? answered Mirabeau.

479. Consider that there are twelve hundred; that they not only speak, but *read* their speeches; and even borrow and steal speeches to read ! With twelve hundred fluent speakers, and their Noah's deluge of vociferous commonplace, silence unattainable may well seem the one blessing of life. But figure twelve hundred pamphleteers, droning forth perpetual pamphlets, and no man to gag them ! Neither, as in the American congress, do the arrangements seem perfect. A senator has not his own desk and newspaper here ; of tobacco (much less of pipes) there is not the slightest provision. Conversation itself has to be transacted in a low tone, with continual interruption ; only "pencil-notes" circulate freely, "in incredible numbers, to the foot of the very tribune."[§] Such work is it, regenerating a nation, perfecting one's theory of irregular verbs !

CHAPTER III.

THE GENERAL OVERTURN.

480. Of the king's court, for the present, there is almost nothing whatever to be said. Silent, deserted are these halls ; royalty languishes forsaken of its war-god and all its hopes, till once the Œil-de-Bœuf rally again. The scepter is departed from King Louis, is gone over to the Salle des Menus, to the Paris town-hall, or one knows not whither. In the

July days, while all ears were yet deafened by the crash of the Bastille, and ministers and princes were scattered to the four winds, it seemed as if the very valets had grown heavy of hearing. Besenval, also in flight toward infinite space, but hovering a little at Versailles, was addressing his majesty personally for an order about post-horses ; when lo, "the valet-in-waiting places himself familiarly between his majesty and me," stretching out his rascal neck to learn what it was. His majesty, in sudden choler, whirled round, made a clutch at the tongs ; "I gently prevented him ; he grasped my hand in thankfulness, and I noticed tears in his eyes."[*]

481. Poor king, for French kings also are men! Louis Fourteenth himself once clutched the tongs, and even smote with them ; but then it was at Louvois, and Dame Maintenon ran up. The queen sits weeping in her inner apartments, surrounded by weak women ; she is "at the height of unpopularity," universally regarded as the evil genius of France. Her friends and familiar counselors have all fled, and fled, surely, on the foolishest errand. The Château Polignac still frowns aloft, on its "bold and enormous cubical rock," amid the blooming champaigns, amid the blue girdling mountains of Auvergne ;[†] but no Duke and Duchess Polignac look forth from it ; they have fled, they have "met Necker at Bâle ;" they shall not return. That France should see her nobles resist the irresistible, inevitable, with the face of angry men, was unhappy, not unexpected ; but with the face and sense of pettish children ? This was her peculiarity. They understood nothing, would understand nothing. Does not, at this hour, a new Polignac, first-born of these two, sit reflective in the castle of Ham,[‡] in an astonishment he will never recover from, the most confused of existing mortals?

482. King Louis has his new ministry, mere popularities ; Old-President Pompignan, Necker coming back in triumph, and other such.[§] But what will it avail him ? As was said, the scepter, all but the wooden gilt scepter, has departed elsewhither. Volition, determination is not in this man ; only innocence, indolence, dependence on all persons but himself, on all circumstances but the circumstances he were lord of. So troublous internally in our Versailles and its work. Beautiful, if seen from afar, resplendent like a sun ; seen near at hand, a mere sun's atmosphere, hiding darkness, confused ferment of ruin !

483. But over France there goes on the indisputablest "destruction of formulas," transactions of realities that follow therefrom. So many millions of persons, all gyved and nigh strangled with formulas, whose life nevertheless, at least the digestion and hunger of it, was real enough ! Heaven has at length sent an abundant harvest; but what profits it the poor man, when earth with her formulas interposes ? Industry, in these times of insurrection, must needs lie dormant ; capital, as usual, not circulating, but stagnating timorously in nooks. The poor man is short of work, is therefore short of money ; nay even had he money, bread is not to be bought for it. Were it plotting of aristocrats, plotting of D'Orléans ; were it brigands, preternatural terror, and the clang of Phœbus Apollo's silver bow —enough, the markets are scarce of grain, plentiful only in tumult. Farmers seem lazy to thresh—being either "bribed," or needing no bribe, with prices ever rising, with perhaps rent itself no longer so pressing. Neither, what is singular, do municipal

---

* "Moniteur," No. 67 (in "Histoire Parlementaire").
† See Toulongeon, l. c. 3.
‡ Dumont, "Souvenirs sur Mirabeau," p. 255.
§ See Dumont (pp. 159–67) ; Arthur Young, etc.

* Besenval, iii. 419.
† Arthur Young, i. 165.
‡ A D 1835.
§ Montgaillard, ii. 108.

enactments "that along with so many measures of wheat you shall sell so many of rye," and other the like, much mend the matter. Dragoons with drawn swords stand ranked among the corn sacks, often more dragoons than sacks.[*] Meal-mobs abound, growing into mobs of a still darker quality.

484. Starvation has been known among the French commonalty before this, known and familiar. Did not we see them, in the year 1775, presenting, in sallow faces, in wretchedness and raggedness, their petition of grievances; and, for answer, getting a brand-new gallows forty feet high? Hunger and darkness, through long years! For look back on that earlier Paris riot, when a great personage, worn out by debauchery, was believed to be in want of blood-baths; and mothers, in worn raiments, yet with living hearts under it, "filled the public places" with their wild Rachel-cries—stilled also by the gallows. Twenty years ago, the friend of men (preaching to the deaf) described the Limousin peasants as wearing a "pain-stricken (souffre-douleur) look," a look *past* complaint, "as if the oppression of the great were like the hail and the thunder, a thing irremediable, the ordinance of nature."[†] And now if, in some great hour, the shock of a falling Bastille should awaken you; and it were found to be the ordinance of art merely, and remediable, reversible!

485. Or has the reader forgotten that "flood of savages," which in sight of the same friend of men, descended from the mountains at Mont d'Or? Lank-haired haggard faces, shapes raw-boned, in high sabots, in woolen jupes, with leather girdles studded with copper nails! They rocked from foot to foot, and beat time with their elbows, too, as the quarrel and battle which was not long in beginning, went on; shouting fiercely, the lank faces distorted into the similitude of a cruel laugh. For they were darkened and hardened; long had they been the prey of excise-men and tax-men, of "clerks with the cold spurt of their pen." It was the fixed prophecy of our old marquis, which no man would listen to, that "such government by blind-man's-buff, stumbling along too far, would end by the general overturn (the culbute générale)!"

486. No man would listen, each went his thoughtless way—and time and destiny also traveled on. The government by blind-man's-buff, stumbling along, has reached the precipice inevitable for it. Dull drudgery, driven on by clerks with the cold dastard spurt of their pen, has been driven—into a communion of drudges! For now, moreover, there have come the strangest confused tidings, by Paris journals with their paper wings, or, still more portentous, where no journals are,[‡] by rumor and conjecture—oppression *not* inevitable, a Bastille prostrate, and the constitution fast getting ready! Which constitution, if it be something and not nothing, what can it be but bread to eat?

487. The traveler, "walking up hill, bridle in hand," overtakes "a poor woman," the image, as most commonly are, of drudgery and scarcity, "looking sixty years of age, though she is not yet twenty-eight." They have seven children, her poor drudge and she, a farm with one cow, which helps to make the children soup, also one little horse, or garron. They have rents and quit-rents, hens to pay this seigneur, oat-sacks to that; king's taxes, statute-labor, church taxes, taxes enough—and think the times inexpressible. She has heard that some *where* in some manner, something is to be done for the poor: "God send it soon, for the dues and taxes crush us down (nous écrasent)!"[§]

* Arthur Young, i. 129, etc.
† Fils Adoptif, "Mémoires de Mirabeau," i. 364-294.
‡ See Arthur Young, i. 137, 150, etc.
§ See "Histoire Parlementaire," ii. 243-46.

Fair prophecies are spoken, but they are not fulfilled. There have been notables, assemblages, turnings-out and comings-in. Intriguing and maneuvering; parlementary eloquence and arguing, Greek meeting Greek in high places, has long gone on, yet still bread comes not. The harvest is reaped and garnered, yet still we have no bread. Urged by despair and by hope, what can drudgery do but rise, as predicted, and produce the general overturn?

488. Fancy, then, some five full-grown millions of such gaunt figures, with their haggard faces (figures hâves); in woolen jupes, with copper-studded leather girths and high sabots, starting up to ask, as in forest-roarings, their washed upper-classes, after long unreviewed centuries, virtually this question: How have ye treated us, how have ye taught us, fed us, and led us, while we toiled for you? The answer can be read in flames, over the nightly summer-sky. *This* is the feeding and leading we have had of you—*emptiness*, of pocket, of stomach, of head and of heart. Behold there is *nothing in us*, nothing but what nature gives her wild children of the desert—ferocity and appetite; strength grounded on hunger. Did ye mark among your rights of man that man was not to die of starvation while there was bread reaped by him? It is among the mights of man.

489. Seventy-two châteaus have flamed aloft in the Mâconnais and Beaujolais alone; this seems the center of the conflagration, but it has spread over Dauphiné, Alsace, the Lyonnaise; the whole south-east is in a blaze. All over the north, from Rouen to Metz, disorder is abroad; smugglers of salt go openly in armed bands, the barriers of towns are burnt, toll-gatherers, tax-gatherers, official persons put to flight. "It was thought," says Young, "the people, from hunger, would revolt;" and we see they have done it. Desperate lackalls, long prowling aimless, now finding hope in desperation itself, everywhere form a nucleus. They ring the church-bell by way of tocsin, and the parish turns out to the work.[*] Ferocity, atrocity, hunger, and revenge, such work as we can imagine!

490. Ill stands it now with the seigneur, who, for example, "has walled up the only fountain of the township," who has ridden high on his chartier and parchments, who has preserved game not wisely, but too well. Churches also, and canonries, are sacked without mercy, which have shorn the flock too close, forgetting to feed it. Woe to the land over which sansculottism, in its day of vengeance, tramps rough-shod—shod in sabots! high bred seigneurs, with their delicate women and little ones, had to "fly half-naked," under cloud of night, glad to escape the flames and even worse. You meet them at the tables-d'hote of inns, making wise reflections or foolish, that "rank is destroyed;" uncertain whither they shall now wend.[†] The métayer will find it convenient to be slack in paying rent. As for the tax-gatherer, he, long hunting as a biped of prey, may now find himself hunted as one; his majesty's exchequer will not "fill up the deficit" this season; it is the notion of many that a patriot majesty, being the restorer of French liberty, has abolished most taxes, though, for their private ends, some men make a secret of it.

491. Where this will end? In the abyss, one may prophesy, whither all delusions are, at all moments, traveling; where this delusion has now arrived. For if there be a faith from of old, it is this, as we often repeat, that no lie can live forever. The very truth has to change its vesture from time to time, and be born again. But all lies have sentence of death written down against them, in heaven's chan-

* See Arthur Young, i. 134.
† See Young, i. 149, etc.

cery itself, and, slowly or fast, advance incessantly toward their hour. "The sign of a grand seigneur being landlord," says the vehement, plain-spoken Arthur Young, "are wastes, landes, deserts, ling; go to his residence, you will find it in the middle of a forest peopled with deer, wild boars, and wolves. The fields are scenes of pitiable management, as the houses are of misery. To see so many millions of hands that would be industrious, all idle and starving; oh, if I were legislator of France for one day, I would make these great lords skip again!"* O Arthur, thou now actually beholdst them *skip*—wilt thou grow to grumble at that too?

492. For long years and generations it lasted, but the time came. Featherbra'n, whom no reasoning and no pleading could touch, the glare of the firebrand had to illuminate; there remained but that method. Consider it, look at it! The widow is gathering nettles for her children's dinner; a perfumed seigneur, delicately lounging in the Œil-de-Bœuf, has an alchemy whereby he will extract from her the third nettle, and name it rent and law; such an arrangement must end. Ought it not? But, oh most fearful is *such* an ending! Let those to whom God, in his great mercy, has granted time and space, prepare another and milder one.

493. To some, it is a matter of wonder that the seigneurs did not do something to help themselves say, combine and arm, for there were a "hundred and fifty thousand of them," all valiant enough. Unhappily, a hundred and fifty thousand, scattered over wide provinces, divided by mutual ill-will, cannot combine. The highest seigneurs, as we have seen, had already emigrated—with a view of putting France to the blush. Neither are arms now the peculiar property of seigneurs, but of every mortal who has ten shillings wherewith to buy a second-hand firelock.

494. Besides, those starving peasants, after all, have not four feet and claws, that you could keep them down permanently in that manner. They are not even of black color; they are mere unwashed seigneurs, and a seigneur, too, has human bowels! The seigneurs did what they could; enrolled in national guards, fled, with shrieks, complaining to heaven and earth. One seigneur, famed Memmay of Quincy, near Vesoul, invited all the rustics of his neighborhood to a banquet, blew up his château and them with gunpowder, and instantaneously vanished, no man yet knows whither.† Some half-dozen years after he came back, and demonstrated that it was by accident.

495. Nor are the authorities idle, though, unluckily, all authorities, municipalities and such-like, are in the uncertain transitionary state, getting regenerated from old monarchic to new democratic; no official yet knows clearly what he is. Nevertheless, mayors old or new, do gather marechaussées, national guards, troops of the line; justice of the most summary sort is not wanting. The electoral committee of Mâcon, though but a committee, goes the length of hanging, for its own behoof, as many as twenty. The prévot of Dauphiné traverses the country "with a movable column," with tipstaves, gallows-ropes; for gallows any tree will serve, and suspend its culprit, or "thirteen" culprits.

496. Unhappy country! How is the fair gold-and-green of the ripe bright year defaced with horrid blackness—black ashes of châteaus, black bodies of gibbeted men! Industry has ceased in it; not sounds of the hammer and saw, but of the tocsin and alarm-drum. The scepter has departed, *whither* one knows not, breaking itself in pieces; here impotent,

there tyrannous. National guards are unskillful and of doubtful purpose, soldiers are inclined to mutiny; there is danger that they two may quarrel, danger that they may *agree*. Strasburg has seen riots; a town-hall torn to shreds, its archives scattered white on the winds, drunk soldiers embracing drunk citizens for three days, and Mayor Dietrich and Marshal Rochambeau reduced nigh to desperation.*

497. Through the middle of all which phenomena is seen, on his triumphant transit—"escorted," through Béfort for instance, "by fifty national horsemen and all the military music of the place"—M. Necker returning from Bâle! Glorious as the meridian, though poor Necker himself partly guesses whither it is leading.† One highest culminating day at the Paris town-hall, with immortal vivats, with wife and daughter kneeling publicly to kiss his hand, with Besenval's pardon granted—but, indeed, revoked before sunset; one highest day, but then lower days, and even lower, down even to lowest! Such magic is in a name, and in the want of a name. Like some enchanted Mambrino's helmet, essential to victory, comes this "savior of France," beshouted, becymbaled by the world, alas! so soon to be *disenchanted*, to be pitched shamefully over the lists as a barber's basin! Gibbon "could wish to show him (in this ejected, barber's basin state) to any man of solidity, who were minded to have the soul burnt out of him, and become a caput mortuum, by ambition, unsuccessful or successful.‡

498. Another small phasis we add, and no more, how, in the autumn months, our sharp-tempered Arthur has been "pestered for some days past," by shot, lead-drops, and slugs, "rattling five or six times into my chaise and about my ears;" all the mob of the country gone out to kill game!§ It is even so. On the cliffs of Dover, over all the marches of France, there appear, this autumn, two signs on the earth—emigrant flights of French seigneurs, emigrant-winged flights of French game! Finished, one may say, or as good as finished, is the preservation of game on this earth, completed for endless time. What part *it* had to play in the history of civilization is played: plaudite; exeat!

499. In this manner does sansculottism blaze up, illustrating many things, producing, among the rest, as we saw, on the 4th of August, that semi-miraculous night of Pentecost in the national assembly; semi-miraculous, which had its causes and its effects. Feudalism is struck dead, not on parchment only, and by ink, but in very fact, by fire—say by self-combustion. This conflagration of the south-east will abate, will be got scattered to the west, or elsewhither; extinguish it will not till the *fuel* be all done.

CHAPTER IV.

IN QUEUE.

500. If we look now at Paris, one thing is too evident: that the bakers' shops have got their queues, or tails, their long strings of purchasers, arranged *in tail*, so that the first come be the first served—were the shop once open! This waiting in tail, not seen since the early days of July, again makes its appearance in August. In time, we shall see it perfected by practice to the rank almost of an art, and the art, or quasi-art, of standing in tail become one of the characteristics of the Parisian people, distinguishing them from all other peoples whatsoever.

---

* Ibid., i. 12, 48, 84, etc.
† "Histoire Parlementaire," ii. 161.
* Arthur Young, i. 141. Dampmartin. "Evénemens qui se sont passés sous mes yeux," i. 105-27.
† "Biographie Universelle," § Necker (by Lally-Tollendal).
‡ Young, i. 176.
§ Gibbon's "Letters."

501. But consider, while work itself is so scarce, how a man must not only realize money, but stand waiting (if his wife is too weak to wait and struggle) for half-days in the tail, till he get it changed for dear bad bread! Controversies, to the length, sometimes of blood and battery, must arise in these exasperated queues. Or if no controversy, then it is but one accordant pange lingua of complaint against the powers that be. France has begun her long curriculum of hungering, instructive and productive beyond academic curriculums, which extends over some seven most strenuous years. As Jean Paul says of his own life, " To a great height shall the business of hungering go."

502. Or consider, in strange contrast, the jubilee ceremonies, for, in general, the aspect of Paris presents these two features, jubilee ceremonials and scarcity of victual. Processions enough walk in jubilee, of young women, decked and dizened, their ribbons all tricolor, moving, with song and tabor, to the shrine of Sainte Geneviève, to thank her that the Bastille is down. The strong men of the market, and the strong women, fail not with their bouquets and speeches. Abbé Fauchet, famed in such work (for Abbé Lefèvre could only distribute powder), blesses tricolor cloth for the national guard, and makes it a national tricolor flag, victorious, or to be victorious, in the cause of civil and religious liberty all over the world. Fauchet, we say, is the man for Te Deums and public consecrations, to which, as in this instance of the flag, our national guard will " reply with volleys of musketry," church and cathedral though it be,* filling Notre Dame with such noisiest fuliginous *Amen*, significant of several things.

503. On the whole, we will say our new Mayor Bailly, our new Commander Lafayette, named also "Scipio-Americanus," have bought their preferment dear. Bailly rides in gilt state-coach, with beefeaters and sumptuousity, Camille Desmoulins, and others, sniffing at him for it Scipio bestrides the "white charger," and waves with civic plumes in sight of all France. Neither of them, however, does it for nothing, but, in truth, at an exorbitant rate. At this rate, namely, of feeding Paris, and keeping it from fighting. Out of the city funds, some 17,000 of the utterly destitute are employed digging on Montmartre, at tenpence a day, which buys them, at market price, almost two pounds of bad bread. They look very yellow when Lafayette goes to harangue them. The town-hall is in travail night and day ; it must bring forth bread, a municipal constitution, regulations of all kinds, curbs on the sansculottic press, above all, bread, bread.

504. Purveyors prowl the country far and wide, with the appetite of lions, detect hidden grain, purchase open grain ; by gentle means or forcible, must and will find grain. A most thankless task, and so difficult, so dangerous, even if a man did gain some trifle by it! On the 19th of August there is food for one day.† Complaints there are that the food is spoiled, and produces an effect on the intestines; not corn but plaster of Paris ! Which effect on the intestines, as well as that " smarting in the throat and palate," a town-hall proclamation warns you to disregard, or even to consider as drastic-beneficial. The Mayor of Saint-Denis, so black was his bread, has, by a dyspeptic populace, been hanged on the lanterne there. National guards protect the Paris corn-market ; first ten suffice, then, 600.‡ Busy are ye, Bailly, Brissot de Warville, Condorcet, and ye others!

505. For, as just hinted, there is a municipal constitution to be made too. The old Bastille electors after some ten days of psalmodying over their glorious victory, began to hear it asked, in a splenetic tone. Who put *you* there ? They accordingly had to give place, not without moanings and audible growlings on both sides, to a new larger body, specially elected for that post. Which new body, augmented, altered, then fixed finally at the number of 300, with the title of town representatives (représentans de la commune), now sits there, rightly portioned into committees, assiduous making a constitution, at all moments when not seeking flour.

506. And such a constitution, little short of miraculous, one that shall "consolidate the revolution ! " The revolution is finished then ? Mayor Bailly and all respectable friends of freedom would fain think so. Your revolution, like jelly sufficiently *boiled*, needs only to be poured into *shapes* of constitution, and " consolidated " therein ? Could it, indeed, contrive to *cool*, which last, however, is precisely the doubtful thing, or even the not doubtful !

507. Unhappy friends of freedom, consolidating a revolution ! They must sit at work there, their pavilion spread on very chaos, between two hostile worlds, the upper court-world, the neither sansculottic one, and, beaten on by both, toil painfully, perilously—doing, in sad literal earnest, " the impossible."

CHAPTER V.

THE FOURTH ESTATE.

508. Pamphleteering opens its abysmal throat wider and wider, never to close more. Our philosophies, indeed, rather withdraw, after the manner of Marmontel, " retiring in disgust the first day." Abbé Raynal, grown gray and quiet in his Marseilles domicile, is little content with this work ; the last literary act of the man will again be an act of rebellion, an indignant " Letter to the Constituent Assembly," answered by " the order of the day." Thus, also, philosophe Morellet puckers discontented brows, being indeed threatened in his benefices by that 4th of August—it is clearly going too far. How astonishing that those " haggard figures in woolen jupes " would not rest as satisfied with speculation and victorious analysis as we!

509. Alas, yes ; speculation, philosophism, once the ornament and wealth of the saloon, will now coin itself into mere practical propositions, and circulate on street and highway, universally, with results! A fourth estate of able editors springs up, increases and multiplies, irrepressible, incalculable. New printers, new journals, and ever new (so prurient is the world) let our 300 curb and consolidate as they can. Loustalot, under the wing of Prudhomme dull-blustering printer, edits weekly his Révolutions de Paris in an acrid, emphatic manner. Acrid, corrosive, as the spirit of sloes and copperas, is Marat—friend of the people—struck already with the fact that the national assembly, so full of aristocrats, "can do nothing," except dissolve itself and make way for a better; that the town-hall representatives are little other than babblers and imbeciles, if not even knaves. Poor is this man, squalid, and dwells in garrets ; a man unlovely to the sense, outward and inward, a man forbid—and is becoming fanatical, possessed with fixed idea. Cruel lusus of nature! Did nature, O poor Marat, in cruel sport, knead thee out of her *leavings* and miscellaneous waste clay, and fling thee forth, stepdame-like, a distraction into this distracted eighteenth century ? Work is appointed thee there, which thou shalt do. The 300 have summoned and will again summon Marat, but always he croaks forth answer sufficient : always he will defy them, or elude them, and endure no gag.

510. Carra, "ex-secretary of a decapitated Hospodar," and then of a necklace-cardinal—likewise of a pamphleteer, adventurer in many scenes and lands—draws nigh to 'Mercier of .the Tableau de Paris, and, with foam on his lips, proposes an Annales Patriques. The Moniteur goes its prosperous way, Barrère "weeps," on paper as yet loyal; Rivarol, Royou are not idle. Deep calls to deep; your domine Salvum fac Regem shall awaken Pange Lingua; with an Ami-du-Peuple there is a king's-friend newspaper, Ami-du-Roi. Camille Desmoulins has appointed himself procureur-général de la lanterne (attorney-general of the lamp-iron), and pleads *not* with atrocity, under an atrocious title; editing weekly his brilliant Revolutions of Paris and Brabant. Brilliant, we say, for if, in that thick murk of journalism, with its dull blustering, with its fixed or loose fury, any ray of genius greet thee, be sure it is Camille's. The thing that Camille touches, he with his light finger adorns; .brightness plays, gentle, unexpected, amid horrible confusions; often is the word of Camille worth reading when no other's is. Questionable Camille, how thou glitterest with a fallen, rebellious, yet still semi-celestial light, as is the starlight on the brow of Lucifer! Son of the morning, into what times and what lands art thou fallen!

511. But in all things there is good—though it be not good for "consolidating revolutions." Thousand wagon-loads of this pamphleteering and newspaper matter lie rotting slowly in the public libraries of our Europe. Snatched from the great gulf, like oysters by bibliomaniac pearl-divers, there must they first *rot*, then what was pearl, in Camille or others, may be seen as such, and continue as such.

512. Nor has public speaking declined, though Lafayette and his patrols look sour on it. Loud always is the Palais Royal, loudest the Café de Foy; such a miscellany of citizens and citizenesses circulating there. "Now and then," according to Camille, "some citizens employ the liberty of the *press* for a private purpose, so that this or the other patriot finds himself short of his watch or pocket-handkerchief!" But for the rest, in Camille's opinion, nothing can be a livelier image of the Roman Forum. "A patriot proposes his motion; if it finds any supporters, they make him mount on a chair and speak. If he is applauded, he prospers and redœts; if he is hissed, he goes his ways." Thus they, circulating and perorating. Tall shaggy Marquis Saint-Huruge, a man that has had losses, and has deserved them, is seen eminent, and also heard. "Bellowing" is the character of his voice, like that of a bull of Bashan, voice which drowns all voices, which causes frequently the hearts of men to leap. Cracked or half-cracked is this tall marquis's head, uncracked are his lungs; the cracked and the uncracked shall alike avail him.

513. Consider further that each of the forty-eight districts has its own committee, speaking and motioning continually, aiding in the search for grain, in the search for a constitution, checking and spurring the poor 300 of the town-hall. That Danton, with a "voice reverberating from the domes," is president of the Cordeliers district, which has already become a Goshen of patriotism. That apart from the "seventeen thousand utterly necessitous, digging on Montmartre," most of whom, indeed, have got passes, and been dismissed into space "with four shillings"—there is a *strike* or union, of domestics out of place, who assemble for public speaking; next, a strike of tailors, for even they will strike and speak; farther, a strike of journeymen cordwainers, a strike of apothecaries, so dear is bread.* All these, having struck, must speak, generally under the open canopy, and

pass resolutions—Lafayette and his patrols watching them suspiciously from the distance.

514. Unhappy mortals, such tugging and lugging, and throttling of one another, to divide, in some not intolerable way, the joint felicity of man in this earth, when the whole lot to be divided is such a "feast of shells!" Diligent are the 300; none equals Scipio-Americanus in dealing with mobs. But surely all these things bode ill for the consolidating of a revolution.

BOOK SEVENTH.

THE INSURRECTION OF WOMEN.

CHAPTER I.

PATROLLOTISM.

515. No, friends, this revolution is not of the consolidating kind. Do not fires, fevers, sown seeds, chemical mixtures, men, events—all embodiments of force that work in this miraculous complex of forces named universe—go on *growing*, through their natural phases and developments, each according to its kind, reach their height, reach their visible decline, finally sink under, vanishing, and what we call *die?* They all grow; there is nothing but what grows, and shoots forth into its special expansion—once give it leave to spring. Observe too that each grows with a rapidity proportioned, in general, to the madness and unhealthiness there is in it, slow regular growth, though this also ends in death, is what we name health and sanity.

516. A sansculottism, which has prostrated bastilles, which has got pike and musket, and now goes burning châteaus, passing resolutions and haranguing under roof and sky, may be said to have sprung, and, by law of nature, must grow. To judge by the madness and diseasedness both of itself and of the soil and element it is in, one might expect the rapidity and monstrosity would be extreme.

517. Many things, too, especially all diseased things, grow by shoots and fits. The first grand fit and shooting-forth of sansculottism was that of Paris conquering its king, for Bailly's figure of rhetoric was all too sad a reality. The king is conquered, going at large on his parole, on condition, say, of absolutely good behavior—which, in these circumstances, will unhappily mean no behavior whatever. A quite untenable position, that of majesty put on its good behaviour! Alas, is it not natural that whatever lives try to keep itself living? Whereupon his majesty's behavior will soon become exceptionable; and so the second grand fit of sansculottism, that of putting him in durance, cannot be distant.

518. Necker, in the national assembly, is making moan as usual about his deficit; barriers and custom-houses burnt, the tax-gatherer hunted, not hunting; his majesty's exchequer all but empty. The remedy is a loan of thirty millions; then, on still more enticing terms, a loan of eighty millions; neither of which loans, unhappily, will the stock-jobbers venture to lend. The stock-jobber has no country except his own black pool of agio.

519. And yet, in those days, for men that have a country, what a glow of patriotism burns in many a heart, penetrating inwards to the very purse! So early as the 7th of August, a don patriotique, "patriotic gift of jewels to a considerable extent," has been solemnly made by certain Parisian women, and solemnly accepted with honorable mention. Whom forthwith all the world takes to imitating and emulating. Patriotic gifts, always with some heroic eloquence, which the president must answer, and the assembly listen to, flow in from far and near in such

---

* "Histoire Parlementaire," ii., 359, 417, 436,

number that the honorable mention can only be performed in "lists published at stated epochs." Each gives what he can. The very cordwainers have behaved munificently. One landed proprietor gives a forest; fashionable society gives its shoe-buckles—takes cheerfully to shoe-ties. Unfortunate-females give what they "have amassed in loving."[*] The smell of all cash, as Vespasian thought, is good.

520. Beautiful, and yet inadequate! The clergy must be "invited" to melt their superfluous church-plate—in the royal mint. Nay, finally, a patriotic contribution, of the forcible sort, has to be determined on, though unwillingly. Let the fourth part of your declared yearly revenue, for this once only, be paid down; so shall a national assembly make the constitution, undistracted, at least, by insolvency. Their own wages, as settled on the 17th of August, are but eighteen francs a day, each man; but the public service must have sinews, must have money. To *appease* the deficit—not to "combler (or choke) the deficit," if you or mortal could! For withal, as Mirabeau was heard saying, "It is the deficit that saves us."

521. Toward the end of August our national assembly in its constitutional labors has got so far as the question of *veto*—shall majesty have a veto on the national enactments, or not have a veto? What speeches were spoken, within doors and without, clear and also passionate logic, imprecations, comminations, gone happily for most part to limbo! Through the cracked brain and uncracked lungs of Saint-Huruge, the Palais Royal rebellows with veto. Journalism is busy; France rings with veto. "I never shall forget," says Dumont, "my going to Paris one of those days with Mirabeau, and the crowd of people we found waiting for his carriage about Le Jay the bookseller's shop. They flung themselves before him, conjuring him, with tears in their eyes, not to suffer the veto absolu. They were in a frenzy. 'Monsieur le Comte, you are the people's father; you must save us; you must defend us against those villains who are bringing back despotism. If the king get his veto, what is the use of national assembly? We are slaves; all is done.'"[†] Friends, *if* the sky fall, there will be catching of larks! Mirabeau, adds Dumont, was eminent on such occasions; he answered vaguely, with a patrician imperturbability, and bound himself to nothing.

522. Deputations go to the Hotel-de-Ville; anonymous letters to aristocrats in the national assembly, threatening that fifteen thousand, or sometimes that sixty-thousand, "will march to illuminate you." The Paris districts are astir, petitions signing; Saint-Huruge sets forth from the Palais Royal with an escort of fifteen-hundred individuals to petition in person. Resolute, or seemingly so, is the tall shaggy marquis, is the Café de Foy; but resolute also is Commandant-General Lafayette. The streets are all beset by patrols; Saint-Huruge is stopped at the Barrière des Bons Hommes; he may bellow like the bulls of Bashan, but absolutely must return. The brethren of the Palais Royal "circulate all night," and make motions under the open canopy, all coffeehouses being shut. Nevertheless Lafayette and the town-hall do prevail; Saint-Huruge is thrown into prison: veto absolu adjusts itself into *suspensive veto*, prohibition not forever, but for a term of time; and this doom's-clamor will grow silent as the others have done.

523. So far has consolidation prospered, though with difficulty, repressing the nether sansculottic world, and the constitution shall be made. With difficulty, amid jubilee and scarcity, patriotic gifts,

bakers's queues, Abbé-Fauchet harangues, with their *amen* of platoon musketry! Scipio-Americanus has deserved thanks from the national assembly and France. They offer him stipends and emoluments to a handsome extent, all which stipends and emoluments he, covetous of far other blessedness than mere money, does, in his chivalrous way, without scruple, refuse.

524. To the Parisian common man, meanwhile, one thing remains inconceivable—that now when the Bastille is down, and French liberty restored, grain should continue so dear. Our rights of man are voted, feudalism and all tyranny abolished; yet behold we stand in queue! It is aristocrat forestallers—a court still bent on intrigues? Something is rotten somewhere.

And yet, alas, what to do? Lafayette, with his patrols, prohibits everything, even complaint. Saint-Huruge and other heroes of the *veto* lie in durance. People's friend Marat was seized; printers of patriotic journals are fettered and forbidden: the very hawkers cannot cry till they get license and leaden badges. Blue national guards ruthlessly dissipate all groups, scour with leveled bayonets the Palais Royal itself. Pass on your affairs along the Rue Taranne, the patrol, presenting his bayonet, cries, *To the left!* Turn into the Rue-Saint-Bénoit, he cries, *To the right!* A judicious patriot (like Camille Desmoulins in this instance) is driven, for quietness sake, to take the gutter.

525. O, much-suffering people, our glorious revolution is evaporating in tricolor ceremonies and complimentary harangues! Of which latter, as Loustalot acridly calculates, "upward of two thousand have been delivered within the last month at the town-hall alone."[*] And our mouths, unfilled with bread, are to be shut, under penalties? The caricaturist promulgates his emblematic tablature: Le Patrouillotisme chassant le Patriotisme (Patriotism driven out by Patrollotism). Ruthless patrols, long superfine harangues, and scanty ill-baked loaves—more like baked bath-bricks—which produce an effect on the intestines! Where will this end? In consolidation.

CHAPTER II.

O RICHARD, O MY KING.

526. For, alas, neither is the town-hall itself without misgivings. The nether sansculottic world has been suppressed hitherto, but then the upper courtworld! Symptoms there are that the Œil-de-Bœuf is rallying.

More than once in the town-hall sanhedrim, often enough from those outspoken bakers'-queues, has the wish uttered itself; O that our restorer of French liberty were here; that he could see with his own eyes, not with the false eyes of queens and cabals, and his really good heart be enlightened! For falsehood still environs him—intriguing Dukes de Guiche, with body-guards, scouts of Bouillé; a new flight of intriguers, now that the old is flown. What else means this advent of the Regiment de Flandre, entering Versailles, as we hear, on the 23d of September, with two pieces of cannon? Did not the Versailles national guard do duty at the Château? Had they not Swiss—Hundred Swiss—gardes-du-corps, body guards, so-called? Nay, it would seem, the number of body-guards on duty has, by a maneuver, been doubled; the new relieving battalion of them arrived at its time, but the old relieved one does not *depart*?

* "Histoire Parlementaire," ii. 427.
† "Souvenirs sur Mirabeau," p. 156.

* "Révolutions de Paris newspaper" (cited in "Histoire Parlementaire," ii. 357).

527. Actually, there runs a whisper through the best-informed upper circles, or a nod still more portentous than ¡whispering, of his majesty's flying to Metz, of a bond (to stand by him therein) which has been signed by noblesse and clergy, to the incredible amount of thirty, or even of sixty thousand. Lafayette coldly whispers it, and coldly asseverates it, to Count d'Estaing, one of the bravest men, quakes to the core lest some lackey overhear it, and tumbles thoughtful, without sleep, all night.* Regiment de Flandre as we said, is clearly arrived. His majesty, they say, hesitates about sanctioning the 4th of August, makes observations, of chilling tenor on the very rights of man! Likewise, may not all persons, the bakers'-queues themselves discern, on the streets of Paris, the most astonishing number of officers on furlough, crosses of St. Louis, and such-like? Some reckon "from a thousand to twelve hundred." Officers of all uniforms, nay, one uniform never before seen by eye—green faced with red! The tricolor cockade is not always visible; but what, in the name of Heaven, may these *black* cockades, which some wear, foreshadow.

528. Hunger whets everything, especially suspicion and indignation. Realities themselves in this Paris, have grown unreal, preternatural. Phantasms once more stalk through the brain of hungry France. O ye laggards and dastards, cry shrill voices from the queues, if ye had the hearts of men, ye would take your pikes and second-hand firelocks, and look into it; not leave your wives and daughters to be starved, murdered, and worse! Peace, women! The heart of man is bitter and heavy; patriotism, driven out by patrollotism, knows not what to resolve on.

529. The truth is, the Œil-de-Bœuf has rallied, to a certain unknown extent. A changed Œil-de-Bœuf; with Versailles national guards, in their tricolor cockades, doing duty there; a court all flaring with tricolor! Yet even to a tricolor court men will rally. Ye loyal hearts, burnt-out seigneurs, rally round your queen! With wishes, which will produce hopes, which will produce attempts!

530. For, indeed, self-preservation being such a law of nature, what can a rallied court do but attempt, and endeavor, or call it *plot*—with such wisdom and unwisdom as it has? They will fly, escorted, to Metz, where brave Bouillé commands; they will raise the royal standard; the bond-signatures shall become armed men. Were not the king so languid! Their bond, if at all signed, must be signed without his privity. Unhappy king, *he* has but one resolution—not to have a civil war. For the rest, he still hunts, having ceased lock-making; he still dozes and digests, is clay in the hands of the potter. Ill will it fare with him, in a world where all is helping itself; where, as has been written, "whosoever is not hammer must be stithy," and "the very hyssop on the wall grows there, in that chink, because the whole universe could not prevent its growing!"

531. But as for the coming up of this Regiment de Flandre, may it not be urged that there were Saint-Huruge petitions, and continual meal-mobs? Undebauched soldiers, be their plot, or only dim elements of a plot, are always good. Did not the Versailles municipality (an old monarchic one, not yet refounded into a democratic) instantly second the proposal? Nay, the very Versailles national guard, wearied with continual duty at the château, did not object; only draper Lecointre, who is now Major Lecointre, shook his head. Yes, friends, surely it was natural this Regiment de Flandre should be sent for, since it

* "Brouillon de Lettre de M d'Estaing à la Reine" (in 'Histoire Parlementaire." iii. 24).

could be got. It was natural that, at sight of military bandoleers, the heart of the rallied Œil-de-Bœuf should revive, and maids of honor and gentlemen of honor speak comfortable words to epauleted defenders and to one another. Natural also, and mere common civility, that the Body-Guards, a regiment of gentlemen, should invite their Flandre brethren to a dinner of welcome! Such invitation, in the last days of September, is given and accepted.

532. Dinners are defined as "the *ultimate* act of communion;" men that can have communion in nothing else, can sympathetically eat together, can still rise into some glow of brotherhood over food and wine. The dinner is fixed on, for Thursday the 1st of October, and ought to have a fine effect. Further, as such dinner may be rather extensive, and even the non-commissioned and the common man be introduced, to see and to hear, could not his majesty's opera apartment, which has lain quite silent ever since Kaiser Joseph was here, be obtained for the purpose? The hall of the opera is granted; the Salon d'Hercule shall be drawing-room. Not only the officers of Flandre, but of the Swiss, of the Hundred Swiss; nay, of the Versailles national guard, such of them as have any loyalty, shall feast; it will be a repast like few.

533. And now suppose this repast, the solid part of it, transacted, and the first bottle over. Suppose the customary loyal toasts drunk, the king's health, the queen's with deafening vivats—that of the nation "omitted," or even "rejected." Suppose champagne flowing, with pot-valorous speech, with instrumental music, empty featherheads growing ever the noisier, in their own emptiness, in each others' noise. Her majesty, who looks unusually sad to-night (his majesty sitting dulled with the day's hunting), is told that the sight of it would cheer her. Behold! She enters there, issuing from her state-rooms, like the moon from clouds, this fairest unhappy queen of hearts; royal husband by her side, young dauphin in her arms! She descends from the boxes, amid splendor and acclaim, walks queen-like round the tables, gracefully escorted, gracefully nodding, her looks full of sorrow, yet of gratitude and daring, with the hope of France on her mother-bosom! And now, the band striking up, O Richard, O mon roi, l'univers t'abandonne (O Richard, O my king, the world is all forsaking thee), could man do no other than rise to height of pity, of loyal valor? Could featherheaded young ensigns do other than, by white Bourbon cockades, handed them from fair fingers, by waving of swords drawn to pledge the queen's health, by trampling of national cockades, by scaling the boxes, whence intrusive murmurs may come, by vociferation, tripudiation, sound, fury and distraction, within doors and without—testify what tempest-tost state of vacuity they are in? Till champagne and tripudiation do their work, and all lie silent, horizontal, passively slumbering with meed-of-battle dreams!

534. A natural repast, in ordinary times a harmless one, now fatal as that of Thyestes, as that of Job's sons, when a strong wind smote the four corners of their banquet-house! Poor ill-advised Marie Antoinette, with a woman's vehemence, not with a sovereign's foresight! It was so natural, yet so unwise. Next day, in public speech of ceremony, her majesty declares herself "delighted with the Thursday."

535. The heart of the Œil-de-Bœuf glows into hope, into daring, which is premature. Rallied maids of honor, waited on by abbés, sew "white cockades," distribute them, with words, with glances, to epauleted youths, who, in return, may kiss, not without

fervor, the fair sewing fingers. Captains of horse and foot go swashing with "enormous white cockade;" nay, one Versailles national captain has mounted the like, so witching were the words and glances, and laid aside his tricolor! Well may Major Lecointre shake his head with a look of severity, and speak audible resentful words. But now a swashbuckler, with enormous white cockade, overbearing the major, invites him insolently, once and then again elsewhere, to recant, and falling that, to duel. Which latter feat Major Lecointre declares that he will not perform, not, at least by any known laws of fence; that he, nevertheless, will, according to mere law of nature, by dirk and blade, "exterminate" any "vile gladiator" who may insult him or the nation—whereupon (for the major is actually drawing his implement) "they are parted," and no weasands slit.*

CHAPTER III.

BLACK COCKADES.

536. But fancy what effect this Thyestes repast, and trampling on the national cockade, must have had in the Salle des Menus, in the famishing bakers'-queues at Paris! Nay, such Thyestes repasts, it would seem, continue. Flandre has given its counter-dinner to the Swiss and Hundred Swiss, then on Saturday there has been another.

537. Yes, here with us is famine, but yonder at Versailles is food, enough and to spare! Patriotism, stands in queue, shivering, hunger-struck, insulted by patrollotism, while bloody-minded aristocrats, heated with excess of high living, trample on the national cockade. Can the atrocity be true? Nay, look—green uniforms faced with red, black cockades —the color of night! Are we to have military onfall, and death also, by starvation? For, behold, the Corbeil corn-boat, which used to come twice a-day, with its plaster-of-Paris meal, now comes only once. And the town-hall is deaf, and the men are laggard and dastard! At the Café de Foy, this Saturday evening, a new thing is seen, not the last of its kind —a woman engaged in public speaking. Her poor man, she says, was put to silence by his district, their presidents and officials would not let him speak. Wherefore she here, with her shrill tongue, will speak, denouncing, while her breath endures, the Corbeil boat, the plaster-of-Paris bread, sacrilegious opera-dinners, green uniforms, pirate aristocrats, and those black cockades of theirs!

538. Truly, it is time for the black cockades at least to vanish. Then patrollotism itself will not protect. Nay, sharp-tempered "M. Tassin," at the Tuileries parade on Sunday morning, forgets all national military rule, starts from the ranks, wrenches down one black cockade which is swashing ominous there, and tramples it fiercely into the soil of France. Patrollotism itself is not without suppressed fury. Also the districts begin to stir; the voice of President Danton reverberates in the Cordeliers; People's-friend Marat has flown to Versailles and back again —swart bird, not of the halcyon kind.*

539. And so patriot meets promenading patriot this Sunday, and sees his own grim care reflected on the face of another. Groups, in spite of patrollotism, which is not so alert as usual, fluctuate deliberative-groups on the bridges, on the quais, at the patriotic cafées. And ever; as any black cockade may emerge,

rises the many-voiced growl and bark, A bas (Down)! All black cockades are ruthlessly plucked off; one individual picks his up again, kisses it, attempts to refix it, but "hundred canes start into the air," and he desists. Still worse went it with another individual. doomed by extempore plebiscitum to the lanterne; saved with difficulty by some active Corps-de-Garde. Lafayette sees signs of an effervescence, which he doubles his patrols, doubles his diligence, to prevent. So passes Sunday the 4th of October, 1789.

540. Sullen is the male heart, repressed by patrollotism; vehement is the female, irrepressible. The public-speaking woman at the Palais Royal was not the only speaking one. Men know not what the pantry is when it grows empty, only house-mothers know. O women, wives of men that will only calculate and not act! Patrollotism is strong, but death by starvation and military onfall is stronger. Patrollotism represses male patriotism; but female patriotism? Will guards named national thrust their bayonets into the bosoms of women? Such thought, or rather such dim, unshaped raw material of a thought, ferments universally under the female night-cap, and by earliest daybreak on slight hint will explode.

CHAPTER IV.

THE MENADS.

541. If Voltaire once, in splenetic humor, asked his countrymen, "But you, Gualches, what have you invented?" they can now answer, The art of insurrection. It was an art needed in these last singular times; an art for which the French nature, so full of vehemence, so free from depth, was, perhaps, of all others the fittest.

Accordingly, to what a height, one may well say of perfection, has this branch of human industry been carried by France within the last half-century! Insurrection, which Lafayette thought might be "the most sacred of duties," ranks now, for the French people, among the duties which they can perform. Other mobs are dull masses, which roll onward with a dull, fierce tenacity, a dull fierce heat, but emit no light-flashes of genius as they go. The French mob, again is among the liveliest phenomena of our world. So rabid, audacious; so clear-sighted, inventive, prompt to seize the moment; instinct with life to its finger-ends! That talent, were there no other, of spontaneously standing in queue, distinguishes, as we said, the French people from all peoples, ancient and modern.

542. Let the reader confess, too, that, taking one thing and another, perhaps few terrestrial appearances are better worth considering than mobs. Your mob is a genuine outburst of nature; issuing from, or communicating with the deepest deep of nature. When so much goes grinning and grimacing as a lifeless formality, and under the stiff buckram no heart can be felt beating, here once more, if nowhere else, is a sincerity and reality. Shudder at it, or even shriek over it, if thou must; nevertheless, consider it. Such a complex of human forces and individualities hurled forth in their transcendental mood, to act and react on circumstances and one another; to work out what it is in them to work. The thing they will do is known to no man, least of all to themselves. It is the inflammablest, immeasurable firework, generating, consuming itself. With what phases, to what extent, with what results it will burn off, philosophy and perspicacity conjecture in vain.

* "Moniteur" (in "Histoire Parlementaire," iii 59); Deux Amis," iii 128–41; Campan, ii. 70–85. etc., etc.

* Camille's newspaper. "Révolution de Paris et de Brabant" (in "Histoire Parlementaire," iii. 108).

543. "Man," as has been written, "is forever interesting to man; nay, properly there is nothing else interesting." In which light also may we not discern why most battles have become so wearisome? Battles in these ages are transacted by mechanism; with the slightest possible development of human individuality or spontaneity men now even die and kill one another in an artificial manner. Battles ever since Homer's time, when they were fighting mobs, have mostly ceased to be worth looking at, worth reading or remembering. How many wearisome bloody battles does history strive to represent, or, even in a husky way, to sing—and she would omit or carelessly slur over this one insurrection of women?

544. A thought, or dim raw material of a thought, was fermenting all night, universally in the female head, and might explode. In squalid garret on Monday morning, maternity awakes to hear children weeping for bread. Maternity must forth to the streets, to the herb-markets and bakers'-queues; meets there with hunger-stricken maternity, sympathetic, exasperative. O we unhappy women! But, instead of bakers'-queues, why not to aristocrats' palaces, the root of the matter. Allons! Let us assemble. To the Hotel-de-Ville, to Versailles, to the lanterne!

545. In one of the guard-houses of the Quartier Saint-Eustache, "a young woman" seizes a drum—for how shall national guards give fire on women, on a young woman. The young woman seizes the drum, sets forth beating it, "uttering cries relative to the dearth of grains." Descend, O mothers, descend, ye Judiths, to food and revenge! All women gather and go; crowds storm all stairs, force out all women; the female insurrectionary force, according to Camille, resembles the English naval one; there is a universal "press of women." Robust dames of the halle, slim mantua-makers, assiduous, risen with the dawn; ancient virginity tripping to matins; the housemaid, with early broom; all must go. Rouse ye, O women; the laggard men will not act; they say we ourselves may act!

546. And so, like snowbreak from the mountains, for every staircase is a melted brook, it storms tumultuous, wild-shrilling, toward the Hotel-de-Ville. Tumultuous, with or without drum-music; for the Faubourg Saint Antoine also has tucked-up its gown, and with besom-staves, fire-irons, and even rusty pistols (void of ammunition), is flowing on. Sounds of it flies with a velocity of sound to the utmost barriers. By seven o'clock, on this raw October morning, fifth of the month, the town-hall will see wonders. Nay, as chance would have it, a male party are already there, clustering tumultuously round some national patrol and a baker who has been seized with short weights. They are there, and have even lowered the rope of the lanterne. So that the official persons have to smuggle forth the short-weighing baker by back-doors, and even send "to all the districts" for more force.

547. Grand it was, says Camille, to see so many Judiths, from 8,000 to 10,000 of them in all, rushing out to search into the root of the matter! Not unfrightful it must have been; ludicro-terrific, and most unmanageable. At such hour the overwatched 300 are not yet stirring, none but some clerks, a company of national guards, and M. de Gouvion, the major-general. Gouvion has fought in America for the cause of civil liberty, a man of no inconsiderable heart, but deficient in head. He is, for the moment, in his back apartment, assuaging Usher Maillard, the Bastille-sergeant, who has come, as too many do

with "representations." The assuagement is still incomplete when our Judiths arrive.

548. The national guards form on the outer stairs, with leveled bayonets; the 10,000 Judiths press up, resistless, with obtestations, with outspread hands—merely to speak to the mayor. The rear forces them; nay, from male hands in the rear stones already fly; the national guard must do one of the two things—sweep the Place de Grève with cannon or else open to right and left. They open; the living deluge rushes in. Through all rooms and cabinets upward to the topmost belfry; ravenous; seeking arms, seeking mayors, seeking justice; while, again, the better-dressed speak kindly to the clerks, point out the misery of these poor women, also their ailments, some even of an interesting sort.*

549. Poor M. de Gouvion is shiftless in this extremity; a man shiftless, perturbed, who will one day commit suicide. How happy for him that Usher Maillard the shifty was there at the moment, though making representations! Fly back, thou shifty Maillard, seek the Bastille company, and, oh, return fast with it; above all, with thy own shifty head! For, behold, the Judiths can find no mayor or municipal; scarcely in the topmost belfry can they find poor Abbé Lefèvre, the powder-distributor. Him, for want of a better, they suspend there in the pale morning light, over the top of all Paris, which swims in one's failing eyes—a horrible end? Nay, the rope broke, as French ropes often did, or else an Amazon cut it. Abbé Lefèvre falls some twenty feet, rattling among the leads, and lives long years after, though always with a "tremblement in the limbs."†

550. And now doors fly under hatchets; the Judiths have broken the armory, have seized guns and cannons, three money-bags, paper-heaps; torches flare: in few minutes, our brave Hotel-de-Ville, which dates from the fourth Henry, will, with all that it holds, be in flames!

CHAPTER V.

USHER MAILLARD.

551. In flames, truly—were it not that Usher Maillard, swift of foot, shifty of head, has returned. Maillard, of his own motion—for Gouvion or the rest would not even sanction him—snatches a drum, descends the porch-stairs, ran-tan, beating sharp, with loud rolls, his rogues'-march: To Versailles! Allons; à Versailles! As men beat on kettle or warming-pan, when angry she-bees, or say, flying desperate wasps, are to be hived; and the desperate insects hear it, and cluster round it—simply as round a guidance, where there was none; so now these Menads round shifty Maillard, riding-usher of the Châtelet. The axe pauses uplifted; Abbé Lefèvre is left half-hanged; from the belfry downward all vomits itself. What rub-a-dub is that? Stanislas Maillard, Bastille hero, will lead us to Versailles? Joy to thee, Maillard, blessed art thou above riding-ushers! Away, then, away!

552. The seized cannon are yoked with seized cart-horses, brown-locked Demoiselle Théroigne, with pike and helmet, sits there as gunneress, "with haughty eye and serene fair countenance;" comparable, some think, to the *Maid* of Orléans, or even recalling "the idea of Pallas Athene."‡ Maillard (for his drum still rolls) is, by heaven-rending acclamation, admitted general. Maillard hastens the languid march.

* "Deux Amis," III. 141-66.
† Dusaulx, "Prise de la Bastille," note, p. 281.
‡ "Deux Amis," III. 157.

Maillard, beating rhythmic, with sharp ran-tan, all along the quais, leads forward with difficulty his Menadic host. Such a host—marched not in silence! The bargeman pauses on the river; all wagoners and coach-drivers fly; men peer from windows—not women, lest they be pressed. Sight of sights; bacchantes, in these ultimate formalized ages! Bronze Henri looks on from his Pont-Neuf; the monarchic Louvre, Medicean Tuileries, see a day like none heretofore seen.

553. And now Maillard has his Menads in the Champs Elysées (fields Tartarean rather), and the Hotel-de-Ville has suffered comparatively nothing. Broken doors, an Abbé Lefèvre, who shall never more distribute powder, three sacks of money, most part of which (for sansculottism, though famishing, is not without honor) shall be returned;* this is all the damage. Great Maillard! A small nucleus of order is round his drum, but his outskirts fluctuate like the mad ocean, for rascality male and female is flowing in on him, from the four winds; guidance there is none but in his single head and two drumsticks.

554. O Maillard, when, since war first was, had general of force such a task before him as thou this day? Walter the Penniless still touches the feeling heart, but then Walter had sanction, had space to turn in, and also his crusaders were of the male sex. Thou, this day, disowned of heaven and earth, art general of Menads. Their inarticulate frenzy thou must, on the spur of the instant, render into articulate words, into actions that are not frantic. Fail in it, this way or that! Pragmatical officiality, with ts penalties and law-books, waits before thee; Menads storm behind. If such hewed off the melodious head of Orpheus, and hurled it into the Peneus waters, what may they not make of thee—thee rythmic merely, with no music but a sheepskin drum! Maillard did not fail. Remarkable Maillard, if fame were not an accident, and history a distillation of rumor, how remarkable wert thou!

555. On the Elysian Fields there is pause and fluctuation; but, for Maillard, no return. He persuades his Menads, clamorous for arms and the arsenal, that no arms are in the arsenal; that an unarmed attitude, and petition to a national assembly, will be the best; he hastily nominates or sanctions generalesses, captains of tens and fifties—and so, in loosest-flowing order, to the rythm of some "eight drums" (having laid aside his own), with the Bastille volunteers bringing up his rear, once more takes the road.

556. Chaillot, which will promptly yield baked loaves, is not plundered; nor are the Sèvres potteries broken. The old madons of Sèvres bridge echo under Menadic feet; Seine river gushes on with his perpetual murmur; and Paris flings after us the boom of tocsin and alarm-drum—inaudible for the present, amid shrill-sounding hosts and the splash of rainy weather. To Mendon, to Saint-Cloud, on both hands, the report of them is gone abroad; and hearths, this evening, will have a topic. The press of women still continues, for it is the cause of all Eve's daughters, mothers that are, or that ought to be. No carriage-lady, were it with never such hysterics, but must dismount, in the mud roads, in her silk shoes, and walk.† In this manner, amid wild October weather, they, a wild unwinged stork-flight, through the astonished country wend their way. Travelers of all sorts they stop, especially travelers or couriers from Paris. Deputy Lechapelier, in his elegant vesture, from his elegant vehicle, looks forth amazed through his spectacles; apprehensive for life—states angrily that he is Patriot-Deputy Lechapelier, and even Old-President Lechapelier, who presided on the night of

* "Histoire Parlementaire," iii. 310.
† "Deux Amis," iii. 159.

Pentecost, and its original member of the Breton Club. Thereupon "rises huge shout of Vive Lechapelier, and several armed persons spring up behind and before to escort him." *

557. Nevertheless, news, dispatches from Lafayette, or vague noise of rumor, have pierced through by side roads. In the national assembly, while all is busy discussing the order of the day; regretting that there should be anti-national repasts in opera-halls, that his majesty should still hesitate about accepting the rights of man, and hang conditions and peradventures on them—Mirabeau steps up to the president, experienced Mounier as it chanced to be, and articulates, in bass undertone, "Mounier, Paris marche sur nous (Paris is marching on us)." "May be (Je n'en sais rien)!" "Believe it or disbelieve it, that is not my concern; but Paris, I say, is marching on us. Fall suddenly unwell; go over to the château; tell them this. There is not a moment to lose."— "Paris marching on us?" responds Mounier, with an atrabiliar accent; "well, so much the better! We shall the sooner be a republic." Mirabeau quits him as one quits an experienced president getting blindfold into deep waters, and the order of the day continues as before.

558. Yes, Paris is marching on us, and more than the women of Paris! Scarcely was Maillard gone, when M. de Gouvion's message to all the districts, and such tocsin and drumming of the générale, began to take effect. Armed national guards from every district, especially the Grenadiers of the Center, who are our old Gardes Françaises, arrive, in quick sequence, on the Place de Grève. An "immense people" is there; Saint-Antoine, with pike and rusty firelock, is all crowding thither, be it welcome or unwelcome. The Center Grenadiers are received with cheering; "It is not cheers that we want," answer they gloomily; "the nation has been insulted; to arms, and come with us for orders!" Ha, sits the wind so? Patriotism and patrollotism are now one!

559. The three hundred have assembled; "all the committees are in activity," Lafayette is dictating dispatches for Versailles, when a deputation of the Center Grenadiers introduces itself to him. The deputation makes military obeisance, and thus speaks, not without a kind of thought in it: "mon général, we are deputed by the six companies of grenadiers. We do not think you a traitor, but we think the government betrays you; it is time that this end. We cannot turn our bayonets against women crying to us for bread. The people are miserable, the source of the mischief is at Versailles; we must go seek the king, and bring him to Paris. We must exterminate (exterminer) the Regiment de Flandre and the Gardes-du-Corps, who have dared to trample on the national cockade. If the king be too weak to wear his crown, let him lay it down. You will crown his son, you will name a council of regency; and all will go better."† Reproachful astonishment paints itself on the face of Lafayette, speaks itself from his eloquent chivalrous lips; in vain. "My general, we would shed the last drop of our blood for you, but the root of the mischief is at Versailles; we must go and bring the king to Paris; all the people wish it (tout le peuple le veut)."

560. My general descends to the outer staircase, and harangues, once more in vain. "To Versailles! To Versailles!" Mayor Bailly, sent for through floods of sansculottism, attempts academic oratory from his gilt state-coach; realizes nothing but infinite hoarse cries of, "Bread! To Versailles!"—and

* Ibid. ii. 177: "Dictionnaire des Hommes Marquans," ii. 379.
† "Deux Amis," iii. 161.

gladly shrinks within doors. Lafayette mounts the white charger, and again harangues, and reharangues, with eloquence, with firmness, indignant demonstration, with all things but persuasion. "To Versailles! To Versailles!" So lasts it, hour after hour—for the space of half a day.

561. The great Scipio-Americanus can do nothing, not so much as escape. "Morbleu, mon général," cry the grenadiers, scrrying their ranks as the white charger makes a motion that way, "you will not leave us, you will abide with us!" A perilous juncture: Mayor Bailly and the municipals sit quaking within doors; my general is prisoner without; the Place de Grève, with its thirty thousand regulars, its whole irregular Saint-Antoine and clear or rusty steel, all hearts set, with a moody fixedness, on one object. Moody, fixed are all hearts; tranquil is no heart—if it be not that of the white charger, who paws there, with arched neck, composedly champing his bit; as if no world, with its dynasties and eras, were now rushing down. The drizzly day bends westward, the cry is still, "To Versailles!"

562. Nay, now, borne from afar, come quite sinister cries, hoarse, reverberating in long-drawn hollow murmurs, with syllables, too, like those of "lanterne!" Or else, irregular sansculottism may be marching off, of itself; with pikes, nay, with cannon. The inflexible Scipio does at length, by aid-de-camp, ask of the municipals whether or not he may go. A letter is handed out to him, over armed heads; sixty thousand faces flash fixedly on his, there is stillness, and no bosom breathes till he have read. By heaven, he grows suddenly pale! Do the municipals permit? "Permit, and even order"—since he can no other. Clangor of approval rends the welkin. To your ranks, then; let us march!

563. It is, as we compute, toward three in the afternoon. Indignant national guards may dine for once from their haversack; dined or undined, they march with one heart. Paris flings up her windows, "claps hands," as the avengers, with their shrilling drums and shalms tramp by; she will then sit pensive, apprehensive, and pass a sleepless night.* On the white charger, Lafayette, in the slowest possible manner going and coming, and eloquently haranguing among the ranks, rolls onward with his thirty thousand. Saint-Antoine, with pike and cannon, has preceded him; a mixed multitude of all and of no arms, hovers on his flanks and skirts; the country once more pauses agape: Paris marche sur nous.

CHAPTER VI.

TO VERSAILLES.

564. For, indeed, about this moment, Maillard has halted his draggled Menads on the last hill-top; and now Versailles, and the château of Versailles, and far and wide the inheritance of royalty, opens to the wondering eye. From far on the right, over Marly and Saint-Germain-en-Laye; round toward Rambouillet, on the left; beautiful all; softly embosomed, as if in sadness, in the dim, moist weather! And near before us is Versailles, new and old, with that broad frondent Avenue de Versailles between—stately-frondent, broad, 300 feet as men reckon, with its four rows of elms; and then the château de Versailles, ending in royal parks and pleasances, gleaming lakelets, arbors, labyrinths, the Ménagerie, and Great and Little Trianon. High-towered dwellings,

leafy pleasant places, where the gods of this lower world abide: whence, nevertheless, black care cannot be excluded; whither Menadic hunger is even now advancing, armed with pike-thyrsi!

565. Yes, yonder, mesdames, where our straight frondent avenue, joined, as you note, by two frondent brother avenues from this hand and from that, spreads out into Place Royal and Palace Forecourt—yonder is the Salle des Menus. Yonder an august assembly sits regenerating France. Forecourt, Grand Court, Court of Marble, court narrowing into court you may discern next, or fancy; on the extreme verge of which that glass-dome, visibly glittering like a star of hope, is the—Œil-de-Bœuf! Yonder, or nowhere in the world is bread baked for us. But, O mesdames, were not one thing good—that our cannons, with Demoiselle Theroigne and all show of war be put to the rear? Submission beseems petitioners of a national assembly; we are strangers in Versailles—whence, too audibly, there comes even now a sound as of tocsin and général! Also to put on, if possible, a cheerful countenance, hiding our sorrows, and even to sing? Sorrow, pitied of the heavens, is hateful, suspicious to the earth. So counsels shifty Maillard, haranguing his Menads on the heights near Versailles.*

566. Cunning Maillard's dispositions are obeyed. The draggled insurrectionists advance up the avenue, "in three columns," among the four elm-rows, "singing 'Henri Quatre,'" with what melody they can, and shouting, Vive le roi. Versailles, though the elm-rows are dripping wet, crowds from both sides, with, "Vivent nos Parisiennes, (Our Paris ones forever!)"

567. Prickers, scouts, have been out toward Paris, as the rumor deepened; whereby his majesty gone to shoot in the woods of Meudon, has been happily discovered, and got home, and the général and tocsin set a-sounding. The Body-Guards are already drawn up in front of the palace-grates, and look down the Avenue de Versailles, sulky, in wet buck-skins. Flandre, too, is there, repentant of the opera-repast. Also dragoons dismounted are there. Finally Major Lecointre, and what can he gather of the Versailles national guard—though it is to be observed, our colonel, that same sleepless Count d'Estaing, giving neither order nor ammunition, has vanished most improperly, one supposes into the Œil-de-Bœuf. Red-coated Swiss stand within the grates, under arms. There likewise, in their inner room, "all the ministers," Saint-Priest, Lamentation Pompignan and the rest, are assembled with M. Necker; they sit with him there; blank, expecting what the hour will bring.‡

568. President Mounier, though he answered Mirabeau with a tant mieux, and affected to slight the matter, had his own forebodings. Surely, for these four weary hours he has reclined not on roses! The order of the day is getting forward; a deputation to his majesty seems proper, that it might please him to grant "acceptance pure and simple" to those constitution-articles of ours; the "mixed qualified acceptance," with its peradventures, is satisfactory to neither gods nor men.

569. So much is clear. And yet there is more, which no man speaks, which all men now vaguely understand. Disquietude, absence of mind, is on every face; members whisper, uneasily come and go; the order of the day is evidently not the day's want. Till at length, from the outer gates, is heard a rustling and justling, shrill uproar and squabbling, muf-

---

* "Deux Amis," iii. 165.

* See "Histoire Parlementaire," iii. 70-117: "Deux Amis," iii. 166-77, etc.

fled by walls, which testifies that the hour is come! Rushing and crushing one hears now; their enter Usher Maillard, with a deputation of fifteen muddy, dripping women—having, by incredible industry, and aid of all the macers, persuaded the rest to wait out of doors. National assembly shall now, therefore, look its august task directly in the face: regenerative constitutionalism has an unregenerate sansculottism bodily in front of it, crying, " Bread ! bread !"

570. Shifty Maillard, translating frenzy into articulation; repressive with the one hand, expostulative with the other, does his best ; and really, though not bred to public speaking, manages rather well. In the present dreadful rarity of grains, a deputation of female citizens has, as the august assembly can discern, come out from Paris to petition. Plots of aristocrats are too evident in the matter : for example, one miller has been bribed " by a bank-note of 200 livres" not to grind, name unknown to the usher, but fact provable, at least indubitable. Further, it seems, the national cockade has been trampled on ; also, there are black cockades, or were. All which things will not an august national assembly, the hope of France, take into its wise immediate consideration ?

571. And Menadic hunger, irrepressible, crying "Black cockades," crying "Bread, bread," adds, after such fashion, Will it not ? Yes, messieurs, if a deputation to his majesty, for the " acceptance pure and simple." seemed proper—how much more now, for ' the afflicting situation of Paris;" for the calming of this effervescence ! President Mounier, with a speedy deputation, among whom we notice the respectable figure of Doctor Guillotin, gets himself forward on march. Vice-president shall continue the order of the day ; Usher Maillard shall stay by him to repress the women. It is four o'clock, of the miserablest afternoon, when Mounier steps out.

572. O experienced Mounier, what an afternoon, the last of thy political existence ! Better had it been to "fall suddenly unwell," while it was yet time. For, behold, the esplanade, over all its spacious expanse, is covered with groups of squalid dripping women, of lank-haired male rascality, armed with axes, rusty pikes, old muskets, iron-shod clubs (batons ferrés, which end in knives or sword-blades, a kind of extempore bill-hook)—looking nothing but hungry revolt. The rain pours, gardes-du-corps go caracoling through the groups " amid hisses," irritating and agitating what is but dispersed here to reunite there.

573. Innumerable squalid women beleaguer the president and deputation, insist on going with him ; has not his majesty himself, looking from the window, sent out to ask what we wanted ? " Bread and speech with the king (Du pain, et parler au roi)," that was the answer. Twelve women are clamorously added to the deputation, and march with it across the esplanade, through dissipated groups, caracoling body-guards, and the pouring rain.

574. President Mounier, unexpectedly augmented by twelve women, copiously escorted by hunger and rascality, is himself mistaken for a group, himself and his women are dispersed by caracolers, rally again with difficulty among the mud.* Finally the grates are opened ; the deputation gets access, with the twelve women, too, in it, of which latter, five shall even see the face of his majesty. Let wet Menadism, in the best spirits it can, expect their return.

* Mounier. "Exposé Justificatif ' (cited in " Deux Amis," ii. 185).

CHAPTER VII.

AT VERSAILLES.

575. But already Pallas Athene (in the shape of Demoiselle Théroigne) is busy with Flandre and the dismounted dragoons. She, and such women as are fittest, go through the ranks, speak with an earnest jocosity, clasp rough troopers to their patriot bosom, crush down spontoons and musketoons with soft arms ; can a man, that were worthy of the name of man, attack furnishing patriot women ?

One reads that Théroigne had bags of money, which she distributed over Flandre—furnished by whom ? Alas, with money-bags, one seldom sits on insurrectionary cannon. Calumnious royalism ! Théroigne had only the limited earnings of her profession of unfortunate-female ; money she had not, but brown locks, the figure of a heathen goddess, and an eloquent tongue and heart.

576. Meanwhile Saint-Antoine, in groups and troops, is continually arriving, wetted, sulky, with pikes and impromptu bill-hooks, driven thus far by popular fixed-idea. So many hirsute figures driven hither in that manner, figures that have come to do they know not what, figures that have come to see it done ! Distinguished among all figures, who is this of gaunt stature, with leaden breast-plate, though a small one ;* bushy in red grizzled locks, nay, with long tile-beard ? It is Jourdan, unjust dealer in mules, a dealer no longer, but a painter's model, playing truant this day. From the necessities of art comes his long tile-beard ; whence his leaden breastplate (unless, indeed, he were some hawker licensed by leaden badge) may have come, will perhaps remain forever a historical problem. Another Saul among the people we discern, " Père Adam (Father Adam)," as the groups name him, to us better known as bull-voiced Marquis Saint Huruge, hero of the veto, a man that has had losses and deserved them. The tall marquis, emitted some days ago from limbo, looks peripatetically on this scene from under his umbrella, not without interest. All which persons and things hurled together as we see; Pallas Athene busy with Flandre, patriotic Versailles national guards short of ammunition, and deserted by D'Estaing, their colonel, and commanded by Lecointre, their major ; then caracoling body-guards, sour, dispirited, with their buckskins wet ; and finally this flowing sea of indignant squalor—may they not give rise to occurrences ?

577. Behold, however, the twelve she-deputies return from the château. Without President Mounier, indeed, but radiant with joy, shouting, " *Life to the king and his house.*" Apparently the news are good, mesdames? News of the best !. Five of us were admitted to the internal splendors, to the royal presence. This slim damsel, " Louison Chabray, worker in sculpture, aged only seventeen," as being of the best looks and address, her we appointed speaker. On whom, and indeed on all of us, his majesty looked nothing but graciousness. Nay, when Louison, addressing him, was like to faint, he took her in his royal arms, and said gallantly, " It was well worth while (Elle en valût bien la peine)." Consider, O women, what a king ! His words were of comfort, and that only ; there shall be provision sent to Paris, if provision is in the world ; grains shall circulate free as air, millers shall grind, or do worse, while their millstones endure, and nothing be left wrong which a restorer of French liberty can right.

* See Weber, ii. 185-231.

578. Good news these, but, to wet Menads, all too incredible! There seems no proof then? *Words* of comfort—they are words only, which will feed nothing. O miserable people, betrayed by aristocrats, who corrupt the very messengers! In his royal arms, Mademoiselle Louison? In his arms? Thou shameless minx, worthy of a name—that shall be nameless! Yes, thy skin is soft; ours is rough with hardship, and well wetted, waiting here in the rain. No children hast thou hungry at home, only alabaster dolls that weep not! The traitress! To the lanterne! And so poor Louison Chabray, no asseveration or shrieks availing her, fair slim damsel, late in the arms of royalty, has a garter round her neck, and furibund amazons at each end, is about to perish so —when two body-guards gallop up, indignantly dissipating, and rescue her. The miscredited twelve hasten back to the château, for an "answer in writing."

579. Nay, behold, a new flight of Menads, with "M. Brunout, Bastille volunteer," as impressed-commandant at the head of it. These also will advance to the grate of the grand court, and see what is toward. Human patience, in wet buckskins, has its limits. Body-guard Lieutenant M. de Savonnières for one moment lets his temper, long provoked, long pent, give way. He not only dissipates these latter Menads, but caracoles and cuts, or indignantly flourishes at M. Brunout, the impressed-commandant, and, finding great relief in it, even chases him, Brunout flying nimbly though in a pirouette manner, and now with sword also drawn. At which sight of wrath and victory, two other body-guards (for wrath is contagious, and to pent body-guards is so solacing) do likewise give way, give chase with brandished saber, and in the air make horrid circles. So that poor Brunout has nothing for it but to retreat with accelerated nimbleness, through rank after rank, parthian-like, fencing as he flies; above all, shouting lustily, "On nous laisse assassiner (They are getting us assassinated)!"

580. Shameful! Three against one! Growls come from the Lecointrian ranks, bellowings—lastly shots. Savonnières's arm is raised to [strike, the bullet of a Lecointrian musket shatters it, the brandished saber jingles down harmless. Brunout has escaped, this duel well ended; but the wild howl of war is everywhere beginning to pipe?

The amazons recoil, Saint-Antoine has its cannon pointed (full of grape-shot); thrice applies the lit flambeau, which thrice refuses to catch—the touchholes are so wetted; and voices cry. "Arrêtez, il n'est pas temps encore (Stop, it is not yet time)!"* Messieurs of the Garde-du-Corps, ye had orders not to fire; nevertheless two of you limp dismounted, and one war-horse' lies slain. Were it not well to draw back out of shot-range, finally to file off—into the interior? If in so filing off, theredid a musketoon or two discharge itself at these armed shopkeepers, hooting and crowing, could man wonder? Draggled are your white cockades of an enormous size, would to heaven they were gotexchanged for tricolor ones! Your buckskins are wet, your hearts heavy. Go, and return not!

581. The body-guards file off as we hint, giving and receiving shots, drawing no life-blood, leaving boundless indignation. Some three times in the thickening dusk, a glimpse of them is seen, at this or the other portal, saluted always with execrations, with the whew of lead. Let but a body-guard show face, he is hunted by rascality—for instance, poor "M. de Moucheton of the Scotch company," owner of the slain war-horse—and has to be smuggled off

* "Deux Amis." II. 192-201.

by Versailles captains. Or rusty fire-locks belch after him, shivering asunder his—hat. In the end, by superior order, the body-guards, all but the few on immediate duty, disappear, or, as it were, abscond, and march, under cloud of night, to Rambouillet.*

582. We remark also that the Versailles have now got ammunition; all afternoon, the official person could find none; till, in these so critical moments, a patriotic sub-lieutenant set a pistol to his ear, and would thank him to find some—which he thereupon succeeded in doing. Likewise that Flandre, disarmed by Pallas Athene, says openly it will not fight with citizens, and for tokens of peace has exchanged cartridges with the Versaillese.

583. Sansculottism is now among mere friends, and can "circulate freely;" indignant at body-guards—complaining also considerably of hunger.

CHAPTER VIII.

THE EQUAL DIET.

584. But why lingers Mounier, returns not with his deputation? It is six, it is seven o'clock, and still no Mounier, no acceptance pure and simple.

And, behold the dripping Menads, not now in deputation but in mass, have penetrated into the assembly, to the shamefulest interruption of public speaking and order of the day. Neither Maillard nor vice-president can restrain them, except within wide limits; not even, except for minutes, can the lion-voice of Mirabeau, though they applaud it; but ever and anon they break in upon the regeneration of France with cries of " Bread; not so much discoursing (Du pain; pas tant de longs discours)!" So insensible were these poor creatures to bursts of parliamentary eloquence!

585. One learns also that the royal carriages are getting yoked, as if for Metz. Carriages, royal or not, have verily showed themselves at the back gates. They even produced, or quoted, a written order from our Versailles municipality—which is a monarchic not a democratic one. However, Versailles patrols drove them in again, as the vigilant Lecointre had strictly charged them to do.

586. A busy man, truly, is Major Lecointre, in these hours. For Colonel d'Estaing loiters invisible in the Œil-de-Bœuf; invisible, or still more questionably *visible* for instants; then also a too loyal municipality requires supervision; no order, civil or military, takes about any of these thousand things! Lecointre is at the Versailles town-hall, he is at the grate of the grand court, communing with Swiss and body-guards. He is in the ranks of Flandre; he is here, he is there; studious to prevent bloodshed, to prevent the royal family from flying to Metz, the Menads from plundering Versailles.

587. At the fall of night, we behold him advance to those armed groups of Saint-Antoine, hovering all too grim near the Salle des Menus. They receive him in a half-circle; twelve speakers behind cannons with lighted torches in hand, the cannon-mouths *toward* Lecointre—a picture for Salvator! He asks, in temperate but courageous language, What they, by this their journey to Versailles, do specially want? The twelve speakers reply, in few words inclusive of much, " Bread, and the end of these brabbles (Du pain, et la fin des affaires)." When the *affairs* will end, no Major Lecointre, nor no mortal, can say; but as to bread, he inquires, How many are you?—learns that they are six hundred, that a loaf each will suffice, and rides off to the municipality to get six hundred loaves.

* Weber, ubi supra.

588. Which loaves, however, a municipality of monarchic temper will not give. It will give two tons of rice rather—could you but know whether it should be boiled or raw. Nay, when this, too, is accepted, the municipals have disappeared—ducked under, as the six-and-twenty long-gowned of Paris did, and, leaving not the slightest vestage of rice, in the boiled or raw state, they there vanish from history!

Rice comes not; one's hope of food is balked, even one's hope of vengeance; is not M. de Moucheton of the Scotch company, as we said, deceitfully smuggled off? Failing all which, behold only M. de Moucheton's slain war-horse, lying on the esplanade there! Saint-Antoine, balked esurient, pounces on the slain war-horse; flays it, roasts it with such fuel, of paling, gates, portable timber, as can be come at, not without shouting; *and*, after the manner of ancient Greek heroes, *they lifted their hands to the daintily readied repast*, such as it might be.* Other rascality prowls discursive, seeking what it may devour. Flandre will retire to its barracks; Lecointre also with his Versailleso—all but the vigilant patrols, charged to be doubly vigilant.

589. So sink the shadows of night, blustering, rainy, and all paths grow dark. Strangest night ever seen in these regions—perhaps since the Bartholomew night, when Versailles, as Bassompierre writes of it, was a *chétif château*. O for the lyre of some Orpheus, to constrain, with touch of melodious strings, these mad masses into order! For here all seems fallen asunder, in wide-yawning dislocation. The highest, as in down-rushing of a world, is come in contact with the lowest; the rascality of France beleaguering the royalty of France; "iron-shod batons" lifted round the diadem, not to guard it! With denunciations of bloodthirsty anti-national body-guards, are heard dark growlings against a queenly name.

590. The court sits tremulous, powerless; varies with the varying temper of the esplanade, with the varying color of the rumors from Paris. Thick-coming rumors, now of peace, now of war. Necker and all the ministers consult, with a blank issue. The Œil-de-Bœuf is one tempest of whispers. We will fly to Metz: we will not fly. The royal carriages again attempt egress—though for trial merely; they are again driven in by Lecointre's patrols. In six hours nothing has been resolved on, not even the acceptance pure and simple.

591. In six hours? Alas, he who, in such circumstances, cannot resolve in six minutes may give up the enterprise; him fate has already resolved for. And Menadism, meanwhile, and sansculottism takes counsel with the national assembly; grows more and more tumultuous there. Mounier returns not, authority nowhere shows itself; the authority of France lies, for the present, with Lecointre and Usher Maillard. This, then, is the abomination of desolation; come suddenly, though long .foreshadowed as inevitable! For, to the blind, all things are sudden. Misery which, through long ages, had no spokesman, no helper. will now be its own helper and speak for itself. The dialect, one of the rudest, is, what it could be, *this*.

592. At eight o'clock there returns to our assembly, not the deputation, but Doctor Guillotin announcing that it will return; also that there is hope of the acceptance pure and simple. He himself has brought a royal letter, authorizing and commanding the freest "circulation of grains." Which royal letter Menadism with its whole heart applauds. Conformably to which the assembly forthwith passes a decree, also

received with rapturous Menadic plaudits. Only could not an august assembly contrive farther to "*fix the price of bread at eight sous the half-quartern, butchers'-meat at six sous the pound;"* which seem fair rates? Such motion do "a multitude of men and women," irrepressible by Usher Maillard, now make—does an august assembly hear made. Usher Maillard himself is not always perfectly measured in speech, but if rebuked, he can justly excuse himself by the peculiarity of the circumstances.*

593. But finally, this decree well passed, and the disorder continuing, and members melting away, and no President Mounier returning—what can the vice-president do but also melt away? The assembly melts; under such pressure, into deliquium; or, as it is officially called, adjourns. Maillard is dispatched to Paris, with the "decree concerning grains" in his pocket, he and some women, in carriages belonging to the king. Thitherward slim Louison Chabray has already set forth, with that "written answer" which the twelve she-deputies returned in to seek. Slim sylph, she has set forth, through the black muddy country; she has much to tell, her poor nerves so flurried, and travels, as indeed to-day on this road all persons do, with extreme slowness. President Mounier has not come, nor the acceptance pure and simple, though six hours with their events have come; though courier on courier reports that Lafayette is coming. Coming with war or with peace? It is time that the château also should determine on one thing or another; that the château also should show itself alive, if it would continue living!

594. Victorious, joyful after such delay, Mounier does arrive at last, and the hard-earned acceptance with him; which now, alas, is of small value. Fancy Mounier's surprise to find his senate, whom he hoped to charm by the acceptance pure and simple, all gone, and in its stead a senate of Menads! For, as Erasmus's ape mimicked, say with wooden splint, Erasmus shaving, so do these amazons hold, in mock majesty, some confused parody of national assembly. They make motions, deliver speeches, pass enactments, productive at least of loud laughter. All galleries and benches are filled; a strong dame of the market is in Mounier's chair. Not without difficulty, Mounier, by aid of maicers and persuasive speaking, makes his way to the female-president; the strong dame, before abdicating, signifies that, for one thing. she and, indeed, her whole senate male and female (for what was one roasted war-horse among so many?) are suffering very considerably from hunger.

595. Experienced Mounier, in these circumstances, takes a twofold resolution—to reconvoke his assembly members by sound of drum; also to procure a supply of food. Swift messengers fly to all bakers, cooks, pastry-cooks, vintners, restorers; drums beat, accompanied with shrill vocal proclamation through all streets. They come; the assembly members come; what is still better, the provisions come. On tray and barrow come these latter; loaves, wine, great store of sausages. The nourishing baskets circulate harmoniously along the benches; *nor*, according to the father of epics, *did any soul lack a fair share of victual* (δαῖτος ἐἴσης), *an equal diet*), highly desirable at the moment.†

596. Gradually some hundred or so of assembly members get edged in, Menadism making way a little, round Mounier's chair; listen to the acceptance pure and simple, and begin, what is the order of the night, "discussion of the penal code." All benches

* Weber; "Deux Amis," etc.

† "Moniteur" (in "Histoire Parlementaire," iii. 105).
‡ "Deux Amis," iii. 208.

are crowded; in the dusky galleries, duskier with unwashed heads, is a strange "coruscation"—of impromptu bill-hooks.* It is exactly five months this day since these same galleries were filled with high-plumed, jeweled beauty, raining bright influences; and now? To such length have we got in regenerating France. Methinks the travail-throes are of the sharpest! Menadism will not be restrained from occasional remarks; asks, "What is the use of penal code? The thing we want is bread." Mirabeau turns round with lion-voiced rebuke; Menadism applauds him, but recommences.

597. Thus they, chewing tough sausages, discussing the penal code, make night hideous. What the issue will be? Lafayette, with his thirty thousand, must arrive first: him, who cannot now be distant, all men expect, as the messenger of destiny.

CHAPTER IX.
LAFAYETTE.

· 598. Toward midnight lights flare on the hill, Lafayette's lights! The roll of his drums comes up the Avenue de Versailles. With peace, or with war? Patience, friends! With neither. Lafayette is come, but not yet the catastrophe.

599 He has halted and harangued so often on the march; spent nine hours on four leagues of road. At Montreuil, close on Versailles, the whole host had to pause, and, with uplifted right hand, in the murk of night, to these pouring skies, swear solemnly to respect the king's dwelling; to be faithful to king and national assembly. Rage is driven down out of sight by the laggard march; the thirst of vengeance slaked in weariness and soaking clothes. Flandre is again drawn out under arms; but Flandre, grown so patriotic, now needs no "exterminating." The way-worn battalions halt in the avenue; they have, for the present, no wish so pressing as that of shelter and rest.

600. Anxious sits President Mounier; anxious the château. There is a message coming from the château, that M. Mounier would please to return thither with a fresh deputation, swiftly; and so at least *unite* our two anxieties. Anxious Mounier does of himself send, meanwhile, to apprise the general that his majesty has been so gracious as to grant us the acceptance pure and simple. The general, with a small advance column, makes answer in passing; speaks vaguely some smooth words to the national president—glances, only with the eye, at that so mixtiform national assembly; then fares forward toward the château. There are with him two Paris municipals; they were chosen from the three hundred for that errand. He gets admittance through the locked and padlocked grates, through sentries and ushers, to the royal halls.

601. The court, male, and female, crowds on his passage, to read their doom on his face, which exhibits, say historians, a mixture "of sorrow, of fervor and valor," singular to behold.† The king, with monsieur, with ministers and marshals, is waiting to receive him, he "is come," in his high-flown, chivalrous way," to offer his head for the safety of his majesty's. The two municipals state the wish of Paris; four things, of quite pacific tenor. First, that the honor of guarding his sacred person be conferred on patriot national guards—say the Center Grenadiers, who, as Gardes Françaises, were wont to have that privilege. Second, that provisions be got if possible. Third, that the prisons, all crowded with po-

litical delinquents may have judges sent them. Fourth, *that it would please his majesty to come and live in Paris.* To all which four wishes, except the fourth, his majesty answers readily, Yes; or indeed may almost say that he has already answered it. To the fourth he can answer only yes or no; would so gladly answer yes *and* no! But, in any case, are not their dispositions, thank heaven, so entirely pacific? There is time for deliberation. The brunt of the danger seems past!

602. Lafayette and D'Estaing settle the watches; Center Grenadiers are to take the guard-room they of old occupied as Gardes Françaises—for, indeed, the Gardes-du-Corps, its late ill-advised occupants, are gone mostly to Rambouillet. That is the order of *this* night; sufficient for the night is the evil thereof. Whereupon Lafayette and the two municipals, with high-flown chivalry, take their leave.

603. So brief has the interview been, Mounier and his deputation were not yet got up. So brief and satisfactory. A stone is rolled from every heart. The fair palace dames publicly declare that this Lafayette,detestable though he be, is their savior for once. Even the ancient vinaigrous tantes admit it—the king's aunts, ancient grain and sisterhood, known to us of old. Queen Marie-Antoinette has been heard often say the like. She alone, among all women and all men, wore a face of courage, of lofty calmness and resolve, this day. She alone saw clearly what she *meant* to do; and Theresa's daughter *dares* do what she means were all France threatening her—abide where her children are, where her husband is.

604. Toward three in the morning all things are settled; the watches set, the Center Grenadiers put into their old guard-room and harangued: the Swiss and new remaining body-guards harangued. The way-worn Paris battalions, consigned to "the hospitality of Versailles," lie dormant in spare-beds, spare-barracks, coffee-houses, empty churches. A troop of them, on their way to the church of Saint-Louis, awoke poor Weber, dreaming troublous, in the Rue Sartory. Weber had his waistcoat-pocket full of balls all day, "two hundred balls, and two *pears* of powder! For waistcoats were waistcoats then, and had flaps down to mid-thigh. So many balls he has had all day, but no opportunity of using them; he turns over now, execrating disloyal bandits, swears a prayer or two, and straight to sleep again.

605. Finally the national assembly is harangued, which, thereupon, on motion of Mirabeau, discontinues the penal code, and dismisses for the night. Menadism, sansculottism, has cowered into guard-houses, barracks of Flandre, to the light of cheerful fire; failing that, to churches, office-houses, sentry-boxes, wheresoever wretchedness can find a lair. The troublous day has brawled itself to rest, no lives yet lost but that of one war-horse. Insurrectionary chaos lies slumbering round the palace, like ocean round a diving-bell, no crevice yet disclosing itself.

606. Deep sleep has fallen promiscuously on the high and on the low, suspending most things, even wrath and famine. Darkness covers the earth. But, far on the north-east, Paris flings up her great yellow gleam, far into the wet black night. For all is illuminated there,as in the old July nights; the streets, deserted, for alarm of war; the municipals all wakeful, patrols hailing, with their hoarse *Who-goes.* There, as we discover, our poor slim Louison Chabray, her poor nerves all fluttered, is arriving about this very hour. There Usher Maillard will arrive, about an hour hence, "toward four in the morning." They report, successively, to a wakeful Hotel-de-Ville what comfort they can: which again, with early dawn, large comfortable placards shall impart to all men.

---

* *Courrier de Provence* (Mirabeau's newspaper). No. 50, p. 19.

† "Mémoire de M. le Comte de Lally-Tollendal" (Janvier 1790), pp 161-165.

607. Lafayette, in the Hotel de Noailles, not far from the château, having now finished haranguing, sits with his officers consulting; at five o'clock the unanimous best counsel is that a man so tost and toiled for twenty-four hours and more, fling himself on a bed, and seek some rest.

608. Thus, then, has ended the first act of the insurrection of women. How it will turn on the morrow? The morrow, as always, is with the Fates! But his majesty, one may hope, will consent to come honorably to Paris; at all events, he can visit Paris. Anti-national body-guards, here and elsewhere, must take the national oath; make reparation to the tricolor; Flandre will swear. There may be much swearing; much public speaking there will infallibly be; and so, with harangues and vows, may the matter in some handsome way wind itself up.

609. Or, alas, may it not be all otherwise, unhandsome; the consent not honorable, but extorted, ignominious? Boundless chaos of insurrection presses slumbering round the palace, like ocean round a diving-bell, and may penetrate at any crevice. Let but that accumulated insurrectionary mass find entrance! Like the infinite inburst of water, or say rather of inflammable, self-igniting fluid—for example, "turpentine-and-phosphorus oil," fluid known to Spinola Sauterre!

CHAPTER X.

THE GRAND ENTRIES.

610. The dull dawn of a new morning, drizzly and chill, had but broken over Versailles when it pleased destiny that a body-guard should look out of window, on the right wing of the château, to see what prospect there was in heaven and in earth. Rascality, male and female, is prowling in view of him. His fasting stomach is, with good cause, sour; he perhaps cannot forbear a passing malison on them, least of all can he forbear answering such.

611. Ill words breed worse, till the worst word come, and then the ill deed. Did the maledicent body-guard, getting (as was too inevitable) better malediction than he gave load his musketoon and threaten to fire; nay actually fire? Were wise who wist! It stands asserted, to us not credibly. But be this as it may, menaced rascality, in whinnying scorn, is shaking at all grates; the fastening of one (some write it was a chain merely) gives way; rascality is in the Grand Court, whinnying louder still.

612. The maledicent body-guard, more body-guards than he, do now give fire; a man's arm is shattered. Lecointre will depose* that "the Sieur Cardine, a national guard without arms, was stabbed." But see, sure enough. poor Jerome l'Héritier. an unarmed national guard, he, too, "cabinet-maker, a saddler's son, of Paris," with the down of youthhood still on his chin—he reels death-stricken, rushes to the pavement, scattering it with his blood and brains! Alleleu! Wilder than Irish wakes rises the howl, of pity, of infinite revenge. In few moments the grate of the inner and inmost court, which they name Court of Marble, this, too, is forced, or surprised, and bursts open; the Court of Marble, too, is overflowed: up the grand staircase, up all stairs and entrances, rushes the living deluge! Deshuttes and Varigny, the two sentry body-guards, are trodden down, or massacred with a hundred pikes. Women snatch their cutlasses. or any weapon, and storm-in Menadic; other women lift the corpse of shot Jerome, lay it down on the marble steps; there shall the livid face and smashed head, dumb forever, *speak*.

* "Déposition de Lecointre" (in "Histoire Parlementaire." iii. 111-15)

613. Woe now to all body-guards; mercy is none for them! Miomandre de Sainte-Marie pleads with soft words on the grand staircase, "descending four steps," to the roaring tornado. His comrades snatch him up by the skirts and belts, literally from the jaws of destruction, and slam-to their door. This also will stand few instants, the panels shivering in like potsherds. Barricading serves not; fly fast, ye body-guards; rabid insurrection, like the hell-hound, chase uproaring at your heels!

614. The terror-struck body-guards fly, bolting and barricading; it follows. Whitherward? Through hall on hall; woe, now! toward the queen's suit of rooms, in the farthest room of which the queen is now fast asleep. Five sentinels rush through that long suit; they are in the anteroom knocking loud: "Save the queen!" Trembling women fall at their feet with tears; are answered, "Yes, we will die; save ye the queen!"

615. Tremble not, women, but haste; for, lo! another voice shouts far through the outermost door, "Save the queen!" and the door is shut. It is brave Miomandre's voice that shouts this second warning. He has stormed across imminent death to do it; fronts imminent death, having done it. Brave Tardivet du Repaire, bent on the same desperate service, was borne down with pikes; his comrades hardly snatched him in again alive. Miomandre and Tardivet—let the names of these two body-guards, as the names of brave men should, live long.

616. Trembling maids of honor, some of whom from afar caught glimpse of Miomandre as well as heard him, hastily wrap the queen—not in robes of state. She flies for her life across the Œil-de-Bœuf, against the main door of which, too, insurrection batters. She is in the king's apartment, in the king's arms; she clasps her children amid a faithful few. The imperial-hearted bursts into mother's tears: "O my friends, save me and my children! (O mes amis, sauvez moi et mes enfans!)" The battering of insurrectionary axes clangs audible across the Œil-de-Bœuf. What an hour!

617. Yes, friends, a hideous, fearful hour, shameful alike to governed and governor, wherein governed and governor ignominiously testify that their relation is at an end. Rage, which had brewed itself in 20,000 hearts for the last four-and-twenty hours, has taken *fire*: Jerome's brained corpse lies there as live coal. It is, as we said, the infinite element bursting in, wild-surging through all corridors and conduits.

618. Meanwhile the poor body-guards have got hunted mostly into the Œil-de-Bœuf. They may die there, at the king's threshold; they can do little to defend it. They are heaping tabourets (stools of honor)-benches, and all movables against the door, at which the axe of insurrection thunders. But did brave Miomandre perish, then, at the queen's outer door? No; he was fractured, slashed, lacerated, left for dead; he has, nevertheless, crawled hither, and shall live, honored of loyal France. Remark, also, in flat contradiction to much which has been said and sung, that insurrection did *not* burst that door he had defended, but hurried elsewhither, seeking new body-guards.*

619. Poor body-guards, with their Thyestes opera-repast! Well for them that Insurrection has only pikes and axes; no right sieging-tools! It shakes and thunders. Must they all perish miserably, and royalty with them? Deshuttes and Varigny, massacred at the first in break, have been beheaded in the Marble Court, a sacrifice to Jerome's manes; Jourdan with the tile-beard did that duty willingly, and asked if there were no more? Another captive they are leading round the corpse with howl-chant-

* Campan. ii. 75-87

ings; may not Jourdan again tuck up his sleeves?

620. And louder and louder rages insurrection within, plundering if it cannot kill; louder and louder it thunders at the Œil-de-Bœuf; what can now hinder its bursting-in? On a sudden it ceases; the battering has ceased! Wild-rushing; the cries grow fainter; there is silence, or the tramp of regular steps; then a friendly knocking: "We are the Center Grenadiers, old Gardes Françaises: open to us, messieurs of the Garde-du-Corps; we have not forgotten how you saved us at Fontenoy!"* The door is opened; enter Captain Gondran and the Center Grenadiers; there are military embracings; there is sudden deliverance from death into life.

621. Strange sons of Adam! It was to "exterminate" these Gardes-du-Corps that the Center Grenadiers left home; and now they have rushed to save them from extermination! The memory of common peril, of old help, melts the rough heart; bosom is clasped to bosom, not in war. The king shows himself one moment through the door of his apartment with: "'Do not hurt my guards!" "Soyons frères! (Let us be brothers!)" cries Captain Gondran, and again dashes off, with leveled bayonets, to sweep the palace clear.

622. Now, too, Lafayette, suddenly roused, not from sleep (for his eyes had. not yet closed), arrives, with passionate, popular eloquence, with prompt military word of command. National guards, suddenly roused by sound of trumpet and alarm drum, are all arriving. The death-melly ceases; the first sky-lambent blaze of insurrection is got damped down; it burns now, if unextinguished yet flameless, as charred coals do, and not inextinguishable. The king's apartments are safe. Ministers, officials, and even some loyal national deputies, are assembling round their majesties. The consternation will, with sobs and confusion, settle down gradually into plan and counsel, better or worse.

623. But glance now for a moment from the royal windows! A roaring sea of human heads, inundating both courts, billowing against all passages: Menadic women, infuriated men, mad with revenge, with love of mischief, love of plunder! Rascality has slipped its muzzle, and now bays, three-throated, like the dog of Erebus. Fourteen body-guards are wounded, two massacred, and, as we saw, beheaded; Jourdan asking, "Was it worth while to come so far for two?" Hapless Deshuttes and Varigny! Their fate surely was sad. Whirled down so suddenly to the abyss, as men are, suddenly, by the wide thunder of the mountain avalanche, awakened not by *them*, awakened far off by others! When the château clock last struck they were pacing languid, with poised musketoon, anxious mainly that the next hour would strike. It has struck, to them inaudible. Their trunks lie mangled, their heads parade, ",on pikes twelve feet long," through the streets of Versailles, and shall, about noon, reach the barriers of Paris—a too ghastly contradiction to the large comfortable placards that have been posted there!

624. The other captive body-guard is still circling the corpse of Jerome amid Indian war-whooping, bloody tile-beard, with tucked sleeves, brandishing his bloody axe, when Gondran and the grenadiers come in sight: "Comrades, will you see a man massacred in cold blood?" "Off, butchers!" answer they, and the poor body-guard is free. Busy runs Gondran, busy run guards and captains, scouring all corridors, dispersing rascality and robbery, sweeping the palace clear. The mangled carnage is removed, Jerome's body to the town-hall for inquest; the fire of insurrection gets damped, more and more, into measurable, manageable heat.

* Toulongeon. i. 144.

625. Transcendent things of all sorts, as in the general outbursts of multitudinous passion, are huddled together; the ludicrous, nay, the ridiculous, with the horrible. Far over the billowy sea of heads may be seen rascality caprioling on horses from the royal stud. The spoilers these; for patriotism is always infected so, with a proportion of mere thieves and scoundrels. Gondran snatched their prey from them in the château, whereupon they hurried to the stables and took horses there. But the generous Diomedes's steeds, according to Weber, disdained such scoundrel-burden, and, flinging up their royal heels, did soon project most of it, in parabolic curves, to a distance, amid peals of laughter, and were caught. Mounted national guards secured the rest.

626. Now, too, is witnessed the touching last-flicker of etiquette, which sinks not here in the Cimmerian world-wreckage without a sign, as the house-cricket might still chirp in the pealing of a trump of doom. "Monsieur," said some master of ceremonies (one hopes it might be De Brézé), as Lafayette, in these fearful moments, was rushing toward the inner royal apartments, "Monsieur, le roi vous accorde les grandes entrées (Monsieur, the king grants you the grand entries)"—not finding it convenient to refuse them!*

CHAPTER XI.

FROM VERSAILLES.

627. However, the Paris national guard, wholly under arms, has cleared the palace, and even occupies the nearer external spaces, extruding miscellaneous patriotism, for most part, into the Grand Court, or even into the Forecourt.

628. The body-guards, you can observe, have now of a verity "hoisted the national cockade," for they step forward to the windows or balconies, hat aloft in hand, on each hat a huge tricolor, and fling over their bandoleers in sign of surrender, and shout, Vive la nation! To which how can the generous heart respond but with Vive le roi; vivent les Gardes-du-Corps? His majesty himself has appeared with Lafayette on the balcony, and again appears: Vive le roi greets him from all throats, but also from some one throat is heard, "Le roi à Paris (The king to Paris)!"

629. Her majesty, too, on demand, shows herself, though there is peril in it: she steps out on the balcony with her little boy and girl. "No children (Point d'enfans)!" cry the voices. She gently pushes back her children, and stands alone, her hands serenely crossed on her breast. "Should I die," she had said, "I will do it." Such serenity of heroism has its effect. Lafayette, with ready wit, in his high-flown, chivalrous way, takes that fair, queenly hand, and, reverently kneeling, kisses it; whereupon the people do shout, Vive la reine. Nevertheless poor Weber "saw" (or even thought he saw, for hardly the third part of poor Weber's experiences, in such hysterical days, will stand scrutiny) "one of these brigands level his musket at her majesty," with or without intention to shoot, for another of the brigands "angrily struck it down."

630. So that all, and the queen herself, nay, the very captain of the body-guards, have grown national! The very captain of the body-guards steps out now with Lafayette. On the hat of the repentant man is an enormous tricolor, large as a soup-platter or sunflower, visible to the utmost Forecourt. He takes the national oath with a loud voice, elevating his hat, at which sight all the army raise their bonnets on their bayonets, with shouts. Sweet is reconcilement to the heart of man. Lafayette has sworn Flandre; he swears the remaining body-guards

* Toulongeon, i. App. 120.

down in the Marble Court; the people clasp them in their arms—O my brothers, why would ye force us to slay you? Behold, there is joy over you as over returning prodigal sons! The poor body-guards, now national and tricolor, exchange bonnets, exchange arms; there shall be peace and fraternity. And still "Vive leroi," and also "Le roi à Paris," not now from one throat, but from all throats as one, for it is the heart's wish of all mortals.

631. Yes, the king to Paris; what else? Ministers may consult and national deputies wag their heads, but there is now no other possibility. You have forced him to go willingly. "At one o'clock!" Lafayette gives audible assurance to that purpose, and universal insurrection, with immeasurable shout and a discharge of all the fire-arms, clear and rusty, great and small, that it has, returns him acceptance. What a sound; heard for leagues—a doom peal! That sound, too, rolls away into the silence of ages. And the château of Versailles stands ever since vacant, hushed-still, its spacious courts grass-grown, responsive to the hoe of the weeder. Times and generations roll on in their confused gulf-current, and buildings, like builders, have their destiny.

632. Till one o'clock, then, there will be three parties, national assembly, national rascality, national royalty, all busy enough. Rascality rejoices; women trim themselves with tricolor. Nay, motherly Paris has sent her avengers sufficient "cart-loads of loaves," which are shouted over, which are gratefully consumed. The avengers, in return, are searching for grain-stores, loading them in fifty wagons, that so a national king, probable harbinger of all blessings, may be the evident bringer of plenty for one.

633. And thus has sansculottism made prisoner its king, revoking his parole. The monarchy has fallen, and not so much as honorably; no, ignominiously; with struggle, indeed, oft-repeated, but then with unwise struggle, wasting its strength in fits and paroxysms, at every new paroxysm foiled more pitifully than before. Thus Broglie's whiff of grape-shot, which might have been something, has dwindled to the pot-valor of an opera repast and "O Richard, O mon roi." Which again we shall see dwindle to a Favras conspiracy, a thing to be settled by the hanging of one chevalier.

634. Poor monarchy! But what save foulest defeat can await that man who wills and yet wills not? Apparently the king either has a right, assertible as such to the death, before God and man, or else he has no right. Apparently the one or the other, could he but know which! May heaven pity him! Were Louis wise he could this day abdicate. Is it not strange so few kings abdicate, and none yet heard of has been known to commit suicide? Fritz the First of Prussia alone tried it, and they cut the rope.[*]

635. As for the national assembly, which decrees this morning that it "is inseparable from his majesty," and will follow him to Paris, there may one thing be noted—its extreme want of bodily health. After the 14th of July there was a certain sickliness observable among honorable members—so many demanding passports on account of infirm health. But now, for these following days, there is a perfect murrain, President Mounier, Lally Tollendal, Clermonte Tonnere, and all constitutional two-chamber royalists needing change of air, as most no-chamber royalists had formerly done.

636. For, in truth, it is the second emigration this, that has now come, most extensive among commons deputies, noblesse, clergy, so that "to Switzerland

alone there go sixty thousand." They will return in the day of accounts! Yes, and have hot welcome. But emigration on emigration is the peculiarity of France. One emigration follows another, grounded on reasonable fear, unreasonable hope, largely also, on childish pet. The high-flyers have gone first, now the lower flyers, and ever the lower will go, down to the crawlers. Whereby, however, cannot our national assembly so much the more commodiously make the constitution, your two-chamber Anglomaniacs being all safe, distant on foreign shores? Abbé Maury is seized and sent back again; he, tough as tanned leather, with eloquent Captain Cazalès and some others, will stand it out for another year.

637. But here, meanwhile, the question arises. Was Philippe D'Orléans seen, this day, "in the Bois de Boulogne, in gray surtout," waiting under the wet, sere foliage what the day might bring forth? Alas! yes the eidolon of him was— in Weber's and other such brains. The Châtelet shall make large inquisition into the matter, examining a hundred and seventy witnesses, and Deputy Chabroud publish his report, but disclose nothing farther.[*] What, then, has caused these two unparalleled October days? For, surely, such dramatic exhibition never yet enacted itself without dramatist and machinist. Wooden Punch emerges not, with his domestic sorrow, into the light of day, unless the wire be pulled; how can human mobs? Was it not D'Orléans, then, and Laclos, Marquis Sillery, Mirabeau, and the sons of confusion, hoping to drive the king to Metz, and gather the spoil? Nay, was it not, quite contrariwise, the Œil-de-Bœuf, body-guard Colonel de Guiche, Minister Saint-Priest, and high-flying loyalists, hoping, also, to drive him to Metz, and try it by the sword of civil war? Good Marquis Toulongeon, the historian and deputy, feels constrained to admit that it was both.[†]

638. Alas! my friends, credulous incredulity is a strange matter. But when a whole nation is smitten with suspicion, and sees a dramatic miracle in the very operation of the gastric juices, what help is there? Such nation is already a mere hypochondriac bundle of diseases, as good as changed into glass: atrahiliar, decadent, and will suffer crises. Is not suspicion itself the one thing to be suspected, as Montaigne feared only fear?

639. Now, however, the short hour has struck. His majesty is in his carriage, with his queen, sister Elizabeth, and two royal children. Not for another hour can the infinite procession get marshaled and under way. The weather is dim, drizzling, the mind confused, the noise great.

640. Professional marches not a few our world has seen—Roman triumphs and ovations, Cabiric cymbal-beatings, Royal progresses, Irish funerals—but this of the French monarchy marching to its bed remained to be seen. Miles long, and of breadth losing itself in vagueness, for all the neighboring country crowds to see. Slow, stagnating along, like shoreless lake, yet with a noise like Niagara, like Babel and bedlam. A splashing and a tramping, a hurrahing, uproaring, musket-volleying—the truest segment of chaos seen in these latter ages! Till slowly it disembogue itself, in the thickening dusk, into expectant Paris, through a double row of faces all the way from Passy to the Hotel-de-Ville.

641. Consider this: Vanguard of national troops, with trains of artillery, of pikemen and pikewomen, mounted on cannons, on carts, hackney-coaches, or on foot, tripudiating, in tricolor ribbons from head to

* Calumnious rumor, current long since, in loose vehicles (Edinburgh Review on "Mémoires de Bastille," for example), concerning Friedrich Wilhelm and his ways, then so mysterious and miraculous to many—not the least truth in it! (Note of 1868.)

* "Rapport de Chabroud' (Moniteur, du 31 Décembre 1789.)
† Toulongeon, i. 150.

heel; loaves stuck on the points of bayonets, green boughs stuck in gun-barrels.* Next, as main-march, "fifty cart-loads of corn," which have been lent, for peace, from the stores of Versailles. Behind which follow stragglers of the Garde-du-Corps, all humiliated, in grenadier bonnets. Close on these comes the royal carriage, come royal carriages, for there are a hundred national deputies, too, among whom sits Mirabeau—his remarks not given. Then, finally, pell-mell, as rear-guard, Fandre, Swiss, Hundred Swiss, other body-guards, brigands, whosoever cannot get before. Between and among all which masses, flows, without limit, Saint-Antoine and the Menadic cohort. Menadic especially about the royal carriage, tripudiating there, covered with tricolor, singing "allusive songs," pointing with one hand to the royal carriage, which the allusions hit, and pointing to the provision-wagons with the other hand, and these words: "Courage, friends! We shall not want bread now; we are bringing you the baker, the bakeress, and the baker's boy (le boulanger, la boulangère, et le petit mitron)."†

642. The wet day draggles the tricolor, but the joy is unextinguishable. Is not all well now? "Ah, madame, notre bonne reine," said some of these strong-women some days hence, "Ah, madame, our good queen, don't be a traitor any more (ne soyez plus traitre), and we will all love you!" Poor Weber went splashing along, close by the royal carriage, with the tear in his eye: "Their majesties did me the honor," or I thought they did it, "to testify from time to time, by shrugging of their shoulders, by looks directed to heaven, the emotions they felt." Thus, like frail cockle, floats the royal life-boat, helmless, on black deluges of rascality.

643. Mercier, in his loose way, estimates the procession and assistants at 200,000. He says it was one

* Mercier. "Nouveau Paris," iii. 21.
† Toulongeon, i. 134-61; "Deux Amis," iii. c. 9; etc., etc

boundless, inarticulate ha-ha—*transcendent* world-laughter, comparable to the saturnalia of the ancients. Why not? Here, too, as we said, is human nature once more human, shudder at it whoso is of shuddering humor—yet, behold, it is human. It has. "swallowed all formulas;" it tripudiates even so. For which reason they that collect vases and antiques, with figures of dancing bacchantes "in wild and all but impossible positions," may look with some interest on it.

644. Thus, however, has the slow-moving chaos, or modern saturnalia of the ancients, reached the barrier, and must halt, to be harangued by Mayor Bailly. Thereafter it has to lumber along, between the double row of faces, in the transcendent, heaven-lashing ha-ha, two hours longer, toward the Hotel-de-Ville. Then, again, to be harangued there by several persons, by Moreau de Saint-Méry, among others—Moreau of the three thousand orders, now national deputy for St. Domingo. To all which poor Louis, "who seemed to experience a slight emotion" on entering this town-hall, can answer only that he "comes with pleasure, with confidence, among his people." Mayor Bailly, in reporting it, forgets "confidence," and the poor queen says eagerly, "Add, with confidence." "Messieurs," rejoins Mayor Bailly, "you are happier than if I had not forgotten."

645. Finally, the king is shown on an upper balcony, by torch-light, with a huge tricolor in his hat, "and all the people," says Weber, "grasped one another's hand," thinking *now*, surely, the new era was born. Hardly till eleven at night can royalty get to its vacant, long-deserted palace of the Tuileries, to lodge there, somewhat in strolling-player fashion. It is Tuesday, the 6th of October, 1789.

646. Poor Louis has two other Paris processions to make, one ludicrous-ignominious like this, the other not ludicrous nor ignominious, but serious, nay sublime.

THE CONSTITUTION:

BOOK FIRST.

THE FEAST OF PIKES.

CHAPTER I.

IN THE TUILERIES.

647. The victim having once got his stroke-of-grace, the catastrophe can be considered as almost come. There is small interest now in watching his long low moans: notable only are his sharper agonies, what convulsive struggle he may make to cast the torture off from him; and then finally the last departure of life itself, and how he lies extinct and ended, either wrapt like Cæsar in decorous mantle-folds, or unseemly sunk together, like one that had not the force even to die.

648. Was French Royalty, when wrenched forth from its tapestries in that fashion, on that 6th of October, 1789, such a victim? Universal France, and Royal Proclamation to all the Provinces, answers anxiously, *No.* Nevertheless one may fear the worst. Royalty was beforehand so decrepit, moribund, there is little life in it to heal an injury. How much of its strength, which was of the imagination merely, has fled; Rascality having looked plainly in the King's face, and not died! When the assembled crows can pluck up their scarecrow, and say to it, Here shalt thou stand and not there; and can treat with it, and make it, from an infinite, a quite finite Constitutional scarecrow,—what is to be looked for? Not in the finite Constitutional scarecrow, but in what still unmeasured, infinite-seeming force may rally round it, is there thenceforth any hope. For it is most true that all available Authority is *mystic* in its conditions, and comes " by the grace of God."

649. Cheerfuller than watching the death-struggles of Royalism will it be to watch the growth and gambolings of Sansculottism; for, in human things, especially in human society, all death is but a death-birth: thus if the scepter is departing from Louis, it is only that, in other forms, other scepters, were it even pike-scepters, may bear sway. In a prurient element, rich with nutritive influences, we shall find that Sansculottism grows lustily, and even frisks in not ungraceful sport: as indeed most young creatures are sportful; nay, may it not be noted further, that as the grown cat, and cat species generally, is the cruelest thing known, so the merriest is precisely the kitten, or growing cat?

650. But fancy the Royal Family risen from its truckle-beds on the morrow of that mad day: fancy the Municipal inquiry, "How would your Majesty please to lodge?"—and then that the King's rough answer, "Each man lodge as he can, I am well enough," is congeed and bowed away, in expressive grius by the Town-hall Functionaries, with obsequious upholsterers at their back; and how the Château of the Tuileries is repainted, regarnished into a golden Royal Residence; and Lafayette with his blue National Guards lies encompassing it, as blue Neptune (in the language of poets) does an island, wooingly. Thither may the wrecks of rehabilitated Loyalty gather, if it will become Constitutional; for Constitutionalism thinks no evil; Sansculottism itself rejoices in the King's countenance. The rubbish of a Menadic Insurrection, as in this ever-kindly world all rubbish can and must be, is swept aside; and so again, on clear arena, and under new conditions, with something eveu of a new stateliness, we begin a new course of action.

651. Arthur Young has witnessed the strangest scene: Majesty walking unattended in the Tuileries Gardens; and miscellaneous tricolor crowds, who cheer it, and reverently make way for it; the very Queen commands at lowest respectful silence, regretful avoidance.[*] Simple ducks, in those royal waters, quackle for crumbs from young royal fingers: the little Dauphin has a little railed garden, where he is seen delving, with ruddy cheeks and flaxen curled hair; also a little hutch to put his tools in, and screen himself against showers. What peaceable simplicity! Is it peace of a Father restored to his children? Or of a Task-master who has lost his whip? Lafayette and the Municipality and universal Constitutionalism assert the former, and do what is in them to realize it. Such Patriotism as snarls dangerously and shows teeth, Patrollotism shall suppress; or far better, Royalty shall soothe down the angry hair of it, by gentle pattings; and, most effectual of all, by fuller diet. Yes, not only shall Paris be fed, but the King's hand be seen in that work. The household goods of the Poor shall, up to a certain amount, by royal bounty, be disengaged from pawn, and that insatiable Mont de Piété shall disgorge; rides in the city with their Vive-le-Roi need not fail; and so, by substance and show, shall Royalty, if man's art can popularize it, be popularized.[†]

652. Or, alas, is it neither restored Father nor diswhipped Task-master that walks there; but an anomalous complex of both these, and of innumerable other heterogenities: reducible to no rubric, if not this newly-devised one; *King Louis Restorer of French Liberty?* Man indeed, and King Louis like other men, lives in this world to make rule out of the ruleless; by his living energy, he shall force the absurd itself to become less absurd. But then if there *be* no living energy; living passively only? King Serpent, hurled into its unexpected watery dominion, did at least bite, and assert credibly that he was there: but as for poor King Log, tumbled hither and thither as thousandfold chance and other will than his might direct, how happy for him that he was indeed wooden; and, doing nothing, could also see and suffer nothing. It is a distracted business.

653. For his French Majesty, meanwhile, one of the worst things is, that he can get no hunting. Alas, no hunting henceforth; only a fatal being-hunted! Scarcely, in the next June weeks, shall he taste again the joys of the game-destroyer; in next

[*] Arthur Young's "Travels," i. 264-280.
[†] "Deux Amis," iii. c. 10.

June, and never more. He sends for his smith-tools; gives in the course of the day, official or ceremonial business being ended, "a few strokes of the file (quelques coups de lime)."* Innocent brother mortal, why wert thou not an obscure substantial maker of locks; but doomed in that other far-seen craft, to be a maker only of world-follies, unrealities; things self-destructive, which no mortal hammering could rivet into coherence!

654. Poor Louis is not without insight, nor even without the elements of will; some sharpness of temper, spurting at times from a stagnating character. If harmless inertness could save him, it were well; but he will slumber and painfully dream, and to *do* aught is not given him. Royalist Antiquarians still show the rooms where Majesty and suit, in these extraordinary circumstances, had their lodging. Here sat the Queen; reading,—for she had her library brought hither, though the King refused his; taking vehement counsel of the vehement uncounseled; sorrowing over altered times; yet with sure hope of better: in her young rosy Boy has she not the living emblem of hope? It is a murky, working sky; yet with golden gleams—of dawn, or of deeper meteoric night? Here again this chamber, on the other side of the main entrance, was the King's: here his Majesty breakfasted, and did official work, here daily after breakfast he received the Queen; sometimes in pathetic friendliness; sometimes in human sulkiness, for flesh is weak; and when questioned about business, would answer: "Madame, your business is with the children." Nay, Sire, were it not better you, your Majesty's self, took the children? So asks impartial History; scornful that the *thicker* vessel was not also the stronger; pity-struck for the porcelain-clay of humanity rather than for the tile-clay, —though indeed *both* were broken!

655. So, however, in this Medicean Tuileries, shall the French King and Queen now sit for one-and-forty months; and see a wild-fermenting France work out its own destiny, and theirs. Months, bleak, ungenial, of rapid vicissitude; yet with a mild pale splendor, here and there · as of an April that were leading to leafiest Summer as of an October that led only to everlasting Frost. Medicean Tuileries, how changed since it was a peaceful Tile-field! Or is the ground itself fate-stricken, accursed; an Atreus's Palace; for that Louvre window is still nigh, out of which a Capet, whipt of the Furies, fired his signal of the Saint Bartholomew! Dark is the way of the Eternal as mirrored in this world of time: God's way is in the sea, and His path in the great deep.

CHAPTER II.

IN THE SALLE DE MANÉGE.

656. To believing Patriots, however, it is now clear that the Constitution will march, *marcher*,—had it once legs to stand on. Quick, then, ye Patriots, bestir yourselves, and make it; shape legs for it! In the Archevéché, or Archbishop's Palace, his Grace himself having fled; and afterward in the Ridinghall, named Manége, close on the Tuileries; there does a National Assembly apply itself to the miraculous work. Successfully, had there been any heaven-scaling Prometheus among them; not successfully, since there was none! There, in noisy debate, for the sessions are occasionally "scandalous," and as many as three speakers have been seen in the Tribune at once,—let us continue to fancy it wearing the slow months.

657. Tough, dogmatic, long of wind is Abbé Maury ; Ciceronian pathetic is Carzalès. Keen-trenchant, on the other side, glitters a young Barnave; abhorrent of sophistry ; shearing, like keen Damascus saber, all sophistry asunder,—reckless what else he shear with it. Simple seemest thou, O solid Dutch-built Pétion ; if solid, surely dull. Nor life-giving is that tone of thine, livelier polemical Rabaut. With ineffable serenity sniffs great Sieyes, aloft, alone ; his Constitution ye may babble over, ye may mar, but can by no possibility mend : is not Polity a science he has exhausted ? Cool, slow, two military Lameths are visible, with their quality sneer, or demi-sneer ; they shall gallantly refund their Mother's Pension, when the Red Book is produced ; gallantly be wounded in duels. A Marquis Toulongeon, whose Pen we yet thank, sits there ; in stoical meditative humor, oftenest silent, accepts what Destiny will send. Thouret and Parlementary Duport produce mountains of Reformed Law ; liberal, Anglomaniac ; available and unavailable. Mortals rise and fall. Shall goose Gobel, for example,—or Gobel, for he is of Strasburg German breed,—be a Constitutional Archbishop ?

658. Alone of all men there, Mirabeau may begin to discern clearly whither all this is tending. Patriotism, accordingly, regrets that his zeal seems to be getting cool. In that famed Pentecost-Night of the 4th of August, when new Faith rose suddenly into miraculous fire, and old Feudality was burnt up, men remarked that Mirabeau took no hand in it ; that, in fact, he luckily happened to be absent. But did he not defend the Veto, nay Veto Absolu ; and tell vehement Barnave that 600 irresponsible senators would make of all tyrannies the insupportablest ? Again, how anxious was he that the King's Ministers should have seat and voice in the National Assembly ;—doubtless with an eye to being Minister himself! Whereupon the National Assembly decides, what is very momentous, that no Deputy shall be Minister; he, in his haughty stormful manner, advising us to make it, "no Deputy called Mirabeau."* A man of perhaps inveterate Feudalisms ; of stratagems ; too often visible leanings toward the Royalist side : a man suspect ; whom Patriotism will unmask ! Thus, in these June days, when the question, *Who shall have right to declare war ?* comes on, you hear hoarse Hawkers sound dolefully through the streets, "Grand Treason of Count Mirabeau, price only one sou;"—because he pleads that it shall be not the Assembly, but the King! Pleads ; nay prevails : for in spite of the hoarse Hawkers, and an endless Populace raised by them to the pitch even of "Lanterne," he mounts the Tribune next day ; grim resolute ; murmuring aside to his friends that speak of danger : "I know it : I must come hence either in triumph, or else torn in fragments :" and it was in triumph that he came.

659. A man stout of heart ; whose popularity is not of the populace, "pas populacière ;" whom no clamor of unwashed mobs without doors, or of washed mobs within, can scare from his way ! Dumont remembers hearing him deliver a Report on Marseilles; "every word was interrupted on the part of the "Coté Droit by abusive epithets ; calumniator, liar, assassin, scoundrel (scélérat) : Mirabeau pauses a moment, and, in a honeyed tone, addressing the most furious, says : 'I wait, Messieurs, till these amenities be exhausted.'"† A man enigmatic, difficult to unmask ! For example, whence comes his money? Can the profit of a Newspaper, sorely eaten into by Dame Le Jay ; can this, and the eighteen

---

* "Le Château des Tuileries, ou récit, etc.," par Rousseau (in "Histoire Parlementaire," iv. 195-219).

* Moniteur, Nos. 65, 86 (29th September, 7th November, 1789).
† Dumont, "Souvenirs," p. 278.

francs a-day your National Deputy has, be supposed equal to this expenditure? House in the Chaussée d'Antin; Country-house at Argenteuil; splendors, sumptuosities, orgies;—living as if he had a mint! All saloons, barred against Adventurer Mirabeau, are flung wide-open to King Mirabeau, the cynosure of Europe, whom female France flutters to behold,—though the Man Mirabeau is one and the same. As for money, one may conjecture that Royalism furnishes it; which if Royalism do, will not the same be welcome, as money always is to him?

660. "Sold," whatever Patriotism thinks, he cannot readily be: the spiritual fire which is in that man; which shining through such confusions is nevertheless Conviction, and makes him strong, and without which he had no strength,—is not buyable nor salable; in such transference of barter, it would vanish and not *be*. Perhaps "paid and not sold (payé pas vendu):" as poor Rivarol, in the unhappier converse way, calls himself "sold and not paid!" A man traveling, comet-like, in splendor and nebulosity, his wild way; whom telescopic Patriotism may long watch, but, without higher mathematics, will not make out. A questionable, most blamable man; yet to us the far notablest of all. With rich munificence, as we often say, in a most blinkard, bespectacled, logic-chopping generation, Nature has gifted this man with an eye. Welcome is his word, there where he speaks and works; and growing ever welcomer; for it alone goes to the heart of the business: logical cobwebbery shrinks itself together; and thou seest a *thing*, how it is, how it may be worked with.

661. Unhappily our National Assembly has much to do: a France to regenerate; and France is short of so many requisites, short even of cash. These same Finances give trouble enough; no choking of the Deficit; which gapes ever, *Give, give!* To appease the Deficit we venture on a hazardous step, sale of the Clergy's Lands and superfluous Edifices; most hazardous. Nay, give the sale, who is to buy them, ready-money having fled? Wherefore, on the 19th day of December, a paper-money of "Assignats," of Bonds secured, or *assigned*, on that Clerico-National Property, and unquestionable at least in payment of that,—is decreed : the first of a long series of like financial performances, which shall astonish mankind. So that now, while old rags last, there shall be no lack of circulating medium : whether of commodities to circulate thereon, is another question. But, after all, does not this Assignat business speak volumes for modern science? Bankruptcy, we may say, was come, as the *end* of all Delusions needs must come: yet how gently, in softening diffusion, in mild succession, was it hereby made to fall;—like no all-destroying avalanche; like gentle showers of a powdery impalpable snow, shower after shower, till all was indeed buried, and yet little was destroyed that could not be replaced, be dispensed with! To such length has modern machinery reached. Bankruptcy, we said, was great; but indeed Money itself is a standing miracle.

662. On the whole, it is a matter of endless difficulty, that of the Clergy. Clerical property may be made the Nation's, and the Clergy hired servants of the State; but if so, is it not an altered Church? Adjustment enough, of the most confused sort, has become unavoidable. Old landmarks, in any sense, avail not in a new France. Nay literally, the very Ground is new divided; your old particolored *Provinces* become new uniform *Departments* Eighty-three in number;—whereby, as in some sudden shifting of the Earth's axis, no mortal knows his new latitude at once. The Twelve old Parlements too, what is to be done with them? The old Parlements are declared to be all "in permanent vacation,"—till once

the new equal-justice, of Departmental Courts, National Appeal-Court, of elective Justices, Justices of Peace, and other Thouret-and-Duport apparatus be got ready. They have to sit there, these old Parlements, uneasily waiting; as it were, with the rope round their neck; crying as they can, *Is there none to deliver us?* But happily the answer being, *None, none,* they are a manageable class, these Parlements. They can be bullied, even, into silence; the Paris Parlement, wiser than most, has never whimpered. They will and must sit there, in such vacation as is fit; their Chamber of Vacation distributes in the interim what little justice is going. With the rope round their neck, their destiny may be succinct! On the 13th of November, 1790, Mayor Bailly shall walk to the Palais de Justice, few even heeding him; and with municipal seal stamp and a little hot wax, seal up the Parlementary Paper-rooms,—and the dread Parlement of Paris pass away, into Chaos, gently as does a dream! So shall the Parlements perish, succinctly, and innumerable eyes be dry.

663. Not so the Clergy. For, granting even that Religion were dead ; that it had died, half-centuries ago, with unutterable Dubois; or emigrated lately to Alsace, with Necklace-Cardinal Rohan; or that it now walked as goblin revenant,with Bishop Talleyrand of Autun; yet does not the Shadow of Religion, the Cant of Religion, still linger? The Clergy have means and material : means, of number, organization, social weight; a material, at lowest, of public ignorance, known to be the mother of devotion. Nay withal, is it incredible that there might, in simple hearts, latent here and there like gold-grains in the mud-beach, still dwell some real Faith in God, of so singular and tenacious a sort that even a Maury or a Talleyrand could still be the symbol for it?—Enough, the Clergy has strength, the Clergy has craft and indignation. It is a most fatal business this of the Clergy. A weltering hydra-coil, which the National Assembly has stirred up about its ears; hissing, stinging; which cannot be appeased, alive; which cannot be trampled dead! Fatal, from first to last! Scarcely after fifteen months' debating, can a *Civil Constitution of the Clergy* be so much as got to paper; and then for getting it into reality! Alas, such Civil Constitution is but an agreement to disagree. It divides France from end to end, with a new split, infinitely complicating all the othersplits:—Catholicism, what of it there is left, with the Cant of Catholicism, raging on the one side, and skeptic Heathenism on the other; both, by contradiction, waxing fanatic. What endless jarring, of Refractory hated Priests, and Constitutional despised ones; of tender consciences, like the King's, and consciences hot-seared, like certain of his People's: the whole to end in Feasts of Reason and a War of La Vendée ! So deep-seated is Religion in the heart of man, and holds of all infinite passions. If the dead echo of it still did so much, what could not the living voice of it once do?

664. Finance and Constitution, Law and Gospel: this surely were work enough ; yet this is not all. In fact, the Ministry, and Necker himself, whom a brass inscription, "fastened by the people over his door-lintel," testifies to be the "Ministre adoré," are dwindling into clearer and clearer nullity. Execution or legislation, arrangement or detail, from their nerveless fingers all drops undone; all lights at last on the toiled shoulders of an august Representative Body. Heavy-laden National Assembly! It has to hear of innumerable fresh revolts, Brigand expeditions; of Châteaux in the West, especially of Charter-Chests, Chartiers, set on fire; for there too the over-loaded Ass frightfully recalcitrates. Of Cities in the South full of heats and jealousies; which will end in

crossed sabers, Marseilles against Toulon, and Carpentras beleaguered by Avignon ;—of so much Royalist collision in a career of Freedom ; nay of Patriot collision, which a mere difference of *velocity* will bring about! Of a Jourdan Coup-tête, who has skulked thitherward, to those southern regions, from the claws of the Châtelet ; and will raise whole scoundrel regiments.

665. Also it has to hear of Royalist Camp of Jalès: Jalès mountain-girdled Plain, amid the rocks of the Cevennes ; whence Royalism, as is feared and hoped, may dash down like a mountain deluge, and submerge France ! A singular thing this Camp of Jalès ; existing mostly on paper. For the Soldiers at Jalès, being peasants or National Guards, were in heart sworn Sansculottes ; and all that the Royalist Captains could do, was, with false words, to keep them, or rather keep the report of them, drawn up there, visible to all imaginations, for a terror and a sign,— if peradventure France might be reconquered by theatrical machinery, by the *picture* of a Royalist Army done to the life !* Not till the third summer was this portent, burning out by fits and then fading, got finally extinguished ; was the old Castle of Jalès, no Camp being visible to the bodily eye, got blown asunder by some National Guards.

666. Also it has to hear not only of Brissot and his *Friends of the Blacks*, but by and by of a whole St. Domingo blazing skyward ; blazing in literal fire, and in far worse metaphorical ; beaconing the nightly main. Also of the shipping interest, and the landed interest, and all manner of interests, reduced to distress. Of Industry everywhere manacled, hindered ; and only Rebellion thriving. Of sub-officers, soldiers and sailors in mutiny by land and water. Of soldiers, at Nanci, as we shall see, needing to be cannonaded by a brave Bouillé. Of sailors, nay the very galley-slaves, at Brest, needing also to be cannonaded, but with no Bonillé to do it. For indeed, to say it in a word, in those days there was *no King* in Israel, and every man did that which was right in his own eyes.†

667. Such things has an august National Assembly, to hear of, as it goes on regenerating France. Sad and stern : but what remedy ? Get the Constitution ready ; and all men will swear to it: for do not "Addresses of adhesion" arrive by the cart-load? In this manner, by Heaven's blessing, and a Constitution got ready, shall the bottomless fire-gulf be vaulted in, with rag-paper ; and Order will wed Freedom, and live with her there,—till it grow too hot for them. O Coté Gauche, worthy are ye, as the adhesive Addresses generally say, to "fix the regards of the Universe ; " the regards of this one poor Planet, at lowest !

668. Nay, it must be owned, the Coté Droit makes a still madder figure. An irrational generation; irrational, imbecile, and with the vehement obstinacy characteristic of that; a generation which will not learn. Falling Bastilles, Insurrections of Women, thousands of smoking Manor-houses, a country bristling with no crop but that of Sansculottic steel : these were tolerably didactic lessons ; but them they have not taught. There are still men, of whom it was of old written, Bray them in a mortar! Or, in milder language, They have *wedded* their delusions: fire nor steel, nor any sharpness of Experience, shall sever the bond ; till *death* do us part ! On such may the Heavens have mercy; for the Earth, with her rigorous Necessity, will have none.

* Dampmartin, "Evénemens," t. 209.
† See "Deux Amis," iii c. 14: iv. c 2. 3. 4. 7. 9. 14. Expedition des Volontaires de Brest sur Lannion; Les Lyonnais Sauveurs des Dauphinois; Massacre au Mans; Troubles du Maine (pamphlets and excerpts in "Histoir Parlementaire," iii. 251; iv. 162-168), etc.

669. Admit, at the same time, that it was most natural. Man lives by Hope : Pandora, when her box of gods'-gifts flew all out, and became gods'-curses, still retained hope. How shall an irrational mortal, when his high-place is never so evidently pulled down, and he, being irrational, is left resourceless, part with the belief that it will be rebuilt ? It would make all so straight again; it seems so unspeakably desirable; so reasonable,—would you but look at it aright! For, must not the thing which was continue to be ; or else the solid World dissolve? Yes, persist, O infatuated Sansculotte of France! Revolt against constituted Authorities ; hunt ont your rightful Seigneurs, who at bottom so loved you, and readily shed their blood for you,—in country's battles as at Rossbach and elsewhere; and, even in preserving game, were preserving *you*, could ye but have understood it; hunt them out, as if they were wild wolves ; set fire to their Châteaus and Chartiers as to wolf-dens ; and what then? Why, then turn every man his hand against his fellow ! In confusion, famine, desolation, regret the days that are gone; rueful recall them, recall us with them. To repentant prayers we will not be deaf.

670. So, with dimmer or clearer consciousness, must the Right Side reason and act. An inevitable position perhaps ; but a most false one for them. Evil, be thou or good : this henceforth must virtually be their prayer. The fiercer the effervescence grows, the sooner will it pass ; for, after all, it is but some mad effervescence ; the World is solid, and cannot dissolve.

671. For the rest, if they have any positive industry, it is that of plots, and back-stairs conclaves. Plots which cannot be executed ; which are mostly theoretic on their part;—for which nevertheless this and the other practical Sieur Angeard, Sieur Maillebois, Sieur Bonne Savardin, gets into trouble, gets imprisoned, and escapes with difficulty. Nay there is a poor practical Chevalier Favras, who, not withont some passing reflex on Monsieur himself, gets hanged for them, amid loud uproar of the world. Poor Favras, he keeps dictating his last will " at the Hotel-de-Ville, through the whole remainder of the day," a weary February day ; offers to reveal secrets, if they will save him ; handsomely declines since they will not; then dies, in the flare of torchlight, with politest composure ; remarking, rather than exclaiming, with outspread hands: "People, I die innocent; pray for me."* Poor Favras;—type of so much that has prowled indefatigable over France, in days now ending; and, in freer field, might have *earned* instead of prowling,—to thee it is no theory!

672. In the Senate-house again, the attitude of the Right Side is that of calm unbelief. Let an august National Assembly make a Fourth-of-August Abolition of Feudality; declare the Clergy State-servants, who shall have wages ; vote Suspensive Vetoes, new Law-Courts; vote or decree what contested thing it will; have it responded to from the four corners of France, nay get King's Sanction, and what other Acceptance were conceivable.—the Right Side, as we find, persists, with imperturbablest tenacity, in considering, and ever and anon shows that it still considers, all these so-called Decrees as mere temporary whims, which indeed stand on paper, but in practice and fact are not, and cannot be. Figure the brass head of an Abbé Maury flooding forth jesuitic eloquence in this strain ; dusky D'Esprémenil, Barrel Mirabeau (probably in liquor), and enough of others, cheering him from the Right ; and, for example, with what visage a sea-green Robespierre eyes him from the Left. And how Sieyes ineffably sniffs on him, or

* See "Deux Amis." iv. c. 14. 7; "Histoire Parlementaire," vi. 384.

does not deign to sniff; and how the Galleries groan in spirit, or bark rabid on him: so that to escape the Lanterne, on stepping forth, he needs presence of mind, and a pair of pistols in his girdle! For he is one of the toughest of men.

673. Here indeed becomes notable one great difference between our two kinds of civil war; between the modern lingual or Parliamentary-logical kind, and the ancient or *manual* kind in the steel battle-field;—much to the disadvantage of the former. In the manual kind, where you front your foe with drawn weapon, one right stroke is final; for, physically speaking, when the brains are out the man does honestly die, and trouble you no more. But how different when it is with arguments you fight! Here no victory yet definable can be considered as final. Beat him down with Parliamentary invective, till sense he fled; cut him in two, hanging one-half on this dilemma-horn, the other on that; blow the brains of thinking-faculty quite out of him for the time; it kills not; he rallies and revives on the morrow; to-morrow he repairs his golden fires! The thing that *will* logically extinguish him is perhaps still a desideratum of Constitutional civilization. For how, till a man know, in some measure, at what point he becomes logically defunct, can Parliamentary Business he carried on, and Talk cease or slake?

674. Doubtless it was some feeling of this difficulty; and the clear insight how little such knowledge yet existed in the French Nation, new in the Constitutional career, and how defunct Aristocrats would continue to walk for unlimited periods, as Partridge the Almanac-maker did,—that had sunk into the deep mind of People's-friend Marat, an eminently practical mind; and had grown there, in that richest putrescent soil, into the most original plan of action ever submitted to a People. Not yet has it grown; but it has germinated, it is growing; rooting itself into Tartarus, branching toward Heaven; the second season hence, we shall see it risen out of the bottomless Darkness, full-grown, into disastrous Twilight,—a Hemlock-tree, great as the world; on or under whose boughs all the People's-friends of the world may lodge. "Two-hundred and sixty thousand Aristocrat heads;" that is the precisest calculation, though one would not stand on a few hundreds; yet we never rise as high as the round 300,000. Shudder at it, O people; but it is as true as that ye yourselves, and your People's-friend, are alive. These prating Senators of yours hover ineffectual on the barren letter, and will never save the Revolution. A Cassandra-Marat cannot do it, with his single shrunk arm; but with a few determined men it were possible. "Give me," said the People's-friend, in his cold way, when young Barbaroux, once his pupil in a course of what was called Optics, went to see him. Give me 200 Naples bravoes, armed each with a good dirk, and a muff on his left arm by way of shield: with them I will traverse France, and accomplish the Revolution."* Nay, be grave, young Barbaroux; For thou seest there is not jesting in those rheumy eyes, in that soot-bleared figure, most earnest of created things; neither indeed, is there madness, of the strait-waistcoat sort.

675. Such produce shall the Time ripen in cavernous Marat, the man forbid; living in Paris cellars, lone as fanatic Anchorite in his Thebaid; say, as far-seen Simon on his Pillar,—taking peculiar views therefrom. Patriots may smile; and, using him as bandog now to be muzzled, now to be let back, name him, as Desmoulins does, "Maximum of Patriotism," and "Cassandra-Marat:" but were it not singular if

this dirk-and-muff plan of his (with superficial modifications) proved to be precisely the plan adopted?

676. After this manner, in these circumstances, do august Senators regenerate France. Nay, they are, in very deed, *believed* to be regenerating it; on account of which great fact, main fact of their history, the wearied eye can never be permitted wholly to ignore them.

677. But, looking away now from these precincts of the Tuileries, where Constitutional Royalty, let Lafayette water it as he will, languishes too like a cut branch; and august Senators are perhaps at bottom only perfecting "their theory of defective verbs,"—how does the young reality, young Sansculottism thrive? The attentive observer can answer: It thrives bravely; putting forth new buds; expanding the old buds into leaves, into boughs. Is not French Existence, as before, most prurient, all *loosened*, most nutrient for it? Sansculottism has the property of growing by what other things die of: by agitation, contention, disarrangement; nay in a word, by what is the symbol and fruit of all these: Hunger.

678. In such a France as this, Hunger as we have remarked, can hardly fail. The Provinces, the Southern Cities feel it in their turn; and what it brings; exasperation, preternatural suspicion. In Paris some halcyon days of abundance followed the Menadic insurrection, with its Versailles grain-carts, and recovered Restore of Liberty; but they could not continue. The month is still October, when famishing Saint-Antoine, in a moment of passion, seizes a poor Baker, innocent "François the Baker;" * and hangs him, in Constantinople wise;—but even this, singular as it may seem, does not cheapen bread! Too clear it is, no Royal bounty, no Municipal dexterity can adequately feed a Bastille-destroying Paris. Wherefore, on view of the hanged Baker, Constitutionalism in sorrow and anger demands "Loi Martiale," a kind of Riot Act;—and indeed gets it most readily, almost before the sun goes down.

679. This is that famed *Martial Law*, with its Red Flag, its "Drapeau Rouge," in virtue of which Mayor Bailly or any mayor, has but henceforth to put on that new *Oriflamme* of his; then to read or mumble something about the King's peace; and, after certain pauses, serve any undispersing Assemblage with musket-shot, or whatever shot will disperse it. A decisive Law; and most just on one proviso: that all Patrollotism be of God, and all mob-assembling be of the Devil;—otherwise not so just. Mayor Bailly, be unwilling to use it! Hang not out that new Oriflamme, *flame* not of *gold* but of the want of gold! The thrice-blessed Revolution is *done*, thou thinkest? If so, it will be well with thee.

680. But now let no mortal say henceforth that an august National Assembly wants riot! all it ever wanted was riot enough to balance Court-plotting; all it now wants, of Heaven or of Earth, is to get its theory of defective verbs perfected.

CHAPTER III.

THE MUSTER.

681. With Famine and a Constitutional theory of defective verbs going on, all other excitement is conceivable. A universal shaking and sifting of French Existence this is: in the course of which, for one thing, what a multitude of low-lying figures are sifted to the top, and set busily to work there!

682. Dog-leech Marat, now far-seen as Simon Stylites, we already know; him and others, raised aloft

---

The mere sample these of what is coming, of what continues coming, upward from the realm of Night! Chaumette, by and by Anaxagoras Chaumette, one already descries: mellifluous in street-groups; not now a sea-boy on the high and giddy mast: a mellifluous tribune of the common people, with long curling locks, on *bournstone* of the thoroughfares; able sub-editor too; who shall rise,—to the very gallows. Clerk Tallien, he also is become sub-editor; shall become able-editor; and more. Bibliopolic Momoro, Typographic Prudhomme see new trades opening. Collot d'Herbois, tearing a passion to rags, pauses on the Thespian boards; listens, with that black bushy head, to the sound of the world's drama: shall the Mimetic become Real? Did ye hiss him, O men of Lyons?* Better had ye clapped!

683. Happy now, indeed, for all manner of *mimetic*, half-original men! Tumid blustering, with more or less of sincerity, which need not be entirely sincere, yet the sincerer the better, is like to go far. Shall we say, the Revolution-element works itself rarer and rarer; so that only lighter and lighter bodies will float in it; till at last the mere blown-bladder is your only swimmer? Limitation of mind, then vehemence, promptitude, audacity, shall all be available; to which add only these two: cunning and good lungs. Good fortune must be presupposed. Accordingly, of all classes the rising one, we observe, is now the Attorney class: witness Bazires, Carriers, Fouquier-Tinvilles, Basoche-Captain Bourdons: more than enough. Such figures shall Night, from her wonder-bearing bosom, emit; swarm after swarm. Of another deeper and deepest swarm, not yet dawned on the astonished eye; of pilfering Candlesnuffers. Thief-valets, disfrocked Capuchins, and so many Héberts, Henriots, Ronsins, Rossignols, let us, as long as possible, forbear speaking.

684. Thus, over France, all stirs that has what the Physiologists call *irritability* in it: how much more all wherein irritability has perfected itself into vitality, into actual vision, and force that can will. All stirs; and if not in Paris, flocks thither. Great and greater waxes President Dantou in his Cordeliers Section; his rhetorical tropes are all "gigantic:" energy flashes from his black brows, menaces in his athletic figure, rolls in the sound of his voice "reverberating from the domes:" this man also, like Mirabeau, has a natural *eye*, and begins to see whither Constitutionalism is tending, though with a wish in it different from Mirabeau's.

685. Remark, on the other hand, how General Dumouriez has quitted Normandy and the Cherbourg Breakwater, to come—whither we may guess. It is his second or even third trial at Paris, since this New Era began; but now it is in right earnest, for he has quitted all else. Wiry, elastic, unwearied man; whose life was but a battle and a march! No, *not* a creature of Choiseul's; "the creature of God and of my sword,"—he fiercely answered in old days. Overfalling Corsican batteries, in the deadly fire-hail; wriggling invincible from under his horse, at Closterkamp of the Netherlands, though tethered with "crushed stirrup-iron and nineteen wounds;" tough minatory, standing at bay, as forlorn hope, on the skirts of Poland; intriguing, battling in cabinet and field; roaming far out, obscure, as King's spiral, or sitting sealed up, enchanted in Bastille; fencing, pamphleteering, scheming and struggling from the very birth of him,† the man has come thus far. How repressed, how irrepressible! Like some incarnate spirit in prison, which indeed he *was;* hewing on granite walls for deliverance; striking fire-flashes

from them. And now has the general earthquake rent his cavern too? Twenty years younger, what might he not have done! But his hair has a shade of gray; his way of thought is all fixed, military. He can *grow* no further, and the new world is in such growth! We will name him, on the whole, one of Heaven's Swiss, without faith; wanting above all things work, work on *any* side. Work also is appointed him; and he will do it.

686. Not from over France only are the unrestful flocking toward Paris; but from all sides of Europe. Where the carcass is thither will the eagles gather. Think how many a Spanish Guzman, Martinico Fournier named "Fournier l'Américain," Engineer Miraude from the very Andes, were flocking or had flocked. Walloon Pereyra might boast of the strangest parentage: him, they say, Prince Kaunitz the Diplomatist heedlessly dropped; like ostrich-eggs to be hatched of Chance,—into an ostrich-*eater!* Jewish or German Freys do business in the great Cesspool of *Agio;* which Cesspool this *Assignat*-fiat has quickened, into a Mother of dead dogs. Swiss Clavière could found no Socinian Genevese Colony in Ireland; but he paused, years ago, prophetic, before the Minister's Hotel at Paris, and said, it was borne on his mind that *he* one day was to be Minister, and laughed.* Swiss Pache, on the other hand, sits sleek-headed, frugal; the wonder of his own alley, and even of neighboring ones, for humility of mind and a thought deeper than most men's: sit there, Tartuffe, till wanted! Ye Italian Durournys, Flemish Prolys, flit hither all ye bipeds of prey! Come whosoever head is hot; thou of mind *ungoverned,* be it chaos as of undevelopment or chaos of ruin; the man who cannot get known, the man who is too well known; if thou have any vendible faculty, nay if thou have but edacity and loquacity, come! They come; with hot unutterabilities in their heart; as Pilgrims toward a miraculous shrine. Nay how many come as vacant Strollers, aimless, of whom Europe is full, merely toward *something!* For benighted fowls, when you beat their bushes, rush toward any light. Thus Frederick Baron Trenck too is here; mazed, purblind, from the cells of Magdeburg; Minotauric cells, and his Ariadne lost! Singular to say, Trenck, in these years, sells wine; not indeed in bottle, but in wood.

687. Nor is our England without her missionaries. She has her life-saving Needham;† to whom was solemnly presented a "civic sword,"—long since rusted into nothingness. Her l'aine: rebellious Staymaker; unkempt; who feels that he, a single Needleman, did, by his "Common-Sense" Pamphlet, free America; that he can and will free all this world: perhaps even the other. Price-Stanhope Constitutional Association sends over to congratulate;‡ welcomes by National Assembly, though they are but a London Club; whom Burke and Toryism eye askance.

688. On thee too, for country's sake, O Chevalier John Paul, be a word spent, or misspent! In faded naval uniform, Paul Jones lingers visible here; like a wine-skin from which the wine is all drawn. Like the ghost of himself! Low is his once loud bruit; scarcely audible, save, with extreme tedium, in ministerial ante-chambers, in this or the other charitable

---

* Buzet, "Mémoires" (Paris, 1823), p. 90.

† Dumouriez, "Mémoires," i. 28, etc.

* Dumont, "Souvenirs sur Mirabeau," p 309

† A trustworthy gentleman writes to me, three years ago, with a feeling which I cannot but respect, that his father, "the late Admiral Nesham" (not *Needham,* as the French journalists give it), is the Englishman meant; and furthermore that the sword is "not rusted at all," but still lies, with the due memory attached to it, in his (the son's) possession at Plymouth, in a clear state. (Note of 1857.)

‡ Moniteur, 10 Novembre, 7 Décembre, 1799.

dining-room, mindful of the past. What changes: culminatings and declinings! Not now, poor Paul, thou lookest wistful over the Solway brine, by the foot of native Criffel, into blue mountainous Cumberland, into blue Infinitude; environed with thrift, with humble friendliness; thyself, young fool, longing to be aloft from it, or even to be away from it. Yes, beyond that sapphire Promontory, which men name St. Bees, which is not sapphire either, but dull sandstone, when one gets *close* to it, there is a world. Which world thou too shalt taste of!—From yonder White Haven rise his smoke-clouds; ominous though ineffectual. Proud Forth quakes at his bellying sails; had not the wind suddenly shifted. Flamborough reapers, home-going, pause on the hill-side; for what sulphur-cloud is that that defaces the sleek sea; sulphur-clouds spitting streaks of fire? A sea cock-fight it is, and of the hottest; where British *Serapis* and French-American *Bon Homme Richard* do lash and throttle each other, in their fashion; and lo the desperate valor has suffocated the deliberate, and Paul Jones too is of the Kings of the Sea!

689. The Euxine, the Meotian waters felt thee next, and long-skirted Turks, O Paul; and thy fiery soul has wasted itself in thousand contractions;—to no purpose. For, in far lands, with scarlet Nassau-Siegens, with sinful Imperial Catherines, is not the heart broken, even as at home with the mean? Poor Paul! hunger and dispiritment track thy sinking foots: once, or at most twice, in this Revolution-tumult the figure of thee emerges; mute, ghost-like, as "with stars dim-twinkling through." And then, when the light is gone quite out, a National Legislature grants "ceremonial funeral!" As good had been the natural Presbyterian Kirk-bell, and six feet of Scottish earth, among the dust of thy loved ones.—*Such* world lay beyond the Promontory of St. Bees. Such is the life of sinful mankind here below.

690. But of all strangers far the notablest for us is Baron Jean Baptiste de Clootz;—or, dropping baptisms and feudalisms, World-Citizen Anacharsis Clootz, from Cleves. Himmark, judicious Reader. Thou hast known his Uncle, sharp-sighted, thoroughgoing Cornelius de Pauw, who mercilessly cuts down cherished illusions; and of the finest antique Spartans will make mere modern cut-throat Mainots.* The like stuff is in Anacharsis: hot metal; full of scoriæ, which should and could have been smelted out, but which will not. He has wandered over this terraqueous Planet; seeking, one may say, the Paradise we lost long ago. He has seen English Burke; has been seen of the Portugal Inquisition; has roamed, and fought, and written; is writing, among other things, "Evidences of the *Mohammedan* Religion." But now, like his Scythian adoptive godfather, he finds himself in the Paris Athens; surely, at last, the haven of his soul. A dashing man, beloved at Patriotic dinner-tables; with gayety, nay with hot mor: headlong, trenchant, of free purse; in suitable costume; though what mortal ever more despised costumes? Under all costumes Anacharsis seeks the man; not Stylites Marat will more freely trample costumes, if they hold no man. This is the faith of Anacharsis: That there is a Paradise discoverable; that all costumes ought to hold men. O Anacharsis, it is a headlong, swift-going faith. Mounted thereon, me seems, thou art bound hastily for the City of *Nowhere;* and wilt *arrive!* At best, we may say, arrive *in good riding attitude;* which indeed is something.

691. So many new persons and new things have come to occupy this France. Her old Speech and Thought, and Activity which springs from these, are

* De Pauw, "Recherches sur les Grecs," etc.

all changing; fermenting toward unknown issues. To the dullest peasant, as he sits sluggish, overtoiled, by his evening hearth, one idea has come: that of Châteaux burnt; of Châteaux combustible. How altered all Coffee-houses, in Province of Capital! The Antre de Procope has now other questions than the Three Stagyrite Unities to settle; not theater-controversies, but a world-controversy: there, in the ancient pig-tail mode, or with modern Brutus's heads, do well-frizzed logicians hold hubbub, and Chaos umpire sits. The ever-enduring melody of Paris Salons has got a new ground-tone: ever-enduring; which has been heard, and by the listening Heaven too, since Julian the Apostate's time and earlier; made now as formerly.

692. Ex-Censor Suard, *Ex-*Censor, for we have freedom of the Press; he may be seen there; impartial, even neutral. Tyrant Grimm rolls large eyes, over a questionable coming Time. Atheist Naigeon, beloved-disciple of Diderot, crows, in his small, difficult way, heralding glad dawn.* But on the other hand, how many Morrellets, Marmontels, who had sat all their life hatching Philosophe eggs, cackle now, in a state bordering on distraction, at the brood they have brought out!† It was so delightful to have one's Philosophe Theorum demonstrated, crowned in the saloons: and now an infatuated people will not continue speculative, but have Practice!

693. There also observe Preceptress Genlis, or Sillery, or Sillery-Genlis,—for our husband is both Count and Marquis, and we have more than one title. Pretentious, frothy; a puritan yet creedless; darkening counsel by words without wisdom! For, it is in that thin element of the Sentimentalist and Distinguished-Female that Sillery-Genlis works; she would gladly be sincere, yet can grow no sincerer than sincere-cant: sincere-cant of many forms, ending in the devotional form. For the present, on a neck still of moderate whiteness, she wears as jewel a miniature Bastille, cut on mere sandstone, but then actual Bastille sandstone. M. le Marquis is one of D'Orléan's errand-men; in National Assembly, and elsewhere. Madame, for her part, trains up a youthful D'Orléans generation in what superfinest morality one can; gives meanwhile rather enigmatic account of fair Mademoiselle Pamela, the daughter whom she has *adopted.* Thus she, in Palais-Royal Saloon;—whither, we remark, D'Orléans himself, spite of Lafayette, has returned from that English "mission" of his: surely no pleasant mission: for the English would not speak to him; and Saint Hannah More of England, so unlike Saint Sillery-Genlis of France, saw him shunned, in Vauxhall [Gardens, like one pest-struck,‡ and his red-blue impassive visage waxing hardly a shade bluer.

CHAPTER IV.

JOURNALISM.

694. As for Constitutionalism, with its National Guards, it is doing what it can; and has enough to do: it must, as ever, with one hand wave persuasively, repressing Patriotism; and keep the other clenched to menace Royalist plotters. A most delicate task; requiring tact.

695. Thus, if People's-friend Marat has to-day his writ of "prise de corps, or seizure of body," served on him, and dives out of sight, to-morrow he is left at large; or is even encouraged, as a sort of bandog

* Ningeon, Adresse à l'Assemblée Nationale (Paris, 1790), sur la liberté des opinions.
† See Marmontel, "Mémoires," passim; Morellet, "Mémoires," etc.
‡ Hannah More's "Life and Correspondence," ii. c. 5.

whose baying may be useful. President Danton, in open Hall, with reverberating voice, declares that, in a case fatal Marat's, "force may be resisted by force." Whereupon the Châtelet serves Danton also with a writ;—which however, as the whole Cordeliers District responds to it, what Constable will be prompt to execute? Twice more, on new occasions, does the Châtelet launch its writ; and twice more in vain: the body of Danton cannot be seized by Châtelet: he unseized, should he even fly for a season, shall behold the Châtelet itself flung into limbo.

696. Municipality and Brissot, meanwhile, are far on with their Municipal Constitution. The Sixty *Districts* shall become forty-eight *Sections*; much shall be adjusted, and Paris have its Constitution. A Constitution wholly Elective; as indeed all French Government shall and must be. And yet, one fatal element has been introduced: that of citoyen actif. No man who does not pay the marc d'argent, or yearly tax equal to three days labor, shall be other than a *passive* citizen: not the slightest vote for him; were he *acting*, all the year round, with sledge-hammer, with forest-leveling axe! Unheard of! cry Patriot Journals. Yes truly, my Patriot Friends, if Liberty, the passion and prayer of all men's souls, means Liberty to send your fifty-thousandth part of a new Tongue-fencer into National Debating-club, then, be the gods witness, ye are hardly entreated. O, if in National *Palaver* (as the Africans name it), such blessedness is verily found, what tyrant would deny it to son of Adam? Nay, might there not be a Female Parliament too, with "screams from the Opposition benches," and the "honorable Member borne out in hysterics?" To a Children's Parliament would I gladly consent, or even lower if ye wished it. Beloved Brothers! Liberty, one may fear, is actually, as the ancient wise men said, of Heaven. On this Earth, where, thinks the enlightened public, did a brave little Dame de Staal (not Necker's Daughter, but a far shrewder than she) find the nearest approach to Liberty? After mature computation, cool as Dilworth's, her answer is, *In the Bastille.*[*] "Of Heaven?" answer many, asking. Woe that they should *ask*; for that is the very misery! "Of Heaven" means much; share in the National Palaver it may, or may as probably *not* mean.

697. One Sansculottic bough that cannot fail to flourish is Journalism. The voice of the People *being* the voice of God, shall not such divine voice make itself heard? To the ends of France; and in as many dialects as when the *first* great Babel was to be built! Some loud as the lion; some small as the sucking dove. Mirabeau himself has his instructive Journal or Journals, with Geneva hodmen working in them; and withal has quarrels enough with Dame le Jay, his Female Bookseller, so ultra-compliant otherwise.†

698. *King's-friend* Royou still prints himself. Barrére sheds tears of loyal sensibility in Break-of-Day Journal, though with declining sale. But why is Fréron so hot, democratic; Fréron, the King's-friend's Nephew. He has it by kind, that heat of his: *wasp* Fréron begot him; Voltaire's Fréron; who fought stinging, while sting and poison-bag were left, were it only as Reviewer, and over Printed Waste-paper. Constant, illuminative, as the nightly lamp-lighter, issues the Moniteur, for it is now become diurnal, with facts and few commentaries, official, safe in the middle;—its Able Editors sunk long since, recoverably or irrecoverably, in deep darkness. Acid Loustalot, with his "vigor," as of young sloes,

shall never ripen, but die untimely: his Prudhomme, whoever, will not let that Révolutions de Paris die; but edit it himself, with much else,—dull-blustering Printer though he be.

699. Of Cassandra-Marat we have spoken often; yet the most surprising truth remains to be spoken: that he actually does not want sense; but, with croaking gelid throat, croaks out masses of the truth, on several things. Nay sometimes, one might almost fancy he had a perception of humor, and were laughing a little far down in his inner man. Camille is wittier than ever, and more outspoken, cynical; yet sunny as ever. A light melodious creature; "born," as he shall yet say with bitter tears, "to write verses;" light Apollo, so clear, soft-lucent, in this war of the Titans, wherein he shall not conquer!

700. Folded and hawked Newspapers exist in all countries; but, in such a Journalistic element as this of France, other and stranger sorts are to be anticipated. What says the English reader to a Journal-Affiche, Placard-Journal; legible to him that has no halfpenny; in bright prismatic colors, calling the eye from afar? Such, in the coming months, as Patriot Associations, public and private, advance, and can subscribe funds, shall plenteously hang themselves out: *leaves*, limed leaves, to catch what they can! The very Government shall have its Pasted Journal; Lonvet, busy yet with a new "charming romance," shall write Sentinelles, and post them with effect; nay Bertrand de Moleville, in his extremity, shall still more cunningly try it.[*] Great is Journalism. Is not every Able Editor a Ruler of the World, being a persuader of it; though self-elected, yet sanctioned, by the sale of his Numbers? Whom indeed the world has the readiest method of deposing, should need be: that of merely doing *nothing* to him; which ends in starvation.

701. Nor esteem it small what those Bill-stickers had to do in Paris: above Three-score of them: all with their cross-poles, haversacks, pastepots; nay with leaden badges, for the Municipality licenses them. A Sacred College, properly of World-rulers' Heralds, though not respected as such in an Era still incipient and raw. They made the walls of Paris didactic, suasive, with an ever-fresh Periodical Literature, wherein he that ran might read: Placard Journals, Placard Lampoons, Municipal Ordinances, Royal Proclamations; the whole other or vulgar Placard-department superadded,—or omitted from contempt! What unutterable things the stone-walls spoke, during these five years! But it is all gone; To-day swallowing Yesterday, and then being in its turn swallowed of To-morrow, even as Speech ever is. Nay what, O thou immortal Man of Letters, is Writing itself but Speech conserved for a time? The Placard Journal conserved it for one day; some Books conserve it for the matter of ten years; nay some for three thousand: but what then? Why, then, the years being all run, it also dies, and the world is rid of it. O, were there not a spirit in the word of man, as in man himself, that survived the audible bodied word, and tended either godward or else devilward forevermore, why should he trouble himself much with the truth of it, or the falsehood of it, except for commercial purposes? His immortality indeed, and whether it shall last half a lifetime or a lifetime and a half; is not that a very considerable thing? Immortality mortality:—there were certain runaways whom Fritz the Great bullied back into the battle with a: "R—, wollt ihr ewig leben (Unprintable Offscouring of Scoundrels, would ye live forever!")

* De Staël, "Mémoires" (Paris, 1821), i. 169–280.
† Dumont, "Souvenirs," 6.

* See Bertrand-Moleville, "Mémoires," ii. 100, etc.

702. This is the Communication of Thought; how happy when there is any Thought to communicate! Neither let the simpler old methods be neglected in their sphere. The Palais-Royal tent, a tyrannous Patrollotism has removed; but can it remove the lungs of man? Anaxagoras Chaumette we saw mounted on bourn-stones, while Tallien worked sedentary at the sub-editorial desk. In any corner of the civilized world, a tub can be inverted, and an articulate-speaking biped mount thereon. Nay, with contrivance, a portable trestle, or folding-stool, can be procured, for love or money; this the paripatetic Orator can take in his hand, and, driven out here, set it up again there: saying mildly, with a Sage Bias, *Omnia mea mecum porto*.

703. Such is Journalism, hawked, pasted, spoken. How changed since One old Métra walked this same Tuileries Garden, in gilt cocked-hat, with Journal at his nose, or held loose-folded behind his back; and was a notability of Paris, "Métra the Newsman;"* and Louis himself was wont to say: Qu'en dit Métra? Since the first Venetian News-sheet was sold for a gazza, or farthing, and named Gazette! We live in a fertile world.

CHAPTER V.

CLUBBISM.

704. Where the heart is full, it seeks, for a thousand reasons, in a thousand ways, to impart itself. How sweet, indispensable, in such cases, is fellowship; soul mystically strengthening soul! The meditative Germans, some think, have been of opinion that Enthusiasm in general means simply excessive Congregating—Schwärmerey, or *Swarming*. At any rate, do we not see glimmering half-red embers, if laid *together*, get into the brightest white glow?

705. In such a France, gregarious Reunions will needs multiply, intensify; French Life will step out of doors, and, from domestic, become a public Club Life. Old Clubs, which already germinated, grow and flourish; new everywhere bud forth. It is the sure symptom of Social Unrest: in such way, most infallibly of all, does Social Unrest exhibit itself; find solacement, and also nutriment. In every French head there hangs now, whether for terror or for hope, some prophetic picture of a New France: prophecy which brings, nay which almost *is*, its own fulfillment; and in all ways, consciously and unconsciously, works toward itself.

706. Observe, moreover, how the Aggregative Principle, let it be but deep enough, goes on aggregating, and this even in a geometrical progression; how when the whole world, in such a plastic time, is forming itself into Clubs, some One Club, the strongest or luckiest, shall by friendly attracting, by victorious compelling, grow ever stronger, till it become immeasurably strong; and all the others, with their strength, be either loving absorbed into it, or hostilely abolished by it. This if the Club-spirit is universal; if the time *is* plastic. Plastic enough is the time, universal the Club-spirit: such an all-absorbing, paramount One Club cannot be wanting.

707. What a progress, since the first salient-point of the Breton Committee! It worked long in secret, not languidly; it has come with the National Assembly to Paris; calls itself *Club*; calls itself, in imitation, as is thought, of those generous Price-Stanhope English who sent over to congratulate, *French Revolution Club*; but soon, with more originality, *Club of Friends of the Constitution*. Moreover it has leased

for itself, at a fair rent, the Hall of the Jacobins Convent, one of our "superfluous edifices;" and does therefrom now, in these spring months, begin shining out on an admiring Paris. And so, by degrees, under the shorter popular title of *Jacobins Club*, it shall become memorable to all times and lands. Glance into the interior; strongly yet modestly benched and seated; as many as Thirteen Hundred chosen Patriots; Assembly Members not a few. Barnave, the two Lameths are seen there; occasionally Mirabeau, perpetually Robespierre; also the ferret-visage of Fouquier-Tinville with other attorneys; Anacharsis of Prussian Scythia, and miscellaneous Patriots, —though all is yet in the most perfectly clean-washed state; decent, nay dignified. President on platform, President's bell are not wanting; oratorical Tribune high-raised; nor strangers' galleries, wherein also sit women. Has any French Antiquarian Society preserved that written Lease of the Jacobins Convent Hall? Or was it, unluckier even than Magna Charta, *clipt* by sacrilegious Tailors? Universal History is not indifferent to it.

708. These Friends of the Constitution have met mainly, as their name may foreshadow, to look after Elections when an Election comes, and procure fit men; but likewise to consult generally that the Common-weal take no damage; one as yet sees not how. For indeed let two or three gather together anywhere, if it be not in Church, where all are bound to the *passive* state; no mortal can say accurately, themselves as little as any, for *what* they are gathered. How often has the broached barrel proved not to be for joy and heart-effusion, but for duel and head breakage; and the promised feast become a Feast of the Lapithæ! This Jacobins Club, which at first shone resplendent, and was thought to be a new celestial Sun for enlightening the Nations, had, as things all have, to work through its appointed phases: it burned unfortunately more and more lurid, more sulphurous, distracted;—and swam at last, through the astonished Heaven, like a Tartarean Portent, and lurid-burning Prison of Spirits in Pain.

709. Its style of eloquence? Rejoice, Reader, that thou knowest it not, that thou canst never perfectly know. The Jacobins published a Journal of Debates, where they that have the heart may examine: impassioned, dull-droning Patriotic eloquence: implacable, unfertile—save for Destruction, which was indeed its work: most wearisome, though most deadly. Be thankful that Oblivion covers so much; that all carrion is by and by buried in the green Earth's bosom, and even makes her grow the greener. The Jacobins are buried; but their work is not; it continues "making the tour of the world," as it can. It might be seen lately, for instance, with bared bosom and death-defiant eye, as far on as Greek Missolonghi; strange enough, old slumbering Hellas was resuscitated, into *somnambulism* which will become clear wakefulness, by a voice from the Rue St. Honoré! All dies, as we often say; except the spirit of man, of what man *does*. Thus has not the very House of the Jacobins vanished: scarcely lingering in a few old men's memories? The St. Honoré Market has brushed it away, and now where dull-droning eloquence, like a Trump of Doom, once shook the world, there is pacific chaffering for poultry and greens. The sacred National Assembly Hall itself has become common ground; President's platform permeable to wain and dust-cart; for the Rue de Rivoli runs there. Verily, at Cock-crow (of this Cock or the other), *all* Apparitions do melt and dissolve in space.

710. The Paris *Jacobins* became "the Mother Society (Société Mère):" and had as many as "three hundred" shrill-tongued daughters in "direct corres-

---

* Dulaure, "Histoire de Paris," viii. 483: Mercier, Nouveau l'aris," etc.

pondence" with her. Of indirectly corresponding, what we may call grand-daughters and minute progeny, she counted "forty-four thousand!"—But for the present we note only two things: the first of them a mere anecdote. One night, a couple of brother Jacobins are door-keepers; for the members take this post of duty and honor in rotation, and admit none that have not tickets: one door-keeper was the worthy Sieur Laïs, a patriotic Opera-singer, stricken in years, whose windpipe is long since closed without result; the other, young, and named Louis Philippe, D'Orléans first-born, has in this latter time, after unheard-of destinies, become Citizen-King, and struggles to rule for a season. All flesh is grass; higher reed-grass, or creeping herb.

711. The second thing we have to note is historical; that the Mother Society, even in this its effulgent period, cannot content all Patriots. Already it must throw off, so to speak, two dissatisfied swarms; a swarm to the right, a swarm to the left. One party, which thinks the Jacobins lukewarm, constitutes itself into *Club of the Cordeliers;* a hotter Club: it is Danton's element; with whom goes Desmoulins. The other party, again, which thinks the Jacobins scalding-hot, flies off to the right, and becomes "Club of 1789, Friends of the *Monarchic* Constitution." They are afterward named "*Feuillans Club;*" their place of meeting being the Feuillans Convent. Lafayette is, or becomes, their chief man; supported by the respectable Patriot everywhere, by the mass of Property and intelligence,—with the most flourishing prospects. They, in these June days of 1790, do, in the Palais Royal, dine solemnly with open windows; to the cheers of the people; with toasts, with inspiriting songs,—with one song at least, among the feeblest ever sung.* They shall, in due time, be hooted forth, over the borders, into Cimmerian Night.

712. Another expressly Monarchic or Royalist Club, "Club des Monarchiens," though a Club of ample funds, and all sitting on damask sofas, cannot realize the smallest momentary cheer; realizes only scoffs and groans;—till, ere long, certain Patriots in disorderly sufficient number, proceed thither, for a night or for nights, and groan it out of pain. Vivacious alone shall the Mother Society and her family be. The very Cordeliers may, as it were, return into her bosom, which will have grown warm enough.

713. Fatal-looking! Are not such Societies an incipient New Order of Society itself? The Aggregative Principle anew at work in a Society grown obsolete, cracked asunder, dissolving into rubbish and primary atoms?

CHAPTER VI.
JE LE JURE.

714. With these signs of the times, is it not surprising that the dominant feeling all over France was still continually Hope? O blessed Hope, sole boon of man: whereby, on his strait prison-walls, are painted beautiful far-stretching landscapes; and into the night of very Death is shed holiest dawn! Thou art to all an indefeasible possession in this God's-world; to the wise a sacred Constantine's-banner, written on the eternal skies; under which they *shall* conquer, for the battle itself is victory to the foolish some secular *mirage,* or shadow of still waters, painted on the parched Earth; whereby at least their dusty pilgrimage, if devious, becomes cheerfuller, becomes possible.

715. In the death tumults of a sinking Society, French Hope sees only the birth-struggles of a new unspeakably better Society and sings, with full assurance of faith, her brisk Melody, which some inspired fiddler has in these very days composed fo her,—the world-famous Ca-ira. Yes; "that will go;" and then there will *come*—? All men hope; even Marat hopes—that Patriotism will take muff and dirk. King Louis is not without hope: in the chapter of chances; in a flight to some Bouillé; in getting popularized at Paris. But what a hoping People he had, judge by the fact, and series of facts, now to be noted.

716. Poor Louis, meaning the best, with little insight and even less determination of his own, has to follow, in that dim wayfaring of his, such signal as may be given him; by back-stairs Royalism, by official or back-stairs Constitutionalism, whichever for the month may have convinced the royal mind. If flight to Bouillé, and (horrible to think!) a *drawing* of the civil sword do hang as theory, portentous in the background, much nearer is this fact of these Twelve Hundred Kings, who sit in the Salle de Manége. Kings uncontrollable by him, hot yet irreverent to him. Could kind management of these but prosper, how much better were it than armed Emigrants, Turin intrigues, and the help of Austria! Nay are the *two* hopes inconsistent? Rides in the suburbs, we have found, cost little; yet they always brought vivats.* Still cheaper is a soft word; such as has many times turned away wrath. In these rapid days, while France is all getting divided into Departments, Clergy about to be remodeled, Popular Societies rising, and Feudalism and so much else is ready to be hurled into the melting-pot,—might not one try?.

717. On the 4th of February, accordingly, M. le Président reads to his National Assembly a short autograph, announcing that his Majesty will step over, quite in an unceremonious way, probably about noon. Think, therefore, Messieurs, what it may mean; especially, how ye will get the Hall decorated a little. The Secretaries' Bureau can be shifted down from the platform; on the President's chair be slipped this cover of velvet, "of a violet color sprigged with gold fleur-de-lis;"—for indeed, M. le Président has had previous notice underhand, and taken counsel with Doctor Guillotin. Then some fraction of "velvet carpet," of like texture and color, cannot that be spread in front of the chair, where the Secretaries usually sit? So has judicious Guillotin advised: and the effect is found satisfactory. Moreover, as it is probable that his Majesty, in spite of the fleur-de-lis velvet, will stand and not sit at all, the President himself, in the interim, presides standing. And so, while some honorable Member is discussing, say, the division of a Department, Ushers announce: "His Majesty!" In person, with small suite, enter Majesty: the honorable Member stops short; the Assembly starts to its feet: the Twelve Hundred Kings "almost all," อุบ pus Galleries no less, do welcome the Restorer of French Liberty with loyal shouts. His Majesty's Speech, in diluted, conventional phraseology, expresses this mainly: That he, most of all Frenchmen, rejoices to see France getting regenerated; is sure, at the same time, that they will deal gently with her in the process, and not regenerate her *roughly.* Such was his Majesty's Speech: the feat he performed was coming to speak it, and going back again.

718. Surely, except to a very hoping People, there was not much here to build upon. Yet what did they not build The fact that the King has spoken, that he has voluntarily come to speak, how inexpressibly encouraging! Did not the glance of his royal countenance, like concentrated sunbeams, kindle all hearts in an august Assembly; nay thereby in an inflammable enthusiastic France? To move

---

* "Histoire Parlementaire," vt. 384.

* See Bertrand-Moleville, L 241, etc.

"Deputation of thanks" can be the happy lot of but one man; to go in such Deputation the lot of not many. The Deputed have gone, and returned with what highest-flown compliment they could; whom a so the Queen met, Dauphin in hand. And still do not our hearts burn with insatiable gratitude; and to one other man a still higher blessedness suggests itself: To move that we all renew the National Oath.

719. Happiness honorable Member, with his word so in season as word seldom was; magic Fugleman of a whole National Assembly, which sat there bursting to do somewhat; Fugleman of a whole on-looking France! The President swears, declares that every one shall swear, in distinct je lé jure. Nay the very Gallery sends him down a written slip signed, with their Oath on it; and as the Assembly now casts an eye that way, the Gallery all stands up and swears again. And then out of doors, consider at the Hotel-de-Ville how Bailly, the great Tennis-Court swearer, again swears, toward nightfall, with all the Municipals, and Heads of Districts assembled there. And "M. Danton suggests that the public would like to partake:" whereupon Bailly, with escort of Twelve, steps forth to the great outer staircase; sways the ebullient multitude with stretched hand; takes their oath, with a thunder of "rolling drums," with shouts that rend the welkin. And on all streets the glad people, with moisture and fire in their eyes, "spontaneously formed groups, and swore one another,"* —and the whole City was illuminated. This was the 4th of February, 1790: a day to be marked white in Constitutional annals.

720. Nor is the illumination for a night only, but partially or totally it lasts a series of nights. For each District, the Electors of each District will swear specially; and always as the District swears it illuminates itself. Behold them, District after District, in some open square, where the Non-Electing People can all see and join: with their uplifted right-hands, and je le jure; with rolling drums, with embracings, and that infinite hurrah of the enfranchised,—which any tyrant that there may be can consider! Faithful to the King, to the Law, to the Constitution which the National Assembly shall make.

721. Fancy, for example, the Professors of Universities parading the streets with their young France, and swearing, in an enthusiastic manner, not without tumult. By a larger exercise of fancy, expand duly this little word: The like was repeated in every Town and District in France! Nay one Patriot Mother, in Lagnon of Brittany, assembles her ten children; and, with her own aged hand, swears them all herself, the high-souled venerable woman. Of all which, moreover, a National Assembly must be eloquently apprized. Such three weeks of swearing! Saw the Sun ever such a swearing people? Have they been hit by a swearing tarantula? No: but they are men and Frenchmen; they have Hope; and, singular to say, they have Faith, were it only in the Gospel according to Jean Jacques. O my Brothers, would to Heaven it were even as ye think and have sworn! But there are Lover's Oaths, which, had they been true as love itself, cannot be kept; not to speak of Dicer's Oaths, also a known sort.

CHAPTER VII.

PRODIGIES.

722. To such lengths had the Contrat Social brought it, in believing hearts. Man, as is well said, lives by faith; each generation has its own faith, more or less; and laughs at the faith of its predecessor,—

* Newspapers (in "Histoire Parlementaire," iv. 445).

most unwisely. Grant indeed that this faith in the Social Contract belongs to the stranger sorts; that an unborn generation may very wisely, if not laugh, yet stare at it, and piously consider. For alas, what is Contract? If all men were such that a mere spoken or sworn Contract would bind them, all men were then true men, and Government a superfluity. Not what thou and I have promised to each other, but what the balance of our forces can make us perform to each other; that, in so sinful a world as ours, is the thing to be counted on. But above all, a People and a Sovereign promising to one another: as if a whole People, changing from generation to generation, nay from hour to hour, could ever by any method be made to speak or promise; and to speak mere solecisms: "We, be the Heavens witness, which Heavens, however, do no miracles now; we, ever-changing Millions, will allow thee, changeful Unit, to force us or govern us!" The world has perhaps seen few faiths comparable to that.

723. So nevertheless had the world then construed the matter. Had they not so construed it, how different had their hopes been, their attempts, their results! But so and not otherwise did the Upper Powers will it to be. Freedom by social Contract: such was verily the Gospel of that Era. And all men had believed in it, as in a Heaven's Glad-tidings men should; and with overflowing heart and uplifted voice clave to it, and stood fronting Time and Eternity on it. Nay smile not; or only with a smile sadder than tears! This too was a better faith than the one it had replaced; than faith merely in the Everlasting Nothing and man's Digestive Power; lower than which no faith can go.

724. Not that such universally prevalent, universally jurant, feeling of Hope could be a unanimous one. Far from that. The time was ominous: social dissolution near and certain; renovation still a problem, difficult and distant, even though sure. But if ominous to some clearest on-looker, whose faith stood not with the one side or with the other, nor in the ever-vexed jarring of Greek with Greek at all,—how unspeakably ominous to dim Royalist participators; for whom Royalism was Mankind's palladium; for whom, with the abolition of Most-Christian Kingship and Most-Talleyrand Bishopship, all loyal obedience, all religious faith was to expire, and final Night envelop the Destinies of Man! On serious hearts, of that persuasion, the matter sinks down deep; prompting, as we have seen, to back-stairs plots, to Emigration with pledge of war, to Monarchic Clubs; nay to still madder things.

725. The Spirit of Prophecy, for instance, had been considered extinct for some centuries: nevertheless these last-times, as indeed is the tendency of last-times, do revive it; that so, of French mad things, we might have sample also of the maddest. In remote rural districts, whither Philosophism has not yet radiated, where a heterodox Constitution of the Clergy is bringing strife round the altar itself, and the very Church-bells are getting melted into small money-coin, it appears probable that the End of the World cannot be far off. Deep-musing atrabiliar old men, especially old women, hint in an obscure way that they know what they know. The Holy Virgin, silent so long, has not gone dumb;—and truly now, if ever more in this world, were the time for her to speak. One Prophetess, though careless Historians have omitted her name, condition and whereabout, becomes audible to the general ear; credible to not a few; credible to Friar Gerle, poor Patriot Chartreux, in the National Assembly itself! She, in Pythoness recitative, with wild-staring eye, sings that there shall be a Sign; that the Heavenly

Sun himself will hang out a Sign, or Mock Sun,—which, many say, shall be stamped with the Head of hanged Favras. List, Dom Gerle, with that poor addled poll of thine; list, O, list;—and hear nothing.*

726. Notable, however, was that "magnetic vellum (vélin magnétique)" of the Sieurs d'Hozier and Petit-Jean, Parlementeers of Rouen. Sweet young D'Hozier, "bred in the faith of his Missal, and of parchment genealogies," and of parchment generally; adust, melancholic, middle-aged Petit-Jean: why came these two to Saint-Cloud, where his majesty was hunting, on the festival of St. Peter and St. Paul; and waited there, in antechambers, a wonder to whispering Swiss, the livelong day; and even waited without the Grates, when turned out; and had dismissed their valets to Paris, as with purpose of endless waiting? They have a magnetic vellum, these two; whereon the Virgin, wonderfully clothing herself in Mesmerean Cagliostric Occult-Philosophy, has inspired them to jot down instructions and predictions for a much-straitened King. To whom, by Higher Order, they will this day present it; and save the Monarchy and World. Unaccountable pair of visual-objects! Ye should be men, and of the Eighteenth Century; but your magnetic vellum forbids us so to interpret. Say, are ye aught? Thus ask the Guard-house Captains, the Mayor of Saint-Cloud; nay, at great length, thus asks the Committee of Researches, and not the Municipal, but the National Assembly one. No distinct answer, for weeks. At last it becomes plain that the right answer is *negative*. Go, ye Chimeras, with your magnetic vellum; sweet young Chimera, adust middle-aged one! The Prison-doors are open. Hardly again shall ye preside the Rouen Chamber of Accounts; but vanish obscurely into Limbo.†

CHAPTER VIII.

SOLEMN LEAGUE AND COVENANT.

727. Such dim masses, and specks of even deepest black, work in that white-hot glow of the French mind, now wholly in fusion and confusion. Old women here swearing their ten children on the new Evangel of Jean Jacques; old women there looking up for Favras's Heads in the celestial Luminary: these *are* preternatural signs, prefiguring somewhat.

728. In fact, to the Patriot children of Hope themselves it is undeniable that difficulties exist: emigrating Seigneurs; Parlements in sneaking but most malicious mutiny (though the rope is round their neck); above all, the most decided "deficiency of grains." Sorrowful; but, to a Nation that hopes, not irremediable. To a Nation which is in fusion and ardent communion of thought; which, for example, on signal of one Fugleman, will lift its right-hand like a drilled regiment, and swear and illuminate, till every village from Ardennes to the Pyrenees has rolled its village-drum, and sent up its little oath, and glimmer of tallow-illumination some fathoms into the reign of Night!

729. If grains are defective, the fault is not of Nature or National Assembly, but of Art and Anti-National Intriguers. Such malign individuals, of the scoundrel species, have power to vex us, while the Constitution is a-making. Endure it, ye heroic Patriots; nay rather, why not cure it? Grains do grow, they lie extant there 'in sheaf or sack'; only that regraters and Royalist plotters, to provoke the People into illegality, obstruct the transport of grains. Quick, ye organized Patriot Authorities, armed Na-

tional Guards, meet together; unite your good-will; in union is tenfold strength: let the concentrated flash of your Patriotism strike stealthy Scoundrelism blind, paralytic, as with a coup de soleil.

730. Under which hat or night-cap of the Twenty-five millions, this pregnant Idea first arose, for in some one head it did rise, no man can now say. A most small idea, near at hand for the whole world: but a living one, fit; and which waxed, whether into greatness or not, into immeasurable size. When a Nation is in this state that the Fugleman can operate on it, what will the word in season, the act in season, not do! It will grow verily, like the Boy's Bean, in the Fairy-Tale, heaven-high, with habitations and adventures on it, in one night. It is nevertheless unfortunately still a Bean (for your long-lived Oak grows *not* so); and the next night, it may lie felled, horizontal, trodden into common mud.— But remark, at least, how natural to any agitated Nation, which has Faith, this business of Covenanting is. The Scotch, believing in a righteous Heaven above them, and also in a Gospel far other than the Jean-Jacques one, swore, in their extreme need, a Solemn League and Covenant,—as Brothers on the forlorn-hope, and imminence of battle, who embrace, looking godward: and got the whole Isle to swear it; and even, in their tough Old-Saxon Hebrew-Presbyterian way, to keep it more or less;—for the thing, as such things are, was heard in Heaven and partially ratified there. neither is it yet dead, if thou wilt look, nor like to die. The French too, with their Gallic-Ethnic excitability and effervescence, have, as we have seen, real Faith, of a sort; they are hard bested, though in the middle of Hope: a National Solemn League and Covenant there may be in France too; under how different conditions; with how different development and issue!

731. Note, accordingly, the small commencement; first spark of a mighty firework: for if the particular *hat* cannot be fixed upon, the particular District can. On the 29th day of last November, were National Guards by the thousand seen filing, from far and near, with military music, with Municipal officers in tri-color sashes, toward and along the Rhone-stream, to the little town of Etoile. There with ceremonial evolution and maneuver, with fanfaronading, musketry salvoes, and what else the Patriot genius could devise, they made oath and obtestation to stand faithfully by one another, under Law and King; in particular, to have all manner of grains, while grains there were, freely circulated, in spite both of robber and regrater. This was the meeting of Etoile, in the mild end of November 1789.

732. But now, if a mere empty Review, followed by Review-dinner, ball, and such gesticulation and flirtation as there may be, interests the happy County-town, and makes it the envy of surrounding County-towns, what much more might this! In a fortnight, larger Montélimart, half ashamed of itself will do as good, and better. On the Plain of Montélimart, or what is equally sonorous, "under the Walls of Montélimart," the 13th of December sees new gathering and obtestation; 6,000 strong; and now indeed, with these three remarkable improvements, as unanimously resolved on there. First, that the men of Montélimart do federate with the already federated men of Etoile. Second, that, implying not expressing the circulation of grain, they " swear in the face of God and their country " with much more emphasis and comprehensiveness, " to obey all decrees of the National Assembly, and see them obeyed till death (jusqu'à la mort)." Third, and most important, that official record of all this be solemnly delivered in, to the National Assembly, to M. de Lafayette, and " to the Restorer of French Liberty; " who

* "Deux Amis." v. 7.
†See "Deux Amis." v. 199.

shall all take what comfort from it they can. Thus, does larger Montélimart vindicate its Patriot importance, and maintain its rank in the municipal scale.*

733. And so, with the New-year, the signal is hoisted : for is not a National Assembly, and solemn deliverance there, at lowest a National Telegraph? Not only grain shall circulate, while there is grain, on highways or the Rhone-waters, over all that South-Eastern region,—where also if Monseigneur d'Artois saw good to break in from Turin, hot welcome might await him ; but whatsoever Province of France is straitened for grain, or vexed with a mutinous Parlement, unconstitutional plotters, Monarchic Clubs, or any other Patriot ailment, can go and do likewise, or even do better. And now, especially, when the February swearing has set them all agog! From Brittany to Burgundy, on most Plains of France, under most City-walls, it is a blaring of trumpets, waving of banners, a Constitutional maneuvering: under the vernal skies, while Nature too is putting forth her green Hopes, under bright sunshine defaced by the stormful East ; like Patriotism victorious, though with difficulty, over Aristocracy and defect of grain! There march and constitutionally wheel, to the ça-ira-ing mood of fife and drum, under their tricolor Municipals, our clear-gleaming Phalanxes ; or halt, with uplifted right-hand, and artillery salvoes that imitate Jove's thunder ; and all the Country, and metaphorically all "the Universe," is looking on. Wholly, in their best apparel, brave men, and beautifully dizened women, most of whom have lovers there ; swearing, by the eternal Heavens and this green-growing all-nutritive Earth, that France is free!

734. Sweetest days, when (astonishing to say) mortals have actually met together in communion and fellowship ; and man, were it only once through long despicable centuries, is for moments verily the brother of man!—And then the Deputations to the National Assembly, with high-flown descriptive harangue ; to M. de Lafayette, and the Restorer; very frequently moreover to the Mother of Patriotism, sitting on her stout benches in that Hall of the Jacobins! The general ear is filled with Federation. New names of Patriots emerge which shall one day become familiar: Boyer-Fonfrède eloquent denunciator of a rebellious Bordeaux Parlement ; Max Isnard eloquent reporter of the Federation of Draguignan ; eloquent pair, separated by the whole breadth of France, who are nevertheless to meet. Ever wider burns the fire of Federation; ever wider and also brighter. Thus the Brittany and Anjou brethren mention a Fraternity of *all* true Frenchmen ; and go the length of invoking "perdition and death" on any renegade : moreover, if in their National-Assembly harangue, they glance plaintively at the marc d'argent which makes so many citizens *passive*, they, over in the Mother-Society, ask, being henceforth themselves "neither Bretons nor Angevins but French," Why all France has not one Federation, and universal Oath of Brotherhood, once for all?† A most pertinent suggestion; dating from the end of March. Which pertinent suggestion the whole Patriot world cannot but catch, and reverberate and agitate till it become *loud*;—which in that case the Town-hall Municipals had better take up, and meditate.

735. Some universal Federation seems inevitable: the Where is given : clearly Paris : only the When, the How? These also productive Time will give; is already giving. For always as the Federative work goes on, it perfects itself, and Patriot genius adds contribution after contribution. Thus, at

* "Histoire Parlementaire," vii. 4.

† Reports, etc. (in "Histoire Parlementaire," ix, 123-147).

Lyons, in the end of the May month, we behold as many as fifty, or some say sixty, thousand, met to federate; and a multitude looking on which it would be difficult to number. From dawn to dusk ! For our Lyons Guardsmen took rank, at five in the bright dewy morning; came pouring in, bright-gleaming, to the Quai de Rhone, to march thence to the Federation-field ; amid wavings of hats and lady-handkerchiefs ; glad shoutings of some 200,000 Patriot voices and hearts; the beautiful and brave ! Among whom, courting no notice, and yet the notablest of all, what queen-like Figure is this: with her escort of house-friends and Champagneux the Patriot Editor; come abroad with the earliest ? Radiant with enthusiasm are those dark eyes, in that strong Minerva-face, looking dignity and earnest joy; joyfulest she where all are joyful. It is Roland de la Platrière's Wife!* Strict elderly Roland, King's Inspector of Manufactures here; and now likewise, by popular choice, the strictest of our new Lyons Municipals : a man who has gained much, if worth and faculty be gain; but, above all things, has gained to wife Philipon the Paris Engraver's daughter. Reader, mark that queenlike burgher-woman: beautiful, Amazonian-graceful to the eye; more so to the mind. Unconscious of her worth (as all worth is), of her greatness, of her crystal clearness; genuine, the creature of Sincerity and Nature, in an age of Artificiality, Pollution and Cant; there, in her still completeness, in her still invincibility, *she*, if thou knew it, is the noblest of all living French-women,—and will be seen, one day. O, blessed rather while *unseen*, even of herself! For the present she gazes, nothing doubting, into this grand theatricality; and thinks her young dreams are to be fulfilled.

736. From dawn to dusk, as we said, it lasts; and truly a sight like few. Flourishes of drums and trumpets are something ; but think of an "artificial Rock fifty feet high," all cut into crag-steps, not without the similitude of "shrubs!" The interior cavity,—for in sooth it is made of deal,—stands solemn, a "Temple of Concord :" on the outer summit rises "a Statue of Liberty," colossal, seen for miles, with her Pike and Phrygian Cap, and civic column : at her feet a country's Altar, "Autel de la Patrie:" —on all which neither deal-timber nor lath-and-plaster, with paint of various colors, have been spared. But fancy then the banners all placed on the steps of the Rock ; high-mass chanted; and the civic oath of fifty thousand : with what volcanic out-burst of sound from iron and other throats, enough to frighten back the very Soane and Rhone; and how the brightest fireworks, and balls, and even re-past closed in that night of the gods!† And so the Lyons Federation vanishes too, swallowed of darkness;—and yet not wholly, for our brave fair Roland was there : also she, though in the deepest privacy, writes her Narrative of it in Champagneux's Courrier de Lyons; a piece which "circulates to the extent of 60,000!" which one would like now to read.

737. But on the whole, Paris, we may see, will have little to devise; will only have to borrow and apply. And then as to the day, what day of all the calender is fit, if the Bastille Anniversary be not? The particular spot too, it is easy to see, must be the Champ-de-Mars; where many a Julian the Apostate has been lifted on bucklers, to France's or the world's sovereignty ; and iron Franks, loud-clanging, have responded to the voice of a Charlemagne ; and from of old mere sublimities have been familiar.

* "Madame Roland," 'Mémoires,' i. (Discours Préliminaire, p. 23).

† "Histoire Parlementaire," xii. 274.

CHAPTER IX.

SYMBOLIC.

738. How natural, in all decisive circumstances, is Symbolic Representation to all kinds of men! Nay, what is man's whole terrestrial Life but a Symbolic Representation, and making visible, of the Celestial invisible Force that is in him? By act and word he strives to do it; with sincerity, if possible; failing that, with theatricality, which latter also may have its meaning. An Almacks Masquerade is not nothing; in more genial ages, your Christmas Guisings, Feasts of the Ass, Abbots of Unreason, were a considerable something: sincere sports they were: as Almacks may still be sincere wish for sport. But what on the other hand, must not sincere earnest have been; say, a Hebrew Feast of tabernacles have been. A whole Nation gathered, in the name of the Highest, under the eye of the Highest; imagination herself flagging under the reality; and all noblest Ceremony as yet not grown ceremonial, but solemn, significant to the outmost fringe! Neither, in modern private life, are theatrical scenes, of tearful women wetting whole ells of cambric in concert, of impassioned bushy-whiskered youth threatening suicide, and such-like, to be so entirely detested: drop thou a tear over them thyself rather.

739. At any rate, one can remark that no Nation will throw by its work, and deliberately go out to make a scene without meaning something thereby. For indeed no scenic individual, with knavish hypo-critical views, will take the trouble to *soliloquize* a scene· and now consider, is not a scenic Nation placed precisely in that predicament of soliloquizing, for its own behoof alone; to solace its own sensibilities, maudlin or other?—Yet in this respect, of readiness for scenes, the difference of Nations, as of men, is very great. If our Saxon Puritanic friends for example, swore and signed their National Covenant, without discharge of gunpowder, or the beating of any drum, in a dingy Covenant-Close of the Edinburgh High-street, in a mean room, where men now drink mean liquor, it was consistent with their ways so to swear it. Our Gallic-Encyclopædic friends, again, must have a Champ-de-Mars, seen of all the world, or universe; and such a Scenic Exhibition, to which the Coliseum Amphitheatre was but a strollers' barn, as this old Globe of ours had never or hardly ever beheld. Which method also we reckon natural, then and there. Nor perhaps was the respective *keeping* of these two Oaths far out of due proportion to such respective display in taking them: inverse proportion, namely. For the theatricality of a People goes in a compound ratio; ratio indeed of their trustfulness, sociability, fervency; but then also of their excitability, of their porosity, not *continent*; or say, of their explosiveness, hot-flashing, but which does not last.

740. How true also, once more, is it that no man or Nation of men, *conscious* of doing a great thing, was ever, in that thing, doing other than a small one! O Champ-de-Mars Federation, with three-hundred drummers, twelve-hundred wind-musicians, and artillery planted on height after height to boom the tidings of it all over France, in few minutes! Could not Atheist-Naigeon contrive to discern, eighteen centuries off, those Thirteen most poor mean-dressed men, at frugal Supper, in a mean Jewish dwelling, with no symbol but hearts god-initiated into the "Divine depth of Sorrow," and a *Do this in remembrance of me;*—and so cease that small difficult crowing of his if he were not doomed to it?

CHAPTER X.

MANKIND.

741. Pardonable are human theatricalities; nay, perhaps touching. like the passionate utterance of a tongue which with sincerity *stammers;* of a head which with insincerity *babbles,*—having gone distracted. Yet, in comparison with unpremeditated outbursts of Nature, such as an Insurrection of women, how foisonless, unedifying, undelightful; like small ale palled, like an effervescence that has effervesced! Such scenes, coming of forethought, were they world-great, and never so cunningly devised, are at bottom mainly pasteboard and paint. But the others are original; emitted from the great ever-living heart of Nature herself: what figure *they* will assume unspeakably significant. To us, therefore, let the French National Solemn League and Federation be the highest recorded triumph of the Thespian Art: triumphant surely, since the whole Pit, which was Twenty-five Millions, not only claps hands, but does itself spring on the boards and passionately set to playing there. And being such, be it treated as such: with sincere cursory admiration; with wonder from afar. A whole nation gone mumming deserves so much; but deserves not that loving minuteness a Menadic Insurrection did. Much more let prior, and as it were rehearsal scenes of Federation come and go, henceforward, as they list; and, on Plains and under City-walls, innumerable regimental bands blare-off into the Inane, without note from us.

742. One scene, however, the hastiest reader will momentarily pause on: that of Anacharsis Clootz and the Collective sinful Posterity of Adam.—For a Patriot Municipality has now, on the 4th of June, got its plan concocted, and got it sanctioned by National Assembly; a Patriot King assenting; to whom, were he even free to dissent, Federative harangues, overflowing with loyalty, have doubtless a transient sweetness. There shall come deputed National Guards, so many in the hundred, from each of the Eighty-three Departments of France. Likewise from all Naval and Military King's Forces shall Deputed quotas come; such Federation of National with Royal Soldier has, taking place spontaneously, been already seen and sanctioned. For the rest, it is hoped, as many as 40,000 may arrive: expenses to be borne by the Deputing District; of all which let District and Department take thought, and elect fit men,—whom the Paris brethren will fly to meet and welcome.

743. Now, therefore, judge if our Patriot artists are busy; taking deep counsel how to make the Scene worthy of a look from the Universe! As many as 15,000 men, spademen, barrow-men, stone-builders, rammers; with their engineers, are at work on the Champ-de-Mars; hollowing it out into a National Amphitheater, fit for such solemnity. For one may hope it will be annual and perennial; a "Feast of Pikes (Fête des Piques), notablest among the high tides of the year: in any case, ought not a scenic Free Nation to have some permanent National Amphitheater? The Champ-de-Mars is getting hollowed out; and the daily talk and the nightly dream in most Parisian heads is of Federation and that only. Federate Deputies are already under way. National Assembly, what with its natural work, what with hearing and answering harangues of these Federates, of this Federation, will have enough to do! Harangue of "American Committee," among whom is that faint figure of Paul Jones as "with the stars dim-twinkling through it,"—come to congratulate us on the prospect of such auspicious day. ☐Ha-

rangue of Bastille Conquerers, come to "renounce" any special recompense, any peculiar place at the solemnity;—since the Center Grenadiers rather grumble. Harangue of "Tennis-Court Club," who enter with far-gleaming Brass-plate, aloft on a pole, and the Tennis-Court Oath engraved thereon; which far-gleaming Brass-plate they purpose to affix solemnly in the Versailles original locality, on the 20th of this month, which is the anniversary, as a deathless memorial, for some years: they will then dine, as they come back, in the Bois de Boulogue;*—cannot, however, do it without apprising the world. To such things does the august National Assembly ever and anon cheerfully listen, suspending its regenerative labors; and with some touch of impromptu eloquence, make friendly reply; as indeed the wont has long been; for it is a gesticulating, sympathetic People, and has a heart, and wears it on its sleeve.

744. In which circumstances, it occurred to the mind of Anacharsis Clootz, that while so much was embodying itself into Club or Committee, and perorating applauded, there yet remained a greater and greatest; of which, if it also took body and perorated, what might not the effect be: Human kind namely, le Genre Humain itself! In what rapt creative moment the Thought rose in Anacharsis's soul; all his throes, while he went about giving shape and birth to it; how he was sneered at by cold worldlings; but did sneer again, being a man of polished sarcasm; and moved to and fro persuasive in coffee-house and soirée, and dived down assiduous-obscure in the great deep of Paris, making his Thought a Fact: of all this the spiritual biographers of that period say nothing. Enough that on the 19th evening of June 1790, the sun's slant rays lighted a spectacle such as our foolish little Planet has not often had to show: Anacharsis Clootz entering the August Salle de Manége, with the Human Species at his heels, Swedes, Spaniards, Polacks; Turks, Chaldeans, Greeks, dwellers in Mesopotamia; behold them all; they have come to claim place in the grand Federation, having an undoubted interest in it.

745 "Our Ambassador titles," said the fervid Clootz; "are not written on parchment, but on the living hearts of all men." These whiskered Polacks, long-flowing turbaned Ishmaelites, astrological Chaldeans, who stand so mute here, let them plead with you, august Senators, more eloquently than eloquence could. They are the mute representatives of their tongue-tied, befettered, heavy-laden Nations; who from out of that dark bewilderment-gaze wistful, amazed, with half-incredulous hope, toward you, and this your bright light of a French Federation: bright particular day-star, the herald of universal day. We claim to stand there, as mute monuments, pathetically adumbrative of much.—From bench and gallery comes "repeated applause;" for what august Senator but is flattered even by the very shadow of Human Species depending on him? From President Sieyes, who presides this remarkable fortnight, in spite of his small voice, there comes eloquent though shrill reply. Anacharsis and the "Foreigners Committee" shall have place in the Federation; on condition of telling their respective Peoples what they see there. In the meantime, we invite them to the "honors of the sitting (honneur de la séance)." A long-flowing Turk, for rejoinder, bows with Eastern solemnity, and utters articulate sounds: but owing to his imperfect knowledge of the French dialect,† his words are like spilt water; the thought he had in him remains conjectural to this day.

746. Anacharsis and Mankind accept the honors of the sitting; and have forthwith, as the old Newspapers still testify, the satisfaction to see several things. First and chief, on the motion of Lameth, Lafayette, Saint-Fargeau and other Patriot Nobles, let the others repugn as they will: all Titles of Nobility, from Duke to Esquire, or lower, are henceforth *abolished*. Then in like manner, Livery Servants, or rather the Livery of Servants. Neither, for the future, shall any man or woman, self-styled noble, be "incensed,"—foolishly fumigated with incense, in Church; as the wont has been. In a word, Feudalism being dead these ten months, why should her empty trappings and scutcheons survive? the very Coats-of-arms will require to be obliterated;—and yet Cassandra-Marat on this and the other coach-panel notices that they "are but painted over," and threaten to peer through again.

747. So that henceforth De Lafayette is but the Sieur Motier, and Saint Fargeau is plain Michel Lepelletier; and Mirabeau soon after has to say huffingly "With your Riquetti you have set Europe at cross-purposes for three days." For his Counthood is not indifferent to this man; which indeed the admiring people treat him with to the last. But let extreme Patriotism rejoice, and chiefly Anacharsis and Mankind; for now it seems to be taken for granted that one Adam is Father of us all!—

748. Such was, in historical accuracy, the famed feat of Anacharsis. Thus did the most extensive of Public Bodies find a sort of spokesman. Whereby at least we may judge of one thing: what a humor the one sniffing, mocking City of Paris and Baron Clootz had got into; when such exhibition could appear a propriety, next door to a sublimity. It is true, Envy did, in after-times, pervert this success of Anacharsis; making him, from incidental "Speaker of the Foreign-Nations Committee," claim to be official permanent "Speaker, Orateur, of the Human Species," which he only deserved to be; and alleging, calumniously, that his astrological Chaldeans, and the rest, were a mere French tag-rag and bobtail disguised for the nonce; and, in short, sneering and fleering at him in *her* cold, barren way: all which however, he, the man he was, could receive on thick enough panoply, or even rebound therefrom, and also go *his* way.

749. Most extensive of Public Bodies, we call it; and also the most unexpected: For who could have thought to see All Nations in the Tuileries Riding-Hall? But so it is; and truly as strange things may happen when a whole People goes mumming and miming. Hast not thou thyself perchance seen diademed Cleopatra, daughter of the Ptolemies, pleading, almost with bended knee, in unheroic tenparlor, or dim-lit retail-shop, to inflexible gross Burghal Dignitary, for leave to reign and die; being dressed for it, and moneyless, with small children; while suddenly Constables have shut the Thespian barn, and her Antony pleaded in vain? Such visual spectra flit across this Earth, if the Thespian Stage be rudely interfered with; but much more, when as was said, Pit jumps on Stage, then is it verily, as in Herr Tieck's Drama, a Verkehrte Welt, or World Topsy-turvied!

750. Having seen the Human Species itself, to have seen the "Dean" of the Human Species "ceased now to be a miracle. Such "Doyen du Genre Humain (Eldest of Men)," had shown himself there, in these weeks: Jean Claude Jacob, a born Serf, deputed from his native Jura Mountains to thank the National Assembly for enfranchising them. On his bleached worn face are plowed the furrowings of 120 years. He has heard dim patois-talk, of immortal Grand-Monarch victories; of a burned Palatinate, as *he*

* See "Deux Amis," v. 122; "Histoire Parlementaire," etc.
† Moniteur, etc. (in "Histoire Parlementaire," xii. 283).

toiled and moiled to make a little speck of this Earth greener; of Cevennes Dragoonings; of Marlborough going to the war. Four generations have bloomed out, and loved and hated, and rustled off; he was forty-six when Louis Fourteenth died. The Assembly, as one man, spontaneously rose, and did reverence to the Eldest of the World; old Jean is to take séance among them, honorably, with covered head. He gazes feebly there, with his old eyes, on that new wonder-scene; dream-like in him, and uncertain, wavering amid fragments of old memories and dreams. For Time is all growing unsubstantial, dream-like; Jean's eyes and mind are weary, and about to close,—and open a far other wonder-scene, which shall be real. Patriot Subscription, Royal Pension was got for him, and he returned home glad; but in two months more he left it all, and went on his unknown way.*

CHAPTER XI.

AS IN THE AGE OF GOLD.

751. Meanwhile to Paris, ever going and returning, day after day, and all day long, toward that Field of Mars, it becomes painfully apparent that the spade-work there cannot be got done in time. There is such an area of it; 300,000 square feet: for from the Ecole Militaire (which will need to be done up in wood with balconies and galleries) westward to the Gate by the River (where also shall be wood, in triumphal arches), we count some thousand yards of length; and for breadth, from this umbrageous Avenue of eight rows, on the South side, to that corresponding one on the North, same thousand feet more or less. All this to be scooped out, and wheeled up in slope along the sides; high enough; for it must be rammed down there, and shaped stair-wise into as many as "thirty ranges of convenient seats," firm-trimmed with turf, covered with enduring timber;—and then our huge pyramidal Fatherland's-Altar (Autel de la Patrie), in the center, also to be raised and stair-stepped. Force-work with a vengeance; it is a World's Amphitheater! There are but fifteen days good: and at this languid rate, it might take half as many weeks. What is singular too, the spadesmen seem to work lazily; they will not work double-tides, even for offer of more wages, though their tide is but seven hours; they declare angrily that the human tabernacle requires occasional rest!

752. Is it Aristocrats secretly bribing? Aristocrats were capable of that. Only six months since, did not evidence get afloat that subterranean Paris, —for we stand over quarries and catacombs, dangerously, as it were midway between Heaven and the Abyss, and are hollow underground,—was charged with gunpowder, which should make us "leap?" Till a Cordeliers Deputation actually went to examine, and found it—carried off again!† An accursed, incurable brood; all asking for "passports," in these sacred days. Trouble, of rioting, château-burning, is in the Limousin and elsewhere; for they are busy! Between the best of Peoples and the best of Restorer Kings they would sow grudges; with what a fiend's grin would they see this Federation, looked for by the Universe, fail!

753. Fail for want of spade-work, however, it shall not. He that has four limbs and a French heart can do spade-work; and will! On the first July Monday, scarcely has the signal-cannon boomed; scarcely have the languescent mercenary Fifteen Thousand laid down their tools, and the eyes of onlookers turned sorrowfully to the still high Sun; when this and the other Patriot, fire in his eye, snatches barrow and mattock, and himself begins indignantly wheeling. Whom scores and then hundreds follow; and soon a volunteer Fifteen Thousand are shoveling and trundling; with the heart of giants: and all in right order, with that extemporaneous adroitness of theirs: whereby *such* a lift has been given, worth three mercenary ones;—which may end when the late twilight thickens, in triumph-shouts, heard or heard of beyond Montmartre!

754. A sympathetic population will *wait*, next day, with eagerness, till the tools are free. Or why wait? Spades elsewhere exist! And so now bursts forth that effulgence of Parisian enthusiasm, good-heartedness and brotherly love; such, if Chroniclers are trustworthy, as was not witnessed since the Age of Gold. Paris, male and female, precipitates itself toward its Southwest extremity, spade on shoulder. Streams of men, without order; or in order, as ranked fellow-craftsmen, as natural or accidental reunions, march toward the Field of Mars. Three-deep these march; to the sound of stringed music; preceded by young girls with green boughs and tricolor streamers: they have shouldered, soldier-wise, their shovels and picks; and with one throat are singing ça-ira. Yes, pardieu ça-ira, cry the passengers on the streets. All corporate Guilds, and public and private Bodies of Citizens, from the highest to the lowest, march; the very Hawkers, one finds, have ceased bawling for one day. The neighboring Villages turn out: their able men come marching, to village fiddle or tambourine and triangle, under their Mayor, or Mayor and Curate, who also walk bespaded, and in tricolor sash. As many as 150,000 workers; nay at certain seasons, as some count, 250,000; for, in the afternoon especially, what mortal but, finishing his hasty day's work, would run! A stirring City: from the time you reach the Place Louis-Quinze, southward over the River, by all Avenues, it is one living throng. So many workers; and no mercenary mock-workers, but real ones that lie freely to it: each Patriot *stretches* himself against the stubborn glebe; hews and wheels with the whole weight that is in him.

755. Amiable infants (aimables enfans)! They do the "police de l'atelier" too, the guidance and governance, themselves; with that ready will of theirs, with that extemporaneous adroitness. It is a true brethren's work; all distinctions confounded, abolished; as it was in the beginning, when Adam himself delved. Long-frocked tonsured Monks, with short-skirted Water-carriers, with swallow-tailed well-frizzled Incroyables of a Patriot turn; dark. Charcoal-men, meal-white Peruke-makers; or Peruke-wearers, for Advocate and 'Judge are there, and all heads of Districts; sober Nuns sisterlike with flaunting Nymphs of the Opera, and females in common circumstances named unfortunate: the patriot Rag-picker, and perfumed dweller in palaces; for Patriotism, like New-birth, and also like death, levels all. The Printers have come marching, Prudhomme's all in Paper-caps with Révolutions de Paris printed on them; as camille notes; wishing that in these great days there should be a Pacte des Ecrivains too, or Federation of Able Editors.* Beautiful to see! The snowy linen and delicate pantaloon alternates with the soiled check-shirt and bushel-breeches; for both have cast their coats, and under both are four limbs and a set of Patriot muscles. There do they pick and shovel; or bend forward, yoked in long strings to box-barrow or overloaded tumbril: joyous, with one mind. Abbé Sieyes is seen pulling, wiry, vehement, if too light for draught; by the side of

---

* "Deux Amis," iv. iii.
† 23d December, 1789 (newspapers in "Histoire Parlementaire," iv. 44).

* See newspapers, etc. (in "Histoire Parlementaire," vi. 381-406.

Beanharnais, who shall get Kings though he be none. Abbé Maury did not pull, but the Charcoalmen brought a mummer guised like him, and he had to pull in effigy. Let no .august Senator disdain the work: Mayor Bailly, Generalissimo Lafayette are there;—and, alas, shall be there *again* another day! The King himself comes to see: sky-rending Vive-le-roi! "and suddenly with shouldered spades they form a guard of honor round him." Whosoever can come comes; to work, or to look, and bless the work.

756. Whole families have come. One whole family we see clearly of three generations; the father picking, the mother shoveling, the young ones wheeling assiduous; old grandfather, hoary with ninety-three years, holds in his arms the youngest of all:* frisky, not helpful this one; who nevertheless may tell it to *his* grandchildren; and how the Future and the Past alike looked on, and with failing or with half-formed voice, faltered their ça-ira. A vintner has wheeled in, on Patriot truck, beverage of wine: "Drink not, my brothers, if ye are not thirsty; that your cask may last the longer:" neither did any drink but men "evidently exhausted." A dapper Abbé looks on sneering: "To the barrow!" cry several whom he, lest a worse thing befall him, obeys: nevertheless one wiser Patriot barrowman, arriving now, interposes his "arrêtez," setting down his .own barrow, he snatches the Abbé's; trundles it fast, like an infected thing, forth of the Champ-de-Mars circuit, and discharges it *there.* Thus too a certain person (of some quality, or private capital, to appearance), entering hastily, flings down his coat, waistcoat and two watches, and is rushing to the thick of the work: "But your watches?" cries the general voice.—"Does one distrust his brothers?" answers he; nor were the watches stolen. How beautiful is noble sentiment: like gossamer gauze, beautiful and cheap; which will stand no tear and wear! Beautiful cheap gossamer gauze, thou film-shadow of a raw material of Virtue, which art *not* woven, nor likely to be, into Duty; thou art better than nothing, and also worse!

757. Young Boarding-school Boys, College Students, about Vive la Nation, and regret that they have yet "only their sweat to give." What say we of Boys? Beautifulest of Hebes; the loveliest of Paris, in their light air-robes, with ribbon-girdle of tricolor, are there; shoveling and wheeling with the rest; their Hebe eyes brighter with enthusiasm, and long hair in beautiful dishevelment; broad-pressed are their small fingers; but they make the patriot barrow go, and even force it to the summit of the slope (with a little tracing, which what man's arm were not too happy to lend?)—then bound down with it again, and go for more; with their long locks and tricolors blown back; graceful as the rosy Hours. O, as that evening Sun fell over the Champ-de-Mars, and tinted with fire the thick umbrageous boscage that shelters it on this hand and on that, and struck direct on those Domes and two-and-forty Windows of the Ecole Militaire, and made them all of burnished gold,—saw he on his wide zodiac road other such sight? A living garden spotted and dotted with such flowerage; all colors of the prism; the beautifulest blent friendly with the usefulest; all growing and working brotherlike there under one warm feeling, were it but for days; once and no second time! But Night is sinking; these Nights, too, into Eternity. The hastiest traveler Versailles-ward has drawn bridle on the heights of Chaillot: and looked for moments over the River; reporting at Versailles what he saw, not without tears.†

758. Meanwhile, from all points of the compass, Federates are arriving: fervid children of the South,

"who glory in their Mirabeau;" considerate North-blooded Mountaineers of Jura; sharp Bretons, with their Gaelic suddenness; Normans, not to be over-reached in bargain: all now animated with one noblest fire of Patriotism. Whom the Paris brethren march forth to receive; with military solemnities, with fraternal embracing, and a hospitality worthy of the heroic ages. They assist at the Assembly's Debates, these Federates; the Galleries are reserved for them. They assist in the toils of the Champ-de-Mars; each new troop will put its hand to the spade; lift a hod of earth on the Altar of the Fatherland. But the flourishes of rhetoric, for it is a gesticulating People; the moral-sublime of those Addresses to an August Assembly, to a Patriot Restorer! Our Breton Captain of Federates kneels even, in a fit of enthusiasm, and gives up his sword; he wet-eyed to a King wet-eyed. Poor Louis! These, as he said afterward, were among the bright days of his life.

759. Reviews also there must be; royal Federate-reviews, with King, Queen and tricolor Court looking on. at lowest, if, as is too common, it rains, our Federate Volunteers will file through the inner gateways, Royalty standing dry. Nay there, should some stop occur, the beautifulest fingers in France may take you softly by the lapelle, and, in mild flute-voice, ask: "Monsieur, of what Province are you?" Happy he who can reply, chivalrously lowering his sword's-point, "Madame, from the Province your ancestors reigned over." He that happy "Provincial Advocate," now Provincial Federate, shall be rewarded by a sun-smile, and such melodious glad words addressed to a King: "Sire, these are your faithful Lorrainers." Cheerier verily in these holidays. is this "sky-blue faced with red" of a National Guardsman, than the dull black and gray of a Provincial Advocate, which in work-days one was used to. For the same thrice-blessed Lorrainer shall, this evening, stand sentry at a Queen's door; and feel that he could die a thousand deaths for her: then again, at the outer gate, and even a third time, she shall see him; nay he will make her do it; presenting arms with emphasis, "making his musket jingle again:" and in her salute there shall again be a sun-smile, and that little blond-locked too hasty Dauphin shall be admonished, "Salute, then, Monsieur; don't be unpolite;" and therewith she, like a bright Sky-wanderer or Planet with her little Moon, issues forth peculiar.*

760. But at night, when Patriot spade-work is over, figure the sacred rites of hospitality! Lepelletier Saint-Fargeau; a mere private-senator, but with great possessions, has daily his "hundred dinner-guests;" the table of Generalissimo Lafayette may double that number. In lowly parlor, as in lofty saloon, the wine-cup passes round; crowned by the smiles of Beauty; be it of lightly tripping Grisette or of high-sailing Dame, for both equally have beauty, and smiles precious to the brave.

<hr>

CHAPTER XII.

SOUND AND SMOKE.

761. And so now, in spite of plotting Aristocrats, lazy hired spademen, and almost of Destiny itself (for there has been much rain too), the Champ-de-Mars, on the 13th of the month, is fairly ready: trimmed, rammed, buttressed with firm masonry; and Patriotism can stroll over it admiring; and as it were rehearsing, for in every head is some unutterable image of the morrow. Pray Heaven there be not clouds. Nay what far worse cloud is this, of a mis-

* Mercier, il. 76, etc.
† Mercier, il. 81.

* Narrative by a Lorraine federate (given in "Histoire Parlementaire," vi.389-391).

guided Municipality that talks of admitting Patriotism to the solemnity by tickets! Was it by tickets we were admitted to the work; and to what brought the work? Did we take the Bastille by tickets? A misguided Municipality sees the error; at late midnight, rolling drums announce to Patriotism starting half out of its bed-clothes, that it is to be ticketless. Pull down thy nightcap therefore; and, with demiarticulate grumble, significant of several things, go pacified to sleep again. To-morrow is Wednesday morning; unforgettable among the fasti of the world.

762. The morning comes, cold for a July one; but such a festivity would make Greenland smile. Through every inlet in that National Amphitheatre (for it is a league in circuit, cut with openings at due intervals), floods-in the living throng; covers, without tumult, space after space. The Ecole Militaire has galleries and overvaulting canopies, wherein Carpentry and Painting have vied, for the Upper Authorities; triumphal arches, at the Gate by the River, bear inscriptions, if weak, yet well-meant and orthodox. Far aloft, over the Altar of the Fatherland, on their tall crane standards of iron, swing pensile our antique Cassolettes or Pans of Incense; dispensing sweet incense-fumes,—unless for the Heathen Mythology, one sees not for whom. Two hundred thousand Patriotic Men; and, twice as good, one hundred thousand Patriotic Women, all decked and glorified as one can fancy, sit waiting in this Champ-de-Mars.

763. What a picture; that circle of bright-dyed Life, spread up there, on its thirty-seated Slope; leaning, one would say, on the thick umbrage of those Avenue Trees, for the stems of them are hidden by the height; and all beyond it mere greenness of Summer Earth, with the gleams of waters, or white sparklings of stone edifices; little circular enamel picture in the center of such a vase—of emerald! A vase not empty: the Invalides Cupolas want not their population, nor the distant Windmills of Montmartre; on remotest steeple and invisible village belfry stand men with spy-glasses. On the heights of Chaillot are many-colored undulating groups; round and far on, over all the circling heights that embosom Paris, it is as one more or less peopled Amphitheater; which the eye grows dim with measuring. Nay heights, as was before hinted, have cannon; and a floating-battery of cannon is on the Seine. When eye fails, ear shall serve; and all France properly is but one Amphitheatre; for in paved town and unpaved hamlet men walk listening; till the muffled thunder sound audible on their horizon, that they too may begin swearing and firing!* But now, to streams of music, come Federates enough,—for they have assembled on the Boulevard Saint-Antoine or thereby, and come marching through the City, with their Eighty-three Department Banners, and blessings not loud but deep; comes National Assembly, and takes seat under its Canopy; comes Royalty, and takes seat on a throne beside it. And Lafayette, on white charger, is here, and all the civic Functionaries; and the Federates form dances, till their strictly military evolutions and maneuvers can begin.

764. Evolutions and maneuvers? Task not the pen of mortal to describe them: truant imagination droops;—declares that it is not worth while. There is wheeling and sweeping, to slow, to quick and double-quick time: Sieur Motier, or Generalissimo Lafayette, for they are one and the same, and he is General of France, in the King's stead, for four-and-twenty hours; Sieur Motier must step forth, with that sublime chivalrous gait of his; solemnly ascend

* "Deux Amis," v. 168.

the steps of the Fatherland's Altar, in sight of Heaven and of the scarcely breathing Earth; and, under the creak of those swinging Cassolettes, "pressing his sword's point firmly there," pronounce the Oath. To King, to Law, and Nation (not to mention "grains," with their circulating), in his own name and that of armed France. Whereat there is wavings of banners, and acclaim sufficient. The National Assembly must swear, standing in its place; the King himself audibly. The king swears; and now be the welkin split with vivats: let citizens enfranchised embrace, each smiting heartily his palm into his fellow's; and armed Federates clang their arms; above all, that floating battery speak! It has spoken,—to the four corners of France. From eminence to eminence bursts the thunder; faint-heard, loud-repeated. What a stone, cast into what a lake; in circles that do not grow fainter. From Arras to Avignon; from Metz to Bayonne! Over Orleans and Blois it rolls, in cannon recitative; Puy bellows of it amid his granite mountains; Pau where is the shell-cradle of Great Henri. At far Marseilles, one can think, the ruddy evening witnesses it; over the deep-blue Mediterranean waters, the Castle of If ruddy-tinted darts forth, from every cannon's mouth, its tongue of fire; and all the people shout: Yes, France is free. O glorious France, that has burst out so; into universal sound and smoke; and attained—the Phrygian Cap of Liberty! In all Towns, Trees of Liberty also may be planted; with or without advantage. Said we not, it was the highest stretch attained by the Thespian Art on this Planet, or perhaps attainable?

765. The Thespian Art, unfortunately, one must still call it; for behold there, on this Field of Mars, the National Banner, before there could be any swearing, were to be all blessed. A most proper operation; since surely without Heaven's blessing bestowed; say even, audibly or inaudibly sought, no Earthly banner or contrivance can prove victorious: but now the means of doing it? By what thrice-divine Franklin thunder-rod shall miraculous fire be drawn out of Heaven: and descend gently, life-giving, with health to the souls of men? Alas, by the simplest: by Two Hundred shaven-crowned Individuals, "in snow-white albs, with tricolor girdles," arranged on the steps of Fatherland's Altar; and, at their head for spokesman, Soul's-Overseer Talleyrand-Perigord! These shall act as miraculous thunder-rod,—to such length as they can. O ye deep azure Heavens, and thou green all-nursing Earth; ye Streams everflowing; deciduous Forests that die and are born again, continually, like the sons of men; stone Mountains that die daily with every rain-shower, yet are not dead and leveled for ages of ages, nor born again (it seems) but with new world-explosions, and such tumultuous seething and tumbling, steam half-way to the Moon; O thou unfathomable mystic All, garment and dwelling-place of the UNNAMED; and thou, articulate-speaking Spirit of Man, who moldest and modelest that Unfathomable Unnamable even as we see,—is not there a miracle: That some French mortal should, we say not have believed, but pretended to imagine he believed that Talleyrand and Two Hundred pieces of white Calico could do it!

766. Here, however, we are to remark with the sorrowing Historians of that day, that suddenly, while Episcopus Talleyrand, long-stoled, with miter and tricolor belt, was yet but hitching up the Altar-steps to do his miracle, the material Heaven grew black; a north-wind, moaning cold moisture, began to sing; and there descended a very deluge of rain. Sad to see! The thirty-staired Seats, all round our Amphitheatre, get instantaneously slated with mere um-

brellas, fallacious when so thick set: our antique Cassolettes become water-pots; their incense-smoke gone hissing, in a whiff of muddy vapor. Alas, instead of *vivats*, there is nothing now but the furious peppering and rattling. From three to four hundred thousand human individuals feel that they have a skin; happily *impervious*. The General's sash runs water: how all military banners droop; and will not wave, but lazily flap, as if metamorphosed into painted tin-banners! Worse far worse these hundred thousand, such is the Historian's testimony, of the fairest of France! Their snowy muslins all splashed and draggled; the ostrich-feather shrunk shamefully to the backbone of the feather: all caps are ruined; innermost pasteboard molten into its original pap: Beauty no longer swims decorated in her garniture, like Love goddess hidden-revealed in her Paphian clouds, but struggles in disastrous imprisonment in it, for "the shape was noticeable;" and now only sympathetic interjections, titterings, te-heeings, and resolute good-humor will avail. A deluge; an incessant sheet of fluid-column of rain,—such that our Overseer's very miter must be filled; not a miter, but a filled and leaky fire-bucket on his reverend head!—Regardless of which, Overseer Talleyrand performs his miracle: the Blessing of Talleyrand, another than that of Jacob, is on all the Eighty-three departmental flags of France; which wave or flap, with such thankfulness as needs. Toward three o'clock, the sun beams out again; the remaining evolutions can be transacted under bright heavens, though with decorations much damaged.[*]

767. On Wednesday our Federation is consummated: but the festivities last out the week, and over into the next. Festivities such as no Bagdad Caliph, or Aladdin with the Lamp, could have equaled. There is a Jousting on the River; with its water-somersets, splashing and ha-ha-ing: Abbé Fauchet, Te Deum Fauchet, preaches, for his part, in the "rotunda of the Corn-Market," a funeral harangue on Franklin; for whom the National Assembly has lately gone three days in black. The Motier and Lepelletier tables still groan with viands; roofs ringing with patriotic toasts. On the fifth evening, which is the Christian Sabbath, there is a universal Ball. Paris, out of doors and in, man, woman and child, is jigging it, to the sound of harp and four-stringed fiddle. The hoariest-headed man will tread one other measure, under this nether Moon; speechless nurselings, *infants*, as we call them *νήπια τέκνα*, crow in arms; and sprawl out numb-plump little limbs,—impatient for muscularity, they know not why. The stiffest balk bends more or less; all joists creak.

768. Or out, on the Earth's breast itself, behold the Ruins of the Bastille. All lamp-lit, allegorically decorated; a Tree of Liberty sixty feet high; and Phrygian Cap on it, of size enormous, under which King Arthur and his round-table might have dined! In the depths of the back-ground is a single lugubrious lamp, rendering dim-visible one of your iron cages, half-buried, and some Prison stones.—Tyranny vanished downward, all gone but the skirt: the rest wholly lamp-festoons, trees real or of pasteboard; in the similitude of a fairy grove; with this inscription, readable to runner: "Ici l'on danse (Dancing Here)." As indeed had been obscurely foreshadowed by Cagliostro,[†] prophetic Quack of Quacks, when he, four years ago, quitted the grim durance;—to fall into a grimmer, of the Roman Inquisition, and not quit it.

769. But, after all, what is this Bastille business to that of the Champs Elysées! Thither, to these Fields

well named Elysian, all feet tend. It is radiant as day with festooned lamps; little oil-cups, like variegated fire-flies, daintily illume the highest leaves: trees there are all sheeted with variegated fire, shedding far a glimmer into the dubious wood. There, under the free sky, do tight-limbed Federates, with fairest newfound sweethearts, elastic as Diana, and not of that coyness and tart humor of Diana, thread their jocund mazes, all through the ambrosial night; and hearts were touched and fired; and seldom surely had our old Planet, in that huge conic Shadow of hers, "which goes beyond the Moon, and is named *Night*," curtained such a Ball-room. O if, according to Seneca, the very gods look down on a good man struggling with adversity, and smile; what must they think of Five-and-twenty million indifferent ones victorious over it,—for eight days and more.

770. In this way, and in such ways, however, has the Feast of Pikes danced itself off: gallant Federates wending homeward, toward every point of the compass, with feverish nerves, heart and head much heated; some of them, indeed, as Dampmartin's elderly respectable friend from Strasburg, quite "burnt out with liquors," and flickering toward extinction.[*] The Feast of Pikes has danced itself off, and become defunct, and the ghost of a Feast;—nothing of it now remaining but this vision in men's memory; and the place that knew it (for the slope of that Champ-de-Mars is crumbled to half the original height††) now knowing it no more. Undoubtedly one of the memorablest National High-tides. Never or hardly ever, as we said, was Oath sworn with such heart-effusion, emphasis and expenditure of joyance; and then it was broken irremediably within year and day. Ah, why? When the swearing of it was so heavenly-joyful, bosom clasped to bosom, and Five-and-twenty million hearts all burning together; O ye inexorable Destinies, why?—Partly *because* it was sworn with such overjoyance; but chiefly, indeed, for an older reason; that Sin had come into the world, and Misery by Sin! These Five-and-twenty millions, if we will consider it, have now henceforth, with that Phrygian Cap of theirs, no force *over* them, to bind and guide; neither *in* them, more than heretofore, is guiding force, or rule of just living: how then, while they all go rushing at such a *pace*, on unknown ways, with no bridle, toward no aim, can hurly-burly unutterable fail? For verily not Federation rose-pink is the color of this Earth and her work: not by outbursts of noble-sentiment, but with far other ammunition, shall a man front the world.

771. But how wise, in all cases, to "husband your fire;" to keep it deep down, rather, as genial radical-heat! Explosions, the forciblest, and never so well directed, are questionable; far oftenest futile, always frightfully wasteful: but think of a man, of a Nation of men, spending its whole stock of fire in one artificial Firework! So have we seen fond weddings (for individuals, like Nations, have their High-tides) celebrated with an outburst of triumph and deray, at which the elderly shook their heads. Better had a serious cheerfulness been; for the enterprise was great. Fond pair! the more triumphant ye feel, and victorious over terrestrial evil, which seems all abolished, the wider-eyed will your disappointment be to find terrestrial evil still extant. "And why extant?" will each of you cry; "Because my false mate has played the traitor: evil was abolished; I, for one, meant faithfully, and did, or would have done!" Whereby the over-sweet moon of honey changes itself into long years of vinegar: perhaps divulsive vinegar, like Hannibal's.

772. Shall we say, then, the French Nation has led

[*] "Deux Amis," v. 143-179.
[†] See his "Lettre au Peuple Français," (London, 1788).

[*] Dampmartin, "Evénemens," 1. 144-184.
[†] Dulaure, "Histoire de Paris," viii. 25.

Royalty, or wooed and teased poor Royalty to lead *her*, to the hymeneal Fatherland's Altar, in such over-sweet manner; and has, most thoughtlessly, to celebrate the nuptials with due shine and demonstration, —burnt her bed?

BOOK SECOND.

NANCI.

CHAPTER I.

BOUILLÉ.

773. Dimly visible, at Metz on the North-Eastern frontier, a certain brave Bouillé, last refuge of Royalty in all straits and meditations of flight, has for many months hovered occasionally in our eye ; some name or shadow of a brave Bouillé: let us now, for a little, look fixedly at him, till he become a substance and person for us. The man himself is worth a glance; his position and procedure there, in these days, will throw light on many things.

774. For it is with Bouillé as with all French Commanding Officers ; only in a more emphatic degree. The grand National Federation, we already guess, was but empty sound, or worse: a last loudest universal *Hep-hep-hurrah*, with full bumpers, in that National Lapithæ-feast of Constitution-making ; as in loud denial of the palpably existing ; as if, with hurrahings, you would shut out notice of the inevitable, already knocking at the gates? Which new National bumper, one may say, can but deepen the drunkenness; and so, the *louder* it swears Brotherhood, will the sooner and the more surely lead to Cannibalism. Ah, under that fraternal shine and clangor, what a deep world of irreconcilable discords lie momentarily assuaged, damp-down for one moment! Respectable military Federates have barely got home to their quarters ; and the inflammablest, " dying, burnt up with liquors and kindness," has not yet got extinct: the shine is hardly out of men's eyes, and still blazes filling all men's memories,— when your discords burst forth again, very considerably darker than ever. Let us look at Bouillé, and see how.

775. Bouillé for the present commands in the garrison of Metz, and far and wide over the East and North ; being indeed, by a late act of Government with sanction of National Assembly, appointed one of our Four supreme Generals. Rochambeau and Mailly, men and Marshals of note in these days, though to us of small moment, are two of his colleagues; tough old babbling Lückner, also of small moment for us, will probably be the third. Marquis de Bouillé is a determined Loyalist; not indeed disinclined to moderate reform, but resolute against immoderate. A man long suspect to Patriotism; who has more than once given the august Assembly trouble ; who would not, for example, take the National Oath, as he was bound to do, but always put it off on this or the other pretext, till an autograph of Majesty requested him to do it as a favor 'There, in this post, if not of honor, yet of eminence and danger, he waits, in a silent concentred manner; very dubious of the future. " Alone," as he says, or alone, of all the old military Notabilities, he has not emigrated ; but thinks always, in attrabiliar moments, that there will be nothing for him too, but to cross the marches. He might cross, say, to Treves or Coblentz, where Exiled Princes will be one day ranking; or say, over into Luxemburg, where old Broglie loiters and languishes. Or is there not the great dim Deep of European Diplomacy ; where your Calonnes, your Breteuils are beginning to hover. dimly discernible?

776. With immeasurable confused outlooks and purposes, with no clear purpose but this of still trying to do his Majesty a service, Bouillé waits; struggling what he can to keep his district loyal, his troops faithful, his garrisons furnished. He maintains, as yet, with his Cousin Lafayette some thin diplomatic correspondence, by letter and messenger ; chivalrous constitutional professions on the one side, military gravity and brevity on the other; which thin correspondence one can see growing ever the thinner and hollower, toward the verge of entire vacuity.[*] A quick, choleric, sharply discerning, stubbornly endeavoring man : with suppressed-explosive resolution, with valor, nay headlong audacity; a man who was more in his place, lion-like defending those Windward Isles, or, as with military tiger-spring, clutching Nevis and Montserrat from the English,—than here in this suppressed condition, muzzled and fettered by diplomatic pack-threads; looking out for a civil war, which may never arrive. Few years ago Bouillé was to have led a French East-Indian Expedition, and reconquered or conquered Pondicherry and the Kingdoms of the Sun : but the whole world is suddenly changed, and be with it; Destiny willed it not in that way, but in this.

CHAPTER II.

ARREARS AND ARISTOCRATS.

777. Indeed, as to the general outlook of things, Bouillé himself augurs not well of it. The French Army, ever since those old Bastille days, and earlier, has been universally in the questionablest state, and growing daily worse. Discipline, which is at all times a kind of miracle, and works by faith, broke down then ; one sees not with what near prospect of recovering itself. The Gardes Françaises played a deadly game ; but how they won it, and wear the prizes of it, all men know. In that general overturn, we saw the hired Fighters refuse to fight. The very Swiss of Château-Vieux, which indeed is a kind of French Swiss, from Geneva and the Pays de Vaud, are understood o have declined. Deserters glided over; Royal-Allemand itself looked disconsolate, though stanch of purpose. In a word, we there saw *Military Rule*, in the shape of poor Besenval with that convulsive unmanageable Camp of his, pass to martyr-days on the Champ-de-Mars ; and then, veiling itself, so to speak, "under cloud of night," depart " down the left bank of the Seine," to seek refuge elsewhere; *this* ground having clearly become too hot for it.

778. But what new ground to seek, what remedy to try? Quarters that 'were "uninfected:" this doubtless, with judicious strictness of drilling, were the plan. Alas, in all quarters and places, from Paris onward to the remotest hamlet, is infection, is seditious contagion: inhaled, propagated by contact and converse, till the dullest soldier catch it! There is speech of men in uniform with men not in uniform; men in uniform read journals, and even write in them.[†] There are public petitions or remonstrances, private emissaries and associations ; there is discontent, jealousy, uncertainty, sullen suspicious humor. The whole French Army, fermenting in dark heat, glooms ominous, boding good to no one.

779. So that, in the general social dissolution and revolt, we are to have this deepest and dismalest kind of it, a revolting soldiery? Barren, desolate

<hr>

[*] Bouillé, "Mémoires" (London, 1797), i. o. 8.
[†] See newspapers of July, 1789 (in "Histoire Parlementaire," ii. 35), etc.

to look upon is this same business of revolt under all its aspects; but how infinitely more so, when it takes the aspect of military mutiny! The very implement of rule and restraint, whereby all the rest was managed and held in order, has become precisely the frightfulest immeasurable implement of misrule; like the element of Fire, our indispensable all-ministering servant, when it gets the *mastery*, and becomes conflagration. Discipline we called a kind of miracle; in fact, is it not miraculous how one man moves hundreds of thousands; each unit of whom, it may ·be, loves him not, and singly fears him not, yet has to obey him, to go hither or go thither, to march and halt, to give death, and even to receive it, as if a Fate had spoken; and the word-of-command becomes, almost in the literal sense, a magic-word?

780. Which magic-word, again, if it be once *forgotten*; the spell of it once broken! The legions of assiduous ministering spirits rise on you now as menacing fiends; your free orderly arena becomes a tumult-place of the Nether Pit, and the hapless magician is rent limb from limb. Military mobs are mobs with muskets in their hands; and also with death hanging over their heads, for death is the penalty of disobedience, and they have disobeyed. And now if all mobs are properly frenzies, and work frantically with mad fits of hot and cold, fierce rage alternating so incoherently with panic terror, consider what your military mob will be, with such a conflict of duties and penalties, whirled between remorse and fury, and, for the hot fit, loaded firearms in its hand! To the soldier himself, revolt is frightful, and oftenest perhaps pitiable; and yet so dangerous, it can only be hated, cannot be pitied. An anomalous class of mortals these poor Hired Killers! With a frankness, which to the Moralist in these times seems surprising, they have sworn to become machines; and nevertheless they are still partly men. Let no prudent person in authority remind them of this latter fact; but always let force, let injustice above all, stop short clearly on *this* side of the rebounding-point! Soldiers, as we often say, do revolt: were it not so, several things which are transient in this world might be perennial.

781. Over and above the general quarrel which all sons of Adam maintain with their lot here below, the grievances of the French soldiery reduce themselves to two. First, that their Officers are Aristocrats; secondly, that they cheat them of their Pay. Two grievances; or rather we might say one, capable of becoming a hundred; for in that single first proposition, that the Officers are Aristocrats, what a multitude of corollaries lie ready! It is a bottomless ever-flowing fountain of grievances this; what you may call a general raw-material of grievance, wherefrom individual grievance after grievance will daily body itself forth. Nay there will even be a kind of comfort in getting it, from time to time, so embodied. Peculation of one's Pay. It is embodied; made tangible, made denounceable; exhalable, if only in angry words.

782. For unluckily that grand fountain of grievances does exist; Aristocrats almost all our Officers necessarily are; they have it in the blood and bone. By the law of the case no man can pretend to be the pitifulest lieutenant of militia till he have first verified, to the satisfaction of the Lion-King, a Nobility of four generations. Not nobility only, but four generations of it: this latter is the improvement hit upon, in comparatively late years, by a certain War-minister much pressed for commissions.* An improvement which did relieve the oppressed War-minister, but which split France still further into yawning contrasts of Commonalty and Nobility, nay of

* Dampmartin. "Evénemens," i. 89.

new Nobility and old; as if already with your new and old, and then with your old, older and oldest, there were not contrasts and discrepancies enough; —the general clash whereof men now see and hear, and in the singular whirlpool, all contrasts gone together to the bottom! Gone to the bottom or going; with uproar, without return, going everywhere save in the Military section of things; and there, it may be asked, can they hope to continue always at the top? Apparently, not.

783. It is true, in a time of external Peace, when there is no fighting, but only drilling, this question, How you rise from the ranks, may seem theoretical rather. But in reference to the Rights of Man it is continually practical. The soldier has sworn to be faithful not to the King only, but to the Law and the Nation. Do our commanders love the Revolution? ask all soldiers. Unhappily no, they hate it, and love the Counter-Revolution. Young epauletted men, with quality-blood in them, poisoned with quality-pride, do sniff openly, with indignation struggling to become contempt, at our Rights of Man, as at some new-fangled cobweb, which shall be brushed down again. Old Officers, more cautious, keep silent, with closed uncurled lips; but one guesses what is passing within. Nay who knows, how, under the plausiblest word of command, might lie Counter-Revolution itself, sale to Exiled Princes and the Austrian Kaiser; treacherous Aristocrats hoodwinking the small insight of us common men?—In such manner works that general raw-material of grievance; disastrous; instead of trust and reverence, breeding hate, endless suspicion, the impossibility of commanding and obeying. And now when this second more tangible grievance has articulated itself universally in the mind of the common man: Peculation of his Pay! Peculation of the despicablest sort does exist, and has long existed; but unless the new-declared Rights of Man, and all rights whatsoever, be a cobweb, it shall no longer exist.

784. The French Military System seems dying a sorrowful suicidal death. Nay more, citizen, as is natural, ranks himself against citizen in this cause. The soldier finds audience, of numbers and sympathy unlimited, among the Patriot lower-classes. Nor are the higher wanting to the officer. The officer still dresses and perfumes himself for such sad unemigrated soirée as there may still be; and speaks his woes,—which woes, are they not Majesty's and Nature's? Speaks, at the same time, his gay defiance, his firm-set resolution. Citizens, still more Citizenesses, see the right and the wrong; not the Military System alone will die by suicide, but much along with it. As was said, there is yet possible a deeper overturn than any yet witnessed: that deepest upturn of the black-burning sulphurous stratum whereon all rests and grows!

785. But how these things may act on the rude soldier-mind, with its military pedantries, its inexperience of all that lies off the parade-ground; inexperience as of a child, yet fierceness of a man, and vehemence of a Frenchman! It is long that secret communings in mess-room and guard-room, sour looks, thousandfold petty vexations between commander and· commanded, measure everywhere the weary military day. Ask Captain Dampmartin; an authentic, ingenious literary officer of horse; who loves the Reign of Liberty, after a sort: yet has had his heart grieved to the quick many times. in the hot South-Western region and elsewhere; and has seen riot, civil battle by daylight and by torchlight, and anarchy hatefuler than death. How insubordinate Troopers, with drink in their heads, meet Captain Dampmartin and another on the ramparts, where there is no escape or side-path; and make military

salute punctually, for we look calm on them; yet make it in a snappish, almost insulting manner; how one morning they "leave all their chamois-shirts" and superfluous buffs, which they are tired of, laid in piles at the Captains' doors; whereat "we laugh," as the ass does eating thistles: nay how they "knot two forage-cords together," with universal noisy cursing, with evident intent to hang the Quartermaster:—all this the worthy Captain, looking on it through the ruddy-and-sable of fond regretful memory, has flowingly written down.* Men growl in vague discontent; officers fling up their commissions and emigrate in disgust.

786. Or let us ask another literary Officer; not yet Captain; Sublieutenant only, in the Artillery Regiment La Fère: a young man of twenty-one; not unentitled to speak; the name of him is *Napoleon Bonaparte.* To such height of Sublieutenancy has he now got promoted, from Brienne School, five years ago; "being found qualified in mathematics by La Place." He is lying at Auxonne, in the West, in these months; not sumptuously lodged—"in the house of a Barber, to whose wife he did not pay the customary degree of respect;" or even over at the Pavillon, in a chamber with bare walls; the only furniture an indifferent "bed without curtains, two chairs, and in the recess of a window a table covered with books and papers; his Brother Louis sleeps on a coarse mattress in an adjoining room." However, he is doing something great: writing his first Book or Pamphlet,—eloquent vehement "Letter to M. Matteo Buttafuoco," our Corsican Deputy, who is not a Patriot, but an Aristocrat unworthy of Deputyship. Joly of Dole is Publisher. The literary Sublieutenant corrects the proofs: "sets out on foot from Auxonne every morning at four o'clock, for Dole: after looking over the proofs, he partakes of an extremely frugal breakfast with Joly, and immediately prepares for returning to his Garrison; where he arrives before noon, having thus walked above twenty miles in the course of the morning."

787. This Sublieutenant can remark that, in drawing-rooms, on streets, on highways, at inns, everywhere men's minds are ready to kindle into a flame. That a Patriot, if he appear in the drawing-room, or amid a group of officers, is liable enough to be discouraged, so great is the majority against him; but no sooner does he get into the street, or among the soldiers, than he feels again as if the whole Nation were with him. That after the famous Oath, "To the King, to the Nation, and Law," there was a great change; that before this, if ordered to fire on the people, he for one would have done it in the King's name; but that after this, in the Nation's name, he would not have done it. Likewise that the Patriot officers, more numerous too in the Artillery and Engineers than elsewhere, were few in number; yet that having the soldiers on their side, they ruled the regiment; and did often deliver the Aristocrat brother officer out of peril and strait. One day, for example, "a member of our own mess roused the mob, by singing, from the windows of our dining-room. 'O Richard, O my King;' and I had to snatch him from their fury."[†]

788. All which let the reader multiply by 10,000; and spread it with slight variations, over all the camps and garrisons of France. The French Army seems on the verge of universal mutiny.

789. Universal mutiny! There is in that what may well make Patriot Constitutionalism and an a pass, be forthwith disbanded, the whole Two Hundred and Eighty Thousand of them; and organized anew.* Impossible this, in so sudden a manner! cry all men. And yet literally, answer we, it is inevitable, in one manner or another. Such an army, with its four-generation Nobles, its peculated Pay, and men knotting forage-cords to hang their Quartermaster, cannot subsist beside such a Revolution. Your alternative is a slow-pining chronic dissolution and new organization; or a swift decisive one; the agonies spread over years, or concentred into an hour. With a Mirabeau for Minister or Governor, the latter had been the choice; with no Mirabeau for Governor, it will naturally be the former.

CHAPTER III.
BOUILLÉ AT METZ.

790. To Bouillé, in his North-Eastern circle, none of these things are altogether hid. Many times flight over the marches gleam out on him as a last guidance in such bewilderment; nevertheless he continues here: struggling always to hope the best, not from new organization, but from happy Counter-Revolution and return to the old. For the rest, it is clear to him that this same National Federation, and universal swearing and fraternizing of People and Soldiers, has done "incalculable mischief." So much that fermented secretly has hereby got vent, and become open: National Guards and Soldiers of the line, solemnly embracing one another on all parade-fields, drinking, swearing patriotic oaths, fall into disorderly street-processions, constitutional unmilitary exclamations and hurrahing. On which account the Regiment Picardie, for one, has to be drawn out in the square of the barracks, here at Metz, and sharply harangued by the General himself; but expresses penitence.[†]

791. Far and near, as accounts testify, insubordination has begun grumbling louder and louder. Officers have been seen shut up in their mess-rooms; assaulted with clamorous demands, not without menaces. The insubordinate ringleader is dismissed with "yellow furlough," yellow infamous thing they call cartouche jaune: but ten new ringleaders rise in his stead, and the yellow cartouche ceases to be thought disgraceful. "Within a fortnight," or at furthest a month, of that sublime Feast of Pikes, the whole French Army, demanding Arrears, forming Reading Clubs, frequenting Popular Societies, is in a state which Bouillé can call by no name but that of mutiny. Bouillé knows it as few do; and speaks by dire experience. Take one instance instead of many.

792. It is still an early day of August, the precise date now undiscoverable, when Bouillé, about to set out for the waters of Aix-la-Chapelle, is once more suddenly summoned to the barracks of Metz. The soldiers stand ranged in fighting order, muskets loaded, the officers all there on compulsion; and required with many-voiced emphasis to have their arrears paid. Picardie was penitent; but we see it has relapsed: the wide space bristles and lours with mere mutinous armed men. Brave Bouillé advances to the nearest Regiment, opens his commanding lips to harangue; obtains nothing but querulous-indignant Assembly shudder. Something behooves to be done; yet what to do no man can tell. Mirabeau proposes even that the Soldiery, having come to such nant discordance, and the sound of so many thousand livres legally due. The moment is trying; there are some 10,000 soldiers now in Metz, and one spirit seems to have spread among them.

* Dampmartin, "Evénemens," i. 122-146.

* Norvins, "Histoire de Napoléon," i. 47; Las Cases "Mémoires" (translated into Hazlitt's "Life of Napoleon," i. 23-31).

† Moniteur, 1790, No. 236.

* Bouillé, "Mémoires," i. 113.

793. Bouillé is firm as the adamant; but what shall he do? A German Regiment, named of Salm, is thought to be of better temper: nevertheless Salm too many have heard of the precept, "Thou shalt not steal," Salm too may know that money is money. Bouillé walks trustfully toward the Regiment de Salm, speaks trustful words; but here again is answered by the cry of forty-four thousand livres odd sous. A cry waxing more and more vociferous, as Salm's humor mounts; which cry, as it will produce no cash or promise of cash, ends in the wide simultaneous whirr of shouldered muskets, and a determined quick-time march on the part of Salm—toward its Colonel's house, in the next street, there to seize the colors and military chest. Thus does Salm, for its part; strong in the faith that meum is not tuum, that fair speeches are not forty-four thousand livres odd sous.

794. Unrestrainable! Salm tramps to military time, quick consuming the way. Bouillé and the officers, drawing sword, have to dash into double-quick pas-de-charge, or unmilitary running; to get the start; to station themselves on the outer stair-case, and stand there with what of death-defiance and sharp steel they have: Salm truculently coiling itself up, rank after rank, opposite them, in such humor as we can fancy, which happily has not yet mounted to the murder-pitch. There will Bouillé stand, certain at least of one man's purpose: in grim calmness, awaiting the issue. What the intrepidest of men and generals can do is done. Bouillé, though there is a barricading picket at each end of the street, and death under his eyes, contrives to send for a Dragoon Regiment with orders to charge: the dragoon officers mount; the dragoon men will not: hope is none there for him. The street, as we say, barricaded; the Earth all shut out, only the indifferent heavenly Vault overhead: perhaps here or there a timorous householder peering out of window, with prayer for Bouillé; copious Rascality, on the pavement, with prayer for Salm: there do the two parties stand;—like chariots locked in a narrow thoroughfare; like locked wrestlers at a dead-grip! For two hours they stand: Bouillé's sword glittering in his hand, adamantine resolution clouding his brow: for two hours by the clocks of Metz. Moody-silent stands Salm, with occasional clangor; but does not fire. Rascality, from time to time, urges some grenadier to level his musket at the General; who looks on it as a bronze general would: and always some corporal or other strikes it up.

795. In such remarkable attitude, standing on that staircase for two hours, does brave Bouillé, long a shadow, dawn on us visibly out of the dimness, and become a person. For the rest, since Salm has not shot him at the first instant, and since in himself there is no variableness, the danger will diminish. The Mayor, "a man infinitely respectable," with his Municipals and tricolor sashes, finally gains entrance; remonstrates, perorates, promises: gets Salm persuaded home to its barracks. Next day, our respectable Mayor lending the money, the officers pay down the half of the demand in ready cash. With which liquidation Salm pacifies itself; and for the present all is hushed up, as much as may be.*

796. Such scenes as this of Metz, or preparations and demonstrations toward such, are universal over France: Dampmartin, with his knotted forage-cords and piled chamois-jackets, is at Strasburg, in the South-East; in those same days or rather nights, Royal Champagne is "shouting Vive la Nation, au diable les Aristocrats, with some thirty lit candles," at Hesdin, on the far North-West. "The garrison of

* Bouillé, i. 140–45.

Bitche," Deputy Rewbell is sorry to state, "went out of the town with drums beating; deposed its officers; and then returned into the town, saber in hand."* Ought not a National Assembly to occupy itself with these objects? Military France is everywhere full of sour inflammatory humor, which exhales itself fuliginously, this way or that: a whole continent of smoking-flax; which, blown on here or there by any angry wind, might so easily start into a blaze, into a continent of fire.

797. Constitutional Patriotism is in deep natural alarm at these things. The august Assembly sits diligently deliberating; dare nowise resolve, with Mirabeau, on an instantaneous disbandment and extinction; finds that a course of palliatives is easier. But at least and lowest, this grievance of the Arrears shall be rectified. A plan much noised of in those days, under the name "Decree of the Sixth of August," has been devised for that. Inspectors shall visit all armies; and, with certain elected corporals and "soldiers able to write," verify what arrears and peculations do lie due, and make them good. Well if in this way the smoky heat be cooled down; if it be not, as we say ventilated overmuch, or, by sparks and collision somewhere, sent up!

CHAPTER IV.

ARREARS AT NANCI.

798. We are to remark, however, that of all districts, this of Bouillé's seems the inflammablist. It was always to Bouillé and Metz that royalty would fly: Austria lies near; here more than elsewhere must the disunited People look over the borders, into a dim sea of Foreign Politics and Diplomacies, with hope or apprehension, with mutual exasperation.

799. It was but in these days that certain Austrian troops, marching peaceably across an angle of this region, seemed an Invasion realized; and there rushed toward Stenai, with musket on shoulder, from all the winds, some thirty thousand National Guards, to inquire what the matter was.† A matter of mere diplomacy it proved; the Austrian Kaiser, in haste to get to Belgium, had bargained for this short cut. The infinite dim movement of European Politics waved a skirt over these spaces, passing on its way; like the passing shadow of a condor, and such a winged flight of thirty thousand, with mixed cackling and crowing, rose in consequence! For, in addition to all; this people, as we said, is much divided: Aristocrats abound; Patriotism has both Aristocrats and Austrians to watch. It is Lorraine, this region; not so illuminated as old France; it remembers ancient Feudalisms; any within man's memory it had a Court and King of its own, or indeed the splendor of a Court and King, without the burden. Then, contrariwise, the Mother Society, which sits in the Jacobins Church at Paris, has Daughters in the Towns here; shrill-tongued, driven acrid: consider how the memory of good King Stanislaus, and ages of Imperial Feudalism, may comport with this New acrid Evangel, and what a virulence of discord there may be! In all which, the Soldiery officers on one side, private men on the other, takes part, and now indeed principal part; a Soldiery, moreover, all the hotter here as it lies the denser, the frontier Province requiring more of it.

800. So stands Lorraine: but the capital City more especially so. The pleasant City of Nanci, which faded Feudalism loves, where King Stanislaus personally dwelt and shone, has an Aristocrat Munici-

* Moniteur (in "Histoire Parlementaire," vii. 29).
† Moniteur, Seance du 9 Aout 1790.

pality, and then also á Daughter Society: it has some 40,000 divided souls of population; and three large Regiments, one of which is Swiss Château-Vieux dear to Patriotism ever since it refused fighting, or was thought to refuse, in the Bastille days. Here unhappily all evil influences seem to meet concentred, here, of all places, may jealousy and heat evolve itself. These many months, accordingly, man has been set against man, Washed against Unwashed; Patriot Soldier against Aristocrat Captain, ever the more bitterly: and a long score of grudges has been running up.

801. Namable grudges, and likewise unnamable: for there is a punctual nature in Wrath; and daily, were there but glances of the eye, tones of the voice, and minutest commissions or omissions, it will jot down somewhat, to account, under the head of sundries, which always swells the sum-total. For example, in April last, in those times of preliminary Federation, when National Guards and Soldiers were everywhere swearing brotherhood, and all France was locally federating, preparing for the National Feast of Pikes, it was observed that these Nanci Officers threw cold water on the whole brotherly business; that they first hung back from appearing at the Nanci Federation; then did appear, but in mere rédingote and undress, with scarcely a clean shirt on; nay that one of them, as the National Colors flaunted by in that solemn moment, did, without visible necessity, take occasion to *spit.*[*]

802. Small "sundries as er journal," but then incessant ones! The Aristocrat Municipality, pretending to be Constitutional, keeps mostly quiet; not so the Daughter of Society, the 5,000 adult male Patriots of the place, still less than 5,000 female: not so the young, whiskered or whiskerless, four-generation Noblesse in epaulettes; the grim Patriot Swiss or Château-Vieux, effervescent infantry of Regiment du Roi, hot troopers of Mestre-de-Camp! Walled Nanci, which stands so bright and trim, with its straight streets, spacious squares, and Stainslaw's Architecture, on the fruitful alluvium of the Meurthe; so bright, amid the yellow corn-fields in these Reaper-Months,—is inwardly but a den of discord, anxiety, inflammability, not far from exploding. Let Bouillé look to it. If that universal military heat, which we liken to a vast continent of smoking flax, do anywhere take fire, his beard, here in Lorraine and Nanci, may the most readily of all get singed by it.

803. Bouillé, for his part, is busy enough, but only with the general superintendence; getting his pacified Salm, and all other still tolerable Regiments, marched out of Metz, to Southward towns and villages; to rural Cantonments as at Vic, Marsal and thereabout, by the still waters; where is plenty of horse-forage, sequestered parade-ground, and the soldier's speculative faculty can be stilled by drilling. Salm, as we said, received only half payment of arrears; naturally not without grumbling. Nevertheless that scene of the drawn sword may, after all, have raised Bouillé in the mind of Salm; for men and soldiers love intrepidity and swift inflexible decision, even when they suffer by it. As indeed is not this fundamentally the quality of qualities for a man? A quality which by itself is next to nothing, since inferior animals, asses, dogs, even mules have it; yet, in due combination, it is the indispensable basis of all.

804. Of Nanci and its heats, Bouillé, commander of the whole, knows nothing special: understands generally that the troops in that City are perhaps the *worst.*[†] The Officers there have it all, as they have long had it, to themselves; and unhappily seem] to

manage it ill. "Fifty yellow furloughs," given out in one batch, do surely betoken difficulties. But what was Patriotism to think of certain light-fencing Fusileers "set on," or supposed to be set on, "to insult the Grenadier-club,—considerate speculative Grenadiers and that reading-room of theirs? With shoutings, with hootings; till the speculative Grenadier drew his side-arms too; and there ensued battery and duels! Nay more, are not swashbucklers of the same stamp "sent out" visibly, or sent out presumably, now in the dress of Soldiers, to pick quarrels with the Citizens; now, disguised as Citizens, to pick quarrels with the Soldiers? For a certain Roussière, expert in fence, was taken in the very fact; four Officers (presumably of tender years) hounding him on, who thereupon fled precipitately! Fence-master Roussière, haled to the guard-house, and sentence of three mouths' imprisonment: but his comrades demanded "yellow furlough" for *him* of all persons; nay thereafter they produced him on parade; capped him in paper-helmet, inscribed *Iscariot*; marched him to the gate of the City; and there sternly commanded him to vanish forevermore.

805. On all which suspicions, accusations, and noisy procedure, and on enough of the like continually accumulating, the Officer could not but look with disdainful indignation; perhaps disdainfully express the same in words, and "soon after fly over to the Austrians."

806. So that when it here, as elsewhere, comes to the question of Arrears, the humor and procedure is of the bitterest: Regiment Mestre-de-Camp getting, amid loud clamor, some three gold louis a-man,—which have, as usual, to be borrowed from the Municipality; Swiss Château-Vieux applying for the like, but getting instead instantaneous courrois, or cat-o'-nine-tails, with subsequent insufferable hisses from the women and children: Regiment du Roi, sick of hope deferred, at length seizing its military chest, and marching to its quarters, but next day marching it back again, through streets all struck silent:—unordered paradings and clamors, not without strong liquor: objurgation, insubordination; your military ranked Arrangement going all (as the Typographers say of set types, in a similar case) rapidly *to pie!*[*] Such is Nanci in these early days of August; the sublime Feast of Pikes not yet a month old.

807. Constitutional Patriotism, at Paris and elsewhere, may well quake at the news. War-Minister Latour du Pin runs breathless to the National Assembly, with a written message that "all is burning, tout brûle, tout presse." The National Assembly, on the spur of the instant, renders such Decret, and "order to submit and repent," as he requires; if it will avail anything. On the other hand, Journalism, through all its throats, gives hoarse outery, condemnatory, elegiac-applausive. The Forty-eight Sections lift up voices; sonorous Brewer, or call him now *Colonel* Santerre, is not silent, in the Faubourg Saint-Antoine. For, meanwhile, the Nanci Soldiers have sent a Deputation of Ten, furnished with documents and proofs; who will tell another story than the "all-is-burning" one. Which deputed Ten, before ever they reach the Assembly Hall, assiduous Latour du Pin picks up, and on warrant of Mayor Bailly, claps in prison! Most 'unconstitutionally; for they had officers' furloughs. Whereupon Saint-Antoine, in indignant uncertainty of the future, closes its shops. In Bouillé a traitor, then, sold to Austria? In that case, these poor private sentinels have revolted mainly out of Patriotism?

808. New Deputation, Deputation of National Guardsmen now, sets forth from Nanci to enlighten

---

[*] "Deux Amis," v. 217.
[†] Bouillé, i. c. 9.

[*] "Deux Amis," v. c. 8.

the Assembly. It meets the old deputed Ten returning, quite unexpectedly *unchanged*: and proceeds thereupon with better prospects; but effects nothing. Deputations, Government Messengers, Orderlies at hand-gallop, Alarms, thousand-voiced Rumors, go vibrating continually; backward and forward,— scattering distraction. Not till the last week of August does M. de Malseigne, selected as Inspector, get down to the scene of mutiny: with Authority, with cash, and "Decree of the Sixth of August." He now shall see these Arrears liquidated, justice done, or at least quashed.

CHAPTER V.

INSPECTOR MALSEIGNE.

809. Of Inspector Malseigne we discern, by direct light, that he is "of Herculean stature;" and infer, with probability, that he is of truculent mustachioed aspect,—for *Royalist* Officers now leave the upper lip unshaven; that he is of indomitable bull-heart; and also, unfortunately, of thick bull-head.

810. On Tuesday, the 24th of August, 1790, he opens session as Inspecting Commissioner; meets those "elected corporals, and soldiers that can write." He finds the accounts of Château-Vieux to be complex; to require delay and reference: he takes to haranguing, to reprimanding; ends amid audible grumbling. Next morning, he resumes session, not at the town-hall as prudent Municipals counselled, but once more at the barracks. Unfortunately Château-Vieux, grumbling all night, will now bear of no delay or reference; from reprimanding on his part, it goes to bullying,—answered with continual cries of " Jugez tout de suite (Judge it at once) ;" whereupon M. de Malseigne will off in a huff. But lo, Château-Vieux, swarming all about the barrack-court, has sentries at every gate; M. de Malseigne, demanding egress, cannot get it, not though Commandant Denoue backs him, can get only " Jugez tout de snite." Here is a nodus !

811. Bull-hearted M. de Malseigne draws his sword; and will force egress. Confused splutter. M. de Malseigne's sword breaks: he snatches Commandant Denoue's: the sentry is wounded. M. de Malseigne, whom one is loth to kill, does force egress,— followed by Château-Vieux all in disarray : a spectacle to Nanci. M. de Malseigne walks at a sharp pace, yet never runs; wheeling from time to time, with menaces and movements of fence; and so reaches Denoue's house, unhurt; which house Château-Vieux, in an agitated manner invests,—hindered as yet from entering, by a crowd of officers formed on the staircase. M. de Malseigne retreats by back ways to the Town-hall, flustered though undaunted; amid an escort of National Guards. From the Town-hall he, on the morrow, emits fresh orders, fresh plans of settlement with Château-Vieux ; to none of which will Château-Vieux listen: whereupon he finally, amid noise enough, emits order that Château-Vieux shall march on the morrow morning, and quarter at Sarre Louis. Château-Vieux flatly refuses marching; M. de Malseigne "takes *act*," due notarial protest, of such refusal,—if happily that may avail him.

812. This is the end of Thursday ; and, indeed, of M. de Malseigne's Inspectorship, which has lasted some fifty hours. To such length, in fifty hours, has he unfortunately brought it. Mestre-de-Camp and Regiment du Roi hang, as it were, fluttering; Château-Vieux is clean gone, in what way we see. Over-night, an Aid-de-Camp of Lafayette's, stationed here for such emergency, sends swift emissaries far and wide to summon National Guards. The slumber of the country is broken by clattering hoofs, by loud fraternal knockings; everywhere the Constitutional Patriot must clutch his 'fighting-gear, and take the road for Nanci.

813. And thus the Herculean Inspector has sat all Thursday, among terror-struck Municipals, a center of confused noise : all Thursday, Friday, and till Saturday toward noon. Château-Vieux, in spite of the notarial protest, will not march a step. As many as 4,000 National Guards are dropping or pouring in, uncertain what is expected of them, still more uncertain what will be obtained of them. For all is uncertainty, commotion, and suspicion: there goes a word that Bouillé, beginning to bestir himself in the rural Cantonments eastward, is but a Royalist traitor; that Château-Vieux and Patriotism are sold to Austria, of which latter M. de Malseigne is probably some agent. Mestre-de-Camp and Roi flutter still more questionably : Château-Vieux, far from marching, "waves red flags out of two carriages," in a passionate manner, along the streets; and next morning answers its Officers: "Pay us, then; and we will march with you to the world's end !"

814. Under which circumstances, toward noon on Saturday, M. de Malseigne thinks it were good perhaps to inspect the ramparts,—on horseback. He mounts, accordingly, with escort of three troopers. At the gate of the City, he bids two of them wait for his return; and with the third, a trooper to be depended upon, he—gallops off for Lunéville ; where lies a certain Carbineer Regiment not yet in a mutinous state! The two left troopers soon get uneasy; discover how it is, and give the alarm. Mestre-de-Camp, to the number of a hundred, saddles in frantic haste, as if sold to Austria; gallops out pell-mell in chase of its Inspector. And so they spur, and the Inspector spurs; careering, with noise and jingle, up the [valley of the River Meurthe, toward Lunéville and the midday sun : through an astonished country ; indeed almost to their own astonishment.

815. What a hunt; Actæon-like:—which Actæon de Malseigne happily *gains*. To arms, ye Carbineers of Lunéville : to chastise mutinous men, insulting your General Officers, insulting your own quarters; —above all things, fire *soon*, lest there be parleying and ye refuse to fire ! The Carbineers fire soon, exploding upon the first strugglers of Mestre-de-Camp; who shriek at the very flash, and fall back hastily on Nanci, in a state not far from distraction. Panic and fury ; sold to Austria without an *if*; so much per regiment, the very sums can be specified ; and traitorous Malseigne is fled ! Help, O Heaven ; help, thou Earth ;—ye unwashed Patriots; ye too are sold. like us !

816. Effervescent Regiment du Roi primes its firelocks, Mestre-de-Camp saddles, wholly Commandant Denoue is seized, is flung in prison with a "canvas-shirt (sarreau de toile)" about him : Château-Vieux burst up the magazines; distributes "3,000 fusils" to a Patriot people: Austria shall have a hot bargain. Alas, the unhappy hunting-dogs, as we said, have *hunted away* their huntsman ; and do now run howling and baying, on what trail they know not; nigh rabid !

817. And so there is tumultuous march of men, through the night: with halt on the heights of Flinval, whence Lunéville can be seen all illuminated. Then there is parley, at four in the morning ; and reparley; finally there is agreement; the Carbineers gave in ; Malseigne is surrendered, with apologies on all sides. After weary confused hours, he is even got under way; the Lunévillers all turning out, in the idle Sunday, to see such departure : home-going of mutinous Mestre-de-Camp with its Inspector captive. Mestre-de-Camp accordingly marches; the

Lunévillers look. See! at the corner of the first street, our Inspector bounds off again, bull-hearted as he is; amid the slash of sabers, the crackle of musketry; and escapes, full gallop, with only a ball-lodged in his buff-*jerkin*. The Herculean man! And yet it is an escape to no purpose. For the Carbineers, to whom after the hardest Sunday's ride on record, he has come circling back, "stand deliberating by their nocturnal watch-fires;" deliberating of Austria, of traitors, and the rage of Mestre-de-Camp. So that, on the whole, the next sight we have is that of M. de Malseigne, on the Monday afternoon, firing bull-hearted through the streets of Nanci; in open carriage, a soldier standing over him with drawn sword; amid the "furies of the women," hedges of National Guards, and confusion of Babel: to the Prison beside Commandant Denoue! That finally is the lodging of Inspector Malseigne.*

818. Surely it is time Bouillé were drawing near. The Country all round, alarmed with watch-fires, illuminated towns, and marching and rout, has been sleepless theseseveral nights. Nanci, with its uncertainNational Guards, with its distributed fusils, mutinous soldiers, black panic and red-hot ire, is not a City but a Bedlam.

CHAPTER VI.

BOUILLE AT NANCI.

819. Haste with help, thou brave Bouillé: if swift help come not, all is now verily "burning;" and may burn,—to what lengths and breadths! Much, in these hours, depends on Bouillé; as it shall now fare with him, the whole future may be this way or be that. If, for example, he were to loiter dubitating, and not come; if he were to come, and fail; the whole Soldiery of France to blaze into mutiny, National Guards going some this way, some that; and Royalism to draw its rapier, and Sansculottism to snatch its pike; and the Spirit of Jacobinism, as yet young, girt with sun-rays, togrow instantaneously mature, grit with hell-fire,—as mortals, in one night of deadly crises, have had their heads turned gray!

820. Brave Bouillé is advancing fast, with the old inflexibility; gathering himself, unhappily "in small affluences," from East, from West and North; and now on Tuesday morning, the last day of the month, he stands all concentred, unhappily still in small force at the village of Frouarde, within some few miles. Son of Adam with a more dubious task before him is not in the world this Tuesday morning. A weltering inflammable sea of doubt and peril, and Bouillé sure of simply one thing, his own determination. Which one thing, indeed, may be worth many. He puts a most firm face on the matter: "Submission, or unsparing battle and destruction; twenty-four hours to make your choice;" this was the tenor of his Proclamation; thirty copies of which he sent yesterday to Nanci:—all which, we find, were intercepted and not posted.†

821. Nevertheless, at half-past eleven this morning, seemingly by way of answer, there does wait on him at Frouarde some Deputation from the mutinous Regiments, from the Nanci Municipals, to see what can be done. Bouillé receives this Deputation "in a large open court adjoining his lodging:" pacified Salm, and the rest, attend also, being invited to do it,—all happily still in the right humor. The Mutineers pronounce themselves with a decisiveness, which to Bouillé seems insolence; and happily to

Salm also. Salm, forgetful of the Metz staircase and saber, demands that the scoundrels "be hanged" there and then. Bouillé represses the hanging; but answers that mutinous Soldiers have one course, and not more than one: To liberate, with heartfelt contrition, Messieurs Denoue and De Malseigne; to get ready forthwith for marching off, whither he shall order; and "submit and repent," as the National Assembly has decreed, as he yesterday did in thirty printed placards proclaim. These are his terms, unalterable as the decrees of Destiny. Which terms as they, the Mutineer deputies, seemingly do not accept, it were good for them to vanish from this spot, and even to do it promptly; with him too, in few instants, the word will be, Forward! The Mutineer deputies vanish, not unpromptly; the Municipal ones, anxious beyond right for their own individualities, prefer abiding with Bouillé.

822. Brave Bouillé, though he puts a most firm face on the matter, knows his position full well: how at Nanci, what with rebellious soldiers, with uncertain National Guards, and so many distributed fusils, their rage and roar some 10,000 fighting men; while with himself is scarcely the third part of that number. In National Guards also uncertain, in more pacified Regiments,—for the present, full of rage, and clamor to march; but whose rage and clamor may next moment take such a fatal *new* figure. On the top of one uncertain billow, therewith to calm billows! Bouillé must "abandon himself to Fortune;" who is said sometimes to favor the brave. At half-past twelve, the Mutineer deputies having vanished, our drums beat; we march; for Nanci! Let Nanci bethink itself, then; for Bouillé has thought and determined.

823. And yet how shall Nanci think: not a City but a Bedlam! Grim Château-Vieux is for defense to the death; forces the Municipality to order, by tap of drum, all citizens acquainted with artillery to turn out, and assist in managing the cannon. On the other hand, effervescent Regiment du Roi is drawn up in its barracks: quite disconsolate, hearing the humor. Salm is in, and ejaculates doefully from its thousand throats: "La loi, la loi (Law, law)!" Mestre-de-Camp blusters, with profane swearing, in mixed terror and furor; National Guards look this way and that, not knowing what to do. What a Bedlam-City: as many plans as heads; all ordering, none obeying: quiet none,—except the Dead, who sleep underground, having *done* their fighting.

824 And, behold, Bouillé proves as good as his word: "at half-past two" scouts report that he is within half a league of the gates; rattling along, with cannon and array; breathing nothing but destruction. A new Deputation, Municipals, Mutineers, Officers, goes out to meet him; with passionate entreaty for yet one other hour. Bouillé grants an hour. Then, at the end thereof, no Denoue or Malseigne appearing as promised, he rolls his drums, and again takes the road. Toward four o'clock the terror-struck Townsmen may see him face to face. His cannons rattle there, in their carriages; his vanguard is within thirty paces of the Gate Stanislaus. Onward like a Planet, by appointed times, by law of Nature! What next? Lo. flag of truce and chamade, conjuration to halt: Malseigne and Denoue are on the street, coming hither; the soldiers all repentant, ready to submit and march! Adamantine Bouillé's look alters not; yet the word *Halt* is given: gladder moment he never saw. Joy of joys! Malseigne and Denoue do verily issue; escorted by National Guards; from streets all frantic, with sale to Austria and so forth: they salute Bouillé, unscathed. Bouillé steps aside to speak with them, and with other heads of the Town there; having already or-

---

* "Deux Amis," v 206-251: newspapers and documents (in "Histoire Parlementaire," vii. 59-162).

* Compare Bouillé. "Mémoires," i. 153-176; "Deux Amis," v. 251-271; "Histoire Parlementaire" ut supra.

dered by what Gates and Routes the mutineer Regiments shall file out.

825. Such colloquy with these two General Officers and other principal Townsmen was natural enough; nevertheless one wishes Bouillé had postponed it, and *not* stepped aside. Such tumultuous inflammable masses, tumbling along, making way for each other; this of keen nitrous oxide, that of sulphurous fire-damp,—were, it not well to stand *between* them, keeping them well separate, till the space he cleared? Numerous stragglers of Château-Vieux and the rest have not marched with their main columns, which are filing out by their appointed Gates, taking station in the open meadows. National Guards are in a state of nearly distracted uncertainty; the populace, armed and unarmed, roll openly delirious,—betrayed, sold to the Austrians, sold to the Aristocrats. There are loaded cannon, with lit matches, among them, and Bonillé's vanguard is halted within thirty paces of the Gate. Command dwells not in that mad inflammable mass; which smolders and tumbles there, in blind smoky rage; which will not open the Gate when summoned; says it will open the cannon's throat sooner!—Cannonade not, O Friends, or be it through my body! cries heroic young Desilles, young Captain of Roi, clasping the murderous engine in his arms, and holding it. Château-Vieux Swiss, by main force, with oaths and menaces, wrench off the heroic youth; who undaunted, amid still louder oaths, seats himself on the touch-hole. Amid still louder oaths, with ever louder clangor,—and, alas, with the loud crackle of first one, and then of three other muskets; which explode into his body: which roll *it* in the dust,—and do also, in the loud madness of such moment, bring lit cannon-match to ready priming: and so, with one thunderous belch of grape shot, blast some fifty of Bouillé's vanguard into air!

826. Fatal! That sputter of the first musket-shot has kindled such a cannon-shot, such a death-blaze; and all is now red-hot madness, conflagration as of Tophet. With demoniac rage, the Bonillé vanguard storms through that Gate Stanislaus; with fiery sweep sweeps Mutiny clear away, to death, or into shelters and cellars, from which latter, again, Mutiny continues firing. The ranked Regiments hear it in their meadow; they rush back again through the nearest Gate; Bouillé gallops in, distracted, inaudible;—and now has begun in Nanci, as in that doomed Hall of the Nibelungen, "a murder grim and great."

827. Miserable: such scene of dismal aimless madness as the anger of Heaven but rarely permits among men! From cellar or from garret, from open street in front, from successive corners of cross-streets on each hand, Château-Vieux and Patriotism keep up the murderous rolling-fire, on murderous not Unpatriotic fires. Your blue National Captain, riddled with balls, one hardly knows on whose side fighting, requests to be laid on the colors to die: the patriotic Woman (name not given, deed surviving) screams to Château-Vieux that it must *not* fire the other cannon: and even flings a pail of water on it, since screaming avails not.* Thou shalt fight; thou shalt not fight; and with whom shalt thou fight! Could tumult awaken the old Dead, Burgundian Charles the Bold might stir from under that Rotunda of his: never since he, raging, sank in the ditches, and lost Life and Diamond, was such a noise heard here.

828. Three thousand, as some count, lie mangled, gory: the half of Château-Vieux has been shot, without need of Court-Martial. Cavalry, of Mestre-de-Camp, or their foes, can do little. Regiment du Roi was persuaded to its barracks; stands there palpitat-

ing. Bouillé, armed with the terrors of the Law, and favored of Fortune, finally triumphs. In two murderous hours, he has penetrated to the grand Squares dauntless, though with loss of forty officers and 500 men: the shattered remnants of Château-Vieux are seeking covert. Regiment du Roi, not effervescent, now, alas no, but *having* effervesced, will offer to ground its arms; will "march in a quarter of an hour." Nay these poor effervesced require "escort" to march with, and get it; though they are thousands strong, and have thirty ball-cartridges a man! The Sun is not yet down, when Peace, which might have come bloodless, has come bloody; the mutinous Regiments are on march, doleful, on their three Routes; and from Nanci rises wail of women and men, the voice of weeping and desolation; the City weeping for its slain who awaken not. These streets are empty but for victorious patrols.

829. Thus has Fortune, favoring the brave, dragged Bouillé, as himself says, out of such a frightful peril "by the hair of the head." An intrepid adamantine man, this Bouillé:—had *he* stood in old Broglie's place in those Bastille days, it might have been all different! He has extinguished mutiny, and immeasurable civil war. Not for nothing, as we see; yet at a rate which he and Constitutional Patriotism consider cheap. Nay, as for Bouillé, he, urged by subsequent contradiction which arose, declares coldly, it was rather against his own private mind, and more by public military rule of duty, that he did extinguish it*—immeasurable civil war being now the only chance. Urged, we say, by subsequent contradiction! Civil war, indeed, is Chaos; and in all vital Chaos there is new order shaping itself free, but what a faith this, that of all new Orders out of Chaos and Possibility of Man and his Universe, Louis Sixteenth and Two-Chamber Monarchy were precisely the one that would shape itself! It is like undertaking to throw deuce-ace, say only five hundred successive times, and *any* other throw to be fatal—for Bouillé. Rather thank Fortune and Heaven, always, thou intrepid Bouillé; and let contradiction go its way! Civil war, conflagrating universally over France at this moment, might have led to one thing or to another thing: meanwhile, to *quench* conflagration, wheresoever one finds it, wheresoever one can; this, in all times, is the rule for man and General Officer.

830. But at Paris, so agitated and divided, fancy how it went, when the continually vibrating Orderlies vibrated *thither* at hand-gallop, with such questionable news! High is the gratulation; and also deep the indignation. An august Assembly, by overwhelming majorities, passionately thanks Bouillé; a King's autograph, the voices of all Loyal, all Constitutional men run to the same tenor. A solemn National funeral-service, for the Law-defenders slain at Nanci, is said and sung in the Champ-de-Mars, Bailly, Lafayette, and National Guards, all except the few that protested, assist. With pomp and circumstance, with episcopal Calicoes in tricolor girdles, Altar of Fatherland smoking with cassolettes, or incense-kettles; the vast Champ-de-Mars wholly hung round with black mort-cloth—which mort-cloth and expenditure Marat thinks had better have been laid out in bread, in these dear days, and given to the hungry living Patriot.† On the other hand, living Patriotism, and Saint-Antoine, which we have seen noisily closing its shops and such-like, assembles now "to the number of 40,000;" and with loud cries, under the very windows of the thanking National Assembly, demands revenge for murdered

---

* "Deux Amis," v. 268.

* "Bouillé, i. 175.
† Ami du Peuple (in "Histoire Parlementaire" ubi supra).

Brothers, judgment on Bouillé, and instant dismissal of War-Minister Latour du Pin.

At sound and sight of which things, if not War-Minister Latour, yet "Adored Minister" Necker sees good, on the 3d of September, 1790, to withdraw softly, almost privily,—with an eye to the "recovery of his health." Home to native Switzerland; not as he last came; lucky to reach it alive! Fifteen months ago, we saw him coming, with escort of horse, with sound of clarion and trumpet; and now, at Arcissur-Aube, while he departs, unescorted, soundless, the Populace and Municipals stop him as a fugitive, are not unlike massacreing him as a traitor; the National Assembly, consulted on the matter, gives him free egress as a nullity. Such an unstable "drift-mold of Accident" is the substance of this lower world, for them that dwell in houses of clay; so, especially in hot regions and times, do the proudest palaces we build of it take wings, and become Sahara sand-palaces, spinning many-pillared in the whirlwind, and bury us under their sand!—

831. In spite of the 40,000, the National Assembly persists in its thanks; and Royalist Latour du Pin continues Minister. The 40,000 assembled next day, as loud as ever; roll toward Latour's Hotel; find cannon on the porch-steps with flambeau lit; and have to retire else-whither, and digest their spleen, or reabsorb it into the blood.

832. Over in Lorraine meanwhile, they of the distributed fusils, ringleaders of Mestre-de-Camp, of Roi, have got marked out for judgment;—yet shall never get judged. Briefer is the doom of Château-Vieux. Château-Vieux is, by Swiss law, given up for instant trial in Court-Martial of its own officers. Which Court-Martial, with all brevity (in not many hours), has hanged some Twenty-three, on conspicuous gibbets; marched some Three-score in chains to the Galleys; and so, to appearance, finished the matter off. Hanged men do cease forever from this Earth; but out of chains and the Galleys there may be resuscitation in triumph. Resuscitation for the chained Hero; and even for the chained Scoundrel or Semi-scoundrel! Scottish John Knox, such World-Hero as we know, sat once nevertheless pulling grim-taciturn at the oar of French Galley, "in the *Water of Lore;*" and even flung their Virgin-Mary over, instead of kissing her,—as a "painted bredd," or timber Virgin, who could naturally swim.* So, ye of Château-Vieux, tug patiently, not without hope!

833. But indeed at Nanci generally, Aristocracy rides triumphant, rough. Bouillé is gone again, the second day; in Aristocrat Municipality, with free course, is as cruel as it had before been cowardly. The Daughter Society, as the mother of the whole mischief, lies ignominiously suppressed; the Prisons can hold no more; bereaved down-beaten Patriotism murmurs, not loud but deep. Here and in the neighboring Towns, "flattened balls" picked from the streets of Nanci are worn at button-holes: balls flattened in carrying death to Patriotism; men wear them there, in perpetual memento of revenge. Mutineer deserters roam the woods; have to demand charity at the musket's end. All is dissolution, mutual rancor, gloom and despair:—till National Assembly Commissioners arrive, with a steady gentle flame of Constitutionalism in their hearts; who gently lift up the down-trodden, gently pull down the too uplifted; reinstate the Daughter Society, recall the mutineer deserter; gradually leveling, strive in all wise ways to smooth and soothe. With such gradual mild leveling on the one side; as with solemn funeral-service, cassolettes, Courts-Martial, National thanks, on the other,—all that Officiality can do is

done. The button-hole will drop its flat ball; the black ashes, as far as many be, get green again.

834. This is the "Affair of Nanci;" by some called the "Massacre of Nanci;"—properly speaking, the unsightly *wrong-side* of that thrice-glorious Feast of Pikes, the right-side of which formed a spectacle for the very gods. Right-side and wrong lie always so near: the one was in July, in August the other! Theaters, the theaters over in London, are bright with their pasteboard simulacrum of that "Federation of the French people," brought out as Drama: this of Nanci, we may say, though not played in any pasteboard Theater, did for many months enact itself, and even walk spectrally, in all French heads. For the news of it fly pealing through all France: awakening, in town and village, in club-room, mess-room, to the utmost borders, some mimic reflex or imaginative repetition to the business; always with the angry questionable assertion: It was right; It was wrong. Whereby come controversies, duels; imbitterment, vain jargon; the hastening forward, the augmenting and intensifying of whatever new explosions lie in store for us.

835. Meanwhile, at this cost or at that, the mutiny, as we say, is stilled. The French Army has neither burst-up in universal simultaneous delirium; nor been at once disbanded, put an end to, and made new again. It must die in the chronic manner, through years, by inches; with partial revolts, as of Brest Sailors or the like, which dare not spread; with men unhappy, insubordinate; officers unhappier, in Royalist mustachioes, taking horse, singly or in bodies, across the Rhine;* sick dissatisfaction, sick disgust on both sides; the Army moribund, fit for no duty: —till it do, in that unexpected manner, phœnix-like, with long throes, get both dead and new-born; then start forth strong, nay stronger and even strongest.

836. Thus much was the brave Bouillé hitherto fated to do. Wherewith let him again fade into dimness; and, at Metz or the rural Cantonments, assiduously drilling, mysteriously diplomatizing, in scheme within scheme, hover as formerly a faint shadow, the hope of Royalty.

BOOK THIRD.

THE TUILERIES.

CHAPTER I.

EPIMENIDES.

837. How true, that there is nothing dead in this Universe; that what we call dead is only changed, its forces working in inverse order! "The leaf that lies rotting in moist winds," says one, "has still force; else how could it *rot?*" Our whole Universe is but an infinite Complex of Forces; thousand-fold, from Gravitation up to Thought and Will; man's Freedom environed with Necessity of Nature: in all which nothing at any moment slumbers, but all is forever awake and busy. The thing that lies isolated inactive thou shalt nowhere discover; seek everywhere, from the granite mountain, slow-moldering since Creation, to the passing cloud-vapor, to the living man; to the action, to the spoken word of man. The word that is spoken, as we know, flies irrevocable; not less, but more, the action that is done. "The gods themselves," sings Pindar, "cannot annihilate the action that is done." No: this once done, is done always; cast forth into endless Time; and, long conspicuous or soon hidden, must verily work and grow forever there, an indestructible new element in the Infinite of Things. Or, indeed, what *is* this Infinite of Things itself which men name

* Knox's "History of the Reformation," b. i.

* See Dampmartin, i. 249, etc., etc.

Universe, but an Action, a sum-total of Actions and Activities? The living ready-made sum-total of these three,—which Calculation cannot add, cannot bring on its tablets; yet the sum, we say, is written visible: All that has been done, All that is doing, All that will be done! Understand it well, the Thing thou beholdest, that Thing is an Action, the product and expression of exerted Force: the All of Things is an infinite conjunction of the verb *To do*. Shoreless Fountain-Ocean of Force, of power to *do;* wherein Force rolls and circles, billowing, many-streamed, harmonious; wide as Immensity, deep as Eternity; beautiful and terrible, not to be comprehended: this is what man names Existence and Universe; this thousand-tinted Flame image at once veil and revelation, reflex such as he, in his poor brain and heart, can paint, of One Unnamable, dwelling in inaccessible light! From beyond the Star-galaxies, from before the Beginning of Days, it billows and rolls,—round *thee*, nay thyself art of it, in this point of Space where thou now standest, in this moment which thy clock measures.

838. Or, apart from all Transcendentalism, is it not a plain truth of sense, which the duller mind can even consider as a truism, that human things wholly are in continual movement, and action and reaction, working continually forward, phasis after phasis, by unalterable laws, toward prescribed issues? How often must we say, and yet not rightly lay to heart, The seed that is sown, it will spring! Given the summer's blossoming, then there is also given the autumnal withering: so is it ordered not with seed-fields only, but with transactions, arrangements, philosophies, societies, French Revolutions, whatsoever man works with in this lower world. The Beginning holds in it the End, and all that leads thereto; as the acorn does the oak and its fortunes. Solemn enough, did we think of it,—which unhappily, and also happily, we do not very much! Thou there canst begin: the Beginning is for thee, and there: but where, and of what sort, and for whom will the End be? All grows, and seeks and endures its destinies: consider likewise how much grows, as the trees do, whether *we* think of it or not. So that when your Epimenides, your somnolent Peter Klaus, since named Rip van Winkle, awakens again, he finds it a changed world. In that seven-years' sleep of his, so much has changed! All that is without us will change while we think not of it; much even that is within us. The truth that was yesterday a restless Problem, has to-day grown a Belief burning to be uttered: on the morrow, contradiction has exasperated it into mad Fanaticism; obstruction has dulled it into sick Inertness; it is sinking toward silence, of satisfaction or resignation. To-day is not Yesterday, for man or for thing. Yesterday there was the oath of Love; to-day has come the curse of Hate. Not willingly: ah no; but it could not help coming. The golden radiance of youth, would it willingly have tarnished itself into the dimness of old age?—Fearful; how we stand enveloped, deep-sunk, in that Mystery of TIME; and are Sons of Time: fashioned and woven out of Time; and on us and on all that we have, or see, or do, is written: Rest not, Continue not, forward to thy doom!

839. But in seasons of Revolution, which indeed distinguish themselves from common seasons by their *velocity* mainly, your miraculous Seven-sleeper might, with miracle enough, awake *sooner:* not by the century, or seven years, need he sleep; often not by the seven months. Fancy, for example, some new Peter Klaus, sated with the jubilee of that Federation day, had lain down, say directly after the Blessing of Talleyrand; and, reckoning it all safe *now*, had fallen composedly asleep under the timber-

work of the Fatherland's Altar; to sleep there, not twenty-one years, but as it were year and day. The cannonading of Nanci, so far off, does not disturb him; nor does the black mort cloth, close at hand, nor the requiems chanted, and minute-guns, incense-pans and concourse right over his head: none of these: but Peter sleeps through them all. Through one circling year, as we say; from July the 14th of 1790, till July the 17th of 1791: but on that latter day, no Klaus, nor most leaden Epimenides, only the Dead could continue sleeping: and so our miraculous Peter Klaus awakens. With what eyes, O Peter! Earth and sky have still their joyous July look, and the Champ-de-Mars is multitudinous with men: but the jubilee-huzzahing has become Bedlam-shrieking, of terror and revenge; not blessing of Talleyrand, or any blessing, but cursing, imprecation, and shrill wail: our cannon-salvoes are turned to sharp shot; for swinging of incense-pans, and Eighty-three Departmental Banners, we have waving of the one sanguineous Drapeau Rouge.—Thou foolish Klaus! The one lay in the other, the one *was* the other *minus* Time; even as Hannibal's rock-rending vinegar lay in the sweet new wine. That sweet Federation was of last year; this sour Divulsion is the self-same substance, only older by the appointed days.

840. No miraculous Klaus or Epimenides sleeps in these times; and yet, may not many a man, if of opacity and levity, act the same miracle in a natural way; we mean, with his eyes open? Eyes has he, but he sees not, except what is under his nose. With a sparkling briskness of glance, as if he not only saw but saw through, such a one goes whisking, assiduous, in his circle of officialities; not dreaming but that *it* is the whole world: as indeed, where your vision terminates, does not inanity begin *there*, and the world's end clearly disclose itself—to you? Whereby our brisk-sparkling assiduous official person (call him, for instance, Lafayette), suddenly startled, after year and day, by huge grape-shot tumult, stares not less astonished at it than Peter Klaus would have done. Such natural-miracle can Lafayette perform; and indeed not he only but most other officials, non-officials, and generally the whole French People can perform it; and do bounce up, ever and anon, like amazed Seven-sleepers awakening; awakening amazed at the noise they themselves *made*. So strangely is Freedom, as we say, environed in Necessity; such a singular Somnambulism, of Conscious and Unconscious, of Voluntary and Involuntary, is this life of man. If anywhere in the world there was astonishment that the Federation Oath went into grape-shot, surely of all persons the French, first swearers and then shooters, felt astonished the most.

841. Alas, offenses must come. The sublime Feast of Pikes with its effulgence of brotherly love, unknown since the Age of Gold, has changed nothing. That prurient heat in 25,000,000 of hearts is not cooled thereby: but is still hot, nay hotter. Lift off the pressure of command from so many millions; all pressure or binding rule, except such melodramatic Federation Oath as they have bound *themselves* with! For *Thou shalt* was from of old the condition of man's being, and his weal and blessedness was in obeying that. Woe for him when, were it on the best of the clearest necessity, rebellion, disloyal isolation, and mere *I will*, becomes his rule! But the Gospel of Jean-Jacques has come, and the first Sacrament of it has been celebrated: all things, as we say, are got into hot and hotter prurience; and must go on pruriently fermenting, in continual change noted or unnoted.

842. "Worn out with disgusts," Captain after Captain, in Royalist mustachioes, mounts his war-horse,

or his Rozinante war-garron, and rides minatory across the Rhine; till all have ridden. Neither does civic Emigration cease; Seigneur after Seigneur must, in like manner, ride or roll; impelled to it, and even compelled. For the very Peasants despise him, in that he dare not join his order and fight.* Can he bear to have a Distaff, a Quenouille sent to him: say in copper-plate shadow, by post; or fixed up in wooden reality over his gate-lintel: as if he were no Hercules, but an Omphale? Such scutcheon they forward to him diligently from beyond the Rhine; till he too bestir himself and march, and in sour humor another Lord of Land is gone, *not* taking the Land with him. Nay, what of Captains and emigrating Seigneurs? There is not an angry word on any of those 25,000,000 French tongues, and indeed not an angry thought in their hearts, but is some fraction of the great Battle. Add many successions of angry words together, you have the manual brawl; add brawls together, with the festering sorrows they leave, and they rise to riots and revolts. One reverent thing after another, ceases to meet reverence; in visible material combustion, château after château mounts up; in spiritual invisible combustion, one authority after another. With noise and glare, or noiselessly and unnoted, a whole Old System of things is vanishing piecemeal: the morrow thou shalt look, and it is not.

CHAPTER II.

THE WAKEFUL.

843. Sleep who will, cradled in hope and short vision, like Lafayette, who "always in the danger done sees the last danger that will threaten him,"— Time is not sleeping, nor Time's seed-field.

844. That sacred Herald's-College of a *new* Dynasty; we mean the Sixty and odd Bill-stickers with their leaden badges, are not sleeping. Daily they, with paste-pot and cross-staff, new-clothe the walls of Paris in colors of the rainbow: authoritative-heraldic, as we say, or indeed almost magical-thaumaturgic; for no Placard-Journal that they paste but will convince some soul or souls of men. The Hawkers bawl; and the Ballad-singers: great Journalism blows and blusters, through all its throats, forth from Paris toward all corners of France, like au Æolus's Cave; keeping all manner of fires.

845. Throats of Journals there are, as men count,† to the number of some Hundred and thirty-three. Of various caliber: from your Cheniers, Gorsases, Camilles, down to your Marat, down now to your incipient Hébert of the Père Duchesne; these blow, with fierce weight of argument or quick light banter, for the Rights of Man: Durosoys, Royous, Peltiers, Sulleaus, equally with mixed tactics (inclusive, singular to say, of much profane Parody),‡ are blowing for Altar and Throne. As for Marat the People's-Friend, his voice is as that of the bull-frog, or bittern by the solitary pools; he, unseen of men, croaks harsh thunder, and that alone continually,—of indignation, suspicion, incurable sorrow. The People are sinking toward ruin, near starvation itself: "My dear friends," cries he, " your indigences is not the fruit of vices nor of idleness; you have a right to life, as good as Louis XVI., or the happiest of the century. What man can say he has a right to dine, when you have no bread?"§ The People sinking on

* Dampmartin, passim.
† Mercier, III. 163.
‡ See "Histoire Parlementaire," vii. 51.
§ Ami du Peuple, No. 306. See other excerpts in "Histoire Parlementaire," viii. 139-149, 428-433; ix. 85-93, etc.

the one hand: on the other hand, nothing but wretched Sieur Motiers, treasonous Riquetti Mirabeaus: traitors, or else shadows and simulacra of Quacks to be seen in high places, look where you will! Men that go mincing, grimacing, with plausible speech and brushed raiment; hollow within: Quacks political, Quacks scientific, academical: all with a fellow-feeling for each other, and kind of Quack public-spirit! Not great Lavoisier himself, or any of the Forty can escape this rough tongue; which wants not fanatic sincerity, nor, strangest of all, a certain rough caustic sense. And then the "3,000 gaming-houses" that are in Paris; cesspools for the scoundrelism of the world; sinks of iniquity and debauchery,—whereas without good morals Liberty is impossible! There, in these Dens of Satan, which one knows, and perseveringly denounces, do Sieur Motier's monchards consort and colleague; battening vampire-like on a People next door to starvation. "O Peuple!" cries he ofttimes, with heart-rending accent. Treason, delusion, vampirism, scoundrelism, from Dan to Beersheba! The soul of Marat is sick with the sight: but what remedy? To erect "800 gibbets," in convenient rows, and proceed to hoisting; "Riquetti on the first of them!" Such is the brief recipe of Marat, Friend of the People.

846. So blow and bluster the 133; nor, as would seem, are these sufficient; for there are benighted nooks in France, to which Newspapers do not reach; and everywhere is "such an appetite for news as was never seen in any country." Let an expeditious Dampmartin, on furlough, set out to return home from Paris,* he cannot get along for "peasants stopping him on the highway; overwhelming him with questions:" the Maître de Poste will not send out the horses till you have well-nigh quarreled with him, but asks always, What news? At Autun, in spite of the dark night and "rigorous frost," for it is now January, 1791, nothing will serve but you must gather your wayworn limbs and thoughts, and "speak to the multitudes from a window opening into the market-place." It is the shortest method: *This*, good Christian people, is verily what an august Assembly seemed to me to be doing; this and no other is the news:

Now my weary lips I close:
Leave me, leave me to repose!

The good Dampmartin!—But, on the whole, are not Nations astonishingly true to their National character; which indeed runs in the blood? Nineteen hundred years ago, Julius Cæsar, with his quick, sure eye, took note how the Gauls waylaid men. "It is a habit of theirs," says he, " to stop travelers, were it even by constraint, and inquire whatsoever each of them may have heard or known about any sort of matter: in their towns, the common people beset the passing trader, demanding to hear from what regions he came, what things he got acquainted with there. Excited by which rumors and hearsays, they will decide about the weightiest matters, and necessarily repent next moment that they did it, on such guidance of uncertain reports, and many a traveler answering with mere fictions to please them, and get off."† Nineteen hundred years; and good Dampmartin, wayworn, in winter frost, probably with scant light of stars and fish-oil, still perorates from the Inn-window! This people is no longer called Gaulish; and it has *wholly* become braccatus, has got breeches, and suffered change enough: certain fierce German Franken came storming over: and, so to speak, vaulted on the back of it; and always after,

* Dampmartin, I. 184.
† "De Bello Gallico," lib. iv. 5.

in their grim tenacious way, have ridden it bridled; for German is, by his very name, *Guerre*-man, or man that *wars* and *gars*. And so the People, as we say, is now called French or Frankish: nevertheless, does not the old Gaulish and Gaelic Celthood, with its vehemence, effervescent promptitude, and what good and ill it had, still vindicate itself little adulterated?—

847. For the rest, that in such prurient confusion, Clubbism thrives and spreads, need not be said. Already the Mother of Patriotism, sitting in the Jacobins, shines supreme over all; and has paled the poor lunar light of that Monarchic Club near to final extinction. She, we say, shines supreme, girt with sunlight, not yet with infernal lightning; reverenced, not without fear, by Municipal Authorities; counting her Barnaves, Lameths, Pétions, of a National Assembly; must gladly of all, her Robespierre. Cordeliers, again, your Hébert, Vincent, Bibliopolist Momoro, groan audibly that a tyrannous Mayor and Sieur Motier harrow them with the sharp tribula of Law, intent apparently to suppress them by tribulation. How the Jacobin Mother Society, as hinted formerly, sheds forth Cordeliers on this hand, and then Feuillans on that; the Cordeliers "an elixir or double distillation of Jacobin Patriotism;" the other a widespread weak dilution thereof: how she will reabsorb the former into her mother bosom, and stormfully dissipate the latter into Nonentity: how she breeds and brings forth Three Hundred Daughter Societies; her endeavorings and continual travail: how, under an old figure, Jacobinism shoots forth organic filaments to the utmost corners of confused dissolved France; organizing it anew:—this properly is the grand fact of the Time.

848. To passionate Constitutionalism, still more to Royalism, which see all their own Clubs fail and die, Clubbism will naturally grow to seem the root of all evil. Nevertheless Clubbism is not death, but rather new organization, and life out of death: destructive, indeed, of the remnants of the Old; but to the New important, indispensable. That man can co-operate and hold communion with man, herein lies his miraculous strength. In hut or hamlet, Patriotism mourns not now like voice in the desert; it can walk to the nearest Town; and there, in the Daughter Society, make its ejaculation into an articulate oration, into an action, guided forward by the Mother of Patriotism herself. All Clubs of Constitutionalists, and such-like, fail, one after another, as shallow fountains: Jacobinism alone has gone down to the deep subterranean lake of waters: and may, unless *filled in*, flow there, copious, continual, like an Artesian well. Till the Great Deep have drained itself up; and all be flooded and submerged, and Noah's Deluge out-deluged!

849. On the other hand, Claude Fauchet, preparing mankind for a Golden Age now apparently just at hand, has opened his Cercle Social, with clerks, corresponding boards, and so forth; in the precincts of the Palais Royal. It is Te-Deum Fauchet: the same who preached on Franklin's Death, in that huge Medicean rotunda of the Halle-aux-bleds. He here, this winter, by Printing-press and melodious Colloquy, spreads bruit of himself to the utmost City-barriers. "Ten thousand persons of respectability" attend there; and listen to this "Procureur-Général de la Vérité (Attorney-General of Truth)," so has he dubbed himself; to his sage Condorcet, or other eloquent coadjutor. Eloquent Attorney-General! He blows out from him, better or worse, what crude or ripe thing he holds: not without result to himself; for it leads to a Bishopric, though only a Constitutional one. Fauchet approves himself a glib-tongued, strong-lunged, whole-hearted human individual: much flowing matter there is, and really of the bet-

ter sort, about Right, Nature, Benevolence, Progress; which flowing matter, whether "it is pan-theistic," or is pot-theistic, only the greener mind, in these days, need examine. Busy Brissot was long ago of purpose to establish precisely some such regenerative *Social Circle*: nay he had tried it in "Newman-street, Oxford-street," of the Fog Babylon; and failed,—as some say, surreptitiously pocketing the cash. Fauchet, not Brissot, was fated to be the happy man; whereat, however, generous Brissot will with sincere heart sing a timber-toned Nunc Domine.* But "10,000 persons of respectability:" what a bulk have many things in proportion to their magnitude! This Cercle Social, for which Brissot chants in sincere timber-tones such Nunc Domine, what is it? Unfortunately wind and shadow. The main reality one finds in it now, is perhaps this· that "an Attorney-General of Truth" did once take shape of a body, as Son of Adam, on our Earth, though but for months or moments; and 10,000 persons of respectability attended, ere yet Chaos and Nox had reabsorbed him.

850. Hundred and thirty-three Paris Journals; regenerative Social Circle; oratory, in Mother and Daughter Societies, from the balconies of Inns, by chimney-nook, at dinner-table,—polemical, ending many times in duel! And ever, like a constant growling accompaniment of bass Discord: scarcity of work, scarcity of food. The winter is hard and cold; ragged Baker's-quenes, like a black tattered flag-of-distress, wave out ever and anon. It is the third of our Hunger-years, this new year of a glorious Revolution. The rich man when invited to dinner, in such distress-seasons, feels bound in politeness to carry his own bread in his pocket, how the poor dine? And your glorious Revolution has done it, cries one. And our glorious Revolution is subtilely, by black traitors worthy of the Lamp-iron, *perverted* to do it, cries another. Who will paint the huge whirlpool within France, all shivered into wild incoherence, whirls? The jarring that went on under every French roof, in every French heart; the diseased things that were spoken, done, the sumtotal whereof is the French Revolution, tongue of man cannot tell. Nor the laws of action that work unseen in the depths of that huge blind Incoherence! With amazement, not with measurement, men look on the Immeasurable; not knowing its laws; *seeing*, with all different degrees of knowledge, what new phases, and results of event, its laws bring forth. France is as a monstrous Galvanic Mass, wherein all sorts of far stranger than chemical galvanic or electric forces and substances are at work; electrifying one another, positive and negative, filling with electri·ity your Leyden-jars,—25,000,000 in number! the jars get full, there will, from time to time, be, on slight hint, an explosion.

CHAPTER III.

SWORD IN HAND.

851. On such wonderful basis, however, has Law, Royalty, Authority, and whatever yet exists of visible Order, to maintain itself, while it can. Here, as in that Commixture of the Four Elements did the Anarch Old, has an august Assembly spread its pavilion; curtained by the dark infinite of discords; founded on the wavering bottomless of the Abyss; and keeps continual hubbub. Time is around it, and Eternity, and the Inane; and it does what it can, what is given it to do.

852. Glancing reluctantly in, once more, we discern little that is edifying: a Constitutional Theory

* See Brissot, *Patriote-Français* newspapers; Fauchet, "Bouche-de-Fer," etc. (excerpted in "Histoire Parlementaire," viii. ix. et seqq).

of Defective Verbs struggling forward, with perseverance, amid endless interruptions: Mirabeau, from his tribune, with the weight of his name and genius, awing-down much Jacobin violence; which in return vents itself the louder over in its Jacobins Hall, and even reads him sharps lectures there.* This man's path is mysterious, questionable; difficult, and he walks without companion in it. Pure Patriotism does not now count him among her chosen; pure Royalism abhors him: yet his weight with the world is overwhelming. Let him travel on, companionless, unwavering, whither he is bound,—while it is yet day with him, and the night has not come.

853. But the chosen band of pure Patriot brothers is small; counting only some thirty, seated now on the extreme tip of the Left, separate from the world. A virtuous Pétion; an incorruptible Robespierre, most consistent, incorruptible of thin acrid men; Triumvirs Barnave, Duport, Lameth, great in speech, thought, action, each according to his kind; a lean old Gupil de Prefeln: on these and what will follow them has pure Patriotism to depend.

854. There too, conspicuous among the Thirty, if seldom audible, Philippe d'Orléans may be seen sitting: in dim fuliginous bewilderment; having, one might say, *arrived* at Chaos! Gleams there are, at once of a Lieutenancy and Regency: debates in the Assembly itself, of succession to the Throne "in case the present Branch should fail," and Philippe, they say, walked anxiously, in silence, through the corridors, till such high argument were done. but it came all to nothing; Mirabeau, glaring into the man, and through him, had to ejaculate in strong untranslatable language: "Ce j—f—ne vaut pas la peine qn'on se donne pour lui." It came all to nothing; and in the meanwhile Philippe's money, they say, is gone! Could he refuse a little cash to the gifted Patriot, in want only of that; he himself in want of all *but* that? Not a pamphlet can be printed without cash; or indeed written without food purchasable by cash. Without cash your hopefulest Projector cannot stir from the spot; individual patriotic or other Projects require cash: how much more do wide-spread Intrigues, which live and exist by cash, lying well-spread, with dragon appetite for cash; fit to swallow Princedoms? And so Prince Philippe, amid his Sillerys, Lacloses and confused Sons of Night, has rolled along: the center of the strangest cloudy coil; out of which has visibly come, as we often say, Epic Preternatural Machinery of *Suspicion*; and *within* which there has dwelt and worked,—what specialities of treason, stratagem, aimed or aimless endeavor toward mischief, no party living (if it be not the presiding Genius of it, Prince of the power of the Air), has now any chance to know. Camille's conjecture is the likliest; that poor Philippe did mount up, a little way, in treasonable speculation, as he mounted formerly in one of the earliest Balloons; but, frightened at the new position he was getting into, had soon turned the cock again, and come down. More fool than he rose! To create Preternatural Suspicion, this was his function in the Revolutionary Epos. But now if he have lost his cornucopia of ready-money, what else had he to lose? In thick darkness, inward and outward, he must welter and flounder on, in that piteous death-element, the hapless man. . Once, or even twice, we shall still behold him emerged; struggling out of the thick death-element: in vain. For one moment, it is the last moment, he starts aloft, or is flung aloft, even into a clearness and a kind of memorability,—to sink then for evermore.

* Camille's Journal (in "Histoire Parlementaire" ix. 366-385).

855. The Coté Droit persists no less, nay with more animation than ever, though hope has now well-nigh fled. Tough Abbé Maury, when the obscure country Royalist grasps his hand with transport of thanks, answers, rolling his indomitable brazen head: "Hélas, Monsieur, all that I do here is as good as simply *nothing*." Gallant Faussigny, visible this one time in history, advance frantic into the middle of the Hall, exclaiming: "There is but one way of dealing with it, and that is to fall sword in hand on those gentry there (sabre à la main sur ces gaillards là),"* frantically indicating one chosen Thirty on the extreme tip of the Left! Whereupon is clangor and clamor, debate, repentance,—evaporation. Things ripen toward downright incompatibility, and what is called "scission:" that fierce theoretic onslaught of Faussigny's was in August, 1790; next August will not have come, till a famed Two Hundred and Ninty-two, the chosen of Royalism, make solemn final "scission" from an Assembly given up to faction; and depart, shaking the dust off their feet.

856. Connected with this matter of sword in hand, there is yet another thing to be noted. Of duels we have sometime spoken. how, in all parts of France, innumerable duels were fought; and argumentative men and messmates, flinging down the wine-cup and weapons of reason and repartee, met in the measured field to part bleeding; or perhaps, *not* to part, but to fall mutually skewered through with iron, their wrath and life ending,—and die as fools die. Long has this lasted, and still lasts. But now it would seem as if in an august Assembly itself, traitorous Royalism in its despair, had taken a new course: that of cutting off Patriotism by systematic duel! Bully swordsmen, "Spadassins" of that party, go swaggering; or indeed they can be had for a trifle of money. "Twelve Spadassins" were *seen*, by the yellow eye of Journalism, "arriving recently out of Switzerland;" also "a considerable number of Assassins (nombre considérable d'assassins), exercising in fencing-schools and at pistol-targets." Any Patriot Deputy of mark can be called out; let him escape one time, or ten times, a time there necessarily is when he must fall, and France mourn. How many cartels has Mirabeau had; especially while he was the People's champion! Cartels by the hundred: which he, since the Constitution must be made first, and his time is precious, answers now always with a kind of stereotype formula: "Monsieur, you are put upon my List; but I warn you that it is long, and I grant no preferences."

857. Then, in Autumn, had we not the Duel of Cazalès and Barnave; the two chief masters of tongue-shot, meeting now to exchange pistol-shot? For Cazalès, chief of the Royalists, whom we call "Blacks or Noirs," said, in a moment of passion, "the Patriots were sheer Brigands," nay in so speaking, he darted, or seemed to dart, a fire-glance specially at Barnave; who thereupon could not but reply by fire-glances —by adjournment to the Bois-du-Boulogne. Barnave's second shot took effect: on Cazalès's *hat*. The "front nook" of a triangular Felt, such as mortals then wore, deadened the ball; and saved that fine hrow from more than temporary injury. But how easily might the lot have fallen the other way, and Barnave's hat not been so good! Patriotism raises its loud denunciation of Duelling in general; petitions an august Assembly to stop such Feudal barbarism by law. Barbarism and solecism: for will it convince or convict any man to blow half an ounce of lead through the head of him? Surely not—Barnave was received at the Jacobins with embraces, yet with rebukes.

* Moniteur. Séance du 21 Août 1790.

858. Mindful of which, and also that his reputation in America was that of headlong foolhardiness rather, and want of brain, not of heart, Charles Lameth does, on the eleventh day of November, with little emotion, decline attending some hot young Gentlemen from Artois, come expressly to challenge him : nay indeed he first coldly engages to attend ; then coldly permits two Friends to attend instead of him, and shame the young Gentlemen out of it, which they successfully do. A cold procedure ; satisfactory to the two Friends, to Lameth and the hot young Gentlemen ; whereby, one might have fancied, the whole matter was cooled down.

859. Not so, however ; Lameth, proceeding to his senatorial duties, in the decline of the day, is met in those Assembly corridors by nothing but Royalist brocards sniffs, huffs and open insults. Human, patience has its limits : "Monsieur," said Lameth, breaking silence to one Lautrec, a man with hunchback, or natural deformity, but sharp of tongue, and a *Black* of the deepest tint, "Monsieur, if you were a man to be fought with !"—"I am one," cries the young Duke de Castries. Fast as fire-flash Lameth replies, "Tout à l'heure (On the instant, then)!" And so, as the shades of dusk thicken in that Bois-de-Boulogne, we behold two men with lion-look, with alert attitude, side foremost, right foot advanced ; flourishing and thrusting, stoccado and passado, in tierce and quart ; intent to skewer one another. See with most skewering purpose, headlong Lameth, with his whole weight, makes a furious lunge ; but deft Castries whisks aside : Lameth skewers only the air, —and slits deep and far, on Castries's sword's-point, his own extended left arm ! whereupon, with bleeding, pallor, surgeon's-lint, and formalities, the Duel is considered satisfactorily done.

860. But will there be no end, then ? Beloved Lameth lies deep-slit, not out of danger. Black traitorous Aristocrats kill the People's defenders, cut up not with arguments, but with rapier-slits And the Twelve Spadassins out of Switzerland, and the considerable number of Assassins exercising at the pistol-target ? So meditates and ejaculates hurt Patriotism, with ever-deepening, ever-widening fervor, for the space of six-and-thirty hours.

861. The thirty-six hours past, on Saturday the 13th, one beholds a new spectacle. The Rue de Varennes, and neighboring Boulevard des Invalides, covered with a mixed flowing multitude the Castries Hotel gone distracted, devil-ridden, belching from every window, "beds with clothes and curtains," plate of silver and gold with filigree, mirrors, pictures, images, commodes, chiffoniers and endless crockery and jingle : amid steady popular cheers, absolutely without theft: for there goes a cry, "He shall be hanged that steals a nail." It is a Plebiscitum, or informed iconoclastic Decree of the Common People in the course of being executed !—The Municipality sit tremulous ; deliberating whether they will hang out the Drapeau Rouge and Martial Law ; National Assembly, part in loud wail, part in hardly suppressed applause ; Abbé Maury unable to decide whether the iconoclastic Plebs amount to 40,000 or to 200,000.

862. Deputations, swift messengers,—for it is at a distance over the River,—come and go. Lafayette and National Guards, though without Drapeau Ronge, get under way ; apparently in no hot haste. Nay, arrived on the scene, Lafayette salutes with doffed hat, before ordering to fix bayonets. What avails it ? The Plebeian "Court of Cessation," as Camille might punningly name it, has done its work ; steps forth, with unbuttoned vest, with pockets turned inside out: sack, and just ravage, not plunder ! With inexhaustible patience, the Hero of two Worlds remonstrates ; persuasively, with a kind of sweet constraint, though also with fixed bayonets, dissipates, hushes down : on the morrow it is once more all as usual.

863. Considering which things, however, Duke Castries may justly "write to the President," justly transport himself across the Marches; to raise a corps, or do what else is in him. Royalism totally abandons that Bobadilian method of contest, and the twelve Spadassins return to Switzerland—or even to Dreamland through the Horn-gate, whichsoever their true home is. Nay Editor Prudhomme is authorized to publish a curious thing. "We are authorized to publish," says he, dull-blustering Publisher, "that M. Boyer champion of good Patriots is at the head of Fifty Spadassinici des or Bully-*killers*. His address is : Passage du Bois-de-Boulogne, Faubourg St. Denis.* One of the strangest Institutes, this of Champion Boyer and the Bully-killers ! Whose services, however, are not wanted ; Royalism having abandoned the rapier method, as plainly impracticable.

CHAPTER IV.

TO FLY OR NOT TO FLY.

864. The truth is, Royalism sees itself verging toward sad extremities; nearer and nearer daily. From over the Rhine it comes asserted that the King in his Tuileries is not free: this the poor King may contradict, with the official mouth, but in his heart feels often to be undeniable. Civil Constitution of the Clergy ; Decree of ejectment against Dissidents from it. not even to this latter, though almost his conscience rebels, can he say Nay ; but, after two months' hesitating, signs this also. It was "on January 21st," of this 1791, that he signed it: to the sorrow of his poor heart yet, on *another* Twenty-first of January ! Whereby come Dissident ejected Priests ; unconquerable Martyrs according to some, incurable chicaning Traitors according to others. And so there has arrived what we once foreshadowed: with Religion, or with the Cant and Echo of Religion, all France is rent asunder in a new rupture of continuity ; complicating, imbittering all the older :—to be cured only by stern surgery, in La Vendée!

865. Unhappy Royalty, unhappy Majesty, Hereditary Representative (Représentant Héréditaire), or howsoever they may name him ; of whom much is expected, to whom little is given ! Blue National Guards encircle that Tuileries ; a Lafayette, thin constitutional Pedant ; clear, thin, inflexible, as water turned to thin ice ; whom no Queen's heart can love. National Assembly, its pavilion spread where we know, sits near by, keeping continual bub-bub. From without, nothing but Nanci Revolts, sack of Castries Hotels, riots and seditions ; riots North and South, at Aix, at Douai, at Bélort, Usez, Perpignan, at Nismes, and that incurable Avignon of the Pope's ; a continual crackling and sputtering of riots from the whole face of France;—testifying how electric it grows. Add only the hard winter, the famished *strikes* of operatives ; that continual running-bass of Scarcity, ground-tone and basis of all other Discords!

866. The plan of Royalty, so far as it can be said to have any fixed plan, is still, as ever, that of flying toward the frontiers. In very truth, the only plan of the smallest promise for it ! Fly to Bouillé ; bristle yourself round with cannon, served by your "40,-000 undebauched Germans :" summon the National Assembly to follow you, summon what of it is Royalist, Constitutional, gainable by money ; dissolve the rest, by grape-shot if need be. Let Jacobinism and Revolt, with one wild wail, fly into Infinite

* "Revolutions de Paris" (in "Histoire Parlementaire," viii. 440).

Space; driven by grape-shot. Thunder over France with the cannon's mouth; commanding, not entreating, that this riot cease. And then to rule afterward with utmost possibleConstitutionality; doing justice, loving mercy; *being* Shepherd of this indigent People, not Shearer merely, and Shepherd's similitude! All this, if ye dare. If ye dare not, then in Heaven's name, go to sleep: other handsome alternative seems none.

867. Nay, it were perhaps possible; with a man to do it. For if such inexpressible whirlpool of Babylonish confusion (which our Era is) cannot be stilled by man, but only by Time and men, a man may moderate its paroxysms, may balance and sway, and keep himself unswallowed on the top of it,—as several men and Kings in these days do. Much is possible for a man; men will obey a man that *kens* and *cans*, and *name* him reverently their *Ken-ning* or King. Did not Charlemagne rule? Consider, too, whether he had smooth times of it; hanging "4,000 Saxons over the Weser-bridge," at one dread swoop! So likewise, who knows but, in this same distracted fanatic France, the right man may verily exist? An olive-complexioned taciturn man; for the present, Lieutenant in the Artillery-service, who once sat studying Mathematics at Brienne! The same who walked in the morning to correct proof-sheets at Dole, and enjoyed a frugal breakfast with M. Joly? Such a one is gone, whither also famed General Paoli his friend is gone, in these very days, to see old scenes in native Corsica, and what Democratic good can be done there.

868. Royalty never executes the evasion plan, yet never abandons it; living in variable hope; undecisive, till fortune shall decide. In utmost secresy, a brisk Correspondence goes on with Bouillé; there is also a plot, which emerges more than once, for carrying the King to Rouen:[*] plot after plot emerging and submerging, like ignes fatui in foul weather, which lead nowhither. "About ten o'clock at night," the Hereditary Representative, in partie quarrée, with the Queen, with Brother Monsieur, and Madame, sits playing "*wisk*," or whist. Usher Campan enters mysteriously, with a message he only half comprehends· How a certain Comte d'Inisdal waits anxious in the outer antechamber; National Colonel, Captain of the watch for this night, is gained over; post-horses ready all the way; party of Noblesse sitting armed, determined; will his Majesty, before midnight, consent to go? Profound silence; Campan waiting with upturned ear. "Did your Majesty hear what Campan said?" asks the Queen, "Yes, I heard," answers Majesty, and plays on. "'Twas a pretty couplet, that of Campan's," hints Monsieur, who at times showed a pleasant wit: Majesty, still unresponsive, plays wisk. "After all, one must say something to Campan," remarks the Queen. "Tell M. d'Inisdal," said the King, and the Queen puts an emphasis on it, "That the King cannot con*sent* to be forced away."—"I see," said D'Inisdal, whisking round, peaking himself into flame of irritancy: "we have the risk; we are to have all the blame if it fail,"[†]—and vanishes, he and his plot, as will-o'-wisps do. The Queen sat till far in the night, packing jewels: but it came to nothing; in that peaked flame of irritancy the will-o'-wisp had gone out.

869. Little hope there is in all this. Alas, with whom to fly? Our loyal Gardes-du-Corps, ever since the Insurrection of Women, are disbanded; gone to their homes; gone, many of them, across the Rhine toward Coblentz and Exiled Princes: brave Mioman-

dre and brave Tardivet, these faithful Two, have received, in nocturnal interview with both Majesties, their viaticum of gold louis, of heartfelt thanks from a Queen's lips, though unluckily his Majesty stood, back to fire, not speaking;[*] and do now dine through the Provinces; recounting hairs-breadth escapes, insurrectionary horrors. Great horrors, to be swallowed yet of greater. But, on the whole, what a falling off from the old splendor of Versailles! Here in this poor Tuileries a National Brewer-Colonel, sonorous Santerre, parades officially behind her Majesty's chair. Our high dignitaries all fled over the Rhine: nothing now to be gained at Court; but hopes, for which life itself must be risked! Obscure busy men frequent the back stairs; with hearsays, wind-projects, unfruitful fanfaronades. Young Royalists, at the Théâtre de Vaudeville, "sing couplets;" if that could do anything. Royalists enough, Captains on furlough, burnt-out Seigneurs, may likewise be met with, "in the Café do Valois, and at Méot the Restaurateur's." There they fan one another into high loyal glow; drink, in such wine as can be procured, confusion to Sansculottism; show purchased dirks, of an improved structure, made to order; and, greatly daring, dine.[†] It is in these places, in these months that the epithet Sansculotte first gets applied to indigent Patriotism; in the last age we had Gilbert Sansculotte, the indigent Poet.[‡] Destitute-of-Breeches: a mournful Destitution; which however, if Twenty millions share it, may become more effective than most Possessions!

870. Meanwhile, amid this vague dim whirl of fanfaronades, wind-projects, poniards made to order, there does disclose itself one punctumsaliens of life and feasibility; the finger of Mirabeau! Mirabeau and the Queen of France have met; have parted with mutual trust! It is strange: secret as the Mysteries; but it is indubitable. Mirabeau took horse, one evening; and rode westward, unattended, to see Friend Clavière in that country-house of his? Before getting to Clavière's, the much-amusing horseman struck aside to a back gate of the Garden of Saint-Cloud: some Duke d'Aremberg, or the like, was there to introduce him; the Queen was not far; on a "round knoll" (rond point), "the highest of the Garden of Saint-Cloud," he beheld the Queen's face; spake with her, alone, under the void canopy of Night. What an interview; fateful, secret for us, after all searching; like the colloquies of the gods![§] She called him "a Mirabeau;" elsewhere we read that she "was charmed with him," the wild submitted Titan; as indeed it is among the honorable tokens of this high ill-fated heart that no mind of any endowment, no Mirabeau, nay no Barnave, no Dumouriez, ever came face to face with her but, in spite of all prepossessions, she was forced to recognize it, to draw nigh to it, with trust. High imperial heart; with the instinctive attraction toward all that had any height! "You know not the Queen," said Mirabeau once in confidence; "her force of mind is prodigious; she is a man for courage."[∥]—And so, under the void Night, on the crown of that knoll, she has spoken with a Mirabeau: he has kissed loyally the queenly hand, and said with enthusiasm: "Madame, the Monarchy is saved!"—Possible? The Foreign Powers, mysteriously sounded, gave favorable guarded response;[¶] Bouillé is at Metz, and could find 40,000 sure Germans. With a Mirabeau

* See "Histoire Parlementaire," vii. 316; Bertrand-Moleville, etc.
† Campan, ii. 105.

* Campan, ii. 199-201.
† Dampmartin, ii. 129.
‡ Mercier, "Nouveau Paris," iii. 204.
§ Campan, ii. c. 17.
∥ Dumont, p. 211.
¶ "Correspondance Secrete" (in "Histoire Parlementaire," viii. 169-173).

for head, and a Bouillé for hand, something verily is possible,—if Fate intervene not.

871. But figure under what thousand-fold wrappages, and cloaks of darkness, Royalty, meditating these things, must involve itself. There are men with "Tickets of Entrance;" there are chivalrous consultings, mysterious plottings. Consider also whether, involve as it like, plotting Royalty can escape the glance of Patriotism; lynx-eyes, by the ten-thousand, fixed on it, which see in the dark! Patriotism knows much: knows the dirks made to order, and can specify the shops; knows Sieur Motier's legions of mouchards; the Tickets of Entrée, and men in black; and how plan of evasion succeeds plan,—or may be supposed to succeed it. Then conceive the couplets chanted at the Théâtre de Vaudeville; or worse, the whispers, significant nods of traitors in mustachioes. Conceive, on the other hand, the loud cry of alarm that came through the Hundred-and-Thirty Journals; the Dionysius-Ear of each of the Forty-eight Sections, wakeful night and day.

872. Patriotism is patient of much: not patient of all. The Café de Procope has sent, visibly along the streets, a Deputation of Patriots, "to expostulate with bad Editors," by trustful word of mouth: singular to see and hear. The bad Editors promise to amend, but do not. Deputations for change of Ministry were many; Mayor Bailly joining even with Cordelier Danton in such; and they have prevailed. With what profit? Of Quacks, willing or constrained to be Quacks, the race is everlasting: Ministers Duportail and Dutertre will have to manage much as Ministers Latour du Pin and Cicé did. So welters the confused world.

873. But now, beaten on forever by such inextricable contradictory influences and evidences, what is the indigent French Patriot, in these unhappy days, to believe and walk by? Uncertainty all: except that he is wretched, indigent; that a glorious Revolution, the wonder of the Universe, has hitherto brought neither Bread nor Peace; being marred by traitors, difficult to discover. Traitors that dwell in dark, invisible there;—or seen for moments, in pallid dubious twilight, stealthily vanishing thither! Preternatural Suspicion once more rules the minds of men.

874. "Nobody here," writes Carra, of the Annales Patriotiques, so early as the first of February, "can entertain a doubt of the constant obstinate project the people have on foot to get the King away; or of the perpetual succession of manœuvres they employ for that." Nobody: the watchful Mother of Patriotism deputed two Members to her Daughter at Versailles, to examine how the matter looked there. Well, and there? Patriotic Carra continues: "The Report of these two deputies we all heard with our own ears last Saturday. They went with others of Versailles, to inspect the King's Stables, also the stables of the whilom Gardes-du-Corps: they found there from seven to eight hundred horses standing always saddled and bridled, ready for the road at a moment's notice. The same deputies, moreover, saw with their own two eyes several Royal Carriages, which men were even then busy loading with large well-stuffed luggage-bags," leather cows, as we call them, "vaches de cuir; the Royal Arms on the panels almost entirely effaced." Momentous enough! Also "on the same day the whole Maréchaussée, or Cavalry Police, did assemble with arms, horses and baggage,"—and disperse again. They want the King over the marches, that so Emperor Leopold and the German Princes, whose troops are ready, may have a pretext for beginning: "this," adds Carra, "is the word of the riddle: this is the reason why our fugi-

tive Aristocrats are now making levies of men on the frontiers; expecting that, one of these mornings, the Executive Chief Magistrate will be brought over to them, and the civil war commence."*

875. If indeed the Executive Chief Magistrate lagged, say in one of these leather cows, were once brought safe over to them! But the strangest thing of all is, that Patriotism, whether barking at a venture, or guided by some instinct of preternatural sagacity, is actually barking aright this time; at something, not at nothing. Bouillé's Secret Correspondence, since made public, testifies as much.

876. Nay, it is undeniable, visible to all, that Mesdames the King's Aunts are taking steps for departure: asking passports of the Ministry, safe-conducts of the Municipality; which Marat warns all men to beware of. They will carry gold with them, "these old Béguines; nay they will carry the little Dauphin, "having nursed a changeling, for some time to leave in his stead!" Besides, they are as some light substance flung up, to show how the wind sits; a kind of proof-kite you fly off to ascertain whether the grand paper-kite, Evasion of the King, may mount!

877. In these alarming circumstances, Patriotism is not wanting to itself. Municipality deputes to the King; Sections depute to the Municipality; a National Assembly will soon stir. Meanwhile, behold, on the 19th of February, 1791, Mesdames, quitting Bellevue and Versailles with all privacy, are off! Toward Rome, seemingly; or one knows not whither. They are not without King's passports, countersigned; and what is more to the purpose, a serviceable Escort. The Patriotic Mayor or Mayorlet of the Village of Moret tried to detain them: but brisk Louis de Narbonne, of the Escort, dashed off at hand-gallop; returned soon with thirty dragoons, and victoriously cut them out. And so the poor ancient women go their way; to the terror of France and Paris, whose nervous excitability is become extreme. Who else would hinder poor Loque and Graille, now grown so old, and fallen into such unexpected circumstances, when gossip itself turning only on terrors and horrors is no longer pleasant to the mind, and you cannot get so much as an Orthodox confessor in peace, —from going what way soever the hope of any solacement might lead them?

878. They go, poor ancient dames,—whom the heart were hard that did not pity: they go; with palpitations, with unmelodious suppressed screeching; all France screeching and cackling, in loud unsuppressed terror, behind and on both hands of them: such mutual suspicion is among men. At Arnay le Duc, above half-way to the frontiers, a Patriotic Municipality and Populace again takes courage to stop them: Louis Narbonne must now go back to Paris, must consult the National Assembly. National Assembly answers, not without an effort, that Mesdames may go. Whereupon Paris rises worse than ever, screeching half-distracted. Tuileries and precincts are filled with women and men, while the National Assembly debates this question of questions; Lafayette is needed at night for dispersing them, and the streets are to be illuminated. Commandant Berthier, a Berthier before whom are great things unknown, lies for the present under blockade at Bellevue in Versailles. By no tactics could he get Mesdames' Luggage stirred from the Courts there; frantic Versaillese women came screaming about him; his very troops cut the wagon-traces; he "retired to the interior," waiting better times.†

879. Nay in these same hours, while Mesdames,

---

* Carra's newspaper, 1st February, 1791 (in "Histoire Parlementaire," ix. 39).
† Campan, ii. 132.

hardly cut ont from Moret by the saber's edge, are driving rapidly, to foreign parts, and not yet stopped at Arnay, their august Nephew poor Monsieur, at Paris, has dived deep into his cellars of the Luxembourg for shelter; and, according to Montgaillard, can hardly be persuaded up again. Screeching multitudes environ that Luxembourg of his; drawn thither by report of his departure; hut at sight and sound of Monsieur, they become crowing multitudes; and escort Madame and him to the Tuileries with vivats.* It is a state of nervous excitability such as few nations know.

CHAPTER V.

THE DAY OF PONIARDS.

880. Or, again, what means this visible reparation of the Castle of Vincennes? Other Jails being all crowded with prisoners, new space is wanted here: that is the Municipal account. For in such changing of Judicatures, Parlements being abolished, and New Courts but just set up, prisoners have accumulated. Not to say that in these times of discord and club-law, offenses and committals are, at any rate, more numerous. Which Municipal account, does it not sufficiently explain the phenomenon? Surely, to repair the Castle of Vincennes was of all enter prises that an enlightened Municipality could undertake the most innocent.

881. Not so, however, does neighboring Saint-Antoine look on it. Saint-Antoine, to whom these peaked turrets and grim donjons, all too near her own dark dwelling are of themselves an offense. Was not Vincennes a kind of minor Bastille? Great Diderot and Philosophes have lain in durance here: great Mirabeau, in d sastrous eclipse, for forty-two months. And now when the old Bastille has become a dancing-ground (had any one the mirth to dance), and its stones are getting built into the Pont Louis-Seize, does this minor, comparative insignificance of a Bastille flank itself with fresh-hewn mullions, spread out tyrannous wings; menacing Patriotism? New space for prisoners: and what prisoners? A D'Orléans, with the chief Patriots on the tip of the Left? It is said, there runs "a subterranean passage" all the way from the Tuileries hither. Who knows? Paris, mined with quarries and catacombs, does hang wondrous over the abyss; Paris was once to be blown up,—though the powder, when we went to look, had got withdrawn. A Tuileries, sold to Austria and Coblentz, should have no subterranean passage. Out of which might not Coblentz or Austria issue, some morning; and with cannon of long range, "foudroyer," bethunder a patriotic Saint-Antoine into smolder and ruin!

882. So meditates the benighted soul of Saint-Antoine, as it sees the aproned workmen, in early spring, busy on these towers. An official-speaking Municipality, a Sieur Motier with his legions of mouchards, deserve no trust at all. Were Patriot Santerre, indeed, Commander! But the sonorous Brewer commands only our own Battalion: of such secrets he can explain nothing, knows, perhaps suspects much. And so the work goes on; and afflicted benighted Saint-Antoine hears rattle of hammers, sees stones suspended in air.†

883. Saint-Antoine prostrated the first great Bastille: will it falter over this comparative insignificance of a Bastille? Friends, what if we took pikes, firelocks, sledge-hammers; and help ourselves!— Speedier is no remedy; nor so certain. On the 28th day of February, Saint-Antoine turns cut, as it has now often done; and, apparently with little super-

fluous tumult, moves eastward to that eye-sorrow of Vincennes. With grave voice of authority, no need of bullying and shouting, Saint-Antoine signifies to parties concerned there, that its purpose is, To have this suspicious Stronghold razed level with the general soil of the country. Remonstrances may be proffered, with zeal, but it avails not. The outer gate goes up, drawbridges tumble; iron windowstanchions, smitten ont with sledge-hammers, become iron-crowbars: it rains a rain of furniture, stone-masses, slates: with chaotic clatter and rattle, Demolition clatters down. And now hasty expresses rush through the agitated streets, to warn Lafayette, and the Municipal and Departmental Authorities; Rumor warns a National Assembly, a Royal Tuileries, and all men who care to hear it: That Saint-Antoine is up; that Vincennes, and probably the last remaining Institution of the Country, is coming down.*

884. Quick then! Let Lafayette roll his drums and fly eastward; for to all Constitutional Patriots this is again bad news. And you, ye Friends of Royalty, snatch your poniards of improved structure, made to order; your sword-canes, secret army, and tickets of entry; quick, by back-stairs passages, rally round the Son of Sixty Kings. An effervescence probably got up by D'Orléans and Company, for the overthrow of Throne and Altar· it is said her Majesty shall be put in prison, put out of the way; what then will *his* Majesty be? Clay for the Sansculottic Potter! Or were it impossible to fly this day; a brave Noblesse suddenly all rallying? Peril threatens, hope invites: Dukes de Villequier, de Duras, Gentlemen of the Chamber give Tickets and admittance; a brave Noblesse is suddenly all rallying. Now were the time to "fall sword in hand on those gentry there," could it be done with effect.

885. The Hero of two Worlds is on his white charger: blue Nationals, horse and foot, hurrying eastward; Santerre, with the Saint-Antoine Battalion, is already there,—apparently indisposed to act. Heavy-laden Hero of two Worlds what tasks are these? The jeerings, provocative gambollings of that Patriot Suburb, which is all ont on the streets now, are hard to endure; unwashed Patriots jeering in sulky sport; one unwashed Patriot "seizing the General by the boot," to unhorse him. Santerre, ordered to fire, makes answer obliquely. "These are the men that took the Bastille;" and not a trigger stirs. Neither dare the Vincennes Magistracy give warrant of arrestment, or the smallest countenance: wherefore the General "will take it on himself" to arrest. By promptitude, by cheerful adroitness, patience and brisk valor without limits, the riot may be again bloodlessly appeased.

886. Meanwhile the rest of Paris, with more or less unconcern, may mind the rest of its business; for what is this but an effervescence, of which there are now so many? The National Assembly, in one of its stormiest moods, is debating a law against Emigration; Mirabeau declaring aloud, "I swear beforehand that I will not obey it." Mirabeau is often at the Tribune this day; with endless impediments from without; with the old unabated energy from within. What can murmurs and clamors, from Left or from Right, do to this man; like Teneriffe or Atlas unremoved? With clear thought; with strong bass voice, though at first low, uncertain, he claims audience, sways the storm of men; anon the sound of him waxes, softens: he rises into far-sounding melody of strength, triumphant, which subdues all hearts; his rude seamed face, desolate, fire-scathed, becomes fire-lit, and radiates: once again men feel, in these

* Montgaillard, ll. 282; "Deux Amis," vi. c. 1.
† Montgaillard, ll. 285.

* "Deux Amis," vi. 11-15; newspapers in "Histoire Parlementaire," ix. 111-117).

beggarly **ages**, what is the potency and omnipotency of man's word on the souls of men. "I will triumph, or be torn in fragments," he was once heard to say. "Silence," he cries now, in strong word of command, in imperial consciousness of strength, "Silence, the thirty voices (Silence aux trente voix)!"—and Robespierre and the Thirty Voices die into mutterings; and the Law is once more as Mirabeau would have it.

887. How different, at the same instant, is General Lafayette's street-eloquence; wrangling with sonorous Brewers, with an ungrammatical Saint-Antoine! Most different, again, from both is the Café-de-Valois eloquence, and suppressed fanfaronade, of this multitude of men with Tickets of Entry; who are now inundating the Corridors of the Tuileries. Such things can go on simultaneously in one City. How much more in one Country; in one Planet with its discrepancies, every Day a mere crackling infinitude of discrepancies,—which nevertheless do yield some coherent net-product, though an infinitesimally small one!

888. But be this as it may, Lafayette has saved Vincennes; and is marching homeward with some dozen of arrested demolitionists. Royalty is not yet saved;—nor indeed specially endangered. But to the King's Constitutional Guard, to these old Gardes Françaises, or Center Grenadiers, as it chanced to be, this affluence of men with Tickets of Entry is becoming more and more unintelligible. Is his Majesty verily for Metz, then: to be carried off by these men, on the spur of the instant? That revolt of Saint-Antoine got up by traitor Royalists for a stalking horse? Keep a sharp outlook, ye Center Grenadiers on duty here: good never came from the "men in black." Nay they have cloaks, rédingotes; some of them leather-breeches, boots,—as if for instant riding! Or what is this that sticks visible from the lapelle of Chevalier de Court?* Too like the handle of some cutting or stabbing instrument! He glides and goes; and still the dudgeon sticks from his left lapelle. "Hold, Monsieur!"—a Center Grenadier clutches him; clutches the protrusive dudgeon, whisks it out in the face of the world; by Heaven, a very dagger; hunting-knife or whatsoever you will call it: fit to drink the life of Patriotism!

889. So fared it with Chevalier de Court, early in the day; not without noise; not without commentaries. And now this continually increasing multitude at nightfall? Have they daggers too? Alas, with them too, after angry parleyings, there has begun a groping and a rummaging; all men in black, spite of their Tickets of Entry, are clutched by the collar, and groped. Scandalous to think of: for always, as the dirk, sword-cane, pistol, or were it but tailor's bodkin, is found on him, and with loud scorn drawn forth from him, he the hapless man in black, is flung all too rapidly down stairs. Flung; and ignominiously descends, head foremost accelerated by ignominious shovings from sentry after sentry; nay, as it is written, by smitings, twitchings,—spurnings à posteriori, not to be named. In this accelerated way emerges uncertain which end uppermost, man after man in black, through all issues, into the Tuileries Garden; emerges, alas, into the arms of an indignant multitude, now gathered and gathering there, in the hour of dusk, to see what is toward, and whether the Hereditary Representative is carried off or not. Hapless men in black; at last *convicted* of poniards made to order; convicted "Chevaliers of the Poniard!" Within is as the burning ship; without is as the deep sea. Within is no help; his Majesty, looking forth, one moment, from his interior sanctuaries, coldly bids all visitors "give up their weapons;" and shuts the door again. The weapons given up form a

* Weber, ii. 286.

heap: the convicted Chevaliers of the Poniard keep descending pell-mell, with impetuous velocity; and at the bottom of all staircases the mixed multitude receive them, hustles, buffets, chases and disperses them.

890. Such sight meets Lafayette, in the dusk of the evening, as he returns, successful with difficulty at Vincennes: Sansculotte Scylla hardly weathered, here is Aristocrat Charybdis gurgling under his lee! The patient Hero of two Worlds almost loses temper. He accelerates, does not retard. the flying Chevaliers; delivers, indeed, this or the other hunted Loyalist of quality, but rates him in bitter words, such as the hour suggested; such as no saloon could pardon. Hero ill-bested; hanging, so to speak, in mid-air; hateful to Rich divinities above; hateful to Indigent mortals below! Duke de Villequier, Gentleman of the Chamber, gets such contumelious rating, in presence of all people there, that he may see good first to exculpate himself in the Newspapers; then, that not prospering, to retire over the frontiers, and begin plotting at Brussels.† His Apartment will stand vacant; usefuller, as we may find, than when it stood occupied.

891. So fly the Chevaliers of the Poniard; hunted of Patriotic men, shamefully in the thickening dusk. A dim miserable business; born of darkness; dying away there in the thickening dusk and dimness. In the midst of which, however, let the reader discern clearly one figure running for its life: Crispin-Catiline d'Esprémênil,—for the last time, or the last but one. It is not yet three years since these same Center Grenadiers, Gardes Françaises then, marched him toward the Calypso Isles, in the gray of the May morning; and he and they have got thus far. Buffetted, beaten down, delivered by popular Pétion, he might well answer bitterly: "And I too, Monsieur have been carried on the People's shoulders."‡ A fact which popular Pétion, if he like, can meditate.

892. But happily, one way and another, the speedy night covers up this ignominious Day of Poniards; and the Chevaliers escape, though maltreated, with torn coat-skirts and heavy hearts, to their respective dwelling-houses. Riot twofold is quelled; and little blood shed, if it be not insignificant blood from the nose; Vincennes stands undemolished, reparable; and the Hereditary Representative has not been stolen, nor the Queen smuggled into Prison. A day long remembered: commented on with loud ha-has and deep grumblings; with bitter scornfulness of triumph, bitter rancor of defeat. Royalism, as usual, imputes it to D'Orléans and the Anarchists intent on insulting Majesty: Patriotism, as usual, to Royalists, and even Constitutionalists, intent on stealing Majesty to Metz: we, also, as usual, to Preternatural Suspicion, and Phœbus Apollo having made himself like the Night.

893. Thus, however, has the reader seen, in an unexpected arena, on this last day of February, 1791, the Three long-contending elements of French Society dashed forth into singular comico-tragical collision; acting and reacting openly to the eye. Constitutionalism, at once quelling Sansculottic riot at Vincennes, and Royalist treachery in the Tuileries, is great, this day, and prevails. As for poor Royalism, tossed to and fro in that manner, its daggers all left in a heap, what can one think of it? Every dog, the Adage says, has its day: *has* it; has had it; or will have it. For the present, the day is Lafayette's and the Constitution's. Nevertheless Hunger and Jacobinism, fast growing fanatical, still work; their day, were they once fanatical, will come. Hitherto,

* "Histoire Parlementaire." ix. 139–148.
† Montgaillard, ii. 286.
‡ See Mercier, ii. 40, 202.

in all tempests, Lafayette, like some divine Sea-ruler, raises his serene-head: the upper Æolus blasts fly back to their caves, like foolish unbidden winds: the under sea-billows they had vexed into froth allay themselves. But if, as we often write, the *submarine* Titanic Fire-powers came into play, the Ocean-bed from beneath being *burst?* If they hurled Poseidon Lafayette and his Constitution out of Space; and, in the Titanic melly, sea were mixed with sky?

CHAPTER VI.

MIRABEAU.

894. The spirit of France waxes ever more acrid, fever-sick: toward the final outburst of dissolution and delirium. Suspicion rules all minds: contending parties cannot now commingle; stand separated sheer asunder, eyeing one another, in most anguish mood, of cold terror, or hot rage. Counter-Revolution, Days of Poniards, Castries Duels; Flight of Mesdames, of Monsieur and Royalty! Journalism shrills ever louder its cry of alarm. The sleepless Dionysius-Ear of the Forty-eight Sections, how feverishly quick has it grown; convulsing with strange pangs the whole sick Body, as in such sleeplessness and sickness the ear will do!

895. Since Royalists got Poniards made to order, and a Sieur Motier is no better than he should be, shall not Patriotism too, even of the indigent sort, have Pikes, second-hand Firelocks, in readiness for the worst? The anvils ring, during this March month, with hammering of Pikes. A Constitutional Municipality promulgated its Placard, that no citizen except the " active " or cash-citizen was entitled to have arms; but there rose, instantly responsive, such a tempest of astonishment from Club and Section, that the Constitutional Placard, almost next morning, had to cover itself up, and die away into inanity, in a second improved edition.* So the hammering continues; as all that it betokens does.

896. Mark, again, how the extreme tip of the Left is mounting in favor, if not in its own National Hall, yet with the Nation, especially with Paris. Far in such universal panic of doubt, the opinion that is sure of itself, as the meagerest opinion may the soonest be, is the one to which all men will rally. Great is Belief, were it never so meager; and leads captive the doubting heart. Incorruptible Robespierre has been elected Public Accuser in our new Courts of Judicature; virtuous Pétion, it is thought, may rise to be Mayor. Cordelier Danton, called also by triumphant majorities, sits at the Departmental Council-table; colleague there of Mirabeau. Of incorruptible Robespierre it was long ago predicted that he might go far, mean meager mortal though he was; for Doubt dwelt not in him.

897. Under which circumstances ought not Royalty likewise to cease doubting, and begin deciding and acting? Royalty has always that sure trump-card in its hand: Flight out of Paris. Which sure trump-card, as we see, keeps ever and anon clutching at, grasping; and swashes it forth tentatively; yet never tables it, still puts it back again. Play it, O Royalty! If there be a chance left, this seems it, and verily the last chance; and now every hour is rendering this a doubtfuler. Alas, one would so fain both fly and not fly; play one's card and have it to play. Royalty, in all human likelihood, will not play its trump-card till the honors, one after one, be mainly lost; and such trumping of it prove to be the sudden finish of the game!

898. Here accordingly a question always arises; of

* Ordonnance du 17 Mars 1791 ("Histoire Parlementaire," ix. 257).

the prophetic sort, which cannot now be answered. Suppose Mirabeau, with whom Royalty takes deep counsel, as with a Prime Minister that cannot yet legally avow himself as such, had got his arrangements *completed?* Arrangements he has; far-stretching plans that dawn fitfully on us, by fragments, in the confused darkness. Thirty Departments ready to sign loyal Addresses, of prescribed tenor; King carried out of Paris, but only to Compiègne and Rouen, hardly to Metz, since, once for all, no Emigrant rabble shall take the lead in it; National Assembly consenting, by dint of loyal Addresses, by management; by force of Bouillé, to hear reason, and follow thither!* Was it so, on *these* terms, that Jacobinism and Mirabeau were then to grapple, in their Hercules-and-Typhon duel; Death inevitable for the one or the other? The duel itself is determined on, and sure: but on what terms; much more with what issue, we in vain guess. It is vague darkness all: unknown what is to be; unknown even what has already been. The giant Mirabeau walks in darkness, as we said; companionless, on wild ways: what his thoughts during these months were, no record of Biographer, nor vague Fils Adoptif, will now ever disclose.

899. To us, endeavoring to cast his horoscope, it of course remains doubly vague. There is one Herculean man; in internecine duel with him, there is Monster after Monster. Emigrant Noblesse return, sword on thigh, vaunting of their Loyalty never sullied; descending from the air, like Harpy-swarms with ferocity, with obscene greed. Earthward there is the Typhon of Anarchy, Political, Religious; sprawling hundred-headed, say with Twenty-five million heads; wide as the area of France; fierce as Frenzy, strong in very Hunger. With these shall the Serpent-queller do battle continually, and expect no rest.

900. As for the King, he as usual will go wavering chameleon-like; changing color and purpose with the color of his environment:—good for no Kingly use, On one royal person, on the Queen only, can Mirabeau perhaps place dependence. It is possible, the greatness of this man, not unskilled too in blandishments, courtiership, and graceful adroitness, might, with most legitimate sorcery, fascinate the volatile Queen, and fix her to him. She has courage for all noble daring; an eye and a heart: the soul of Theresa's daughter. "Faut-il donc. Is it fated then," she passionately writes to her Brother, "that I with the blood I am come of, with the sentiments I have' must live and die among such mortals?"† Alas' poor Princess, Yes. "She is the only man," has Mirabeau observes, "whom his Majesty has about him." Of one other man Mirabeau is still surer; of himself. There lie his resources; sufficient or insufficient.

901. Dim and great to the eye of Prophecy looks that future. A perpetual life-and-death battle; confusion from above and from below;—mere confused darkness for us; with here and there some streak of faint lurid light. We see a King perhaps laid aside; not tonsured.—tonsuring is out of fashion now,—but say sent away anywhither, with handsome annual allowance, and stock of smith-tools. We see a Queen and Dauphin, Regent and Minor; a Queen "mounted on horseback," in the din of battles, with Moriamur pro rege nostro! "Such a day," Mirabeau writes, "may come."

902. Din of battles, wars more than civil, confusion from above and from below: in such environment the eye of Prophecy sees Comte de Mirabeau, like some Cardinal de Retz, stormfully maintain himself; with head all-devising, heart all-daring, i

* See "Fils Adoptif," vii. l. 6; Dumont, c. 11, 12, 14.
† "Fils Adoptif," ubi supra.

not victorious, yet unvanquished, while life is left him. The specialties and issues of it, no eye or Prophecy can guess at: it is clouds, we repeat, and tempestuous night; and in the middle of it, now visible, far-darting, now laboring in eclipse, is Mirabeau indomitably struggling to be Cloud-Compeller! —One can say that, had Mirabeau lived, the History of France and of the World had been different. Further, that the man would have needed, as few men ever did, the whole compass of that same "Art of Daring (Art d'Oser)," which he so prized; and likewise that he, above all men then living, would have practiced and manifested it. Finally, that some substantiality, and no empty simulacrum of a formula, would have been the result realized by him, a result you could have loved, a result you could have hated; by no likelihood, a result you could only have rejected with closed lips, and swept into quick forgetfulness forever. Had Mirabeau lived one other year.

CHAPTER VII.

DEATH OF MIRABEAU.

903. But Mirabeau could not live another year, any more than he could live another thousand years. Men's years are numbered and the tale of Mirabeau's was now complete. Important or unimportant; to be mentioned in World-History for some centuries, or not to be mentioned there beyond a day or two, —it matters not to peremptory Fate. From amid the press of ruddy busy Life, the Pale Messenger beckons silently: wide-spreading interests, projects, salvation of French Monarchies, what thing soever man has on hand, he must suddenly quit it all, and go. Wert thou saving French Monarchies: wert thou blacking shoes on the Pont Neuf! The most important of men cannot stay; did the World's History depend on an hour, that hour is not to be given. Whereby, indeed, it come that these same *would-have-beens* are mostly a vanity; and the World's History could never in the least be what it would, or might, or should, by any manner of potentiality, but simply and altogether what it *is*.

904 The fierce wear and tear of such an existence has wasted out the giant oaken strength of Mirabeau. A fret and fever that keeps heart and brain on fire; excess of effort, of excitement; excess of all kinds: labor incessant, almost beyond credibility! "If I had not lived with him," says Dumont, "I never should have known what a man can make of one day, what things may be placed within the interval of twelve hours. A day for this man was more than a week or a month is for others: the mass of things he guided on together was prodigious; from scheming to the executing not a moment lost."—"Monsieur le Comte" said his Secretary to him once, "what you require is impossible."—"Impossible!"—answered he starting from his chair, "Ne me dites jamais ce bête de mot (Never name to me that blockhead of a word)."* And the social repasts; the dinner which he gives as Commandant National Guards, which "cost five hundred pounds;" alas "the Syreus of the Opera;" and all the ginger that is hot in the mouth: —down what a course is this man hurled! Cannot Mirabeau stop; cannot he fly, and save himself alive? No! there is a Nessus-Shirt on this Hercules; he must storm and burn there without *rest*, till he be consumed. Human strength, never so Herculean, has its measure. Herald shadows flit pale across the fire-brain of Mirabeau; heralds of the pale repose. While he tosses and storms, straining every nerve, in that sea of ambition and confusion, there comes, somber and still, a

*Dumont, p. 311.

monition that for him the issue of it will be swift death.

905. In January last you might see him as President of the Assembly; "his neck wrapt in linen cloths, at the evening session:" there was sick heat of the blood, alternate darkening and flashing in the eyesight; he had to apply leeches, after the morning labor, and preside bandaged. "At parting he embraced me," says Dumont, "with an emotion I had never seen in him: 'I am dying, my friend, dying as by slow fire; we shall perhaps not meet again. When I am gone, they will know what the value of me was. The miseries I have held back will burst from all sides on France.'"* Sickness gives louder warning; but cannot be listened to. On the 27th day of March, proceeding toward the Assembly, he had to seek rest and help in Friend de Lamarck's by the road; and lay there, for an hour, half-fainted, stretched on a sofa. To the Assembly nevertheless he went, as if in spite of Destiny itself; spoke, loud and eager, five several times; then quitted the Tribune—forever. He steps out, utterly exhausted, into the Tuileries Gardens; many people press round him, as usual, with applications, memorials; he says to the Friend who was with him:"Take me out of this!"

906. And so, on the last day of March, 1791, endless anxious multitudes beset the Rue de la Chaussée d'Antin; incessantly inquiring within door there, in that House numbered, in our time, 42, the overwearied giant has fallen down, to die.† Crowds of all parties and kinds; of all ranks from the king to the meanest man! The King sends publicly twice a-day to inquire; privately besides: from the world at large there is no end of inquiring. "A written bulletin is handed out every three hours," is copied and circulated; in the end, it is printed. The People spontaneously keep silence; no carriage shall enter with its noise; there is crowding pressure; but the Sister of Mirabeau is reverently recognized, and has free way made for her. The People stand mute, heart-stricken; to all it seems as if a great calamity were nigh: as if the last man of France, who could have swayed these coming troubles, lay there at hand-grips with the unearthly power.

907. The silence of a whole People, the wakeful toil of Cabanis Friend and Physician, skills not: on Saturday the second day of April, Mirabeau feels that the last of the Days has risen for him; that on this day he has to depart and be no more. His death is Titanic, as his life has been! Lit up, for the last time, in the glare of coming dissolution, the mind of the man is all glowing and burning: utters itself in sayings, such as men long remember. He longs to live, yet acquiesces in death, argues not with the inexorable. His speech is wild and wondrous: unearthly Phantasms dancing now their torch-dance round his soul; the soul itself looking out, fire-radiant, motionless, girt together for that great hour! At times comes a beam of light from him on the world he is quitting. "I carry in my heart the death-dirge of the French Monarchy; the dead remains of it will now be the spoil of the factious." Or again, when he heard the cannon fire, what is characteristic too: "Have we the Achilles's Funeral already?" So likewise, while some friend is supporting him: "Yes, support that head; would I could bequeath it to thee!" For the man dies as he has lived; self-conscious, conscious of a world looking on. He gazes forth on the young Spring, which for him will never be summer. The Sun has risen; he says, "Si ce n'est pas là Dieu, c'est du moins son cousin germain."‡—Death has mastered the outworks; power

*Dumont, p. 307.
† "Fils Adoptif," viii 420-470.
‡ "Fils Adoptif," viii 450: "Journal de la maladie et de la mort de Mirabeau," par P. J. G. Cabanis (Paris, 1803).

of speech is gone; the citadel of the heart still hold-ing out: the moribund giant, passionately, by sign, demands paper and pen; writes his passionate de-mand for opium, to end these agonies. The sorrow-ful Doctor shakes his head: "Dormir (To sleep)," writes the other, passionately pointing at it! So dies a gigantic Heathen and Titan; stumbling blindly, undismayed, down to his rest. At half-past eight in the morning Doctor Petit, standing at the foot of the bed, says, "Il ne souffre plus." His suffering and his working are now ended.

908. Even so, ye silent Patriot multitudes, all ye men of France; this man is rapt away from you. He has fallen suddenly, without bending till he broke; as a tower falls, smitten by sudden lightning. His word ye shall hear no more, his guidance follow no more. The multitudes depart, heart-struck; spread the sad tidings. How touching is the loyalty of men to their Sovereign Man! All theaters, public amusements close; no joyful meeting can be held in these nights, joy is not for them: the People break in upon private dancing-parties, and sullenly com-mand that they cease. Of such dancing-parties ap-parently but two came to light; and these also have gone out. The gloom is universal; never in this City was such sorrow for one death; never since that old night when Louis XII. departed, "and the Crieurs des Corps went sounding their bells and cry-ing along the streets: Le bon roi Louis, père du peuple, est mort (The good King Louis, Father of the People, is dead)!"[*] King Mirabeau is now the lost King; and one may say with little exaggeration, all the People mourns for him.

909. For three days there is low wide moan; weep-ing in the National Assembly itself. The streets are all mournful; orators mounted on the bornes, with large silent audience, preaching the funeral sermon of the dead. Let no coachman whip fast, distrac-tively with his rolling wheels, or almost at all, through these groups! His traces may be cut; himself and his fare, as incurable Aristocrats, hurled sulkily into the kennels. The bourn-stone orators speak as it is given them; the Sansculottic People, with its rude soul, listens eager,—as men will to any Sermon, or Sermo, when it is a spoken Word meaning a Thing, and not a Babblement meaning No-thing. In the Restaurateur's of the Palais-Royal, the waiter re-marks, "Fine weather, Monsieur:"—"Yes, my friend," answers the ancient Man of Letters, "very fine; but Mirabeau is dead." Hoarse rhythmic threno-dies come also from the throats of ballad-singers; are sold on gray-white paper at a son each.[†] But of Portraits, engraved, painted, hewn and written; of Eulogies, Reminiscences, Biographies, nay Vaude-villes, Dramas and Melodramas, in all Provinces of France, there will, through these coming months, be the due immensurable crop; thick as the leaves of Spring. Nor, that a tincture of burlesque might be in it, is Gobel's Episcopal Mandement wanting; goose Gobel, who has just been made Constitutional Bishop of Paris. A Mandement wherein Ça ira al-ternates very strangely with Nomine Domini, and you are, with a grave countenance, invited to "re-joice at possessing in the midst of you a body of Pre-lates created by Mirabeau, zealous followers of his doctrine, faithful imitators of his virtues.[‡] So speaks, and cackles manifold, the Sorrow of France; wail-ing articulately, inarticulately, as it can, that a Sov-ereign Man is snatched away. In the National As-sembly, when difficult questions are astir, all eyes

will "turn mechanically to the place where Mirabeau sat,"—and Mirabeau is absent now

910. On the third evening of the lamentation, the 4th of April, there is solemn Public Funeral; such as deceased mortal seldom had. Procession of a league in length; of mourners reckoned loosely at 100,000. All roofs are thronged with on-lookers, all windows, lamp-irons, branches of trees. "Sadness is painted on every countenance; many persons weep. There is double hedge of National Guards; there is National Assembly in a body; Jacobin Society, and Societies; King's Ministers, Municipals, and all Notabilities, Patriot or Aristocrat. Bouillé is notice-able there, "with his hat on;" says, hat drawn over his brow, hiding many thoughts! Slow-wending, in religious silence, the Procession of a league in length, under the level sun-rays, for it is five o'clock, moves and marches; with its sable plumes; itself in a re-ligious silence; but, by fits with the muffled roll of drums, by fits with some long-drawn wail of music, and strange new clangor of trombones, and metallic dirge-voice: amid the infinite hum of men. In the Church of Saint-Eustache, there is funeral oration by Cerutti; and discharge of fire-arms, which "brings down pieces of the plaster." Thence, forward again to the Church of Sainte-Geneviève; which has been consecrated, by superior decree, on the spur of this time, into a Pantheon for the Great Men of the Fatherland (Aux Grands Hommes la Patrie récon-naissante). Hardly at midnight is the business done; and Mirabeau left in his dark dwelling: first tenant of that Fatherland's Pantheon.

911. Tenant, alas, who inhabits but at will, and shall be cast out. For, in these days of convulsion and dejection, not even the dust of the dead is per-mitted to rest. Voltaire's bones are, by and by, to be carried from their stolen grave in the Abbey of Scel-lières, to an eager stealing grave, in Paris his birth-city: all mortals processioning and perorating there; cars drawn by eight white horses, goadsters in classi-cal costume, with fillets and wheat-ears enough;— though the weather is of the wettest.[*] Evangelist Jean Jacques too, as is most proper, must be dug up from Ermenonville, and processioned, with pomp, with sensibility, to the Pantheon of the Fatherland.[†] He and others: while again Mirabeau, we say, is cast forth from it, happily incapable of being re-placed; and rests now, irrecognizable, reburied hastily at dead of night "in the central part of the Church-yard Sainte-Catherine, in the Suburb Saint-Marceau," to be disturbed no farther.

912. So blazes out, far-seen, a Man's Life, and be-sides ashes and a caput mortuum, in this World-Pyre, which we name French Revolution: not the first that consumed itself there; nor, by thousands and many millions, the last! A man who "had swallowed all formulas;" who, in these strange times and circumstances, felt called to live Titanically, and also to die so. As he, for his part, had swallowed all formulas, what Formula is there, never so compre-hensive, that will express truly the plus and the minus of him, give us the accurate net-result of him? There is hitherto none such. Moralities not a few must shriek condemnatory over this Mirabeau; the Morality by which he could be judged has not yet got uttered in the speech of men. We will say this of him again: That he is a Reality and no Simula-crum; a living Son of Nature our general Mother; not a hollow Artifice, and mechanism of Convention-alities, son of nothing, brother to nothing. In which little word, let the earnest man, walking sorrowful in a world mostly of "Stuffed Clothes-suits," that

---

* Hénault, "Abrégé Chronologique," p. 429.

† "Fils Adoptif," viii. l. 10; newspapers and excerpts (in "Histoire Parlementaire," ix. 366–402).

‡ "Histoire Parlementaire," ix. 405.

* Moniteur, du 13 Juillet 1791.

† Ibid. du 15 Septembre 1794. See also du 30 Aout, etc., 1791.

chatter and grin meaningless on him, quite *ghastly* to the earnest soul,—think what significance there is!

913. Of men who, in such sense, are alive, and see with eyes, the number is now not great. It may be well, if in this huge French Revolution itself, with its all-developing fury, we find some. Three Mortals driven rabid we find; sputtering the acridest logic; baring their breast to the battle-hail, their neck to the guillotine :—of whom it is so painful to say that they too are still, in good part, manufactured Formalities, not Facts but Hearsays!

914. Honor to the strong man in these ages who has shaken himself loose of shams, and is something. For in the way of being *worthy*, the first condition surely is that one *be*. Let Cant cease, at all risks and at all costs: till Cant cease, nothing else can begin. Of human Criminals, in these centuries, writes the Moralist, I find but one unforgivable: the Quack, "Hateful to God," as divine Dante sings, "and to the Enemies of God.

"'A Dio spiacente ed a' nemici sui!'"

915. But whoever will, with sympathy, which is the first essential toward insight, look at this questionable Mirabeau, may find that there lay verily in him, as the basis of all, a Sincerity, great free Earnestness; nay, call it Honesty; for the man did before all things see, with that clear flashing vision, into what *was*, into what existed as fact; and did, with his wild heart, follow that and no other. Whereby on what ways soever he travels and struggles, often enough falling, he is still a brother man. Hate him not; thou canst not hate him! Shining through such soil and tarnish and now victorious effulgent, and oftenest struggling eclipsed, the light of genius itself is in this man; which was never yet base and hateful; but at worst was lamentable, lovable with pity. They say that he was ambitious, that he wanted to be Minister. It is most true. And was he not simply the one man in France who could have done any good as Minister? Not vanity alone, not pride alone; far from that! Wild burstings of affection were in this great heart; of fierce lightning and soft dew of pity. So sunk bemired in wretchedest defacements, it may be said of him, like the Magdalen of old, that he loved much; his Father, the harshest of old crabbed men, he loved with warmth, with veneration.

916. Be it that his falls and follies are manifold,—as himself often lamented even with tears.[*] Alas, is not the Life of every such man already a poetic Tragedy; made up "of Fate and of one's own Deservings," of Schicksal and eigene Schuld; full of the elements of Pity and Fear? This brother man if not Epic for us, is Tragic; if not great, is large; large in his qualities, world-large in his destinies. Whom other men, recognizing him as such, may, through long times, remember, and draw nigh to examine and consider: these, in their several dialects, will say of him and sing of him,—till the right thing be said; and so the Formula that *can* judge him be no longer an undiscovered one.

917. Here then the wild Gabriel Honoré drops from the tissue of our History; not without a tragic farewell. He is gone; the flower of the wild Riquetti or Arrighetti kindred; which seems as if in him, with one last effort, it had done its best, and then expired, or sunk down to the undistinguished level. Crabbed old Marquis Mirabeau, the Friend of Men, sleeps sound. The Bailli Mirabeau, worthy Uncle, will soon die forlorn alone. Barrel Mirabeau already gone across the Rhine, his Regiment of Emigrants will drive nigh desperate. "Barrel Mirabeau," says a biographer of his, "went indignantly across the Rhine, and drilled Emigrant Regiments. But as

[*] Dumont, p. 287.

he sat one morning in his tent, sour of stomach doubtless and of heart, meditating in Tartarean humor on the turn things took, a certain Captain or Subaltern demanded admittance on business. Such Captain is refused; he again demands, with refusal; and then again; till Colonel Viscount Barrel Mirabeau, blazing up into a mere burning brandy-barrel, clutches his sword, and tumbles out on this canaille of an intruder,—alas, on the canaille of an intruder's sword-point, who had drawn with swift dexterity; and dies, and the Newspapers name it *apoplexy* and *alarming accident*." So die the Mirabeaus.

918. New Mirabeaus one hears not of: the wild kindred, as we said, is gone out with its greatest. As families and kindreds sometimes do; producing after long ages of unnoted notability, some living quintessence of all the qualities they had, to flame forth as a man world-noted; after whom they rest as if exhausted; the scepter passing to others. The chosen Last of the Mirabeaus is gone; the chosen man of France is gone. It was he who shook old France from its basis; and, as if with his single hand, has held it toppling there, still unfallen. What things depended on that one man! He is as a ship suddenly shivered on sunk rocks: much swims on the waste waters, far from help.

BOOK FOURTH.

VARENNES.

CHAPTER I.

EASTER AT SAINT-CLOUD.

919. The French Monarchy may now therefore be considered as, in all human probability, lost; as struggling henceforth in blindness as well as weakness, the last light of reasonable guidance having gone out. What remains of resources their poor Majesties will waste still further, in uncertain loitering and wavering. Mirabeau himself had to complain that they only gave him half confidence, and always had some plan within his plan. Had they fled frankly with him to Rouen or anywhither, long ago! They may fly now with chance immeasurably lessened; which will go on lessening toward absolute zero. Decide, O Queen; poor Louis can decide nothing: execute this flight-project, or at least abandon it. Correspondence with Bouillé there has been enough; what profits consulting and hypotheses, while all around is in fierce activity of practice? The Rustic sits waiting till the river run dry: alas, with you it is not a common river, but a Nile Inundation; snows melting in the unseen mountains; till all, and you where you sit, be submerged.

920. Many things invite to flight. The voice of Journals invites; Royalist Journals proudly hinting it as a threat, Patriot Journals rabidly denouncing it as a terror. Mother Society, waxing more and more emphatic, invites ;—so emphatic that, as was prophesied, Lafayette and your limited Patriots have ere long to branch off from her, and form themselves into Feuillans; with infinite public controversy; the victory in which, doubtful though it look, will remain with the unlimited Mother. Moreover, ever since the Day of Poniards, we have seen unlimited Patriotism openly equipping itself with arms. Citizens denied "activity," which is facetiously made to signify a certain weight of purse, cannot buy blue uniforms, and be Guardsmen; but man is greater than blue cloth; man can fight, if need be, in multiform cloth, or even almost without cloth,—as Sans-culotte. So pikes continue to be hammered, whether those Dirks of improved structure with barbs be "meant for the West-India market," or not meant

Men beat, the wrong way, their plowshares into swords. Is there not what we may call an "Austrian Committee" (Comité Autrichien), sitting daily and nightly in the Tuileries? Patriotism, by vision and suspicion, knows it too well! If the King fly, will there not be Aristocrat-Austrian invasion; butchery; replacement of Feudalism; wars more than civil? The hearts of men are saddened and maddened.

921. Dissident Priests likewise give trouble enough. Expelled from their Parish Churches, where Constitutional Priests, elected by the Public have replaced them, these unhappy persons resort to, Convents of Nuns, or other such receptacles; and there, on Sabbath, collecting assemblages of Anti-Constitutional individuals, who have grown devout all on a sudden,* they worship or pretend to worship in their strait-laced contumacious manner; to the scandal of Patriotism. Dissident Priests, passing along with their sacred wafer for the dying, seem wishful to be massacred in the streets; wherein Patriotism will not gratify them. Slighter palm of martyrdom, however, shall not be denied; martyrdom not of massacre, yet of fustigation. At the refractory places of worship, Patriot men appear; Patriot women with strong hazel wands, which they apply. Shut thy eyes, O Reader; see not this misery, peculiar to these later times,—of martydom without sincerity, with only cant and contumacy! A dead Catholic Church is not allowed to lie dead; no, it is *galvanized* into the detestablest death-life; whereat Humanity, we say, shuts its eyes. For the Patriot women take their hazel wands, and fustigate, amid laughter of bystanders, with alacrity: broad bottom of Priests; alas, Nuns too, reversed and cotillons retroussés! The National Guard does what it can; Municipality "invokes the Principles of Toleration;" grants Dissident worshipers the Church of the Théatins: promising protection. But it is to no purpose: at the door of that Théatins Church appears a Placard, and suspended atop, like Plebeian Consular fasces—a Bundle of Rods! The Principles of Toleration must do the best they may: but no Dissident man shall worship contumaciously; there is a Plebiscitum to that effect; which, though unspoken, is like the laws of the Medes and Persians. Dissident contumacious Priests ought not to be harbored, even in private, by any man: the Club of the Cordeliers openly denounces Majesty himself as doing it.†

922. Many things invite to flight: but probably this thing above all others, that it has become impossible! On the 15th of April, notice is given that his Majesty, who has suffered much from catarrh lately, will enjoy the Spring weather, for a few days, at Saint-Cloud. Out at Saint-Cloud? Wishing to celebrate his Easter, his Pâques, or Pasch, there; with refractory Anti-Constitutional Dissidents?— wishing rather to make off for Compiègne, and thence to the Frontiers? As were, in good sooth, perhaps feasible, or would once have been; nothing but some two chasseurs attending you; chasseurs easily corrupted! It is a pleasant possibility, execute it or not. Men say there are 30,000 Chevaliers of the Poniard lurking in the woods there: lurking in the woods, and 30,000,—for the human Imagination is not fettered. But now, how easily might these, dashing out on Lafayette, snatch off the Hereditary Representative; and roll away with him, after the manner of a whirl-blast, whither they listed!—Enough, it were well the King did not go. Lafayette is forewarned and forearmed: but, indeed, is the risk his only; or his and all France's?

923. Monday the 18th of April is come; the Easter Journey to Saint-Cloud shall take effect. National Guard has got its orders; a First Division, as Advanced Guard, has even marched, and probably arrived. His Majesty's Maison-bouche, they say, is all busy stewing and frying at Saint-Cloud; the King's dinner not far from ready there. About one o'clock the Royal Carriage, with its eight royal blacks, shoots stately into the Place du Carrousel: draws up to receive its royal burden. But hark! from the neighboring Church of Saint-Roch, the tocsin begins ding-donging. Is the King stolen, then; is he going; gone! Multitudes of persons crowd the Carrousel: the Royal Carriage still stands there, —and, by Heaven's strength, shall stand!

924. Lafayette comes up, with aids-de-camp and oratory; pervading the groups: "Taisez-vous," answer the groups; "the King shall not go." Monsieur appears, at an upper window: 10,000 voices bray and shriek, "Nous ne voulons pas que la Roi parte." Their Majesties have mounted. Crack go the whips; but twenty Patriot arms have seized each of the eight bridles: there is rearing, rocking, vociferation; not the smallest headway. In vain does Lafayette fret, indignant; and perorate and strive: Patriots in the passion of terror bellow round the Royal Carriage; it is one bellowing sea of Patriot terror run frantic. Will Royalty fly off toward Austria; like a lit rocket, toward endless Conflagration of Civil War? Stop it, ye Patriots, in the name of Heaven! Rude voices passionately apostrophize Royalty itself. Usher Campan, and other the like official persons, pressing forward with help or advice, are clutched by the sashes, and hurled and whirled, in a confused perilous manner, so that her Majesty has to plead passionately from the carriage-window.

925. Order cannot be heard, cannot be followed; National Guards know not how to act. Center Grenadiers, of the Observatoire Battalion, are there; not on duty, alas, in quasi-mutiny; speaking rude disobedient words; threatening the mounted Guards with sharp shot if they hurt the people. Lafayette mounts and dismounts; runs haranguing, panting; on the verge of despair. For an hour and three-quarters; "seven quarters of an hour," by the Tuileries Clock! Desperate Lafayette will open a passage, were it by the cannon's mouth, if his Majesty will order. Their Majesties, counselled to it by Royalist friends, by Patriot foes, dismount; and retire in, with heavy indignant heart; giving up the enterprise. Maison-bouche may eat that cooked dinner themselves: his Majesty shall not see Saint-Cloud this day,—nor any day.*

926. The pathetic fable of imprisonment in one's own Palace has become a sad fact, then? Majesty complains to Assembly; Municipality deliberates, proposes to petition or address; Sections respond with sullen brevity of negation. Lafayette flings down his commission; appears in civic pepper-and-salt frock; and cannot be flattered back again; not in less than three days; and by unheard-of entreaty; National Guards kneeling to him, and declaring that it is not sycophancy, that they are free men kneeling here to the *Statue of Liberty*. For the rest, those Center Grenadiers of the Observatoire are disbanded,—yet indeed are re-enlisted, all but fourteen, under a new name, and with new quarters. The King must keep his Easter in Paris; meditating much on this singular posture of things; but as good as determined now to fly from it, desire being whetted by difficulty.

* Toulongeon, i. 262.
† Newspapers of April and June, 1791 (in "Histoire Parlementaire," ix. 449; x. 217).

* "Deux Amis," vi. c. 1.; "Histoire Parlementaire," ix. 407-414.

CHAPTER. II.

EASTER AT PARIS.

927. For above a year, ever since March, 1790, it would seem, there has hovered a project of Flight before the royal mind; and ever and anon has been condensing itself into something like a purpose; but this or the other difficulty always vaporized it again. It seems so full of risks, perhaps of civil war itself; above all, it cannot be done without effort. Somnolent laziness will not serve: to fly, if not in a leather vache, one must verily stir oneself. Better to adopt that Constitution of theirs; execute it so as to show all men that it is *inexecutable*? Better or not so good: surely it is *easier*. To all difficulties you need only say, There is a lion in the path, behold your Constitution will not act! For a somnolent person it requires no effort to counterfeit death,—as Dame de Staël and Friends of Liberty can see the King's Government long doing, *faisant la mort*.

928. Nay now, when desire whetted by difficulty has brought the matter to a head, and the royal mind no longer halts between two, what can come of it? Grant that poor Louis were safe with Bouillé, what, on the whole, could he look for there? Exasperated Tickets of Entry answer: Much, all. But cold Reason answer: Little, almost nothing. Is not loyalty a law of Nature? ask the Tickets of Entry. Is not love of your King, and even death for him, the glory of all Frenchmen,—except these few Democrats? Let Democrat Constitution-builders see what they will do without their Keystone; and France rend its hair having lost the Hereditary Representative!

929. Thus will King Louis fly; one sees not reasonably toward what. As a maltreated Boy, shall we say, who, having a Stepmother, rushes sulky into the wide world; and will wring the paternal heart? —Poor Louis escapes from known unsupportable evils, to an unknown mixture of good and evil, colored by Hope. He goes, as Rabelais did when dying, to seek a great May-be; Je vais chercher un grand Peutêtre! As not only the sulky Boy but the wise grown Man is obliged to do, so often, in emergencies.

930. For the rest, there is still no lack of stimulants, and step-dame maltreatments, to keep one's resolutions at the due pitch. Factious disturbances cease not; as indeed how can they, unless authoritatively *conjured*, in a Revolt which is by nature bottomless? If the ceasing of faction be the price of the King's somnolence, he may awake when he will and take wing.

931. Remark, in any case, what somersets and contortions a dead Catholicism is making,—skillfully galvanized: hideous, and even piteous to behold! Jurant and Dissident, with their shaved crowns, argue, frothing everywhere; or, are ceasing to argue, and stripping for battle. In Paris was scourging while need continued; contrariwise, in the Morbihan of Brittany, without scourging, armed Peasants are up, roused by pulpit-drum, they know not why. General Dumouriez, who has got missioned thitherward, finds all in sour heat of darkness; finds also that explanation and conciliation will still do much.*

932. But again, consider this: that his Holiness, Pius Sixth, has seen good to excommunicate Bishop Talleyrand! Surely, we will say then, considering it, there is no living or dead Church in the Earth that has not the indubitablest right to excommunicate Talleyrand. Pope Pius has right and might in his way. But truly so likewise has Father Adam,

ci-devant Marquis Saint-Huruge, in his way. Behold, therefore, on the 4th of May, in the Palais Royal, a mixed loud-sounding multitude; in the middle of whom, Father Adam, bull-voiced Saint-Huruge, in white hat, towers visible and audible. With him it is said, walks Journlist Gorsas,walk many others of the washed sort; for no authority will interfere. Pius Sixth, with his plush and tiara, and power of the Keys, they bear aloft: of natural size,—made of lath and combustible gum. Royou, the King's Friend, is borne too in effigy; with a pile of Newspaper King's-Friends, condemned Numbers of the Ami-du-Roi; fit fuel of the sacrifice. Speeches are spoken; a judgment is held, a doom proclaimed, audible in bull-voice, toward the four winds. And thus, amid great shouting, the holocaust is consummated, under the summer sky; and our lath-and-gum holiness, with the attendent victims, mounts up in flame, and sinks down in ashes; a decomposed Pope: and right or might, among all the parties, has better or worse accomplished itself, as it could.* But, on the whole, reckoning from Martin Luther in the Market-place of Wittenberg to Marquis Saint-Huruge in this Palais Royal of Paris, what a journey have we gone; into what strange territories has it carried us! No Authority can now interfere: Nay, Religion herself mourning for such things, may after all ask, What have *I* to do with them?

933. In such extraordinary manner does dead Catholicism somerset and caper, skillfully galvanized. For does the reader inquire into the subject-matter of controversy in this case; what the difference between Orthodoxy or *My-doxy* and Heterodoxy or *Thy-doxy* might here be? My-doxy is, that an august National Assembly can equalize the extent of Bishoprics; that an equalized Bishop, his Creed and Formularies being left quite as they were, can swear Fidelity to King. Law, and Nation, and so become a constitutional Bishop. Thy-doxy, if thou be Dissident, is that he cannot; but that he must become an accursed thing. Human ill-nature needs but some Homoiousian *iota*, or even the pretence of one; and will flow copiously through the eye of a needle : thus always must mortals go jargoning and fuming.

And, like the ancient Stoics in their porches,
With fierce dispute maintain their churches.

This Auto-da-fé of Saint-Huruge's was on the Fourth of May, 1791. Royalty sees it; but says nothing.

CHAPTER III.

COUNT FERSEN.

934. Royalty, in fact, should, by this time, be far on with its preparations. Unhappily much preparation is needful. Could a Hereditary Representative be carried in leather vache, how easy were it! But it is not so.

935. New Clothes are needed; as usual, in all Epic transactions, were it in the grimmest iron ages; consider "Queen Chrimhilde, with her sixty sempstresses," in that iron *Nibelungen Song*! No Queen can stir without new clothes. Therefore, now, Dame Campan whisks assiduous to this mantua-maker and to that; and there is clipping of frocks and gowns, upper clothes and under, great and small; such a clipping and sewing as—might have been dispensed with. Moreover, her Majesty cannot go a step anywhither without her Nécessaire; dear Nécessaire, of inlaid ivory and rosewood; cunningly devised; which holds perfumes, toilet-implements, infinite small queenlike furnitures: necessary to terrestrial

---

* "Deux Amis." v. 410-421; Dumouriez, ii. c. 5.

* "Histoire Parlementaire," x. 90-102.

life. Not without a cost of some five hundred louis, of much precious time, and difficult hoodwinking which does not blind, can this same Necessary of life be forwarded by the Flanders Carriers,—never to get to hand.* All which, you would say, augurs ill for the prospering of the enterprise. But the whims of women and queens must be humored.

936. Bouillé, on his side, is making a fortified Camp at Montmédi; gathering Royal-Allemand, and all manner of other German and true French Troops thither, "to watch the Austrians." His Majesty will not cross the frontiers, unless on compulsion. Neither shall the Emigrants be much employed, hateful as they are to all people.† Nor shall old war-god Broglie have any hand in the business; but solely our brave Bouillé; to whom, on the day of meeting, a Marshal's Baton shall be delivered, by a rescued King, amid the shouting of all the troops. In the meanwhile, Paris being so suspicious, were it not perhaps good to write your Foreign Ambassadors an ostensible Constitutional Letter; desiring all Kings and men to take heed that King Louis loves the Constitution, that he has voluntarily sworn, and does again swear, to maintain the same, and will reckon those his enemies who effect to say otherwise? Such a Constitutional Circular is dispatched by Couriers, is communicated confidentially to the Assembly, and printed in all Newspapers; with the finest effect.‡ Simulation and dissimulation mingle extensively in human affairs.

937. We observe, however, that Count Fersen is often using his Ticket of Entry; which surely he has clear right to do. A gallant Soldier and Swede, devoted to this fair Queen;—as indeed the Highest Swede now is. Has not King Gustav, famed fiery Chevalier du Nord, sworn himself, by the old laws of chivalry, her Knight? He will descend on fire-wings, of Swedish musketry, and deliver her from these foul dragons,—if, alas, the assassin's pistol intervene not!

938. But, in fact, Count Fersen does seem a likely young soldier, of alert decisive ways: he circulates widely, seen, unseen; and has business on hand. Also Colonel the Duke de Choiseul, nephew of Choiseul the great, of Choiseul the now deceased; he and Engineer Goguelat are passing and repassing between Metz and the Tuileries: and Letters go in cipher,—one of them, a most important one, hard to decipher; Fersen having ciphered it in haste.§ As for Duke de Villequier, he is gone ever since the Day of Poniards; but his Apartment is useful for her Majesty.

939. On the other side, poor Commandant Guivon, watching at the Tuileries, second in National command, sees several things hard to interpret. It is the same Gouvion who sat, long months ago, at the Town-hall, gazing helpless into that Insurrection of Women; motionless, as the brave stabled steed when conflagration rises, till Usher Maillard snatched his drum. Sincerer Patriot there is not; but many a shiftier. He, if Dame Campan gossip credibly, is paying some similitude of love-court to a certain false Chambermaid of the Palace, who betrays much to him: the Nécessaire, the clothes, the packing of jewels,∥—could he understand it when betrayed. Helpless Gouvion gazes with sincere glassy eyes into it; stirs up his sentries to vigilance; walks restless to and fro; and hopes the best.

940. But, on the whole, one finds that, in the second week of June, Colonel de Choiseul is privately

* Campan, ii. c. 18.
† Bouillé, "Mémoires," ii. c. 10.
‡ Moniteur, Séance du 23 Avril 1791.
§ Choiseul, "Relation du Départ de Louis XVI." (Paris, 1822), p. 39.
∥ Campan, ii. 141.

in Paris; having come "to see his children." Also that Fersen has got a stupendous new Coach built of the kind named Berline; done by the first artists; according to a model: they bring it home to him, in Choiseul's presence; the two friends take a proof-drive in it, along the streets; in meditative mood; then send it up to "Madame Sullivan's, in the Rue de Clichy," far North, to wait there till wanted. Apparently a certain Russian Baroness de Korff, with Waiting-woman, Valet, and two Children, will travel homeward with some state: in whom these young military gentlemen take interest? A Passport has been procured for her; and much assistance shown, with Coach-builders and such-like;—so helpful-polite are young military men. Fersen has likewise purchased a Chaise fit for two, at least for two waiting-maids; further, certain necessary horses; one would say, he is himself quitting France, not without delay? We observe finally that their Majesties, Heaven willing, will assist at Corpus-Christi Day, this blessed Summer Solstice, in Assumption Church, here at Paris, to the joy of all the world. For which same day, moreover, brave Bouillé, at Metz, as we find, has invited a party of friends to dinner; but indeed is gone from home, in the interim, over to Montmédi.

941. These are of the Phenomena, or visual Appearances, of this wide-working terrestrial world: which truly is all phenomenal, what they call spectral: and never rests any moment: one never at any moment can know why.

942. On Monday night, the 20th of June, 1791, about eleven o'clock, there is many a hackney-coach, and glass-coach (carrosse de remise), still rumbling, or at rest, on the streets of Paris. But of all glass-coaches, we recommend this to thee, O Reader, which stands drawn up in the Rue de l'Echelle, hard by the Carrousel and outgate of the Tuileries; in the Rue de l'Echelle that then was; "opposite Ronsin the saddler's door," as if waiting for a fare there! Not long does it wait: a hooded Dame, with two hooded Children has issued from Villequier's door, where no sentry walks, into the Tuileries Court-of-Princes; into the Carrousel: into the Rue de l'Echelle; where the Glass-coachman readily admits them; and again waits. Not long; another Dame, likewise hooded or shrouded, leaning on a servant, issues in the same manner; bids the servant good-night; and is, in the same manner, by the Glass-coachman, cheerfully admitted. Whither go so many Dames? 'Tis his Majesty's Couchée, Majesty just gone to bed, and all the Palace-world is retiring home. But the Glass-coachman still waits; his fare seemingly incomplete.

943. By and by, we note a thick-set Individual, in round hat and peruke, arm-in-arm with some servant, seemingly of the Runner or Courier sort; he also issues through Villequier's door; starts a shoe-buckle as he passes one of the sentries, stoops down to clasp it again; is however by the Glass-coachman, still more cheerfully admitted. And *now*, is his fare complete? Not yet; the Glass-coachman still waits. —Alas! and the false Chambermaid has warned Gouvion that she thinks the Royal Family will fly this very night; and Gouvion, distrusting his own glazed eyes, has sent express for Lafayette; and Lafayette's Carriage, flaring with lights, rolls this moment through the inner Arch of the Carrousel,— where a Lady shaded in broad gypsy-hat, and leaning on the arm of a servant, also of the Runner or Courier sort, stands aside to let it pass, and has even the whim to touch a spoke of it with her badine,— light little magic rod which she calls badine, such as the Beautiful then wore. The flare of Lafayette's Carriage rolls past: all is found quiet in the Court-

of-princes; sentries at their post; Majesties' Apartments closed in smooth rest. Your false Chambermaid must have been mistaken? Watch thou, Gouvion, with Argus's vigilance; for, of a truth, treachery is within these walls.

944. But where is the Lady that stood aside in gypsy-hat, and touched the wheel-spoke with her badine? O Reader, that Lady that touched the wheel-spoke was the Queen of France! She has issued safe through that inner Arch, into the Carrousel itself; but not into the Rue de l'Echelle. Flurried by the rattle and rencounter, she took the right hand, not the left; neither she nor her Courier knows Paris; he indeed is no Courier, but a loyal stupid ci-devant Body-guard disguised as one. They are off, quite wrong, over the Pont Royal and River; roaming disconsolate in the Rue du Bac; far from the Glass-coachman, who still waits. Waits, with flutter of heart; with thoughts—which he must button close up, under his jarvie-surtout!

945. Midnight clangs from all the City-steeples; one precious hour has been spent so; most mortals are asleep. The Glass-coachman waits; and in what mood! A brother jarvie drives up, enters into conversation; is answered cheerfully in jarvie-dialect: the brothers of the whip exchange a pinch of snuff;* decline drinking together; and part with good-night. Be the Heavens blest! here at length is the Queen-lady, in gypsy-hat; safe after perils, who has had to inquire her way. She, too, is admitted; her Courier jumps aloft, as the other, who is also a disguised Body-guard, has done; and now, O Glass-coachman of a thousand,—Count-Fersen, for the Reader sees it is thou,—drive!

946. Dust shall not stick to the hoofs of Fersen; crack! crack! the Glass-coach rattles, and every soul breathes lighter. But is Fersen on the right road? North-eastward, to the Barrier of Saint-Martin and Metz Highway, thither were we bound: and lo, he drives right Northward! The royal Individual, in round hat and peruke, sits astonished; but right or wrong, there is no remedy. Crack, crack, we go incessant, through the slumbering City. Seldom, since Paris rose out of mud, or the Long-haired Kings went in Bullock-carts, was there such a drive. Mortals on each hand of you, close by, stretched out horizontal, dormant; and we alive and quaking! Crack, crack, through the Rue de Grammont; across the Boulevard; up the Rue de la Chaussée d'Antin,—these windows, all silent, of Number 42, were Mirabeau's. Toward the Barrier, not of Saint-Martin, but of Clichy on the utmost North! Patience, ye royal Individuals; Fersen understands what he is about. Passing up the Rue de Clichy, he alights for one moment at Madame Sullivan's: "Did Count Fersen's Coachman get the Baroness de Korff's new Berline?" —"Gone with it an hour-and-half ago," grumbles responsive the drowsy Porter.—"C'est bien." Yes, it is well;—though had not such hour-and-half been lost, it were still better. Forth therefore, O Fersen, fast, by the Barrier de Clichy; then Eastward along the Outer Boulevard, what horses and whipcord can do!

947. Thus Fersen drives, through the ambrosial night. Sleeping Paris is now all on the right-hand of him; silent except for some snoring hum: and now he is Eastward as far as the Barrier de Saint-Martin, looking earnestly for Baroness de Korff's Berline. This Heaven's Berline he at length does descry, drawn up with its six horses, his own German Coachman waiting on the box. Right, thou good German; now haste, whither thou knowest?—And as for us of the

*Weber, ii. 340-342; Choiseul, pp. 44-56.

Glass-coach, haste too, O haste; much time is already lost! The august Glass-coach fare, six Insides, hastily packs itself into the new Berline; two Body-guard Couriers behind. The Glass-coach itself is turned adrift, it heads toward the City; to wander whither it lists,—and be found next morning tumbled in a ditch. But Fersen is on the new box, with its brave new hammer-cloths; flourishing his whip; he bolts forward toward Bondy. There a third and final Body-guard Courier of ours ought surely to be, with post-horses ready-ordered. There likewise ought that purchased Chaise, with the two Waiting-maids and their bandboxes, to be; whom also her Majesty could not travel without. Swift, thou deft Fersen, and may the Heavens turn it well!

948. Once more, by Heaven's blessing, it is all well. Here is the sleeping Hamlet of Bondy; Chaise with Waiting-women; horses all ready, and postillions with their churn-boots, impatient in the dewy dawn. Brief harnessing done, the postillions with their churn-boots vault into the saddles; brandish circularly their little noisy whips. Fersen, under his jarvie-surtout, bends in lowly silent reverence of adieu; royal hands wave speechless inexpressible response; Baroness de Korff's Berline, with the Royalty of France, bounds off: forever, as it proved. Deft Fersen dashes obliquely Northward, through the country, toward Bougret; gains Bougret, finds his German Coachman and chariot waiting there; cracks off, and drives undiscovered into unknown space. A deft active man, we say; what he undertook to do is nimbly and successfully done.

949. And so then the Royalty of France is actually fled? This precious night, the shortest of the year, it flies, and drives! Baroness de Korff is, at bottom, Dame de Tourzel, Governess of the Royal Children: she who came hooded with the two hooded little ones; little Dauphin; little Madame Royale, known long afterward as Duchesse d'Angoulême. Baroness de Korff's *Waiting-maid* is the Queen in gypsy-hat. The royal individual in round hat and peruke, he is *Valet* for the time being. That other hooded Dame, styled *Traveling-companion*, is kind Sister Elizabeth; she had sworn, long since, when the Insurrection of Women was, that only death should part her and them. And so they rush there, not too impetuously, through the Wood of Bondy:—over a Rubicon in their own and France's History.

950. Great; though the future is all vague! If we reach Bouillé? If we do not reach him? O Louis! and this all round thee is the great slumbering Earth (and overhead, the great watchful Heaven); the slumbering Wood of Bondy,—where Longhaired Childeric Donothing was struck through with iron;* not unreasonably, in a world like ours. These peaked stone-towers are Raincy; towers of wicket D'Orléans. All slumbers save the multiplex rustle of our new Berline. Loose-skirted scarecrow of an Herb-merchant, with his ass and early greens, toilsomely plodding, seems the only creature we meet. But right ahead the great North-east sends up evermore his gray brindled dawn: from dewy branch, birds here and there, with short deep warble, salute the coming Sun. Stars fade out, and Galaxies; Street-lamps of the City of God. The Universe, O my brothers, is flinging wide its portals for the Levee of the GREAT HIGH KING. Thou, poor King Louis, farest nevertheless, as mortals do, toward Orient lands of Hope; and the Tuileries with *its* Levees, and France and the Earth itself, is but a larger kind of dog-hutch,—occasionally going rabid.

*Hénault, "Abrégé Chronologique," p. 36.

CHAPTER IV.

ATTITUDE.

951. But in Paris, at six in the morning; when some Patriot Deputy, warned by a billet, awoke Lafayette, and they went to the Tuileries?—Imagination may paint, but words cannot, the surprise of Lafayette; or with what bewilderment helpless Gouvion rolled glassy Argus's eyes, discerning now that his false Chambermaid had told true!

952. However, it is to be recorded that Paris, thanks to an august National Assembly, did, on this seeming doomsday, surpass itself. Never, according to Historian eye-witnesses, was there seen such au "imposing attitude."* Sections all " in permanence;" our Town-hall too, having first, about ten o'clock, fired three solemn alarm-cannons: above all, our National Assembly! National Assembly, likewise permanent, decides what is needful; with unanimous consent, for the Coté Droit sits dumb, afraid of the Lanterne. Decides with a calm promptitude, which rises toward the sublime. One must needs vote, for the thing is self-evident, that his Majesty has been *abducted*, or spirited away, "enlevé," by some person or persons unknown: in which case, what will the Constitution have us do? Let us return to first principles, as we always say: "revenons aux principes."

953. By first or by second principles, much is promptly decided: Ministers are sent for, instructed how to continue their functions; Lafayette is examined; and Gouvion, who gives a most helpless account, the best he can. Letters are found written: one Letter, of immense magnitude; all in his Majesty's hand, and evidently of his Majesty's own composition; addressed to the National Assembly. It details with earnestness, with a childlike simplicity, what woes his Majesty has suffered. Woes great and small: A Necker seen applauded, a Majesty not; then insurrection; want of due furniture in Tuileries Palace, want of due cash in Civil List; *general* want of cash, of furniture and order; anarchy everywhere: Deficit never yet, in the smallest, "choked or comblé:"—wherefore, in brief, his Majesty has retired toward a place of Liberty; and leaving Sanctions, Federation, and what Oaths there may be, to shift for themselves, does now refer—to what, thinks an august Assembly? To that " Declaration of the 23d of June," with its "Seul il fera (He alone will make his People happy.") As if *that* were not buried, deep enough, under two irrevocable Twelve months, and the wreck and rubbish of a whole Feudal World! This strange autograph Letter the National Assembly decides on printing; on transmitting to the Eighty-three Departments, with exegetic commentary, short but pithy. Commissioners also shall go forth on all sides; the People be exhorted; the Armies be increased; care taken that the Commonweal suffer no damage.—And now, with a sublime air of calmness, nay of-indifference, we "pass to the order of the day!"

954. By such sublime calmness, the terror of the People is calmed. These gleaming Pike-forests, which bristled fateful in the early sun, disappear again; the far-sounding Street-orators cease, or spout milder. We are to have a civil war, let us have it then. The King is gone; but National Assembly, but France and we remain. The People also takes a great attitude; the People also is calm; motionless as a couchant lion. With but a few *broolings*, some waggings of the tail; to show what it *will* do! Cazalès, for instance, was beset by street-groups, and cries of

Lanterne; but National Patrols easily delivered him. Likewise all King's effigies and statues, at least stucco ones, get abolished. Even King's names; the word Roi fades suddenly out of all shop-signs; the Royal Bengal Tiger itself, on the Boulevards, becomes the National Bengal one, Tiger National.*

955. How great is a calm couchant People! On the morrow, men will say to one another: "We have no King, yet we slept sound enough." On the morrow, fervent Achille de Châtelet, and Thomas Paine the rebellious Needleman, shall have the walls of Paris profusely plastered with their Placard; announcing that there must be a *Republic*.† Need we add, that Lafayette too, though at first menaced by Pikes, has taken a great attitude, or indeed the greatest of all? Scouts and Aides-de-camp fly forth, vague, in quest and pursuit; young Romœuf toward Valenciennes, though with small hope.

956. Thus Paris; sublimely calmed, in its bereavement. But from the Messageries Royales, in all Mail-bags, radiates forth far-darting the electric news: Our Hereditary Representative is flown. Laugh, black Royalists: yet be it in your sleeve only; lest Patriotism notice, and waxing frantic, lower the Lanterne! In Paris alone is a sublime National Assembly with its calmness; truly, other places must take it as they can: with open mouth and eyes; with panic cackling, with wrath, with conjecture. How each one of those dull leathern Diligences, with its leathern bag and "The King is fled," furrows up smooth France as it goes; through town and hamlet, ruffles the smooth public mind into quivering agitation of death-terror; then lumbers on, as if nothing had happened! Along all highways; toward the utmost borders; till all France is ruffled, —roughened up (metaphorically speaking) into one enormous, desperate minded, red guggling Turkey Cock!

957. For example, it is under cloud of night that the leathern Monster reaches Nantes; deep sunk in sleep. The word spoken rouses all Patriot men: General Dumonriez, enveloped in roquelaures, has descend from his bedroom; finds the street covered with "four or five thousand citizens in their shirts."‡ Here and there a faint farthing rushlight, hastily kindled; and so many swart-featured haggard faces with nightcaps pushed back; and the more or less flowing drapery of nightshirt. open-mouthed till the General say his word! And overhead, as always, the Great Bear is turning so quiet round Boötes; steady, indifferent as the leathern Diligence itself. Take comfort, ye men of Nantes; Boötes and the steady Bear are turning; ancient Atlantic still sends his brine, loud-billowing, up your Loire stream; brandy shall be hot in the stomach: this is not the Last of the Days, but one before the Last.— The fools! If they knew what was doing, in these very instants, also by candle-light, in the far North-east!

958. Perhaps, we may say, the most terrified man in Paris or France is—who thinks the Reader?—sea-green Robespierre. Double paleness, with the shadow of gibbets and halters, over-casts the sea-green features: it is too clear to him that there is to be "a Saint-Bartholomew of Patriots," that in four-and-twenty hours he will not be in life. These horrid anticipations of the soul he is heard uttering at Pétion's: by a notable witness. By Madame Roland, namely; her whom we saw last year, radiant at the Lyons Federation. These four months, the Rolands have been in Paris; arranging with Assembly Committees the Municipal affairs of Lyons, affairs all sunk in debt;

* "Deux Amis.' vi. 67-178; Toulongeon. ii. 1-38; Camille, Prudhomme, and editors (in "Histoire Parlementaire." x. 240-144).

* "Walpoliana."
† Dumont, c. 16.
‡ Dumouriez, "Mémoires," ii. 109.

—communing, the while, as was most natural, with the best Patriot to be found here, with our Brissots, Pétious, Buzots, Robespierres: who were wont to come to us, says the fair Hostess, four evenings in the week. They, running about, busier than ever this day, would fain have comforted the sea-green man; spake of Achille de Châtelet's Placard; of a Journal to be called The Republican; of preparing men's minds for a Republic. "A Republic?" said the Sea-green, with one of his dry husky, unsportful laughs, "What is that?"[*] O sea-green Incorruptible, thou shalt see!

CHAPTER V.

THE NEW BERLINE.

959. But scouts, all this while, and aids-de-camp, have flown forth faster then the leathern Diligences. Young Romœuf, as we said, was off early toward Valenciennes: distracted Villagers seize him, as a traitor with a finger of his own in the plot; drag him back to the Town-hall; to the National Assembly, which speedily grants a new passport. Nay now, that same scarecrow of an Herb-merchant with his ass has bethought him of the grand new Berline seen in the Wood of Bondy; and delivered evidence of it:[†] Romœuf, furnished with new passport, is sent forth with double speed on a hopefuler track; by Bondy, Claye and Châlons, toward Metz, to track the new Berline; and gallops (à franc étrier).

960. Miserable new Berline! Why could not Royalty go in some old Berline similar to that of other men? Flying for life, one does not stickle about his vehicle. Monsieur, in a commonplace travelling-carriage is off Northwards; Madame, his Princess, in another, with variation of route: they cross one another while changing horses, without look of recognition; and reach Flanders, no man questioning them. Precisely in the same manner, beautiful Princess de Lamballe set off, about the same hour; and will reach England safe:—would she had continued there! The beautiful, the good, but the unfortunate reserved for a frightful end!

961. All runs along, unmolested, speedy, except only the new Berline. Huge leathern vehicle:—huge Argosy, let us say, or Acapulco ship; with its heavy stern-boat af Chaise-and-pair; with its three yellow Pilot-boats of mounted Body-guard Couriers, rocking aimless round it and ahead of it, to bewilder, not to guide! It lumbers along, lurchingly with stress, at a snail's pace; noted of all the world. The Body-guard Couriers, in their yellow liveries, go prancing and clattering; loyal but stupid; unacquainted with all things. Stoppages occur; and breakages, to be repaired at Etoges. King Louis, too, will dismount, will walk up hills, and enjoy the blessed sunshine:—with eleven horses and double drink-money, and all furtherances of Nature and Art, it will be found that Royalty, flying for life, accomplishes Sixty-nine miles in Twenty-two incessant hours. Slow Royalty! And yet not a minute of these hours but is precious: on minutes hang the destinies of Royalty now.

962. Readers, therefore, can judge in what humor Duke de Choiseul might stand waiting, in the village of Pont-de-Sommevelle, some leagues beyond Châlons, hour after hour, now when the day bends visibly westward. Choiseul drove out of Paris, in all privity, ten hours before their Majesties' fixed time; his Hussars, led by Engineer Goguelat, are here duly, come "to escort a Treasure that is expected;" but, hour after hour, is no Baroness de

Korff's Berline. Indeed, over all that North-east Region, on the skirts of Champagne and of Lorraine, where the great Road runs, the agitation is considerable. For all along, from this Pont-de-Sommevelle North-eastward as far as Montmédi, at Post-villages and Towns, escorts of Hussars and Dragoons do lounge waiting; a train or chain of Military Escorts; at the Montmédi end of it our brave Bouillé: an electric thunder-chain; which the invisible Bouillé, like a Father Jove, holds in his hand—for wise purposes! Brave Bouillé has done what man could; has spread out his electric thunder-chain of Military Escorts, onward to the threshold of Châlons: it waits but for the new Korff Berline; to receive it, escort it, and, if need be, bear it off in whirlwind of military fire. They lie and lounge there, we say, these fierce Troopers; from Montmédi and Stenai, through Clermont, Sainte-Menehould to utmost Pont-de-Sommevelle, in all Post-villages; for the route shall avoid Verdun and great Towns: they loiter impatient, "till the Treasure arrive.

963. Judge what a day this is for brave Bouillé: perhaps the first day of a new glorious life; surely the last day of the old! Also, and indeed still more, what a day, beautiful and terrible, for your young full-blooded Captains: your Dandoins, Comte de Damas, Duke de Choiseul, Engineer Goguelat, and the like; intrusted with the secret!—Alas, the day bends ever more westward; and no Korff Berline comes to sight. It is four hours beyond the time, and still no Berline. In all Village-streets, Royalist Captains go lounging, looking often Paris-ward; with face of unconcern, with heart full of black care: rigorous Quartermasters can hardly keep the private dragoons from cafés and dram-shops.[*] Dawn on our bewilderment, thou new Berline; dawn on us, thou Sun-Chariot of a new Berline, with the destinies of France!

964. It was of his Majesty's ordering, this military array, of Escorts: a thing solacing the Royal imagination with a look of security and rescue; yet, in reality, creating only alarm, and where there was otherwise no danger, danger without end. For each Patriot, in these Post-villages, asks naturally: This clatter of cavalry, and marching and lounging of troops, what means it? To escort a Treasure? Why escort, when no Patriot will steal from the Nation; or where is your Treasure?—There has been such marching and countermarching: for it is another fatality, that certain of these Military Escorts came out so early as yesterday; the 19th not the 20th of the month being the day first appointed; which her Majesty, for some necessity or other, saw good to alter. And now consider the suspicious nature of Patriotism; suspicions, above all, of Bouillé the Aristocrat; and how the sour doubting rumour has had leave to accumulate and exacerbate for four-and-twenty hours!

965. At Pont-de-Sommevelle, these Forty foreign Hussars of Goguelat and Duke Choiseul are becoming an unspeakable mystery to all men. They lounged long enough, already, at Sainte-Menehould; lounged and loitered till our National Volunteers there, all risen into hot wrath of doubt, "demanded 300 fusils of their Town-hall," and got them. At which same moment too, as it chanced, our Captain Dandoins was just coming in, from Clermont with his troop, at the other end of the Village. A fresh troop; alarming enough; though happily they are only Dragoons and French! So that Goguelat with his Hussars had to ride, and even to do it fast; till here at Pont-de-Sommevelle, where Choiseul lay waiting, he found resting-place. Resting-place as on

* Madame Roland, ii. 70.
† Moniteur, etc., (in "Histoire Parlementaire" x. 244–253).

* "Déclaration du Sieur La Gache du Régiment Royal-Dragons" (in Choiseul, pp. 125–139).

burning marle. For the rumor of him flies abroad; and men run to and fro in fright and anger: Châlons sends forth exploratory pickets of National Volunteers toward this hand; which meet exploratory pickets, coming from Sainte-Menehould, on that. What is it, ye whiskered Hussars, men of foreign guttural speech; in the name of Heaven, what is it that brings you? A treasure?—exploratory pickets shake their heads. The hungry Peasants, however, know too well what Treasure it is; Military seizure for rents, feudalities; which no Bailiff could make us pay! This they knew;—and set to jingling their Parish-bell by way of tocsin; with rapid effect! Choiseul and Goguelat, if the whole country is not to take fire, must needs, be there Berline, be there no Berline, saddle and ride.

966. They mount; and this parish tocsin happily ceases. They ride slowly Eastward; toward Sainte-Menehould; still hoping the Sun-Chariot of a Berline may overtake them. Ah me, no Berline! And near now is that Sainte-Menehould, which expelled us in the morning, with its "three hundred national fusils;" which looks, belike, not too lovingly on Captain Dandoins and his fresh Dragoons, though only French:—which, in a word, one dare not enter a *second* time, under pain of explosion! With rather heavy heart, our Hussar Party strikes off to the left; through by-ways, through pathless hills and woods; they, avoiding Sainte-Menehould and all places which have seen them heretofore, will make direct for the distant Village of Varennes. It is probable they will have a rough evening ride.

967. This first military post, therefore, in the long thunder-chain, has gone off with no effect; or with worse, and your chain threatens to entangle itself! —The Great Road, however, is got hushed again into a kind of quietude, though one of the wakefulest. Indolent Dragoons cannot by any Quartermaster, be kept altogether from the dram-shop; where Patriots drink, and will even treat, eager enough for news Captains, in a state near distraction, beat the dusky highway, with a face of indifference; and no Sun-Chariot appears. Why lingers it? Incredible, that with eleven horses, and such yellow Couriers and furtherances, its rate should be under the weightiest dray-rate, some three miles an hour! Alas, one knows not whether it ever even got out of Paris;— and yet also one knows not whether, this very moment, it is not at the Village-end! One's heart flutters on the verge of unutterabilities.

CHAPTER VI.

OLD-DRAGOON DROUET.

968. In this manner, however, has the Day bent downward. Wearied mortals are creeping home from their field-labor; the village-artisan eats with relish his supper of herbs, or has strolled forth to the village-street for a sweet mouthful of air and human news. Still summer-eventide everywhere! The great Sun hangs flaming on the utmost Northwest; for it is his longest day this year. The hill tops rejoicing will ere long be at their ruddiest and blush Good-night. The thrush, in green dells, on long-shadowed leafy spray, pours gushing his glad serenade, to the babble of brooks grown audibler; silence is stealing over the Earth. Your dusty Mill of Valmy, as all other mills and drudgeries, may furl its canvas, and cease swashing and circling. The swinkt grinders in this Treadmill of an Earth have ground out another Day: and lounge there, as we say, in village-groups; movable, or ranked on social stone-seats;* their children, mischievous imps,

* "Rapport de M. Remy (in Choiseul, p. 140).

sporting about their feet. Unnotable hum of sweet human gossip rises from this Village of Sainte-Menehould, as from all other villages. Gossip mostly sweet, unnotable; for the very Dragoons are French and gallant; nor as yet has the Paris-and-Verdun Diligence, with its leathern bag, rumbled in, to terrify the minds of men.

969. One figure nevertheless we do note at the last door of the Village: that figure in loose-flowing night-gown, of Jean Baptiste Drouet, Master of the Post here. An acrid choleric man, rather dangerous looking; still in the prime of life, though he has served, in his time, as a Cédon Dragoon. This day, from an early hour Drouet got his cholerstirred, and has been kept fretting. Hussar Goguelat in the morning saw good, by way of thrift, to bargain with his own Inn-keeper, not with Drouet regular Maître de Post, about some gig-horse for the sending back of his gig; which thing Drouet perceiving came over in red ire, menacing the Inn-keeper, and would not be appeased. Wholly an unsatisfactory day. For Drouet is an acrid Patriot too, was at the Paris Feast of Pikes: and what do these Bouillé soldiers mean? Hussars,—with their gig, and a vengeance to it!— have hardly been thrust out, when Dandoins and his fresh Dragoons arrive from Clermont, and stroll. For what purpose? Choleric Drouet steps out and steps in, with long-flowing night-gown; looking abroad, with that sharpness of faculty which stirred choler gives to man.

970. On the other hand, mark Captain Dandoins on the street of that same Village; sauntering with a face of indifference, a heart eaten of black care! For no Korff Berline makes its appearance. The great Sun flames broader toward setting: one's heart flutters on the verge of dread unutterabilities.

971. By Heaven! here is the yellow Body-guard Courier; spurring fast in the ruddy evening light! Steady, O Dandoins, stand with inscrutable indifferent face; though the yellow blockhead spurs past the Post-house; inquires to find it; and stirs the Village, all delighted with his fine livery.—Lumbering along with its mountains of bandboxes, and Chaise behind, the Korff Berline rolls in; huge Acapulco ship with its Cock-boat, having got thus far. The eyes of the Villagers look enlightened, as such eyes do when a coach-transit, which is an event, occurs for them. Strolling Dragoons respectfully, so fine are the yellow liveries, bring hand to helmet; and a Lady in gypsy-hat responds with a grace peculiar to her.* Dandoins stands with folded arms, and what look of indifference and disdainful garrison-air a man can, while the heart is like leaping out of him. Curled disdainful mustachio; careless glance—which however surveys the Village-groups, and does not like them. With his eye he bespeaks the yellow Courier, Be quick, be quick! Thick-headed Yellow cannot understand the eye; comes up mumbling, to ask in words: seen of the Village!

972. Nor is Postmaster Drouet unobservant all this while: but steps out and steps in, with his long-flowing night-gown, in the level sunlight; prying into several things. When a man's faculties, at the right time, are sharpened by choler, it may lead to much. That Lady in slouched gipsy-hat, though sitting back in the Carriage, does she not resemble some one we have seen, some time;—at the Feast of Pikes or elsewhere? And this Grosse-Tête in round hat and peruke, which, looking rearward, pokes itself out from time to time, methinks there are features in it——? Quick, Sieur Guillaume, Clerk of the Directoire, bring me a new Assignat! Drouet scans the new Assignat; compares the Paper-money Picture with the Gross Head in round hat there: by Day

* "Déclaration de La Gache" (in Choiseul, ubi supra).

and Night! you might say the one was an attempted Engraving of the other. And this march of Troops; this sauntering and whispering,—I see it!

973. Drouet Postmaster of this Village, hot Patriot, Old-Dragoon of Condé, consider, therefore, what thou wilt do. And fast, for behold the new Berline, expeditiously yoked, cracks whipcord, and rolls away!—Drouet dare not, on the spur of the instant, clutch the bridles in his own two hands ; Dandoins, with broadsword, might hew you off. Our poor Nationals, not one of them here, have 300 fusils, but then no powder: besides one is not sure, only morally certain. Drouet, as an adroit Old-Dragoon of Condé, does what is advisablest; privily bespeaks Clerk Guillaume, Old-Dragoon of Condé be too; privily, while Clerk Guillaume is saddling two of the fleetest horses, slips over to the Town-hall to whisper a word; then mounts with Clerk Guillaume; and the two bound eastward in pursuit, to *see* what can be done.

974. They bound eastward, in sharp trot: their moral-certainty permeating the Village, from the Town-hall outward, in busy whispers. Alas! Captain Dandoins orders his Dragoons to mount; but they, complaining of long fast, demand bread-and-cheese first;—before which brief repast can be eaten, the whole Village is permeated; not whispering now, but blustering and shrieking! National Volunteers, in hurried muster, shriek for gunpowder; Dragoons halt beween Patriotism and Rule of the Service, between bread-and-cheese and fixed bayonets: Dandoins hands secretly his Pocket-book, with its secret dispatches, to the rigorous Quartermaster: the very Ostlers have stable-forks and flails. The rigorous Quartermaster, half-saddled, cuts out his way with the sword's edge, amid leveled bayonets, amid Patriot vociferations, adjurations, flail-strokes; and rides frantic;*—few or even none follow him; the rest, so sweetly constrained, consenting to stay there.

975. And thus the new Berline rolls; and Drouet and Guillaume gallop after it, and Dandoins's Troopers or trooper gallops after them; and Sainte-Menehould, with some leagues of the King's Highway, is in explosion;—and your Military thunder-chain has gone off in a self-destructive manner; one may fear, with the frightfulest issues.

CHAPTER VII

THE NIGHT OF SPURS.

976. This comes of mysterious Escorts, and a new Berline with eleven horses: "He that has a secret should not only hide it, but hide that he has it to bide." Your first Military Escort has exploded self-destructive; and all Military Escorts, and a suspicious Country will now be up, explosive; comparable *not* to victorious thunder. Comparable, say rather, to the first stirring of an Alpine Avalanche; which, once stir it, as here at Sainte-Menehould, will spread, —all round, and on and on, as far as Stenai; thundering with wild ruin, till Patriot Villagers. Peasantry, Military Escorts, new Berline and Royalty are down, jumbling in the Abyss!

977. The thick shades of Night are falling. Postillions crack and whip: the Royal Berline is through Clermont, where Colonel Comte de Damas got a word whispered to it; is safe through, toward Varennes; rushing at the rate of double drink-money: an Unknown, "Inconnu on horseback" shrieks earnestly some hoarse whisper, not audible, into the rushing Carriage-window, and vanishes, left in the night.† August Travelers palpitate; nevertheless overwear-

* "Déclaration de La Gache" (in Choiseul, p. 134).
† Campan, ii. 159.

ied Nature sinks every one of them into a kind of sleep. Alas! and Drouet and Clerk Guillaume spur; taking side-roads, for shortness, for safety; scattering abroad that moral-certainty of theirs; which flies, a bird of the air carrying it!

978. And your rigorous Quartermaster spurs; awakening hoarse trumpet-tone,—as here at Clermont, calling out Dragoons gone to bed. Brave Colonel de Damas has them mounted, in part, these Clermont men; young Cornet Remy dashes off with a few. But the Patriot Magistracy is out here at Clermont too; National Guards shrieking for ball-cartridges; and the Village "illuminates itself;"—deft Patriots springing out of bed; alertly, in shirt or shift, striking a light; sticking up each his farthing candle, or penurious oil-cruse, till all glitters and glimmers; so deft are they! A camisado, or shirt-tumult, everywhere: storm-bell set a-ringing; village drum beating furious générale, as here at Clermont, under illumination; distracted Patriots pleading and menacing! Brave young Colonel de Damas, in that uproar of distracted Patriotism, speaks some fire-sentences to what Troopers he has: "Comrades insulted at Sainte-Menehould: King and Country calling on the brave;" then gives the fire-word, "Draw swords." Whereupon, alas, the Troopers only *smite* their sword-handles, driving them farther home! "To me, whoever is for the King!" cries Damas in despair, and gallops, he with some poor loyal Two, of the Subalteru sort, into the bosom of the Night.*

979. Night unexampled in the Clermontais; shortest of the year; remarkablest of the century; Night deserving to be named of Spurs! Cornet Remy, and those few he dashed off off with, has missed his road; is galloping for hours toward Verdun; then, for ours, across hedged country, through roused hamlets, toward Varennes. Unlucky Cornet Remy; unluckier Colonel Damas, with whom there ride desperate only some loyal Two! More ride not of that Clermont Escort: of other Escorts, in other Villages, not even Two may ride; but only all curvet and prance,—impeded by storm-bell and your Village illuminating itself.

980. And Drouet rides and Clerk Guillaume; and the country runs.—Goguelat and Duke Choiseul are plunging through morasses, over cliffs, over stock and stone, in the shaggy woods of the Clermontais; by tracks; or trackless, with guides; Hussars tumbling into pitfalls, and lying "swooned three-quarters of an hour," the rest refusing to march without them. What an evening ride from Pont-de-Sommeville; what a thirty hours, since, Choiseul quitted Paris, with Queen's-valet Leonard in the chaise by him! Black Care sits behind the rider. Thus go they plunging; rustle the owlet from his branchy nest; champ the sweet-scented forest-herb, queen-of-the-meadows *spilling* her spikenard; and frighten the car of Night. But hark! toward twelve o'clock, as one guesses, for the very stars are gone out: sound of the tocsin from Varennes? Checking bridle, the Hussar Officer listens: "Some fire undoubtedly!"—yet rides on, with double breathlessness, to verify.

981. Yes, gallant friends that do your utmost, is a certain sort of fire: difficult to quench.—The Korff Berline, fairly ahead of all this riding Avalanche, reached the little paltry Village of Varennes about eleven o'clock; hopeful, in spite of that hoarse whispering Unknown. Do not all Towns now lie behind us; Verdun avoided, on our right? Within wind of Bouillé himself, in a manner; and the darkest of midsummer nights favoring us! And so we halt on the hilltop at the South end of the Village; expect-

* "Procès-verbal du Directoire du Clermont" (in Choiseul, pp. 189-195).

ing our relay; which young Bouillé, Bouillé's own son, with his Escort of Hussars, was to have ready; for in this Village was no Post. Distracting to think of: neither horse nor Hussar is here! Ah, and stout horses, a proper relay belonging to Duke Choiseul, do stand at bay, but in the Upper Village over the Bridge; and we know not of them. Hussars likewise do wait, but drinking in the taverns. For indeed it is six hours beyond the time; young Bouillé, silly stripling, thinking the matter over for this night, has retired to bed. And so our yellow Couriers, inexperienced, must rove, groping, bungling, through a Village mostly asleep: Postillions will not, for any money, go on with the tired horses; not, at least without refreshment; not they, let the Valet in round hat argue as he likes.

982. Miserable! "For five-and-thirty minutes" by the King's watch, the Berline is at a dead stand: Round-hat arguing with Churn-boots; tired horses slobbering their meal-and-water: yellow Couriers groping, bungling;—young Bouillé asleep, all the while, in the Upper Village, and Choiseul's fine team standing there at bay. No help for it; not with a king's ransom; the horses deliberately slobber, Round-hat argues, Bouillé sleeps. And mark now, in the thick night, do not two Horsemen, with jaded trot, come clank-clanking; and start with half-pause, if one noticed them, at sight of this dim mass of a Berline, and its dull slobbering and arguing; then prick off faster, into the village? It is Drouet, he and Clerk Guillaume! Still ahead, they two, of the whole riding hurly-burly; unshot though some brag of having chased them. Perilous is Drouet's errand also; But he is an Old-Dragoon, with his wits shaken thoroughly awake.

983. The Village of Varennes lies dark and slumberous; a most unlevel Village, of inverse saddle-shape, as men write. It sleeps; the rushing of the River Aire singing lullaby to it. Nevertheless from the Golden Arm, Bras d'Or Tavern, across that sloping Market-place, there still comes shine of social light; comes voice of rude drovers, or the like, who have not yet taken the stirrup-cup; Boniface Le Blanc, in white apron, serving them: cheerful to behold. To this Bras d'Or Drouet enters, alacrity looking through his eyes; he nudges Boniface, in all privacy, 'Camarade, es-tu bon Patriote, (Art thou a good Patriot)?"—"Si je suis!" answers Boniface.—"In that case," eagerly whispers Drouet—what whisper is needful, heard of Boniface alone.[*]

984. And now see Boniface Le Blanc bustling as he never did for the jolliest toper. See Drouet and Guillaume, dexterous Old-Dragoons, instantly down blocking the bridge, with a "furniture-wagon they find there," with whatever wagons, tumbrils, barrels, barrows their hands can lay hold of;—till no carriage can pass. Then swiftly, the Bridge once blocked, see them take station hard by, under Varennes Archway: joined by Le Blanc, Le Blanc's Brother, and one or two alert Patriots he has roused. Some half-dozen in all, with National muskets, they stand close, waiting under the Archway, till that same Korff Berline rumble up.

985. It rumbles up: Alte là! lanterns flash out from under coat-skirts, bridles chuck in strong fists, two National muskets level themselves fore and aft through the two Coach-doors: "Mesdames, your Passports?—Alas, alas! Sieur Sausse, Procureur of the Township, Tallow-chandler also and Grocer, is there, with official grocer-politeness; Drouet with fierce logic and ready wit:—The respected Traveling Party, be it Baroness de Korff's or persons of still higher consequence, will perhaps please to rest itself in M. Sausse's till the dawn strike up!

[*] "Deux Amis," vi. 139–173.

986. O Louis; O hapless Marie-Antoinette, fated to pass thy life with such men! Phlegmatic Louis, art thou but lazy semi-animate phlegm, then, to the center of thee? King, Captain-General, Sovereign Frank! if thy heart ever formed, since it began beating under the name of heart, any resolution at all, be it now then, or never in this world:—"Violent nocturnal individuals, and if it were persons of high consequence? And if it were the King himself? Has the King not the power, which all beggars have, of traveling unmolested on his own Highway? Yes: it is the King; and tremble ye to know it! The King has said, in this one small matter; and in France, or under God's Throne, is no power that shall gainsay. Not the King shall ye stop here under this your miserable Archway; but his dead body only, and answer it to Heaven and Earth. To me, Body-guards; l'ostillions, en avant!"—One fancies in that case the pale paralysis of these two Le Blanc musketeers; the drooping of Drouet's under-jaw; and how Procureur Sausse had melted like tallow in furnace-heat; Louis faring on; in some few steps awakening Young Bouillé, awakening relays and Hussars: triumphant entry, with cavalcading high-brandishing Escort, and Escorts, into Montmedi; and the whole course of French History different!

987. Alas, it was not *in* the poor phlegmatic man. Had it been in him, French History had never come under this Varennes Archway to decide itself.—He steps out: all step out. Procureur Sausse gives his grocer-arms to the Queen and Sister Elizabeth; Majesty taking the two children by the hand. And thus they walk, coolly back, over the Market-place to Procureur Sausse's; mount into his small upper story: where straightway his Majesty "demands refreshments." Demands refreshments, as is written; gets bread-and-cheese with a bottle of Burgundy; and remarks, that it is the best Burgundy he ever drank!

988. Meanwhile the Varennes Notables, and all men, official and non-official, are hastily drawing-on their breeches; getting their fighting gear. Mortals half-dressed tumble out barrels, lay felled trees; scouts dart off to all the four winds,—the tocsin begins clanging, "the Village illuminates itself." Very singular: how these little Villages do manage, so adroit are they, when startled in midnight alarm of war. Like little adroit municipal rattlesnakes suddenly awakened: for their storm-ell rattles and rings; their eyes glisten luminous (with tallow-light), as in rattlesnake ire; and the Village will sting. Old-Dragoon Drouet is our engineer and generalissimo; valiant as a Ruy Diaz: now or never, ye Patriots, for the soldiery is coming; massacre by Austrians, by Aristocrats, wars more than civil, it all depends on you and the hour!—National Guards rank themselves, half-buttoned: mortals, we say still only in breeches, in under-petticoat, tumble out barrels and lumber, lay felled trees for barricades: the Village will sting. Rabid Democracy, it would seem, is *not* confined to Paris, then? Ah no, whatsoever Courtiers might talk; too clearly no. This of dying for one's King is grown into a dying for one's self, *against* the King, if need be.

989. And so our riding and running Avalanche and Hurly-burly has *reached* the Abyss, Korff Berline foremost; and may pour itself thither, and jumble: endless! For the next six hours, need we ask if there was a clattering far and wide? Clattering and tocsining and hot tumult, over all the Clermontais, spreading through the Three-Bishoprics: Dragoon and Hussar Troops galloping on roads and no-roads; National Guards arming and starting in the dead of night; tocsin after tocsin transmitting the alarm: In some forty minutes, Goguelat and Choiseul, with

their wearied Hussars, reach Varennes. Ah, it is no fire, then; or a fire difficult to quench! They leaf the tree-barricades, in spite of National sergeant; they enter the village, Choiseul instructing his Troopers how the matter really is; who respond interjectionally, in their glutteral dialect, " Der Konig ; die Koniginn!" and seem stanch. These now, in their stauch humor, will, for one thing, beset Procureur Sausse's house. Most beneficial: had not Drouet stornfully ordered otherwise; and even bellowed, in his extremity, " Cannoneers, to your guns!" —two old honeycomed Field-pieces, empty of all but cobwebs; the rattle whereof, as the Cannoneers with assured countenance trundled them up, did nevertheless abate the Hussar ardor, and produce a respectfuler ranking farther back. Jugs of wine, handed over the ranks,—for the German throat too has sensibility,—will complete the business. When Engineer Gognelat, some hour or so afterward, steps forth, the response to him is—a hiccuping Vive la Nation!

990. What boots it? Gognelat, Choiseul, now also Count Damas, and all the Varennes Officiality are with the King; and the King can give no order, form no opinion but sits there, as he has ever done, like clay on potter's wheel; perhaps the absurdest of all pitiable and pardonable clay-figures that now circle under the Moon. He will go on, next morning, and take the National Guard *with* him; Sausse permitting! Hapless Queen: with her two children laid there on the mean bed, old Mother Sausse kneeling to Heaven, with tears and an audible prayer, to bless them ; imperial Marie-Antoinette near kneeling to Son Sausse and Wife Sausse, amid candle-boxes and treacle-barrels,—in vain! There are 3,000 National Guards got in ; before long they will count 10,000: tocsins spreading like fire on dry heath, or far faster.

991. Young Bouillé, roused by this Varennes tocsin, has taken horse, and—fled toward his Father. Thitherward also rides, in an almost hysterically desperate manner, a certain Sieur Aubriot, Choiseul's Orderly ; swimming dark rivers, our Bridge being blocked ; spurring as if the Hell-hunt were at his heels.* Through the village of Dun, he galloping still on, scatters the alarm ; at Dun, brave Captain Deslons and *his* Escort of a Hundred saddle and ride, Deslons too gets into Varenne; leaving his Hundred outside, at the tree-barricade; offers to cut King Louis out, if he will order it : but unfortunately "the work *will* prove hot ;" whereupon King Louis has "no orders to give."†

992. And so the tocsin clangs, and Dragoons gallop, and can do nothing, having galloped: National Guards stream in like the gathering of ravens : your exploding Thunder-chain, falling Avalanche, or what else we liken it to, does play, with a vengeance,—up now as far as Stenai and Bouillé himself.‡ Brave Bouillé, son of the whirlwind, he saddles Royal-Allemand: speaks fire-words, kindling heart and eyes; distributes twenty-five gold-louis a company: —Ride, Royal-Allemand, long-famed: no Tuileries Charge and Necker-Orléans Bust-Procession; a very King made captive, and world all to win!—Such is the Night deserving to be named of Spurs.

993. At six o'clock two things have happened. Lafayette's Aid-de-camp, Romœuf, riding a franc étrier, on that old Herb-merchant's route, quickened during the last stages, has got to Varennes; where the 10,000 now furiously demand, with fury of panic terror, that Royalty shall forthwith return Parisward, that there be not infinite bloodshed. Also, on the other

side, "English Tom," Choiseul's jokei, flying with that Choiseul relay, has met Bouillé on the heights of Dun; the adamantine brow flushed with dark thunder; thunderous rattle of Royal-Allemand at his heels. English Tom answers as he can the brief question, How it is at Varennes?—then asks in turn What he, English Tom, with M. de Choiseul's horses is to do, and whither to ride?—To the Bottomless Pool! answers a thunder-voice; then again speaking and spurring, orders Royal-Allemand to the gallop ; and vanishes, swearing (en jurant).* 'Tis the last of our brave Bouillé. Within sight of Varennes, he having drawn bridle, calls a council of officers; finds that it is in vain. King Louis has departed, consenting: amid the clangor of universal stormbell ; amid the tramp of 10,000 armed men, already arrived ; and say, of 60,000 flocking thither. Brave Deslons, even without " orders," darted at the River Aire with his Hundred;† swam one branch of it, could not the other and stood there, dripping and panting, with inflated nostril; the 10,000 answering him with a shout of mockery, the new Berline lumbering Parisward its weary inevitable way. No help, then, in Earth; nor, in an age not of miracles, in Heaven!

994. That night, " Marquis de Bouillé and twenty-one more of us rode over the Frontiers: the Bernardine monks at Orval in Luxemburg gave us supper and lodging."‡ With little of speech, Bouillé rides: with thoughts that do not brook speech. Northward, toward uncertainty, and the Cimmerian Night: toward West-Indian Isles, for with thin Emigrant delirium the son of the whirlwind cannot act; toward England, toward premature Stoical death; not toward France any more. Honor to the Brave; who, be it in this quarrel or in that, *is* a substance and articulate-speaking piece of human Valor, not a fanfaronading hollow Spectrum and squeaking and gibbering Shadow! One of the few Royalist Chief-actors this Bouillé, of whom so much can be said.

995. The brave Bouillé too, then, vanishes from the tissue of our Story. Story and tissue, faint ineffectual Emblem of that grand Miraculous Tissue, and Living Tapestry named *French Revolution,* which did weave itself then in very fact, "on the loud-sounding LOOM OF TIME!" The old Brave drop out from it, with their strivings; and new acrid Drouets, of new strings and color, come in·—as in the manner of that weaving.

CHAPTER VIII
THE RETURN.

996. So, then, our grand Royalist Plot, of Flight to Metz, has *executed* itself. Long hovering in the background, as a dread royal *ultimatum,* it has rushed forward in its terrors; verily to some purpose. How many Royalist Plots and Projects, one after another, cunningly-devised, that were to explode like powder-mines and thunder-claps; not one solitary Plot of which has issued otherwise! Powder-mine of a Séance Royale on the 23d of June, 1789, which exploded as we then said, "through the touch-hole ;" which next, your war-god Broglie having reloaded it, brought a Bastille about your ears. Then came fervent Opera-Repast, with flourishing of sabers, and *O Richard, O my King ;* which aided by Hunger produces Insurrection of Women, and Pallas, Athene, in the shape of Demoiselle Théroigne. Valor profits not ; neither has fortune smiled on fanfaronade. The Bouillé Armament ends as the Broglie one has done. Man after man spends himself in this cause, only to

---

* "Rapport de M. Aubriot (in Choiseul, pp. 150-157).
† "Extrait d'un Rapport de M. Deslons" (in Choiseul, pp. 164-167).
‡ Bouillé, ii. 74-76.

* "Déclaration du Sieur Thomas" (in Choiseul, p. 183.
† Weber, ii. 886.
‡ Aubriot, ut suprà, p. 156.

work it quicker ruin; it seems a cause doomed, forsaken of Earth and Heaven.

997. On the 6th of October gone a year, King Louis escorted by Demoiselle Théroigne and some two hundred thousand, made a Royal Progress and Entrance into Paris, such as man had never witnessed; we propesied him Two more such; and accordingly another of them, after this Flight to Metz, is now coming to pass. Théroigne will not escort here; neither does Mirabeau now "sit in one of the accompanying carriages." Mirabeau lies dead, in the Pantheon of Great Men. Théroigne lies living, in dark Austrian Prison; having gone to Liège, professionally, and been seized there. Bemurmured now by the hoarse-flowing Danube: the light of her Patriot Supper-parties gone quite out; so lies Théroigne: she shall speak with the Kaiser face to face, and return. And France lies—how! Fleeting Time shears down the great and the little; and in two years alters many things.

998. But at all events, here, we say, is a second Ignominious Royal Procession, though much altered; to be witnessed also by its hundreds of thousands. Patience, ye Paris Patriots; the Royal Berline is returning. Not till Saturday: for the Royal Berline travels by slow stages; amid such loud-voiced confluent sea of National Guards, sixty thousand as they count; amid such tumult of all people. Three National-Assembly Commissioners, famed Barnave, famed Pétion, generally respectable Latour-Manbourg, have gone to meet it; of whom the two former ride in the Berline itself beside Majesty, day after day. Latour, as a mere respectability, and man of whom all men speak well, can ride in the rear, with Dame de Tourzel and the Soubrettes.

999. So on Saturday evening, about seven o'clock. Paris by hundreds, of thousands is again drawn up: not now dancing the tricolor joy-dance of hope; nor as yet dancing in fury-dance of hate and revenge: but in silence, with vague look of conjecture, and curiosity mostly scientific. A Saint-Antoine Placard has given notice this morning that "whosoever insults Louis shall be caned, whosoever applauds him shall be hanged." Behold then, at last, that wonderful New Berline; encircled by blue National sea with fixed bayonets, which flows slowly, floating it on, through the silent assembled hundreds of thousands. Three yellow Couriers sit atop bound with ropes: Pétion, Barnave, their Majesties, with sister Elizabeth, and the children of France, are within.

1000. Smile of embarrassment, or cloud of dull sourness, is on the broad phlegmatic face of his majesty; who keeps declaring to the successive Official persons, what is evident, "Eh bien, me voilà (Well here you have me);" and what is not evident, "I do assure you I did not mean to pass the frontiers;" speeches natural for that poor Royal Man; which Decency would veil. Silent is her Majesty, with a look of grief and scorn: natural for that Royal Woman. Thus lumbers and creeps the ignominious Royal Procession, through many streets, amid a silent-gazing people: comparable, Mercier thinks,* to some Procession du Roi de Basoche; or say, Procession of King Crispin, with his Dukes of Sutormania and royal blazonry of Cordwainery. Except indeed that this is *not* comic; ah no, it is comico-tragic; with bound Couriers and a Doom hanging over it; most fantastic, yet most miserably real. Miserablest flebile ludibrium of a Pickle-herring Tragedy! It sweeps along there, in most ungorgeous pall, through many streets in the dusty summer evening; gets itself at length wriggled out of sight; vanishing in the Tuileries Palace,—toward its doom, of slow torture, pine forte et dure.

1001. Populace, it is true, seizes the three rope-bound yellow Couriers; will at least massacre *them.* But our august Assembly, which is sitting at this great moment, sends out Deputation of rescue; and the whole is got huddled up. Barnave, "all dusty," is already there, in the National Hall; making brief discreet address and report. As indeed, through the whole Journey, this Barnave has been most discreet, sympathetic; and has gained the Queen's trust, whose noble instinct teaches her always who is to be trusted. Very different from heavy Pétions; who, if Campan speak truth, ate his luncheon, comfortably filled his wine-glass, in the Royal Berline; flung out his chicken-bones past the nose of Royalty itself; and, on the King's saying, "France cannot be a Republic," answered, "No, it is not ripe yet." Barnave is henceforth a queen's adviser, if advice could profit: and her Majesty astonishes Dame Campan by signifying almost a regard for Barnave; and that, in a day of retribution and Royal triumph, Barnave shall *not* be executed.*

1002. On Monday night Royalty went; on Saturday evening it returns: so much, within one short week, has Royalty accomplished for itself. The Pickle-herring Tragedy has vanished in the Tuileries Palace, toward "pain strong and hard." Watched, fettered and humbled, as Royalty never was. Watched even in its sleeping-apartments and inmost recesses: for it has to sleep with door set ajar, blue National Argus watching, his eye fixed on the Queen's curtains; nay, on one occasion, as the Queen cannot sleep, he offers to sit by her pillow, and converse a little!†

CHAPTER IX.

SHARP SHOT.

1003. In regard to all which this most pressing question arises: What is to be done with it? Depose it! resolutely answer Robespierre and the thorough-going few. For, truly, with a King who runs away, and needs to be watched in his very bedroom that he may stay and govern you, what other reasonable thing can be done? Had Philip d'Orléans not been a caput mortuum! But of himknown as one defunct, no man now dreams. Depose it not; say that it is inviolable, that it was spirited away, was enlevé; at any cost of sophistry and solecism, re-establish it! so answer with loud vehemence all manner of Constitutional Royalists; as all your pure Royalists do naturally likewise, with low vehemence, and rage compressed by fear, still more passionately answer. Nay Barnave and the two Lameths, and what will follow them, do likewise answer so. Answer with their whole might; terror-struck at the unknown Abysses on the verge of which, driven thither by themselves mainly, all now reels ready to plunge.

1004. By mighty effort and combination, this latter course is the course fixed on; and it shall by the strong arm, if not by the clearest logic, be made good. With the sacrifice of all their hard-earned popularity this notable Triumvirate, says Toulongeon, "set the Throne up again, which they had so toiled to overturn: as one might set up an overturned pyramid, on its vertex;" to stand so long as it is *held.*

1005. Unhappy France; unhappy in King, Queen and Constitution; one knows not in which unhappiest! Was the meaning of our so glorious French Revolution this, and no other, That when Shams and Delusions, long soul-killing, had become body-killing, and got the length of Bankruptcy and Inanition, a great People rose and, with one voice, said, in the name of the Highest: *Shams shall be no more?* So many sorrows and bloody horrors, endured, and to be yet endured through dismal coming centuries, were they not the heavy price paid and payable for the same. Total Destruction of Shams from among men? And now, O Barnave Triumvirate! is it in such *double*-distilled Delusion, and Sham even of a Sham, that an effort of this kind will rest acquiescent? Messieurs of the popular Triumvirate, never! —But, after all, what can poor popular Triumvirates, and fallible august Senators, do? They can, when the truth is all too horrible, stick their heads ostrich-like into what sheltering Fallacy is nearest; and wait there, a posteriori.

1006. Readers who saw the Clermontais and Three-Bishoprics gallop in the Night of Spurs; Diligences ruffling up all France into one terrific terrified Cock of India; and the town of Nantes in its shirt,—may fancy what an affair to settle this was. Robespierre, on the extreme Left, with perhaps Pétion and lean old Goupil, for the very Triumvirate has defalcated, are shrieking hoarse; drowned in Constitutional clamor. But the debate and arguing of a whole Nation; the bellowings through all Journals, for and against; the reverberant voice of Danton; the Hyperion shafts of Camille, the porcupine-quills of implacable Marat:—conceive all this.

1007. Constitutionalists in a body, as we often predicted, do now recede from the Mother Society, and become Feuillans; threatening her with inanition, the rank and respectability being mostly gone. Petition after Petition, forwarded by Post, or borne in Deputation, comes praying for Judgment and Déchéance, which is our name for Deposition; praying, at lowest, for Reference to the Eighty-three Departments of France. Hot Marseillese Deputation comes declaring, among other things: "Our Phocean Ancestors flung a Bar of Iron into the Bay at their first landing; this Bar will float again on the Mediterranean brine before we consent to be slaves." All this for four weeks or more, while the matter still hangs doubtful; Emigration streaming with double violence over the frontiers;* France, seething in fierce agitation of this question and prize-question: What is to be done with the fugitive Hereditary Representative?

1008. Finally, on Friday the 15th of July, 1791, the National Assembly decides; in what negatory manner we know. Whereupon the Theaters all close, the Bourn-stones and Portable-chairs begin spouting. Municipal Placards flaming on the walls, and Proclamations published by sound of trumpet, "invite to repose;" with small effect. And so, on Sunday the 17th, there shall be a thing seen, worthy of remembering. Scroll of a Petition, drawn up by Brissots, Dantons, by Cordeliers, Jacobins; for the thing was infinitely shaken and manipulated, and many had a hand in it: such Scroll lies now visible, on the wooden framework of the Fatherland's Altar, for signature. Unworking Paris, male and female, is crowding thither, all day, to sign or to see. Our fair Roland herself the eye of History can discern there "in the morning;"† not without interest. In few weeks the fair Patriot will quit Paris; yet perhaps only to return.

1009. But what with sorrow of balked Patriotism, what with closed theaters, and Proclamations still publishing themselves by sound of trumpet, the fervor of men's minds, this day is great. Nay, over and above, here has fallen out an incident, of the nature of Farce-Tragedy and Riddle; enough to stimulate

all creatures. Early in the day, a Patriot (or some say, it was a Patriotess, and indeed the truth is undiscoverable), while standing on the firm deal-board of Fatherland's Altar, feels suddenly, with indescribable torpedo-shock of amazement, his boot-sole pricked through from below; clutches up suddenly this electrified boot-sole and foot; discerns next instant—the point of a gimlet or brad-awl playing up, through the firm deal-board, and now hastily drawing itself back! Mystery, perhaps Treason? The wooden frame-work is impetuously broken up; and behold, verily a mystery; never explicable fully to the end of the world! Two human individuals, of mean aspect, one of them with a wooden leg, lie ensconced there, gimlet in hand; they must have come in over-night; they have a supply of provisions,—no "barrel of gunpowder" that one can *see*; they affect to be asleep; look blank enough, and give the lamest account of themselves. "Mere curiosity; they were boring up, to get an eye-hole; to see, perhaps,' with lubricity,' whatsoever, from that *new* point of vision could be seen:"—little that was edifying, one would think! But indeed what stupidest thing may not human Dullness, Pruriency, Lubricity, Chance and the Devil, choosing Two out of Half-a-million idle human heads, tempt them to?*

1010. Sure enough, the two human individuals with their gimlet are there. Ill-starred pair of individuals! For the result of it all is, that Patriotism, fretting itself, in this state of nervous excitability, with hypotheses, suspicions and reports, keeps questioning these two distracted human individuals, and again questioning them; claps them into the nearest Guard-house, clutches them out again; one hypothetic group snatching them from another; till finally, in such extreme state of nervous excitability, Patriotism hangs them as spies of Sieur Motier; and the life and secret is choked out of them forevermore. Forevermore, alas! Or is a day to be looked for when these two evidently mean individuals, who are human nevertheless, will become Historical Riddles; and, like him of the *Iron Mask* (also a human individual, and evidently nothing more),—have their Dissertations? To us this only is certain, that they had a gimlet, provisions and a wooden leg; and have died there on the Lanterne, as the unluckiest fools might die.

1011. And so the signature goes on, in a still more excited manner. And Chaumette, for Antiquarians possess the very Paper to this hour,†—has signed himself" in a flowing saucy hand slightly leaned;" and Hébert, detestable Père Duchesne, as if "an inked spider had dropped on the paper;" Usher Maillard also has signed, and many Crosses, which cannot write. And Paris, through its thousand avenues, is welling to the Champ-de-Mars and from it, in the utmost excitability of humor; central Fatherland's Altar quite heaped with signing Patriots and Patriotesses; the Thirty benches and whole internal Space crowded with on-lookers, with comers and goers; one regurgitating whirlpool of men and women in their Sunday clothes. All which a Constitutional Sieur Motier sees; and Bailly, looking into it with his long visage made still longer. Auguring no good; perhaps Déchéance and Deposition after all! Stop it, ye Constitutional Patriots; fire itself is quenchable,—yet only quenchable at *first*.

1012. Stop it, truly: but how stop it? Have not the first free People of the Universe a right to petition?—Happily, if also unhappily, here is one proof of riot: these two human individuals hanged at the Lanterne. Proof, O trencherous Sieur Motier? Were

---

* Bouillé, ii. 101.
† "Histoire Parlementaire." xi. 104-107

* "Histoire Parlementaire." xi. 104-107.
† Histoire Parlementaire, xi. 113, etc.

they not two human individuals sent thither by *thee* to be hanged ; to be a pretext for thy bloody Drapeau Rouge ? This question shall many a Patriot, one day, ask, and answer affirmatively, strong in Preternatural Suspicion.

1013. Enough, toward half-past seven in the evening, the mere natural eye can behold this thing ; Sieur Motier, with Municipals in scarf, with blue National Patrollotism, rank after rank, to the clang of drums, wending resolutely to the Champ-de-Mars ; Mayor Bailly, with elongated visage, bearing, as in sad duty bound, the Drapeau Rouge. Howl of angry derision rises in treble and bass from a hundred thousand throats, at the sight of Martial Law ; which nevertheless, waving its Red sanguinary Flag, advances there, from the Gros-Caillou Entrance ; advances, drumming and waving, toward Altar of Fatherland. Amid still wilder howls, with objurgation, obtestation ; with flights of pebbles and mud, saxa et fæces , with crackle of a pistol-shot :—finally with volley-fire of Patrollotism ; leveled muskets ; roll of volley on volley ! Precisely after one year and three days, our sublime Federation Field is wetted, in this manner, with French blood.

1014. Some "Twelve unfortunately shot," reports Bailly, counting by units ; but Patriotism counts by tens and even by hundreds. Not to be forgotten, nor forgiven ! Patriotism flies, shrieking, execrating. Camille ceases journalizing, this day ; great Danton with Camille and Fréron have taken wing, for their life ; Marat burrows deep in the Earth, and is silent. Once more Patrollotism has triumphed ; one other time ; but it is the last.

This was the Royal Flight to Varennes. Thus was the Throne overturned thereby ; but thus also was it victoriously set up again—on its vertex ; and will stand while it can be held.

BOOK FIFTH.

PARLIAMENT FIRST.

CHAPTER I.

GRANDE ACCEPTATION.

1015. In the last nights of September, when the autumnal equinox is past, and gray September fades into brown October, why are the Champs Elysées illuminated ; why is Paris dancing, and flinging fireworks ? They are gala-nights, these last of September ; Paris may well dance, and the Universe : the Edifice of the Constitution is completed ! Complete ; nay *revised*, to see that there was nothing insufficient in it, solemnly proffered to his Majesty ; solemnly accepted by him, to the sound of cannon-salvoes, on the 14th of the month. And now by such illumination, jubilee, dancing and fire-working, do we joyously handsel the new Social Edifice, and first raise heat and reek there, in the name of Hope.

1016. The Revision, especially with a throne standing on its vertex, has been a work of difficulty, of delicacy. In the way of propping and buttressing, so indispensable now, something could be done ; and yet, as is feared, not enough. A repentant Barnave Triumvirate, our Rabauts, Duports, Thourets, and indeed all Constitutional Deputies did strain every nerve but the Extreme Left was so noisy ; the People were so suspicious, clamorous to have the work ended ; and then the loyal Right Side sat feeble-petulant all the while, and as it were pouting and petting, unable to help, had they even been willing. The Two Hundred and Ninety had solemnly made scission, before that, and departed, shaking the dust off their feet. To such transcendency of fret, and

desperate hope that worsening of the bad might the sooner end it and bring back the good, had our unfortunate loyal Right Side now come !*

1017 However, one finds that this and the other little prop has been added, where possibility allowed. Civil-list and Privy-purse were from of old well cared for. King's Constitutional Guard, Eighteen hundred loyal men from the Eighty-three Departments, under a loyal Duke de Brissac ; this, with trustworthy Swiss besides, is of itself something. The old loyal Body-guards are indeed dissolved, in name as well as in fact ; and gone mostly toward Coblentz. But now also those Sansculottic violent Gardes Françaises, or Center Grenadiers, shall have their mittimus : they do ere long, in the Journals, not without a hoarse pathos, publish their farewell ; "wishing all aristocrats the graves in Paris which to us are denied."† They depart, these first Soldiers of the Revolution ; they hover very dimly in the distance for about another year ; till they can be remodeled, new-named, and sent to fight the Austrians ; and then History beholds them no more. A most notable Corps of men ; which has its place in World-History ;—though to us, so is History written, they remain mere rubrics of men ; nameless ; a shaggy Grenadier Mass, crossed with buff-belts. And yet might we not ask : What Argonauts, what Leonidas Spartans had done such a work ? Think of their destiny : since that May morning, some three years ago, when they, unparticipating, trundled off D'Esprémenil to the Calypso Isles ; since that July evening, some two years ago, when they, participating and sacreing with knit brows, poured a volley into Besenval's Prince de Lambesc ! History waves them her mute adieu.

1018. So that the Sovereign Power, these Sansculottic Watch-dogs, more like wolves, being leashed and led away from his Tuileries, breathes freer. The Sovereign Power is guarded henceforth by a loyal Eighteen Hundred ;—whom Contrivance, under various pretexts, may gradually swell to 6,000 ; who will hinder no journey to Saint-Cloud. The sad Varennes business has been soldered up ; cemented, even in the blood of the Champ-de-Mars, these two months and more ; and indeed ever since, as formerly, Majesty has had its privileges, its "choice of residence," though, for good reasons, the royal mind "prefers continuing in Paris." Poor royal mind, poor Paris ; that have to go mumming : enveloped in speciosities, in falsehood which knows itself false ; and to enact mutually your sorrowful farce-tragedy, being bound to it ; and on the whole, to hope always in spite of hope !

1019. Nay, now that his Majesty has accepted the Constitution, to the sound of cannon-salvoes, who would not hope ? Our good King was misguided, but he meant well. Lafayette has moved for an Amnesty, for universal forgiving and forgetting of Revolutionary faults ; and now surely the glorious Revolution, cleared of its rubbish, is complete ! Strange enough, and touching in several ways, the old cry of Vive le Roi once more rises round King Louis the Hereditary Representative. Their Majesties went to the Opera ; gave money to the Poor : the Queen herself, now when the Constitution is accepted, hears voice of cheering. Bygone shall be bygone ; the New Era *shall* begin ! To and fro, amid those lamp-galaxies of the Elysian Fields, the Royal Carriage slowly wends and rolls ; everywhere with vivats, from a multitude striving to be glad. Louis looks out, mainly on the variegated lamps and gay human groups, with satisfaction enough for the hour. In her Majesty's face, " under that kind grace-

---

* Toulongeon, ii. 56, 59.
† "Histoire Parlementaire," xiii. 73.

ful smile a deep sadness is legible."* Brilliancies of valor and of wit stroll here observant: a Dame de Staël, leaning most probably on the arm of her Narbonne. She meets Deputies; who have built this Constitution; who saunter here with vague communings, not without thoughts whether it will stand. But as yet melodious fiddle-strings twang and warble everywhere, with the rhythm of light fantastic feet; long lamp-galaxies fling their colored radiance: and brass-lunged Hawkers elbow and bawl, "Grande Acceptation, Constitution Monarchique:" it behooves the Son of Adam to hope. Have not Lafayette, Barnave, and all Constitutionalists set their shoulders handsomely to the inverted pyramid of a throne? Feuillans, including almost the whole Constitutional Respectability of France, perorate nightly from their tribune: correspond through all Post-offices: denouncing unquiet Jacobinism; trusting well that its time is nigh done. Much is uncertain, questionable: if the Hereditary Representative be wise and lucky, may one not, with a sanguine Gaelic temper, hope that he will get in motion better or worse; that is wanting to him will gradually be gained and added?

1020. For the rest, as we must repeat, in this building of the Constitutional Fabric, especially in this Revision of it, nothing that one could think of to give it new strength, especially to steady it, to give it permanence, and even eternity, has been forgotten. Biennial Parliament, to be called legislative, Assemblée Législative; with 745 members, chosen in a judicious manner by the "active citizens" alone, and even by electing of electors still more active: this, with privileges of Parliament, shall meet, self-authorized if need be, and self-dissolved; shall grant money-supplies and talk; watch over the administration and authorities; discharge forever the functions of a Constitutional Great Council, Collective Wisdom and National Palaver—as the Heavens will enable. Our First biennial Parliament, which indeed has been a choosing since early in August, is now as good as chosen. Nay it has mostly got to Paris: it arrived gradually;—not without pathetic greeting to its venerable Parent, the now moribund Constituent; and sat there in the Galleries, reverently listening; ready to begin, the instant the ground were clear.

1021. Then as to changes in the Constitution itself? This, impossible for any Legislative or common biennial Parliament, and possible solely for some resuscitated Constituent or National Convention, is evidently one of the most ticklish points. The august moribund Assembly debated it for four entire days. Some thought a change, or at least a reviewal and new approval, might be admissible in thirty years; some even went lower, down to twenty, nay to fifteen. The august Assembly had once decided for thirty years; but it revoked that, on better thoughts; and did not fix any date of time, but merely some vague outline of a posture of circumstances, and, on the whole, left the matter hanging.† Doubtless a National Convention can be assembled even within the thirty years: yet one may hope, not; but that Legislatives, biennial Parliaments of the common kind, with their limited faculty, and perhaps quiet successive additions thereto, may suffice for generations, or indeed while computed Time runs.

1022. Furthermore, be it noted that no member of this Constituent has been, or could be, elected to the new Legislative. So noble-minded were these Law-makers! cry some; and Solon-like would banish themselves. So splenetic! cry more: each grudging the other, none daring to be outdone in self-denial by the other. So unwise in either case! an-

swer all practical men. But consider this other self-denying ordinance, That none of us can be King's Minister, or accept the smallest Court Appointment, for the space of four, or at lowest (and on long debate and Revision) for the space of two years! So moves the incorruptible sea-green Robespierre: with cheap magnanimity he; and none dare to be outdone by him. It was such a law, not superfluous then, that sent Mirabeau to the gardens of Saint-Cloud, under cloak of darkness, to that colloquy of the gods; and thwarted many things. Happily and unhappily there is no Mirabeau now to thwart.

1023. Welcomer meanwhile, welcome surely to all right hearts, is Lafayette's chivalrous Amnesty. Welcome too is that hard-wrung Union of Avignon; which has cost us, first and last, "thirty sessions of debate," and so much else; may it at length prove lucky! Rousseau's statute is decreed: virtuous Jean-Jacques, Evangelist of the Contrat Social. Not Drouet of Varennes; not worthy Lataille, master of the old world famous Tennis-Court in Versailles, is forgotten; but each has his honorable mention, and due reward in money.* Whereupon, things being all so neatly winded up, and the Deputations, and Messages, and royal and other ceremonials having rustled by: and the King having now affectionately perorated about peace and tranquillization, and members having answered "Oui! oui!" with effusion, even with tears,—President Thouret, he of the Law Reforms, rises, and, with a strong voice, utters these memorable last-words · "The National Constituent Assembly declares that it has finished its mission; and that its sittings are all ended." Incorruptible Robespierre, virtuous Pétion, are borne home on the shoulders of the people; with vivats heaven-high. The rest glide quietly to their respective places of abode. It is the last afternoon of September, 1791; on the morrow morning the new Legislative will begin.

1024. So, amid glitter of illuminated streets and Champs Elysées, and crackle of fire-works and glad deray, has the first National Assembly vanished; dissolving, as they well say, into blank Time; and is no more. National Assembly is gone, its work remaining; as all Bodies of men go, and as man himself goes: it had its beginning, and must likewise have its end. A Phantasm-Reality born of Time, as the rest of us are; flitting ever backward now on the tide of Time; to be long remembered of men. Very strange Assemblages, Sanhedrims, Amphictyonic, Trades-Unions, Ecumenic Councils, Parliaments and Congresses, have met together on this Planet, and dispersed again; but a stranger Assemblage than this august Constituent, or with a stranger mission, perhaps never met there. Seen from the distance, this also will be a miracle. Twelve Hundred human individuals, with the Gospel of Jean-Jacques Rousseau in their pocket, congregating in the name of 25,000,000, with full assurance of faith, to "make the Constitution:" such sight, the acme and main product of the Eighteenth Century, our World can witness once only. For Time is rich in wonders, in monstrosities most rich; and is observed never to repeat himself, or any of his Gospels:—surely least of all, this Gospel according to Jean-Jacques. Once it was right and indispensable, since such had become the Belief of men; but once also is enough.

1025. They have made the Constitution, these Twelve Hundred Jean-Jacques Evangelists; not without results. Near twenty-nine months they sat, with various capacity;—always, we may say, in that capacity of car-borne Carroccio, and miraculous Standard of the Revolt of Men, as a Thing high and lifted up; whereon whosoever looked might hope healing. They have seen much. cannons leveled on

* De Staël, "Considérations," i. c. 23.
† "Choix de Rapports," etc. (Paris, 1825), vi. 230-317.

* Moniteur (in "Histoire Parlementaire," xi. 473.)

them; then suddenly, by interposition of the Powers, the cannons drawn back; and a war-god Broglie vanishing, in thunder *not* his own, amid the dust and down-rushing of a Bastille and Old Feudal France. They have suffered·somewhat; Royal Session, with rain and Oath of the Tennis-Court; Nights of Pentecost; Insurrections of Women. Also have they not done somewhat? Made the Constitution, and managed all things the while; passed, in these twenty-nine months, "twenty-five hundred Decrees," which on the average is some three for each day, including Sundays! Brevity, one finds, is possible, at times: had not Moreau de St. Méry to give 3,000 votes before rising from his seat?—There was valor (or value) in these men; and a kind of faith were it only faith in this, That cobwebs are not cloth; that a Constitution could be made. Cobwebs and chimeras ought verily to disappear; for a Reality there is. Let formulas, soul-killing, and now grown body-killing, insupportable, begone, in the name of Heaven and Earth!—Time, as we say, brought forth these Twelve Hundred; Eternity was before them, Eternity behind: they worked, as we all do, in the confinence of Two Eternities; what was given them. Say not that it was nothing they did. Consciously they did somewhat; unconsciously how much! They had their giants and their dwarfs, they accomplished their good and their evil; they are gone, and return no more. Shall they not go with our blessing, in these circumstances; with our mild farewell?

1026. By post, by diligence, on saddle or sole; they are gone: toward the four winds. Not a few over the marches, to rank at Coblentz. Thither wended Maury, among others; but in the end toward Rome, —to be clothed there in red Cardinal plush; in falsehood as in a garment; pet son (her *last* born?) of the Scarlet Woman. Talleyrand-Perigord, excommunicated Constitutional Bishop, will make his way to London: to be Ambassador, spite of the Self-denying Law; brisk young Marquis Chauvelin acting as Ambassador's-Cloak. In London too, one finds Pétion the virtuous; harangued and haranguing, pledging the wine-cup with Constitutional Reform-Clubs, in solemn tavern-dinner: Incorruptible Robespierre retires for a little to native Arras: seven short weeks of quiet; the last appointed him in the world. Public Accuser in the Paris Department, acknowedged high-priest of the Jacobins; the glass of incorruptible thin Patriotism, for his narrow emphasis is loved of all the narrow,—this man seems to be rising, somewhither? He sells his small heritage at Arras; accompanied by a Brother and a Sister, he returns scheming out with resolute timidity a small sure destiny for himself and them, to his old lodging, at the Cabinet-maker's, in the Rue St. Honoré: O resolute-tremulous incorruptible sea-green man, toward *what* a destiny!

1027. Lafayette, for his part, will lay down the command. He retires Cincinnatus-like to his hearth and farm; but soon leaves them again. Our National Guard, however, shall henceforth have no one Commandant; but all Colonels shall command in succession. month about. Other Deputies we have met, or Dame de Staël has met, "sauntering in a thoughtful manner;" perhaps uncertain what to do. Some, as Barnave, the Lameths, and their Duport, will continue here in Paris; watching the new biennial Legislative, Parliament the First; teaching it to walk, if so might be: and the Court to lead it.

1028. Thus these . sauntering in a thoughtful manner; travellug by post or diligence,—whither Fate beckons. Giant Mirabeau slumbers in the Pantheon of Great Men. and France? and Europe?—the brasslunged Hawkers sing "Grand Acceptation, Monarchic Constitution" through these gay crowds: the

Morrow, grandson of Yesterday, must be what it can, as To-day its father is. Our new biennial Legislative begins to constitute itself on the 1st of October, 1791.

CHAPTER II.

THE BOOK OF THE LAW.

1029. If the august Constituent Assembly itself, fixing the regards of the Universe, could, at the present distance of time and place, gain comparatively small attention from us, how much less can this poor Legislative! It has its Right Side and its Left; the less Patriotic and the more, for Aristocrats exist not here or now: it spouts and speaks; listens to Reports, reads Bills and Laws; works in its vocation, for a season: but the History of France, one finds, is seldom or never there. Unhappy Legislative, what can History do with it; if not drop a tear over it, almost in silence? First of the two-year Parliaments of France which, if Paper Constitution and oft-repeated National Oath could avail aught, were to follow in softly-strong indissoluble sequence while time ran,—it had to vanish dolefully within *one* year: and there came no second like it. Alas! your biennial Parliaments in endless indissoluble sequence, they and all that Constitutional Fabric, built with such explosive Federation Oaths, and its top stone brought out with dancing and variegated radiance, went to pieces, like frail crockery, in the crash of things; and already, in eleven short months, were in that Limbo near the Moon, with the ghosts of other Chimeras. There, except for rare specific purposes, let them rest, in melancholy peace.

1030. On the whole, how unknown is a man to himself; or a public Body of men to itself! Æsop's fly sat on the chariot-wheel, exclaiming, What a dust I do raise! Great Governors, clad in purple with fasces and insignia, are governed by their valets, by the pouting of their women and children; or, in Constitutional countries, by the paragraphs of their Able Editors. Say not, I am this or that; I am doing this or that! For thou knowest *it* not, thou knowest only the name it as yet goes by. A purple Nebuchadnezzar rejoices to feel himself now verily Emperor of this great Babylon which he has builded; and *is* a nondescript biped-quadruped, on the eve of a seven-years' course of grazing! These 745 elected individuals doubt not but they are the first biennial Parliament, come to govern France by parliamentary eloquence: and they *are* what? And they have come to do what? Things foolish and not wise!

1031. It is much lamented by many that this First Biennial had no members of the old Constituent in it, with their experience of parties and parliamentary tactics; that such was their foolish Self-denying Law. Most surely, old members of the Constituent had been welcome to us here. But, on the other hand, what old or what new members of any Constituent under the Sun could have effectually profited? There are first biennial Parliaments so postured as to be, in a sense, *beyond* wisdom; where wisdom and folly differ only in degree, and wreckage and dissolution are the appointed issue for both.

1032. Old-Constituents, your Barnaves, Lameths and the like, for whom a special Gallery has been set apart, where they may sit in honor and listen, are in the habit of sneering at these new Legislators;* but let not us! The poor 745 sent together by the active citizens of France, are what they could be; do what is fated them. That they are of Patriot temper we can well understand. Aristocrat Noblesse had fled over the marches, or sat brooding silent in their unburnt Châteaus; small prospect had they in Primary Electoral Assemblies. What with Flights to Va-

* Dumouriez, ii. 150, etc.

rennes, what with Days of Poniards, with plot after plot, the People are left to themselves; the People must needs choose Defenders of the People, such as can be had. Choosing, as *they* also will ever do, "if not the ablest man, yet the man ablest to be chosen !" Fervor of character, decided Patriot-Constitutional feeling; these are qualities: but free utterance, mastership in tongue-fence; this is the quality of qualities. Accordingly one finds, with little astonishment, in this First Biennial, that as many as 400 Members are of the Advocate or Attorney species. Men who can speak, if there be aught to speak: nay here are men also who can think, and even act. Candor will say of this ill-fated First French Parliament, that it wanted not its modicum of talent, its modicum of honesty; that it, neither in the one respect nor in the other, sank below the average of Parliaments, but rose above the average. Let average Parliaments, whom the world does *not* guillotine, and cast forth to long infamy, be thankful not to themselves but to their stars!

1033. France, as we say, has once more done what it could: fervid men have come together from wide separation; for strange issues. Fiery Max Isnard is come, from the utmost South-east: fiery Claude Fauchet, Te-Deum Fauchet Bishop of Calvadoes, from the utmost North-west. No Mirabeau now sits here who has swallowed formulas: our only Mirabeau now is Danton, working as yet out of doors; whom some call "Mirabeau of the Sansculottes."

1034. Nevertheless we have our gifts,—especially of speech and logic. An eloquent Vergniaud we have; most-mellifluous yet most impetuous of public speakers; from the region named Gironde, of the Garonne: a man unfortunately of indolent habits; who will sit playing with your children when he ought to be scheming and perorating. Sharp bustling Guadet; considerate grave Gensonué; kind-sparkling mirthful young Ducos; Valazé doomed to a sad end : all these likewise are of that Gironde or Bourdeaux region: men of fervid Constitutional principles; of quick talent, irrefragable logic, clear respectability; who will have the Reign of Liberty establish itself, but only by respectable methods. Round whom others of like temper will gather; known by and by as Girondins, to the sorrowing wonder of the world. Of which sort note Condorcet, Marquis and Philosopher; who has worked at much, at Paris Municipal Constitution, Differential Calculus, Newspaper Chronique de Paris, Biography, Philosophy; and now sits here as two-years' Senator: a notable Condorcet, with stoical Roman face and fiery heart: "volcano hid under snow ;" styled likewise, in irreverent language, "mouton enragé," peaceablest of creatures bitten rabid ! Or note lastly, Jean-Pierre Brissot; whom Destiny, long working noisily with him, has hurled hither, say to have done with him. A biennial Senator he too; nay, for the present, the king of such. Restless, scheming, scribbling Brissot; who took to himself the style *De Warville*, heralds know not in the least why ;—unless it were that the father of him did, in an unexceptionable manner, perform Cookery and Vintnery in the Village of *Ouarville*? A man of the windmill species, that grinds always, turning toward all winds : not in the steadiest manner.

1035. In all these men there is talent, faculty to work ; and they will do it: working and shaping, not *without* effect, though alas, not in marble, only in quick-sand !—But the highest faculty of them all remains yet to be mentioned; or indeed has yet to unfold itself for mention: Captain Hippolyte Carnot, sent hither from the Pas de Calais; with his cold mathematical head, and silent stubbornness of will; iron Carnot, far-planning, imperturbable, unconquerable; who, in the hour of need, shall not be found wanting. His hair is yet black : and it shall grow gray, under many kinds of fortune, bright and troublous; and with iron aspect this man shall face them all.

1036. Nor is Coté Droit, and band of King's friends wanting: Vauhlanc, Dumas, Jaucourt the honored Chevalier ; who love Liberty, yet with Monarchy over it; and speak fearlessly according to that faith ; —whom the thick-coming hurricanes will sweep away. With them let a new military Theodore Lameth be named :—were it only for his two Brothers' sake, who look down on him, approvingly there, from the Old Constituents' Gallery. Frothy professing Pastorets, honey-mouthed conciliatory Lamourettes, and speechless nameless individuals sit plentiful, as Moderates in the middle. Still less is a Coté Gauche wanting: extreme left ; sitting on the topmost benches, as if aloft on its speculatory Height or *Mountain*, which will become a practical fulminatory Height, and make the name of Mountain famous-infamous to all times and lands.

1037. Honor waits not on this mountain; nor as yet even loud dishonor. Gifts it boasts not, nor graces, of speaking or of thinking; solely this one gift of assured faith, of audacity that will defy the Earth and the Heavens. Foremost here are the Cordelier Trio: hot Merlin from Thionville, hot Bazaire, Attorneys both; Chabot, disfrocked Capuchin, skillful in agio. Lawyer Lacroix, who wore once as subaltern the single epaulet, has loud lungs and a hungry heart. There too is Couthon, little dreaming *what* he is :—whom a sad chance has paralyzed in the lower extremities. For, it seems, he sat once a whole night, not warm in his true-love's bower (who indeed was by law another's), but sunken to the middle in a cold peat-bog, being hunted out from her: quaking for his life, in the cold quaking morass;* and goes now on crutches to the end. Cambon likewise. in whom slumbers undeveloped such a finance-talent for printing of Assignats; Father of Paper-money; who, in the hour of menace shall utter this stern sentence, "War to the Manorhouse, peace to the Hut (Guerre aux Châteaux, paix aux Chaumières) !"† Lecointre, the intrepid Draper of Versailles, is welcome here ; known since the Opera-Repast and Insurrection of Women. Thuriot, too; Elector Thuriot, who stood in the embrasures of the Bastille, and saw Saint-Antoine rising in mass; who has many other things to see. Last and grimmest of all, note old Ruhl, with his brown dusky face and long white hair; of Alsatian Lutheran breed ; a man whom age and book-learning have not taught ; who, haranguing the old men of Rheims, shall hold up the Sacred Ampulla (Heaven-sent, wherefrom Clovis and all Kings have been anointed) as a mere worthless oil-bottle, and dash it to sherds on the pavement there; who, alas, shall dash much to sherds, and finally his own wild head by pistolshot, and so end it.

1038. Such lava welters red-hot in the bowels of this Mountain; unknown to the world and to itself; A mere commonplace Mountain hitherto; distinguished from the Plain chiefly by its superior *barrenness*, its baldness of look : at the utmost it may, to the most observant, perceptibly *smoke*. For as yet all lies so solid, peaceable; and doubts not as was said, that it will endure while Time runs. Do not all love Liberty and the Constitution ? All heartily —and yet with degrees. Some, as Chevalier Jarcourt and his Right Side, may love Liberty less than Royalty, were the trial made; others, as Brissot and his Left Side, may love it more than Royalty. Nay again, of these latter some may love Liberty more

* Dumouriez, ii. 370.
† "Choix de Rapports," xi. 25.

than Law itself: others not more. Parties *will* unfold themselves; no mortal as yet knows how. Forces work within those men and without: dissidence grows opposition: ever widening: waxing into incompatibility and internecine feud; till the strong is abolished by a stronger; himself in his turn by a strongest! Who can help it? Jaucourt and his Monarchists, Feuillans, or Moderates; Brissot and his Brissotins, Jacobins, or Girondins; these with the Cordelier Trio, and all men, must work what is appointed them, and in the way appointed them.

1039. And to think what fate these poor Seven-Hundred and Forty-five are assembled, most unwittingly, to meet! Let no heart be so hard as not to pity them. Their soul's wish was to live and work as the First of the French Parliaments; and make the Constitution march. Did they not, at their very installment, go through the most affecting Constitutional ceremony, almost with tears? The Twelve eldest are sent solemnly to fetch the Constitution itself, the printed Book of the Law. Archivist Camus, an Old-Constituent appointed Archivist, he and the Ancient Twelve, amid blare of military pomp and clangor, enter, bearing the divine Book: and President and all Legislative Senators, laying their hand on the same, successively take the Oath, with cheers and heart-effusion, universal three-times-three.* In this manner they begin their Session. Unhappy mortals! For, that same day, his Majesty having received their Deputation of Welcome, as seemed, rather drily, the Deputation cannot but feel slighted, cannot but lament such slight: and thereupon our cheering swearing First Parliament sees itself, on the morrow, obliged to explode into fierce retaliatory sputter of anti-royal Enactment as to how they, for their part, will receive Majesty: and how Majesty shall not be called Sire any more, except they please: and then, on the following day, to recall this enactment of theirs, as too hasty, and a mere sputter, though not unprovoked.

1040. An effervescent well-intentioned set of Senators; too combustible, where continual sparks are flying! Their History is a series of sputters and quarrels; true desire to do their function, fatal impossibility to do it. Denunciations, reprimandings of King's Ministers, of traitors supposed and real: hot rage and fulmiuation against fulminating Emigrants; terror of Austrian Kaiser, of "Austrian Committee" in the Tuileries itself; rage and haunting terror, haste and doubt and dim bewilderment!—Haste, we say: and yet the Constitution had provided against haste. No Bill can be passed till it have been printed, till it have been thrice read, with intervals of eight days;—"unless the Assembly shall beforehand decree that there is urgency." Which accordingly the Assembly, scrupulous of the Constitution, never omits to do: Considering this, and also considering that, and then that other, the Assembly decrees always "qu'il y a urgence;" and thereupon "the assembly, having decreed that there is urgence," is free to decree—what indispensable distracted thing seems best to it. Two thousand and odd decrees, as men reckon, within Eleven months!† The haste of the Constituent seemed great; but this is treble-quick. For the time itself is rushing treble-quick; and they have to keep pace with that. Unhappy Seven Hundred and Forty-five: true-patriotic, but so combustible; being fired, they must needs fling fire: Senate of touchwood and rockets, in a world of smoke-storm, with sparks wind-driven continually flying!

1041. Or think, on the other hand. looking forward some months, of that scene they call Baiser de La-

mourette! The dangers of the country are now grown imminent, immeasurable; National Assembly, hope of France, is divided against itself. In such extreme circumstances, honey-mouthed Abbé Lamourette, new Bishop of Lyons, rises, whose name, l'amourette, signifies *the sweetheart*, or Delilah doxy,—he rises, and with pathetic honeyed eloquence, calls on all august Senators to forget mutual griefs and gudges, to swear a new oath, and unite as brothers. Whereupon they all, with vivats, embrace and swear; Left Side confounding itself with Right; barren Mountain rushing down to fruitful Plain, Pastoret into the arms of Condorcet, injured to the breast of injurer, with tears: and all swearing that whosoever wishes either Feuillant Two-Chamber Monarchy or Extreme-Jacobin Republic, or anything but the Constitution and that only, shall be anathema maranatha.* Touching to behold! For, literally on the morrow morning, they must again quarrel, driven by Fate; and their sublime reconcilement is called derisively the Baiser de L'amourette, or Delilah Kiss.

1042. Like fated Eteocles-Polynices Brothers, embracing though in vain; weeping that they must not love, that they must hate only, and die by each other's hands! Or say, like doomed Familiar Spirits; ordered, by Art Magic under penalties, to do a harder than twist ropes of sand: "to make the Constitution march." If the Constitution would but march! Alas, the Constitution will not stir. It falls on its face; they tremblingly lift it on end again: march, thou gold Constitution! The Constitution will not march.—"He shall march, by——!" said kind Uncle Toby, and even swore. The Corporal answered mournfully: "He will never march in this world."

1043. A Constitution, as we often say, will march when it images, if not the old Habits and Beliefs of the Constituted, then accurately their Rights, or better indeed their Mights;—for these two, well understood, are they not one and the same? The old Habits of France are gone: her new Rights and Mights are not yet ascertained, except in Paper-theorem, nor can be, in any sort till she have *tired*. Till she have measured herself, in fell death-grip, and were it in utmost preternatural spasm of madness, with Principalities and Powers, with the upper and the under, internal and external; with the Earth and Tophet and the very Heaven! Then will she know.—Three things bode ill for the marching of this French Constitution: the French People; the French King; thirdly, the French Noblesse and an assembled European World.

CHAPTER III.

AVIGNON.

1044. But quitting generalities, what strange Fact is this, in the far South-west, toward which the eyes of all men do now, in the end of October, bend themselves? A tragical combustion, long smoking and smoldering unluminous, has now burst into flame there.

1045. Hot is that Southern Provençal blood; alas, collisions as was once said, must occur in a career of Freedom; different directions will produce such; nay different *velocities* in the same direction will! To much that went on there, History, busied elsewhere, would not specially give heed: to troubles of Uzez, troubles of Nismes, Protestant and Catholic, Patriot and Aristocrat; to troubles of Marseilles, Montpellier, Arles; to Aristocrat Camp of Jalès, that wondrous real-imaginary Entity, now fading pale-dim, then always again glowing forth deep-hued (in the imagination mainly);—ominous magical, "an Aris-

---

* Moniteur, Séance du 4 Octobre, 1791.
† Montgaillard. iii. 1, 237.

* Moniteur, Séance du 6 Juillet, 1792.

tocrat *picture* of war done naturally!" All this was a tragical deadly combustion, with plot and riot, tumult by night and by day; but a *dark* combustion, not luminous, not noticed; which now, however, one cannot help noticing.

1046. Above all places, the unluminous combustion in Avignon and the Comtat Venaissin was fierce. Papal Avignon, with its Castle rising sheer over the Rhone-stream; beautifulest Town, with its purple vines and gold-orange groves; why must foolish old rhyming Réné, the last Sovereign of Provence, bequeath it to the Pope and Gold Tiara, not rather to Louis Eleventh with the Leaden Virgin in his hatband? For good and for evil! Popes, Antipopes, with their pomp, have dwelt in that Castle of Avignon rising sheer over the Rhone-stream; there Laura de Sade went to hear mass; her Petrarch twanging and singing by the Fountain of Vaucluse hard by, surely in a most melancholy manner. This was in the old days.

1047. And now in these new days such issues do come from a squirt of the pen by some foolish rhyming Réné, after centuries,—this is what we have: Jourdan Coupe-tête, leading to siege and warfare an Army, from three to fifteen thousand strong, called the Brigands of Avignon; which title they themselves accept, with the addition of an epithet, "The *brave* Brigands of Avignon!" It is even so. Jourdan the Headsman fled hither from that Châtelet Inquest, from that Insurrection of Women; and began dealing in madder: but the scene was rife in other than dye-stuffs; so Jourdan shut his madder-shop, and has risen, for he was the man to do it. The tile-beard of Jourdan is shaven off; his fat visage has got coppered and studded with black carbuncles; the Silenus trunk is swollen with drink and high living: he wears blue National uniform with epaulets, "an enormous saber, two horse-pistols crossed in his belt, and two smaller sticking from his pockets;" styles himself General, and is the tyrant of men.* Consider this one fact, O Render; and what sort of facts must have preceded it, must accompany it! Such things come of old Réné; and of the question which has risen, Whether Avignon cannot now cease wholly to be Papal, and become French and free?

1048. For some twenty-five months the confusion has lasted. Say three months of arguing; then seven of raging; then finally some fifteen months now of fighting, and even of hanging. For already in February, 1790, the Papal Aristocrats had set up four gibbets, for a sign; but the people rose in June, in retributive frenzy; and, forcing the public Hangman to act, hanged four Aristocrats, on each Papal gibbet a Papal Haman. Then were Avignon Emigrations, Papal Aristocrats emigrating over the Rhone River; demission of Papal Consul, flight, victory; re-entrance of Papal Legate, truce, and new onslaught; and the various turns of war. Petitions there were to National Assembly; Congresses of Townships three-score and odd Townships voting for French Reunion and the blessings of Liberty; while some twelve of the smaller, manipulated by Aristocrats, gave vote the other way: with shrieks and discord! Township against Township, Town against Town: Carpentras, long jealous of Avignon, is now turned out in open war with it;—and, Jourdan Coupe-tête, your first General being killed in mutiny, closes his dye-shop; and does there visibly with siege-artillery, above all with bluster and tumult, with the "brave Brigands of Avignon," beleaguer the rival Town, for two months, in the face of the world.

1049. Fents were done, doubt it not, far-famed in Parish History: but to Universal History unknown. Gibbets we see rise, on one side and on the other; and

* Dampmartin, "Evénemens," i. 287.

wretched carcasses swinging there, a dozen in the row; wretched Mayor of Vaison buried before dead.* The fruitful seed-fields lie unreaped, the vineyards trampled down; there is red cruelty, madness of universal choler and gall. Havoc and anarchy everywhere; a combustion most fierce, but *unlucent*, not to be noticed here!—Finally, as we saw, on the 14th of September last, the National Constituent Assembly, —having sent Commissioners and heard them;† having heard Petitions, held Debates, month after month ever since August. 1789; and on the whole "spent thirty sittings" on this matter,—did solemnly decree that Avignon and the Comtat were incorporated with France, and his Holiness the Pope should have what indemnity was reasonable.

1050. And so hereby all is amnestied and finished? Alas, when madness of choler has gone through the blood of men, and gibbets have swung on this side and on that, what will a Parchment Decree and Lafayette Amnesty do? Oblivious Lethe flows not *abore* ground! Papal Aristocrats and Patriot Brigands are still an eye-sorrow to each other; suspected, suspicions, in what they do and forbear. The august Constituent Assembly is gone but a fortnight, when, on Sunday the Sixteenth morning of October, 1791, the unquenched combustion suddenly becomes luminous. For Anti-constitutional Placards are up, and the Statue of the Virgin is said to have shed tears, and grown red.‡ Wherefore, on that morning, Patriot l'Escuyer, one of our "six leading Patriots," having taken counsel with his brethren and General Jourdan, determines on going to Church, in company with a friend or two: not to hear mass, which he values little; but to meet all the Papalists there in a body, nay to meet that same weeping Virgin, for it is the Cordeliers Church; and give them a word of admonition. Adventurous errand; which has the fatalest issue! What L'Escuyer's word of admonition might be, no History records; but the answer to it was a shrieking howl from the Aristocrat Papal worshipers, many of them women. A thousand-voiced shriek and menace; which, as L'Escuyer did not fly, became a thousand-handed hustle and jostle, a thousand-footed kick, with tumblings and tramplings, with the pricking of sempstress stilettoes, scissors and female pointed instruments. Horrible to behold; the ancient Dead, and Petrarchan Laura, sleeping round it there:§ high Altar and burning tapers looking down on it; the Virgin quite tearless, and of the natural stone-color!—L'Escuyer's friend or two rush off, like Job's Messengers, for Jourdan and the National Force. But heavy Jourdan will seize the Town-Gates first; does not run treble-fast, as he might: on arriving at the Cordeliers Church, the Church is silent, vacant; L'Escuyer, all alone, lies there, swimming in his blood, at the foot of the high Altar; pricked with scissors, trodden, massacred;— gives one dumb sob, and gasps out his miserable life forevermore.

1051. Sight to stir the heart of any man; much more of many men, self-styled Brigands of Avignon! The corpse of L'Escuyer, stretched on a bier, the ghastly head girt with laurel, is borne through the streets; with many-voiced unmelodious Nenia; funeral-wail still deeper than it is loud! The copper-face of anarchy, of bereft Patriotism, has grown black. Patriot Municipality dispatches official Narrative and tidings to Paris; orders numerous or innumerable arrestments for inquest and perquisition.

* Reyharoux "Mémoires," p. 26.
† Bescêne Desmaisons, ' Compte rendu à l'Assembléo Nationale, 10 Septembre. 1791 (Choix des Rapports," vii. 273-293).
‡ "Procès-verbal de la Commune d'Avignon," etc., (in "Histoire Parlementaire," xii. 419-423).
§ Ugo Foscolo, Essay on Petrarch," p. 35.

Aristocrats male and female are haled to the Castle; lie crowded in subterranean dungeons there, bemoaned by the hoarse rushing of the Rhone; cut out from all help.

1052. So lie they: waiting inquest and perquisition. Alas, with a Jourdan Headsman for Generalissimo, with his copper-face grown black, and armed Brigand Patriots chanting their Nenia, the inquest is likely to be brief. On the next day and the next, let Municipality consent or not, a Brigand Court-Martial establishes itself in the subterranean stories of the Castle of Avignon; Brigand Executioners, with naked saber, waiting at the door for a Brigand verdict. Short judgment, no appeal! There is Brigand wrath and vengence; not unrefreshed by brandy. Close by is the dungeon of the Glacière, or Ice-Tower: there may be deeds done—? For which language has no name!—Darkness and the shadow of horrid cruelty envelopes these Castle Dungeons, that Glacière Tower: clear only that many have entered, that few have returned. Jourdan and the Brigands supreme now over Municipals, over all authorities Patriot or Papal, reign in Avignon, waited on by Terror and Silence.

1053. The result of all which is, that, on the 15th of November, 1791, we behold friend Dampmartin, and subalterns beneath him, and General Choisi above him, with Infantry and Cavalry, and proper cannon-carriages rattling in front, with spread banners, to the sound of fife and drum wend, in a deliberate formidable manner, toward that sheer Castle Rock, toward those broad gates of Avignon; three new National-Assembly Commissioners following at safe distance, in the rear.* Avignon, summoned in the name of Assembly and Law, flings its Gates wide open: Choisi with the rest, Dampmartin and the "Bons Enfans (Good Boys) of Baufremont,"—so they name these brave Constitutional Dragoons, known to them of old,—do enter, amid shouts and scattered flowers. To the joy of all honest persons; to the terror only of Jourdan Headsman and the Brigands. Nay next we behold carbuncled swollen Jourdan himself show copper-face, with saber and four pistols; affecting to talk high; engaging, meanwhile, to surrender the Castle that instant. So the Choisi Grenadiers enter with him there. They start and stop, passing that Glacière, snuffing its horrible breath; with wild yells, with cries of "Cut the Butcher down!"—and Jourdan has to whisk himself through secret passages, and instantaneously vanish.

1054. Be the mystery of iniquity laid bare, then! A Hundred and Thirty Corpses, of men, nay of women and even children (for the trembling mother, hastily seized, could not leave her infant), lie heaped in that Glacière; putrid, under putridities: the horror of the world. For three days there is mournful lifting out, and recognition; amid the cries and movements of a passionate Southern people, now kneeling in prayer, now storming in wild pity and rage: lastly there is solemn sepulture, with muffled drums, religious requiem, and all the people's wail and tears. Their Massacred rest now in holy ground; buried in one grave.

1055. And Jourdan Coupe-tête? Him also we behold again, after a day or two: in flight, through the most romantic Petrarchan hill-country; vehemently spurring his nag; young Ligonnet, a brisk youth of Avignon, with Choisi Dragoons, close in his rear. With such swollen mass of a rider no nag can run to advantage. The tired nag, spur-driven, does take the River Sorgne; but sticks in the middle of it; firm on that chiaro fondo di Sorga; and will proceed no further for spurring! Young Ligonnet dashes up; the Copper-face menaces and bellows,

*Dampmartin, i. 251-294.

draws pistol, perhaps even snaps it; is nevertheless seized by the collar; is tied firm, ankles under horse's belly, and ridden back to Avignon, hardly to be saved from massacre on the streets there.*

1056. Such is the combustion of Avignon and the South-west, when it becomes luminous. Long loud debate is in the august Legislative, in the Mother Society, as to what now shall be done with it. Amnesty, cry eloquent Vergniaud and all Patriots: let there be mutual pardon and repentance; restoration, pacification, and, if so might anyhow be, an end! Which vote ultimately prevails. So the South-west smolders and welters again in an "Amnesty," or Non-remembrance,which, alas, cannot *but* remember, no Lethe flowing above ground! Jourdan himself remains unhanged; gets loose again, as one not yet gallows-ripe; nay, as we transiently discern from the distance, is "carried in triumph through the cities of the South."† What things men carry!

1057. With which transient glimpse, of a Copper-faced Portent faring in this manner through the cities of the South, we must quit these regions;—and let them smolder. They want not their Aristocrats; prond old Nobles, not yet emigrated. Arles has its "Chiffonne," so, in symbolical cant, they name that Aristocrat Secret-Association; Arles has its pavements piled up, by and by, into Aristocrat barricades. Against which Rebecqui, the hot-clear Patriot, must lead Marseillese with cannon. The Bar of Iron has not yet risen to the top in the Bay of Marseilles; neither have these hot Sons of the Phoceans submitted to be slaves. By clear management and hot instance, Rebecqui dissipates that Chiffonne, without bloodshed; restores the pavement of Arles. He sails in Coast-barks, this Rebecqui, scrutinizing suspicious Martello-towers, with the keen eye of Patriotism; marches overland with dispatch, singly, or in force; to City after City; dim scouring far and wide;‡—argues, and if it must be, fights. For there is much to do; Jalès itself is looking suspicion. So that Legislator Fauchet, after debate on it, has to propose Commissioners and a Camp on the Plain of Beaucaire; with or without result.

1058. Of all which, and much else, let us note only this small consequence, that young Barbaroux, Advocate, Town-Clerk of Marseilles, being charged to have these things remedied, arrives at Paris in the month of February, 1792. The beautiful and brave: young Spartan, ripe in energy, not ripe in wisdom; over whose black doom there shall flit nevertheless a certain ruddy fervor, streaks of bright Southern tint, not wholly swallowed of Death! Note also that the Rolands of Lyons are again in Paris; for the second and final time. King's Inspectorship is abrogated at Lyons, as elsewhere; Roland has his retiring-pension to claim, if attainable; has Patriot friends to commune with; at lowest, has a Book to publish. That young Barbaroux and the Rolands came together; that elderly Spartan Roland liked, or even loved the young Spartan, and was loved by him, one can fancy: and Madame——? Breathe not, thou'poison-breath' Evil-speech! That soul is taintless, clear as the mirror-sea. And yet if they two did look into each other's eyes, and each, in silence, in tragical renunciance, did find that the other was all-too lovely? Honi soit! She calls him "beautiful as Antinous;" he "will speak elsewhere of that astonishing woman." —A Madame d'Udon (or some such name, for Dumont does not recollect quite clearly) gives copious breakfast to the Brissotin Deputies and us Friends of Freedom, at her House in the Place Vendome; with temporary celebrity, with graces and wreathed

* Dampmartin, ut supra.
† "Deux Amis" (Paris, 1797), vii. pp. 59-71.
‡ Barbaroux, p. 21; "Histoire Parlementaire," xiii. 421-424.

smiles; not without cost. There, amid wide babble and jingle, our plan of Legislative Debate is settled for the day, and much counseling·held. Strict Roland is secu there, but does not go often.*

CHAPTER IV.

NO SUGAR.

1059. Such are our onward troubles; seen in the Cities of the South; extant, seen or unseen, in all cities and districts, North as well as South. For in all are Aristocrats, more or less malignant; watched by Patriotism; which again, being of various shades, from light Fayettist-Feuillant down to deep-somber Jacobin, has to watch even *itself.*

1060. Directories of Departments, what we call County Magistracies, being chosen by Citizens of a too "active" class, are found to pull one way : Municipalities, Town Magistracies, to pull the other way. In all places too are Dissident Priests; whom the Legislative will have to deal with : contumacious individuals, working on that angriest of passions; plotting, enlisting for Coblentz; or suspected of plotting: fuel of a universal unconstitutional heat. What to do with them ? They may be conscientious as well as contumacious : gently they should be dealt with, and yet it must be speedily. In unilluminated La Vendée the simple are like to be seduced by them ; many a simple peasant, a Cathelineau wool-dealer wayfaring meditative with his wool-packs, in these hamlets, dubiously shakes his head ! Two Assembly Commissioners went thither last Autumn ; considerate Gensonné, not yet called to be a senator ; Gallois, an editorial man. These Two, consulting with General Dumouriez, spake and worked softly, with judgment ; they have hushed down the irritation, and produced a soft Report—for the time.

1061. The General himself doubts not in the least but he can keep peace there ; being an able man. He passes these frosty months among the pleasant people of Niort, occupies "tolerably handsome apartments in the Castle of Niort," and tempers the minds of men.† Why is there but one Dumouriez ? Elsewhere you find, South or North, nothing but untempered obscure jarring, which breaks forth ever and anon into open clangor of riot. Southern Perpignan has its tocsin, by torchlight ; with rushing and onslaught : Northern Caen, not less, by daylight ; with Aristocrats ranged in arms at places of Worship; Departmental compromise proving impossible , breaking into musketry and a plot discovered ‡‡ Add Hunger too : for bread, always dear, is getting dearer: not so much as Sugar can be had ; for good reasons. Poor Simoneau, Mayor of Etampes, in this Northern region, hanging out his Red Flag in some riot of grains, is trampled to death by a hungry exasperated People. What a trade this of Mayor, in these times! Mayor of Saint-Denis hung at the Lanterne, by Suspicion and Dyspepsia, as he saw long since ; Mayor of Vaison, as we saw lately buried before dead ; and now this poor Simoneau the Tanner, of Etampes,—whom legal Constitutionalism will not forget.

1062. With factions, suspicions, want of bread and sugar, it is verily what they call déchiré, torn asunder, this poor country : France and all that is French. For, over seas too come bad news. In black Saint-Domingo, before that variegated Glitter in the Champs Elysées was lit for an accepted Constitution, there had risen, and was burning contemporary with it, quite another variegated Glitter and Nocturnal Fulgor, had we known it : of molasses and ardent-spirits; of sugar-boileries, plantations, furniture, cat-

tle and men : sky-high; the Plain of Cap Français one huge whirl of smoke and flame !

1063. What a change here, in those two years; since that first "Box of Tricolor Cockades" got through the Custom-house, and atrabiliar Creoles too rejoiced that there was a leveling of Bastilles ! Leveling is comfortable, as we often say : leveling, yet only down to oneself. Your pale-white Creoles have their grievances :—and your yellow Quarteroons ? And your dark-yellow Mulattoes ? And your Slaves soot-black ? Quarteroon Ogé, Friend of our Parisian-Brissotin *Friends of the Blacks*, felt, for his share too, that Insurrection was the most sacred of duties. So the tricolor Cockades had fluttered and swashed only some three months on the Creole hat, when Ogé's signal-conflagrations went aloft; with the voice of rage and terror. Repressed, doomed to die, he took black powder or seed-grains in the hollow of his hand, this Ogé ; sprinkled a film of white ones on the top, and said to his Judges, "Behold they are white ;" then *shook* his hand, and said, "Where are the whites (Où sont les blancs) ?"

1064. So now, in the Autumn of 1791, looking from the sky-windows of Cap Français, thick clouds of smoke girdle our horizon, smoke in the day, in the night fire; preceded by fugitive shrieking white women, by Terror and Rumor. Black demonized squadrons are massacring and harrying, with nameless cruelty. They fight and fire " from behind thickets and coverts," for the Black man loves the Bush; they rush to the attack, thousands strong, with brandished cutlasses and fusils, with caperings, shoutings, and vociferation.—which, if the White Volunteer Company stands firm, dwindle into staggerings, into quick gabblement, into panic flight at the first volley, perhaps before it.* Poor Ogé could be broken on the wheel; this fire-whirlwind too can he abated, driven up into the Mountains : but Saint-Domingo is *shaken*, as Ogé's seed-grains were : shaking, writhing in long horrid death-throes, it is Black without remedy ; and remains, as African Hayti, a monition to the world.

1065. O my Parisian Friends, is not *this*, as well as Regraters and Feuillant Plotters, one cause of the astonishing dearth of Sugar ? The Grocer, palpitant, with drooping lip, sees his Sugar taxed ; weighed out by female Patriotism, in instant retail; at the inadequate rate of twenty-five sous, or thirteen pence a pound. "Abstain from it ?" Yes, ye Patriot Sections, all ye Jacobins, abstain ! Louvet and Collot-d'Herbois so advise; resolute to make the sacrifice ; though "how shall literary men do without coffee ?" Abstain, with an oath ; that is the surest !†

1066. Also, for like reason, must not Brest and the Shipping Interest languish ? Poor Brest languishes, sorrowing, not without spleen ; denounces an Aristocrat Bertrand-Moleville, traitorous Aristocrat Marine-Minister. Do not her Ships and King's Ships lie rotting piecemeal in harbor; Naval Officers mostly fled, and on furlough too, with pay? Little stirring there; if it be not the Brest Galleys, whip-driven, with their Galley-Slaves,—alas, with some forty of our hapless Swiss Soldiers of Château-Vieux, among others ! These Forty Swiss, too mindful of Nanci, do now, in their red wool caps, tug sorrowfully at the oar ; looking into the Atlantic brine, which reflects only their own sorrowful shaggy faces ; and seem forgotten of Hope.

1067. But, on the whole, may we not say, in figurative language, that the French Constitution which shall march is very *rheumatic*, full of shooting internal pains, in joint and muscle; and will not march without difficulty?

---

* Dumont, "Souvenirs," p. 374.
† Dumouriez, ii. 129.
‡ "Histoire Parlementaire." xii. 131, 141; xiii. 114, 417.

* "Deux Amis," x. 157.
† "Débats des Jacobins" etc.("Histoire Parlementaire," xiii. 171, 92-98).

CHAPTER V.

KINGS AND EMIGRANTS.

1068. Extremely rheumatic Constitutions have been known to march, and keep on their feet; though in a staggering sprawling manner, for long periods, in virtue of one thing only· that the *Head* were healthy But this head of the French Constitution! What King Louis is and cannot help being, Readers already know A King who cannot take the Constitution, nor reject the Constitution: nor do anything at all, but miserably ask. What shall I do? A King environed with endless confusions, whose own mind is no germ of order. Haughty implacable remnants of Noblesse struggling with humiliated repentant Barnave-Lameths· struggling in that obscure element of fetchers and carriers, of Half-pay braggarts from the Café Valois, of Chambermaids whisperers, and subaltern officious persons; fierce, Patriotism looking on all the while, more and more suspicious, from without. what, in such struggle can they do? At best, *cancel* one another, and produce *zero* Poor King· Barnave and your Senatorial Jaucourts speak earnestly into this ear, Bertrand-Moleville, and Messenger from Coblentz, speak earnestly into that: the poor Royal head turns to the one side and to the other side; can turn itself fixedly to no side. Let Decency drop a veil over it: sorrier misery was seldom enacted in the world. This one small fact, does it not throw the saddest light on much? The Queen is lamenting to Madame Campan: "What am I to do?" When they, these Barnaves, get us advised to any step which the noblesse do not like, then I am pouted at; nobody comes to my card-table; the King's Conchee is solitary."* In such a case of dubiety, what *is* one to do? Go inevitably to the ground!

1069. The King has accepted this Constitution, knowing beforehand that it will not serve he studies it, and executes it in the hope mainly that it will be found inexecutable. King's Ships lie rotting in harbor, their officers gone the Armies disorganized, robbers scour the Highways which wear down unrepaired, all Public Service lies slack and waste, the Executive makes no effort, or an effort only to throw the blame on the Constitution. Shamming death, "faisant la mori!" What Constitution, use it in this manner, can march? "Grow to disgust the Nation," it will truly,† unless *you* first grow to disgust the Nation! It is Bertrand de Moleville's plan, and his Majesty's, the best they can form.

1070 Or if, after all, this best-plan proved too slow, proved a failure? Provident of that too, the Queen, shrouded in deepest mystery, "writes all day, in cipher, day after day, to Coblentz," Engineer Goguelat, he of the *Night of Spurs*, whom the Lafayette Amnesty has delivered from Prison, rides and runs. Now and then, on fit occasion, a Royal familiar visit can be paid to that Salle de Manége, an affecting encouraging Royal Speech (sincere, doubt it not, for the moment) can be delivered there, and the Senators all cheer and almost weep;—at the same time Mallet du Pan has visibly ceased editing, and invisibly bears abroad a King's Autograph, soliciting help from the Foreign Potentates.‡ Unhappy Louis, *do* this thing or else that other,—if thou couldst!

1071. The thing which the King's Goverment did do was to stagger distractedly from contradiction to contradiction; and wedding Fire to Water, envelop itself in hissing and ashy steam. Danton and needy corruptible Patriots are sopped with presents of cash:

they accept the sop; they rise refreshed by it, and travel their own way.* Nay the King's Government did likewise hire Hand-clappers, or claqueurs, persons to applaud. Subterranean-Rivarol has 1500 Men in King's pay, at the rate of some £10,000 sterling pre month; what he calls "a staff of genius;" Paragraph-writers, Placard Journalists. "280 Applauders, at three shillings a day;" one of the strangest Staffs ever commanded by· man. The muster rolls and account-books of which still exist.† Bertrand-Moleville himself, in a way he thinks very dexterous, contrives to pack the Galleries of the Legislatives; gets Sansculottes hired to go thither, and applaud at a signal given, they fancying it was Pétion that bade them a device which was not detected for almost a week. Dexterous enough; as if a man, finding the Day fast decline, should determine on altering the Clock-hand . *that* is a thing possible for him.

1072. Here too let us note an unexpected apparition of Philippe d'Orléans, at court· his last at the Levee of any King. D'Orléans, some time in the winter months seemingly, has been appointed to that old first-coveted rank of Admiral,—though only over ships rotting in port. The wished-for comes too late! However, he waits on Bertrand-Moleville to give thanks: nay to state that he would willingly thank his Majesty in person; that, in spite of all the horrible things men have said and sung, he is far from being his Majesty's enemy; at bottom, how far! Bertrand delivers the message, brings about the royal Interview, which does pass to the satisfaction of his Majesty ; D'Orléans seeming clearly repentant, determined to turn over a new leaf. And yet, next Sunday, what do we see? "Next Sunday," says Bertrand, "he came to the King's Levee; but the Courtier, ignorant of what had passed, the Crowd of Royalists who were accustomed to resort thither on that day specially to pay their court, gave him the most humiliating reception. They came pressing round him ; managing, as if by mistake, to tread on his toes, to elbow him toward the door, and not let him enter again. He went down stairs to her Majesty's Apartments, where cover was laid ; so soon as he shewed face, sounds rose on all sides, "*Messieurs, take care of the dishes*,"as if he had carried poison in his pockets. The insults, which his presence everywhere excited, forced him to retire without having seen the Royal Family, the crowd followed him to the Queen's staircase ; in descending, he received a spitting (crachat) on the head, and some others on his clothes. Rage and spite were seen visibly painted on his face :"‡ as indeed how could they miss to be? He imputes it all to the King and Queen, who know nothing of it, who are even much grieved at it ; and so descends to his Chaos again. Bertrand was there at the Château that day himself, and an eye-witness to these things.

1073. For the rest, Non-jurant Priests, and the repression of them, will distract the King's conscience ; Emigrant Princes and Noblesse will force him to double-dealing : there must be *veto* on *veto* ; amid the ever-waxing indignation of men. For Patriotism, as we said, looks on from without, more and more suspicious. Waxing tempest, blast after blast, of Patriotic indignation, from without; dim inorganic whirl of Intrigues, Fatuities, within! Inorganic fatuous ; from which the eye turns away De Staël intrigues for her so gallant Narbonne, to get him made War-Minister; and ceases not, having got him made. The King shall fly to Rouen ; shall there, with the gallant Narbonne, properly "modify the Constitution." This is the same brisk Narbonne,

* Campan, ii. 177, 202.
† Bertrand-Moleville, i. c. 4.
‡ Bertrand-Moleville, i. 370.

* Ibid., i. c 17.
† Montgaillard, III. 41.
‡ Bertrand-Moleville, i. 177.

who, last year, cut out from their entanglement, by force of dragoons, those poor fugitive Royal Aunts: men say he is at bottom their Brother, or even *more*, so scandalous is scandal. He drives now, with his De Staël, rapidly to the Armies, to the Frontier Towns; produces rose-colored Reports, not too credible; perorates, gesticulates; wavers poising himself on the top, for a moment, seen of men : then tumbles, dismissed, washed away by the Time-flood.

1074. Also the fair Princess de Lamballe intrigues, bosom-friend of her Majesty: to the angering of Patriotism. Beautiful Unfortunate, why did she ever return from England ? Her small silver-voice what can it profit in that piping of the black World-tornado ? Which will whirl *her*, poor fragile Bird of Paradise, against grim rocks. Lamballe and De Staël intrigue visibly, apart or together : but who shall reckon how many others, and in what infinite ways, invisibly ! Is there not what one may call an ' Austrian Committee," sitting invisible in the Tuileries; center of an invisible Anti-National Spider-web, which, for we sleep among mysteries, stretches its threads to the ends of the Earth ? Journalist Carra has now the clearest certainty of it : to Brissotin Patriotism, and France generally, it is growing more and more probable.

1075. O Reader, hast thou no pity for this Constitution ? Rheumatic shooting pains in its members; pressure of hydrocephale and hysteric vapors on its Brain · a Constitution divided against itself; which will never march, hardly even stagger ? Why were not Drouet and Procureur Sausse in their beds, that unblessed Varennes Night ? Why did they not, in the name of Heaven, let the Korff Berline go whither it listed ? Nameless incoherency, incompatibility, perhaps prodigies at which the world still shudders, had been spared.

1076. But now comes the third thing that bodes ill for the marching of this French Constitution . besides the French People, and the French King, there is thirdly—the assembled European World. It has become necessary now to look at that also. Fair France is so luminous : and round and round it, is troublous : Cimmerian Night. Calonnes, Breteuils hover dim, far-flown ; overnetting Europe with intrigues. From Turin to Vienna ; to Berlin, and utmost Petersburg in the frozen North ! Great Burke has raised his great voice long ago ; eloquently demonstrating that the end of an Epoch is come, to all appearance the end of Civilized Time. Him many answer: Camille Desmoulins, Clootz Speaker of Mankind, Paine the rebellious Needleman, and honorable Gaelic Vindicators in that country and in this; but the great Burke remains unanswerable; " the Age of Chivalry *is* gone," and could not but go, having now produced the still more indomitable Age of Hunger. Altars enough, of the Dubois-Rohan sort, changing to the Gobel-and-Talleyrand sort, are faring by rapid transmutations to—shall we say, the right Proprietor of them ? French Game and French Game-Preservers did alight on the Cliffs of Dover, with cries of distress. Who will say that the end of much is not come ? A set of mortals has risen, who believe that Truth is not a printed Speculation, but a practical Fact; that Freedom and Brotherhood are possible in this Earth, supposed always to be Belial's, which " the Supreme Quack" was to inherit! Who will say that Church, State, Throne, Altar are not in danger; that the sacred Strongbox itself, last Palladium of effete Humanity, may not be blasphemously blown upon, and its padlocks undone?

1077. The poor Constituent Assembly might act with what delicacy and diplomacy it would; declare that it abjured meddling with its neighbors, foreign conquest, and so forth , but from the first this thing was to be predicted : that old Europe and new France could not subsist *together*. A Glorious Revolution, oversetting State-Prisons and Feudalism ; publishing, with outburst of Federative Cannon, in face of all the Earth, that Appearance is not Reality, how shall it subsist amid Governments which, if Appearance is *not* Reality, are—one knows not what ? In death-feud, and internecine wrestle and battle, it shall subsist with them ; not otherwise.

1078. Rights of Man, printed on Cotton Handkerchiefs, in various dialects of human speech, pass over to the Frankfort Fair.* What say we, Frankfort Fair ? They have crossed Euphrates, and the fabulous Hydaspes ; wafted themselves beyond the Ural, Altai, Himalaya, struck off from wood stereotypes, in angular Picture-writing, they are jabbered and jingled of in China and Japan. Where will it stop ? Kien-Lung smells mischief; not the remotest Dalai-lama shall knead his dough-pills in peace—Hateful to us, as is the Night! Bestir yourselves, ye Defenders of Order ! They do bestir themselves : all Kings and Kinglets, with their spiritual temporal array, are astir, their brows clouded with menace. Diplomatic emissaries fly swift ; Conventions, privy Conclaves assemble ; and wise wigs wag, taking what council they can.

1079. Also, as we said, the Pamphleteer draws pen, on this side and that : zealous fists beat the Pulpit-drum.* Not without issue! Did not iron Birmingham, shouting " Church and King," itself knew not why, burst out, last July, into rage, drunkenness and fire; and your Priestleys, and the like, dining there on that Bastille day, get the maddest singeing-scandalous to consider ! In which same days, as we can remark, High Potentates, Austrian and Prussian, with Emigrants, were faring toward Pilnitz in Saxony ; there, on the 27th of August, they, keeping to themselves what farther "secret Treaty" there might or might not be, did publish their hopes and their threatenings, their Declaration that it was, " the common cause of Kings."

1080. Where a will to quarrel is, there is a way. Our readers remember that Pentecost-Night, 4th of August, 1789, when Feudalism, fell in a few hours? The National Assembly, in abolishing Feudalism, promised that " compensation" should be given ; and did endeavor to give it. Nevertheless the Austrian Kaiser answers that his German Princes, for their part, cannot be unfeudalized, that they have Possessions in French Alsace, and Feudal Rights secured to them, for which no conceivable compensation will suffice. So, this of the Possessioned Princes, " Princes, Possessionés," is bandied from Court to Court ; covers acres of diplomatic paper at this day : a weariness to the world. Kaunitz argues from Vienna ; Delessart responds from Paris, though perhaps not sharply enough. The Kaiser and his Possessioned Princes, will too evidently come and *take* compensation,—so much as they can get. Nay might one not *partition* France, as we have done Poland, and are doing ; and so pacify it with a vengeance ?

1081 From South to North ! For actually it is " the common cause of Kings." Swedish Gustav, sworn Knight of the Queen of France, will lead Coalesced Armies;—had not Ankarstrom treasonously shot him ; for indeed there were griefs nearer home.† Austria and Prussia speak at Pilnitz; all men intensely listening. Imperial Rescripts have gone out from Turin ; there will be secret Convention at Vienna. Catherine of Russia beckons approvingly ; will help, were she ready. Spanish Bourbon stirs amid his pillows ; from him too, even from him shall there come help. Lean Pitt, "the Minister of Pre-

* Toulongeon, i. 256.
† 30th March, 1792 (" Annual Register," p. it).

paratives," looks out from his watch-tower in Saint James's, in a suspicious manner. Councilors plotting, Calonnes dim-hovering;—alas, Sergeants rub-a-dubbing openly through al manner of German market towns, collecting ragged valor!* Look where you will, immeasurable Obscurantism is girdling this fair France; which, again, will not be girdled by it. Europe is in travail; pang after pang; what a shriek was that of Pilnitz! The birth will be WAR.

1082. Nay, the worst feature of the business is this last, still to be named; the Emigrants at Coblentz. So many thousands ranking there, in bitter hate and menace: King's Brothers, all Princes of the Blood except wicked D'Orléans; your dueling De Castries, your eloquent Cazalès; bull-headed Malseigne, a war-god Broglie; Distaff Seigneurs, insulted Officers, all that have ridden across the Rhine-stream;—D'Artois welcoming Abbé Maury with a kiss, and clasping him publicly to his own royal heart! Emigration, flowing over the Frontiers, now in drops, now in streams, in various humors of fear, of petulance, rage and hope, ever since those Bastille days when D'Artois went, "to shame the citizens of Paris,"—has swollen to the size of a Phenomenon for the world. Coblentz is become a small extra-national Versailles; a Versailles in partibus; briguing, intriguing, favoritism, strumpetocracy itself, they say, goes on there; all the old activities, on a small scale, quickened by hunger Revenge.

1083. Enthusiasm, of loyalty, of hatred and hope, has risen to a high pitch; as, in any Coblentz tavern you may hear, in speech and in singing. Maury assists in the interior Council: much is decided on: for one thing, they keep lists of the dates of your emigrating; a month sooner, or a month later, determines your greater or your less right to the coming Division of the Spoil. Cazalès himself, because he had occasionally spoken with a Constitutional tone, was looked on coldly at first: so pure are our principles.† And arms are a-hammering at Liége; "3,000 horses" ambling hitherward from the Fairs of Germany: Cavalry enrolling; likewise Foot-soldiers, "in blue coat, red waistcoat and nankeen trousers."‡ They have their secret domestic correspondences, as their open foreign: with disaffected Crypto-Aristocrats, with contumacious Priests, with Austrian Committee in the Tuileries. Deserters are spirited over by assiduous crimps; Royal-Allemand is gone almost wholly. Their route of march, toward France and the Division of the Spoil, is marked out, were the Kaiser once ready. "It is said they mean to poison the sources; but," adds Patriotism making report of it, "they will not poison the source of Liberty;" whereat on applaudit (we cannot but applaud). Also they have manufactories of False Assignats: and men that circulate in the interior, distributing and disbursing the same; one of these we denounce now to Legislative Patriotism: "a man Lebrun by name; about thirty years of age, with blonde hair and in quantity; has," only for the time being surely, "a black-eye (œil poché); goes in a wiski with a black horse,"§ always keeping his Gig!

1084. Unhappy Emigrants, it was their lot, and the lot of France! They are ignorant of much that they should know: of themselves, of what is around them. A Political Party that knows not when it is beaten, may become one of the fatulest of things, to itself, and to all. Nothing will convince these men

that they cannot scatter the French Revolution at the first blast of their war-trumpet; that the French Revolution is other than a blustering Effervescence, of brawlers and spouters, which, at the flash of chivalrous broadswords, at the rustle of gallows-ropes, will burrow itself, in dens the deeper the welcomer. But, alas, what man does know and measure himself, and the things that are round him;—else where were the need of physical fighting at all? Never, till they are cleft asunder, can these heads believe that a Sansculottic arm has any vigor in it: cleft asunder, it will be too late to believe.

1085. One may say, without spleen against his poor erring brothers of any side, that above all other mischiefs, this of the Emigrant Nobles acted fatally on France. Could they have known, could they have understood! In the beginning of 1789, a splendor and a terror still surrounded them: the Conflagration of their Châteaus, kindled by months of obstinacy, went out after the 4th of August; and might have continued out, had they at all known what to defend, what to relinquish as indefensible. They were still a graduated Hierarchy of Authorities, or the accredited similitude of such; they sat there, uniting King with Commonality; transmitting and translating gradually, from degree to degree, the command of the one into the obedience of the other rendering command and obedience still possible. Had they understood their place, and what to do in it, this French Revolution, which went forth explosively in years and in months, might have spread itself over generations; and not a torture-death but a quiet euthanasia have been provided for many things.

1086. But they were proud and high, these men: they were not wise to consider. They spurned all from them in disdainful hate, they drew the sword and flung away the scabbard. France has not only no Hierarchy of Authorities, to translate command into obedience; its Hierarchy of Authorities has fled to the enemies of France; calls loudly on the enemies of France to interfere armed, who want but a pretext to do that. Jealous Kings and Kaisers might have looked on long, meditating interference, yet afraid and ashamed to interfere: but now do not the King's Brothers, and all French Nobles, Dignitaries and Authorities that are free to speak, which the King himself is not,—passionately invite us, in the name of Right and of Might? Ranked at Coblentz, from 15,000 to 20,000 stand now brandishing their weapons, with the cry: On, on! Yes, Messieurs, you shall on;—and divide the spoil according to your dates of emigrating.

1087. Of all which things a poor Legislative Assembly, and Patriot France, is informed by denunciant friend, by triumphant foe. Sulleau's Pamphlets, of the Rivarol Staff of Genius, circulate: heralding supreme hope. Durosoy's Placards tapestry the walls; Chant du Coq crows day, pecked at by Tallien's, Ami des Citoyens. King's-Friend Royou, Ami du Roi, can name, in exact arithmetical ciphers, the contingents of the various Invading Potentates; in all, 419,000 Foreign fighting men, with 15,000 Emigrants. Not to reckon these your daily and hourly desertions, which an Editor must daily record, of whole Companies, and even Regiments, crying Vive le Roi, Vive le Reine, and marching over with banners spread:*—lies all, and wind yet to Patriotism not wind; nor, alas, one day, to Royou! Patriotism, therefore, may brawl and babble yet a little while; but its hours are numbered: Europe is coming with 419,000 and the Chivalry of France; the gallows, one may hope, will get its own.

---

* Toulongeon, II. 100-117.

† Montgaillard, III. 5-17; Toulongeon, ubi supra.

‡ See "Histoire Parlementaire." xiii, 11-38, 41-41, 258, etc.

§ Moniteur. Séance du 2 Novembre, 1771 (Histoire Parlementaire,' xii. 212).

* Ami du Roi newspaper (in "Histoire Parlementaire," xiii. 175.)

CHAPTER VI.

BRIGANDS AND JALES.

1088. We shall have War, then; and on what terms! With an Executive "pretending," really with less and less deceptiveness now, "to be dead;" casting even a wishful eye toward the enemy: on such terms we shall have War.

1089. Public Functionary in vigorous action there is none; if it be not Rivarol with his Staff of Genius and 280 Applauders. The Public service lies waste; the very Tax-gatherer has forgotten his cunning: in this and the other Provincial Board of Management (Directoire de Département) it is found advisable to *retain* what Taxes you can gather, to pay your own inevitable expenditures. Our Revenue is Assignats; emission on emission of Paper-money. And the Army; our Three grand Armies, of Rochambeau, of Lückner, of Lafayette? Lean, disconsolate hover these Three grand Armies, watching the frontiers there; three Flights of long-necked Cranes in molting-time ;—wrecked, disobedient, disorganized; who never saw fire; the old Generals and Officers gone across the Rhine. War-Minister Narbonne, he of the rose-colored Reports, solicits recruitment, equipments, money, always money; threatens, since he can get none, to "take his sword," which belongs to himself, and go serve his country with that.*

1090. The question of questions is: What shall be done? Shall we, with a desperate defiance which Fortune sometimes favors, draw the sword at once, in the face of this inrushing world of Emigration and Obscurantism; or wait, and temporize and diplomatize, till, if possible, our resources mature themselves a little? And yet again, are our resources growing toward maturity; or growing the *other* way? Dubious: the ablest Patriots are divided; Brissot and his Brissotins, or Girondins, in the Legislative, cry aloud for the former defiant plan; Robespierre, in the Jacobins, pleads as loud for the latter dilatory one: with responses, even with mutual reprimands; distracting the Mother of Patriotism. Consider also what agitated Breakfasts there may be at Madame d'Udon's in the Place Vendome! The alarm of all men is great. Help, ye Patriots; and O at least agree; for the hour presses. Frost was not yet gone, when in that "tolerably handsome apartment of the Castle of Niort," there arrived a Letter. General Dumouriez must to Paris. It is War-Minister Narbonne that writes; the General shall give counsel about many things.† In the month of February, 1792, Brissotin friends welcome their Dumouriez Polymetis,—comparable really to an antique Ulysses in modern costume; quick, elastic, shifty, insuppressible, a "many-counseled man."

1091. Let the Reader fancy this fair France with a whole Cimmerian Europe girdling her, rolling in on her, black, to burst in red thunder of War; fair France herself hand-shackled and foot-shackled in the weltering complexities of this Social Clothing, or Constitution, which they have made for her; a France that, in such Constitution, cannot march! And Hunger too; and plotting Aristocrats, and excommunicating Dissident Priests: "the man Lebrun by name" urging his black wiski visible to the eye; and still more terrible in his invisibility, Engineer Goguelat, with Queen's cipher, riding and running!

1092. The excommunicatory Priests give new trouble in the Maine and Loire; La Vendée, our Cathelineau the wool-dealer, has not ceased grumbling and rumbling. Nay behold! Jalès itself once more: how often does that real-imaginary Camp of

the Fiend require to be extinguished! For near two years now, it has waned faint and again waxed bright, in the bewildered soul of Patriotism: actually, if Patriotism knew it, one of the most surprising products of Nature working with Art. Royalist Seigneurs, under this or the other pretext, assemble the simple people of these Cevennes Mountains; men not unused to revolt, and with heart for fighting, could their poor heads be got persuaded. The Royalist Seigneur harangues; harping mainly on the religious string: "True Priests maltreated, false Priests intruded, Protestants (once dragooned) now triumphing, things sacred given to the dogs;" and so produces, from the pious Mountaineer throat, rough growlings ·—"Shall we not testify, then, ye brave hearts of the Cevennes; march to the rescue? Holy Religion; duty to God and the King?"—"Si fait, si fait (Just so, just so)," answer the brave hearts always: "Mais il y a de bien bonnes choses dans la Révolution (But there are main good things in the Revolution too)!"—And so the matter, cajole as we may, will only turn on its axis, not stir from the spot, and remains theatrical merely.*

1093. Nevertheless deepen your cajolery, harp quick and quicker, ye Royalist Seigneurs; with a dead-lift effort you may bring it to that. In the month of June next, this Camp of Jalès will step forth as a theatricality suddenly become real; 2,000 strong, and with the boast that it is 70,000: most strange to see; with flags flying, bayonets fixed; with Proclamation, and d'Artois Commission of civil war! Let some Rebecqui, or other the like hot-clear Patriot; let some "Lieutenant-Colonel Aubry," if Rebecqui is busy elsewhere, raise instantaneus National Guards, and disperse and dissolve it: and blow the Old Castle asunder,† that so, if possible, we hear of it no more!

1094. In the Months of February and March, it is recorded, the terror, especially of rural France, had risen even to the transcendental pitch : not far from madness. In Town and Hamlet is rumor, of war, massacre: that Austrians, Aristocrats, above all, that *The Brigands* are close by. Men quit their houses and huts; rush fugitive, shrieking, with wife and child, they know not whither. Such a terror, the eye-witnesses say, never fell on a Nation; nor shall again fall, even in Reigns of Terror expressly so-called. The countries of the Loire, all the Central and South-east regions, start up distracted. "Simultaneously as by an electric shock;"—for indeed grain too gets scarcer and scarcer. "The people barricade the entrances of Towns, pile stones in the upper stories, the women prepare boiling water; from moment to moment, expecting the attack. In the Country, the alarm-bell rings incessant; troops of peasants, gathered by it, scour the highways, seeking an imaginary enemy. They are armed mostly with scythes stuck in wood; and, arriving in wild troops at the barricaded Towns, are themselves sometimes taken for Brigands."‡

1095. So rushes old France: old France is rushing *down*. What the end will be is known to no mortal; that the end is near all mortals may know.

CHAPTER VII.

CONSTITUTION WILL NOT MARCH.

1096. To all which our poor Legislative, tied up by an unmarching Constitution, can oppose nothing, by way of remedy, but mere bursts of parliamentary eloquence! They go on, debating, denouncing, ob-

---

* Moniteur, Seance du 23 Janvier, 1792; "Biographie des Ministres," § Narbonne.
† Dumouriez, ii. c. 6.

* Dampmartin, i. 201.
† Moniteur Séance du 15 Juillet, 1792.
‡ Newspapers, etc. (in "Histoire Parlementaire," xii. 325).

jurgating : loud weltering Chaos,which devours *itself.*

1097. But their 2,000 and odd Decrees? Reader, these happily concern not thee, nor me. Mere Occasional-Decrees, foolish and not foolish ; sufficient for *that* day was its own evil ! Of the whole 2,000 there are not now half a score, and those mostly blighted in the bud by royal *Veto*, that will profit or disprofit us. On the 17th of January, the Legislative, for one thing, got its High Court, its Haute Cour, set up at Orléans. The theory had been given by the Constituent, in May last, but this is the reality : a Court for the trial of Political Offences : a Court that cannot want work. To this it was decreed that there needed no royal Acceptance, therefore that there could be no *Veto*. Also Priests can now be married ; ever since last October. A Patriotic adventurous Priest had made bold to marry himself then ; and not thinking this enough, came to the bar with his new spouse, that the whole world might hold honeymoon with him, and a Law be obtained.

1098. Less joyful are the Laws again Refractory Priests ; and yet not less needful ! Decrees on Priests and decrees on Emigrants ; these are the two brief Series of Decrees, worked out with endless debate, and then canceled by *Veto*, which mainly concerns us here. For an august National Assembly must needs conquer these Refractories, Clerical or Laic, and thumbscrew them into obedience : and behold, always as you turn your legislative thumbscrew, and will press and even crush till Refractories give way, —King's *Veto* steps in with magical paralysis ; and your thumbscrew, hardly squeezing, much less crushing, does not act.

1099. Truly a melancholy Set of Decrees, a pair of Sets ; paralyzed by *Veto !* First, under date the 28th of October, 1791, we have legislative proclamation, issued by herald and bill-sticker ; inviting Monsieur, the King's Brother, to return within two months, under penalties. To which invitation Monsieur replies nothing ; or indeed replies by Newspaper Parody, inviting the august Legislative "to return to common sense within two months," under penalties. Whereupon the Legislative must take stronger measures. So, on the 9th of November, we declare all Emigrants to be "suspect of conspiracy ; and, in brief, to be "outlawed," if they have not returned at New-year's day :—Will the King say *Veto ?* That "triple impost" shall be levied on these men's Properties, or even their Properties be "put in sequestration," one can understand. But farther, on New-year's day itself, not an individual having "returned," we declare, and with fresh emphasis some fortnight later again declare, That Monsieur is *déchu*, forfeited of his eventual Heirship to the Crown : nay more, that Condé, Calonne, and a considerable List of others are accused of high treason ; and shall be judged by our High Court of Orléans : *Veto !*—Then again as to Non-jurant Priests : it was decreed in November last, that they should forfeit what Pensions they had ; be " put under inspection, under *surveillance*," and, if need were, be banished : *Veto !* A still sharper turn is coming ; but to this also the answers will be, *Veto.*

1100. *Veto* after *Veto ;* your thumbscrew paralyzed ! Gods and men may see that the Legislative is in a false position. As, alas, who is in a true one ? Voices already murmur for a "National Convention."* This poor Legislative, spurred and stung into action by a whole France and a whole Europe, cannot act : can only objurgate and perorate ; with stormy "motions," and motion in which is no *way*, with effervescence, with noise and fuliginous fury !

1101. What scenes in that National Hall ! President jingling his inaudible bell ; or, as utmost signal

* Decembre, 1791 ("Histoire Parlementaire," xii. 257.)

of distress clapping on his hat ; "the tumult subsiding in twenty minutes," and this or the other indiscreet Member sent to the Abbaye Prison for three days ! Suspected Persons must be summoned and questioned : old M. de Sombreuil of the Invalides has to give account of himself, and why he leaves his Gates open. Unusual smoke rose from the Sevres Pottery, i..dicating conspiracy ; the Potters explained that it was Necklace-Lamotte's *Mémoires*, bought up by her Majesty, which they were endeavoring to suppress by fire,*—which nevertheless he that runs may still read.

1102. Again, it would seem, Duke de Brissac and the King's Constitutional-Guard are "making cartridges secretly in the cellars :" a set of Royalists pure and impure ; black cut-throats many of them, picked out of gaming-houses and sinks ; in all 6,000 instead of Eighteen hundred ; who evidently gloom on us every time we enter the Château.† Wherefore, with infinite debate, let Brissac and King's Guard be *disbanded*. Disbanded accordingly they are ; after only two months of existence, for they did not get on foot till March of this same year. So ends briefly the King's new Constitutional Maison Militaire ; he must now be guarded by mere Swiss and blue Nationals again. It seems the lot of Constitutional things. New Constitutional Maison Civile he would never even establish, much as Barnave urged it ; old resident Duchesses sniffed at it, and held aloof ; on the whole her Majesty thought it not worth while, the Noblesse would so soon be back triumphant.‡

1103. Or, looking still into this National Hall and its scenes, behold Bishop Torné, a Constitutional Prelate, not of severe morals, demanding that "religious costumes and such caricatures" be abolished. Bishop Torné warms, catches fire ; finishes by untying, and indignantly flinging on the table, as if for gage or bet, his own pontifical cross. Which cross, at any rate, is instantly covered by the cross or Te-Deum Fauchet, then by other crosses and insignia, till all are stripped : this clerical Senator clutching off his skull-cap, that other his frill collar,—lest Fanaticism return on us.§

1104. Quick is the movement here ! And then so confused, unsubstantial, you might call it almost *spectral :* pallid, dim, inane, like the Kingdom's of Dis ! Unruly Linguet, shrunk to a kind of specter for us, pleads here some cause that he has : amid rumor and interruption, which excel human patience ; he " tears his papers, and withdraws," the irascible adust little man. Nay honorable Members will tear their papers, being effervescent : Merlin of Thionville tears his papers, crying : " So, the People cannot be saved by *you !*" Nor are Deputations wanting : " Deputations of Sections ; generally with complaint and denouncement, always with Patriot fervor of sentiment : Deputation of Women, pleading that they also may be allowed to take Pikes, and exercise in the Champ-de Mars. Why not, ye Amazons, if it be in you ? Then occasionally, having done our message and got answer, we " defile through the Hall singing çn-ira ;" or rather roll and whirl through it, " dancing our ronde patriotique the while,"—our new Carmagnole, or Pyrrhic war-dance and liberty-dance. Patriot Huguenin, Ex-Advocate, Ex-Carbineer, Ex-Clerk of the Barriers, comes deputed, with Saint-Antoine at his heels ; denouncing Anti-patriotism, Famine, Forestallment and Man-eaters ; asks an august Legislative : " Is there not a *tocsin in your hearts* against these mangeurs d'hommes !"||

* Moniteur. Séance du 28 Mai, 1792; Campan, ii. 196.
† Dumouriez, ii. 168.
‡ Campan. ii. c. 19
§ Moniteur. du 7 Avril. 1792: "Deux Amis." vii. 111.
|| See Moniteur Séances (in "Histoire Parlementaire," xiii. xiv.)

1105. But above all things, for this is a continual business, the Legislative has to reprimand the King's Ministers. Of his Majesty's Ministers we have said hitherto, and say, next to nothing. Still more spectral these! Sorrowful; of no permanency any of them, none at least since Montmorin vanished: the "eldest of the King's Council" is occasionally not ten days old.* Feuillant-Constitutional, as your respectable Cahier de Gerville, as your respectable unfortunate Delessarts : or Royalists-Constitutional, as Montmorin last Friend of Necker, or Aristocrat, as Bertrand-Moleville : they flit there phantomlike, in the huge simmering confusion; poor shadows, dashed in the racking winds; powerless, without meaning;—whom the human memory need not charge itself with.

1106. But how often, we say, are these poor Majesty's Ministers summoned over; to be questioned, tutored; nay threatened, almost bullied! They answer what, with adroitest simulation and casuistry, they can : of which a poor Legislative knows not what to make. One thing only is clear, That Cimmerian Europe is girdling us in; that France (not actually dead, surely ?) cannot march. Have a care, ye Ministers! Sharp Guadet transfixes you with cross-questions, with sudden Advocate-conclusions; the sleeping tempest that is in Vergniaud can be awakened. Restless Brissot brings up Reports, Accusations, endless thin Logic; it is the man's highday even now. Condorcet redacts, with his firm pen, our "Address of the Legislative Assembly to the French Nation."† Fiery Max Isnard, who, for the rest, will "carry not fire and Sword" on those Cimmerian Enemies, "but Liberty,"—is for declaring "that we hold Ministers responsible; and that by responsibility we mean death (nous entendons la mort)."

1107. For verily it grows serious: the time presses, and traitors there are. Bertrand-Moleville has a smooth tongue, the known Aristocrat; gall in his heart. How his answers and explanations flow ready; jesuitic, plausible to the ear! But perhaps the notablest is this, which befell once when Bertrand had done answering and was withdrawn. Scarcely had the august Assembly begun considering what was to be done with him, when the Hall fills with *smoke.* Thick sour smoke: no oratory, only wheezing and barking; irremediable; so that the august Assembly has to adjourn!‡ A miracle? Typical miracle? One knows not · only this one seems to know, that "the Keeper of the Stoves *was appointed* by Bertrand" or by some underling of his !—O fuliginous confused Kingdom of Dis, with thy Tantalus-Ixion toils, with thy angry Fire-floods, and Streams named of Lamentation, why hast thou not thy Lethe too, that so one might *finish* ?

CHAPTER VIII.

THE JACOBINS.

1108. Nevertheless let not Patriotism despair. Have we not, in Paris at least, a virtuous Pétion, a wholly Patriotic Municipality ? Virtuous Pétion, ever since November, is Mayor of Paris : in our Municipality, the Public, for the Public is now admitted too, may behold an energetic Danton; farther an epigrammatic slow-sure Manuel; a resolute unrepentant Billaud-Varennes, of Jesuit breeding; Tallien able-editor, and nothing but Patriots, better or worse. So ran the November Elections : to the joy of most citizens; nay the very Court supported Pétion rather

than Lafayette. And so Bailly and his Feuillants, long waning like the Moon, had to withdraw then; making some sorrowful obeisance,* into extinction : —or indeed into worse, into lurid half-light, grimmed by the shadow of that Red Flag of theirs, and bitter memory of the Champ-de-Mars. How swift is the progress of things and men ! Not now does Lafayette, as on that Federation-day, when *his* noon was, "press his sword firmly on the Fatherland's Altar," and swear in sight of France : ah no; he, waning and setting ever since that hour, hangs now, disastrous, on the edge of the horizon ; commanding one of those Three molting Crane-flights of Armies, in a most suspected, unfruithful, uncomfortable manner.

1109. But, at worst, cannot Patriotism, so many thousand strong in this Metropolis of the Universe, help itself? Has it not right-hands, pikes ? Hammering of Pikes, which was not to be prohibited by Mayor Bailly, has been sanctioned by Mayor Pétion; sanctioned by Legislative Assembly. How not, when the King's so-called Constitutional Guard "was making cartridges in secret ?" Changes are necessary for the National Guard itself; this whole Feuillant-Aristocrat Staff of the Guard must be disbanded. Likewise, citizens without uniform may surely rank in the Guard, the pike beside the musket, in such a time: the "active" citizen and the passive who can fight for us, are they not both welcome?—O my Patriot friends, indubitably Yes! Nay the truth is, Patriotism throughout, were it never so white-frilled, logical, respectable, must either lean itself heartily on Sansculottism, the black, bottomless ; or else vanish, in the frightfulest way, to Limbo! Thus some, with upturned nose, will altogether sniff and disdain Sansculottism; others will lean heartily on it ; nay others again will lean what we call *heartlessly* on it: three sorts ; each sort with a destiny corresponding.

1110. In such point of view, however, have we not for the present a Volunteer Ally, stronger than all the rest; namely, Hunger? Hunger; and what rushing of Panic Terror this and the sum-total of our other miseries may bring! For Sansculottism grows by what all other things die of. Stupid Peter Baille almost made an epigram, though unconsciously, and with the Patriot world laughing not at it but at him, when he wrote: "Tout va bien ici, le pain manque (All goes well here, food is not to be had)."†

1111. Neither, if you knew it, is Patriotism without her Constitution that *can* march; her not impotent Parliament; or call it Ecumenic Council, and General-Assembly of the Jean-Jacques Churches: the MOTHER SOCIETY, namely! Mother Society with her three hundred full-grown Daughters; with what we can call little Grand-daughters trying to walk, in every village of France, numerable, as Burke thinks, by the hundred thousand. This is the true Constitution ; made not by Twelve hundred august Senators, but by Nature herself; and has grown, unconsciously, out of the wants and the efforts of these 25,000,000 of men. They are "Lords of the Articles," our Jacobins; they originate debates for the Legislative : discuss Peace and War ; settle beforehand what the Legislative is to do. Greatly to the scandal of philosophical men, and of most Historians;—who do in that judge naturally, and yet not wisely. A Governing Power must exist: your other powers here are simulacra; this power is *it.*

1112. Great is the Mother Society; she has had the honor to be denounced by Austrian Kaunitz;‡

---

* Dumouriez, ii. 137.
† 16th February, 1792 ("Choix des Rapports," viii. 375-698).
‡ Courrier de Paris, 14 Janvier, 1792 (Gorsas's newspaper), n "Histoire Parlementaire," xiii. 83.

* "Discours de Bailly, Réponse de Pétion" (Moniteur du 20 Novembre, 1791).
† Barbaroux, p. 94.
‡ Moniteur, Séance du 20 Mars, 1792.

and is all the dearer to Patriotism. By fortune and valor she has extinguished Feuillantism itself, at least the Feuillant Club. This latter, high as it once carried its head, she, on the 18th of February, has the satisfaction to see shut, extinct; Patriots having gone thither, with tumult, to hiss it out of pain. The Mother Society has enlarged her locality, stretches now over the whole nave of the Church. Let us glance in, with the worthy Toulongeon, our old Ex-Constituent Friend, who happily has eyes to to see. "The nave of the Jacobins Church," says he, "is changed into a vast Circus, the seats of which mount up circularly like an amphitheater to the very groin of the domed roof. A high Pyramid of black marble, built against one of the walls, which was formerly a funeral monument, has alone been left standing; it serves now as back to the Office-bearers' Bureau. Here on an elevated Platform sit President and Secretaries, behind and above them the white Busts of Mirabeau, of Franklin, and various others, nay finally of Marat. Facing this is the Tribune, raised till it is midway between floor and groin of the dome, so that the speaker's voice may be in the center. From that point thunder the voices which shake all Europe: down below, in silence, are forging the thunderbolts and the fire-brands. Penetrating into this huge circuit, where all is out of measure, gigantic, the mind cannot repress some movement of terror and wonder; the imagination recalls those dread temples which Poetry, of old, had consecrated to the Avenging Deities."[*]

1113. Scenes too are in this Jacobin Amphitheater, —had History time for them. Flags of the "Three Free Peoples of the Universe," trinal brotherly flags of England, America, France, have been waved here in concert; by London Deputation, of Whigs or *Wighs* and their Club, on this hand, and by young French Citoyennes on that; beautiful sweet-tongued Female Citizens, who solemnly sent over salutation and brotherhood, also Tricolor stitched by their own needle, and finally Ears of Wheat; while the dome re-bellows with Vivent les trois peuples libres! from all throats:—a most dramatic scene. Demoiselle Théroigne recites, from that Tribune in mid-air, her persecutions in Austria; comes leaning on the arm of Joseph Chénier, Poet Chénier, to demand Liberty for the hapless Swiss of Château-Vieux.[†] Be of hope, ye forty Swiss; tugging there, in the Brest waters; *not* forgotten!

1114. Deputy Brissot perorates from that Tribune; Desmoulins, our wicked Camille, interjecting audibly from below, "Coquin!" Here though oftener in the Cordeliers, reverberates the lion-voice of Danton; grim Billaud-Varennes is here; Collot d'Herbois pleading for the forty Swiss, tearing a passion to rags, Apophthegmatic Manuel winds up in this pithy way: "A Minister must perish!"—to which the Amphitheater responds: "Tous, Tous (All, All)!" But Chief Priest and Speaker of this place, as we said, is Robespierre, the long-winded incorruptible man. What spirit of Patriotism dwelt in men in those times, this one fact, it seems to us. will evince: that 1,500 human creatures, not bound to it, sat quiet under the oratory of Robespierre; nay listened nightly, hour after hour, applausive; and gaped as for the word of life. More insupportable individual, one would say, seldom opened his mouth in any Tribune. Acrid, implacable-impotent; dull-drawling, barren as the Harmattan wind. He pleads, in endless earnest-shallow speech, against immediate War, against Woolen Caps or Bonnets Rouges, against many things; and is the Trismegistus and Dalai-Lama of Patriot men. Whom nevertheless a shrill-voiced little man, yet with fine eyes and a broad beautifully sloping brow, rises respectfully to controvert; he is, say the Newspaper Reporters, "M. Louvet, Author of the charming Romance of Faublas." Steady, ye Patriots! Pull not *yet* two ways; with a France rushing panic-stricken in the rural districts, and a Cimmerian Europe storming in on you!

CHAPTER IX.

MINISTER ROLAND.

1115. About the vernal equinox, however, one unexpected gleam of hope does burst forth on Patriotism: the appointment of a thoroughly Patriot Ministry. This also his Majesty, among his innumerable experiments of wedding fire to water, will try. Quod bonum sit. Madame d'Udon's Breakfasts have jingled with a new significance; not even Genevese Dumont but had a word in it. Finally, on the 15th and onward to the 23d day of March, 1792, when all is negotiated,—this is the blessed issue; this Patriot Ministry that we see.

1116. General Dumouriez, with the Foreign Portfolio, shall ply Kaunitz and the Kaiser, in another style than did poor Delessarts; whom indeed we have sent to our High Court of Orléans for his sluggishness. War-Minister Narbonne is washed away by the Time-flood: poor Chevalier de Grave, chosen by the Court, is fast washing away; then shall auste-re Servan, able Engineer-Officer, mount suddenly to the War Department. Genevese Clavière sees an omen realized: passing the Finance Hotel, long years ago, as a poor Genevese exile, it was borne wondrously on his mind that *he* was to be Finance-Minister; and now he is it;—and his poor Wife, given up by the Doctors, rises and walks, not the victim of nerves but their vanquisher.[*] And above all, our Minister of the Interior? Roland de la Platrière, he of Lyons! So have the Brissotins, public or private Opinion, and Breakfasts in the Place Vendome, decided it. Strict Roland, compared to a Quaker endimanché, or Sunday Quaker, goes to kiss hands at the Tuileries, in round hat and sleek hair, his shoes tied with mere ribbon or ferrat. The Supreme Usher twitches Dumouriez aside: "Quoi, Monsieur! No buckles to his shoes?"—"Ah, Monsieur," answers Dumouriez, glancing toward the ferrat: "All is lost (Tout est perdu."[†]

1117. Thus and so our fair Roland removes from her upper-floor in the Rue Saint-Jacques, to the sumptuous saloons once occupied by Madame Necker. Nay still earlier, it was Calonne that did all this gilding; it was he who ground these lusters, Venetian mirrors; who polished this inlaying, this veneering and ormoulu; and made it, by rubbing of the proper *lamp*, an Aladdin's Palace:—and now behold, he wanders dim-flitting over Europe; half-drowned in the Rhine-stream, scarcely saving his Papers! Vos non vobis.—The fair Roland, equal to either fortune, has her public Dinner on Fridays, the Ministers all there in a body: she withdraws to her desk (the cloth once removed), and seems busy writing; nevertheless loses no word: if, for example, Deputy Brissot and Minister Clavière get too hot in argument, she, not without timidity, yet with a cunning gracefulness, will interpose. Deputy Brissot's head, they say, is getting giddy, as feeble heads do.

1118. Envious men insinuate that the Wife Roland is Minister, and not the Husband: it is happily the worse they have to charge her with. For the rest,

---

[*] Toulongeon. ii. 124.
[†] "Débats des Jacobins" ("Histoire Parlementaire," xiii. 259, etc.)

[*] Dumont, c. 20, 21.
[†] Madame Roland, ii. 80-115.

let whose head soever be getting giddy, it is not this brave woman's. Serene and queenly here, as she was of old in her own hired garret of the Ursulines Convent! She who has quietly shelled French-beans for her dinner; being led to that, as a young maiden. by quiet insight and computation; and knowing what that was, and what she was: such a one will also look quietly on ormoulu and veneering, not ignorant of these either. Calonne did the veneering: he gave dinners here, old Besenval diplomatically whispering to him; and was great. yet Calonne we saw at last "walk with long strides." Necker next; and where now is Necker? Up also a swift change has brought hither; a swift change will send us hence. Not a Palace but a Caravansary!

1119. So wags and wavers this unrestful World, day after day, month after month. The streets of Paris, and all Cities, roll daily their oscillatory flood of men; which flood does nightly disappear, and lie hidden horizontal in beds and truckle-beds; and awakes on the morrow to new perpendicularity and movement. Men go their roads, foolish or wise;— Engineer Goguelat to and fro, bearing Queen's cipher. A Madame de Staël is busy; cannot clutch her Narbonne from the Time-flood: a Princess de Lamballe is busy; cannot help her Queen. Barnave, seeing the Feuillants dispersed, and Coblentz so brisk, begs by way of final recompense to kiss her Majesty's hand; "augurs not well of her new course;" and retires home to Grenoble, to wed an heiress there. The Café Valois and Méot the Restaurateur's hear daily gasconade; loud babble of Half-pay Royalists, with or without poniards. Remnants of Aristocrat saloons call the new Ministry Ministère-Sansculotte. A Louvet, of the Romance Faublas, is busy in the Jacobins. A Cazotte, of the Romance Diable Amoureux, is busy elsewhere: better wert thou quiet, old Cazotte; it is a world, this, of magic become *real!* All men are busy; doing they only half guess what: —flinging seeds, of tares mostly, into the "Seed-field of TIME;" this, by and by, will declare wholly what.

1120. But Social Explosions have in them something dread, and as it were mad and magical; which indeed Life always secretly has: thus the dumb Earth (says Fable), if you pull her mandrake-roots, will give a demonic mad-making *moan*. These Explosions and Revolts ripen, break forth like dumb dread Forces of Nature; and yet they are Men's forces; and yet *we* are part of them: the Dæmonic that is in man's life has burst out on us, will sweep us too away!—One day here is like another, and yet it is not like but different. How much is growing, silently resistless, at all moments! Thoughts are growing; forms of Speech are growing, and Customs and even Costumes; still more visibly are actions and transactions growing, and that doomed Strife of France with herself and with the whole world.

1121. The word *Liberty* is never named now except in conjunction with another; *Liberty* and *Equality*. In like manner, what, in a reign of Liberty and Equality. can these words, "Sir," "Obedient Servient," "Honor to be," and such-like, signify? Tatters and fibres of old Feudality; which, were it only in the Grammatical province, ought to be rooted out! The Mother Society has long since had proposals to that effect: these she could not entertain; not, at the moment. Note too how the Jacobin Brethren are mounting new Symbolical headgear: the Woolen Cap or Night-Cap, bonnet de laine, better known as bonnet rouge, the color being *Red*. A thing one wears not only by way of Phrygian Cap-of-Liberty, but also for convenience-sake, and then also in compliment to the Lower-class Patriots and Bastille Heroes; for the Red Night-cap combines all three properties. Nay

cockades themselves begin to be made of wool, of tricolor yarn: the ribbon-cockade, as a symptom of Feuillant Upper-class temper, is becoming suspicious. Signs of the times.

1122. Still more, note the travail-throes of Europe: or rather note the birth she brings; of the successive throes and shrieks, of Austrian and Prussian Alliance, of Kaunitz Anti-Jacobin Dispatch, of French Ambassadors cast out, and so forth, were long to note. Dumouriez corresponds with Kaunitz, Metternich, or Cobentzel, in another style than Delessarts did. Strict becomes stricter; categorical answer, as to this Coblentz work and much else, shall be given. Failing which? Failing which, on the 20th day of April, 1792, King and Ministers step over to the Salle de Menége; promulgate how the matter stands; and poor Louis, "with tears in his eyes," propose that the Assembly do now decree War. After due eloquenc, War is decreed that night.

1123. War, indeed! Paris came all crowding, full of expectancy, to the morning, and still more to the evening, session. D'Orléans with his two sons is there; looks on wide-eye, from the opposite gallery.* Thou canst look, O Philippe: it is a War big with issues, for thee and for all men. Cimmerian Obscurantism and this thrice-glorious Revolution shall wrestle for it, then: some Four-and-Twenty years; in immeasurable Briareus wrestle; trampling and tearing; before they can come to any, not agreement, but compromise, and approximate ascertainment each of what is in the other.

1124. Let our Three Generals on the Frontiers look to it, therefore: and poor Chevalier de Grave, the War-Minister, consider what he will do. What is in the three Generals and Armies we may guess. As for poor Chevalier de Grave, he, in this whirl of things all coming to a press and pinch upon him, loses head, and merely whirls with them, in a totally distracted manner; signing himself at last, " De Grave, *Mayor of Paris;*" whereupon he demits, returns over the Channel, to walk in Kensington Gardens;† and austere Servan, the able Engineer-Officer, is elevated in his stead. To the post of Honor? To that of Difficulty, at least.

CHAPTER X.
PETION-NATIONAL-PIQUE.

1125. And yet, how, on dark bottomless Cataracts there plays the foolishest fantastic-colored spray and shadow; hiding the Abyss under vapory rainbows! Alongside of this discussion, as to Austrian-Prussian War, there goes on not less but more vehemently a discussion, Whether the Forty or Two-and-forty Swiss of Châteaux-Vieux shall be liberated from the Brest Galleys? And then, Whether, being liberated, they shall have a public Festival, or only private ones?

1126. Théroigne, as we saw, spoke; and Collot took up the tale. Has not Bouillé's final display of himself, in that final Night of Spurs, stamped your aso-clled "Revolt of Nanci" into a "Massacre of Nanci," for all Patriot judgments? Hateful is that massacre; hateful the Lafayette-Feuillant "public thanks" given for it! For indeed, Jacobin Patriotism and dispersed Feuillantism are now at death-grips; and do fight with all weapons, even with scenic shows. The walls of Paris, accordingly, are covered with Placard and Counter-Placard, on the subject of Forty Swiss blockheads. Journal responds to Journal; Player Collot to Poetaster Roucher; Joseph Chénier the Jacobin, squire of Théroigne, to his brother André the Feuillant; Mayor Pétion to

* "Deux Amis." vii. 148-166.
† Dumont, c. 19, 21.

Dupont de Nemours: and for the space of two months, there is nowhere peace for the thought of man,—till this thing be settled.

1127. Gloria in excelsis! The Forty Swiss are at last got "amnestied," Rejoice, ye Forty; doff your greasy wool Bonnets, which shall become Caps of Liberty The Brest Daughter Society welcomes you from on board, with kisses on each cheek: your iron Hand-cuffs are disputed as Relics of Saints; the Brest Society indeed can have one portion, which it will beat into Pikes, a sort of Sacred Pikes. but the other portion must belong to Paris, and be suspended from the dome thereat, along with the Flags of the Three Free Peoples! Such a goose is man; and cackles over plush-velvet Grand Monarques and woolen Galley-slaves; over everything and over nothing,—and will cackle with his whole soul, merely if others cackle!

1128. On the 9th morning of April, these Forty Swiss blockheads arrive. From Versailles; with vivats heaven-high; with affluence of men and women. To the Town-hall we conduct them; nay to the Legislative itself, though not without difficulty. They are harangued, bedinnered, begifted,—the very Court, *not* for conscience-sake, contributing something; and their Public Festival shall be next Sunday. Next Sunday accordingly it is.* They are mounted into a "triumphal Car resembling a ship;" are carted over Paris, with the clang of cymbals and drums, all mortals assisting applausive; carted to the Champ-de-Mars and Fatherland's Altar· and finally carted, for Time always brings deliverance,—into invisibility forever more.

1129. Whereupon dispersed Feuillantism, or that Party which loves Liberty yet *not* more than Monarchy, will likewise have its Festival: Festival of Simoneau, unfortunate Mayor of Etampes,[who died for the Law; most surely for the Law, though Jacobinism disputes; being trampled down with his Red Flag in the riot about grains. At which Festival the Public again assists, *un*applausive: not we.

1130. On the whole, Festivals are not wanting; beautiful rainbow-spray when all is now rushing treble-quick toward its Niagara Fall. National Repasts there are; countenanced by Mayor Pétion; Saint-Antoine, and the Strong Ones of the Halles defiling through Jacobin Club, "their felicity," according to Santerre, "not perfect otherwise;" singing many-voiced their ça-ira, dancing their ronde patriotique. Among whom one is glad to discern Saint-Huruge, expressly "in white hat," the Saint-Christopher of the Carmagnole. Nay a certain Tambour, or National Drummer, having just been presented with a little daughter, determines to have the new French-woman christened, on Fatherland's Altar, then and there. Repast once over, he accordingly has her christened; Fauchet the Te-Deum Bishop acting in chief, Thuriot and honorable persons standing gossips: by the name Pétion-National-Pique!† Does this remarkable Citizeness, now past the meridian of life, still walk the Earth? Or did she die perhaps of teething? Universal History is not indifferent.

CHAPTER XI.

THE HEREDITARY REPRESENTATIVE.

1131. And yet it is not by carmagnole-dances, and singing of ça-ira, that the work can be done. Duke Brunswick is not dancing carmagnoles, but has his drill-sergeants busy.

* Newspapers of February, March, April, 1792; Iambe d'André Chénier "Sur la Fête des Suisses;" etc.. etc., (in "Histoire Parlementaire," xiii. xiv.).
† Patriote-Française (Brissot's newspaper), in "Histoire Parlementaire," xiii. 451.

1132. On the Frontiers, our Armies, be it treason or not, behave in the worst way. Troops badly commanded, shall we say? Or troops intrinsically bad? Unappointed, undisciplined, mutinous; that, in a thirty-years peace, have never seen fire? In any case, Lafayette's and Rochambeau's little clutch, which they made at Austrian Flanders, has prospered as badly as clutch need do: soldiers starting at their own shadow; suddenly shrieking, "On nous trahit," and flying off in wild panic, at or before the first shot;—managing only to hang some two or three prisoners they had picked up, and massacre their own Commander, poor Theobald Dillon, driven into a granary by them in the town of Lille.

1133. And poor Gouvion. he who sat shiftless in that Insurrection of Women! Gouvion quitted the Legislative Hall and Parliamentary duties in disgust and despair, when those Galley-slaves of Château-Vieux were admitted there. He said, "Between the Austrians and the Jacobins, there is nothing but a soldier's death for it;* and so, "in the dark stormy night," he has flung himself into the throat of the Austrian cannon, and perished in the skirmish at Maubeuge on the 9th of June. Whom Legislative Patriotism shall mourn, with black mort-cloths and melody in the Champ-de-Mars; many a Patriot shiftier, truer none. Lafayette himself is looking altogether dubious; in place of beating the Austrians, is about writing to denounce the Jacobins. Rochambeau, all disconsolate, quits the service: there remains only Lückner, the babbling old Prussian Grenadier.

1134. Without Armies, without Generals! And the Cimmerian Night *has* gathered itself; Brunswick preparing his proclamation; just about to march! Let a Patriot ministry and Legislative see, what in these circumstances it will do? Suppress eternal enemies, for one thing, answers the Patriot Legislative, and proposes, on the 24th of May, its Decree for the Banishment of Priests. Collect also some nucleus of determined internal friends, adds War-Minister Servan; and proposes, on the 7th of June, his Camp of 20,000. Twenty thousand National Volunteers: Five out of each Canton, picked Patriots, for Roland has charge of the Interior: they shall assemble here in Paris; and for a defense, cunningly devised, against foreign Austrians and domestic *Austrian Committee* alike. So much can a Patriot Ministry and Legislative do.

1135. Reasonable and cunningly devised as such Camp may, to Servan and Patriotism appear, it appears not so to Feuillantism : to that Feuillant-Aristocrat Staff of the Paris Guard: a Staff one would say again, which will need to be *dissolved*. These men see, in this proposed Camp of Servan's, an offense: and even, as they pretend to say, an insult. Petitions there come, in consequence. from blue Feuillants in epaulets; ill received. Nay, in the end, there comes one petition call "of the 8,000 National Guards:" so many names are on it, including women and children. Which famed petition of the 8,000 is indeed received and the Petitioners, all under arms, are admitted to the honors of the sitting,—if honors or even if sitting there be; for the instant their bayonets appear at the one door, the Assembly "adjourns", and begins to flow out at the door.†

1136. Also, in these same days, it is lamentable to see how National Guards, escorting Fête-Dieu or Corpus-Christi ceremonial, do collar and smite down any Patriot that does not uncover as the Hostie passes. They clap their bayonets to the breast of Cattle-butcher Legendre, a known Patriot ever since the Bastille days; and threaten to butcher him;

* Toulongeon, ii. 149.
† Moniteur, Séance du 10 Juin 1792.

though he sat quite respectfully, he says, in his Gig, at a distance of fifty paces, waiting till the thing were by. Nay orthodox females were shrieking to have down the Lanterne on him.*

1137. To such height has Feuillantism gone in his Corps. For, indeed, are not their officers creatures of the chief Feuillant, Lafayette? The Court too has, very naturally, been tampering with them; caressing them, ever since that dissolution of the so-called Constitutional Guard. Some Battalions are altogether "Pétris (kneaded full)" of Feuillantism, mere Aristocrats at bottom: for instance, the Battalion of the Filles-Saint-Thomas, made up of your Bankers, Stock-brokers, and other Full-purses of the Rue Vivienne. Our Worthy old Friend Weber, Queen's Foster-brother Weber, carries a musket in that Battalion,—one may judge with what degree of Patriotic intention.

1138. Heedless of all which, or rather heedful of all which, the Legislative, backed by Patriot France and the feeling of Necessity, decrees this Camp of 20,000 Decisive though conditional Banishment of malign Priests it has already decreed.

1139 It will now be seen, therefore, Whether the Hereditary Representative is for us or against us? Whether or not, to all our other woes, this intolerablest one is to be added: which renders us not a menaced Nation in extreme jeopardy and need, but a paralytic Solecism of a Nation, sitting wrapped as in dead cerements, of a Constitutional-Vesture that were no other than a winding-sheet, our right hand glued to our left: to wait there, writhing and wriggling, unable to stir from the spot till in Prussian rope we mount to the gallows? Let the Hereditary Representative consider it well The Decree of Priests? The Camp of 20,000?—By Heaven, he answers, Veto! Veto!—Strict Rolupd hands-in his Letter to the King; or rather it was Madame's Letter, who wrote it all at a sitting; one of the plainest-spoken Letters ever handed-in to any King. This plain-spoken Letter King Louis has the benefit of reading overnight. He reads, inwardly digests, and next morning, the whole Patriot Ministry finds itself turned out. It is the 13th of June, 1792.†

1140. Dumouriez the many-counseled, he, with one Duranthon, called Minister of Justice, does indeed linger for a day or two; in rather suspicious circumstances; speaks with the Queen, almost weeps with her; but in the end, he too sets off for the Army, leaving what Un-Patriot or Semi-Patriot Ministry and Ministries can now accept the helm to accept it. Name them not; new quick-changing Phantasms, which shift like magic-lantern figures; more spectral than ever.

1141. Unhappy Queen, unhappy Louis! The two Vetos were so natural: are not the Priests martyrs; also friends? This Camp of 20,000, could it be other than of stormfulest Sansculottes? Natural: and yet to France, unendurable. Priests that co-operate with Coblentz must go elsewhither with their martyrdom: stormful Sansculottes, these and no other kind of creatures will drive back the Austrians. If thou prefer the Austrians, then, for the love of Heaven, go join them. If not, join frankly with what will oppose them to the death. Middle course is none.

1142. Or, alas, what extreme course was there left now for a man like Louis? Underhand Royalists, Ex-Minister Bertrand-Moleville, Ex-Constituent Malonet, and all manner of unhelpful individuals, advise and advise. With face of hope turned now on the Legislative Assembly, and now on Austria and Cob-

lentz, and round generally on the Chapter of Chances an ancient Kingship, is reeling and spinning, one knows not whitherward, on the flood of things.

CHAPTER XII.

PROCESSION OF THE BLACK BREECHES.

1143 But is there a thinking man in France who, in these circumstances, can persuade himself that the Constitution will march? Brunswick is stirring; he, in few days now, will march. Shall France sit still, wrapped in dead cerements and grave-clothes, its right hand glued to its left, till the Brunswick Saint-Bartholomew arrive: till France be as Poland, and its Rights of Man become a Prussian Gibbet?

1144. Verily it is a moment frightful for all men. National Death; or else some preternatural convulsive outburst of National Life,—that same demonic outburst! Patriots whose audacity has limits had, in truth, better retire like Barnave; court private felicity at Grenoble. Patriots whose audacity has no limits must sink down into the obscure; and, daring and defying all things, seek salvation in stratagem, in Plot of Insurrection Roland and young Barbaroux have spread out the Map of France before them, Barbaroux says "with tears:" they consider what Rivers, what Mountain-ranges are in it: they will retire behind this Loire-stream, defend these Auvergne stone-labyrinths; save some little sacred Territory of the Free; die at least in their last ditch. Lafayette indites his emphatic Letter to the Legislative against Jacobinism;* which emphatic Letter will not heal the unhealable.

1145. Forward, ye Patriots whose audacity has no limits, it is you now that must either do or die! The sections of Paris sit in deep counsel; send out Deputation after Deputation to the Salle de Manége, to petition and denounce. Great is their ire against tyrannous Veto, Austrian Committee, and the combined Cimmerian Kings. What boots it? Legislative listens to the "tocsin in our hearts;" grants us honors of the sitting, sees us defile with jingle and fanfaronade; but the Camp of 20,000, the Priest-Decree, be-vetoed by Majesty, are become impossible for Legislative. Fiery Isnard says, "We will have Equality, should we descend for it to the tomb." Vergniaud utters, hypothetically, his stern Ezekiel-visions of the fate of Anti-national Kings. But the question is: Will hypothetic prophecies, will jingle and fanfaronade demolish the Veto; or will the Veto, secure in its Tuileries Château, remain undemolishable by these? Barbaroux, dashing away his tears, writes to the Marseilles Municipality, that they must send him "600 men who know how to die (qui savant mourir)."† No wet-eyed message this, but a fire-eyed one,—which will be obeyed!

1146. Meanwhile the 20th of June is nigh, anniversary of the world-famous Oath of the Tennis-Court: on which day, it is said, certain citizens have in view to plant a Mai or Tree of Liberty in the Tuileries Terrace of the Feuillants, perhaps also to petition the Legislative and Hereditary Representative about these Vetoes,—with such demonstration, jingle and evolution, as may seem profitable and practicable. Sections have gone singly, and jingled and evolved, but if they all went, or great part of them, and there, planting their Mai in these alarming circumstances, sounded the tocsin in their hearts.

1147 Among King's Friends there can be but one opinion as to such a step: among Nation's Friends there may be two. On the one hand, might it not hy possibility scare away these unblessed Vetos? Private Patriots and even Legislative Deputies may

* "Débats des Jacobins" (in "Histoire Parlementaire," xiv. 429).
† Madame Roland, II. 115.

* Moniteur, Séance du 18 Juin 1792
† Barbaroux, p 40.

have each his own opinion, or own no-opinion: but the hardest task falls evidently on Mayor Pétion and the Municipals, at once Patriots and Guardians of the public Tranquillity. Hushing the matter down with the one hand; tickling it up with the other! Mayor Pétion and Municipality may lean this way; Department-Directory with Procureur-Syndic Rœderer, having a Feuillant tendency, may lean that. On the whole, each man must act according to his own opinion or to his two opinions; and all manner of influences, official representations cross one another in the foolishest way. Perhaps after all, the Project, desirable and yet not desirable, will dissipate itself, being run athwart by so many complexities; and come to nothing?

1148.· Not so; on the Twentieth morning of June, a large Tree of Liberty, Lombardy Poplar by kind, lies visibly tied on its car, in the Suburb Saint-Antoine. Suburb Saint-Marceau too, in the uttermost Southeast, and all that remote Oriental region, Pikemen and Pikewomen, National Guards, and the unarmed curious are gathering,—with the peaceablest intentions in the world. A tricolor Municipal arrives; speaks. Tush, it is all peaceable, we tell thee, in the way of Law: are not Petitions allowable, and the Patriotism of Mais? The tricolor Municipal returns without effect: your Sansculottic rills continue flowing, combining into brooks: toward noontide, led by tall Santerre in blue uniform, by tall Saint-Huruge in white hat, it moves westward, a respectable river, or complication of still-swelling rivers.

1149. What Processions have we not seen: Corpus-Christi and Legendre waiting in his Gig; Bones of Voltaire with bullock-chariots, and goadsmen in Roman Costume; Feasts of Château-Vieux and Simoneau; Gouvion Funerals, Rousseau Sham-funeral, and the Baptism of Pétion-National-Pike! Nevertheless this Procession has a character of its own. Tricolor ribbons streaming aloft from Pike-heads; iron-shod batons; and emblems not a few; among which see specially these two, of the tragic and the untragic sort: a Bull's Heart transfixed with iron, bearing this epigraph, "Cœur d'Aristocrate (Aristocrat's heart);" and, more striking still, properly the standard of the host, a pair of old Black Breeches (silk, they say), extended on cross-staff, high overhead, with these memorable words "Tremblez, tyrans; voilà les Sansculottes (Trembling, tyrants; here are the Sans-indispensables)!" Also, the Procession trails two cannons.

1150. Scarfed-tricolor Municipals do now again meet it, in the Quai Saint-Bernard, and plead earnestly, having called halt. Peaceable, ye virtuous tricolor Municipals, peaceable are we as the sucking dove. Behold our Tennis-Court Mai. Petition is legal; and as for arms, did not an august Legislative receive the so-called 8,000 in arms, Feuillants though they were? Our Pikes, are they not of National Iron? Law is our father and mother, whom we will not dishonor; but Patriotism is our own soul. Peaceable, ye virtuous Municipals;—and on the whole, limited as to time! Stop we cannot; march ye with us.—The Black Breeches agitate themselves, impatient; the cannon-wheels grumble: the many-footed Host tramps on.

1151. How it reached the Salle de Manége, like an ever-waxing river; got admittance after debate; read its Address, and defiled, dancing and ça-ira-ing, led by tall sonorous Santerre and tall sonorous Saint-Huruge: how it flowed, not now a waxing river but a shut Caspian lake, round all Precincts of the Tuileries, the front Patriot squeezed by the rearward against barred iron Grates, like to have the life squeezed out of him, and looking too into the dread

throat of cannon, for national Battalions stand ranked within: how tricolor Municipals ran assiduous, and Royalists with Tickets of Entry; and both Majesties sat in the interior surrounded by men in black: all this the human mind shall fancy for itself, or read in old newspapers, and Syndic Rœderer's "Chronicle of Fifty Days."*

1152. Our Mai is planted; if not in the Feuillants Terrace, whither is no ingate, in the then Garden of the Capuchins, as near as we could get. National Assembly has adjourned till the Evening Session· perhaps this shut lake, finding no ingate, will retire to its sources again, and disappear in peace? Alas, not yet rearward still presses on; rearward knows little what pressure is in the front. One would wish, at all events, were it possible, to have a word with his Majesty first!

1153. The shadows fall longer, eastward; it is four o'clock · will his Majesty not come out? Hardly he! in that case, Commandant Santerre, Cattle-butcher Legendre, Patriot Huguenin with the tocsin in his heart, they, and others of authority, will enter *in*. Petition and request to wearied uncertain National Guard; louder and louder petition; backed by the rattle of our two cannons! The reluctant Grate opens: endless Sansculottic multitudes flood the stairs; knock at the wooden guardian of your privacy. Knocks, in such case, grow strokes, grow smashings· the wooden guardian flies in shivers. And now ensues a Scene over which the world has long wailed; and not unjustly for a sorrier spectacle, of Incongruity frouting Incongruity, and as it were recognizing themselves incongruous, and staring stupidly in each other's face, the world seldom saw.

1154. King Louis, his door being beaten on, opens it; stands with free bosom; asking, "What do you want?" The Sansculottic flood recoils awe-struck; returns however, the rear pressing on the front, with cries of "Veto! Patriot Ministers! Remove Veto!" —which things, Louis valiantly answers, this is not the time to do, nor this the way to ask him to do. Honor what virtue is in a man. Louis does not want courage; he has even the higher kind called moral-courage; though only the passive half of that. His few National Grenadiers shuffle back with him, into the embrasure of a window: there he stands, with unimpeachable passivity, amid the shouldering and the braying; a spectacle to men. They hand him a red Cap of Liberty; he sets it quietly on his head, forgets it there. He complains of thirst; half-drunk Rascality offers him a bottle, he drinks it. "Sire, do not fear," says one of his Grenadiers. "Fear?" answers Louis "feel then," putting the man's hand on his heart. So stands Majesty in Red Woolen Cap; black Sansculottism weltering round him, far and wide, aimless, with inarticulate dissonance, with cries of "Veto! Patriot Ministers!"

1155. For the space of three hours or more! The National Assembly is adjourned; tricolor Municipals avail almost nothing: Mayor Pétion tarries absent; Authority is none. The Queen with her Children and Sister Elizabeth, in tears and terror not for themselves only, are sitting behind barricaded tables and Grenadiers, in an inner room. The Men in black have all wisely disappeared. Blind lake of Sansculottism welters stagnant through the King's Château, for the space of three hours.

1156. Nevertheless all things do end. Vergniaud arrives with Legislative Deputation, the Evening Session having now opened. Mayor Pétion has arrived; is haranguing, " lifted on the shoulders of two

* Rœderer, etc., etc. (in "Histoire Parlementaire," xv. 96-194).

Grenadiers." In this uneasy attitude and in others, at various places without and within, Mayor Pétion harangues; many men harangue: finally Commandant Santerre defiles; passes out, with his Sansculottism, by the opposite side of the Château. Passing through the room where the Queen, with an air of dignity and sorrowful resignation, sat among the tables and Grenadiers, a woman offers her too a Red Cap; she holds it in her hand, even puts it on the little Prince Royal. "Madame," said Santerre, "this People loves you more than you think."*—About eight o'clock the Royal Family fall into each other's arms amid "torrents of tears." Unhappy Family! Who would not weep for it, were there not a whole world to be wept for?

1157. Thus has the Age of Chivalry gone, and that of Hunger come. Thus does all-needing Sansculottism look in the face of its Roi, Regulator, King or Able-man; and find that *he* has nothing to give it. Thus do the two Parties, brought face to face after long centuries, stare stupidly at one another, "*This, verily, am I; but good Heaven, is that Thou?*—and depart, not knowing what to make of it. And yet, Incongruities having recognized themselves to be incongruous, something must be made of it. The Fates know what.

1158. This is the world-famous 20th of June, more worthy to be called the *Procession of the Black Breeches*. With which, what we had to say of this First French biennial Parliament, and its products and activities, may perhaps fitly enough terminate.

BOOK SIXTH.

THE MARSEILLESE.

CHAPTER I.
EXECUTIVE THAT DOES NOT ACT.

1159. How could your paralytic National Executive be put "in action," in any measure, by such a 20th of June as this? Quite contrariwise: a large sympathy for Majesty so insulted arises everywhere; expresses itself in Addresses, Petitions, "Petition of the 20,000 inhabitants of Paris," and such-like among all Constitutional persons; a decided rallying round the throne.

1160. Of which rallying it was thought King Louis might have made something. However, he does make nothing of it, or attempt to make; for indeed his views are lifted beyond domestic sympathy and rallying, over to Coblentz mainly. Neither in itself is this same sympathy worth much. It is sympathy of men who believe still that the Constitution can march. Wherefore the old discord and ferment, of Feuillant sympathy for Royalty, and Jacobin sympathy for Fatherland, acting against each other from within; with terror of Coblentz and Brunswick acting from without:—this discord and ferment must hold on its course, till a catastrophe do ripen and come. One would think, especially as Brunswick is near marching, such catastrophe cannot now be distant. Busy, ye Twenty-five French Millions; ye foreign Potentates, minatory Emigrants, German drill-sergeants; each do what his hand findeth! Thou, O Reader, at such safe distance, wilt see what they make of it among them.

1161. Consider, therefore, this pitiable 20th of June as a futility; no catastrophe, rather a catastasis, or heightening. Do not its Black Breeches wave there, in the Historical Imagination, like a melancholy flag of distress; soliciting help, which no mortal can give? Soliciting pity, which thou wert hard-hearted not to give freely, to one and all! Other such flags, or what

are called Occurrences, and black or bright symbolic Phenomena will flit through the Historical Imagination; these, one after one, let us note, with extreme brevity.

1162. The first phenomenon is that Lafayette at the Bar of the Assembly; after a week and day. Promptly on hearing of this scandalous 20th of June, Lafayette had quitted his Command on the North Frontier, in better or worse order; and got hither, on the 28th, to repress the Jacobins: not by letter now; but by Petition, and weight of character, face to face. The august Assembly finds the step questionable; invites him meanwhile to the honors of the sitting.* Other honor, or advantage, there unhappily came almost none; the Galleries all growling; fiery Isnard glooming; sharp Guadet not wanting in sarcasms.

1163. And out of doors, when the sitting is over, Sieur Resson, keeper of the Patriot Café in these regions, hears in the street a hurly-burly; steps forth to look, he and his Patriot customers: it is Lafayette's carriage, with a tumultuous escort of blue Grenadiers, Cannoneers, even Officers of the Line, hurrahing and capering round it. They make a pause opposite Sieur Resson's door; wag their plumes at him; nay, shake their fists, bellowing A bas les Jacobins! but happily pass on without onslaught. They pass on, to plant a Mai before the General's door, and bully considerably. All which the Sieur Resson cannot but report with sorrow, that night, in the Mother Society.† But what no Sieur Resson nor Mother Society can do more than guess is this, That a council of rank Feuillants, your unabolished Staff of the Guard and who else has status and weight, is in these very moments privily deliberating at the General's: Can we not put down the Jacobins by force? Next day, a Review shall be held, in the Tuileries Gardens, of such as will turn out, and try. Alas, says Toulongeon, hardly a hundred turned out. Put it off till to-morrow, then, to give better warning. On the morrow, which is Saturday, there turn out "some thirty;" and depart shrugging their shoulders.‡ Lafayette promptly takes carriage again; returns musing on many things.

1164. The dust of Paris is hardly off his wheels, the summer Sunday is still young, when Cordeliers in deputation pluck up that Mai of his: before sunset, Patriots have burnt him in effigy. Louder doubt and louder rises, in Section, in National Assembly, as to the legality of such unbidden Anti-jacobin visit on the part of a General: doubt swelling and spreading all over France, for six weeks or so; with endless talk about usurping soldiers, about English Monk, nay about Cromwell: O thou poor *Grandison*-Cromwell!—What boots it? King Louis himself looked coldly on the enterprise: colossal Hero of two Worlds, having weighed himself in the balance, finds that he is become a gossamer Colossus, only some thirty turning out.

1165. In a like sense, with a like issue, works our Department-Directory here at Paris; who, on the 6th of July, take upon them to suspend Mayor Pétion and Procureur Manuel from all civic functions, for their conduct, replete, as is alleged, with omissions and commissions, on that delicate 20th of June. Virtuous Pétion sees himself a kind of martyr, or pseudo-martyr, threatened with several things; drawls out due heroical lamentation; to which Patriot Paris and Patriot Legislative duly respond. King Louis and Mayor Pétion have already had an interview on that business of the 20th; an interview and dialogue, distinguished by frankness on both sides; ending on

---

* Toulongeon, ii. 173; Campan, ii. c. 20.

* Moniteur, Séance du 28 Juin 1792.
† "Débats des Jacobins" ("Histoire Parlementaire," xv. 236.
‡ Toulongeon, ii. 180. See also Dampmartin, ii. 161.

King Louis's side with the words " Taisez-vous (Hold your peace)."

1166 For the rest, this of suspending our Mayor does seem a mistimed measure. By ill chance, it came out precisely on the day of that famous baiser de l'amourette, or miraculous reconciliatory Delilah-Kiss, which we spoke of long ago. Which Delilah-Kiss was thereby quite hindered effect. For now his Majesty has to write, almost that same night, asking a reconciled Assembly for advice! the reconciled Assembly will not advise; will not interfere. The King confirms the suspicion; then perhaps, but not till then will the Assembly interfere, the noise of Patriot Paris getting loud. Whereby your Delilah-Kiss, such was the destiny of Parliament First, becomes a Philistine Battle!

1167. Nay there goes a word that as many as Thirty of our chief Patriot Senators are to be clapped in prison, by mittimus and indictment of Feuillant Justices (Juges de Paix); who here in Paris were well capable of such a thing. It was but in May last that Juge-de-Paix Larivière, on complaint of Bertrand-Moleville touching that Austrian Committee, made bold to launch his mittimus against three heads of the Mountain, Deputies Bazire, Chabot, Merlin, the Cordelier Trio; summoning them to appear before him, and show where that Austrian Committee was, or else suffer the consequences. Which mittimus the Trio, on their side, made bold to fling in the fire, and valiantly pleaded privilege of Parliament. So that, for his zeal without knowledge, poor Justice Larivière now sits in the prison of Orléans, waiting trial from the Haute Cour there. Whose example, may it not deter other rash Justices; and so this word of the Thirty arrestments continue a word merely?

1168. But on the whole, though Lafayette weighed so light, and has had his Mai plucked up, Official Feuillantism falters not a whit; but carries its head high, strong in the letter of the law. Feuillants all of these men, a Feuillant Directory; founding on high character, and such-like; with Duke de la Rochefoucault for President,—a thing which may prove dangerous for him! Dim now is the once bright Anglomania of these admired Noblemen. Duke de Liancourt offers, out of Normandy where he is Lord-Lieutenant, not only to receive his Majesty, thinking of flight thither, but to lend him money to enormous amounts. Sire, it is not a Revolt, it is a Revolution; and truly no rose-water one! Worthier Noblemen were not in France nor in Europe than those two· but the time is crooked, quick-shifting, perverse; what straightest course will lead to any goal, in it?

1169. Another phasis which we note, in these early July days, is that of certain thin streaks of Federate National Volunteers wending from various points toward Paris, to hold a new Federation-Festival, or Feast of Pikes, on the Fourteenth there. So has the National Assembly wished it, so has the Nation willed it. In this way, perhaps, may we still have our Patriot Camp in spite of Veto. For cannot these Fédérés, having celebrated their Feast of Pikes, march on to Soissons; and, there being drilled and regimented, rush to the Frontiers, or whither we like? Thus were the one Veto cunningly alluded!

1170. As indeed the other Veto, about Priests, is also like to be eluded: and without much cunning. For Provincial Assemblies, in Calvados as one instance, are proceeding, on their own strength, to judge and banish Antinational Priests. Or still worse, without Provincial Assembly, a desperate People, as at Bordeaux, can " hang two of them on the Lanterne," on the way toward judgment.[*] Pity

* " Histoire Parlementaire." xvi. 259.

for the spoken Veto, when it cannot become an acted one!

1171. It is true, some ghost of a War-minister, or Home-minister, for the time being, ghost whom we do not name, does write to Municipalities and King's Commanders, that they shall, by all conceivable methods, obstruct this Federation, and even turn back the Fédérés by force of arms; a message which scatters mere doubt, paralysis and confusion; irritates the poor Legislature: reduces the Fédérés, as we see, to thin streaks. But being questioned, this ghost and the other ghosts, What it is then that they propose to do for saving the country ?—they answer, that they cannot tell; that indeed they, for their part, have, this morning, resigned in a body; and do now merely respectfully take leave of the helm altogether. With which words they rapidly walk out of the hall (sorteut brusquement de la salle), the " Galleries cheering loudly," the poor Legislature sitting "for a good while in silence!"[*] Thus do Cabinet-ministers themselves, in extreme cases, strike work, one of the strangest omens. Other complete Cabinet-ministry there will not be; only fragments, and these changeful, which never get completed; spectral Apparitions that cannot so much as appear! King Louis writes that he now views this Federation Feast with approval; and will himself have the pleasure to take part in the same.

1172. And so these thin streaks of Fédérés wend Paris-ward through a paralytic France. Thin grim streaks: not thick joyful ranks, as of old to the first Feast of Pikes! No these poor Federates march now toward Austria and Austrian Committee; toward jeopardy and forlorn hope; men of hard fortune and temper, not rich in the world's goods. Municipalities paralyzed by War-minister, are shy of affording cash, it may be, your poor Federates cannot arm themselves, cannot march, till the Daughter Society of the place open her pocket and subscribe. There will not have arrived, at the set day, 3,000 of them in all. And yet, thin and feeble as these streaks of Federates seem, they are the only thing one discerns moving with any clearness of aim in this strange scene Angry buzz and simmer; uneasy tossing and moaning of a huge France, all enchanted, spell-bound by unmarching Constitution into frightful conscious and unconscious Magnetic-sleep; which frightful Magnetic-sleep must now issue soon in one of two things: Death or Madness! The Fédérés carry mostly in their pocket some earnest cry and Petition, to have the " National Executive put in action;" or as a step toward that, to have the King's Déchéance (King's Forfeiture), or at least his Suspension, pronounced. They shall be welcome to the Legislative, to the Mother of Patriotism: and Paris will provide for their lodging.

1173. Déchéance, indeed: and what next? A France spell-free, a Revolution saved; and anything and all things next! so answer grimly Danton and the unlimited Patriots, down deep in their subterranean region of Plot, whither they have now dived. Déchéance, answers Brissot with the limited: and if next the little Prince Royal were crowned, and some Regency of Girondins and recalled Patriot Ministry set over him? Alas, poor Brissot; looking, as indeed poor man does always, on the nearest morrow as his peaceable promised land; deciding what must reach to the world's end, yet with an insight that reaches not beyond his own nose! Wiser are the unlimited subterranean Patriots, who with light for the hour itself, leave the rest to the gods.

1174. Or were it not, as we now stand, the probablest issue of all, that Brunswick, in Coblentz, just gathering his huge limbs toward him to rise, might

* Moniteur, Séance du Juillet 1792.

arrive first; and stop both Déchéance, and theorizing on it? Brunswick, is on the eve of marching; with 80,000, they say; fell Prussians, Hessians, feller Emigrants: a General of the Great Frederick, with such an army. And our Armies? And our Generals? As for Lafayette, on whose late visit a Committee is sitting and all France is jarring and censuring, he seems readier to fight *us* than fight Brunswick. Lückner and Lafayette pretend to be interchanging corps, and are making movements, which Patriotism cannot understand. This only is very clear, that their corps go marching and shuttling, in the interior of the country; much nearer Paris than formerly! Lückner has ordered Dumouriez down to him; down from Maulde, and the Fortified Camp there. Which order the many-counseled Dumouriez, with the Austrians hanging close on him, he busy meanwhile training a few thousands to stand fire and be soldiers, declares that, come of it what will, he cannot obey.* Will a poor Legislative, therefore, sanction Dumouriez; who applies to it, "not knowing whether there is any War-ministry?" Or sanction Lückner and these Lafayette movements?

1175. The poor Legislative knows not what to do. It decrees, however, that the Staff of the Paris Guard, and indeed all such Staffs, for they are Feuillants mostly, shall be broken and replaced. It decrees earnestly: in what manner one can declare, that the *Country is in Danger.* And finally, on the 11th of July, the morrow of that day when the Ministry struck work, it decrees that *the Country be,* with all dispatch, *declared in Danger.* Whereupon let the King sanction; let the Municipality take measures: if such Declaration will do service, *it* need not fail.

1176. In Danger truly, if ever Country was! Arise, O Country; or be trodden down to ignominious ruin! Nay, are not the chances a hundred to one that no rising of the Country will save it; Brunswick, the Emigrants, and Feudal Europe drawing nigh?

CHAPTER II.

LET US MARCH.

1177. But, to our minds. the notablest of all these moving phenomena is that of Barbaroux's "600 Marseillese who know how to die."

Prompt to the request of Barbaroux, the Marseilles Municipality has got these men together: on the fifth morning of July, the Townhall says, "Marchez. abattez le Tyran (March, strike down the Tyrant),"† and they, with grim appropriate "Marchons," are marching. Long journey, doubtful errand; Enfans de la Patrie, may a good genius guide you! Their own wild heart and what faith it has will guide them: and is not that the monition of some genius, better or worse? Five-hundred and Seventeen able men, with Captains of fifties and tens; well armed all, musket on shoulder, saber on thigh: nay they drive three pieces of cannon: for who knows what obstacles may occur? Municipalities there are, paralyzed by War-minister; Commandants with orders to stop even Federation Volunteers; good, when sound arguments will not open a Town-gate, if you have a petard to shiver it! They have left their sunny Phocean City and Seahaven, with its bustle and its bloom: the thronging *Course,* with high frondent Avenues, pitchy dock-yards, almond and olive groves, orange-trees on house-tops, and white glittering bastides that crown the hills, are all behind them. They wend on their wild way, from the extremity of French land. through unknown cities, toward an unknown destiny; with a purpose that they know,

* Dumouriez, ii. 1. 5.
† Dampmartin, ii. 153.

1178. Much wondering at this phenomenon, and how, in a peaceable trading City, so many householders or hearth-holders do severally fling down their crafts and industrial tools; gird themselves with weapons of war, and set out on a journey of 600 miles, to "strike down the tyrant,"—you search in all Historical Books, Pamphlets and Newspapers, for some light on it: unhappily without effect. Rumor and Terror precede this march; which still echo on you: the march itself an unknown thing. Weber, in the back-stairs of the Tuileries, has understood that they were Forçats, Galley-slaves and mere scoundrels, these Marseillese; that, as they marched through Lyons, the people shut their shops; —also that the number of them was some 4,000. Equally vague is Blanc Gilli, who likewise murmurs about Forçats and danger of plunder.* Forçats they were not; neither was there plunder or danger of it. Men of regular life, or of the best-filled purse, they could hardly be; the one thing needful in them was that they "knew how to die." Friend Dampmartin saw them, with his own eyes, march "gradually" through his quarters at Villefranche in the Beaujolais: but saw in the vaguest manner; being indeed preoccupied; and himself minded for marching just then—across the Rhine. Deep was his astonishment to think of such a march, without appointment or arrangement, station or ration; for the rest, it was "the same men he had seen formerly" in the troubles of the South; "perfectly civil;" though his soldiers could not be kept from talking a little with them.†

1179. So vague are all these; Moniteur, "Histoire Parlementaire" are as good as silent: garrulous History, as is too usual, will say nothing where you most wish her to speak! If enlightened Curiosity ever get sight of the Marseilles Council-Books, will it not perhaps explore this strangest of Municipal procedures, and feel called to fish-up what of the Biographies, creditable or discreditable, of these 517, the stream of Time has not yet irrevocably swallowed?

1180. As it is, these Marseillese remain inarticulate, undistinguishable in feature; a black-browed Mass, full of grim fire, who wend there, in the hot sultry weather: very singular to contemplate. They wend; amid the infinitude of doubt and dim peril; they not doubtful: Fate and Feudal Europe, having decided, come girdling in from without; they, having also decided, do march within. Dusty of face, with frugal refreshment. they plod onward; unweariable, not to be turned aside. Such march will not become famous. The Thought, which works voiceless in this black-browed mass, an inspired Tyrtæan Colonel, Rouget de Lille, whom the Earth still holds,‡ has translated into grim melody and rhythm; into his *Hymn* or March *of the Marseillese:* luckiest musical composition ever promulgated. The sound of which will make the blood tingle in men's veins; and whole Armies and assemblages will sing it, with eyes weeping and burning, with hearts defiant of Death, Despot and Devil.

1181. One sees well. these Marseillese will be too late for the Federation Feast. In fact, it is not Champ-de-Mars Oaths that they have in view. They have quite another feat to do: a paralytic National Executive to set in action. They must "strike down" whosoever "Tyrant," or Martyr-Fainéant, there may be who paralyzes it; strike and be struck; and on the whole prosper, and know how to die.

* See Barbaroux, "Mémoires" (note in pp. 40, 41).
† Dampmartin, ubi suprà.—As to Dampmartin himself and what became of him farther, see "Mémoires," de la Comtesse de Lichtenau," écrite par elle-même; traduits do l'Allemand (à Londres 1809), i. 200-207; ii. 78-91.
‡ A. D. 1836.

CHAPTER III.

SOME CONSOLATION TO MANKIND.

1182. Of the Federation Feast itself we shall say almost nothing. There are tents pitched in the Champ-de-Mars; tent for National Assembly: tent for Hereditary Representative,—who indeed is there too early, and has to wait long in it. · There are Eighty-three symbolic Departmental Trees-of-Liberty; trees and mais enough: beautifulest of all, there is one huge mai, hung round with effete Scutcheons, Emblazonries and Genealogy-books, nay better still, with Lawyers's-bags, "sacs de procédure," which shall be burnt. The Thirty seat-rows of that famed Slope are again full; we have a bright Sun; and all is marching, streamering and blaring: but what avails it? Virtuous Mayor Pétion, whom Feuillantism had suspended, was reinstated only last night, by Decree of the Assembly. Men's humor is of the sourest. Men's hats have on them, written in chalk, "Vive Pétion;" and even, "Pétion or death (Pétion ou la Mort)."

1183. Poor Louis, who has waited till five o'clock before the Assembly would arrive, swears the Nation Oath this time, with a quilted cuirass under his waistcoat which will turn pistol-bullets.* Madame de Staël, from that Royal Tent, stretches out the neck in a kind of agony, lest the waving multitude which received him may not render him back alive. No cry of Vive le Roi salutes the ear; cries only of Vive Pétion; Pétion ou la mort. The National Solemnity is as it were huddled by, each cowering off almost before the evolutions are gone through. The very Mai with its Scutcheons and Lawyer's-bags is forgotten, stands unburnt; till "certain Patriot Deputies," called by the people, set a torch to it, by way of voluntary after-piece. Sadder Feast of Pikes no man ever saw.

1184. Mayor Pétion, named on huts, is at his zenith in this Federation: Lafayette again is close upon his nadir. Why does the storm-bell of Saint-Roch speak out, next Saturday; why do the citizens shut their shops?† It is Sections defiling, it is fear of effervescence. Legislative Committee, long deliberating on Lafayette and that Anti-jacobin visit of his reports this day, that there is "*not* ground for Accusation!" Peace, ye Patriots, nevertheless; and let that tocsin cease: the Debate is not finished, nor the Report accepted; but Brissot, Isnard and the Mountain will sift it, and resift it, perhaps for some three weeks longer.

1185. So many bells, storm-bells, and noises do ring;—scarcely audible; one drowning the other. For example: in this same Lafayette tocsin, of Saturday, was there not withal some faint bob-minor, and Deputation of Legislative, ringing the Chevalier Paul Jones to his long rest; tocsin or dirge now all one to him! , Not ten days hence Patriot Brissot, beshouted this day by the Patriot Galleries, shall find himself begroaned by them, on account of his limited Patriotism; nay pelted at while perorating, and "hit with two prunes."‡ It is a distracted empty-sounding world; of bob-minors and bob-majors, of triumph and terror, of rise and fall!

1186. The more touching is this other Solemnity, which happens on the morrow of the Lafayette tocsin: Proclamation that the *Country is in Danger.* Not till the present Sunday could such Solemnity be. The Legislative decreed it almost a fortnight ago; but Royalty and the ghost of a Ministry held back as they could. Now however, on this Sunday, 22d day of July, 1792, it will hold back no longer;

* Campan, ii. c. 20; De Staël, ii. c. 7.
† Moniteur, Séance du 21 Juillet 170.
‡ "Histoire Parlementaire," xvi. 183

and the Solemnity in very deed is. Touching to behold! Municipality and Mayor have on their scarfs; cannon-salvo booms alarm from the Pont Neuf, and single-gun at intervals all day. Guards are mounted, scarfed Notabilities, Halberdiers, and a Cavalcade; with streamers, emblematic flags; especially with one huge Flag, flapping mournfully Citoyens, la Patrie est en Danger. They roll through the streets, with stern-sounding music, and slow rattle of hoofs; pausing at set stations, and with doleful blast of trumpet singing out through Herald's throat, what the Flag says to the eye: "Citizens, our Country is in Danger!"

1187. Is there a man's heart that bears it without a thrill? The many-voiced responsive hum or bellow of these multitudes is not of triumph; and yet it is a sound deeper than triumph. But when the long Cavalcade and Proclamation ended; and our huge Flag was fixed on the Pont-Neuf, another like it on the Hotel-de-Ville, to wave there till better days; and each Municipal sat in the center of his Section, in a Tent raised in some open square, Tents surmounted with flags of Patrie en Danger, and topmost of all a Pike and Bonnet Rouge; and, on two drums in front of him, there lay a plank-table, and on this an open Book, and a Clerk sat, like recording-angel, ready to write the lists, or as we say to enlist! O, then, it seems, the very gods might have looked down on it. Young Patriotism, Culottic and Sanscullottic, rushes forward emulous: That is my name; name, blood and life is all my country's; why have I nothing more! Youths of short stature weep that they are below size. Old men come forward, a son in each hand. Mothers themselves will grant the son of their travail; send him, though with tears. And the multitude bellows Vive la Patrie, far reverberating. And fire flashes in the eyes of men;—and at eventide, your Municipal returns to the Town-hall followed by his long train of Volunteer valor; hands-in his List; says proudly, looking round. This is my days harvest.* They will march, on the morrow, to Soissons; small bundle holding all their chattels.

1188. So, with Vive la Patrie, Vive la Liberté, stone Paris reverberates like Ocean in his caves; day after day, Municipals enlisting in tricolor Tent; the Flag flapping on Pont-Neuf and Town-hall, Citoyens, la Patrie est en Danger. Some 10,000 fighters, without discipline but full of heart, are on march in few days. The like is doing in every Town of France. Consider, therefore, whether the Country will want defenders, had we but a National Executive? Let the Sections and Primary Assemblies, at any rate, become Permanent! They do become Permanent, and sit continually in Paris, and over France, by Legislative Decree, dated Wednesday the 25th.†

1189. Mark contrariwise how, in these very hours, dated the 25th, Brunswick "shakes himself (s'ébranle)" in Coblentz; and takes the road! Shakes himself indeed; one spoken word becomes such a shaking. Successive, simultaneous dirl of 30,000 muskets shouldered; prance and jingle of 10,000 horsemen, fanfaronading Emigrants in the van; drum, kettledrum; noise of weeping, swearing; and the immeasurable lumbering clank of baggage-wagons and camp-kettles that groan into motion: all this is, Brunswick shaking himself; not without all this does the one man march, "covering a space of forty miles." Still less without his Manifesto, dated, as we say, the 25th; a State-Paper worthy of attention!

1190. By this Document, it would seem great things are in store for France. The universal French People shall now have permission to rally round Brunswick and his Emigrant Seigneurs; tyranny of

* "Tableau, de la Révolution." § Patrie en Danger.
† Moniteur, Séance du 25 Juillet 1792.

a Jacobin Faction shall oppress them no more; but they shall return, and find favor with their own good King; who, by Royal Declaration (three years ago) of the 23d of June, said that he would himself make them happy. As for National Assembly, and other Bodies of men invested with some temporary shadow of authority, they are charged to maintain the King's Cities and Strong Places intact, till Brunswick arrive to take delivery of them. Indeed, quick submission may extenuate many things; but to this end it must be quick. Any National Guard or other unmilitary person found resisting in arms shall be "treated as a traitor;" that is to say, hanged with promptitude. For the rest, if Paris, before Brunswick gets thither, offer any insult to the King; or, for example, suffer a Faction to carry the King away elsewhither; in that case, Paris shall be blasted asunder with cannon-shot and "military execution." Likewise all other Cities, which may witness, and not resist to the uttermost, such forced-march of his Majesty, shall be blasted asunder; and Paris and every City of them, starting-place, course and goal of said sacrilegious forced-march, shall, as rubbish and smoking ruin, lie there for a sign. Such vengeance were indeed signal "an insigne vengeance :"—O Brunswick, what words thou writest and blusterest! In this Paris, as in old Nineveh, are so many score thousands that know not the right hand from the left, and also much cattle. Shall the very milk-cows, hard-living cadgers'-asses, and poor little canary birds die?

1191. Nor is Royal and Imperial Prussian-Austrian Declaration wanting: setting forth, in the amplest manner, their Sans-souci-Schönbrunn version of this whole French Revolution, since the first beginning of it; and with what grief these high heads have seen such things done under the Sun. However, "as some small consolation to mankind,"[*] they do now dispatch Brunswick; regardless of expense, as one might say, or of sacrifices on their own part; for is it not the first duty to console men?

1192. Serene Highnesses, who sit there protocoling and manifestoing, and consoling mankind! how were it if, for once in the thousand years, your parchments, formularies and reasons of state were blown to the four winds; and Reality Sans-indispensables stared you, even you, in the face; and Mankind said for itself what the thing was that would console it?

CHAPTER IV.

SUBTERRANEAN.

1193. But judge if there was comfort in this to the Sections all sitting permanent; deliberating how a National Executive could be put in action!

High rises the response, not of cackling terror but of crowing counter-defiance, and Vive la Nation; young Valor streaming toward the Frontiers; Patrie en Danger mutely beckoning on the Pont-Neuf. Sections are busy, in their permanent Deep; and down, lower still, works unlimited Patriotism, seeking salvation in plot. Insurrection, you would say, becomes once more the sacredest of duties? Committee, self-chosen, is sitting at the Sign of the Golden Sun; Journalist Carra, Camille Desmoulins, Alsatian Westermann friend of Danton, American Fournier of Martinique;—a Committee not unknown to Mayor Pétion, who, as an official person, must sleep with one eye open. Not unknown to Procureur Manuel; least of all to Procureur-Substitute Danton! He, wrapped in darkness, being also official, bears it on his giant shoulders; cloudy invisible Atlas of the whole.

1194. Much is invisible; the very Jacobins have

[*] "Annual Register," (1792), p. 236.

their reticences. Insurrection is to be: but when? This only we can discern, that such Fédérés as are not yet gone to Soissons, as indeed are not inclined to go yet, "for reasons," says the Jacobin President, "which it may be interesting not to state,"—have got a *Central Committee* sitting close by, under the roof of the Mother Society herself. Also, what in such ferment and danger of effervescence is surely proper, the Forty-eight Sections have got their Central Committee; intended "for prompt communication." To which Central Committee the Municipality, anxious to have it at hand, could not refuse an Apartment in the Hotel-de-Ville.

1195. Singular City! For overhead of all this, there is the customary baking and brewing; Labor hammers and grinds. Frilled promenaders saunter under the trees; white-muslin promenaderess, in green parasol, leaning on your arm. Dogs dance, and shoe-blacks polish, on that Pont-Neuf itself, where Fatherland is in danger. So much goes its course;—and yet the course of all things is nigh altering and ending.

1196. Look at that Tuileries and Tuileries Garden. Silent all as Sahara; none entering save by ticket! They shut their Gates, after the Day of the Black Breeches; a thing they had the liberty to do. However, the National Assembly grumbled something about Terrace of the Feuillants, how said Terrace lay contiguous to the back-entrance to their Salle, and was partly *National* Property; and so now National Justice has stretched a Tricolor Ribbon athwart it, by way of boundary-line; respected with splenetic strictness by all Patriots. It hangs there, that Tricolor boundary-line; carries "satirical inscriptions on cards," generally, in verse; and all beyond this is called Coblentz, and remains vacant; silent as a fateful Golgotha; sunshine and umbrage alternating on it in vain. Fateful Circuit: what hope can dwell in it? Mysterious Tickets of Entry introduce themselves; speak of Insurrection very imminent. Rivarol's Staff of Genius had better purchase blunderbusses; Grenadier bonnets, red Swiss uniforms may be useful. Insurrection will come; but likewise will it not be met? Staved off, one may hope, till Brunswick arrive?

1197. But consider withal if the Bourn-stones and Portable-chairs remain silent; if the Herald's College of Bill-Stickers sleep! Louvet's Sentinel warns gratis on all walls; Suleau is busy; *People's-Friend* Marat and *King's-Friend* Royou croak and counter-croak. For the man Marat, though long hidden since that Champ-de-Mars Massacre, is still alive. He has lain, who knows in what cellars; perhaps in Legendre's; fed by a steak of Legendre's killing; but since April, the bull-frog voice of him sounds again; hoarsest of earthly cries. For the present, black terror haunts him: O brave Barbaroux, wilt thou not smuggle me to Marseilles, "disguised as a jockey?"[*] In Palais Royal and all public places, as we read, there is sharp activity; private individuals haranguing that Valor may enlist; haranguing that the Executive may be put in action. Royalist Journals ought to be solemnly burnt: argument thereupon; debates, which generally end in single-stick (coupes de cannes).[†] Or think of this; the hour midnight; place Salle de Manége; august Assembly just adjourning; "Citizens of both sexes enter in a rush, exclaiming, *Vengeance; they are poisoning our Brothers ;*"—baking brayed-glass among their bread at Soissons! Vergniaud has to speak soothing words, How Commissioners are already sent to investigate this brayed-glass, and do what is needful therein; till the rush

[*] Barbaroux, p. 60.

[†] Newspaper, narrative, and documents ("Histoire Parlementaire," xv. 240; xvi. 399).

of Citizens "makes profound silence;" and goes home to its bed.

1198. Such is Paris; the heart of France like to it. Preternatural suspicion, doubt, disquietude, nameless anticipation, from shore to shore:—and those black-browed Marseillese [marching, dusty, unwearied, through the midst of it; not doubtful they. Marching to the grim music of their hearts, they consume continually the long road, these three weeks and more; heralded by Terror and Rumor. The Brest Fédérés arrive on the 26th; through hurrahing streets. Determined men are these also, bearing or not bearing the Sacred Pikes of Château-Vieux; and on the whole decidedly disinclined for Soissons as yet Surely the Marseillese Brethren do draw nigher all days.

CHAPTER V.

AT DINNER.

1199. It was a bright day for Charenton, that 29th of the month, when the Marseilles Brethren actually came in sight. Barbaroux, Santerre and Patriots have gone out to meet the grim Wayfarers. Patriot clasps dusty Patriot to his bosom; there is foot-washing and refection: "dinner of twelve-hundred covers at the Blue Dial (Cadran Bleu);" and deep interior consultation, that one wots not of.* Consultation indeed which comes to little; for Santerre, with an open purse, with a loud voice, has almost no head. Here, however, we repose this night; on the morrow is public entry into Paris.

1200. Of which public entry the Day-Historians, *Diurnalists*, or Journalists as they call themselves, have preserved record enough. How Saint-Antoine male and female, and Paris generally, gave brotherly welcome, with bravo and hand-clapping, in crowded streets; and all passed in the peaceablest manner;—except it might be our Marsaillese pointed out here and there a ribbon-cockade, and beckoned that it should be snatched away, and exchanged for a wool one; which was none. How the Mother Society in a body has come as far as the Bastille-ground, to embrace you. How you then wend onward, triumphant, to the Town-hall, to be embraced by Mayor Pétion; to put down your muskets in the Barracks of Nouvelle France, not far off:—then toward the appointed Tavern in the Champs Elysées, to enjoy a frugal Patriot repast.‡

1201. Of all which the indignant Tuileries may, by its Tickets of Entry, have warning. Red Swiss look doubly sharp to their Château-Grates;—though surely there is no danger? Blue Grenadiers of the Filles-Saint-Thomas Section are on duty there this day: men of Agio, as we have seen; with stuffed purses, ribbon-cockades; among whom serves Weber. A party of these latter, with Captains, with sundry Feuillant Notabilities, Moreau de Saint-Méry of the three-thousand orders, and others, have been dining, much more respectably, in a Tavern hard by. They have dined, and are now drinking Loyal-Patriotic toasts; while the Marseillese, *National*-Patriotic merely, are about sitting down to their frugal covers of delf. How it happened remains to this day undemonstrable; but the external fact is, certain of these Filles-Saint-Thomas Grenadiers do issue from their Tavern perhaps touched, surely not yet muddled with any liquor they have had;—issue in the professed intention of testifying to the Marseillese, or to the multitude of Paris Patriots who stroll in these spaces, That they, the Filles-Saint-Thomas

men, if well seen into, are not a whit less Patriotic than any other class of men whatever.

1202. It was a rash errand! For how can the strolling multitude credit such a thing; or do other indeed than hoot at it, provoking and provoked?—till Grenadier sabers stir in the scabbard, and thereupon a sharp shriek, rises: "A nous, Marseillais (Help, Marseillese)?" Quick as lightning, for the frugal repast is not yet served, that Marseillese Tavern flings itself open: by door, by window; running, bounding, vault forth the 517 undined Patriots; and, saber flashing from thigh, are on the scene of controversy. Will ye parley, ye Grenadier Captains and Official Persons; "with faces grown suddenly pale," the Deponents say?* Advisabler were instant moderately swift retreat! The Filles-Saint-Thomas men retreat, back foremost; then, alas, face foremost, at treble-quick time; the Marseillese, according to a Deponent, "clearing the fences and ditches after them, like lions: Messieurs, it was an imposing spectacle."

1203. Thus they retreat, the Marseillese following. Swift and swifter, toward the Tuileries: where the Drawbridge receives the bulk of the fugitives; and, then suddenly drawn up, saves them; or else the green mud of the Ditch does it. The bulk of them; not all; ah, no! Moreau de Saint-Méry, for example, being too fat, could not fly fast; he got a stroke, *flat*-stroke only, over the shoulder-blades, and fell prone;—and disappears there from the History of the Revolution. Cuts also there were, pricks in the posterior fleshly parts; much rending of skirts, and other discrepant waste. But poor Sublieutenant Duhamel, innocent Change-broker, what a lot for him! He turned on his pursuer, or pursuers, with a pistol; he fired and missed; drew a second pistol, and again fired and missed; then ran: unhappily in vain. In the Rue Saint-Florentin, they clutched him; thrust him through, in red rage: that was the end of the New Era, and of all Eras, to poor Duhamel.

1204. Pacific readers can fancy what sort of grace-before-meat this was to frugal Patriotism. Also how the Battalion of the Filles-Saint-Thomas "drew out in arms," luckily without farther result; how there was accusation at the Bar of the Assembly, and counter-accusation and defense: Marseillese challenging the sentence of a free jury-court,—which never got impaneled. We ask rather, What the upshot of all these distracted wildly-accumulating things may, by probability, be? Some upshot; and the time draws nigh! Busy are Central Committees, of Fédérés at the Jacobins Church, of Sections at the Town-hall; Reunion of Carra Camille and Company at the Golden Sun. Busy; like submarine deities, or call them mud-gods, working there in deep murk of waters; till the thing be ready.

1205. And how your National Assembly, like a ship water-logged, helmless, lies tumbling; the Galleries, of shrill women, of Fédérés with sabers, bellowing down on it, not unfrightful;—and waits where the waves of chance may please to strand it; suspicious, nay on the Left-side, conscious, what submarine explosion is meanwhile a-charging! Petition for King's Forfeiture rises often there: Petition from Paris Section, from Provincial Patriot Towns; "from Alençon, Briançon, and the Traders at the Fair of Beaucaire." Or what of these? On the 3d of August, Mayor Pétion and the Municipality come petitioning for Forfeiture: they openly, in their tricolor Municipal scarfs. Forfeiture is what all Patriots now want and expect. All Brissotins want Forfeiture; with the little Prince Royal for King, and us for Protector over him. Emphatic Fédérés ask the Legislature:

---

* "Deux Amis," viii. 90-101.

‡ "Histoire Parlementaire," xvi. 196. See Barbaroux, pp. 51-55.

* Moniteur, Séances du 30, du 31 Juillet 1792 ("Histoire Parlementaire," xvi. 197-210).

"Can you save us, or not?" Forty-seven Sections have agreed to Forfeiture; only that of the Filles-Saint-Thomas pretending to disagree. Nay Section Mauconseil declares Forfeiture to be, properly speaking, come; Mauconseil, for one, "does from this day," the last of July, "cease allegiance to Louis," and take minute of the same before all men. A thing blamed aloud; but which will be praised aloud; and the name *Mauconseil* (of Ill-counsel), be thenceforth changed to *Bonconseil* (of Good-counsel).

1206. President Danton, in the Cordeliers Section, does another thing: invites all Passive Citizens to take place among the Active in Section-business, one peril threatening all. Thus he, though an official person; cloudy Atlas of the whole. Likewise he manages to have that black-browed Battalion of Marseillese shifted to new Barracks, in his own region of the remote Southeast. Sleek Chaumette, cruel Billaud, Deputy Chabot the Disfrocked, Huguenin with the tocsin in his heart, will welcome them there. Wherefore again and again, "O Legislators, can you save us or not?" Poor Legislators; volcanic Explosion charging under it! Forfeiture shall be debated on the 9th of August; that miserable business of Lafayette may be expected to terminate on the eighth.

1207. Or, will the humane Reader glance into the Levee-day of Sunday the fifth? The last Levee! Not for a long time, "never," says Bertrand-Moleville, had a Levee been so brilliant, at least so crowded. A sad presaging interest sat on every face; Bertrand's own eyes were filled with tears. For indeed, outside of that Tricolor Ribbon on the Feuillants Terrace, Legislature is debating, Sections are defiling, all Paris is astir this very Sunday, demanding Déchéance.* Here, however, within the ribbon, a grand proposal is on foot, for the hundredth time, of carrying his Majesty to Rouen and the Castle of Gaillon. Swiss at Courbevoye are in readiness; much is ready; Majesty himself seems almost ready. Nevertheless, for the hundredth time, Majesty, when near the point of action, draws back; writes, after one has waited, palpitating, an endless summer day, that "he has reason to believe the Insurrection is not so ripe as you suppose." Whereat Bertrand-Moleville breaks forth "into extremity at once of spleen and despair (d'humor et de désespoir)."†

CHAPTER VI.

THE STEEPLES AT MIDNIGHT.

1208. For, in truth, the Insurrection is just about ripe. Thursday is the 9th of the month August: if Forfeiture be not pronounced by the Legislature that day, we must pronounce it ourselves.

Legislature? A poor water-logged Legislature can pronounce nothing. On Wednesday the 8th, after endless oratory once again, they cannot even pronounce Accusation against Lafayette: but absolve him,—hear it, Patriotism!—by a majority of two to one. Patriotism hears it; Patriotism, hounded-on by Prussian Terror, by Preternatural Suspicion, roars tumultuous round the Salle de Manége all day: insults many leading Deputies, of the absolvent Rightside; nay chases them, collars them with loud menace: Deputy Vaublanc, and others of the like are glad to take refuge in Guard-houses, and escape by the back window. And so, next day, there is infinite complaint; Letter after Letter from insulted Deputy; mere complaint, debate and self-canceling jargon: the sun of Thursday sets like the others, and no Forfeiture pronounced. Wherefore in fine, To your tents, O, Israel!

* "Histoire Parlementaire," xvi. 337–339.
† Bertrand-Moleville, "Memoires," ii. 129.

1209. The Mother Society ceases speaking; groups cease haranguing Patriots, with closed lips now, "take one another's arm;" walk off, in rows, two and two, at a brisk business-pace; and vanish afar in the obscure places of the East.* Santerre is ready; or we will make him ready. Forty-seven of the Forty-eight Sections are ready; nay Filles-Saint-Thomas itself turns up the Jacobins side of it, turns down the Feuillant side of it, and is ready too. Let the unlimited Patriot look to his weapon, be it pike, be it firelock; and the Brest brethren,—above all, the black-browed Marseillese prepared themselves for the extreme hour! Syndic Rœderer knows, and laments or not as the issue may turn, that "5,000 ball-cartridges, within these few days, have been distributed to Fédérés, at the hotel-de-Ville."†

1210. And ye likewise, gallant gentlemen, defenders of Royalty, crowd ye on your side to the Tuileries. Not to a levee: no, to a Couchée; where much will be put to bed. Your Tickets of Entry are needful; needfuler your blunderbusses!—They come and crowd, like gallant men who also know how to die: old Maillé the Camp-Marshal has come, his eyes gleaming once again, though dimmed by the rheum of almost four-score years. Courage, Brothers! We have a thousand red Swiss; men staunch of heart, steadfast as the granite of their Alps. National Grenadiers are at least friends of Order; Commandant Mandat breathes loyal ardor, will "answer for it on his head." Mandat will, and his staff; for the staff, though there stands a doom and Decree to that effect, is happily never yet dissolved.

1211. Commandant Mandat has corresponded with Mayor Pétion; carries a written Order from him these three days, to repel force by force. A squadron on the Pont-Neuf with cannon shall turn back these Marseillese coming across the River: a squadron at the Town-hall shall cut Saint-Antoine in two, "as it issues from the Arcade Saint-Jean;" drive one half back to the obscure East, drive the other half forward "through the Wickets of the Louvre." Squadrons not a few, and mounted squadrons; squadrons in the Palais Royal, in the Place Vendome; all these shall charge, at the right moment; sweep this street, and then sweep that. Some new 20th of June we shall have; only still more ineffectual? Or probably the Insurrection will not dare to rise at all? Mandat's Squadrons, Horse-gendarmerie and blue Guards march, clattering, tramping; Mandat's Cannoneers rumble. Under cloud of night; to the sound of his générale, which begins drumming when men should go to bed. It is the 9th night of August, 1792.

1212. On the other hand, the Forty-eight Sections correspond by swift messengers; are choosing each their "three Delegates with full power." Syndic Rœderer, Mayor Pétion are sent for to the Tuileries: courageous Legislators, when the drum beats danger, should repair to their Salle. Demoiselle Théroigne has on her grenadier-bonnet, short-skirted riding-habit; two pistols garnish her small waist, and saber hangs in baldric by her side.

1213. Such a game is playing in this Paris Pandemonium, or City of All the Devils!—And yet the Night, as Mayor Pétion walks here in the Tuileries Garden, "is beautiful and calm;" Orion and Pleiades glitter down quite serene. Pétion has come forth, the "heat" inside was so oppressive.‡ Indeed, his Majesty's reception of him was of the roughest; as it well might be. And now there is no outgate; Mandat's blue Squadrons turn you back at every

* "Deux Amis," viii. 129–188.
† Rœderer à la Barre (Seance du 9 Aout, in " Histoire Parlementaire," xvi 393).
‡ Rœderer, 'Chronique de Cinquante Jours; Recit de Petion.' Town hall records, etc., in "Histoire Parlementaire," xvi. 399–466).

Grate; nay the Filles-Saint-Thomas Grenadiers give themselves liberties of tongue, How a virtuous Mayor "shall pay for it, if there-be mischief," and the like: though others again are full of civility. Surely if any man in France is in straits this night, it is Mayor Pétion; bound, under pain of death, one may say, to smile dexterously with the one side of his face, and weep with the other;—death if he do it not dexterously enough! Not till four in the morning does a National Assembly, hearing of his plight, summon him over "to give account of Paris;" of which he knows nothing: whereby, however, he shall get home to bed, and only·his gilt coach be left. Scarcely less delicate is Syndic Rœderer's task; who must wait, whether he will lament or not, till he see the issue. Janus Bifrons, or Mr. *Facing-both-ways*, as vernacular Bunyan has it! They walk there, in the meanwhile, these two Januses, with others of the like double conformation; and "talk 'of indifferent matters."

1214. Rœderer, from time to time, steps in: to listen, to speak; to send for the Department- Directory itself. he their Procureur Syndic not seeing how to act. The Apartments are all crowded; some 700 gentlemen in black elbowing, bustling; red Swiss standing like rocks: ghost, or partial-ghost of a Ministry, with Rœderer and advisers, hovering round their Majesties; old Marshal Maillé kneeling at the King's feet to say, He and these gallant gentlemen are come to die for him. List! through the placid midnight; clang of the distant storm-bell! So, in very sooth: steeple after steeple takes up the wondrous tale. Black Courtiers listen at the windows, opened for air; discriminate the steeple-bells:* this is the tocsin of Saint-Roch; that again, is it not Saint-Jacques, named de la Bouc'ierie? Yes, Messieurs! . Or even Saint-Germain l'Auxerrois, hear ye *it* not? The same metal that rang storm, 220 years ago; but by a Majesty's order then; on Saint-Bartholomew's Eve!†—So go to the steeple-bells; which Courtiers can discriminate. Nay, mescems, there is the Town-hall itself; we know it by its sound! Yes, Friends, that is the Town-hall, discoursing so, to the Night. Miraculously; by miraculous metal-tongue and man's arm: Marat himself, if you knew it, is pulling at the rope there! Marat is pulling; Robespierre lies deep, invisible for the next forty hours; and some men have heart, and some have as good as none, and not even frenzy will give them any.

1215. What struggling confusion. as the issue slowly draws on; and the doubtful Hour, with pain and blind struggle, brings forth its Certainty, never to be abolished!—The Full-power Delegates, three from each Section, a Hundred and forty-four in all, got gathered at the Town-hall, about midnight. Mandat's Squadron, stationed there, did not hinder their entering: are they not the "Central Committee of the Sections" who sit here usually; though in greater number to-night? They are there: presided by confusion, Irresolution, and the Clack of Tongues. Swift scouts fly; Rumor buzzes, of black Courtiers, red Swiss, of Mandat and his Squadrons that shall charge. Better put off the Insurrection? Yes, put it off. Ha, Hark! Saint-Antoine booming out eloquent tocsin of its own accord!—Friends, no: ye cannot put off the Insurrection; but must put it on, and live with it, or die with it.

1216. Swift now, therefore: let these actual Old Municipals, on sight of the Full-powers, and mandate of the Sovereign elective People, lay down their functions: and this New Hundred and Forty-four take them up! Will ye nill ye, worthy Old Municipals, go ye must. Nay is it not a happiness for many

a Municipal that he can wash his hands of such a business; and sit there paralyzed, unaccountable, till the hour do bring forth; or even go home to his night's rest?* Two only of the Old, or at most three, we retain: Mayor Pétion, for the present walking in the Tuileries; Procureur Manuel; Procureur-Substitute Danton, invisible Atlas of the whole. And so, with our Hundred and Forty-four, among whom are a Tocsin-Huguenin, a Billaud, a Chaumette; and Editor-Tallies, and Fabre d'Eglantines, Sergents, Panises; and in brief, either emergent or else emerged and full-blown, the entire Flower of unlimited Patriotism: ¡have we not, as by magic, made a New Municipality; ready to act in the unlimited manner; and declare itself roundly, "in a state of Insurrection!"—First of all, then, be Commandant Mandat sent for, with that Mayor's-Order of his; also let the New Municipals visit those Squadrons that were to charge; and let the storm-bell ring its loudest;—and, on the whole, Forward, ye Hundred and Forty-four; retreat is now none for you!

1217. Reader, fancy not, in thy languid way, that Insurrection is easy. Insurrection is difficult: each individual uncertain even of his next neighbor; totally uncertain of his distant neighbors, what strength is with him, what strength is against him; certain only that, in case of his failure, his individual portion is the gallows! Eight hundred thousand heads, and in each of them a separate estimate of these uncertainties, a separate theorem of action conformable to that: out of so many uncertainties, does the certainty, and inevitable net-result never to be abolished, go on, at all moments, bodying itself forth;—leading thee also toward civic crowns or an ignominious noose.

1218. Could the Reader take an Asmodeus'sFlight, and waving open all roofs and privacies, look down from the Tower of Notre Dame, what a Paris were it! Of treble-voice whimperings or vehemence, of bass-voice growlings, dubitations; Courage screwing itself to desperate defiance; Cowardice trembling silent within barred doors;—and all round, Dullness calmly snoring; for much Dullness, flung on its mattresses, always sleeps. O, between the clangor of these high-storming tocsins and that snore of Dullness, what a gamut: of trepidation, excitation, desperation; and above it mere Doubt, Danger, Atropos and Nox!

1219. Fighters of this Section draw out; hear that the next Section does not: thereupon draw in. Saint-Antoine, on this side the River, is uncertain of Saint-Marceau on that. Steady only is the snore of Dullness, are the 600 Marseillese that know how to die. Mandat, twice summoned to the Town-hall, has not come. Scouts fly incessant, in distracted haste; and the many-whispering voices of Rumor. Théroigne and unofficial Patriots flit, dim-visible, exploratory, far and wide; like night-birds on the wing. Of Nationals some 3,000 have followed Mandat and his générale; the rest follow each his own theorem' of the uncertainties; theorem, that one should march rather with Saint-Antoine: innumerable theorems, that in such a case the wholesomest were *sleep.* And so the drums beat, in mad fits, and the storm-bells peal. Saint-Antoine itself does but draw out and draw in: Commandant Santerre, over there, cannot believe that the Marseillese and Saint-Marceau will march. Thou laggard sonorous Beer-vat with the loud voice and timber-head, is it time now to palter? Alsatian Westermann clutches him by the throat with drawn saber: whereupon the Timberheaded believes. In this manner wanes the slow night; amid fret, uncertainty and tocsin: all men's humor rising to the hysterical pitch; and nothing done.

1220. However, Mandat, on the third summons, does come;—come, unguarded; astonished to find the Municipality *new*. They question him straitly on that Mayor's-Order to resist force by force; on that strategic scheme of cutting Saint-Antoine in two halves: he answers what he can: they think it were right to send this strategic National Commandant to the Abbaye Prison, and let a Court of Law decide on him. Alas, a Court of Law, not Boot-Law but primeval Club-Law, crowds and jostles out of doors; all fretted to the hysterical pitch; cruel as Fear blind as the Night: such Court of Law, and no other, clutches poor Mandat from his constables: beats him down, massacres him, on the steps of the Town-hall. Look to it, ye new Municipals; ye People, in a state of Insurrection! Blood is shed, blood must be answered for;—alas, in such hysterical humor, more blood will flow: for it is as with the Tiger in that; he has only to begin.

1221. Seventeen Individuals have been seized in the Champs Elysées, by exploratory Patriotism; they flitting dim-visible, by it flitting dim-visible. Ye have pistols, rapiers, ye Seventeen? One of those accursed "false Patrols;" that go marauding, with Anti-National intent; seeking what they can spy, what they can spill! The Seventeen are carried to the nearest Guard-house; eleven of them escape by back passages. "How is this?" Demoiselle Théroigne appears at the front entrance, with saber, pistols and a train; denounces treasonous connivance; demands, seizes, the remaining six, that the justice of the People be not trifled with. Of which six two more escape in the whirl and debate of the Club-Law Court; the last unhappy Four are massacred, as Mandat was: Two ex-Body-guards: one dissipated Abbé; one Royalist Pamphleteer, Sulleau, known to us by name, Able Editor and wit of all work. Poor Sulleau: his "Acts of the Apostles." and brisk Placard-Journals (for he was an able man) come to Finis, in this manner: and questionable jesting issues suddenly in horrid earnest! Such doings usher-in the dawn of the 10th of August, 1792.

1222. Or think what a night the poor National Assembly has had: sitting there, "in great paucity," attempting to debate;—quivering and shivering; pointing toward the thirty-two azimuths at once, as the magnet-needle does when thunder-storm is in the air! If the Insurrection come? If it come, and fail? Alas, in that case, may not black Courtiers with blunderbusses, red Swiss with bayonets rush over, flushed with victory, and ask us: Thou undefinable, waterlogged, self-distractive, self-destructive Legislative, what dost thou here *unsunk?*—Or figure the poor National Guards bivouacking in "temporary tents" there; or standing ranked, shifting from leg to leg, all through the weary night; New tricolor Municipals ordering one thing, old Mandat Captains ordering another. Procureur Manuel has ordered the cannons to be withdrawn from the Pont-Neuf; none ventured to disobey him. It seems certain, then, the old staff, so long doomed, has finally been dissolved, in these hours; and Mandat is not our Commandant now, but Santerre? Yes, friends: Santerre henceforth,—surely Mandat no more! The Squadrons that were to charge see nothing certain, except that they are cold, hungry, worn down with watching: sadder to slay French brothers; sadder to be slain by them. Without the Tuileries Circuit, and within it, sour uncertain humor sways these men: only the red Swiss stand steadfast. Them their officers refresh now with a slight wetting of brandy; wherein the

Nationals, too far gone for brandy, refuse to participate.

1223. King Louis meanwhile had laid him down for a little sleep; his wig when he reappeared had lost the powder on one side.* Old Marshal Maillé and the gentlemen in black rise always in spirits, as the Insurrection does not rise; there goes a witty saying now, "Le tocsin ne rend pas," The tocsin, like a dry milk-cow, does not yield. For the rest, could not one proclaim Martial Law? Not easily; for now, it seems, Mayor Pétion is gone. On the other hand, our Interim Commandant, poor Mandat being off "to the Hotel-de-Ville," complains that so many Courtiers in black encumber the service, are an eye-sorrow to the National Guards. To which her Majesty answers with emphasis, That they will obey all, will suffer all, that they are sure men these.

1224. And so the yellow lamp-light dies out in the gray of morning, in the King's Palace, over such a scene. Scene of jostling, elbowing, of confusion, and indeed conclusion, for the thing is about to end. Rœderer and spectral Ministers jostle in the press; consult, in side-cabinets, with one or with both Majesties. Sister Elizabeth takes the Queen to the window: "Sister, see what a beautiful sunrise," right over the Jacobins Church and that quarter! How happy if the tocsin did not yield! But Mandat returns not; Pétion is gone: much hangs wavering in the invisible Balance. About five o'clock, there rises from the Garden a kind of sound; as of a shout which had become a howl, and instead of Vive le Roi were ending in Vive la Nation. "Mon Dieu!" ejaculates a spectral Minister, "what is he doing down there!" For it is his Majesty, gone down with old Marshal Maillé to review the troops; and the nearest companies of them answer *so*. Her Majesty bursts into a stream of tears. Yet on stepping from the cabinet, her eyes are dry and calm, her look is even cheerful. "The Austrian lip, and the aquiline nose, fuller than usual, gave to her countenance," says Peltier,† "something of majesty, which they that did not see her in those moments cannot well have an idea of." O thou Theresa's Daughter!

King Louis enters much blown with the fatigue; but for the rest with his old air of indifference. Of all hopes now, surely the joyfulest were, that the tocsin did not yield.

CHAPTER VII.

THE SWISS.

1225. Unhappy Friends, the tocsin does yield, has yielded! Lo ye, how with the first sun rays its Ocean-tide, of pikes, and fusils, flows glittering from the far East;—immeasurable: born of the Night! They march there, the grim host; Saint-Antoine on this side the River; Saint-Marceau on that, the black-browed Marseillese in the van. With hum, and grim murmur, far-heard; like the Ocean-tide, as we say: drawn up, as if by Luna and Influences, from the great Deep of Waters, they roll gleaming on; no King, Canute or Louis, can bid them roll back. Wide-eddying side-currents, of on-lookers, roll hither and thither, unarmed, not voiceless; they, the steel host, roll on. New-Commandant Santerre, indeed, has taken seat at the Town-hall, rest there, in his half-way-house. Alsatian Westermann, with flashing saber, does not rest; nor the Sections, nor the Marseillese, nor Demoiselle Théroigne; but roll continually on.

1226. And now, where are Mandat's Squadrons that

---

* Rœderer, ubi suprá.
† In Toulongeon. ii 241.

were to charge? Not a Squadron of them stirs: or
they stir in the wrong direction, out of the way;
their officers glad that they will do even that. It is
to this hour uncertain whether the Squadron on the
Pont-Neuf made the shadow of resistance, or did not
make the shadow: enough, the black-browed Marseillese, and Saint-Marceau following them, do cross
without let; do cross, in sure hope now of Saint-
Antoine and the rest; do billow on, toward the Tuileries, where their errand is. The Tuileries, at sound
of them, rustles responsive: the red Swiss look to
their priming; Courtiers in black draw their blunderbusses, rapiers, poniards, some have even fire-shovels;
every man his weapon of war.

1227. Judge if, in these circumstances, Syndic
Rœderer felt easy! Will the kind Heavens open no
middle-course of refuge for a poor Syndic who halts
between two? If indeed his Majesty would consent
to go over to the Assembly! His Majesty, above all
her Majesty, cannot agree to that. Did her Majesty
answer the proposal with a "Fi donc;" did she say
even, she would be nailed to the walls sooner? Apparently not. It is written also that she offered the
King a pistol: saying, Now or else never was the
time to show himself. Close eye-witnesses did not
see it, nor do we. They saw only that she was queen-
like, quiet; that she argued not, upbraided not, with
the Inexorable; but, like Cæsar in the Capitol,
wrapped her mantle, as it beseems Queens and Sons
of Adam to do. But thou, O Louis! of what stuff
art thou at all? Is there no stroke in thee, then, for
Life and Crown? The silliest hunted deer dies not
so. Art thou the languidest of all mortals; or the
mildest-minded? Thou art the worst-starred.

1228. The tide advances; Syndic Rœderer's and
all men's straits grow straiter and straiter. Fremescent clangor comes from the armed Nationals in the
Court; far and wide the infinite hubbub of tongues.
What counsel? And the tide is now nigh! Messengers, forerunners speak hastily through the outer
Grates; bold parley sitting astride the walls. Syndic Rœderer goes out and comes in. Cannoneers ask
him: Are we to fire against the people? King's
Ministers ask him: Shall the King's House be
forced? Syndic Rœderer has a hard game to play.
He speaks to the Cannoneers with eloquence, with
fervor; such fervor as a man can, who has to blow
hot and cold in one breath. Hot and cold, O Rœderer?
We, for our part, cannot live *and* die? The Cannoneers, by way of answer, fling down their linstocks.
—Think of this answer, O King Louis, and King's
Ministers; and take a poor Syndic's safe middle-
course, toward the Salle de Manége. King Louis
sits, his hands leant on his knees, body bent forward:
gazes for a space fixedly on Syndic Rœderer; then
answers, looking over his shoulder to the Queen:
Marchons! They march; King Louis, Queen, Sister
Elizabeth, the two royal children and governess;
these, with Syndic Rœderer, and Officials of the Department; amid a double rank of National Guards.
The men with blunderbusses, the steady red Swiss
gaze mournfully, reproachfully; but hear only these
words from Syndic Rœderer: "The King is going to
the Assembly; make way." It has struck eight, on
all clocks, some minutes ago: the King has left the
Tuileries—forever.

1229. O ye stanch Swiss, ye gallant gentlemen in
black, for what a cause are ye to spend and be spent!
Look out from the western windows ye may see
King Louis placidly hold on his way; the poor little
Prince Royal "sportfully kicking the fallen leaves."
Fremescent multitude on the Terrace of the Feuillants whirls parallel to him; one man in it, very
noisy, with a long pole: will they not obstruct the
outer Staircase, and back-entrance of the Salle, when

it comes to that? King's Guards can go no farther
than the bottom step there. Lo, Deputation of Legislators come out; he of the long pole is stilled by
oratory; Assembly's Guards join themselves to
King's Guards, and all may mount in this case of
necessity; the outer Staircase is free, or passable.
See, Royalty ascends; a blue Grenadier lifts the poor
little Prince Royal from the press; Royalty has entered in. Royalty has vanished forever from your
eyes.—And ye? Left standing there, amid the
yawning abysses, and earthquake of Insurrection;
without course; without command: if ye perish, it
must be as more than martyrs, as martyrs who are
now without a cause! The black Courtiers disappear mostly; through such issues as they can. The
poor Swiss know not how to act; one duty only is
clear to them, that of standing by their post; and
they will perform that.

1230. But the glittering steel tide has arrived; it
beats now against the Château barriers and eastern
Courts; irresistible, loud-surging far and wide;—
breaks in, fills the Court of the Carrousel, black-
browed Marseillese in the van. King Louis gone,
say you; over to the Assembly! Well and good:
but till the Assembly pronounce Forfeiture of him,
who boots it? Our post is in that Château or stronghold of his; there till then must we continue.
Think, ye stanch Swiss, whether it were good that
grim murder began, and brothers blasted one another
in pieces for a stone edifice?—Poor Swiss! they
know not how to act! from the southern windows,
some fling cartridges, in sign of brotherhood; on the
eastern outer-staircase, and within through long
stairs and corridors, they stand firm-ranked, peaceable and yet refusing to stir. Westermann speaks to
them in Alsatian German, Marseillese plead, in hot
Provençal speech and pantomime; stunning hubbub
pleads and threatens, infinite, around. The Swiss
stand fast, peaceable and yet immovable; red granite
pier in that waste-flashing sea of steel.

1231. Who can help the inevitable issue; Marseillese and all France on this side; granite Swiss on
that? The pantomime grows hotter and hotter;
Marseillese sabers flourishing by way of action; the
Swiss brow also clouding itself, the Swiss thumb
bringing its firelock to the cock. And hark! high
thundering above all the din, three Marseillese cannon from the Carrousel, pointed by a gunner of bad
aim, come rattling over the roofs! Ye Swiss, therefore: *Fire!* The Swiss fire; by volley, by platoon,
in rolling-fire: Marseillese men not a few, and "a
tall man that was louder than any," lie silent,
smashed upon the pavement;—not a few Marseillese,
after the long dusty march, have made halt *here*.
The Carrousel is void; the black tide recoiling;
"fugitives rushing as far as Saint-Antoine before
they stop." The Cannoneers without linstock have
squatted invisible, and left their cannon; which the
Swiss seize.

1232. Think what a volley: reverberating doomful
to the four corners of Paris, and through all hearts;
like the clang of Bellona's thongs! The black-
browed Marseillese, rallying on the instant, have become black Demons that know how to die. Nor is
Brest behindhand; nor Alsatian Westermann; Demoiselle Théroigne is Sibyl Théroigne: Vengeance,
Victoire ou la mort! From all Patriot artillery,
great and small; from Feuillants Terrace, and all
terraces and places of the wide-spread Insurrectionary sea, there roars responsive a red blazing whirlwind. Blue Nationals, ranked in the Garden, cannot
help their muskets going off *against* Foreign murderers. For there is a sympathy in muskets, in
heaped masses of men: nay, are not Mankind, in
whole, like tuned strings, and a cunning infinite con-

cordance and unity; you smite one string, and all strings will begin sounding,—in soft sphere-melody, in deafening screech of madness! Mounted Gendarmerie gallop distracted; are fired on merely as a thing running: galloping over the Pont Royal, or one knows not whither. The brain of Paris, brain-fevered in the center of it here, has gone mad; what you call, taken fire.

1233. Behold, the fire slackens not; nor does the Swiss rolling-fire slacken from within. Nay they clutched cannon, as we saw; and now, from the other side, they clutch three pieces more; alas, cannon without linstock; nor will the steel-and-flint answer, though they try it.* Had it chanced to answer! Patriot onlookers have their misgivings; one strangest Patriot onlooker thinks that the Swiss, had they a commander, would beat. He is a man not unqualified to judge; the name of him Napoleon Bonaparte.† And onlookers, and women, stand gazing, and the witty Dr. Moore of Glasgow among them, on the other side of the River: cannon rush rumbling past them, pause on the Pont Royal; belch out their iron entrails there, against the Tuileries and at every new belch, the women and onlookers "shout and clap hands."‡ City of all the Devils! In remote streets, men are drinking breakfast coffee; following their affairs; with a start now and then, as some dull echo reverberates a note louder. And here? Marseillese fall wounded, but Barbaroux has surgeons; Barbaroux is close by, managing, though underhand and under cover Marseillese fall death-struck; bequeath their firelock, specify in which pocket are the cartridges, and die murmuring, "Revenge me, Revenge thy country!" Brest Fédéré Officers, galloping in red coats, are shot as Swiss. Lo you, the Carrousel has burst into flame! —Paris Pandemonium! Nay the poor City, as we said, is in fever-fit and convulsion: such crisis has lasted for the space of some half hour.

1234. But what is this that, with Legislative Insignia, ventures through the hubbub and death-hail, from the back-entrance of the Manège? Toward the Tuileries and Swiss. written Order from his Majesty to cease firing! O ye hapless Swiss, why was there no order not to begin it? Gladly would the Swiss cease firing: but who will bid mad Insurrection cease firing? To Insurrection you cannot speak; neither can it, hydra-headed, hear. The dead and dying, by the hundred, lie all around; are borne bleeding through the streets, toward help; the sight of them, like a torch of the Furies, kindling Madness. Patriot Paris roars; as the bear bereaved of her whelps. On, ye Patriots: Vengeance! Victory or death! There are men seen, who rush on, armed only with walking-sticks!§ Terror and Fury rule the hour.

1235. The Swiss, pressed on from without, paralyzed from within, have ceased to shoot: but not to be shot. What shall they do? Desperate is the moment. Shelter or instant death: yet How, Where? One party flies out by the Rue de l'Echelle; is destroyed utterly, "en entier." A second, by the other side, throws itself into the Garden; "hurrying across a keen fusillade;" rushes suppliant into the National Assembly: finds pity and refuge in the back benches there. The third, and largest, darts out in column, 300 strong, toward the Champs Elysées: "Ah, could we but reach Courbevoye, where other Swiss are!" Woe! see, in such fusillade the column "soon

breaks itself by diversity of opinion," into distracted segments, this way and that;—to escape in holes, to die fighting from street to street. The firing and murdering will not cease; not yet for long. The red Porters of Hotels are shot at, be they Suisse by nature, or Suisse only in name. The very Firemen, who pump and labor on that smoking Carrousel are shot at: why should the Carrousel not burn? Some Swiss take refuge in private houses; find that mercy too does still dwell in the heart of man. The brave Marseillese are merciful. late so wroth, and labor to save. Journalist Gorsas pleads hard with infuriated groups. Clemence, the Wine-merchant, stumbles forward to the Bar of the Assembly, a rescued Swiss in his hand; tells passionately how he rescued him with pain and peril, how he will henceforth support him, being childless himself; and falls a-swoon round the poor Swiss's neck: amid plaudits. But the most are butchered, and even mangled. Fifty (some say Four-score) were marched as prisoners, by National Guards, to the Hotel-de-Ville: the ferocious people bursts through on them, in the Place-de-Grève; massacres them to the last man. "O People, envy of the universe!" People, in mad Gaelic effervescence!

1236. Surely few things in the history of carnage are painfuler. What ineffaceable red streak, flickering so sad in the memory, is that, of this poor column of red Swiss "breaking itself in the confusion of opinions," dispersing, into blackness and death! Honor to you, brave men; honorable pity, through long times! Not martyrs were ye, and yet almost more. He was no King of yours, this Louis; and he forsook you like a King of shreds and patches; ye were but sold to him for some poor sixpence a day; yet would ye work for your wages, keep your plighted word. The work now was to die; and ye did it. Honor to you, O Kinsmen; and may the old Deutsch Biederkeit and Tapferkeit, and Valor which is *Worth* and *Truth.* be they Swiss, be they Saxon, fail in no age! Not bastards; true-born were these men: sons of the men of Sempach, of Murten, who knelt, but not to thee, O Burgundy!—Let the traveler, as he passes through Lucerne, turn aside to look a little at their monumental Lion; not for Thorwaldsen's sake alone. Hewn out of living rock, the Figure rests there, by the still Lake-waters, in lullaby of distant-tinkling rance-des-vaches, the granite Mountains dumbly keeping watch all round; and, though inanimate speaks.

CHAPTER VIII.
CONSTITUTION BURST IN PIECES.

1237. Thus is the 10th of August won and lost. Patriotism reckons its slain by the thousand on thousand, so deadly was the Swiss fire from these windows; but will finally reduce them to some Twelve-hundred. No child's-play was it;—nor is it! Till two in the afternoon the massacring, the breaking and the burning has not ended; nor the loose Bedlam shut itself again.

1238. How deluges of frantic Sansculottism roared through all passages of this Tuileries. ruthless in vengeance; how the Valets were butchered, hewn down; and Dame Campan saw the Marseillese saber flash over her head, but the Black-browed said, "Va-t-en (Get thee gone)," and flung her from him unstruck;* how in the cellars wine-bottles were broken. wine-butts were staved-in and drunk; and upward to the very garrets, all windows tumbled out their precious royal furnitures; and, with gold mirrors, velvet curtains, down of ript feather-beds, and dead bodies of men, the Tuileries was like no

* "Deux Amis," viii. 179-188.
† See "Histoire Parlementaire." xvii; Las Cases, etc.
‡ Moore, "Journal during a Residence in France," (Dublin. 1793) 1 26.
§ "Histoire Parlementaire," ubi suprà. "Rapport du Capitaine des Cannoniers, Rapport du Commandant," etc. (ibid., xvii. 300-318).

* Campan. ii. c. 21.

Garden of the Earth:—all this let him who has a taste for it see amply in Mercier, in acrid Montgaillard, or Beaulieu of the "Deux Amis." A hundred and eighty bodies of Swiss lie piled there; naked, unremoved till the second day. Patriotism has torn their red coats into snips; and marches with them at the Pike's point: the ghastly bare corpses lie there, under the sun and under the stars; the curious of both sexes crowding to look. Which let not us do. Above a hundred carts, heaped with Dead, fare toward the Cemetery of Sainte-Madeleine; bewailed, bewept; for all had kindred, all had mothers, if not here, then there. It is one of those Carnage-fields, such as you read of by the name "Glorious Victory," brought home in this case to one's own door.

1239. But the black-browed Marseillese have struck down the tyrant of the Château. He is struck down; low, and hardly again to rise. What a moment for an august Legislative was that when the Hereditary Representative entered, under such circumstances; and the Grenadier, carrying the little Prince Royal out of the press, set him down on the Assembly-table! A moment,—which one had to smooth-off with oratory; waiting what the next would bring! Louis said few words: "He was come hither to prevent a great crime; he believed himself safer nowhere than here." President Verguiaud answered briefly, in vague oratory as we say, about "defense of Constituted Authorities," about dying at our post.* And so King Louis sat him down; first here, then there; for a difficulty arose, the Constitution not permitting us to debate while the King is present: finally he settles himself with his family in the "Loge of the Logographe," in the Reporter's-Box of a Journalist; which is beyond the enchanted Constitutional Circuit, separated from it by a rail. To such Lodge of the Logographe, measuring some ten feet square, with a small closet at the entrance of it behind, is the King of broad France now limited: here can he and his sit pent, under the eyes of the world, or retire into their closet at intervals; for the space of sixteen hours. Such quite peculiar moment has the Legislative lived to see.

1240. But also what a moment was that other, few minutes later, when the three Marseillese cannon went off and the Swiss rolling-fire and universal thunder, like the crack of Doom, began to rattle! Honorable Members start to their feet; stray bullets singing epicedium even here, shivering-in with window-glass and jingle. "No, this is our post; let us die here!" They sit therefore, like stone Legislators. But may not the Loge of the Logographe be forced from behind? Tear down the railing that divides it from the enchanted Constitutional Circuit! Ushers tear and tug; his Majesty himself aiding from within: the railing gives way; Majesty and Legislative are united in place, unknown Destiny hovering over both.

1241. Rattle, and again rattle, went the thunder; one breathless wide-eyed messenger rushing in after another: King's order to the Swiss went out. It was a fearful thunder; but as we know, it ended. Breathless messengers, fugitive Swiss, denunciatory Patriots, trepidation; finally tripudiation!—Before four o'clock much has come and gone.

1242. The New Municipals have come and gone; with three Flags, Liberté, Egalité, Patrie, and the clang of vivats. Verguiaud, he who as President few hours ago talked of dying for Constituted Authorities, has moved, as Committee Reporter, that the Hereditary Representative *be suspended*; that a NATIONAL CONVENTION do forthwith assemble to say what farther! An able Report: which the President

* Moniteur, Séance du 10 Aout 1792.

must have had ready in his pocket? A President, in such cases, must have much ready, and yet not ready; and Janus-like look before and after.

1243. King Louis listens to all; retires about midnight "to three little rooms on the upper floor;" till the Luxembourg be prepared for him, and "the safeguard of the Nation." Safer if Brunswick were once here! Or, alas, not so safe? Ye hapless discrowned heads! Crowds came, next morning, to catch a glimpse of them, in their three upper rooms. Montgaillard says the august Captives wore an air of cheerfulness, even of gayety; that the Queen and Princess Lamballe, who had joined her overnight, looked out of the opened window, "shook powder from her hair on the people below, and laughed."* He is an acrid distorted man.

1244. For the rest, one may guess that the Legislative, above all that the New Municipality continues busy. Messengers, Municipal or Legislatives, and swift dispatches rush off to all corners of France; full of triumph, blended with indignant wail, for Twelve-hundred have fallen. France sends up its blended shout responsive; the 10th of August shall be as the 14th of July, only bloodier and greater. The Court has conspired? Poor Court: the Court has been vanquished; and will have both the scath to bear and the scorn. How the statues of Kings do now all fall? Bronze Henri himself, though he wore a cockade once, jingles down from the Pont Neuf, where Patrie floats *in danger*. Much more does Louis Fourteenth, from the Place Vendome, jingle down; and even breaks in falling. The curious can remark, written on his horse's shoe: "12 Août, 1682;" a Century and a day.

1245. The 10th of August was Friday. The week is not done, when our old Patriot Ministry is recalled, what of it can be got: strict Roland, Genevese-Clavière; add heavy Monge the Mathematician, once a stone-hewer; and, for Minister of Justice,—Danton, "led hither," as himself says, in one of his gigantic figures, "through the breach of Patriot cannon!" These, under Legislative Committees, must rule the wreck as they can: confusedly enough; with an old Legislative water-logged, with a new Municipality so brisk. But National Convention will get itself together; and *then!* Without delay, however, let a new Jury-Court and Criminal Tribunal be set up in Paris, to try the crimes and conspiracies of the Tenth. High Court of Orléans is distant, slow; the blood of the Twelve-hundred Patriots, whatever become of other blood, shall be inquired after. Tremble, ye Criminals and Conspirators; the Minister of Justice is Danton! Robespierre too, after the victory, sits in the New Municipality; insurrectionary "improvised Municipality," which calls itself Council General of the Commune.

1246. For three days now, Louis and his Family have heard the Legislative Debates in the Lodge of the Logographe; and retired nightly to their small upper rooms. The Luxembourg and safeguard of the Nation could not be got ready: nay, it seems the Luxembourg has too many cellars and issues: no Municipality can undertake to watch it. The compact Prison of the Temple, not so elegant indeed, were much safer. To the Temple, therefore! On Monday, 13th day of August, 1792, in Mayor Pétion's carriage, Louis and his sad suspended Household fare thither; all Parisout to look at them. As they pass through the Place Vendome, Louis Fourteenth's Statue lies broken on the ground. Pétion is afraid the Queen's looks may be thought scornful, and produce provocation; she casts down her eyes, and does not look at all. The "press is prodigious," but quiet: here and there, it shouts.

* Montgaillard, ii. 135-167.

Vive la Nation: but for most part gazes in silence. French Royalty vanishes within the gates of the Temple; these old peaked Towers, like peaked extinguisher or Bonsoir, do cover it up:—from which same Towers, poor Jacques Molay and his Templars were burnt out, by French Royalty, five centuries since. Such are the turns of Fate below. Foreign Ambassadors, English Lord Gower have all demanded passports; aredriving indignantly toward their respective homes.

1247. So, then, the Constitution is over? Forever and a day! Gone is that, wonder of the Universe; First biennial Parliament, water-logged, waits only till the Convention come; and will then sink to endless depths. One can guess the silent rage of Old-Constituents, Constitution-builders, extinct Feuillants, men who though, the Constitution would march! Lafayette rises to the altitude of the situation; at the head of his Army. Legislative Commissioners are posting toward him and it, on the Northern Frontier, to congratulate and perorate; he orders the Municipality of Sedan to arrest these Commissioners, and keep them strictly in ward as Rebels, till they say farther. The Sedan Municipals obey.

1248. The Sedan Municipals obey; but the Soldiers of the Lafayette Army? The Soldiers of the Lafayette Army have, as all Soldiers have, a kind of dim feeling that they themselves are Sansculottes in buff belts; that the victory of the 10th of August is also a victory for them. They will not rise and follow Lafayette to Paris; they will rise and send him thither! On the 18th, which is but next Saturday, Lafayette, with some two or three indignant Staff-officers, one of whom is Old-Constituent Alexander de Lameth, having first put his Lines in what order he could,—rides swiftly over the marches toward Holland. Rides, alas, swiftly into the claws of Austrians! He, long wavering, trembling on the verge of the Horizon, has set, in Olmütz Dungeons; this History knows him no more. Adieu, thou Hero of two Worlds; thinnest, but compact honor-worthy man! Through long rough night of captivity, through other tumults, triumphs and changes, thou wilt swing well, "fast-anchored to the Washington Formula;" and be the Hero and Perfect character, were it only of one idea. The Sedan Municipals repent and protest; the Soldiers shout Vive la Nation. Dumouriez Polymetis, from his Camp at Maulde, sees himself made Commander-in-Chief.

1249. And, O Brunswick! what sort of "military execution" will Paris merit now? Forward, ye well-drilled exterminatory men; with your artillery-wagons, and camp-kettles jingling. Forward, tall chivalrous King of Prussia; fanfaronading Emigrants and war-god Broglie, "for some consolation to mankind," which verily is not without need of some.

THE GUILLOTINE.

BOOK FIRST.

SEPTEMBER.

CHAPTER I.

THE IMPROVISED COMMUNE.

1250. Ye have roused her, then, ye Emigrants and Despots of the world: France is roused! Long have ye been lecturing and tutoring this poor Nation, like cruel uncalled-for pedagogues, shaking over her your ferulas of fire and steel; it is long that ye have pricked and filliped and affrighted her, there as she sat helpless in her dead cerements of a Constitution, you gathering on her from all lands, with your armaments and plots, your invadings and truculent bullyings;—and lo now, ye have pricked her to the quick, and she is up, and her blood is up. The dead cerements are rent into cobwebs, and she fronts you in that terrible strength of Nature, which no man has measured, which goes down to Madness and Tophet: see now how ye will deal with her.

1251. This month of September, 1792, which has become one of the memorable months of History, presents itself under two most diverse aspects: all of black on the one side, all of bright on the other. Whatsoever is cruel in the panic frenzy of 25,000,000 men, whatsoever is great in the simultaneous death-defiance of 25,000,000 men, stand here in abrupt contrast, near by one another. As indeed is usual when a man, how much more when a Nation of men, is hurled suddenly beyond the limits. For Nature, as green as she looks, rests everywhere on dread foundations were we farther down; and Pan, to whose music the Nymphs dance, has a cry in him that can drive all men distracted.

1252. Very frightful it is when a Nation, rending asunder its Constitutions and Regulations which were grown dead cerements for it, becomes transcendental; and must now seek its wild way through the New, Chaotic,—where Force is not distinguished into Bidden and Forbidden, but Crime and Virtue welter unseparated,—in that domain of what is called the Passions; of what we call the Miracles and the Portents! It is thus that, for some three years to come, we are to contemplate France, in this final Third Part of our History. Sansculottism reigning in all its grandeur and in all its hideousness; the Gospel (God's-message) of Man's Rights, Man's mights or strengths, once more preached irrefragably abroad; along with this, and still louder for the time, the fearfulest Devil's-Message of Man's weaknesses and sins;—and all on such a scale, and under such aspect: cloudy "death-birth of a world:" huge smoke-cloud, streaked with rays as of heaven on one side; girt on the other as with hell-fire! History tells us many things: but for the last thousand years and more, what thing has she told us of a sort like this? Which therefore let us two, O Reader, dwell on willingly, for a little; and from its endless significance endeavor to extract what may, in present circumstances, be adapted for us.

1253. It is unfortunate, though very natural, that the history of this Period has so generally been written in hysterics. Exaggeration abounds, execration, wailing; and, on the whole, darkness. But thus too, when foul old Rome had to be swept from the Earth, and those Northmen, and other horrid sons of Nature, came in, "swallowing formulas," as the French now do, foul old Rome screamed execratively her loudest: so that the true shape of many things is lost for us. Attila's Huns had arms of such length that they could lift a stone without stooping. Into the body of the poor Tartars execrative Roman History intercalated an alphabetic letter; and so they continue Tartars, of fell Tartarean nature, to this day. Here, in like manner, assert as we will in these multiform innumerable French Records, darkness too frequently covers, or sheer distraction bewilders. One finds it difficult to imagine that the Sun shone in this September month, as he does in others. Nevertheless it is an indisputable fact that the Sun did shine; and there was weather and work—nay as to that, very bad weather for harvest-work! An unlucky Editor may do his utmost; and after all require allowances.

1254. He had been a wise Frenchman, who, looking close at hand on this waste aspect of France all stirring and whirling, in ways new, untried, had been able to discern where the cardinal movement lay; which tendency it was that had the rule and primary direction of it then! But at forty-four years' distance, it is different. To all men now, two cardinal movements or grand tendencies, in the September whirl, have become discernible enough; that stormful affluence toward the Frontiers; that frantic crowding toward Town-houses and Council-halls in the interior. Wild France dashes, in desperate death-defiance, toward the Frontiers, to defend itself from foreign Despots; crowds toward Town-hall and Election Committee-rooms, to defend itself from domestic Aristocrats. Let the Reader conceive well these two cardinal movements; and what side-currents and endless vortexes might depend on these. He shall judge too, whether, in such sudden wreckage of all old Authorities, such a pair of cardinal movements, half-frantic in themselves, could be of soft nature? As in dry Sahara, when the winds waken and lift and winnow the immensity of sand! The air itself (Travelers say) is a dim sand-air; and dim looming through it, the wonderfulest uncertain colonnades of Sand-Pillars rush whirling from this side and from that, like so many mad Spinning-Dervishes, of a hundred feet in stature; and dance their huge Desert-waltz there!—

1255. Nevertheless, in all human movements, were they but a day old, there is order, or the beginning of order. Consider two things in this Sahara-waltz of the French 25,000,000; or rather one thing and one hope of a thing; the *Commune* (Municipality) of Paris which is already here; The National Convention, which shall in a few weeks be here. The Insurrectionary Commune, which, improvising itself on the eve of the 10th of August, worked this ever-memorable Deliverance by explosion, must needs rule over it,—till the Convention meet. This Commune, which they may well call a spontaneous or "improvised" Commune, is, for the present, sovereign of France. The Legislative, deriving its authority from the Old, how can it now have authority when the Old is exploded by insurrection? As a floating piece of wreck, certain things, persons and interests may still cleave to it: volunteer defenders, riflemen or pikemen in green uniform, or red nightcap (of bonnet rouge), defile before it daily, just on the wing toward Brunswick; with the brandishing of arms; always with some touch of Leonidas-eloquence, often with a fire of daring that threatens to out-Herod Herod, the Galleries, "especially the ladies, never done with applauding."[*] Addresses of this or the like sort can be received and answered in the hearing of all France; The Salle de Manége is still useful as a place of proclamation. For which use, indeed, it now chiefly serves. Vergniaud delivers spirit-stirring orations; but always with a prophetic sense only, looking toward the coming Convention. "Let our memory perish," crys Vergniaud; "but let France be free!" whereupon they all start to their feet, shouting responsive: "Yes, yes, *périsse notre mémoire, pourvu que la France soit libre!*"[†] Disfrocked Chabot adjures Heaven that at least we may "have done with Kings;" and fast as powder under spark, we all blaze-up once more, and with waved hats shout and swear: "Yes, nous le jurons; plus de

rois!"[*] All which, as a method of proclamation, is very convenient.

1256. For the rest,'that our busy Brissots, rigorous Rolands, men who once had authority, and now have less and less; men who love law, and will have even an Explosion explode itself as far as possible according to rule, do find this state of matters most unofficial-unsatisfactory,—is not to be denied. Complaints are made; attempts are made: but without effect. The attempts even recoil; and must be desisted from, for fear of worse: the scepter has departed from this Legislative once and always. A poor Legislative so hard was fate, had let itself be hand-gyved, nailed to the rock like an Andromeda, and could only wail there to the Earth and Heavens; miraculously a winged Perseus (or Improvised Commune) has drawn out of the void Blue, and cut her loose: but whether now is it she, with her softness and musical speech, or is it he, with his hardness and sharp falchion and ægis, that shall have casting-vote? Melodious *agreement* of vote; this were the rule! But if otherwise, and votes diverge, then surely Andromeda's part is to weep,—if possible, tears of gratitude alone.

1257. Be content, O France, with this Improvised Commune, such as it is! It has the implements, and has the hands: the time is not long. On Sunday the 26th of August, our Primary Assemblies shall meet, begin electing of Electors; on Sunday the 2d of September (may the day prove lucky!) the Electors shall begin electing Deputies; and so an all-healing National Convention will come together. No mare d'argent, or distinction of Active and Passive, now insults the French Patriot: but there is universal suffrage, unlimited liberty to choose. Old-Constituents, Present-Legislators, all France is eligible. Nay it may be said, the flower of all the Universe (de l'Univers) is eligible; for in these very days we, by act of Assembly, "naturalize" the chief Foreign Friends of Humanity: Priestley, burnt out for us in Birmingham; Klopstock, a genius of all countries; Jeremy Bentham, useful Jurisconsult; distinguished Paine, the rebellious Needleman;—some of whom may be chosen. As is most fit; for a Convention of this kind. In a word, 745 unshackled sovereigns, admired of the universe, shall replace this hapless impotency of a Legislative,—out of which, it is likely, the best Members, and the Mountain in mass, may be re-elected. Roland is getting ready the Salle des Cent Suisses, as preliminary rendezvous for them; in that void Palace of the Tuileries, now void and National, and not a Palace, but a Caravansary.

1258. As for the Spontaneous Commune, one may say that there never was on Earth a stranger Town-Council. Administration, not of a great City, but of a great Kingdom in a state of revolt and frenzy, this is the task that has fallen to it. Enrolling, provisioning, judging; devising, deciding, doing, endeavoring to do: one wonders the human brain did not give way under all this, and reel. But happily human brains have such a talent of taking up simply what they can carry, and ignoring all the rest: leaving all the rest, as if it were not there! Whereby somewhat is verily shifted for; and much shifts for itself. This Improvised Commune walks along, nothing doubting; promptly making front, without fear or flurry, at what moment soever, to the wants of the moment. Were the world on fire, one improvised tricolor Municipal has but one life to lose. They are the elixir and chosen-men of Sansculottie Patriotism; promoted to the forlorn-hope; unspeakable victory or a high gallows, this is their meed. They sit there, in the Town-hall, these astonishing

---

tricolor Municipals: in Council General; in Committee of Watchfulness (de Surveillance, which will ever become de Salut Public, of Public Salvation), or what other Committees and Subcommittees are needful;—managing infinite Correspondence; passing infinite Decrees: one hears of a Decree being "the ninety-eight of the day." Ready! is the word. They carry loaded pistols in their pocket; also some improvised luncheon by way of meal. Or indeed, hy and by, traiteurs contract for the supply of repasts, to be eaten on the spot,—too lavishly, as it was afterward grumbled. Thus they; girt in their tricolor sashes; Municipal note-paper in the one hand, fire arms in the other. They have their Agents out all over France; speaking in town-houses, market-places, highways and byways: agitating, urging to arm; all hearts tingling to hear. Great is the fire of Anti-aristocrat eloquence: nay some, as Bibliopolic Momoro, seem to hint afar off at something which smells of agrarian Law, and a surgery of the over-swoln dropsical strong-box itself, ·whereat indeed the bold Bookseller runs the risk of being hanged, and Ex-Constituent Buzot has to smuggle him off.*

1259. Governing Persons, were they never so insignificant intrinsically, have for most part plenty of Memoir-writers; and the curious, in after-times, can learn minutely their goings out and comings in: which, as men always love to know their fellow-men in singular situations, is a comfort, of its kind. Not so with these Governing Persons, now in the Town-hall! And yet what most original fellow-man, of the Governing sort, high-chancellor, king, kaiser, secretary of the home or the foreign department, ever showed such a phasis as Clerk Tallien, Procureur Manuel, future Procureur Chaumette, here in this Sand-waltz of the Twenty-five millions now do? O brother mortals,—thou Advocate Panis, friend of Danton, kinsman of Santerre; Engraver Sergent; since called *Agate* Sergent; thou Huguenin, with the tocsin in thy heart! But, as Horace says, they wanted the sacred memoir-writer (sacro vate): and we know them not. Men bragged of August and its doings, publishing them in high places; but of this September none now or afterwards would brag. The September world remains dark, fuliginous, as Lapland witch-midnight;—from which, indeed, very strange shapes will evolve themselves.

1260. Understand this, however: that incorruptible Robespierre is not wanting, now when the brunt of battle is past; in a stealthy way the sea-green man sits there, his feline eyes excellent in the twilight, Also understand this other, a single fact worth many: that Marat is not only there, but has a seat of honor assigned him, a tribune particulière. How changed for Marat; lifted from his dark cellar into this luminous "peculiar tribune!" All dogs have their day; even rabid dogs. Sorrowful, incurable Philoctetes Marat; without whom Troy cannot be taken! Hither, as a main element of the Governing Power, has Marat been raised. Royalist types, for we have "suppressed" innumerable Durosoys, Royous, and even clapt them in prison,—Royalist types replace the worn types often snatched from a People's-Friend in old ill days. In our "peculiar tribune" we write and redact: Placards, of due monitory terror; Amis-du-Peuple (now under the name of Journal de la République); and sit obeyed of men. "Marat," says one, "is the conscience of the Hotel-de-Ville." *Keeper*, as some call it, of the Sovereign's Conscience; which surely in such hands will not lie hid in a napkin!

1261. Two great movements, as we said, agitate this distracted National mind: a rushing against domestic Traitors, a rushing against foreign Despots. Mad movements both, restrainable by no known rule;

strongest passions of human nature driving them on love, hatred, vengeful sorrow, braggart Nationality also vengeful,—and pale Panic over all! Twelve-hundred slain Patriots, do they not, from their dark catacombs there, in Death's dumb-show, plead (O ye Legislators) for vengeance! Such was the destructive rage of these Aristocrats on the ever-memorable 10th. Nay, apart from vengeance, and with an eye to Public Salvation only, are there not still, in this Paris (in round numbers) "30,000 Aristocrats," of the most malignant humor; driven now to their last trump-card?—Be patient, ye Patriots: our new High Court, "Tribunal of the Seventeenth," sits; each Section has sent Four Jurymen; and Danton, extinguishing improper judges, improper practices wheresoever found, is "the same man you have known at the Cordeliers." With such a Minister of Justice, shall not Justice be done?—Let it be swift, then, answers universal Patriotism; swift and sure!—

1262. One would hope, this Tribunal of the Seventeenth is swifter than most. Already on the 21st, while our Court is but four days old, Collenot d'Angremont, "the Royalist enlister" (crimp crobaucheur), dies by torchlight. For, lo, the great Guillotine, wondrous to behold, now stands there; the Doctor's *Idea* has become Oak and Iron; the huge cyclopean axe "falls in its grooves like the ram of the Pile-engine," swiftly snuffing out the light of men! "Mais vous, Gualches, what have you invented?" *This!*—Poor old Laport, Intendent of the Civil List, follows next; quietly, the mild old man. Then Durosoy, Royalists Placarder, "cashier of all the Anti-revolutionists of the interior:" he went rejoicing; said that a Royalist like him ought to die, of all days, on this day, the 25th or St. Louis's Day. All these have been tried, cast,—the Galleries shouting approval; and handed over to the Realized Idea, within a week. Besides those whom we have acquitted, the Galleries murmuring, and have dismissed; or even have personally guarded back to Prison, as the Galleries took to howling, and even to menacing and elbowing.* Languid this Tribunal is not.

1263. Nor does the other movement slacken; the rushing against foreign Despots. Strong forces shall meet in death-grip; drilled Europe against mad undrilled France; and singular conclusions will be tried. —Conceive therefore, in some faint degree, the tumult that whirls in this France, in this Paris! Placards from Section, from Commune, from Legislative, from the individual Patriot, flame monitory on all walls. Flags of danger to Fatherland wave at the Hotel-de-Ville; on the Pont-Neuf—over the prostrate Statues of Kings. There is universal enlisting, urging to enlist; there is tearful-boastful leave-taking; irregular marching on the Great North-eastern Road. Marseillese sing their wild *To arms*, in chorus; which now all men, all women and children have learnt, and sing chorally, in Theaters, Boulevards, Streets; and the heart burns in every bosom: Aux armes! Marchons!—Or think how your Aristocrats are skulking into covert; how Bertrand-Moleville lies hidden in some garret "in Aubry-le-boucher Street, with a poor surgeon who had known me." Dame de Staël has secreted her Narbonne, not knowing what in the world to make of him. The Barriers are sometimes open, oftenest shut; no passports to be had; Town-hall Emissaries, with the eyes and claws of falcons, flitting watchful on all points of your horizon! In two words: Tribunal of the Seventeenth, busy under 'howling Galleries; Prussian Brunswick, "over a space of forty miles," with his war-tumbrils, and sleeping thunders, and 'Briarean "sixty-six thousand"† right hands,—coming, coming!

---

* "Mémoires de Buzot" (Paris, 1823), p. 85.

* Moore's "Journal," l. 159-168.
† See Toulongeou, "Histoire de France," B. c. 5.

1264. O Heavens, in these latter days of August, he is come! Durosoy was not yet guillotined when news had come that the Prussians were harrying and ravaging about Metz; in some four days more, one hears that Longwi, our first strong-place on the borders, is fallen " in fifteen hours." Quick therefore, O ye improvised Municipals ; quick, and ever quicker! —the improvised Municipals make front to this also. Enrollment urges itself ; and clothing, and arming. Our very officers have now " wool epaulets ; " for it is the reign of Equality, and also of Necessity. Neither do men now *monsieur* and *sir* one another ; **citoyen** (citizen) were suitabler ; we even say *thou*, as " the free peoples of Antiquity did : " so have Journals and the Improvised Commune suggested ; which shall be well.

1265. Infinitely better, meantime, could we suggest, where arms are to be found. For the present, our Citoyens chant chorally *To arms* ; and have no arms! Arms are searched for ; passionately ; there is joy over any musket. Moreover, intrenchments shall be made round Paris : on the slopes of Montmartre men dig and shovel ; though even the simple suspect this to be desperate. They dig ; Tricolor sashes speak encouragement and *well-speed-ye*. Nay finally " Twelve Members of the Legislative go daily," not to encourage only, but to bear a hand, and delve : it was decreed with acclamation. Arms shall either be provided ; or else the ingenuity of men crack itself, and become fatuity. Lean Beaumarchais, thinking to serve the Fatherland, and do a stroke of trade in the old way, has commissioned 60,000 stand of good arms out of Holland : would to Heaven, for Fatherland's sake and his, they were come! Meanwhile railings are torn up ; hammered into pikes ; chains themselves shall be welded together into pikes. The very coffins of the dead are raised ; for melting into balls. All Church-bells must down into the furnace to make cannon ; all Church-plate into the mint to make money. Also, behold the fair swan-bevies of Citoyennes that have alighted in Churches, and sit there with swan-neck,—sewing tents and regimentals! Nor are Patriotic Gifts wanting, from those that have aught left ; nor stingily given : the fair Villaumes, mother and daughter, Milliners in the Rue St. Martin, give a " silver thimble, and a coin of fifteen sous (sevenpence half-penny)," with other similar effects ; and offer, at least the mother does, to mount guard. Men who have not even a thimble, give a thimbleful,—were it but of invention. One Citoyen has wrought out the scheme of a wooden cannon ; which France shall exclusively profit by, in the first instance. It is to be made of *staves*, by the coopers ;—of almost boundless caliber, but uncertain as to strength! Thus they : hammering, scheming, stitching, founding, with all their heart and with all their soul. Two bells only are to remain in each Parish,—for tocsin and other purposes.

1266. But mark also, precisely while the Prussian batteries were playing their briskest at Longwi in the North-east, and our dastardly Lavergne saw nothing for it but surrender,—south-westward, in remote, patriarchal La Vendée, that sour ferment about Nonjuring Priests, after long working, is ripe, and explodes : at the wrong moment for us! And so we have " 8,000 peasants at Châtillon-sur-Sèvre " who will not be balloted for soldiers ; will not have their Curates molested. To whom Bonchamps, Larochejaquelins, and Seigneurs enough of a Royalist turn, will join themselves ; with Stofflets and Charettes ; with Heroes and Chouan Smugglers ; and the loyal warmth of a simple people, blown to flame and fury by theological and seignorial bellows! So that there shall be fighting from behind ditches, death-volleys bursting out of thickets and ravines of rivers ;

huts burning, feet of the pitiful women hurrying to refuge with their children on their back, seed-fields fallow, whitened with human bones ;—" 80,000, of all ages, ranks, sexes, flying at once across the Loire," with wail borne far on the winds : and in brief, for years coming, such a suit of scenes as glorious war has not offered in these late ages, not since our Albigenses and Crusadings were over,—save indeed some chance Palatinate, or so, we might have to " burn," by way of exception. The " 80,000 at Châtillon " will be got dispelled for the moment ; the fire scattered, not extinguished. To the dints and bruises of outward battle there is to be added henceforth a deadlier internal gangrene.

1267. This rising in La Vendée reports itself at Paris on Wednesday the 29th of August :—just as we had got our Electors elected ; and, in spite of Brunswick and Longwi, were hoping still to have a National Convention, if it pleased Heaven. But indeed otherwise this Wednesday is to be regarded as one of the notablest Paris had yet seen : gloomy tidings come successively, like Job's messengers ; are met by gloomy answers. Of Sardinia rising to invade the South-east, and Spain threatening the South, we do not speak. But are not the Prussians masters of Longwi (treacherously yielded, one would say) ; and preparing to besiege Verdun? Clairfait and his Austrians are encompassing Thionville ; darkening the North. Not Metzland now, but the Clermontais is getting harried : flying hulans and hussars have been seen on the Châlons road, almost as far as Sainte-Menehould. Heart, ye Patriots ; if ye lose heart, ye lose all!

1268. It is not without a dramatic emotion that one reads in the Parliamentary Debates of this Wednesday evening " past seven o'clock," the scene with the military fugitives from Longwi. Wayworn, dusty, disheartened, these poor men enter the Legislative, about sunset or after ; give the most pathetic detail of the frightful pass they were in : Prussians billowing round by the myriad, volcanically spouting fire for fifteen hours : we, scattered sparse on the ramparts, hardly a cannoneer to two guns ; our dastard Commandant Lavergne nowhere showing face ; the priming would not catch ; there was no powder in the bombs,—what could we do? " Mourir (Die)!" answer prompt voices ;[*] and the dusty fugitives must shrink elsewhither for comfort.—Yes, Mourir, that is now the word. Be Longwi a proverb and a hissing among French strong-places : let it (says the Legislative) be obliterated rather, from the shamed face of the Earth ;—and so there has gone forth Decree, that Longwi shall, were the Prussians once out of it, " be razed," and exist only as plowed ground.

1269. Nor are the Jacobins milder ; as how could they, the flower of Patriotism? Poor Dame Lavergne, wife of the poor Commandant, took her parasol one evening, and escorted by her Father came over to the Hall of the mighty Mother ; and " reads a memoir tending to justify the Commandant of Longwi." Lafarge, President, makes answer : " Citoyenne, the nation will judge Lavergne ; the Jacobins are bound to tell him the truth. He would have ended his course there (terminé sa carrière), if he had loved the honor of his country."[†]

CHAPTER II.

DANTON.

1270. But better than razing of Longwi, or rebuking poor dusty soldiers or soldiers' wives, Danton had come over, last night, and demanded a Decree to *search* for arms, since they were not yielded volun-

* "Histoire Parlementaire," xvii. 146.
† "Histoire Parlementaire," xix. 500.

tarily. Let "Domiciliary visits," with rigor of authority, be made to this end. To search for arms; for horses,—Aristocratism rolls in its carriage, while Patriotism cannot trail its cannon. To search generally for munitions of war, " in the houses of persons suspect,"—and even, if it seem proper, to seize and imprison the suspect persons themselves! In the Prisons their Plots will be harmless; in the Prisons they will be as hostages for us, and not without use. This Decree the energetic Minister of Justice demanded last night, and got; and this same night it is to be executed; it is being executed at the moment when these dusty soldiers get saluted with Mourir. Two-thousand stand of arms, as they count, are foraged in this way; and some 400 head of new Prisoners; and, on the whole, such a terror and damp is struck through the Aristocrat heart, as all but Patriotism, and even Patriotism were it out of this agony, might pity. Yes, Messieurs! if Brunswick blast Paris to ashes, he probably will blast the Prisons of Paris too: pale Terror, if we have got it, we will also give it, and the depth of horrors that lie in it; the same leaky bottom, in these wild waters, bears us all.

1271. One can judge what stir there was now among the "30,000 Royalists:" how the Plotters, or the accused of Plotting, shrank each closer into his lurking-place,—like Bertrand-Moleville,looking eager toward Longwi, hoping the weather would keep rigid. Or how they dressed themselves in valet's clothes, like Narbonne, and "got to England as Dr. Bollman's famulus;" how Dame de Staël bestirred herself, pleading with Manuel as a Sister in Literature, pleading even with Clerk Tallien; a prey to nameless chagrins !* Royalist Peltier, the Pamphleteer, gives a touching Narrative (not deficient in height of coloring) of the terrors of that night. From five in the afternoon, a great city is struck suddenly silent; except for the beating of drums, for the tramp of marching feet; and ever and anon the dread thunder of the knocker at some door, a Tricolor Commissioner with his blue Guards (black-guards!) arriving. All Streets are vacant, says Peltier; beset by Guards at each end : all Citizens are ordered to be within doors. On the River float sentinel barges, lest we escape by water; the Barriers hermetically closed. Frightful! The Sun shines: serenely westering, in smokeless mackerel-sky; Paris is as if sleeping, as if dead:— Paris is holding its breath, to see what stroke will fall on it. Poor Peltier! "Acts of Apostles," and all jocundity of Leading-Articles, are gone out, and it is become bitter earnest instead; polished satire changed now into course pike-points (hammered out of railing); all logic reduced to this one primitive thesis, An eye for an eye, a tooth for a tooth !—Peltier, dolefully aware of it, ducks low; escapes unscathed to England; to urge there the inky war anew;—to have Trial by Jury, in due season, and deliverance by young Whig eloquence, world-celebrated for a day.

1272. Of "30,000" naturally great multitudes were left unmolested : but, as we said, some 400. designated as " persons suspect," were seized ; and an unspeakable terror fell on all. Woe to him who is guilty of plotting, of Anti-civism, Royalism, Feuillantism; who, guilty or not guilty, has an enemy in his Section to call him guilty! Poor old M. de Cazotte is seized his young loved Daughter with him, refusing to quit him. Why, O Cazotte, wouldst thou quit romancing and " Diable Amoureux," for such reality as this? Poor old M. de Sombreuil, he of the Invalides, is seized; a man seen askance by Patriotism ever since the Bastille days; whom also a fond Daughter will not quit. With young tears hardly

suppressed, and old wavering weakness rousing itself once more,—O my brothers, O my sisters!

1273. The famed and named go; the nameless, if they have an accuser. Necklace Lamotte's Husband is in these Prisons (she long since squelched on the London Pavements); but gets delivered. Gross de Morande, of the Courrier de l'Europe hobbles distractedly to and fro there: but they let him hobble out ; on right nimble crutches;—his hour not being yet come. Advocate Maton de la Varenne, very weak in health, is snatched off from mother and kin ; Tricolor Rossignol (journeyman goldsmith and scoundrel lately, a risen man now) remembers an old Pleading of Maton's! Jourgniac de Saint-Méard goes ; the brisk frank soldier : he was in the mutiny of Nanci, in that "effervescent Regiment du Roi,"—on the wrong side. Saddest of all: Abbé Sicard goes; a Priest who could not take the Oath, but who could teach the Deaf and Dumb : in his Section one man, he says, had a grudge at him; one man, at the fit hour, launches an arrest against him; which hits. In the Arsenal quarter, there are dumb hearts making wail, with signs, with wild gestures; he their miraculous healer and speech-bringer is rapt away.

1274. What with the arrestments on this night of the 29th, what with those that have gone on more or less, day and night ever since the 10th, one may fancy what the Prisons now were. Crowding and confusion ; jostle, hurry, vehemence and terror! Of the poor Queen's Friends, who had followed her to the Temple, and been committed elsewhither to Prison, some, as Governess de Tourzelle, are to be let go : one, the poor Princess de Lamballe, is not let go; but waits in the strong rooms of La Force there, what will betide farther.

1275. Among so many hundreds whom the launched arrest hits, who are rolled off to Town-hall or Section-hall, to preliminary Houses of Detention, and hurled in thither as into cattle-pens, we must mention one other : Caron de Beaumarchais, Author of "Figaro"; vanquisher of Maupeou Parlements and Goezman hell-dogs; once numbered among the demigods; and now—? We left him in his culminant state; what dreadful decline is this, when we again catch a glimpse of him! "At midnight" (it was but the 12th of August yet), "the servant, in his shirt," with wide-staring eyes, enters your room:—Monsieur, rise, all the people are come to seek you; they are knocking, like to break-in the door! "And they were in fact knocking in a terrible manner (d'une façon terrible). I fling on my coat, forgetting even the waistcoat, nothing on my feet but slippers; and say to him"—And he, alas, answers mere negatory incoherences, panic interjections. And through the shutters and crevices, in front or rearward, the dull street-lamps disclose only streetfuls of haggard countenances; clamorous, bristling with pikes : and you rush distracted from an outlet, finding none ;—and have to take refuge in the crockery-press, down stairs; and stand there, palpitating in that imperfect costume, lights dancing past your key-hole, tramp of feet overhead, and the tumult of Satan, "for four hours and more!" And old ladies, of the quarter, started up (in my way at their next morning) ; rang for their bonnes and cordial-drops, with shrill interjections: and old gentlemen, in their shirts, "leapt garden-walls;" flying while none pursued; one of whom unfortunately broke his leg.* Those 60,000 stand of Dutch Arms (which never arrive), and the bold stroke of trade, have turned out so ill!—

1276. Beaumarchais escaped for this time ; but not for the next time, ten days after. On the evening of the 29th he is still in that chaos of the Prisons, in

* De Staël, "Considérations sur la Révolution," ii. 67-81.

* Beaumarchais' Narrative, "Mémoires sur les Prisons," (Paris, 1823), i. 179-190.

saddest wrestling condition; unable to get justice, even to get audience; "Panis scratching his head" when you speak to him, and making off. Nevertheless let the lover of "Figaro" know that Procureur Manuel, a Brother in Literature, found him, and delivered him once more. But how the lean demigod, now shorn of his splendor, had to lurk in barns, to roam over harrowed fields, pauting for life; and to wait under eaves-drops, and sit in darkness "on the Boulevard amid paving-stones and boulders," longing for one word of any Minister, or Minister's Clerk, about those accursed Dutch muskets, and getting none,—with heart fuming in spleen, and terror, and suppressed canine-madness; alas, how the swift sharp hound, once fit to be Diana's, breaks his old teeth now, gnawing mere whinstones; and must "fly to England;" and returning from England, must creep into the corner, and lie quiet, toothless (moneyless),—all this let the lover of "Figaro" fancy, and weep for. We here, without weeping, not without sadness, wave the withered tough fellow-mortal our farewell. His "Figaro" has returned to the French stage; nay is, at this day, sometimes named the best piece there. And indeed, so long as Man's Life can ground itself only on artificiality and aridity; each new Revolt and Change of Dynasty turning up only a new stratum of *dry-rubbish*, and no *soil* yet coming to view,—may it not be good to protest against such a Life, in many ways, and even in the "Figaro" way?

CHAPTER III.

DUMOURIEZ.

1277. Such are the last days of August, 1792; days gloomy, disastrous and of evil omen. What will become of this poor France? Dumouriez rode from the Camp of Maulde, eastward to Sedan, on Tuesday last, the 28th of the month; reviewed that so-called Army left forlorn there by Lafayette: the forlorn soldiers gloomed on him; were heard growling on him "This is one of them, ce b—e là, that made War be declared."[*] Unpromising Army! Recruits flow in, filtering through Dépot after Dépot; but recruits merely: in want of all; happy if they have so much as arms. And Longwi has fallen basely; and Brunswick, and the Prussian King, with his 60,000, will beleaguer Verdun; and Clairfait and Austrians press deeper in, over the Northern marches: 150,000 as fear counts, 80,000 as the returns show, do hem us in; Cimmerian Europe behind them. There is Castries-and-Broglie chivalry; Royalist foot "in red facing and nankeen trousers;" breathing death and the gallows.

1278. And lo, finally, at Verdun, on Sunday the 2d of September, 1792, Brunswick is here. With his King and 60,000, glittering over the heights, from beyond the winding Meuse River, he looks down on us, on our "high citadel" and all our confectionary ovens (for we are celebrated for confectionary); has sent courteous summons, in order to spare the effusion of blood!—Resist him to the death? Every day of retardation precious? How, O General Beaurepaire (asks the amazed Municipality), shall we resist him? We, the Verdun Municipals, see no resistance possible. Has he not 60,000, and artillery without end? Retardation, Patriotism is good; but so likewise is peaceable baking of pastry, and sleeping in whole skin.—Hapless Beaurepaire stretches out his hands, and pleads passionately, in the name of country, honor, of Heaven and of Earth: to no purpose. The Municipals have, by law, the power of ordering it;—with an Army offered by Royalism or Crypto-Royalism, such a Law seemed needful: and they order it, as pacific Pastry-cooks, not as heroic Patriots would,—To surrender! Beaurepaire strides home, with long steps: his valet, entering the room, sees him "writing eagerly," and withdraws. His valet hears then, in few minutes, the report of a pistol: Beaurepaire is lying dead; his eager writing had been a brief suicidal farewell. In this manner died Beaurepaire, wept of France; buried in the Pantheon, with honorable Pension to his Widow, and for Epitaph these words, *He chose Death rather than yield to Despots.* The Prussians, descending from the heights, are peaceable masters of Verdun.

1279. And so Brunswick advances, from stage to stage: who shall now stay him,—covering forty miles of country? Foragers fly far; the villages of the North-east are harried; your Hessian forager has only "three sous a day:" the very Emigrants, it is said, will take silver-plate,—by way of revenge. Clermont, Sainte-Menehould, Varennes especially, ye Towns of the *Night of Spurs*, tremble ye! Procureur Sausse and the Magistracy of Varennes have fled; brave Boniface le Blanc of the Bras d'Or is to the woods: Mrs. le Blanc, a young woman fair to look upon, with her young infant, has to live in greenwood, like a beautiful Bessy Bell of Song, her bower thatched with rushes; catching permature rheumatism.[*] Clermont may ring the tocsin now, and illuminate itself! Clermont lies at the foot of its *Cow* (or *Vache*, so they name that Mountain), a prey to the Hessian spoiler; its fair women, fairer than most, are robbed; not of life, or what is dearer, yet of all that is cheaper and portable; for Necessity, on three half-pence a day, has no law. At Sainte-Menehould the enemy has been expected more than once,—our Nationals all turning out in arms; but was not yet seen. Postmaster Drouet he is not in the woods, but minding his Election; and will sit in the Convention, notable King-taker, and bold Old-Dragoon as he is.

1280. Thus on the North-east all roams and runs; and on a set day, the *date* of which is irrecoverable by History, Brunswick "has engaged to dine in Paris," —the Powers willing. And at Paris, in the center, it is as we saw; and in La Vendée South-west, it is as we saw; and Sardinia is in the South-east, and Spain in the South, and Clairfait with Austria and sieged Thionville is in the North;—and all France leaps distracted, like the winnowed Sahara waltzing in sand colonnades! More desperate posture no country ever stood in. A country, one would say, which the Majesty of Prussia (if it so pleased him) might partition and clip in pieces, like a Poland; flinging the remainder to poor Brother Louis,—with directions to keep it quiet, or else *we* will keep it for him!

1281. Or perhaps the Upper Powers, minded that a new Chapter in Universal History shall begin here and not farther on, may have ordered it all otherwise? In that case, Brunswick will not dine in Paris on the set day; nor, indeed, one knows not when!—verily, amid this wreckage, where poor France seems grinding itself down to dust and bottomless ruin, who knows what miraculous salient-point of Deliverance and New-life may have already come into existence there; and be already working there, though as yet human eye discern it not! On the night of that same 28th of August, the unpromising Review-day in Sedan, Dumouriez assembles a Council of War at his lodgings there. He spreads out the map of this forlorn war-district; Prussians here, Austrians there; triumphant both, with broad highway, and little hindrance, all the way to Paris: we scattered, helpless, here and there: what to advise? The Generals,

---

[*] Dumouriez, "Mémoires," ii. 383.

[*] Helen Maria Williams, "Letters from France" (London, 1791-1793), iii. 96.

strangers to Dumouriez, look blank enough; know not well what to advise,—if it be not retreating, and retreating till our recruits accumulate; till perhaps the chapter of chances turn up some leaf for us; or Paris, at all events, be sacked at the latest day possible. The many-counseled; who "has not closed an eye for three nights," listens with little speech to these long, cheerless speeches: merely watching the speaker, that he may know him; then wishes them all good-night;—but beckons a certain young Thouvenot, the fire of whose looks had pleased him, to wait a moment. Thouvenot waits; Voilà, says Polymetis, pointing to the map! That is the Forest of Argonne, that long strip of rocky Mountain and wild Wood: forty miles long; with but five, or say even three practicable passes through it: this, for they have forgotten it, might one not still seize, though Clairfait sits so nigh? Once seized ;—the Champagne called the Hungry (or worse, Champagne Pouilleuse) on their side of it; the fat Three Bishoprics, and willing France on ours; and the Equinox rains not far :—this Argonne "might be the Thermopylæ of France !"[*]

1282. O brisk Dumouriez Polymetis with thy teeming head, may the gods grant it !—Polymetis, at any rate, folds his map together, and flings himself on bed; resolved to try, on the morrow morning. With astucity, with swiftness, with audacity! One had need to be a lion-fox, and have luck on one's side.

CHAPTER IV.
SEPTEMBER IN PARIS.

1283. At Paris, by lying Rumor which proved prophetic and veridical, the fall of Verdun was known some hours *before* it happened. It is Sunday the 2d of September; handiwork hinders not the speculations of the mind. Verdun gone (though some still deny it); the Prussians in full march, with gallows-ropes, with fire and faggot! Thirty thousand Aristocrats within our own walls, and but the merest quarter-tithe of them yet put in Prison! Nay there goes a word that even these will revolt. Sieur Jean Julien, wagoner of Vaugirard,[†] being set in the Pillory last Friday, took all at once to crying, That he would be well revenged ere long; that the King's Friends in Prison would burst out, force the Temple, set the King on horseback, and, joined by the unimprisoned, ride rough-shod over us all. This the unfortunate wagoner of Vaugirard did bawl, at the top of his lungs; when snatched off to the Town-hall, he persisted in it, still bawling; yesternight, when they guillotined him, he died with the froth of it on his lips.[‡] For a man's mind padlocked to the Pillory, may go mad; and all men's minds may go mad and "believe him," as the frenetic will do, "*because* it is impossible."

1284. So that apparently the knot of the crisis and last agony of France is come? Make front to this, thou Improvised Commune, strong Danton, whatsoever man is strong! Readers can judge whether the Flag of Country in Danger flapped soothingly or distractively on the souls of men that day.

1285. But the Improvised Commune, but strong Danton is not wanting, each after his kind. Huge Placards are getting plastered to the walls; at two o'clock the storm-bell shall be sounded, the alarm cannon fired; all Paris shall rush to the Champ-de-Mars, and have itself enrolled. Unarmed, truly, and undrilled; but desperate, in the strength of

* Dumouriez, ii. 391.

† Moore, i. 178.

‡ "Histoire Parlementaire," xvii. 409.

frenzy. Haste, ye men; ye very women, offer to mount guard and shoulder the brown musket: weak clucking-hens, in a state of desperation, will fly at the muzzle of the mastiff; and even conquer him,—by vehemence of character! Terror itself, when once grown transcendental, becomes a kind of courage; as frost sufficiently intense according to Poet Milton, will *burn*.—Danton, the other night, in the Legislative Committee of General Defense, when the other Ministers and Legislators had all opined, said, It would not do to quit Paris, and fly to Saumur; that they must abide by Paris; and take such attitude at would put their enemies in fear,—*faire peur*; a word of his which has been often repeated, and reprinted —in italics.[*]

1286. At two of the clock, Beaurepaire, as we saw, has shot himself at Verdun; and, over Europe, mortals are going in for afternoon sermon. But at Paris, all steeples are clangoring not for sermon; the alarm-gun booming from minute to minute; Champ-de-Mars and Fatherland's Altar boiling with desperate terror-courage: what a miserere going up to Heaven from this once Capital of the Most Christian King! The Legislative sits in alternate awe and effervescence; Vergniaud proposing that Twelve shall go and dig personally on Montmartre; which is decreed by acclaim.

1287. But better than digging personally with acclaim, see Danton enter;—the black brows clonded, the colossus figure tramping heavy; grim energy looking from all features of the rugged man! Strong is that grim Son of France and Son of Earth; a Reality and not a Formula he too: and surely now if ever, being hurled *low* enough, it is on the Earth and on Realities that he rests. "Legislators !" so speaks the stentor-voice, as the Newspapers yet preserve it for us, " it is not the alarm-cannon that you hear: it is the pas-de-charge against our enemies. To conquer them, to hurl them back, what do we require? Il nous faut de l'audace, et encore de l'audace, et toujours de l'audace (To dare, and again to dare, and without end to dare)!"[†]—Right so, thou brawny Titan; there is nothing left for thee but that. Old men, who heard it, will still tell you how the reverberating voice made all hearts swell, in that moment; and braced them to the sticking-place; and thrilled abroad over France, like electric virtue, as a word spoken in season.

1288. But the Commune, enrolling in the Champ-de-Mars? But the Committee of Watchfulness, become now Committee of Public Salvation; whose conscience is Marat? The Commune enrolling enrolls many; provides tents for them in that Mars-Field, that they may march with dawn on the morrow: praise to this part of the Commune! To Marat and the Committee of Watchfulness not praise;—not even blame, such as could be meted out in these insufficient dialects of ours; expressive silence rather ! Lone Marat, the man forbid, meditating long in his Cellars of refuge, on his Stylites Pillar, could see salvation in one thing only: in the fall of "260,000 Aristocrat heads." With so many score of Naples Bravoes, each a dirk in his right-hand, a muff on his left, he would traverse France, and do it. But the world laughed, mocking the severe-benevolence of a People's-Friend; and his idea could not become an action, but only a fixed-idea: Lo, now, however, he has come down from his Stylites Pillar to a Tribune particulière; here now, without the dirks, without the *muffs* at least, were it not grown possible,—now in the knot of the crisis, when salvation or destruction hangs in the hour !

1289. The Ice-Tower of Avignon was noised of

* "Biographie des Ministres" (Bruxelles, 1825), p. 96.

† Moniteur (in "Histoire Parlementaire," xvii. 347).

sufficiently, and lives in all memories; but the authors were not punished: nay we saw Jourdan Coupe-tête, borne on men's shoulders, like a copper Portent, "traversing the cities of the South."—What phantasms, squalid-horrid, shaking their dirk and muff, may dance through the brain of a Marat; in this dizzy pealing of tocsin-miserere and universal frenzy, seek not to guess, O Reader! Nor what the cruel Billaud "in his short brown coat" was thinking; nor Sergent, not yet Agate-Sergent; nor Panis the confidant of Danton;—nor, in a word, how gloomy Orcus does breed in her gloomy womb and fashion her monsters and prodigies of Events, which thou seest her visibly bear! Terror is on these Streets of Paris; terror and rage, tears and frenzy: tocsin-miserere pealing through the air; fierce desperation rushing to battle; mothers, with streaming eyes and wild hearts, sending forth their sons to die. "Carriage-horses are seized by the bridle," that they may draw cannon; "the traces cut, the carriages left standing." In such tocsin-miserere, and murky bewilderment of Frenzy, are not Murder, Até and all Furies near at hand? On slight hint—who knows on how slight?—may not Murder come; and with *her* snaky-sparkling head, illuminate this murk!

1290. How it was and went, what part might be premeditated, what was improvised and accidental, man will never know, till the great Day of Judgment make it known. But with a Marat for a keeper of the Sovereign's Conscience—And we know what the ultima ratio of Sovereigns, when they are driven to it, is! In this Paris there are as wicked men, say a hundred or more, as exist in all the earth: to be hired, and set on; to set on, of their own accord, unhired.—And yet we will remark that premeditation itself is not performance, is not surety of performance : that it is perhaps, at most, surety of *letting* whosoever wills perform. From the purpose of crime to the act of crime there is an abyss; wonderful to think of. The finger lies on the pistol; but the man is not yet a murderer: nay his whole nature staggering at such consummation, is there not a confused pause rather,—one last instant of possibility for him? Not yet a murderer; it is at the mercy of light trifles whether the most fixed idea may not yet become unfixed. One slight twitch of a muscle, the death-flash bursts; and he is it; and will for Eternity be it; and Earth has become a penal Tartarus for him; his horizon girdled now not with golden hope, but with red flames of remorse; voices from the depths of Nature sounding, Woe, woe, on him!

1291. Of such stuff are we all made; on such powder-mines of bottomless guilt and criminality,—"if God restrained not," as is well said,—does the purest of us walk. There are depths in man that go to the length of lowest Hell, as there are heights that reach highest Heaven;—for are not both Heaven and Hell made out of him, made by him, everlasting Miracle and Mystery as he is?—But looking on this Champ-de-Mars, with its tent-buildings and frantic enrollments; on this murky-simmering Paris, with its crammed Prisons (supposed about to burst), with its tocsin-miserere, its mothers' tears, and soldiers' farewell shoutings,—the pious soul might have prayed, that day that God's grace would restrain, and greatly restrain; lest on slight heat or hint, Madness, Horror and Murder rose, and this Sabbath-day of September became a Day black in the Annals of men.

1292. The tocsin is pealing its loudest, the clocks inaudibly striking *Three*, when poor Abbé Sicard, with whom thirty other Nonjurant Priests, in six carriages, fare along the streets, from their preliminary House of Detention at the Town-hall, westward toward the Prison of the Abbaye. Carriages enough stand deserted on the streets; these six move on,—through angry multitudes, cursing as they move. Accursed Aristocrat Tartuffes, this is the pass ye have brought us to! And now ye will break the Prisons, and set Capet Veto on horseback to ride over us? Out upon you, Priests of Beelzebub and Moloch: of Tartuffery Mammon and the Prussian Gallows,—which ye name Mother-Church and God!—Such reproaches have the poor Nonjurants to endure, and worse; spoken-in on them by frantic Patriots, who mount even on the carriage-steps : the very Guards hardly refraining. Pull up your carriage-blinds?—No! answers Patriotism clapping its horny paw on the carriage-blind, and crushing it down again. Patience in oppression has limits : we are close on the Abhaye, it has lasted long : a poor Nonjurant, of quicker temper, smites the horny paw with his cane; nay, finding solacement in it, smites the unkempt head, sharply and again more sharply, twice over,—seen clearly of us and of the world. It is the last that we see clearly. Alas, next moment the carriages are locked and blocked in endless raging tumults, in yells deaf to the cry for mercy, which answer the cry for mercy with saber-thrusts through the heart.* The thirty Priests are torn out, are massacred about the Prison Gate, one after one,—only the poor Abbé Sicard, whom one Moton, a watchmaker, knowing him, heroically tried to save and secrete in the prison, escapes to tell;—and it is Night and Orcus: and Murder's snaky-sparkling head *has* risen in the murk!—

1293. From Sunday afternoon (exclusive of intervals and pauses not final) till Thursday evening, there follow consecutively a Hundred Hours. Which hundred hours are to be reckoned with the hours of the Bartholomew Butchery, of the Armagnac Massacres, Sicilian Vespers, or whatsoever is savagest in the annals of this world. Horrible the hour when man's soul, in its paroxysm, spurns asunder the barriers and rules; and shows what dens and depths are in it! For Night and Orcus, as we say, as was long prophesied, have burst forth, here in this Paris, from their subterranean imprisonment : hideous, dim-confused; which it is painful to look on; and yet which cannot, and indeed which should not, be forgotten.

1294. The Reader, who looks earnestly through this dim Phantasmagory of the Pit, will discern few fixed certain objects; and yet still a few. He will observe, in this Abbaye Prison, the sudden massacre of the Priests being once over, a strange Court of Justice, or call it Court of Revenge and Wild-Justice, swiftly fashion itself, and take seat round a table, with the Prison Registers spread before it ;—Stanislas Maillard, Bastille hero, famed leader of the Menads, presiding. O Stanislas, one hoped to meet thee elsewhere than here; thou shifty Riding-Usher, with an inkling of Law! This work also thou hadst to do; and then—to depart forever from our eyes. At La Force, at the Châtelet, the Conciergerie, the like Court forms itself, with the like accompaniments: the thing that one man does, other men can do. There are some Seven Prisons in Paris, full of Aristocrats with conspiracies;—nay not even Bicêtre and Salpêtrière shall escape, with their Forgers of Assignats: and there are seventy times 700 Patriot hearts in a state of frenzy. Scoundrel hearts also there are; as perfect, say, as the Earth holds,—if such are needed. To whom, in this mood, law is as no law; and killing, by what name soever called, is but work to be done.

1295. So sit these sudden Courts of Wild-Justice, with the Prison Registers before them: unwonted

---

* Félémhesi (anagram for Méhée Fils), "La Vérité tout entière sur les varis auteurs de la journée du 2 Septembre 1792 (reprinted in "Histoire Parlementaire," xviii. 156-181), p. 167.

wild tumult howling all round; the Prisoners in dread expectancy within. Swift: a name is called; bolts jingle, a Prisoner is there. A few questions are put; swiftly this sudden Jury decides: Royalist Plotter or not? Clearly not; in that case, let the Prisoner be enlarged with Vive la Nation. Probably yes; then still, Let the Prisoner be enlarged, but without Vive la Nation; or else it may run, Let the Prisoner be conducted to La Force. At La Force again their formula is, Let the Prisoner be conducted to the Abbaye—"To La Force, then!" Volunteer bailiffs seize the doomed man; he is at the outer gate; "enlarged," or "conducted," not into La Force, but into a howling sea; forth, under an arch of wild sabres, axes and pikes; and sinks, hewn asunder. And another sinks, and another; and there forms itself a piled heap of corpses, and the kennels begin to run red. Fancy the yells of these men, their faces of sweat and blood; the crueller shrieks of these women, for there are women too; and a fellow-mortal hurled naked into it all! Jourgniac, de Saint Méard has seen battle, has seen an effervescent Regiment du Roi in mutiny; but the bravest heart may quail at this. The Swiss Prisoners, remnants of the 10th of August, "clasped each other spasmodically, and hung back; gray veterans crying: ' Mercy, Messieurs; ah, mercy!' But there was no mercy. Suddenly, however, one of these men steps forward. He had on a blue frockcoat; he seemed about thirty, his stature was above common, his look noble and martial. 'I go first,' said he, 'since it must be so: adieu!' Then dashing his hat sharply behind him: ' Which way?' cried he to the Brigands: ' Show it me, then.' They open the folding gate; he is announced to the multitude. He stands a moment motionless; then plunges forth among the pikes, and dies of a thousand wounds."[*]

1296. Man after man is cut down; the sabers need sharpening, the killers refresh themselves from wine-jugs. Onward and onward goes the butchery; the loud yells wearying down into bass growls. A somber-faced shifting multitude looks on; in dull approval, or dull disapproval; in dull recognition that it is Necessary. "An Anglais in drab great-coat" was seen, or seemed to be seen, serving liquor from his own dram-bottle;—for what purpose, "if not set on by Pitt," Satan and himself know best! Witty Dr. Moore grew sick on approaching, and turned into another street.[†]—Quick enough goes this Jury-Court; and rigorous. The brave are not spared, nor the beautiful, nor the weak. Old M. de Montmorin, the Minister's Brother, was acquitted by the Tribunal of the Seventeenth; and conducted back, elbowed by howling galleries; but is not acquitted here. Princess de Lamballe has lain down on bed: "Madame, you are to be removed to the Abbaye." "I do not wish to remove; I am well enough here." There is a need-be for removing. She will arrange her dress a little, then; rude voices answer, " You have not far to go." She too is led to the hell-gate; a manifest Queen's-Friend. She shivers back, at the sight of bloody sabers; but there is no return. Onward! That fair kind head is cleft with the axe; the neck is severed. That fair body is cut in fragments; with indignities, and obscene horrors of mustachio grands-lèvres, which human nature would fain find incredible,—which shall be read in the original language only. She was beautiful, she was good, she had known no happiness. Young hearts, generation after generation, will think with themselves: O worthy of worship, thou king-descended, god-descended, and poor sister-woman! why was not I there; and some Sword Balmung or Thor's Hammer in my hand?

[*] Félémhesl. "La Vérité tout entière" (ut supra), p. 173.
[†] Moore's "Journal," i. 185-195.

Her head is fixed on a pike; paraded under the windows of the Temple, that a still more hated, a Marie Antoinette, may see. One Municipal, in the Temple with the Royal Prisoners at the moment, said, " Look out." Another eagerly whispered, "Do not look." The circuit of the Temple is guarded, in these hours, by a long stretched tricolor ribbon: terror enters, and the clangor of infinite tumult, hitherto not regicide, though that too may come.

1297. But it is more edifying to note what thrillings of affection, what fragments of wild virtues turn up in this shaking asunder of man's existence; for of these too there is a proportion. Note old .Marquis Cazotte: he is doomed to die; but his young Daughter clasps him in her arms, with an inspiration of eloquence, with a love which is stronger than very death: the heart of the killers themselves is touched by it; the old man is spared. Yet he was guilty, if plotting for his King is guilt: in ten days more a Court of Law condemned him, and he ,had to die elsewhere; bequeathing his Daughter a lock of his old gray hair. Or note old M. de Sombreuil, who also had a Daughter:—My Father is not an Aristocrat: O good gentlemen, I will swear it, and testify it, and in all ways prove it; we are not; we hate Aristocrats! "Wilt thou drink Aristocrats' blood?" The man lifts blood (if universal Rumor can be credited);[*] the poor maiden does drink. "This Sombreuil is innocent, then!" Yes, indeed,—and now note, most of all how the bloody pikes, at this news, do rattle to the ground; and the tiger-yells become bursts of jubilee over a brother saved; and the old man and his daughter are clasped to bloody bosoms, with hot tears, and borne home in triumph of Vive la Nation, the killers refusing even money! Does it seem strange, this temper of theirs? It seems very certain, well proved by Royalist testimony in other instances;[†] and very significant.

CHAPTER V.

A TRILOGY.

1298. As all Delineation, in these ages, were it never so Epic, "speaking itself and not singing itself," must either found on Belief a provable Fact, or have no foundation at all (nor, except as floating cobweb, any existence at all),—the Reader will perhaps prefer to take a glance with the very eyes of eye-witnesses; and see, in that way, for himself, how it was. Brave Jourgniac, innocent Abbé Sicard, judicious Advocate Maton, these, greatly compressing themselves, shall speak, each an instant. Jourgniac's " Agony of Thirty-eight Hours " went through " above a hundred editions," though intrinsically a poor work. Some portion of it may go through above the hundred-and-first, for want of a better.

1299. " Toward seven o'clock" (Sunday night at the Abbaye; for Jourgniac goes by dates): " We saw two men enter, their hands bloody and armed with sabers; a turnkey, with a torch, lighted them; he pointed to the bed of the unfortunate Swiss, Reding. Reding spoke with a dying voice. One of them paused; but the other cried, Allons done; lifted the unfortunate man; carried him out on his back to the street. He was massacred there.

1300. " We all looked at one another in silence, we clasped each other's hands. Motionless, with fixed eyes, we gazed on the pavement of our prison; on which lay the moonlight, checkered with the triple stancheons of our windows."

1301. " Three in the morning: They were breaking

[*] Dulaure, "Esquisses historiques des principaux événiemens de la Révolution," ii. 200 (cited in Montgaillard ii. 205).
[†] Bertrand Moleville ("Mémoires particuliers," ii. 133), etc., etc.

in one of the prison-doors. We at first thought they were coming to kill us in our room; but heard, by voices on the staircase, that it was a room where some Prisoners had barricaded themselves. They were all butchered there, as we shortly gathered."

1302. " *Ten o'clock :* The Abbé Lefant and the Abbé de Chapt-Rastignac appeared in the pulpit of the Chapel, which was our prison ; they had entered by a door from the stairs. They said to us that our end was at hand ; that we must compose ourselves, and receive their last blessing. An electric movement, not to be defined, threw us all on our knees, and we received it. These two white-haired old men, blessing us from their place above; death hovering over our heads, on all hands environing us; the moment is never to be forgotten. Half an hour after, they were both massacred, and we heard their cries."[*]— Thus Jourgniac in his " Agony " in the Abbaye: how it ended with Jourgniac, we shall see anon.

1303. But now let the good Maton speak, what he, over in La Force, in the same hours, is suffering and witnessing. This " Résurrection " by him is greatly the best, the least theatrical of these Pamphlets; and stands testing by documents:

1304. " Toward seven o'clock," on Sunday night, " prisoners were called frequently, and they did not reappear. Each of us reasoned, in his own way, on this singularity: but our ideas became calm, as we persuaded ourselves that the Memorial I had drawn up for the National Assembly was producing effect."

1305. " At one in the morning, the grate which led to our quarter opened anew. Four men in uniform, each with a drawn saber and blazing torch, came up to our corridor, preceded by a turnkey ; and entered an apartment close to ours, to investigate a box there, which we heard them break up. This done, they stept into the gallery, and questioned the man Cuissa, to know where Lamotte " (Necklace's Widower) " was." Lamotte, they said, had some months ago, under pretext of a treasure he knew of, swindled a sum of three-hundred livres from one of them, inviting him to dinner for that purpose. The wretched Cuissa, now in their hands, who indeed lost his life this night, answered trembling, That he remembered the fact well, but could not tell what was become of Lamotte. Determined to find Lamotte, and confront him with Cuissa, they rummaged, along with this latter, through various other apartments; but without effect, for we heard them say : ' Come search among the corpses, then ; for, nom de Dieu ! we must find where he is.' "

1306. " At this same time, I heard Louis Bardy, the Abbé Bardy's name called : he was brought out ; and directly massacred, as I learnt. He had been accused, along with his concubine, five or six years before, of having murdered and cut in pieces his own Brother, Auditor of the Chambre des Comptes of Montpellier; but had, by his subtlety, his dexterity, nay his eloquence, outwitted the judges, and escaped.

1307. " One may fancy what terror those words, ' Come search among the corpses, then,' had thrown me into. I saw nothing for it now but resigning myself to die. I wrote my last-will; concluding it by a petition and adjuration, that the paper should be sent to its address. Scarcely had I quitted the pen, when there came two other men in uniform; one of them, whose arm and sleeve up to the very shoulder, as well as his saber, were covered with blood, said, He was as weary as a hodman that had been beating plaster."

1308. " Baudin de la Chenaye was called sixty years of virtues could not save him. They said

A l'Abbaye: he passed the fatal outer-gate; gave a cry of terror, at sight of the heaped corpses; covered his eyes with his hands, and died of innumerable wounds. At every new opening of the grate, I thought I should hear my own name called, and see Rossignol enter."

1309. " I flung off my nightgown and cap; I put on a coarse unwashed shirt, a worn frock without waistcoat, an old round hat: these things I had sent for, some days ago, in the fear of what might happen."

1310. " The rooms of this corridor had been all emptied but ours. We were four together; whom they seemed to have forgotten: we addressed our prayers in common to the Eternal to be delivered from this peril."

1311. " Baptiste the turnkey came up by himself, to see us. I took him by the hands; I conjured him to save us; promised him a hundred louis, if he would conduct me hither. A noise coming from the grates made him hastily withdraw.

1312. " It was the noise of some dozen or fifteen men, armed to the teeth ; as we, lying flat to escape being seen, could see from our windows. ' Up stairs !' said they : ' Let not one remain.' I took out my penknife ; I considered where I should strike myself," — but reflected " that the blade was too short," and also " on religion."

1313. Finally, however, between seven and eight o'clock in the morning, enter four men with bludgeons and sabers!—" To one of whom Gérard my comrade whispered, earnestly, apart. During their colloquy I searched everywhere for shoes, that I might lay off the Advocate pumps (pantoufles de Palais) I had on," but could find none.—" Constant, called le Sauvage, Gérard, and a third whose name escapes me, they let clear off : as for me, four sabers were crossed over my breast, and they led me down. I was brought to their bar; to the Personage with the scarf, who sat as judge there. He was a lame man, of tall lank stature. He recognized me on the streets and spoke to me, seven months after. I have been assured that he was son of a retired attorney, and named Chepy. Crossing the Court called Des Nourrices, I saw Manuel haranguing in tricolor scarf." The trial, as we see, ends in acquittal and *resurrection.*[*]

1314. Poor Sicard, from the violin of the Abbaye, shall say but a few words ; true-looking, though tremulous. Toward three in the morning, the killers bethink them of this little violon ; and knock from the court. " I tapped gently, trembling lest the murderers might hear, on the opposite door, where the Section Committee was sitting : they answered gruffly, that they had no key. There were three of us in this violon : my companions thought they perceived a kind of loft overhead. But it was very high ; only one of us could reach it by mounting on the shoulders of both the others. One of them said to me, that my life was usefuller than theirs ; I resisted, they insisted : no denial ! I fling myself on the neck of these two deliverers :· never was scene more touching. I mount on the shoulders of the first, then on those of the second, finally on the loft: and address to my two comrades the expression of a soul overwhelmed with natural emotions."[†]

1315. The two generous companions, we rejoice to find, did not perish. But it is time that Jourgniac de Saint-Méard should speak his last words, and end this singular trilogy. The night had become day; and the day has again become night. Jourgniac,

---

[*] Jourgniac Saint Méard, "Mon Agonie de trente-huit heures" (reprinted in "Histoire Parlementaire," xviii. 103-126).

[*] Maton de la Varenne, "Ma Résurrection" (in "Histoire Parlementaire" xviii. 135-158).
[†] Abbé Sicard, "Relation adressée h un de ses amis (in "Histoire Parlementaire," xviii. 90-100).

worn down with uttermost agitation, was fallen asleep, and had a cheering dream: he had also contrived to make acquaintance with one of the volunteer bailiffs, and spoken in native Provençal with him. On Tuesday, about one in the morning this *Agony* is reaching its crisis.

1316. "By the glare of two torches, I now descried the terrible tribunal, where lay my life or my death. The President, in gray coat, with a saber at his side, stood leaning with his hands against a table, on which were papers, an ink-stand, tobacco-pipes and bottles. Some ten persons were around, seated or standing; two of whom had jackets and aprons: others were sleeping stretched on benches. Two men, in bloody shirts, guarded the door of the place; an old turnkey had his hand on the lock. In front of the President three men held a Prisoner, who might be about sixty" (or seventy: he was old Marshal Maillé, of the Tuileries and August Tenth). "They stationed me in a corner; my guards crossed their sabers on my breast. I looked on all sides for my Provençal: two National Guards, one of them drunk, presented some appeal from the Section of Croix Rouge in favor of the Prisoner; the man in Gray answered: 'They are useless, these appeals for traitors.' Then the Prisoner exclaimed: 'It is frightful; your judgment is a murder.' The President answered: 'My hands are washed of it; take M. Maillé away.' They drove him into the street; where through the opening of the door, I saw him massacred.

1317. "The President sat down to write; registering, I suppose, the name of this one whom they had finished; then I heard him say, 'Another (A un autre)!'

"Behold me then haled before this swift and bloody judgment-bar, where the best protection was to have no protection; and all resources of ingenuity became null if they were not founded on truth. Two of my guards held me each by a hand, the third by the collar of my coat. 'Your name, your profession?' said the President. 'The smallest lie ruins you,' added one of the Judges.—'My name is Jourgniac Saint-Méard; I have served, as an officer, twenty years: and I appear at your tribunal with the assurance of an innocent man, who therefore will not lie.'—'We shall see that,' said the President. 'Do you know why you are arrested?'—'Yes, Monsieur le Président; I am accused of editing the Journal De la Cour et de la Ville. But I hope to prove the falsity'"—But no; Jourgniac's proof of the falsity, and defense generally, though of excellent result as a defense, is not interesting to read. It is long-winded; there is a loose theatricality in the reporting of it, which does not amount to unveracity, yet which tends that way. We shall suppose him, successful, beyond hope, in proving and disproving; and skip largely,—to the catastrophe almost at two steps.

1318. "'But after all,' said one of the Judges, 'there is no smoke without kindling: tell us why they accuse you of that.'—'I was about to do so,'"—Jourgniac does so: with more and more success.

"'Nay,' continued I, 'they accuse me even of recruiting for the Emigrants!' At these words there arose a general murmur. 'O Messieurs, Messieurs!' I exclaimed, raising my voice, 'it is my turn to speak; I beg M. le Président to have the kindness to maintain it for me; I never needed it more.'—'True enough, true enough,' said almost all the Judges with a laugh: 'Silence!'

1319. "While they were examining the testimonials I had produced, a new Prisoner was brought in, and placed before the President. 'It was one Priest more,' they said, 'whom they had ferreted out of the

Chapelle.' After very few questions: 'A la Force!' He flung his breviary on the table; was buried forth, and massacred. I reappeared before the tribunal.

1320. "'You tell us always,' cried one of the Judges, with a tone of impatience, 'that you are not this, that you are not that; what are you, then?'—'I was an open Royalist.'—There arose a general murmur; which was miraculously appeased by another of the men, who had seemed to take an interest in me: 'We are not here to judge opinions, said he, 'but to judge the results of them.' Could Rousseau and Voltaire both in one, pleading for me, have said better?—'Yes, Messieurs,' cried I, 'always till the 10th of August I was an open Royalist. Ever since 'the 10th of August that cause has been finished. I am a Frenchman, true to my country. I was always a man of honor.'

1321. "'My soldiers never distrusted me. Nay, two days before that business of Nanci, when their suspicion of their officers was at its height, they chose me for commander, to lead them to Lunéville, to get back the prisoners of the Regiment Mestre-de-Camp, and seize General Malseigne.'" Which fact there is, most luckily, an individual present who by a certain token can confirm.

1322. "The President, this cross-questioning/being over, took off his hat and said: 'I see nothing to suspect in this man: I am for granting him his liberty. Is that your vote?' To which all the Judges answered: 'Oui, Oui; it is just!'"

1323. And there arose vivats within doors and without; "escort of three," amid shoutings and embracings: thus Jourgniac escaped from jury-trial and the jaws of death.* Maton and Sicard did, either by trial and no bill found, lank President Chepy finding "absolutely nothing;" or else by evasion, and new favor of Moton the brave watchmaker, likewise escape; and were embraced and wept over, weeping in return, as they well might.

1324. Thus they three, in wondrous trilogy, or triple soliloquy, uttering simultaneously, through the dread night-watches, their Night-thoughts,—grown audible to us! They Three are become audible: but the other "Thousand and Eighty-nine, of whom 202 were Priests," who also had Night-thoughts, remain inaudible; choked forever in black Death. Heard only of President Chepy and the Man in Gray!—

CHAPTER VI.
THE CIRCULAR.

1325. But the Constituted Authorities, all this while? The Legislative Assembly; the Six Ministers; the Town-hall; Santerre with the National Guard?—It is very curious to think what a City is Theaters, to the number of some twenty-three, were open every night during these prodigies; while right arms here grew weary with slaying, right arms there were twiddle-deeing on melodious catgut: at the very instant when Abbé Sicard was clambering up his second pair of shoulders three-men high, 500,000 human individuals were lying horizontal, as if nothing were amiss.

1326. As for the poor Legislative, the scepter had departed from it. The Legislative did send Deputation to the Prisons, to these Street-Courts; and poor M. Dusaulx did harangue there; but produced no conviction whatsoever: nay at last, as he continued haranguing, the Street-Court interposed, not without threats: and he had to cease, and withdraw. This is the same poor worthy old M. Dusaulx who told

* "Mon Agonie" (ut suprà. "Histoire Parlementaire," xviii. 128).

or indeed almost sang (though with cracked voice), the *Taking of the Bastille* to our satisfaction, long since. He was wont to announce himself, on such and all occasions, as the *Translator of Juvenal.* "Good Citizens, you see before you a man who loves his country, why is the Translator of Juvenal," said he once.—"Juvenal!" interrupts Sansculottism: "Who the devil is Juvenal? One of your sacrés Aristocrates? To the Lanterne!" From an orator of this kind, conviction was not to be expected. The Legislative had much ado to save one of its own Members, or ex-Members, Deputy Jouneau, who chanced to be lying in arrest for mere Parliamentary delinquencies, in these Prisons. As for poor old Dusaulx and Company, they returned to the Salle de Manége, saying, "It was dark; and they could not see well what was going on."*

1327. Roland writes indignant messages, in the name of Order, Humanity and the Law; but there is no Force at his disposal. Santerre's National Force seems lazy to rise; though he made requisitions, he says,—which always dispersed again. Nay did not we, with Advocate Maton's eyes, see "men in uniform" too, with their "sleeves bloody to the shoulder?" Pétion goes in tricolor scarf; speaks "the austere language of the law;" the killers give up, while he is there; when his back is turned, recommence. Manuel too in scarf we, with Maton's eyes, transiently saw haranguing, in the Court called of Nurses (Cour des Nourrices). On the other hand, cruel Billaud, likewise in scarf, "with that small puce coat and black wig we are used to, on him,"† audibly delivers, "standing among corpses," at the Abbaye, a short but ever-memorable harangue, reported in various phraseology, but always to this purpose: "Brave Citizens, you are extirpating the Enemies of Liberty: you are at your duty. A grateful Commune and Country would wish to recompense you adequately; but cannot, for you know its want of funds. Whoever shall have worked (travaillé) in a Prison shall receive a draft of one louis, payable by our cashier. Continue your work."‡ The Constituted Authorities are of yesterday: all pulling different ways: there is properly no Constituted Authority, but every man in his own King; and all are kinglets, belligerent, allied, or armed-neutral, without king over them.

1328. "Oh everlasting infamy," exclaims Montgaillard, "that Paris stood looking on in stupor for four days, and did not interfere!" Very desirable indeed that Paris had interfered; yet not unnatural that it stood even so, looking on in stupor. Paris is in death-panic, the enemy and gibbets at its door: whosoever in Paris has the heart to front death, finds it more pressing to do it fighting the Prussians, than fighting the killers of Aristocrats. Indignant abhorrence, as in Roland, may be here; gloomy sanction, premeditation or not, as in Marat and Committee of Salvation, may be there; dull disapproval, dull approval, and acquiescence in Necessity and Destiny, is the general temper. The Sons of Darkness, "two hundred or so," risen from their lurking-places, have scope to do their work. Urged on by fever-frenzy of Patriotism, and the madness of terror:—urged on by lucre, and the gold louis of wages? Nay, not lucre; for the gold watches, rings, money of the Massacred, are punctually brought to the Town-hall, by Killers sans-indispensables, who higgle afterward for their twenty shillings of wages; and Sergent sticking an uncommonly fine agate on his finger (fully "meaning to account for it") becomes *Agate-*Sergent. But the temper, as we say, is

dull acquiescence. Not till the Patriotic or Frenetic part of the work is finished for want of material; and Sons of Darkness, bent clearly on lucre alone, begin wrenching watches and purses, brooches from ladies' necks, "to equip volunteers," in daylight, on the streets,—does the temper from dull grow vehement; does the Constable raise his truncheon, and striking heartily (like a cattle-driver in earnest) beat the "course of things" back into its old regulated drove-roads. The Garde-Meuble itself was surreptitiously plundered, on the 17th of the month, to Roland's new horror; who anew bestirs himself, and is, as Sieyes says, "the veto of scoundrels," Roland veto des coquins.*

1329. This is the September Massacre, otherwise called "Severe Justice of the People." These are the Septemberers (Septembriseurs), a name of some note and lucency,—but lucency of the nether-fire sort; very different from that of our Bastille Heroes, who shone, disputable by no Friend of Freedom, as in Heavenly-light radiance: to such phasis of the business have we advanced since then! The numbers massacred are in the Historical *fantasy,* "between two and three thousand;" or indeed they are upward of 6,000," for Peltier (in vision) saw them massacring the patients, of the Bicêtre Madhouse "with grape-shot;" nay finally they are "12,000" and odd hundreds,—not more than that.† In Arithmetical ciphers, and Lists drawn up by accurate Advocate Maton, the number, including 202 priests, three "persons unknown," and "one thief killed at the Bernadins," is as above hinted, 1089,—not less than that.

1330. A Thousand and eighty-nine lie dead, 260 heaped carcasses on the Pont au Change" itself;—among which, Robespierre pleading afterward will "nearly weep" to reflect that there was said to be one slain innocent.‡ One; not two, O thou sea-green Incorruptible? If so, Themis Sansculotte must be lucky; for she was brief!—In the dim Registers of the Town-hall, which are preserved to this day, men read, with a certain sickness of heart, items and entries not usual in Town Books: "To workers employed in preserving the salubrity of the air in the Prisons, and persons who presided over these dangerous operations," so much,—in various items, nearly £700 sterling. To carters employed to "the Burying-grounds of Clamart, Montrouge and Vangirard," at so much a journey, per cart; this also is an entry. Then so many francs and odd sous "for the necessary quantity of quicklime!"§ Carts go along the streets; full of stript human corpses, thrown pell-mell; limbs sticking up:—seest thou that cold Hand sticking up, through the heaped embrace of brother corpses, in its yellow paleness, in its cold rigor; the palm opened toward Heaven, as if in dumb prayer, in expostulation de profundis, Take pity on the Sons of Men!—Mercier saw it, as he walked down "the Rue Saint-Jacques from Montrouge, on the morrow of the Massacres:" but not a Hand; it was a Foot,—which he reckons still more significant, one understands not well why. Or was it at the Foot of one *spurning* Heaven? Rushing, like a wild diver, in disgust and despair, toward the depths of Annihilation? Even there shall His hand find thee, and His right hand hold thee,—surely for right not for wrong, for good not evil! "I saw that Foot," says Mercier; "I shall know it again at the great Day of Judgment, when the Eternal, throned on his

* Moniteur, Debate of 2d September, 1792.
† Méhée Fils (ut suprà, in "Histoire Parlementaire," xviii. p. 189).
‡ Montgaillard, iii. 191.

* Helen Maria Williams, iii. 27.
† See "Histoire Parlementaire," xvii. 421, 422.
‡ Moniteur of 6th November (Debate of 5th November, 1793).
§ "Etats des sommes payées par la Commune de Paris," ("Histoire Parlementaire," xviii. 211).

thunders, shall judge both Kings and September-berers."*

1331. That a shriek of inarticulate horror rose over this thing, not only from French Aristocrats and Moderates, but from all Europe, and has prolonged itself to the present day, was most natural and right. The thing lay done, irrevocable; a thing to be counted beside some other things, which lie very black in our Earth's Annals; yet which will not erase therefrom. For man, as was remarked, has transcendentalism in him; standing, as he does, poor creature, every way "in the confluence of Infinitudes;" a mystery to himself and others; in the center of two Eternities, of three Immensities,—in the intersection of primeval Light with the everlasting Dark!—Thus have there been, especially by vehement tempers reduced to a state of desperation, very miserable things done. Sicilian Vespers, and "8,000 slaughtered in two hours," are a known thing. Kings themselves, not in desperation, but only in difficulty, have sat hatching; for year and day (nay De Thou says for seven years), their Bartholomew Business; and then, at the right moment, also on an Autumn Sunday, this very Bell (they say it is the identical metal) of Saint-Germain l'Auxerrois was set a-pealing—with effect.† Nay the same black boulder-stones of these Paris Prisons have seen Prison-massacres before now: men massacring countrymen, Burgundies massacring Armagnacs, whom they had suddenly imprisoned, till, as now, there were piled heaps of carcasses, and the streets ran red;—the Mayor Pétion of the time speaking the austere language of the law, and answered by the Killers, in old French (it is some 400 years old): "Maugré bieu, Sire,—(Sir God's malison) on your 'justice,' your 'pity,' your 'right reason.' Cursed be of God whoso shall have pity on these false traitorous Armagnacs, English ; dogs they are; they have destroyed us, wasted this realm of France, and sold it to the English."‡ And so they slay, and fling aside the slain, to the extent of "1518, among whom are found four Bishops of false and damnable counsel, and two Presidents of Parlement." For though it is not Satan's world this that we live in, Satan always has his place in it (under-ground properly): and from time to time bursts up. Well may mankind shriek, inarticulately anathematizing as they can. There are actions of such emphasis that no shrieking can be too emphatic for them. Shriek ye; acted have they.

1332. Shriek who might in this France, in this Legislative or Paris Town-hall, there are Ten Men who do not shriek. A Circular goes out from the Committee of Salut Public, dated 3d of September, 1792; directed to all Town-halls: a State-paper too remarkable to be overlooked. "A part of the ferocious conspirators detained in the Prisons," it says, "have been put to death by the People; and we cannot doubt but the whole Nation, driven to the edge of ruin by such endless series of treasons will make haste to adopt *this* means of public salvation: and all Frenchmen will cry as the men of Paris: We go to fight the enemy; but we will not leave robbers behind us, to butcher our wives and children." To which are legibly appended these signatures: Panis; Sergent: Marat, Friend of the People :⁂ with Seven others;—carried down thereby, in a strange way, to the late remembrance of Antiquarians. We remark, however, that their Circular rather recoiled on themselves. The Town-halls made no use of it, even the

distracted Sansculottes made little; they only howled and bellowed, but did not bite. At Rheims "about eight persons" were killed; and two afterward were hanged for doing it. At Lyons, and a few other places, some attempt was made; but with hardly any effect, being quickly put down.

1333. Less fortunate were the Prisoners of Orléans was the good Duke de la Rochefoucault. He journeying, by quick stages, with his Mother and Wife, toward the Waters of Forges, or some quieter country, was arrested at Gisors; conducted along the streets, amid effervescing multitudes, and killed dead "by the stroke of a paving-stone hurled through the coach-window." Killed as a once Liberal now Aristocrat; Protector of Priests, Suspender of Virtuous Pétions, and most unfortunate Hot-grown-cold, detestable to Patriotism. He dies, lamented of Europe; his blood spattered the cheeks of his old Mother, ninety-three years old.

1334. As for the Orléans Prisoners, they are State Criminals:· Royalist Ministers, Delessarts, Montmorins; who have been accumulating on the High Court of Orléans, ever since that Tribunal was set up. Whom now it seems good that we should get transferred to our New Paris Court of the Seventeenth; which proceeds far quicker. Accordingly hot Fournier from Martinique, Fournier l'Américain, is off missioned by Constituted Authority; with stanch National Guards, with Lazouski the Pole; sparingly provided with road-money. These, through bad quarters, through difficulties, perils, for Authorities cross each other in this time,—do triumphantly bring off the Fifty or Fifty-three Orléans Prisoners toward Paris; where a swifter Court of the Seventeenth will do justice on them.* But lo, at Paris, in the interim, a still swifter and swiftest Court of the *Second*, and of *September*, has instituted itself· enter not Paris, or that will judge you!—What shall hot Fournier do? It was his duty, as volunteer Constable, had he been a perfect character, to guard those men's lives never so Aristocratic, at the expense of his own valuable life never so Sansculottic, till some Constituted Court had disposed of them. But he was an imperfect. character and Constable; perhaps one of the more imperfect.

1335. Hot Fournier, ordered to turn hither by one Authority, to turn thither by another Authority, is in a perplexing multiplicity of orders; but finally he strikes off for Versailles. His Prisoners fare in tumbrils, or open carts, himself and Guards riding and marching around: and at the last village, the worthy Mayor of Versailles comes to meet him, anxious that the arrival and locking-up were well over. It is Sunday, the 9th day of the month. Lo, on entering the Avenue of Versailles, what multitudes, stirring, swarming in the September sun, under the dull-green September foliage; the Four-rowed Avenue all humming and swarming, as if the Town had emptied itself! Our tumbrils roll heavily through the living sea; the Guards and Fournier making way with ever more difficulty; the Mayor speaking and gesturing his persuasivest; amid the inarticulate growling hum, which growls ever the deeper even by hearing itself growl, not without sharp yelping here and there:—Would to God we were out of this strait place, and wind and separation had cooled the heat, which seems about igniting here!

1336. And yet if the wide Avenue is too strait, what will the Street de Surintendance be, at leaving of the same ? At the corner of Surintendance Street, the compressed yelpings become a continuous yell: savage figures spring on the tumbril-shafts; first sprays of an endless coming tide? The Mayor pleads,

---

* Mercier, "Nouveaux Paris," vi. 21.
† 9th to 13th September, 1572 (Dulaure, "Histoire de Paris," iv. 289).
‡ Dulaure, iii. 494.
⁂ "Histoire Parlementaire," xvii. 433.

* Ibid. xvii. 434.

pushes, half-desperate; is pushed; carried off in men's arms: the savage tide has entrance, has mastery. Amid horrid noise, and tumult as of fierce wolves, the Prisoners sink massacred,—all but some eleven, who escaped into houses, and found mercy. The Prisons, and what other Prisoners they held, were with difficulty saved. The stript clothes are burnt in bonfire; the corpses lie heaped in the ditch on the morrow morning.* All France, except it be the Ten Men of the Circular and their people, moans and rages, inarticulately shrieking; all Europe rings.

1337. But neither did Danton shriek; though, as Minister of Justice, it was more his part to do so. Brawny Danton is in the breach, as of stormed Cities and Nations; amid the sweep of Tenth-of-August cannon, the rustle of Prussian gallows-ropes, the smiting of September sabers; destruction all round him, and the rushing down of worlds: Minister of Justice is his name; but Titan of the Forlorn Hope, and Enfant Perdu of the Revolution, in his quality, —and the man acts according to that. "We must put our enemies in fear!" Deep fear, is it not, as of its own accord, falling on our enemies? The Titan of the Forlorn Hope, he is not the man that would swiftest of all prevent its so falling. Forward, thou Titan of an Enfant Perdu; thou must dare and again dare, and without end dare; there is nothing left for thee but that! "Que mon nom soit flétri (Let my name be blighted):" what am I? The Cause alone is great; and shall live, and not perish.—So, on the whole, here too is a Swallower of Formulas; of still wider gulp than Mirabeau: this Danton, Mirabeau of the Sansculottes. In the September days, this Minister was not heard of as co-operating with strict Roland; his business might lie elsewhere,—with Brunswick and the Hotel-de-Ville. When applied to by an official person, about the Orléans Prisoners, and the risks they ran, he answered gloomily, twice over, "Are not these men guilty?"—When pressed, he "answered in a terrible voice," and turned his back.† A thousand slain in the Prisons; horrible if you will; but Brunswick is within a day's journey of us; and there are Five-and-twenty Millions yet, to slay or to save. Some men have tasks,—fruitfuler than ours! It seems strange, but is not strange, that this Minister of Moloch-Justice, when any suppliant for a friend's life got access to him, was found to have human compassion; and yielded and granted "always;" "neither did one personal enemy of Danton perish in these days."‡

1338. To shriek, we say; when certain things are acted, is proper and unavoidable. Nevertheless, articulate speech, not shrieking, is the faculty of man: when speech is not yet possible, let there be, with the shortest delay, at least—silence. Silence, accordingly, in this forty-fourth year of the business, and eighteen hundred and thirty-sixth of an "Era called Christian as lucus à non," is the thing we recommend and practice. Nay, instead of shrieking more, it were perhaps edifying to remark, on the other side, what a singular thing Customs (in Latin, Mores) are; and how fitly the Virtue, Vir-tus, Manhood or Worth, that is in a man, is called his Morality or Customariness. Fell Slaughter, one of the most authentic products of the Pit you would say, once give it Customs, becomes War, with Laws of War; and is Customary and Moral enough; and red individuals carry the tools of it girt round their haunches, not without an air of pride,—which do thou nowise blame. While, see! so long as it is but dressed in hodden or russet;

and Revolution, less frequent than War, has not yet got its Laws of Revolution, but the hodden or russet individuals are Uncustomary—O shrieking beloved brother blockheads of Mankind, let us close those wide mouths of ours; let us cease shrieking, and begin considering!

CHAPTER VII.

SEPTEMBER IN ARGONNE.

1339. Plain, at any rate, is one thing: that the *fear*, whatever of fear those Aristocrat enemies might need, has been brought about. The matter is getting serious, then! Sansculottism too has become a Fact, and seems minded to assert itself as such? This huge moon-calf of Sansculottism, staggering about, as young calves do, is not mockable only, and soft like another calf; but terrible too, if you prick it; and, through its hideous nostrils, blows fire!—Aristocrats, with pale panic in their hearts, fly toward covert; and a light rises to them over several things; or rather a confused transition toward light, whereby for the moment darkness is only darker than ever. But what will become of this France? Here is a question! France is dancing its desert-waltz, as Sahara does when the winds waken; in whirl-blasts 25,000,000 in number; waltzing toward Town-halls, Aristocrat Prisons and Election Committee-rooms; toward Brunswick and the frontiers; toward a New Chapter of Universal History; if indeed it be not the *Finis*, and winding-up of that!

1340. In Election Committee-rooms there is now no dubiety; but the work goes bravely along. The Convention is getting chosen,—really in a decisive spirit; in the Town-hall we already date *First year of the Republic*. Some 200 of our best Legislators may be re-elected, the Mountain bodily: Robespierre, with Mayor Pétion, Buzot, Curate Grégoire, Rabaut, some three-score Old-Constituents; though we once had only "thirty voices." All these; and along with them, friends long known to Revolutionary fame: Camille Desmoulins, though he stutters in speech; Manuel, Tallien and Company; Journalists Gorsas, Carra, Mercier, Louvet of Faublas; Clootz, Speaker of Mankind; Collot d'Herbois, tearing a passion to rags; Fabre d'Eglantine, speculative Pamphleteer; Legendre, the solid Butcher: nay Marat, though rural France can hardly believe it, or even believe that there *is* a Marat, except in print. Of Minister Danton, who will lay down his Ministry for a Membership, we need not speak. Paris is fervent; nor is the Country wanting to itself. Barbaroux, Rebecqui, and fervid Patriots are coming from Marseilles. Seven hundred and forty-five men, (or indeed forty-nine, for Avignon now sends Four) are gathering: so many are to meet; not so many are to part!

1341. Attorney Carrier from Aurillac, Ex-Priest Lebon from Arras, these shall both gain a *name*. Mountainous Auvergne re-elects her Romme; hardy tiller of the soil, once Mathematical Professor, who, unconscious, carries in petto a remarkable *New Calendar*, with Messidors, Pluvioses, and such-like;— and having given it well forth. shall depart by the death they call *Roman*. Sieyes Old-Constituent comes; to make new Constitutions as many as wanted: for the rest, peering out of his clear cautious eyes, he will cower low in many an emergency, and find silence safest. Young Saint-Just is coming, deputed by Aisne in the North; more like a Student than a Senator; not four-and-twenty yet, who has written Books; a youth of slight stature, with mild mellow voice, enthusiast olive-complexion and long black hair. Féraud, from the far valley D'Aure in the folds of the Pyrenees, is coming; an ardent Republican; doomed to fame, at least in death.

---

* "Pièces officielles relatives au massacre des Prisonniers à Versailles" (in "Histoire Parlementaire," xviii. 236-249.
† "Biographie des Ministres," p. 97.
‡ Ibid. p. 103.

1342. All manner of Patriot men are coming: Teachers, Husbandmen, Priests and Ex-Priests, Traders, Doctors; above all, Talkers, or the Attorney species. Man-midwives, as Levasseur of the Sarthe, are not wanting. Nor Artists: gross David, with the swoln cheek, has long painted, with genius in a state of convulsion; and will now legislate. The swoln cheek, choking his words in the birth, totally disqualifies him as an orator; but his pencil, his head, his gross hot heart, with genius in a state of convulsion, will be there. A man bodily and mentally swoln-cheeked, disproportionate; flabby-large, instead of great; weak withal as in a state of convulsion, not strong in a state of composure: so let him play his part. Nor are naturalized Benefactors of the Species forgotten: Priestly, elected by the Orne Department, but declining; Paine the rebellious Needleman, by the Pas de Calais, who accepts.

1343. Few Nobles come, and yet not none. Paul-François Barras, "noble as the Barrases, old as the rocks of Provence;" he is one. The reckless, shipwrecked man: flung ashore on the coast of the Maldives long ago, while sailing and soldiering as Indian Fighter: flung ashore since then, as hungry Parisian pleasure-hunter and half-pay, on many a Circe Island, with temporary enchantment, temporary conversion into beasthood and hoghood,—the remote Var Department has now sent him hither. A man of heat and haste; defective in utterance; defective indeed in anything to utter; yet not without a certain rapidity of glance, a certain swift transient courage; who in these times, Fortune favoring, may go far. He is tall, handsome to the eye, " only the complexion a little yellow ;" but " with a robe of purple, with a scarlet cloak and plume of tricolor, on occasions of solemnity," the man will look well.* Lepelletier Saint-Fargeau, Old-Constituent, is a kind of noble, and of enormous wealth ; he too has come hither :—to have the Pain of Death abolished? Hapless Ex-Parlementeer! Nay among our Sixty Old-Constituents see Philippe d'Orléans, a Prince of the Blood! Not now D'Orleans: for, Feudalism being swept from the world, he demands of his worthy friends the Electors of Paris, to have a new name of their choosing; whereupon Procureur Manuel, like an antithetic literary man, recommends Equality, Égalité. A Philippe Égalité therefore will sit, seen of the Earth and Heaven.

1344. Such a Convention is gathering itself together. Mere angry poultry in moulting season ; whom Brunswick's grenadiers and cannoneers will give short account of. Would the weather, as Bertrand always praying, only mend a little!†

1345. In vain, O Bertrand! The weather will not mend a whit: nay even if it did? Dumouriez Poly-metis, though Bertrand knows it not, started from brief slumber at Sedan, on that morning of the 29th of August; with stealthiness, with promptitude, audacity. Some three mornings after that, Brunswick, opening wide eyes, perceives the Passes of the Argonne all seized; blocked with felled trees, fortified with camps; and that it is a most shifty swift Dumouriez this, who has outwitted him!

1346. The maneuver may cost Brunswick " a loss of three weeks," very fatal in these circumstances. A Mountain-wall of forty miles lying between him and Paris: which he should have preoccupied;—which how now to get possession of? Also the rain it raineth every day; and we are in a hungry Champagne Pouilleuse, a land flowing only with ditchwater. How to cross this Mountain-wall of the Argonne; or what in the world to do with it?—There are marchings and wet splashings by steep

paths, with sackerments and guttural interjections; forcings of Argonne Passes,—which unhappily will not force. Through the woods, volleying War reverberates, like huge gong-music, or Moloch's kettledrum, borne by the echoes; swoln torrents boil angrily round the foot of rocks, floating pale carcasses of men. In vain! Islettes Villages, with its church-steeple, rises intact in the Mountain-pass, between the embosoming heights; your forced marchings and climbings have become forced slidings and tumblings back. From the hill-tops thou seest nothing but dumb crags, and endless wet moaning woods; the Clermont Vache (huge Cow that she is) disclosing herself* at intervals; flinging off her cloud-blanket, and soon taking it on again, drowned in the pouring Heaven. The Argonne Passes will not force: you must skirt the Argonne: go round by the end of it.

1347. But fancy whether the Emigrant Seigneurs have not got their brilliancy dulled a little; whether that " Foot Regiment in red-facings with nankeen trousers " could be in field-day order! In place of gasconading, a sort of desperation, and hydrophobia from excess of water, is threatening to supervene. Young Prince de Ligne, son of that brave literary De Ligne the Thunder-god of Dandies, fell backward ; shot dead in Grand-Pré, the Northmost of the Passes: Brunswick is skirting and rounding, laboriously, by the extremity of the South. Four days; days of a rain as of Noah,—without fire, without food! For fire you cut down green trees, and produce smoke; for food you eat green grapes, and produce colic, pestilential dysentery δλέχοντα δὲ λαοί. And the Peasants assassinate us, they do not join us; shrill women cry shame on us, threaten to draw their very scissors on us! O ye hapless dullen-bright Seigneurs, and hydrophobic splashed Nankeens;—but O, ten times more, ye poor sackermenting ghastly-visaged Hessians and Hulans, fallen on your backs; who had no call to die there, except compulsion and three half-pence a-day! Nor has Mrs. le Blanc of the Golden Arm a good time of it, in her bower of dripping rushes. Assassinating Peasants are hanged; Old-Constituent Honorable Members, though of venerable age, ride in carts with their hands tied: these are the woes of war.

1348. Thus they; sprawling and wriggling, far and wide, on the slopes and passes of the Argonne;—a loss to Brunswick of five-and-twenty disastrous days. There is wriggling and struggling; facing, backing and right-about facing ; as the positions shift, and the Argonne gets partly rounded, partly forced:—but still Dumouriez, force him, round him as you will, sticks like a rooted fixture on the ground; fixture with many hinges ; wheeling now this way, now that ; showing always new front, in the most unexpected manner; nowise consenting to take himself away. Recruits stream up on him; full of heart; yet rather difficult to deal with. Behind Grand-Pré for example, Grand-Pré which is on the wrong-side of the Argonne, for we are now forced and rounded, —the full heart, in one of those wheelings and showings of new front, did as it were overset itself, as full hearts are liable to do; and there rose a shriek of sauve qui peut, and a death-panic which had nigh ruined all! So that the General had to come galloping; and, with thunder-words, with gesture, stroke of drawn sword even, check and rally, and bring back the sense of shame;—nay, to seize the first shriekers and ringleaders; "shave their heads and eyebrows," and pack them forth in the world as a sign. Thus too (for really the rations are short, and wet camping with hungry stomach brings bad humor) there

---

is like to be mutiny. Whereupon again Dumouriez "arrives at the head of their line, with his staff, and an escort of a hundred hussars. He had placed some squadrons behind them, the artillery in front; he said to them: 'As for you, for I will neither call your citizens, nor soldiers, nor my men (ni mes enfans), you see before you this artillery, behind you this cavalry. You have dishonored yourselves by crimes. If you amend, and grow to behave like this brave Army which you have the honor of belonging to, you will find in me a good father. But plunderers and assassins I do not suffer here. At the smallest mutiny I will have you shivered in pieces (hacher en pièces). Seek out the Scoundrels that are among you, and dismiss them yourselves; I hold you responsible for them.'"*

1349. Patience, O Dumouriez! This uncertain heap of shriekers, mutineers, were they once drilled and inured, will become a phalanxed mass of Fighters; and wheel and whirl, to order, swiftly like the wind or the whirlwind : tanned mustachio-figures; often bare-foot, even bare-backed ; with sinews of iron : who require only bread and gunpowder : very Sons of Fire, the adroitest, hastiest, hottest ever seen perhaps, since Attila's time. They may conquer and overrun amazingly, much as that same Attila did ;—whose Attila's Camp and Battle-field thou now seest, on this very ground,† who, after sweeping bare the world, was, with difficulty, and days of tough fighting, checked here by Roman Ætius and Fortune; and his dust-cloud made to vanish in the East again !—

1350. Strangely enough, in this shrieking Confusion of a Soldiery, which we saw long since fallen; all suicidal collision,—at Nanci, or on the streets of Metz, where brave Bouillé stood with drawn sword; and which has collided and ground itself to pieces worse and worse ever since, down now to such a state; in this shrieking Confusion, and not elsewhere, lies the first germ of returning Order for France ! Round which, we say, poor France nearly all ground down suicidally likewise into rubbish and Chaos, will be glad to rally; to begin growing, and new-shaping her inorganic dust; very slowly, through centuries, through Napoleons, Louis Philippes, and other the like media and phases,—into a new, infinitely preferable France, we can hope!—

1351. These wheelings and movements in the region of the Argonne, which are all faithfully described by Dumouriez himself, and more interesting to us than Hoyle's or Philidor's best Game of Chess, let us nevertheless, O Reader, entirely omit;—and hasten to remark two things : the first a minute private, the second a large public thing. Our minute private thing is : the presence, in the Prussian host, in that war-game of the Argonne, of a certain Man, belonging to the sort called Immortal; who, in days since then, is becoming visible more and more in that character, as the Transitory more and more vanishes: for from of old it was remarked that when the Gods appear among men, it is seldom in recognizable shape; thus Admetus's neat-herds give Apollo a draught of their goat-skin whey-bottle (well if they do not give him strokes with their ox-rungs) not dreaming that he is the Sun-god! This man's name is Johann Wolfgang von Goethe. He is Herzog Weimar's Minister, come with the small contingent of Weimar ; to do insignificant unmilitary duty here; very irrecognizable to nearly all! He stands at present, with drawn bridle, on the height near Sainte-Menehould, making an experiment on the "cannon-fever;" having ridden thither against persuasion, into the dance and firing of the cannon-balls with a scientific desire to understand what that same cannon-fever may be: "The

sound of them," says he, "is curious enough ; as if it were compounded of the humming of tops, the gurgling of water and the whistle of birds. By degrees you get a very uncommon sensation; which can only be described by similitude. It seems as if you were in some place extremely hot, and at the same time were completely penetrated by the heat of it; so that you feel as if you and this element you are in were perfectly on a par. The eye-sight loses nothing of its strength or distinctness; and yet it is as if all things had got a kind of brown-red color, which makes the situation and the object still more impressive on you."*

1352. This is the cannon-fever, as a World-Poet feels it.—A man entirely irrecognizable ! In whose irrecognizable head, meanwhile there verily is the spiritual counterpart (and call it complement) of this same huge Death-Birth of the World: which now effectuates itself, outwardly in the Argonne, in such cannon-thunder ; inwardly, in the irrecognizable head, quite otherwise than by thunder ! Mark that man, O Reader, as the memorablest of all the memorable in this Argonne Campaign. What we say of him is not dream, nor flourish of rhetoric, but scientific historic fact ; as many men, now at this distance, see or begin to see.

1353. But the large public thing we had to remark is this : That the 20th of September, 1792, was a raw morning covered with mist; that from three in the morning, Sainte-Menehould, and those Villages and homesteads we know of old, were stirred by the rumble of artillery-wagons, by the clatter of hoofs and many-footed tramp of men: all manner of military, Patriot and Prussian, taking up positions, on the Heights of La Lune and other Heights; shifting and shoving,—seemingly in some dread chess-game; which may the Heavens turn to good ! The Miller of Valmy has fled dusty under ground; his Mill were it never so windy, will have rest to-day. At seven in the morning the mist clears off: see Kellermann, Dumouriez's second in command, with "eighteen pieces of cannon," and deep-serried ranks, drawn up round that same silent Windmill, on his knoll of strength ; Brunswick, also with serried ranks and cannon, glooming over to him from the Height of La Lune ; only the brook and its little dell now parting them.

1354. So that the much-longed-for has come at last! Instead of hunger and dysentery, we shall have sharp shot; and then !—Dumouriez, with force and firm front, looks on from a neighboring height ; can help only with his wishes, in silence. Lo, the eighteen pieces do bluster and bark, responsive to the bluster of La Lune ; and thunder-clouds mount into the air : and echoes roar through all dells, far into the depths of Argonne Wood (deserted now) ; and limbs and lives of men dissipated, this way and that. Can Brunswick make an impression on them ? The dulled-bright Seigneurs stand biting their thumbs: these Sansculottes seem *not* to fly like poultry ! Toward noontide a cannon shot blows Kellermann's horse from under him; there bursts a powder-cart high into the air, with knell heard over all : some swagging and swaying observable ; —Brunswick will try! "Camarades," cries Kellermann, "Vive la Patrie ! Allons vaincre pourelle (Come let us conquer for her)." "Live the Fatherland !" rings responsive to the welkin. like rolling-fire from side to side : our ranks are as firm as rocks; and Brunswick may recross the dell, ineffectual ; regain his old position on La Lune ; not unbattered by the way. And so, for the length of a September day,—with bluster and bark : with bellow far-echoing ! The cannonade lasts till sunset; and no impression made. Till an hour after

---

* Dumouriez, "Mémoires," (ii. 55.
† Helen Maria Williams, (ii. 32.

* Goethe, "Campagne in Frankreich" (Werke, xxx. 73.)

sunset, the few remaining Clocks of the District striking Seven; at this late time of day Brunswick tries again. With not a whit better fortune! He is met by rock-ranks, by shouts of Vive la Patrie; and driven back, not unbattered. Whereupon he ceases; retires "to the Tavern of La Lune;" and sets to raising a redoubt lest *he* be attacked!

1355. Verily so, ye dulled-bright Seigneurs, make of it what ye may. Ah, and France does not rise round us in mass: and the Peasants do not join us but assassinate us: neither hanging nor any persuasion will induce them! They have lost their old distinguishing love of King and King's cloak,—I fear, altogether; and will even fight to be rid of it: that seems now their humor. Nor does Austria prosper, nor the siege of Thionville. The Thionvillers, carrying their insolence to the epigrammatic pitch, have put a Wooden Horse on their walls, with a bundle of Hay hung from him, and this Inscription: "When I finish my hay, you will take Thionville."* To such height has the frenzy of mankind risen.

1356. The trenches of Thionville may shut; and what though those of Lille open? The Earth smiles not on us, nor the Heaven; but weeps and blears itself, in sour rain, and worse. Our very friends insult us; we are wounded in the house of our friends: "His Majesty of Prussia had a great-coat, when the rain came; and (contrary to all known laws) he put it on, though our two French Princes, the hope of their country, had none!" To which indeed; as Goethe admits, what answer could be made?†—Cold and Hunger and Affront, Colic and Dysentery and Death; and we here, cowering *redoubted*, most unredoubtable, amid the "tattered corn-shocks and deformed stubble;" on the splashy Height of La Lune, round the mean Tavern de la Lune!—

1357. This is the Cannonade of Valmy; wherein the World-Poet experimented on the cannon-fever; wherein the French Sansculottes did not fly like poultry. Precious to France! Every soldier did his duty, and Alsatian Kellermann (how preferable to old Lückner the dismissed!) began to become greater; and Égalité Fils (Equality Junior), a light gallant Field-Officer, distinguished himself by intrepidity: —it is the same intrepid individual who now, as Louis Philippe, without the Equality, struggles, under sad circumstances, to be called King of the French for a season.

CHAPTER VIII.

EXEUNT.

1358. But this 20th of September is otherwise a great day. For, observe, while Kellermann's horse was flying blown from under him at the Mill of Valmy, our new National Deputies, that shall be a NATIONAL CONVENTION, are hovering and gathering about the Hall of the Hundred Swiss: with intent to constitute themselves!

1359. On the morrow, about noontide, Camus the Archivist is busy "verifying their powers;" several hundreds of them already here. Whereupon the Old Legislative comes solemnly over, to merge its old ashes phœnix-like in the body of the new;—and so forthwith, returning all solemnly back to the Salle de Manége, there sits a National Convention, 749 complete, or complete enough; presided by Pétion; —which proceeds directly to do business. Read that reported afternoon's debate, O Reader: there are few debates like it: dull reporting Moniteur itself becomes more dramatic than a very Shakespeare. For epigrammatic Manuel rises, speaks strange things; how the President shall have a guard of honor, and

lodge in the Tuileries:—*rejected*. And Danton rises and speaks; and Collot d'Herbois rises, and Curate Grégoire, and lame Couthon of the Mountain rises; and in rapid Melibœan stanzas, only a few lines each, they propose motions not a few: That the cornerstone of our new Constitution is, Sovereignty of the People; that our Constitution shall be accepted by the People or be null; further that the people ought to be avenged, and have right Judges; that the Imposts must continue till new order; that Landed and other Property be sacred forever; finally that "Royalty from this day is abolished in France:"—*Decreed* all, before four o'clock strike, with acclamation of the world!* The tree was all so ripe; only shake it, and there fall such yellow cart-loads.

1360. And so over in the Valmy Region, as soon as the news come, what stir is this, audible, visible from our muddy Heights of La Lune?† Universal shouting of the French on their opposite hill-side; caps raised on bayonets: and a sound as of République: Vive la République borne dubious on the winds!—On the morrow morning, so to speak, Brunswick slings his knapsacks before day, lights any fires he has; and marches without tap of drum. Dumouriez finds ghastly symptoms in that camp; "latrines full of blood!"‡ The chivalrous King of Prussia.—for he, as we saw, is here in person,—may long rue the day: may look colder than ever on these dulled-bright Seigneurs, and French Princes their Country's hope;—and, on the whole, put on his great-coat without ceremony, happy that he has one. They retire, all retire with convenient dispatch, through a Champagne trodden into a quagmire, the wild weather pouring on them: Dumouriez, through his Kellermanns and Dillons, pricking them a little in the hinder parts. A little, not much; now pricking, now negotiating: for Brunswick has his eyes opened; and the Majesty of Prussia is a repentant Majesty.

1361. Nor has Austria prospered; nor the Wooden Horse of Thionville bitten his hay; nor Lille City surrendered itself. The Lille trenches opened on the 29th of the month; with balls and shells, and red-hot balls; as if not trenches but Vesuvius and the Pit had opened. It was frightful, say all eyewitnesses; but it is ineffectual. The Lillers have risen to such temper; especially after these news from Argonne and the East. Not a Sans-indispensables in Lille that would surrender for a King's ransom. Red-hot balls rain, day and night, "6,000," or so, and bombs "filled internally with oil of turpentine which splashes up in flame;"—mainly on the dwellings of the Sansculottes and Poor; the streets of the Rich being spared. But the Sansculottes get water-pails; form quenching-regulations: "The ball is in Peter's house!" "The ball is in John's!" They divide their lodging and substance with each other; shout Vive la République; and faint not in heart. A ball thunders through the main chamber of the Hotel-de-Ville while the Commune is there assembled: "We are in permanence," says one coldly, proceeding with his business; and the ball remains permanent too, sticking in the wall, probably to this day.§

1362. The Austrian Archduchess (Queen's Sister) will herself see red artillery fired: in their overhaste to satisfy an Archduchess, "two mortars explode and kill thirty persons." It is in vain; Lille, often burning, is always quenched again: Lille will not yield. The very boys deftly wrench the matches out of fallen bombs: "a man clutches a rolling ball

* "Histoire Parlementaire," xix. 177.
† Goethe, xxx. 49.

* "Histoire Parlementaire," xix. 19.
† Williams. iii. 71.
‡ 1st October. 1792; Dumouriez, iii. 73.
§ "Bombardement de Lille" (in "Histoire Parlementaire," xx. 63-71).

with his hat, which takes fire; when cool, they crown it with a bonnet rouge." Memorable also be that nimble Barber, who when the bomb burst beside him, snatched up a sherd of it, introduced soap and lather into it, crying "Voilà mon plat à barbe (My new shaving-dish)!" and shaved "fourteen people" on the spot. Bravo, thou nimble shaver; worthy to shave old spectral Red-cloak, and find treasures!—On the eighth day of this desperate siege, the 6th day of October, Austria, finding it fruitless, draws off, with no pleasurable consciousness; rapidly, Dumouriez tending thitherward; and Lille, too, black with ashes and smoulder, but jubilant sky-high, flings its gates open. The Plat à barbe became fashionable; "no Patriot of an elegant turn," says Mercier several years afterward, "but shaves himself out of the splinter of a Lille bomb."

1363. Quid multa (Why many words)? The Invaders are in flight; Brunswick's Host, the third part of it gone to death, staggers disastrous along the deep highways of Champagne; spreading out also into "the fields of a tough spongy red-colored clay:" —"like Pharaoh through a Red Sea of Mud," says Goethe; "for here also lay broken chariots, and riders and foot seemed sinking around."* On the eleventh morning of October, the World-Poet, struggling Northward out of Verdun, which he had entered Southward, some five weeks ago, in quite other order, discerned the following Phenomenon and formed part of it:

1364. "Toward three in the morning, without having had any sleep, we were about mounting our carriage, drawn up at the door; when an insuperable obstacle disclosed itself: for there rolled on already, between the pavement-stones which were crushed up into a ridge on each side, an uninterrupted column of sick-wagons through the Town, and all was trodden as into a morass. While we stood waiting what could be made of it, our Landlord and Knight of Saint-Louis pressed past us, without salutation." He had been a Calonne's Notable in 1787, an Emigrant since; had returned to his home, jubilant, with the Prussians: but must now forth again into the wide world, "followed by a servant carrying a little bundle on his stick."

1365. "The activity of our alert Lisieux shone eminent, and on this occasion too brought us on: for he struck into a small gap of the wagon-row; and held the advancing team back till we, with our six and our four horses, got intercalated; after which, in my light little coachlet, I could breath freer. We were now under way; at a funeral pace, but still under way. The day broke; we found ourselves at the outlet of the Town, in a tumult and turmoil without measure. All sorts of vehicles, few horsemen, innumerable foot-people, were crossing each other on the great esplanade before the Gate. We turned to the right, with our Column, toward Estain, on a limited highway, with ditches at each side. Self-preservation, in so monstrous a press, knew now no pity, no respect of aught.

Not far before us there fell down a horse of an ammunition-wagon; they cut the traces, and let it lie. And now as the three others could not bring their load along, they cut them also loose, tumbled the heavy-packed vehicle into the ditch; and with the smallest retardation, we had to drive on right over the horse, which was just about to rise; and I saw too clearly how its legs, under the wheels, went crashing and quivering.

1366. "Horse and foot endeavored to escape from the narrow laborious highway into the meadows; but these too were rained to ruin; overflowed by full ditches, the connection of the foot-paths everywhere

* "Campagne in Frankreich." p. 109.

interrupted. Four gentlemen-like, handsome, well-dressed French soldiers waded for a time beside our carriage; wonderfully clean and neat: and had such art of picking their steps, that their foot-gear testified no higher than the ankle to the muddy pilgrimage these good people found themselves engaged in.

1367. "That under such circumstances one saw, in ditches, in meadows, in fields and crofts, dead horses enough, was natural to the case: by and by, however, you found them also flayed, the fleshy parts even cut away; sad token of the universal distress.

1368. "Thus we fared on; every moment in danger, at the smallest stoppage on our own part, of being ourselves tumbled overboard; under which circumstances, truly, the careful dexterity of our Lisieux could not be sufficiently praised. The same talent showed itself at Estain; where we arrived toward noon; and descried, over the beautiful well-built little Town, through streets and on squares, around and beside us, one sense-confusing tumult: the mass rolled this way and that; and, all struggling forward, each hindered the other. Unexpectedly our carriage drew up before a stately house in the market-place; master and mistress of the mansion saluted us in reverent distance." Dexterous Lisieux, though we knew it not, had said we were the King of Prussia's Brother!

1369. "But now, from the ground-floor windows, looking over the whole market-place, we had the endless tumult lying, as it were, palpable. All sorts of walkers, soldiers in uniform, marauders, stout but sorrowing citizens and peasants, women and children, crushed and jostled each other, amid vehicles of all forms: ammunition-wagons, baggage-wagons; carriages, single, double, and multiplex; such hundred-fold miscellany of teams, requisitioned or lawfully owned, making way, hitting together, hindered each other, rolled here to right and to left. Horned-cattle too were struggling on; probably herds that had been put in requisition. Riders you saw few; but the elegant carriages of the Emigrants, many-colored, lackered, gilt and silvered, evidently by the best builders, caught your eye.*

1370. "The crisis of the strait, however, arose farther on a little; where the crowded market-place had to introduce itself into a street,—straight indeed and good, but proportionately far too narrow. I have, in my life, seen nothing like it: the aspect of it might perhaps be compared to that of a swollen river which has been raging over meadows and fields, and is now again obliged to press itself through a narrow bridge, and flow on in its bounded channel. Down the long street, all visible from our windows, there swelled continually the strangest tide: a high double-seated traveling coach towered visible over the flood of things. We thought of the fair Frenchwomen we had seen in the morning. It was not they, however; it was Count Haugwitz; him you could look at, with a kind of sardonic malice, rocking onward, step by step, there."†

1371. In such untriumphant Procession has the Brunswick Manifesto issued! Nay in worse, "in negotiation with these miscreants,"—the first news of which produced such a revulsion in the Emigrant nature, as put our scientific World-Poet "in fear for the wits of several."‡ There is no help: they must fare on, these poor Emigrants, angry with all persons and things, and making all persons angry in the hapless course they struck into. Landlord and landlady testify to you, at tables-d'hote, how insupportable

* See "Hermann und Dorothea" (also by Goethe), Buch "Kalliope."

† "Campagne in Frankreich." Goethe's "Werke" (Stuttgart, 1829). xxx. 133-137.

‡ "Campagne in Frankreich." Goethe's "Werke." xxx. 153.

these Frenchmen are: how, in spite of such humiliation, of poverty and probable beggary, there is ever the same struggle for precedence, the same forwardness and want of discretion. High in honor; at the head of the table, you with your own eyes observe not a Seigneur, but the automaton of a Seigneur fallen into dotage; still worshiped, reverently waited on and fed. In miscellaneous seats is a miscellany of soldiers, commissaries, adventurers; consuming silently their barbarian victuals. "On all brows is to be read a hard destiny; all are silent, for each has his own sufferings to bear, and looks forth into misery without bounds." One hasty wanderer, coming in, and eating without ungraciousness what is set before him, the landlord lets off almost scotfree. "He is," whispered the landlord to me, "the first of these cursed people I have seen condescend to taste our German black bread."*

1372. And Dumouriez is in Paris; lauded and feasted; paraded in glittering saloons, floods of beautifulest blonde-dresses and broadcloth-coats flowing past him, endless, in admiring joy. One night, nevertheless, in the splendor of one such scene, he sees himself suddenly apostrophized by a squalid unjoyful Figure, who has come in uninvited, nay despite of all lackeys: an unjoyful Figure! The Figure is come "in express mission from the Jacobins," to inquire sharply, better then than later, touching certain things: "Shaven eyebrows of Volunteer Patriots, for instance?" Also, "your threats of shivering in pieces?" Also, "why you have not chased Brunswick hotly enough?" Thus, with sharp cronk, inquires the Figure.—"Ah, c'est vous qu'on appelle Marat (You are he they call Marat)!" answers the General, and turns coldly on his heel.†—"Marat!" The blonde-gowns quiver like aspens; the dress coats gather round; Actor Talma (for it is his house), Actor Talma, and almost the very chandelier-lights are blue: till this obscene Spectrum, swart unearthly Visual-Appearance, vanish, back into his native Night.

1373. General Dumouriez, in few brief days, is gone again, toward the Netherlands; will attack the Netherlands, winter though it be. And General Montesquiou, on the South-east, has driven in the Sardinian Majesty; nay, almost without a shot fired, has taken Savoy from him, which longs to become a piece of the Republic. And General Custine, on the North-east, has dashed forth on Spires and its Arsenal; and then on Electoral Mentz, not uninvited, wherein are German Democrats and no shadow of an Elector now: so that in the last days of October, Frau Forster, a daughter of Heyne's, somewhat democratic, walking out of the Gate of Mentz with her Husband, finds French Soldiers playing at bowls with cannon-balls there. Forster trips cheerfully over one iron bomb, with "Live the Republic!" A black-bearded National Guard answers, "Elle vivra bien sans vous (It will probably live independently of you)."‡

BOOK SECOND.
REGICIDE.

CHAPTER I.
THE DELIBERATIVE.

1374. France therefore has done two things very completely: she has hurled back her Cimmerian Invaders far over the marches; and likewise she has

* "Campagne in Frankreich," Goethe's Werke, p. 210-212.
† Dumouriez, iii 115 —Marat's account, in the "Débats des Jacobins" and Journal de la République ("Histoire Parlementaire," xix. 817-821), agrees to the turning on the heel, but strives to interpret it differently.
‡ Johann Georg Forster's "Briefwechsel" (Leipzig, 1829), i. 88.

shattered her own internal Social Constitution, even to the minutest fiber of it, into wreck and dissolution. Utterly it is all altered: from King down to Parish Constable, all Authorities, Magistrates, Judges, persons that bore rule, have had, on the sudden, to alter themselves, so far as needful; or else, on the sudden, and not without violence, to be altered; a Patriot "Executive Council of Ministers," with a Patriot Danton in it, and then a whole Nation and National Convention, have taken care of that. Not a Parish Constable, in the farthest hamlet, who has said De par le Roi, and shown loyalty, but must retire, making way for a new improved Parish Constable who can say De par la République.

1375. It is a change such as History must beg her readers to imagine, undescribed. An instantaneous change of the whole body-politic, the soul-politic being all changed; such a change as few bodies, politic or other, can experience in this world. Say, perhaps, such as poor Nymph Semele's body did experience, when she would needs, with woman's humor, see her Olympian Jove as very Jove:—and so stood, poor Nymph, this moment Semele, next moment not Semele, but Flame and a Statue of red-hot Ashes! France has looked upon Democracy; seen it face to face.—The Cimmerian Invaders will rally, in humbler temper, with better or worse luck: the wreck and dissolution must reshape itself into a social Arrangement as it can and may. But as for this National Convention, which is to settle everything, if it do, as Deputy Paine and France generally expects, get all finished "in a few months," we shall call it a most deft Convention.

1376. In truth, it is very singular to see how this mercurial French People plunges suddenly from Vive-le-Roi to Vive la République; and goes simmering and dancing, shaking off daily (so to speak), and trampling into the dust, its old social garnitures, ways of thinking, rules of existing; and cheerfully dances toward the Ruleless, Unknown, with such hope in its heart, and nothing but *Freedom, Equality, and Brotherhood* in its mouth. Is it two centuries, or is it only two years, since all France roared simultaneously to the welkin, bursting forth into sound and smoke at its *Feast of Pikes,* "Live the Restorer of French Liberty?" Three short years ago there was still Versailles and Œil-de-Bœuf: now there is that watched Circuit of the Temple, girt with dragons eyed Municipals, where, as in its final limbo, Royalty lies extinct. In the year 1789, Constituent Deputy Barrère "wept," in his Break-of-Day Newspaper, at sight of a reconciled King 1 ·uis; and now in 1792, Convention Deputy Barrère, perfectly tearless, may be considering, whether the reconciled King Louis shall be guillotined or not!

1377. Old garnitures and social ventures drop off, (we say) so fast, being indeed quite decayed, and are trodden under the National dance. And the new vestures, where are they; the new modes and rules? Liberty, Equality, Fraternity: not vestures, but the wish for vestures! The Nation is for the present, figuratively speaking, *naked;* it has no rule or vesture; but is naked,—a Sansculottic Nation.

1378. So far therefore, and in such manner, have our Patriot Brissots, Guadets triumphed. Vergniaud's Ezekiel-visions of the fall of thrones and crowns, which he spake hypothetically and prophetically in the Spring of the year, have suddenly come to fulfillment in the Autumn. Our eloquent Patriots of the Legislative, like strong Conjurors, by the word of their mouth, have swept Royalism with its old modes and formulas to the winds; and shall now govern a France free of formulas. Free of formulas! And yet man lives not except with formulas; with customs, *ways* of doing and living: no text truer than this; which will hold true from the Tea-table and Tailor's shop-board up to the High Senate-houses, Solemn Temples; nay through all provinces of Mind and Imagination, onwards to the outmost confines of articulate Being,—Ubi homines sunt modi sunt. There are modes wherever there are men. It is the deepest law of man's nature; whereby man is a craftsman and " tool-using animal;" not the slave of Impulse, Chance and brute Nature, but in some measure their lord. Twenty-five millions of men, suddenly stript bare of their modi, and dancing them down in that manner, are a terrible thing to govern!

1379. Eloquent Patriots of the Legislative, meanwhile, have precisely this problem to solve. Under the name and nickname of "statesmen (hommes d'état)," of "moderate men (modérantins)," of Brissotins, Rolandins, finally of Girondins, they shall become world-famous in solving it. For the 25,000,000 are Gallic effervescent too;—filled both with hope of the unutterable, of universal Fraternity and Golden Age; and with terror of the unutterable, Cimmerian Europe all rallying on us. It is a problem like few. Truly, if man, as the Philosophers brag, did to any extent look before and after, what, one may ask, in many cases would become of him? What, in this case, would become of these 749 men? The Convention, seeing clearly before and after, were a paralyzed Convention. Seeing clearly to the length of its own nose, it is not paralyzed.

1380. To the Convention itself neither the work nor the method of doing it is doubtful! To make the Constitution; to defend the Republic till that be made. Speedily enough, accordingly, there has been a " Committee of the Constitution " got together. Sieyes, Old-Constituent, Constitution-builder by trade; Condorcet, fit for better things; Deputy Paine, foreign Benefactor of the Species, with that " red carbuncled face and the black beaming eyes ;" Hérault de Séchelles, Ex-Parlementeer, one of the handsomest men in France; these, with inferior guildbrethren, are girt cheerfully to the work; will once more "make the Constitution;" let us hope, more effectually than last time. For that the Constitution can be made, who doubts,—unless the Gospel of Jean Jacques came into the world in vain? True, our last Constitution did tumble within the year, so lamentably. But what then: except sort the rubbish and boulders, and build them up again better? "Widen your basis," for one thing,—to Universal Suffrage, if need be; exclude, rotten materials, Royalism and such-like, for another thing. And in brief, build, O unspeakable Sieyes and Company, unwearied! Frequent perilous down-rushing of scaffolding and rubble-work, be that an irritation, no discouragement. Start ye always again, clearing aside the wreck; if with broken limbs, yet with whole hearts; and build, we say, in the name of Heaven,—till either the work do stand; or else mankind abandon it, and the Constitution-builders be paid off, with laughter and tears? One good time, in the course of Eternity, it was appointed that this Social Contract too should try itself out. And so the Committee of Constitution shall toil: with hope and faith;—with no disturbance from any reader of these pages.

1381. To make the Constitution, then, and return home joyfully in a few months; this is the prophecy our National Convention gives of itself; by this scientific programme shall its operations and events go on. But from the best scientific programme, in such a case, to the actual fulfillment, what a difference! Every reunion of men, is it not, as we often say, a reunion of incalculable Influences; every unit of it a microcosm of Influences:—of which how shall Science calculate to prophesy? Science, which cannot, with all its calculuses, differential, integral and

of variations, calculate the Problem of Three gravitating Bodies, ought to hold her peace here, and say only: In this National Convention there are 749 very singular Bodies, that gravitate and do much else;—who, probably in an amazing manner, will work the appointment of Heaven.

1382. Of National Assemblages, Parliaments, Congresses, which have long sat, which are of saturine temperament; above all, which are not " dreadfully in earnest;" something may be computed or conjectured: yet even these are a kind of Mystery in progress,—whereby accordingly we see the Journalist Reporter find livelihood: even these joit madly out of the ruts, from time to time. How much more a poor National Convention, of French vehemence; urged on at such velocity; without routine, without rut, track or landmark, and dreadfully in earnest every man of them! It is a Parliament literally such as there was never elsewhere in the world. Themselves are new, unarranged; they are the Heart and presiding center of a France fallen wholly into maddest disarrangement. From all cities, hamlets, from the utmost ends of this France with its 25,000,-000 vehement souls, thick-streaming influences stormin on that same Heart, in the Salle de Manége, and storm-out again: such fiery venous-arterial circulation is the function of that Heart. Seven-hundred and Forty-nine human individuals, we say, never sat together on our Earth under more original circumstances. Common individuals most of them, or not far from common: yet in virtue of the position they occupied, so notable. How, in this wild piping of the whirlwind of human passions, with death, victory, terror, valor, and all height and all depth pealing and piping, these men, left to their own guidance, will speak and act?

1383. Readers know well that this French National Convention (quite contrary to its own Programme) became the astonishment and horror of mankind; a kind of Apocalyptic Convention, or black *Dream become real;* concerning which History seldom speaks except in the way of interjection: how it covered France with woe, delusion and delirium; and from its bosom there went forth Death on the pale Horse. To hate this poor National Convention is easy; to praise and love it has not been found impossible. It is, as we say, a Parliament in the most original circumstances. To us, in these pages, be it as a fuliginous fiery mystery, where Upper has met Nether, and in such alternate glare and blackness of darkness poor bedazzledr mortals know not which is Upper, which is Nether; but rage and plunge distractedly, as mortals in that case will do. A Convention which has to consume itself, suicidally; and become dead ashes—with its World! Behooves us, not to enter exploratively its dim embroiled deeps; yet to stand with unwavering eyes, looking how it welters; what notable phases and occurrences it will successively throw up.

1384. One general superficial circumstance we remark with praise: the force of Politeness. To such depth has the sense of civilization penetrated man's life; no Drouet, no Legendre, in the maddest tug of war, can altogether shake it off. Debates of Senates dreadfully in earnest are seldom given frankly to the world; else perhaps they would surprise it. Did not the Grand Monarque himself once chase his Louvois with a pair of brandished tongs? But reading long volumes of these Convention Debates, all in a foam with furious earnestness, earnest many times to the extent of life and death, one is struck rather with the degree of contjmence they manifest in speech; and how in such wild ebullition, there is still a kind of polite rule struggling for mastery, and the forms of social life, never altogether disappear.

These men, though the menace with clenched right-hands, do not clutch one another by the collar; they draw no daggers, except for oratorical purposes, and this not often: profane swearing is almost unknown, though the Reports are frank enough; we find only one or two oaths, oath by Marat, reported in all.

1385. For the rest, that there is "effervescence" who doubts? Effervescence enough; Decrees passed by acclamation to-day, repealed by vociferation to-morrow; temper fitful, most rotatory-changeful, always headlong! The "voice of the orator is covered with rumors;" a hundred "honorable Members rush with menaces toward the Left side of the Hall;" President has "broken three bells in succession,"—claps on his bat, as signal that the country is near ruined. A fiercely effervescent Old-Gallic Assemblage!—Ah, how the loud sick sounds of Debate, and of Life, which is a *debate*, sink silent, one after another: so loud now, and in a little while so low! Brennus, and those antique Gael Captains, in their way to Rome, to Galatia and such places, whither they were in the habit of marching in the most fiery manner, had Debates as effervescent, doubt it not; though no Moniteur has reported them. They scolded in Celtic Welsh, those Brennuses; neither were they Sansculotte; nay rather breeches (braceæ, say of felt or rough-leather) were the only thing they had; being, as Livy testifies, naked down *to* the haunches:—and, see, it is the same sort of work and of men still, now when they have got coats, and speak nasally a kind of broken Latin! But, on the whole, does not TIME envelop this present National Convention; as it did those Brennuses, and ancient august Senates in felt breeches? Time surely: and also Eternity. Dim dusk of Time,—or noon which will be dusk; and then there is night, and silence; and Time with all its sick noises is swallowed in the still sea. Pity thy brother, O son of Adam! The angriest frothy jargon that he utters, is it not properly the whimpering of an infant which cannot *speak* what ails it, but is in distress clearly, in the inwards of it; and so must squall and whimper continually, till its Mother take it, and it get—to sleep!

1386. This Convention is not four days old, and the melodious Melibœan stanzas that shook down Royalty are still fresh in our ear, when there bursts out a new diapason,—unhappily, of Discord, this time. For speech has been made of a thing difficult to speak of well: the September Massacres. How deal with these September Massacres; with the Paris Commune that presided over them ? A Paris Commune hateful-terrible; before which the poor effete Legislative had to quail, and sit quiet. And now if a young omnipotent Convention will not so quail and sit, what steps shall it take? Have a Departmental Guard in its pay, answer the Girondins and Friends of Order! A Guard of National Volunteers, missioned from all the Eighty-three or Eighty-five Departments, for that express end; these will keep Septemberers, tumultuous Communes in a due state of submissiveness, the Convention in a due state of sovereignty. So have the Friends of Order answered, sitting in Committee, and reporting; and even a Decree has been passed of the required tenor. Nay certain Departments, as the Var or Marseilles, in mere expectation and assurance of a Decree, have their contingent of Volunteers already on march; brave Marseilles, foremost on the 10*th* of August, will not be hindmost here: "Fathers gave their sons a musket and twenty-five louis," says Barbaroux," "and bade them march."

1387. Can anything be properer? A Republic that will found itself on justice must needs investigate September Massacres; a Convention calling itself National, ought it not to be guarded by a Na-tional force?—'Alas, Reader, it seems so to the eye: and yet there is much to be said and argued. Thou beholdest here the small beginning of a Controversy, which mere logic will not settle. Two small well-springs, September, Departmental Guard, or rather at bottom they are but one and the same small well-spring; which will swell and widen into waters of bitterness; all manner of subsidiary streams and brooks of bitterness flowing in, from this side and that; till it become a wide river of bitterness, of rage and separation,—which can subside only into the Catacombs. This Departmental Guard, decreed by overwhelming majorities, and then repealed for peace's sake, and not to insult Paris, is again decreed more than once; nay it is partially executed, and the very men that are to be of it are seen visibly parading the Paris streets,—shouting once, being overtaken with liquor: "A bas Marat (Down with Marat)!"* Nevertheless, decreed never so often, it is repealed just as often; and continues, for some seven months an angry noisy Hypothesis only: a fair Possibility struggling to become a Reality, but which shall never be one; which, after endless struggling, shall, in February next, sink into sad rest,—dragging much along with it. So singular are the ways of men and honorable Members.

1388. But on this fourth day of the Convention's existence, as we said, which is the 25th of September, 1792, there comes Committee Report on that Decree of the Departmental Guard, and speech of repealing it; there come denunciations of Anarchy, of a Dictatorship,—which let the incorruptible Robespierre consider: there comes denunciations of a certain Journal de la République, once called Ami de Peuple; and so thereupon there comes, visibly stepping up, visibly standing aloft on the Tribune, ready to speak,—the Bodily Spectrum of People's-Friend Marat! Shriek, ye 749; it is verily Marat, he and not another. Marat is no phantasm of the brain, or mere lying impress of Printer's Types; but a thing material, of joint and sinew, and a certain small stature; ye behold him there, in his blackness, in his dingy squalor, a living fraction of Chaos and Old-Night; visibly incarnate, desirous to speak. "It appears," says Marat to the shrieking Assembly, "that a great many persons here are enemies of mine."—"All! all!" shriek hundreds of voices: enough to drown any People's-Friend. But Marat will not drown; he speaks and croaks explanation; croaks with such reasonableness, air of sincerity, that repentant pity smothers anger, and the shrieks subside, or even become applauses. For this Convention is unfortunately the crankest of machines: it shall be pointing eastward with stiff-violence this moment; and then do but touch some spring dexterously, the whole machine, clattering and jerking seven-hundred-fold, will whirl with huge crash, and, next moment, is pointing westward! Thus Marat, absolved and applauded, victorious in this turn of fence, is, as the Debate goes on, prickt at again by some Dexterous Girondin; and then the shrieks rise anew, and Decree of Accusation is on the point of passing; till the dingy People's-Friend bobs aloft once more; croaks once more persuasive stillness, and the Decree of Accusation sinks. Whereupon he draws forth—a Pistol; and setting it to his Head, the seat of such thought and prophecy, says: "If they had passed their Accusation Decree, he, the People's-Friend, would have blown his brains out." A People's-Friend has that faculty in him. For the rest, as to this of the 260,000 Aristocrat Heads, Marat candidly says, "Cest là mon avis (Such is my opinion)." Also is it not indisputable: "No power on Earth can prevent me from seeing into traitors,

* "Histoire Parlementaire," xx. 184.

and unmasking them,"—by my superior originality of mind?* An honorable member like this Friend of the People few terrestrial Parliaments have had.

1389. We observe, however, that this first onslaught by the Friends of Order, as sharp and prompt as it was, has failed. For neither can Robespierre, summoned out by talk of Dictatorship, and greeted with the like rumor on showing himself, be thrown into Prison, into Accusation; not though Barbaroux openly bear testimony against him, and sign it on paper. With such sanctified meekness does the Incorruptible lift his sea-green cheek to the smiter; lift his thin voice, and with jesuitic dexterity plead, and prosper; asking at last, in a prosperous manner: "But what witnesses has the Citoyen Barbaroux to support his testimony?" "Moi!" cries hot Rebecqui, standing up, striking his breast with both hands, and answering "Me!"† Nevertheless the Sea-green pleads again, and makes it good, the long hurly-burly, "personal merely," while so much public matter lies fallow, has ended in the order of the day. O Friends of the Gironde, why will you occupy our august sessions with mere paltry Personalities, while the grand Nationality lies in such a state?—The Gironde has touched, this day, on the foul black-spot of its fair Convention Domain; has trodden on it, and yet *not* trodden it down. Alas, it is a *well-spring*, as we said, this black-spot; and will not tread down!

CHAPTER II.

THE EXECUTIVE.

1390. May we not conjecture therefore that round this grand enterprise of Making the Constitution, there will, as heretofore, very strange embroilments gather, and questions and interests complicate themselves; so that after a few or even several months, the Convention will not have settled everything? Alas, a whole tide of questions comes rolling, boiling; growing ever wider, without end! Among which, apart from this question of September and Anarchy, let us notice three, which emerge oftener than the others, and promise to become Leading Questions: Of the Armies; of the Subsistences; thirdly, of the Dethroned King.

1391. As to the Armies, Public Defense must evidently be put on a proper footing; for Europe seems coalescing itself again; one is apprehensive even England will join it. Happily Dumouriez prospers in the North;—nay, what if he should prove *too* prosperous, and become Liberticide, Murderer of Freedom!—Dumouriez prospers, through this winter season; yet not without lamentable complaints. Sleek Pache, the Swiss School-master, he that sat frugal in his Alley, the wonder of neighbors, has got lately—whither thinks the Reader? To be Minister of War! Madame Roland, struck with his sleek ways, recommended him to her husband as Clerk; the sleek Clerk had no need of salary, being of true Patriotic temper; he would come with a bit of bread in his pocket, to save dinner and time; and munching incidentally, do three men's work in a day; punctual, silent, frugal,—the sleek Tartuffe that he was. Wherefore Roland, in the late Overturn, recommended him to be War-Minister. And now, it would seem, he is secretly undermining Roland; playing into the hands of your hotter Jacobins and September Commune; and cannot, like strict Roland, be the Veto des Coquins!‡

1392. How the sleek Pache might mine and undermine, one knows not well; this however one does know: that his War-Office has become a den of thieves and confusion, such as all men shudder to behold. That the Citizen Hassenfratz, as Head-Clerk, sits there in bonnet rouge, in rapine, in violence, and some Mathematical calculation; a most insolent, red-nightcapped man. That Pache munches his pocket-loaf, amid head-clerks and sub-clerks, and has spent all the War-Estimates. That Furnishers scour in gigs, over all districts of France, and drive bargains. And lastly that the Army gets next to no furniture: no shoes, though it is winter; no clothes; some have not even arms; "In the Army of the South," complains an honorable Member, "there are 30,000 pairs of breeches wanting,"—a most scandalous want.

1393. Roland's strict soul is sick to see the course things take: but what can he do? Keep his own Department strict; rebuke, and repress whosoever possible; at lowest, complain. He can complain in Letter after Letter, to a National Convention, to France, to Posterity, the Universe; grow ever more querulous-indignant;—till at last, may he not grow wearisome? For is not this continual text of his, at bottom, a rather barren one: How astonishing that in a time of Revolt and abrogation of all Law but Cannon Law, there should be such Unlawfulness? Intrepid Veto-of-Scoundrels, narrow-faithful, respectable, methodic man, work thou in that manner, since happily it is thy manner, and wear thyself away: though ineffectual, not profitless in it—then nor *now!*—The brave Dame Roland, bravest of all French women, begins to have misgivings: The figure of Danton has too much of the "Sardanapalus character," at a Republican Rolandin Dinner-table: Clootz, Speaker of Mankind, proses and staff about a Universal Republic, or union of all Peoples and Kindreds in one and the same Fraternal Bond; of which Bond, how it is to be *tied*, one unhappily sees not.

1394. It is also an indisputable, unaccountable or accountable fact, that Grains are becoming scarcer and scarcer. Riots for grain, tumultuous Assemblages demanding to have the price of grain fixed, abound far and near. The Mayor of Paris and other poor Mayors are like to have their difficulties. Pétion was re-elected Mayor of Paris; but has declined; being now a Convention Legislator. Wise surely to decline: for, besides this of Grains and all the rest, there is in these times an Improvised Insurrectionary Commune passing into an Elected one; getting their accounts settled,—not without irritancy! Pétion has declined: nevertheless many do covet and canvass. After months of scrutinizing, balloting, arguing and jargoning, one Doctor Chambon gets the post of honor: who will not long keep it; but be, as we shall see, literally *crushed* out of it.*

1395. Think also if the private Sansculotte has not his difficulties, in a time of dearth! Bread, according to the People's-Friend, may be some "six sous per pound, a day's wages some fifteen;" and grim winter here. How the Poor Man continues living, and so seldom starves; by miracle! Happily, in these days, he can enlist, and have himself shot by the Austrians, in an unusually satisfactory manner: for the Rights of Man.—But Commandant Santerre, in this so straitened condition of the flour-market, and state of Equality and Liberty, proposes, through the Newspapers, two remedies, or at least palliatives: *First*, that all classes of men should live two days of the week on potatoes; then, *second*, that every man should hang his dog. Hereby, as

---

* Moniteur newspaper, Nos. 271, 290, 294. Année première; Moore's, "Journal," ii. 21, 157, etc., (which, however, may perhaps, as in similar cases, be only a copy of the newspaper).

† Moniteur, ut suprà: Séance du 25 Septembre.

‡ Madame Roland, "Mémoires," ii. 287, etc.

* "Dictionnaire des Hommes Marquans." § Chambon-

the Commandant thinks, the saving, which indeed he computes to so many sacks, would be very considerable. Cheerfuler form of inventive-stupidity than Commandant Santerre's dwells in no human soul. Inventive-stupidity, imbedded in health, courage and good-nature: much to be commended. "My whole strength," he tells the Convention once, "is day and night, at the service of my fellow-citizens if they find me worthless, they will dismiss me; I will return and brew beer.*

1396. Or figure what correspondences a poor Roland, Minister of the Interior, must have, on this of Grains alone! Free-trade in Grain, impossibility to fix the Prices of Grain; on the other hand, clamor and necessity to fix them: Political Economy lecturing from the Home Office, with demonstration clear as Scripture;—ineffectual for the empty National Stomach. The Mayor of Chartres, like to be eaten himself, cries to the Convention; the Convention sends honorable Members in Deputation; who endeavor to feed the multitude by miraculous spiritual methods; but cannot. The multitude, in spite of all Eloquence, come hellowing round; will have the Grain-Prices fixed, and at moderate elevation; or else —the honorable Deputies hanged on the spot! The honorable Deputies reporting this business admit that on the edge of horrid death, they did fix, or effect to fix the Price of Grain: for which, be it also noted, the Convention, a Convention that will not be trifled with, sees good to reprimand them.†

1397. But as to the origin of these Grain-Riots, is it not most probably your secret Royalists again? Glimpses of Priests were discernible in this of Chartres,—to the eye of Patriotism. Or indeed may not "the root of it all lie in the Temple Prison, in the heart of a perjured King" well as we guard him?‡ Unhappy perjured King!—And so there shall be Bakers' Queues by and by, more sharp-tempered than ever: on every Baker's door-rabbet an iron ring, and coil of rope; whereon, with firm grip, on this side and that, we form our Queue: but mischievous deceitful persons cut the rope, and our Queue becomes a ravelment; wherefore the coil must be made of iron chain.§ Also there shall be Prices of Grain well fixed; but then no grain purchasable by them: bread not to be had except by Ticket from the Mayor, few ounces per mouth-daily; after long swaying, with firm grip, on the chain of the Queue. And Hunger shall stalk direful; and Wrath and Suspicion, whetted to the Preternatural pitch, shall stalk; as those other preternatural "shapes of Gods in their wrathfulness" were discerned stalking, "in glare and gloom of that fire ocean," when Troy Town fell!—

CHAPTER III.

DISCROWNED.

1398. But the question more pressing than all on the Legislator, as yet, is this third: What shall be done with King Louis?

King Louis, now King and Majesty to his own family alone, in their own Prison Apartment alone, has, for months past, been mere Louis Capet and the Traitor Veto with the rest of France. Shut in his Circuit of the Temple, he has heard and seen the loud whirl of things; yells of September Massacres Brunswick war-thunders dying off in disaster and discomfiture: he passive, a spectator merely; waiting whither it would please to whirl with him. From the neighboring windows; the curious, not

without pity, might see him walk daily, at a certain hour, in the Temple Garden, with his Queen, Sister and two Children, all that now belongs to him on this earth.* Quietly he walks and waits: for he is not of lively feelings, and is of a devout heart. The wearied Irresolute has, at least, no need of resolving now. His daily meals, lessons to his Son, daily walk in the Garden, daily game at ombre or draughts fill up the day: the morrow will provide for itself.

1399. The morrow indeed; and yet how? Louis asks, How? France, with perhaps still more solicitude, asks How? A King dethroned by insurrection is verily not easy to dispose of. Keep him prisoner, he is a secret center for the Disaffected, for endless plots, attempts and hopes of theirs. Banish him, he is an open center for them; his royal war-standard, with what of divinity it has, unrolls itself, summoning the world. Put him to death? A cruel questionable extremity that too: and yet the likeliest in these extreme circumstances, of insurrectionary men, whose own life and death lies naked: accordingly it is said, from the last step of the throne to the first of the scaffold there is short distance.

1400. But, on the whole, we will remark here that this business of Louis looks altogether different now, as seen over Seas and at the distance of forty-four years, from what it looked then, in France, and struggling confused all round one. For indeed it is a most lying thing that same Past Tense always: so beautiful, sad, almost Elysian-sacred, "in the moonlight of Memory," it seems; and seems only. For observe. always one most important element is surreptitiously (we not noticing it) withdrawn from the Past Time: the haggard element of Fear! Not there does Fear dwell, nor Uncertainty, nor Anxiety; but it dwells here; haunting us, tracking us; runlike an accursed ground-discord through all the music tones of our Existence;—making the Tense a mere Present one! Just so is it with this of Louis. Why smite the fallen? Ask Magnanimity, out of danger now. He has fallen so low this once-high man; no criminal nor traitor, how far from it; but the unhappiest of Human Solecisms, whom if abstract Justice had to pronounce upon, she might well become concrete Pity, and pronounce only sobs and dismissal!

1401. So argues retrospective Magnanimity: but Pusillanimity, present, prospective? Reader, thou hast never lived, for months, under the rustle of a National Sahara-waltz. Twenty-five millions running distracted to fight Brunswick! Knights Errant themselves, when they conquered Giants, usually slew the Giants; quarter was only for other Knights Errant, who knew courtesy and the laws of battle. The French Nation, in simultaneous, desperate dead-pull and as if by miracle of madness, has pulled down the most dread Goliath, huge with the growth of ten centuries; and cannot believe, though his giant bulk, covering acres, lies prostrate, bound with peg and pack-thread, that he will not rise again, man-devouring; that the victory is not partly a dream. Terror has its skepticism; miraculous victory its rage of vengeance. Then as to criminality, is the prostrated Giant, who will devour us if he rise, an innocent Giant? Curate Grégoire, who indeed is now Constitutional Bishop Grégoire, asserts, in the heat of eloquence, that Kingship by the very nature of it is a crime capital; that King's Houses are as wild-beasts dens.† Lastly consider this: that there is on record a Trial of Charles First! This printed "Trial of Charles First" is sold and read everywhere at present.†—Quel spectacle! Thus did the English.

* Moniteur (in " Histoire Parlementaire," xx. 412).
† " Histoire Parlementaire," xx. 431–440.
‡ "Histoire Parlementaire," xx. 409.
§ Mercier, "Nouveau Paris."

* Moore, i. 123; ii. 224, etc.
† Monitour, Séance du 21 Septembre, An 1er (1792).

at present.*—Quel spectacle! Thus did the English People judge their Tyrant, and become the first of Free Peoples: which feat, by the grace of Destiny, may not France now rival? Skepticism of terror, rage of miraculous victory, sublime spectacle to the universe,—all things point one fatal way.

1402. Such leading questions, and their endless incidental ones,—of September Anarchists and Departmental Guard; of Grain-Riots, plaintive Interior Ministers; of Armies, Hassenfratz dilapidations: and what is to be done with Louis,—beleaguer and embroil this Convention; which would so gladly make the Constitution rather. All which questions, too, as we often urge of such things, are in *growth;* they grow in every French head; and can be *seen* growing also, very curiously, in this mighty welter of Parliamentary Debate, of Public Business which the Convention has to do. A question emerges, so small at first; is put off, submerged; but always re-emerges bigger than before. It is curious, indeed an indescribable sort of growth;which such things have.

1403 We perceive, however, both by its frequent re-emergence and by its rapid enlargement of bulk, that this Question of King Louis will take the lead of all the rest. And truly, in that case, it will take the *lead* in a much deeper sense. For as Aaron's Rod swallowed all the other serpents; so will this Foremost Question, whichever may get foremost, absorb all other questions and interests; and from it and the decision of it will they all, so to speak, be *born,* or new-born, and have shape, physiognomy and destiny corresponding. It was appointed of Fate that, in this wide-weltering, strangely growing, monstrous stupendous imbroglio of Convention Business, the grand First Parent of all the questions, controversies, measures and enterprises which were to be evolved there to the world's astonishment, should be this Question of King Louis.

CHAPTER IV.

THE LOSER PAYS.

1404. The 6th of November, 1792, was a great day for the Republic: outwardly, over the Frontiers; inwardly, in the Salle de Manége.

Outwardly, for Dumouriez,overrunning the Netherlands, did, on that day, come in contact with Saxe-Teschen and the Austrians; Dumouriez wide-winged, they wide-winged; at and around the village of Jemappes, near Mons. And fire-hail is whistling, far and wide there, the great guns playing, and the small; so many green Heights getting fringed and manned with red Fire. And Dumouriez is swept back on this wing, and swept back on that, and is like to be swept back utterly; when he rushes up in person, the prompt Polymetis; speaks a prompt word or two; and then, with clear tenor-pipe, "uplifts the Hymn of the Marseillese (entonna la Marseillaise),"† 10,000 tenor or bass pipes joining; or say, some 40,000 in all; for every heart leaps at the sound; and so with rhythmic march melody, waxing ever quicker, to double and to treble quick, they rally, they advance, they rush, death-defying, man-devouring; carry batteries, redoubts, whatsoever is to be carried; and, like the fire whirlwind, sweep all manner of Austrians from the scene of action. Thus, through the hands of Dumouriez, may Rouget de Lille, in figurative speech, he said to have gained, miraculously, like another Orpheus, by his Marseillese fiddle-strings (fidibus canoris), a Victory of Jemappes; and conquered the Low Courtries.

1405. Young General Égalité, it would seem, shone

brave among the bravest on this occasion. Doubtless a brave Égalité;—whom however does not Dumouriez rather talk of oftener than need were? The Mother Society has her own thoughts. As for the elder Égalité, he flies low at the time; appears in the Convention for some half-hour daily, with rubicund, pre-occupied or impassive quasi-contemptuous countenance; and then takes himself away.* The Netherlands are conquered, at least overrun. Jacobin missionaries, your Prolys, Perciras, follow in the train of the Armies; also Convention Commissioners, melting church-plate, revolutionizing and remodeling,—among whom Danton, in brief space does immensities of business: not neglecting his own wages and trade-profits, it is thought Hassenfratz dilapidates at home; Dumouriez grumbles and they dilapidate abroad: within the walls there is sinning and without the walls there is sinning. .

1406. But in the Hall of the Convention, at the same hour with this victory of Jemappes, there, went another thing forward: Report, of great length from the proper appointed Committee, on the crimes of Louis. The Galleries listen breathless; take comfort, ye Galleries: Deputy Valazé, Reporter on this occasion, thinks Louis very criminal: and that, if convenient, he should be tried,—poor Girondin Valazé, who may be tried himself, one day! Comfortable so far. Nay here comes a second Committee-reporter, Deputy Mailhe, with a Legal Argument, very prosy to read now, very refreshing to hear then, That by the Law of the Country, Louis Capet was only called Inviolable by a figure of rhetoric; but at bottom was perfectly violable, triable: that he can, and even should be tried. This Question of Louis, emerging so often as an angry, confused possibility, and submerging again, has emerged now in an articulate shape.

1407. Patriotism growls indignant joy. The so-called reign of Equality is not a mere name, then but a thing! Try Louis Capet? scornfully ejaculates. Patriotism. Mean criminals go to the gallows for a purse cut; and this chief criminal, guilty of a France cut; of a France slashed asunder with Clotho-scissors and Civil war; with his victims "1200 on the Tenth of August alone" lying low in the Catacombs, fattening the passes of Argonne Wood, of Valmy and far Fields; *he,* such chief criminal. shall not even come to the bar?—For, alas, O Patriotism! add we, it was from of old said, *The loser pays!* It is he who has to pay *all* scores, run up by whomsoever: on him must all breakages and charges fall; and the 1200 on the Tenth of August are not rebel traitors, but victims and martyrs: such is the law of quarrel.

1408. Patriotism, nothing doubting, watches over this Question of the trial, now happily emerged in an articulate shape; and will see it to maturity, if the gods permit. With a keen solicitude Patriotism, watches; getting ever keener, at every new difficulty, as Girondins and false brothers interpose delays; till it get a keenness as of fixed-idea, and will have this Trial and no earthly thing instead of it,—if Equality be not a name. Love of Equality; then skepticism of terror, rage of victory, sublime spectacle to the universe: all these things are strong.

But indeed this Question of the Trial, is it not to all persons a most grave one; filling with dubiety many a Legislative head! Regicide? asks the Gironde Respectability. To kill a king, and become the horror of respectable notions and persons? But then also, to save a king; to lose one's footing with the decided Patriot; the undecided Patriot, though never so respectable, being mere hypothetic froth and no footing?—The dilemma presses sore; and between the horns of it you wriggle round and round. Deci-

* Moore's "Journal," II. 165.
† Dumouriez. "Mémoires," III. 174.

* Moore, II. 148.

sion is nowhere, save in the Mother Society and her Sons. These have decided, and go forward: the others wriggle round uneasily within their dilemma-horns, and make way nowhither.

CHAPTER V.

STRETCHING OF FORMULAS.

1409. But how this Question of the Trial grew laboriously, through the weeks of gestation, now that it has been articulated or conceived, were superfluous to trace here. It emerged and submerged among the infinite of questions and embroilments. The Veto of Scoundrels writes plaintive Letters as to Anarchy; "concealed Royalists," aided by Hunger, produce Riots about Grain. Alas, it is but a week ago, these Girondins made a new fierce onslaught on the September Massacres!

1410. For, one day, among the last of October, Robespierre, being summoned to the tribune by some new hint of that old calumny of the Dictatorship, was speaking and pleading there, with more and more comfort to himself; till rising high in heart, he cried out valiantly: Is there any man here that dare specifically accuse me? "Moi!" exclaimed one. Pause of deep silence: a lean angry little Figure, with broad bald brow, strode swiftly toward the tribune, taking papers from its pocket: "I accuse thee, Robespierre,"—I, Jean Baptiste Louvet! The sea-green became tallow-green; shrinking to a corner of the tribune: Danton cried, "Speak, Robespierre, there are many good citizens that listen;" but the tongue refused its office. And so Louvet, with a shrill tone, read and recited crime after crime: dictatorial temper, exclusive popularity, bullying at elections, mob-retinue, September Massacres;—till all the Convention shrieked again, and had almost indicted the Incorruptible there on the spot. Never did the Incorruptible run such a risk. Louvet, to his dying day, will regret that the Gironde did not take a bolder attitude, and extinguish him there and then.

1411. Not so, however: the Incorruptible, about to be indicted in this sudden manner, could not be refused a week of delay. That week be is not idle; nor is the Mother Society idle,—fierce-tremulous for her chosen son. He is ready at the day with his written Speech; smooth as a Jesuit Doctor's; and convinces some. And now? Why now lazy Vergniaud does not rise with Demosthenic thunder; poor Louvet, unprepared, can do little or nothing: Barrère proposes that these comparatively despicable "personalities" be dismissed by order of the day! Order of the day it accordingly is. Barbaroux cannot even get'a hearing; not though he rush down to the Bar, and demand to be heard there as a petitioner.* The Convention, eager for public business (with that first articulate emergence of the Trial just coming on), dismisses these comparative misères and despicabilities: splenetic Louvet must digest his spleen, regretfully, forever: Robespierre, dear to Patriotism, is dearer for the dangers he has run.

1412. This is the second grand attempt of our Girondin Friends of Order to extinguish that black spot in their domain; and we see they have made it far blacker and wider than before! Anarchy, September Massacre: it is a thing that lies hideous in the general imagination; very detestable to the undecided Patriot, of Respectability: a thing to be harped on as often as need is. Harp on it, denounce it, trample it, ye Girondin Patriots:—and yet behold, the black

spot will not trample down; it will only, as we say, trample blacker and wider: fools, it is no black spot of the surface, but a well-spring of the deep! Consider rightly, it is the Apex of the everlasting Abyss, this black spot, looking up as water through thin ice;—say, as the region of Nether Darkness through your thin film of Gironde Regulation and Respectability: trample it not, lest the film break, and then—!

1413. The truth is, if our Gironde understanding of it, where were French Patriotism, with all its eloquence, at this moment, had not that same great Nether Deep, of Bedlam, Fanaticism and Popular wrath and madness, risen unfathomable on the Tenth of August? French Patriotism were an eloquent Reminiscence; swinging on Prussian gibbets. Nay, where, in few months, were it still, should the same great Nether Deep subside?—Nay, as readers of Newspapers pretend to recollect, this hatefulness of the September Massacre is itself partly an afterthought; readers of the Newspapers can quote Gorsas and various Brissotins approving of the September Massacre, at the time it happened; and calling it a salutary vengeance.* So that the real grief, after all, were not so much righteous horror, as grief that one's own power was departing? Unhappy Girondins!

1414. In the Jacobin Society, therefore, the decided Patriot complains that here are men who with their private ambitions and animosities will ruin Liberty, Equality and Brotherhood, all three they check the spirit of Patriotism; throw stumbling-blocks in its way; and instead of pushing on, all shoulders at the wheel, will stand idle there, spitefully clamoring what foul ruts there are, what rude jolts we give! To which the Jacobin Society answers with angry roar;—with angry shriek, for there are Citoyennes too, thick crowded in the galleries here. Citoyennes who bring their scam with them, or their knitting-needles; and shriek or knit as the case needs; famed Tricoteuses, Patriot knitters; Mère Duchesse, or the like Deborah and Mother of the Faubourgs, giving the key-note. It is a changed Jacobin Society; and a still changing. Where Mother Duchess sits, authentic Duchesses have sat. High-rouged dames went once in jewels and spangles; now, instead of jewels, you may take the knitting-needles and leave the rouge: the rouge will gradually give place to natural brown, clean washed or even unwashed: and Demoiselle Théroigne herself get scandalously fustigated. Strange enough; it is the same tribune raised in mid-air, where a high Mirabeau, a high Barnave and Aristocrat Lameths once thundered; whom gradually your Brissots, Guadets, Vergniauds, a hotter style of Patriots in bonnet rouge, did displace; red heat, as one may say, superseding light. And now your Brissots in turn, and Brissotins, Rolandins, Girondins, are becoming supernumerary; must desert the sittings, or be expelled: the light of the Mighty Mother is burning not red but blue!—Provincial Daughter Societies loudly disapprove these things; loudly demand the swift reinstatement of such eloquent Girondins, the swift "erasure of Marat (radiation de Marat)." The Mother Society, so far as natural reason can predict, seems ruining herself. Nevertheless she has at all crisis seemed so; she has a preternatural life in her, and will not ruin.

1415. But, in a fortnight more, this great Question of the Trial, while the fit Committee is assiduously but silently working on it, receives an unexpected stimulus. Our readers remember poor Louis's turn for smith work: how, in old happier days a certain Sieur Gamain of Versailles was wont to come over and instruct him in lock-making;—often scolding

---

* Louvet, "Mémoires," (Paris, 1823), p. 52; Moniteur (Séance du 29 Octobre, 5 Novembre. 1792); Moore, ii. 178 etc.

* See "Histoire Parlementaire," xvii. 401; newspapers by Gorsas and others (cited ibid. 428).

him, they say, for his numbness. By whom, nevertheless, the royal Apprentice had learned something of that craft. Hapless Apprentice; perfidious Master-Smith! For now, on this 20th of November, 1792, dingy Smith Gamain comes over to the Paris Municipality, over to Minister Roland, with hints that he, Smith Gamain, knows a thing; that, in May last, when traitorous Correspondence was so brisk, he and the royal Apprentice fabricated an "Iron Press (Armoire de Fer)," cunningly inserting the same in a wall of the royal chamber in the Tuileries; invisible under the wainscot; where doubtless it still sticks! Perfidious Gamain, attended by the proper Authorities, finds the wainscot panel which none else can find; wrenches it up; discloses the Iron Press,—full of Letters and Papers? Roland clutches them out; conveys them over in towels to the fit assiduous Committee, which sits hard by, in towels we say, and without notarial inventory; an oversight on the part of Roland.

1416. Here, however, are Letters enough : which disclose to a demonstration the Correspondence of a traitorous self-preserving Court; and this not with Traitors only, but even with Patriots so-called ! Barnave's treason, of Correspondence with the Queen, and friendly advice to her, ever since that Varennes Business, is hereby manifest : how happy that we have him, this Barnave, lying safe in the Prison of Grenoble, since September last, for he had long been suspect! Talleyrand's treason, many a man's treason, if not manifest hereby, is next to it. Mirabeau's treason : wherefore his Bust in the Hall of the Convention "is veiled with gauze," till we ascertain. Alas, it is too ascertainable! His Bust in the Hall of the Jacobins, denounced by Robespierre from the tribune in mid-air, is not veiled, it is instantly broken to shreds; a Patriot mounting swiftly with a ladder, and shivering it down on the floor;—it and others : amid shouts.* Such is *their* recompense and amount of wages, at this date : on the principle of supply and demand. Smith Gamain, inadequately recompensed for the present, comes, some fifteen months after, with a humble Petition; setting forth that no sooner was that important Iron Press finished off by him, than (as he now bethinks himself) Louis gave him a large glass of wine. Which large glass of wine did produce in the stomach of Sieur Gamain the terriblest effects, evidently tending toward death, and was then brought up by an emetic; but has, notwithstanding, entirely ruined the constitution of Sieur Gamain; so that he cannot work for his family (as he now bethinks himself). The recompense of *which* is "Pension of 1200 francs," and "honorable mention." So different is the ratio of demand and supply at different times.

1417. Thus, amid obstructions and stimulating furtherances, has the Question of the Trial to grow; emerging and submerging; fostered by solicitous Patriotism. Of the orations that were spoken on it, of the painfully devised Forms of Process for managing it, the Law Arguments to prove it lawful, and all the infinite floods of Juridical and other ingenuity and oratory, be no syllable reported in this History. Lawyer ingenuity is good : but what can it profit here? If the truth must be spoken, O august Senators, the only law in this case is : Væ victis (The loser pays)! Seldom did Robespierre say a wiser word than the hint he gave to that effect, in his oration, That it was needless to speak of Law; that here, if never elsewhere, our Right was Might. An oration admired almost to ecstacy by the Jacobin Patriot: who shall say that Robespierre is not a thorough-going man; bold in Logic at least? To

* "Journal des Débats des Jacobins" (in "Histoire Parlementaire," xxii. 296).

the like effect, or still more plainly, spake young Saint-Just, the black-haired, mild-toned youth. Danton is on mission in the Netherlands, during this preliminary work. The rest, far as one reads, welter amid Law of Nations, Social Contract, Juristics, Syllogistics; to us barren as the East wind. In fact, what can be more unprofitable than the sight of 649 ingenious men struggling with their whole force and industry, for a long course of weeks, to do at bottom this; To stretch out the old Formula and Law Phrascology, so that it may cover the new, contradictory, entirely *uncoverable* Thing? Whereby the poor Formula does but *crack*, and one's honesty along with it! The thing that is palpably *hot*, burning, wilt thou prove it, by syllogism, to be a freezing-mixture? This of stretching out Formulas till they crack, is, especially in, times of swift change, one of the sorrowfulest tasks poor Humanity has.

CHAPTER VI.

AT THE BAR.

1418. Meanwhile, in a space of some five weeks, we have got to another emerging of the Trial, and a more practical one than ever.

On Tuesday, 11th of December, the King's Trial has *emerged*, very decidedly : into the streets of Paris; in the shape of that green Carriage of Mayor Chambon, within which sits the King himself, with attendants, on his way to the Convention Hall! Attended, in that green carriage, by Mayors Chambon, Procureurs Chaumette; and outside of it, by Commandants Santerre, with cannon, cavalry, and double row of infantry; all Sections under arms, strong Patrols scouring all streets; so fares he, slowly through the dull drizzling weather: and about two o'clock we behold him, "in walnut-colored great-coat (redingote noisette)," descending through the Place Vendôme, toward that Salle de Manége; to be indicted, and judicially interrogated. The mysterious Temple Circuit has given up its secret; which now, in this walnut-colored coat, men behold with eyes. The same bodily Louis who was once Louis the Desired, fares there : hapless King, he is getting now toward port; his deplorable farings and voyagings draw to a close. What duty remains to him henceforth, that of placidly enduring, he is fit to do.

1419. The singular Procession fares on ; in silence, says Prudhomme, or amid growlings of the Marseillese Hymn ; in silence, ushers itself into the Hall of the Convention, Santerre holding Louis's arm with his hand. Louis looks round him, with composed air, to see what kind of Convention and Parliament it is. Much changed indeed :—since February gone two years, when our Constituent, then busy, spread fleur-de-lis velvet for us; and we came over to say a kind word here, and they all started up swearing Fidelity ; and all France started up swearing, and made it a Feast of Pikes; which has ended in this! Barrère, who once "wept" looking up from his Editor's-Desk, looks down now from his President's-Chair, with a list of Fifty-seven Questions; and says, dry-eyed : "Louis, you may sit down." Louis sits down : it is the very seat, they say, same timber and stuffing, from which he accepted the Constitution, amid dancing and illumination, autumn gone a year. So much woodwork remains identical; so much else is not identical. Louis sits and listens, with a composed look and mind.

1420. Of the Fifty-seven Questions we shall not give so much as one. They are questions captiously embracing all the main Documents seized on the 10th of August, or found lately in the Iron Press; embracing all the main incidents of the Revolution History; and they ask, in substance, this: Louis, who wert King, art thou not guilty to a certain extent, by act and written document, of trying to continue King? Neither in the Answers is there much notable. Mere quiet negations, for most part; an accused man standing on the simple basis of *No:* 1 do not recognize that document; I did not do that act; or did it according to tne law that then was. Whereupon the Fifty-seven Questions, and Documents to the number of 162, being exhausted in this manner, Barrère finishes, after some three hours, with his: "Louis, I invite you to withdraw."

1421. Louis withdraws, under Municipal escort into a neighboring Committee-room; having first, in leaving the bar, demanded to have Legal Counsel. He declines refreshment, in this Committee-room; then, seeing Chaumette busy with a small loaf which a grenadier had divided with him, says, he will take a bit of bread. It is five o'clock; and he had breakfasted but slightly, in a morning of such drumming and alarm. Chaumette breaks his half-loaf: the King eats of the crust; mounts the green Carriage, eating; asks now, What he shall do with the crumb? Chaumette's clerk takes it from him; flings it out into the street. Louis says, It is pity to fling out bread, in a time of dearth. "My grandmother," remarks Chaumette, "used to say to me, Little boy, never waste a crumb of bread; you cannot make one." "Monsieur Chaumette," answers Louis, "your grandmother seems to have been a sensible woman."* Poor innocent mortal; so quietly he waits the drawing of the lot;—fit to do this at least well; Passivity alone, without Activity, sufficing for it! He talks once of traveling over France by and by, to have a geographical and topographical view of it; being from of old fond of geography.—The Temple Circuit again receives him, closes on him; gazing Paris may retire to its hearths and coffee-houses, to its clubs and theaters: the damp Darkness has sunk, and with it the drumming and patroling of this strange Day.

1422. Louis is now separated from his Queen and Family; given up to his simple reflections and resources. Dull lie these stone walls round him; of his loved ones none with him. "In this state of uncertainty," providing for the worst, he writes his Will: a Paper which can still be read; full of placidity, simplicity, pious sweetness. The Convention, after debate, has granted him Legal Counsel, of his own choosing. Advocate Target feels himself "too old," being turned of fifty-four; and declines. He had gained great honor once, defending Rohan the Necklace-Cardinal; but will gain none here. Advocate Tronchet, some ten years older, does not decline. Nay behold, good old Malesherbes steps forward voluntarily; to the last of his fields, the good old hero! He is gray with seventy years: he says, "I was twice called to the Council of him who was my Master, when all the world coveted that honor; and I owe him the same service now, when it has become one which many reckon dangerous." These two, with a younger Desèze, whom they will select for pleading, are busy over that Fifty-and-seven-fold Indictment, over the Hundred and Sixty-two Documents; Louis aiding them as he can.

1423. A great Thing is now therefore in open progress; all men, in all lands watching it. By what Forms and Methods shall the Convention acquit itself, in such manner that there rest not on it even the suspicion of blame? Difficult that will be! The Convention, really much at a loss, discusses and deliberates. All day from morning to night, day after day, the Tribune drones with oratory on this matter; one must stretch the old Formula to cover the new Thing. The Patriots of the Mountain, whetted ever

* Prudhomme's newspaper (in "Histoire Parlementaire," xxi. 314).

keener, clamor for dispatch above all; the only good Form will be a swift one. Nevertheless the Convention deliberates; the Tribune drones,—drowned indeed in tenor, and even in treble, from time to time; the whole Hall shrilling up round it into pretty frequent wrath and provocation. It has droned and shrilled well-nigh a fortnight, before we can decide, this shrillness getting ever shriller, That on Wednesday, 26th of December, Louis shall appear and plead. His Advocates complain that it is fatally soon; which they well might as Advocates: but without remedy; to Patriotism it seem endlessly late.

1424. On Wednesday therefore, at the cold dark hour of eight in the morning, all Senators are at their post. Indeed they warm the cold hour, as we find, by a violent effervescence, such as is too common now; some Louvet or Buzot attacking some Tallien, Chabot; and so the whole Mountain effervescing against the whole Gironde. Scarcely is this done, at nine, when Louis and his three Advocates, escorted by the clang of arms and Santerre's National force, enter the Hall.

1425. Desèze unfolds his papers; honorably fulfilling his perilous office, pleads for the space of three hours. An honorable Pleading," composed almost overnight;" courageous yet discreet; not without ingenuity, and soft pathetic eloquence; Louis fell on his neck, when they had withdrawn, and said with tears, "Mon pauvre Desèze!" Louis himself, before withdrawing, had added a few words, "perhaps the last he would utter to them;" how it pained his heart, above all things, to be held guilty of that bloodshed on the 10th of August; or of ever shedding or wishing to shed French blood. So saying, he withdrew from that Hall;—having indeed finished his work there. Many are the strange errands he has had thither; but this strange one is the last.

1426. And now, why will the Convention loiter? Here is the Indictment and Evidence; here is the Pleading: does not the rest follow of itself? The Mountain, and Patriotism in general, clamors still louder for dispatch; for Permanent-session, till the task be done. Nevertheless a doubting, apprehensive Convention decides that it will still deliberate first; that all Members, who desire it, shall have leave to speak.—To your desks, therefore, ye eloquent Members! Down with your thoughts, your echoes and hearsays of thoughts; now is the time to show oneself; France and the Universe listens! Members are not wanting: Oration, spoken Pamphlet follows spoken Pamphlet, with what eloquence it can: President's List swells ever higher with names claiming to speak; from day to day, all days and all hours, the constant Tribune drones;—shrill Galleries supplying, very variably; the tenor and treble. It were a dull tone otherwise.

1427. The Patriots, in Mountain and Galleries, or taking counsel nightly in Section-house, in Mother Society, amid their shrill Tricoteuses, have to watch lynx-eyed; to give voice when needful; occasionally very loud. Deputy Thuriot, he who was Advocate Thuriot, who was Elector Thuriot, and from the top of the Bastille saw Saint-Antoine rising like the ocean; this Thuriot can stretch a Formula as heartily as most men. Cruel Billaud is not silent, if you incite him. Nor is cruel Jean-Bon silent; a kind of Jesuit he too;—write him not, as the Dictionaries too often do, Jamhon, which signifies mere *Ham!*

1428. But on the whole, let no man conceive it possible that Louis is not guilty. The only question for a reasonable man is or was: Can the Convention judge Louis? Or must it be the whole People; in Primary Assembly, and with delay? Always delay ye Girondins, false hommes d'état! so bellows Patriotism, its patience almost failing.—But indeed, if we consider it, what shall these poor Girondins do? Speak their conviction that Louis is a Prisoner of War; and cannot be put to death without injustice, solecism, peril? Speak such conviction; and lose utterly your footing with the decided Patriot! Nay properly it is not even a conviction, but a conjecture and dim puzzle. How many poor Girondins are sure of but one thing: That a man and Girondin ought to *have* footing somewhere, and to stand firmly on it; keeping well with the Respectable Classes! *This* is what conviction and assurance of faith they have. They must wiggle painfully between their dilemma-horns.*

1429. Nor is France idle, nor Europe. It is a Heart this Convention, as we said, which sends our influences, and receives them. A King's Execution, call it Martyrdom, call it Punishment, were an influence!—Two notable influences this Convention has already sent forth over all Nations; much to its own detriment. On the 19th of November, it emitted a Decree, and has since confirmed and unfolded the details of it, That any Nation which might see good to shake off the fetters of Despotism was thereby, so to speak, the Sister of France, and should have help and countenance. A Decree much noised of by Diplomatists, Editors, International Lawyers; such a Decree as no living Fetter of Despotism, nor Person in Authority anywhere, can approve of! It was Deputy Chambon the Girondin who propounded this Decree;—at bottom perhaps as a flourish of rhetoric.

1430. The second influence we speak of had a still poorer origin: in the restless loud-rattling slightly-furnished head of one Jacob Dupont from the Loire country. The Convention is speculating on a plan of National Education: Deputy Dupont in his speech says, " I am free to avow, M. le Président, that I for my part am an Atheist,†—thinking the world might like to know that. The French world received it without commentary; or with no audible commentary, so *loud* was France otherwise. The Foreign world received it with confutation, with horror and astonishment;‡ a most miserable influence this' And now if to these two were added a third influence and sent pulsing abroad over all the Earth: that of Regicide?

1431. Foreign Courts interfere in this Trial of Louis; Spain, England: not to be listened to; though they come, as it were, at least Spain comes, with the olive-branch in one hand, and the sword without scabbard in the other. But at home too, from out of this circumambient Paris and France, what influences come thick-pulsing! Petitions flow in; pleading for equal justice, in a reign of so-called Equality. The living Patriot pleads;—O ye National Deputies, do not the dead Patriots plead? The Twelve-hundred that lie in cold obstruction, do not they plead; and petition, in Death's dumb show, from their narrow house there, more eloquently than speech? Crippled Patriots hop on crutches round the Salle de Manége, demanding justice. The Wounded of the 10th of August, the Widows and Orphans of the Killed petition in a body; and hop and defile, eloquently mute, through the Hall: one wounded Patriot, unable to hop, is borne on his bed thither, and passes shoulder-high, in the horizontal posture.§ The Convention Tribune, which has paused at such sight, commences again,—droning mere Juristic Oratory. But out of doors Paris and is piping ever higher. Bull-voiced St.-Huruge is

heard, and the hysteric eloquence of Mother Duchess; " Varlet, Apostle of Liberty," with pike and red cap, flies hastily, carrying his oratorical folding-stool. Justice on the Traitor! cries all the Patriot world. Consider also this other cry, heard, loud on the streets: " Give us Bread, or else kill us!" Bread and Equality; Justice on the Traitor, that we may have Bread!

1432. The Limited or undecided Patriot is set against the Decided. Mayor Chambon heard of dreadful rioting at the Théâtre de la Nation: it had come to rioting, and even to fist-work, between the Decided and the Undecided, touching a new Drama called "Ami des Lois " (" Friend of the Laws)." One of the poorest Dramas ever written: but which had didactic applications in it wherefore powdered wigs of Friends of Order and black hair of Jacobin heads are flying there; and Mayor Chambon hastens with Santerre, in hopes to quell it. Far from quelling it, our poor Mayor gets so " squeezed," says the Report, and likewise so blamed and bullied, say we,—that he, with regret, quits the brief Mayoralty altogether, " his lungs being affected." This miserable " Ami des Lois " is debated of in the Convention itself; so violent, mutually-enraged, are the Limited Patriots and the Unlimited.*

1433. Between which two classes, are not Aristocrats enough, and Crypto-Aristocrats, busy? Spies running over from London with important Packets; spies pretending to run! One of the latter, Viard was the name of him, pretended to accuse Roland, and even the Wife of Roland: to the joy of Chabot and the Mountain. But the wife of Roland came, being summoned, on the instant, to the Convention Hall; came, in her high clearness; and, with few clear words, dissipated this Viard into despicability and air; all Friends of Order applauding.† So, with Theater-riots, and "Bread, or else kill us;" with Rage, Hunger, preternatural Suspicion, does this wild Paris pipe. Roland grows ever more querulous, in his Messages and Letters; rising almost to the hysterical pitch. Marat, whom no power on Earth can prevent seeing into traitors and Rolands, takes to bed for three days; almost dead, the invaluable People's-friend, with heart-break, with fever and headache: "O Peuple babillard, si tu savais agir—People of Babblers, if thou couldst but *act!*"

1434. To crown all, victorious Dumouriez, in these New-year's days, is arrived in Paris;—one fears for no good. He pretends to be complaining of Minister Pache, and Hassenfratz dilapidations; to be concerting measures for the spring Campaign: one finds him much in the company of the Girondins. Plotting with them against Jacobinism, against Equality and the punishment of Louis? We have Letters of his to the Convention itself. Will he act the old Lafayette part, this new victorious General? Let him withdraw again; not undenounced.‡

1435. And still in the Convention Tribune, it drones continually, mere Juristic Eloquence, and Hypothesis without action; and there are still fifties on the President's List. Nay these Gironde Presidents give their own party preference: we suspect they play foul with the List; men of the Mountain cannot be heard. And still it drones, all through December into January and a New-year; and there is no end! Paris pipes round it; multitudinous; ever higher, to the note of the whirlwind. Paris will "bring cannon from Saint-Denis;" there is talk of "shutting the Barriers,"—to Roland's horror.

1436. Whereupon, behold, the Convention Tribune suddenly ceases droning; we cut short, be on the

---

* See extracts from their newspapers, in "Histoire Parlementaire," xxi. 1-38, etc.

† Moniteur Séance du 14 Decembre 1792.

‡ Mrs. Hannah More. "Letter to Jacob Dupont" (London, 1793); etc , etc.

§ "Histoire Parlementaire." xxii. 131; Moore, etc.

* " Histoire Parlementaire," xxiii. 31, 48, etc.

† Moniteur, Séance du 7 Decembre 1792.

‡ Dumouriez, "Mémoires," iii. c. 4

List who likes; and *make* end. On Tuesday next, the 15th of January, 1793, it shall go to the Vote, name by name; and one way or other, this great game play itself out!

CHAPTER VII.

THE THREE VOTINGS.

1437. Is Louis Capet guilty of conspiring against Liberty? Shall our Sentence be itself final, or need ratifying by Appeal to the People? If guilty, what punishment? This is the form agreed to, after uproar and "several hours of tumultuous indecision:" these are the Three successive Questions, whereon the Convention shall now pronounce. Paris floods round their Hall; multitudinous, many-sounding. Europe and all Nations listen for their answer. Deputy after Deputy shall answer to his name: Guilty or Not Guilty.

1438. As to the Guilt, there is, as above hinted, no doubt in the mind of Patriot men. Overwhelming majority pronounces Guilt; the unanimous Convention votes for Guilt, only some feeble twenty-eight voting not Innocence, but refusing to vote at all. Neither does the Second Question prove doubtful, whatever the Girondins might calculate. Would not Appeal to the People be another name for civil war? Majority of two to one answers that there shall he no Appeal: this also is settled. Loud Patriotism, now at ten o'clock, may hush itself for the night; and retire to its bed not without hope. Tuesday has gone well. On the morrow comes, What Punishment? On the morrow is the tug of war.

1439. Consider therefore if, on this Wednesday morning, there is an affluence of Patriotism; if Paris stands a-tiptoe, and all Deputies are at their post! Seven-hundred and Forty-nine honorable Deputies; only some twenty absent on mission, Duchâtel and some Seven others absent by sickness. Meanwhile expectant Patriotism and Paris standing a-tiptoe have need of patience. For this Wednesday again passes to debate ,and effervescence; Girondins proposing that a "majority of three-fourths" shall be required; Patriots fiercely resisting them. Danton, who has just got back from mission in the Netherlands, does obtain "order of the day" on this Girondin proposal; nay he obtains farther that we decide sans désemparer, in Permanent-session, till we have done.

1440. And so, finally, at eight in the evening this Third stupendous Voting, by roll-call, or appel nominal, does begin. What punishment? Girondins undecided, Patriots decided, men afraid of Royalty, men afraid of Anarchy, must answer here and now. Infinite Patriotism, dusky in the lamp-light, floods all corridors, crowds all galleries; sternly waiting to hear. Shrill-sounding Ushers 'summon you by Name and Department; you must rise to the Tribune and say.

1441. Eye-witnesses have represented this scene of the Third Voting, and of the votings that grew out of it,—a scene protracted, like to be endless, lasting, with few brief intervals, from Wednesday till Sunday morning,—as one of the strangest seen in the Revolution. Long night wears itself into day, morning's paleness is spread over all faces; and again the wintry shadows sink, and the dim lamps are lit: but through day and night and the vicissitudes of hours, Member after Member is mounting continually those Tribune-steps; pausing aloft there, in the clearer upper light, to speak his Fate-word; then diving down into the dusk and throng again. Like Phantoms in the hour of midnight; most spectral, pandemonial! Never did President Vergniaud, or any terrestrial President, superintend the like. A King's

Life, and so much else that depends thereon, hangs trembling in the balance. Man after man mounts; the buzz hushes itself till he have spoken: Death; Banishment; Imprisonment till the Peace. Many say, Death; with what cautious well-studied phrases and paragraphs they could devise, of explanation, of enforcement, of faint recommendation to mercy. Many too say, Banishment; something short of Death. The balance trembles, none can yet guess whitherward. Whereat anxious Patriotism bellows; irrepressible by Ushers.

1442. The poor Girondins, many of them, under such fierce bellowing of Patriotism, say Death; justifying, motivant, that most miserable word of theirs by some brief casuistry and jesuitry. Vergniaud himself says, Death; justifying by jesuitry. Rich Lepelletier Saint-Fargeau had been of the Noblesse, and then of the Patriot Left Side, in the Constituent; and had argued and reported, there and elsewhere, not a little, *against* Capital Punishment: nevertheless he now says, Death; a word which may cost him dear. Manuel did surely rank with the Decided in August last; but he has been sinking and backsliding ever since September and the scenes of September. In this Convention, above all, no word he could speak would find favor; he says now, Banishment; and in mute wrath quits the place forever,—much hustled in the corridors. Philippe Égalité votes, in his soul and conscience, Death: at the sound of which and of whom, even Patriotism shakes its head: and there runs a groan and shudder through this Hall of Doom. Robespierre's vote cannot be doubtful; his speech is long. Men see the figure of shrill Sieyes ascend; hardly pausing, passing merely, this figure says, "La Mort sans phrase (Death without phrases);" and fares onward and downward. Most spectral, pandemonial!

1443. And yet if the Reader fancy it of a funereal, sorrowful or even grave character, he is far mistaken: "the Ushers in the 'Mountain quarter,' says Mercier, " had become as Box-keepers at the Opera;" opening and shutting of Galleries for privileged persons, for "D'Orléans Égalité's mistresses," or other high-dizened women of condition, rustling with laces and tricolor. Gallant Deputies pass and repass thitherward, treating them with ices, refreshments and small talk; the high-dizened heads beck responsive; some have their card and pin, pricking down the Ayes and Noes, as at a game of Rouge-et-Noir. Farther aloft reigns Mère Duchesse with her unrouged Amazons; she cannot be prevented making long Ha-has, when the vote is not La Mort. In these Galleries there is refection, drinking of wine and brandy "as in open tavern (en pleine tabagie)." Betting goes on in all coffee-houses of the neighborhood. But within doors, fatigue, impatience, uttermost weariness sits now on all visages; lighted up only from time to time by turns of the game. Members have fallen asleep; Ushers come and awaken them to vote: other Members calculate whether they shall not have time to run and dine. Figures rise, like phantoms, pale in the dusky lamp-light, utter from this Tribune, only one word: Death. "Tout est optique," says Mercier, "The world is all an optical shadow."[*] Deep in the Thursday night, when the Voting is done, and Secretaries are summing it up, sick Duchâtel, more spectral than another, comes borne on a chair, wrapped in blankets, in "nightgown and nightcap," to vote for Mercy: one vote it is thought may turn the scale.

1444. Ah no! In profoundest silence, President Vergniaud, with a voice full of sorrow, has to say: "I declare, in the name of the Convention, that the

* Mercier, "Nouveau Paris," vi. 156-159; Montgaillard, iii. 348-387; Moore, etc.

punishment it pronounces on Louis Capet is that of Death." Death by a small majority of Fifty-three. Nay, If we deduct from the one side, and add to the other, a certain Twenty-six, who said Death but coupled some faintest ineffectual surmise of mercy in it, the majority will be but One.

1445. Death is the sentence; but its execution? It is not executed yet! Scarcely is the vote declared when Louis's Three Advocates enter; with Protest in his name, with demand for Delay, for Appeal to the People. For this do Desèze and Trouchet plead, with brief eloquence: brave old Malesherbes pleads for it with eloquent want of eloquence, in broken sentences, in embarrassment and sobs; that brave time-honored face, with its gray strength, its broad sagacity and honesty, is mastered with emotion, melts into dumb tears.*—They reject the Appeal to the People; that having been already settled. But as to the Delay, what they call Sursis, it shall be considered; shall be voted for to-morrow; at present we adjourn. Whereupon Patriotism " hisses" from the Mountain; but a "tyrannical majority" has so decided, and adjourns.

1446. There is still this fourth Vote, then, growls indignant Patriotism:—this vote, and, who knows what other votes, and adjournments of voting; and the whole matter still hovering hypothetical! And at every new vote those Jesuit Girondins, even they who voted for Death, would so fain find a loop-hole! Patriotism must watch and rage. Tyrannical adjournments there have been; one, and now another at midnight on plea of fatigue,—all Friday wasted in hesitation and higgling; in re-counting of the votes, which are found correct as they stood! Patriotism bays fiercer than ever; Patriotism, by long watching, has become red-eyed, almost rabid.

1447. "Delay: yes or no?" men do vote it finally, all Saturday, all day and night. Men's nerves are worn out, men's hearts are desperate; now shall it end. Vergniaud, spite of baying, ventures to say, Yes, Delay; though he had voted Death. Philippe Egalité says, in his soul and conscience, No. The next Member mounting: "Since Philippe says No, I for my part say Yes (Moi je dis Oni)." The balance still trembles. Till finally, at three o'clock on Sunday morning, we have: No Delay, by a Majority of Seventy: Death within four-and-twenty hours!

1448. Garat, Minister of Justice, has to go to the Temple with this stern message: he ejaculates repeatedly, "Quelle commission affreuse (What a frightful function!")† Louis begs for a Confessor; for yet three days of life, to prepare himself to die. The Confessor is granted; the three days and all respite are refused.

1449. There is no deliverance, then? Thick stone walls answer, None. Has King Louis no friends? Men of action, of courage grown desperate, in this his extreme need? King Louis's friends are feeble and far. Not even a voice in the coffee-houses rises for him. At Méot the Restaurateur's no Captain, Dampmartin now dines; or sees death-doing whiskerandoes on furlough exhibit daggers of improved structure. Méot's gallant Royalists on furlough are far across the marches; they are wandering distracted over the world: or their bones lie whitening Argonne Wood. Only some weak Priests "leave Pamphlets on all the bourn-stones," this night calling for a rescue: calling for the pious women to rise; or are taken distributing Pamphlets, and sent to prison.‡

1450. Nay there is one death-door, of the ancient Méot sort, who, with effort, has done even less and worse: slain a Deputy, and set all the Patriotism of

Paris on edge! It was five on Saturday evening when Lepelletier Saint-Fargeau, having given his vote, No Delay, ran over to Février's in the Palais Royal to snatch a morsel of dinner. He had dined and was paying. A thickset man " with black hair and blue beard," in a loose kind of frock, stept up to him: it was, as Février and the bystanders bethought them, one Pâris of the old King's-Guard. "Are you Lepelletier?" asks he.—"Yes."—"You voted in the King's Business—?"—"I voted Death." —"Scélérat, take that!" cries Pâris, flashing out a saber from under his frock, and plunging it deep in Lepelletier's side. Février clutches him: but he breaks off; is gone.

1451. The voter Lepelletier lies dead; he has expired in great pain, at one in the morning:—two hours before that Vote of No Delay was fully summed up. Guardsman Pâris is flying over France: cannot be taken; will be found some months after, self-shot in a remote inn.*—Robespierre sees reason to think that Prince d'Artois himself is privately in Town; that the Convention will be butchered in the lump. Patriotism sounds mere wail and vengeance; Santerre doubles and trebles all his patrols. Pity is lost in 'rage and fear; and Convention has refused the three days of life and all respite.

CHAPTER VIII.

PLACE DE LA RÉVOLUTION.

1452. To this conclusion, then hast thou come, O hapless Louis! The Son of Sixty Kings is to die on the Scaffold by form of Law. Under Sixty Kings this same form of Law, form of Society, has been fashioning itself together these thousand years; and has become, one way and other, a most strange Machine. Surely, if needful, it is also frightful, this Machine; dead, blind; not what it should be; which with swift stroke, or cold slow torture, has wasted the lives and souls of innumerable men. And behold now a King himself, or say rather King-hood in his person, is to expire here in cruel tortures,—like a Phalaris shut the belly of his own red-heated Brazen Bull! It is ever so; and thou shouldst know it, O haughty tyrannous man: injustice breeds injustice; curses and falsehoods do verily return "always home," wide as they may wander. Innocent Louis bears the sins of many generations: he too experiences that man's tribunal is not in this Earth; that if he had no Higher one, it were not well with him.

1453. A King dying by such violence appeals impressively to the imagination; as the like must do, and ought to do. And yet at bottom it is not the King dying, but the man! Kingship is a coat: the grand loss is of the skin. The man from whom you take his Life, to him can the whole combined world do more? Lally went on his hurdle; his mouth filled with a gag. Miserablest mortals, doomed for picking pockets, have a whole five-act Tragedy in them, in that dumb pain, as they go to the gallows, unregarded; they consume the cup of trembling down to the lees. For Kings and for beggars, for the justly doomed and the unjustly, it is a hard thing to die. Pity them all: thy utmost pity, with all aids and appliance and throne-and-scaffold contrasts, how far short is it of the thing pitied!

1454. A Confessor has come: Abbé Edgeworth, of Irish extraction, whom the king knew by good report, has come promptly on this solemn mission. Leave the Earth alone, then, thou hapless King; it with its malice will go its way, thou also canst go thine. A hard scene yet remains the parting with our loved ones. Kind hearts, environed in the same

---

* Moniteur (in "Histoire Parlementaire," xxiii. 210). See Boissy d'Anglas, "Vie de Malesherbes," ii. 139.

† "Biographie des Ministres," p. 157.

‡ See Prudhomme's newspaper, Révolutions de Paris in "Histoire Parlementaire," xxiii. 316).

---

* "Histoire Parlementaire," xxii. 275, 318; Felix Lepelletier, "Vie de Michel Lepe letier son Frère," p. 61, etc. Fé ix, with due love of the miraculous, will have it that the suicide in the inn was not Paris, but some double-ganger of his.

grim peril with us; to be left *here !* Let the Reader look with the eyes of Valet Cléry through these glass-doors, where also the Municipality watches; and see the cruelest of scenes:

1455. At half-past eight, the door of the ante-room opened: the Queen appeared first, leading her Son by the hand; then Madame Royale and Madame Elizabeth: they all flung themselves into the arms of the King. Silence reigned 'for some minutes; interrupted only by sobs. The Queen made a movement to lead his Majesty toward the inner room, where M. Edgeworth was waiting unknown to them: 'No,' said the King, 'let us go into the dining-room; it is there only that I can see you. They entered there; I shut the door of it, which was of glass. The King sat down, the Queen on his left hand, Madame Elizabeth on his right, Madame Royale almost in front; the young Prince remained standing between his Father's legs. They all leaned toward him, and often held him embraced. This scene of woe lasted an hour and three-quarters; during which we could hear nothing; we could see only that always when the King spoke, the sobbing of the Princesses redoubled, continued for some minutes; and that then the King began again to speak.*" And so our meetings and our partings do now end! The sorrows we gave each other; the poor joys we faithfully shared, and all our lovings and our sufferings, and confused toilings under the earthly Sun, are over. Thou good soul, I shall never, never through all ages of Time, see thee any more!—NEVER! O Reader, knowest thou that hard word?

1456. For nearly two hours this agony lasts; then they tear themselves asunder. "Promise that you will see us on the morrow." He promises:—Ah yes, yes; yet once, and go now, ye loved ones; cry to God for yourselves and me!—It was a hard scene, but it is over. He will not see them on the morrow. The Queen, in passing through the anteroom, glanced at the Cerberus Municipals; and, with woman's vehemence, said through her tears, "Vous êtes tous des scélérats."

King Louis slept sound, till five in the morning, when Cléry, as he had been ordered, awoke him. Cléry dressed his hair: while this went forward, Louis took a ring from his watch, and kept trying it on his finger; it was his wedding-ring, which he is now to return to the Queen as a mute farewell. At half-past six, he took the Sacrament, and continued in devotion, and conference with Abbé Edgeworth. He will not see his Family: it were too hard to bear.

1457. At eight, the Municipals enter, the King gives them his Will, and messages and effects; which they, at first, brutally refuse to take charge of: he gives them a roll of gold pieces, 125 louis; these are to be returned to Malesherbes, who had lent them. At nine, Santerre says the hour is come. The King begs yet to retire for three minutes. At the end of three minutes, Santerre again says the hour is come. 'Stamping on the ground with his right-foot, Louis, answers: 'Partons (Let us go).' "—How the rolling of those drums come in through the Temple bastions and bulwarks, on the heart of a queenly wife; soon to be a widow! He is gone, then, and has not seen us? A Queen weeps bitterly; a King's Sister and Children. Over all these Four doors Death also hover; all shall perish miserably save one; she, as Duchesse d'Angoulême, will live,—not happily.

1458. At the Temple Gate were some faint cries, perhaps from voices of pitiful women: "Grâce! Grâce!" Through the rest of the streets there is silence as of the grave. No man not armed is al-

lowed to be there: the armed, did not even pity dare not express it, each man overawed by all his neighbors. All windows are down, none seen looking through them. All shops are shut. No wheel-carriage rolls, this morning, in these streets but one only. Eighty-thousand armed men stand ranked, like armed statues of men; cannons bristle, cannoneers with match burning, but no word or movement: it is as a city enchanted into silence and stone; one carriage with its escort, slowly rumbling, is the only sound. Louis reads, in his Book of Devotion, the Prayers of the Dying: clatter of death-march falls sharp on the ear, in the great silence; but the thought would fain struggle heavenward, and forget the Earth.

1459. As the Clocks strike ten, behold the Place de la Révolution, once Place de Louis Quinze; the Guillotine, mounted near the old Pedestal where once stood the Statue of that Louis! Far round, all bristles with cannons and armed men: spectators crowding in the rear; D'Orléans Égalité there in carbrolet. Swift messengers, hoquetons, speed to the Town-hall, every three minutes: near by it is the Convention sitting—vengeful for Lepelletier. Heedless of all, Louis reads his Prayers of the Dying; not till five minutes yet has he finished, then the Carriage opens. What temper he is in? Ten different witnesses will give ten different accounts of it. He is in the collision of all tempers; arrived now at the black Mahlstrom and descent of Death: in sorrow, in indignation, in resignation struggling to be resigned. "Take care of M. Edgeworth," he straitly charges the Lieutenant who is sitting with them: then they two descend.

1460. The drums are beating· "Taisez-vous (Silence)!" he cries "in a terrible voice (d'une voix terrible)." He mounts the scaffold, not without delay; he is in puce coat, breeches of gray, white stockings. He strips off the coat; stands disclosed in a sleeve-waistcoat of white flannel. The Executioners approach to bind him, he spurns, resists; Abbé Edgeworth has to remind him how the Saviour, in whom men trust, submitted to be bound. His hands are tied, his head bare; the fatal moment is come. He advances to the edge of the Scaffold, "his face very red," and says; "Frenchmen, I die innocent: it is from the Scaffold and near appearing before God that I tell you so. I pardon my enemies; I desire that France————" A General on horseback, Santerre or another, prances out, with uplifted hand: "Tambours!" The drums drown the voice. "Executioners, do your duty!" The Executioners, desperate lest themselves be murdered (for Santerre and his Armed Ranks will strike, if they do not), seize the hapless Louis: six of them desperate, him singly desperate, struggling there; and bind him to their plank. Abbé Edgeworth, stooping, bespeaks him: "Son of Saint Louis, ascend to Heaven." The Axe clanks down; a King's Life is shorn away. It is Monday, the 21st of January, 1793. He was aged Thirty-eight years, four months and twenty-eight days.†

1461. Executor Samson shows the Head: fierce shouts of Vive la République rises, and swells; caps raised on bayonets, hats waving: students of the College of Four Nations take it up, on the far Quais; fling it over Paris. D'Orléans drives off in his cabriolet: the Town-hall Councilors rub their hands, saying. "It is done, It is done." There is dipping of handkerchiefs, of pike-points in the blood. Headsman Samson, though he afterward denied it,† sells locks

---

* Cléry's "Narrative" (London, 1798), cited in Weber, iii. 312.

* Newspapers, municipal records, etc., etc. (in "Histoire Parlementaire," xxiii. 298-349): "Deux Amis," ix. 369-373; Mercier, "Nouveau Paris," iii. 3-8.
† His letter in the newspapers (" Histoire Parlementaire," ubi suprà).

of the hair: fractions of the puce coat are long after worn in rings.†—And so, in some half-hour it is done; and the multitude has all departed. Pastry-cooks, coffee-sellers, milkmen sing out their trivial quotidian cries: the world wags on, as if this were a common day. In the coffee-houses that evening, says Prudhomme, Patriot shook hands with Patriot in a more cordial manner than usual. Not till some day after, according to Mercier, did public men see what a grave thing it was.

1462. A grave thing it indisputably is; and will have consequences. On the morrow morning, Roland, so long steeped to the lips in disgust and chagrin, sends in his demission. His accounts lie all ready, correct in black-on-white to the utmost farthing; these he wants but to have audited, that he might retire to remote obscurity, to the country and his books. They will never be audited, those accounts; he will never get retired thither.

1463. It was on Tuesday that Roland demitted. On Thurday comes Lepelletier St. Fargeau's Funeral, and passage to the Pantheon of Great Men. Notable as the wild pageant of a winter day. The Body is borne aloft, half-bare; the winding-sheet disclosing the death wound saber and bloody clothes parade themselves; a "lugubrious music" wailing harsh unanime. Oak-crowns showered down from windows; President Vergniaud walks there, with Convention and Jacobin Society, and all Patriots of every color all mourning brother-like.

1464. Notable also for another thing this Burial of Lepelletier: it was the last act these men ever did with concert! All parties and figures of Opinion, that agitate this distracted France and its Convention, now stand, as it were, face to face, and dagger to dagger; the King's Life, round which they all struck and battled, being hurled down. Dumouriez, conquering Holland, growls ominous discontent, at the head of Armies. Men say Dumouriez will have a King; that young D'Orléans Égalité shall be his King. Deputy Fauchet, in the Journal des Amis, curses his day, more bitterly than Job did; invokes the poniards of Regicides, of "Arras Vipers" or Robespierres, of Pluto Dantons, of horrid Butchers Legendre and Simulacra d'Herbois, to send him swiftly to another world than theirs.† This is Te-Deum Fauchet, of the Bastille Victory, of the Cercle Social. Sharp was the death-hail rattling round one's Flag-of-truce, on that Bastille day; but it was soft to such wreckage of high Hope as this: one's New Golden Era going down on leaden dross, and sulphurous black of the Everlasting Darkness!

1465. At home this Killing of a King has divided all friends; and abroad it has united all enemies. Fraternity of People, Revolutionary Propagandism; Atheism, Regicide; total destruction of social order in this world! All Kings; and lovers of Kings, and haters of Anarchy, rant in colition; as in a war for life. England signifies to Citizen Chauvelin, the Ambassador or rather Ambassador's-Cloak, that he must quit the country in eight days. Ambassador's-Cloak and Ambassador, Chauvelin and Talleyrand, depart accordingly. Talleyrand,* implicated in that Iron Press of the Tuileries, thinks it safest to make for America.

1466. England has cast out the Embassy; England declares war,—being shocked principally, it would seem, at the condition of the River Scheldt. Spain declares war; being shocked principally at some other thing; which doubtless the Manifesto indicates.§ Nay we find it was not England that declared war first; or

Spain first, that France herself declares war first on both of them;*— a point of immense Parliamentary and Journalistic interest in those days, but which has become of no interest whatever in these. They all declare war. The sword is drawn, the scabbard thrown away. It is even as Danton said, in one of all-too gigantic figures: "The coalesced Kings threaten us; we hurl at their feet, as gage of battle the Head of a King."

BOOK THIRD.

THE GIRONDINS.

CHAPTER I.

CAUSE AND EFFECT.

1467. This huge Insurrectionary Movement, which we liken to a breaking-out of Tophet and the Abyss, has swept away Royalty, Aristocracy, and a King's life. The question is, What will it next do; how will it henceforth shape itself? Settle down into a reign of Law and Liberty; according as the habits, persuasions and endeavors of the educated, moneyed, respectable class prescribe? That is to say: the volcanic lava-flood, bursting up in the manner described, will explode and flow according to Girondin Formula and pre-established rule of Philosophy? If so, for our Girondin friends it will be well.

1468. Meanwhile were not the prophecy rather, that as no external force, Royal or other, now remains which could control this Movement, the Movement will follow a course of its own; probably a very original one! Further, that whatsoever man or men can best interpret the inward tendencies it has, and give them voice and activity, will obtain the lead of it? For the rest, that as a thing *without* order, a thing proceeding from beyond and beneath the 'region of order, it must work and welter, not as a Regularity but as a Chaos; destructive and self-destructive; always till something that *has* order arise, strong enough to bind it into subjection again? Which something, we may farther conjecture, will not be a Formula, with philosophical propositions and forensic eloquence; but a Reality, probably with a sword in its hand?

1469. As for the Girondin Formula, of a respectable Republic for the Middle Classes, all manner of Aristocracies being now sufficiently demolished, there seems little reason to expect that the business will stop there. *Liberty, Equality, Fraternity*, these are the words; enunciative and prophetic. Republic for the respectable washed Middle Classes, how can that be the fulfillment thereof? Hunger and nakedness, and nightmare oppression lying heavy on 25,000,000 hearts; this, not the wounded vanities or contradicted philosophies of philosophical Advocates, rich Shop-keepers, rural Noblesse, was the prime mover in the French Revolution; as the like will be in all such Revolutions, in all countries. Feudal Fleur-de-lis-had become an insupportably bad marching-banner, and needed to be torn and trampled; but Money-bag of Mammon (for that, in these times, is what the respectable Republic for the Middle Classes will signify) is a still worse, while it lasts. Properly, indeed, it is the worst and basest of all banners and symbols of dominion among men; and indeed is possible only in a time of general Atheism, and Unbelief in anything save in brute Force and Sensualism; pride of birth, pride of office, any known kind of pride being a degree better than purse pride. Freedom, Equality, Brotherhood: not in the Money-bag, but far elsewhere, will Sansculottism seek these things.

---

* Forster's "Briefwechsel," i. 473.
† "Histoire Parlementaire," ubi suprà.
‡ "Annual Register" of 1793, pp. 114–128.
§ 23d March ("Annual Register," p. 161).

* 1st February: 7th March (Moniteur of these dates).

1470. We say therefore that an Insurrectionary France, loose of control from without, destitute of supreme order from within, will form one of the most tumultuous Activities ever seen on this Earth; such as no Girondin Formula can regulate. An immeasurable force, made up of forces manifold, heterogeneous, compatible and incompatible. In plainer words, this France must needs split into Parties; each of which seeking to make itself good, contradiction, exasperation will arise; and Parties on Parties find that they cannot work together, cannot exist together.

1471. As for the number of Parties, there will, strictly counting, be as many Parties as there are opinions. According to which rule, in this National Convention itself, to say nothing of France generally, the number of Parties ought to be 749; for every unit entertains his opinion. But now, as every unit has at once an individual nature or necessity to follow his own road, and a gregarious nature or necessity to see himself traveling by the side of others,—what can there be but dissolutions, precipitations, endless turbulence of attracting and repelling; till once the master-element get evolved, and this wild alchemy arrange itself again?

1472. To the length of 749 Parties, however, no Nation was ever yet seen to go. Nor indeed much beyond the length of Two Parties; two at a time:—so invincible is man's tendency to unite, with all the invincible divisiveness he has! Two Parties, we say, are the usual number at one time: let these two fight it out, all minor shades of party rallying under the shade likest them; when the one has fought down the other, then it, in its turn, may divide, self-destructive; and so the process continue, as far as needful. This is the way of Revolutions, which spring up as the French one has done; when the so-called Bonds of Society snap asunder; and all Laws that are not Laws of Nature become naught and Formulas merely.

1473. But, quitting these somewhat abstract considerations, let History note this concrete reality which the streets of Paris exhibit, on Monday the 25th of February, 1793. Long before daylight that morning, these streets are noisy and angry. Petitioning enough there has been; a Convention often solicited. It was but yesterday there came a Deputation of Washerwomen with Petition; complaining that not so much soap could be had; to say nothing of bread, and condiments of bread. The cry of women, round the Salle de Manége, was heard plaintive: "Du pain et du savon (Bread and soap)."*

1474. And now from six o'clock, this Monday morning, one perceives the Baker's Queues unusually expanded, angrily agitating themselves. Not the Baker alone, but two Section Commissioners to help him, manage with difficulty the daily distribution of loaves. Soft-spoken assiduous, in the early candle-light, are Baker and Commissioners: and yet the pale chill February sunrise discloses an unpromising scene. Indignant Female Patriots, partly supplied with bread, rush now to the shops, declaring that they will have groceries. Groceries enough: sugar-barrels rolled forth into the street, Patriot Citoyennes weighing it out at a just rate of eleven-pence a pound; likewise coffee-chests, soap-chests, nay cinnamon and cloves-chests, with aquavitæ and other forms of alcohol,—at a just rate, which some do not pay; the pale-faced Grocer silently wringing his hands! What help? The distributive Citoyennes are of violent speech and gesture, their long Eumenides-hair hanging out of curl; nay in their girdles pistols are seen sticking: some, it is even said have

*Moniteur, etc. (" Histoire Parlementaire.' xxiv. 332-848).

beards,—male Patriots in petticoats and mob-cap. Thus, in the street of Lombards, in the street of Five-Diamonds, street of Pulleys, in most streets of Paris does it effervesce, the live-long day; no Municipality, no Mayor Pache, though he was War-Minister lately, sends military against it, or aught against it but persuasive-eloquence, till seven at night, or later.

1475. On Monday gone five weeks, which was the 21st of January, we saw Paris, beheading its King, stand silent, like a petrified City of Enchantment: and now on this Monday it is so noisy, selling sugar! Cities, especially Cities in Revolution, are subject to these alternations; the secret courses of civic business and existence effervescing and efflorescing, in this manner, as a concrete Phenomenon to the eye. Of which Phenomenon, when secret existence becoming public effloresces on the street, the philosophical cause and effect is not so easy to find. What, for example, may be the accurate philosophical meaning and meanings of this sale of sugar? These things that have become visible in the street of Pulleys and over Paris, whence are they, we say; and whither?—

1476. That Pitt has a hand in it, the gold of Pitt: so much, to all reasonable Patriot men, may seem clear. But then, through what agents of Pitt? Varlet, Apostle of Liberty, was discerned again of late, with his pike and red nightcap. Deputy Marat published in his Journal, this very day, complaining of the bitter scarcity, and sufferings of the people, till he seemed to get wroth: "If your Rights of Man were anything but a piece of written paper, the plunder of a few shops, and a forestaller or two hung up at the door-lintels, would put an end to such things.* Are not these, say the Girondins, pregnant indications? Pitt has bribed the Anarchists; Marat is the agent of Pitt: hence this sale of sugar. To the Mother Society, again, it is clear that the scarcity is factitious: is the work of Girondins, and such-like; a set of men sold partly to Pitt; sold wholly to their own ambitions and hard-hearted pedantries; who will not fix the grain-prices, but prate pedantically of free-trade; wishing to starve Paris into violence, and embroil it with the Departments: hence this sale of sugar.

1477. And, alas, if to these two notabilities, of a Phenomenon and such Theories of a Phenomenon, we add this third notability. That the French Nation has believed, for several years now, in the possibility, nay certainty and near advent. of a universal Millennium, or reign of Freedom, Equality, Fraternity, wherein man should be the brother of man, and sorrow and sin flee away? Not bread to eat, nor soap to wash with; and the reign of Perfect Felicity ready to arrive, due always since the Bastille fell! How did our hearts burn within us, at that Feast of Pikes, when brother flung himself on brother's bosom; and in sunny jubilee, 25,000,000 burst forth into sound and cannon-smoke! Bright was our Hope then, as sunlight; red-angry is our Hope now, as consuming fire. But, O Heavens, what enchantment is it, or devilish legerdemain, of such effect, that Perfect Felicity, always within arm's length, could never be laid hold of, but only in her stead Controversy and Scarcity? This set of traitors after that set! Tremble, ye traitors; dread a People which calls itself patient, long-suffering; but which cannot always submit to have its pocket picked, in this way,—of a Millennium!

1478. Yes, Reader, here is the miracle. Out of that putrescent rubbish of Skepticism, Sensualism, Sentimentalism, hollow Machiavelism, such a Faith has verily risen; flaming in the heart of a People.

* " Histoire Parlementaire," xxiv. 353-356.

A whole People, awakening as it were to conscious-ness in deep misery, believes that it is within reach of a Fraternal Heaven-ou-Earth. With longing arms, it struggles to embrace the Unspeakable; cannot embrace it, owing to certain causes.—Seldom do we find that a whole People can be said to have any Faith at all; except in things which it can eat and handle. Whensoever it gets any Faith, its history becomes spirit-stirring, noteworthy. But since the time when steel Europe shook itself simultaneously at the word of Hermit Peter, and rushed toward the Sepulcher where God had lain, there was no uni-versal impulse of Faith that one could note. Since Protestantism went silent, no Luther's voice, no Zisca's drum any longer proclaiming that God's Truth was *not* the Devil's Lie; and the Last of the Cameronians (Renwick was the name of him; honor to the name of the brave!) sank, shot, on the Castle-hill of Edinburgh, there was no partial impulse of Faith among Nations. Till now, behold, once more, this French Nation believes! Herein, we say, in that astonishing Faith of theirs, lies the miracle. It is a Faith undoubtedly of the more prodigious sort, even among Faiths; and will embody itself in prodi-gies. It is the soul of that world-prodigy named French Revolution; whereat the world still gazes and shudders.

1479 But, for the rest, let no man ask History to explain by cause and effect how the business pro-ceeded henceforth. This battle of Mountain and Gironde, and what follows, is the battle of Fanati-cisms and Miracles; unsuitable for cause and effect. The sound of it, to the mind, is as a hubbub of voices in distraction; little of articulate is to be gathered by long listening and studying: only battle-tumult, shouts of triumph, shrieks of despair. The Mount-ain has left no Memoirs; the Girondins have left Memoirs, which are too often little other than long-drawn Interjections, of *Woe is me, and Cursed be ye.* So soon as History can philosophically delineate the conflagration of a kindled Fire-ship, she may try this other task. Here lay the bitumen-stratum, there the brimstone one, so ran the vein of powder, of nitre, terebinth and foul grease this, were she inquisitive enough, History might partly know. But how they acted and reacted below decks, one fire-stratum playing into the other, by its nature and the art of man, now when all hands ran raging, and the flames lashed high over shrouds and topmast this let not History attempt.

1480 The Fire-ship is old France, the old French Form of Life, her crew a Generation of men. Wild are their cries and their ragings there, like spirits tormented in that flame But, on the whole, are they not *gone,* O Reader? Their Fire-ship and they, frightening the world, have sailed away; its flames and its thunders quite away, into the Deep of Time. One thing therefore History will do: pity them all; for it went hard with them all. Not even the sea-green Incorruptible but shall have some pity, some human love, though it takes an effort. And, now, so much once thoroughly attained, the rest will become easier To the eye of equal brotherly pity, innu-merable perversions dissipate themselves; exaggera-tions and execrations fall off, of their own accord Standing wistfully on the saf. shore, we will look, and see, what is of interest to us, what is adapted to us.

CHAPTER II.

CULOTTIC AND SANSCULOTTIC.

1481 Gironde and Mountain are now in full quar-rel; their mutual rage, says Toulongeon, is growing a " pale " rage. Curious, lamentable. all these men

have the word Republic on their lips; in the heart of every one of them is a passionate wish for some-thing which he calls Republic: yet see their death-quarrel! So, however, are men made. Creatures who live in confusion; who, once thrown together, can readily fall into that confusion of confusions which quarrel is, simply because their confusions differ from one another; still more because they seem to differ! Men's words are a poor exponent of their thought; nay their thought itself is a poor exponent of the inward unnamed Mystery, wherefrom both thought and action have their birth. No man can explain himself, can get himself explained; men see not one another, but distorted phantasms which they call one another; which they hate and go to battle with: for all battle is well said to be *misunderstand-ing.*

1482. But indeed that similitude of the Fire-ship; of our poor French brethren, so fiery themselves, working also in an *element* of fire, was not insignifi-cant. Consider it well, there is a shade of the truth in it. For a man once committed headlong to re-publican or any other Transcendentalism, and fight-ing and fanaticising amid a Nation of his like, be-comes as it were enveloped in an ambient atmos-phere of Transcendentalism and Delirium: his indi-vidual self is lost in something that is not himself, but foreign though inseparable from him. Strange to think of, the man's cloak still seems to hold the same man: and yet the man is not there, his voli-tion is not there; nor the source of what he will do and devise; instead of the man and his volition there is a piece of Fanaticism and Fatalism incar-nated in the shape of him. He, the hapless incar-nated Fanaticism, goes his road; no man can help him, he himself least of all. It is a wonderful, tragical predicament;—such as human language, unused to deal with these things, being contrived for the uses of common life, struggles to shadow out in figures. The ambient element of material fire is not wilder than this of Fanaticism; nor, though visible to the eye, is it more real. Volition bursts forth involuntary-voluntary; rapt along; the movement of free human minds becomes a raging tornado of fatalism, blind as the winds; and Mountain and Gironde, when they recover themselves, are alike astounded to see *where* it has flung and dropt them. To such height of miracle can men work on men; the Conscious and the Unconscious blended inscru-tably in this our inscrutable Life; endless Necessity environing Freewill!

1483. The weapons of the Girondins are Political Philosophy, Respectability and Eloquence. Elo-quence, or call it rhetoric, really of a superior order; Vergniaud, for instance, turns a period as sweetly as any man of that generation. The weapons of the Mountain are those of mere Nature: Audacity and Impetuosity which may become Ferocity, as of men complete in *their* determination, in their conviction; nay of men, in some cases, who as Septemberers must either prevail or perish. The ground to be fought for is Popularity: farther you may either seek Popu-larity with the friends of Freedom and Order, or with the friends of Freedom Simple: to seek it with both has unhappily become impossible. With the former sort; and generally with the Authorities of the Departments, and such as read Parliamentary Debates, and are of Respectability, and of a peace-loving moneyed nature, the Girondins carry it. With the extreme Patriot again, with the indigent Millions, especially with the Population of Paris who do not read so much as hear and see, the Giron-dins altogether lose it, and the Mountain carries it.

1484. Egoism, nor meanness of mind, is not want-ing on either side. Surely not on the Girondin side;

where in fact the instinct of self-preservation, too prominently unfolded by circumstances, cuts almost a sorry figure; where also a certain finesse, to the length even of shuffling and shamming, now and then shows itself. They are men skillful in Advocate-fence. They have been called the Jesuits of the Revolution;* but that is too hard a name. It must be owned likewise that this rude blustering Mountain has a sense in it of what the Revolution means; which these eloquent Girondins are totally void of Was the Revolution made, and fought for, against the world, these four weary years, that a Formula might be substantiated; that Society might become methodic, demonstrable by logic; and the old Noblesse with their pretensions vanish? Or ought it not withal to bring some glimmering of light and alleviation to the 25,000,000, who sat in darkness, heavy-laden, till they rose with pikes in their hands? At least and lowest, one would think, it should bring them a proportion of bread to live on? There is in the Mountain here and there; in Marat People's-friend; in the incorruptible Sea-green himself, though otherwise so lean and formulary, a heartfelt knowledge of this latter fact;—without which knowledge all other knowledge here is naught, and the choicest forensic eloquence is as sounding brass and a tinkling cymbal. Most cold, on the other hand, most putronizing, unsubstantial is the tone of the Girondins toward "our poorer brethren;"—those brethren whom one often hears of under the collective name of "the masses," as if they were no persons at all, but mounds of combustible explosive material, for blowing down Bastilles with! In very truth, a Revolutionist of this kind, is he not a Solecism? Disowned by Nature and Art; deserving only to be erased, and disappear! Surely, to our poorer brethren of Paris, all this Girondin patronage sounds deadening and killing: if fine-spoken and incontrovertible in logic, then all the falser, all the hatefuler in fact.

1485. Nay doubtless, pleading for Popularity, here among our poorer brethren of Paris, the Girondin has a hard game to play. If he gain the ear of the Respectable at a distance, it is by insisting on September and such-like; it is at the expense of this Paris where he dwells and perorates. Hard to perorate in such an auditory! Wherefore the question arises: Could not we get ourselves out of this Paris? Twice or oftener such an attempt is made. If not we ourselves, thinks Guadet, then at least our Suppléans might do it. For every Deputy has his Suppléant, or Substitute, who will take his place if need be: might not these assemble, say at Bourges, which is a quiet episcopal Town, in quiet Berri, forty good leagues off? In that case, what profit were it for the Paris Sansculottery to insult us; our Suppléans sitting quiet in Bourges, to whom we could run? Nay, even the Primary electoral Assemblies, thinks Guadet, might be reconvoked, and a New Convention got, with new orders from the Sovereign People; and right glad were Lyons, were Bourdeaux, Rouen, Marseilles, as yet Provincial Towns, to welcome us in their turn, and become a sort of Capital Towns; and teach these Parisians reason.

1486. Fond schemes; which all misgo! If decreed, in heat of eloquent logic, to-day, they are repealed, by clamor and passionate wider considerations, on the morrow.† Will you, O Girondins, parcel us into separate Republics, then; like the Swiss, like your Americans; so that there be no Metropolis or indivisible French Nation any more? Your Departmental Guard seemed to point that way! Federal Republic? Federalist? Men and Knitting-women

repeat Fédéraliste, with or without much Dictionary-meaning; but go on repeating it, as is usual in such cases, till the meaning of it becomes almost magical, fit to designate all mystery of Iniquity; and Fédéraliste has grown a word of Exorcism and Apage-Satanas. But furthermore, consider what "poisoning of public opinion" in the Departments, by these, Brissot, Gorsas, Caritat-Condorcet Newspapers! And then also what counter-poisoning, still feller in quality, by a Père Duchesne of Hébert, brutalest Newspaper yet published on Earth; by a Rougiff of Guffroy; by the "incendiary leaves of Marat"! More than once, on complaint-given and effervescence rising, it is decreed that a man cannot both be Legislator and Editor; that he shall choose between the one function and the other.* But this too, which indeed could help little, is revoked or eluded; remains a pious wish mainly.

1487. Meanwhile, as the sad fruit of such strife, behold, O ye National Representatives, how, between the friends of Law and the friends of Freedom everywhere, mere heats and jealousies have arisen; fevering the whole Republic! Department, Provincial Town is set against Metropolis, Rich against Poor, Culottic against Sansculottic, man against man. From the Southern Cities come Addresses of an almost inculpable character; for Paris has long suffered Newspaper calumny. Bourdeaux demands a reign of Law and Respectability, meaning Girondism, with emphasis. With emphasis Marseilles demands the like. Nay, from Marseilles there come two Addresses: one Girondin; one Jacobin Sansculottic. Hot Rebecqui, sick of this Convention-work, has given place to his Substitute, and gone home; where also, with such jarrings, there is work to be sick of.¶

1488. Lyons, a place of Capitalists and Aristocrats, is in still worse state; almost in revolt. Chalier the Jacobin Town-Councilor has got, too literally, to daggers-drawn with Nièvre-Chol the Modératin Mayor; one of your Moderate, perhaps Aristocrat, Royalist or Federalist Mayors! Chalier, who pilgrimed to Paris "to behold Marat and the Mountain," has verily kindled himself at their sacred ran: for on the 6th of February last, History or Rumor has seen him haranguing his Lyons Jacobins in a quite transcendental manner, with a drawn dagger in his hand; recommending (they say) sheer September methods, patience being worn out; and that the Jacobin Brethren should, impromptu, work the Guillotine themselves! One sees him still, in Engravings; mounted on a table; foot advanced, body contorted; a bald, rude, slope-browed, infuriated visage of the canine species, the eyes starting from their sockets; in his puissant right-hand the brandished dagger, or horse-pistol, as some give it; other dog-visages kindling under him:—a man not likely to end well! However, the Guillotine was not got together impromptu, that day, "on the Pont Saint-Clair," or elsewhere; but indeed continued lying rusty in its loft: Nièvre-Chol† with military went about, rumbling cannon, in the most confused manner; and the "900 prisoners" received no hurt. So distracted is Lyons grown, with its cannons rumbling. Convention Commissioners must be sent thither forthwith: if even they can appease it, and keep the Guillotine in its loft.

1489. Consider finally if, on all these mad jarrings of the Southern Cities, and of France generally, a traitorous Crypto-Royalist class is not looking and watching; ready to strike in, at the right season! Neither is there bread; neither there soap; see the Patriot women selling out sugar, at a just rate

---

* Dumouriez, "Mémoires," iii. 314.
† Moniteur, 1793, No. 140, etc.

* "Histoire Parlementaire." xxv. 25, etc.
† "Histoire Parlementaire." xxiv. 385-393; xxvi. 229, etc.

of twenty-two sous per pound! Citizen Representatives, it were verily well that your quarrels finished, and the reign of Perfect Felicity began.

CHAPTER III.

GROWING SHRILL.

1490. On the whole, one cannot say that the Girondins are wanting to themselves, so far as good-will might go. They prick assiduously into the sore-places of the Mountain; from principle, and also from Jesuitism.

1491. Besides September, of which there is now little to be made except effervescence, we discern two sore-places where the Mountain often suffers: Marat, and Orléans Egalité. Squalid Marat, for his own sake and for the Mountain's, is assaulted ever and anon; held up to France, as a squalid blood-thirsty Portent, inciting to the pillage of the shops; of whom let the Mountain have the credit! The Mountain murmurs, ill at ease: this "Maximum of Patriotism," how shall they either own him or disown him? As for Marat personally, he, with his fixed-idea, remains invulnerable to such things; nay the People's Friend is very evidently rising in importance, as his befriended People rises. No shrieks now, when he goes to speak: occasional applauses rather, furtherance which breeds confidence. The day when the Girondins proposed to "decree him accused" (décréter d'accusation, as they phrase it) for that February Paragraph, of "hanging up a Forestaller or two at the door-lintels," Marat proposes to have *them* "decreed insane;" and, descending the Tribune-steps, is heard to articulate these most unsenatorial ejaculations, "Les cochons, les imbécilles (Pigs, idiots)!" Oftentimes he croaks harsh sarcasm, having really a rough rasping tongue, and a very deep fund of contempt for fine outsides; and once or twice, he even laughs, nay "explodes into laughter (rit aux éclats)," at the gentilities and superfine airs of these Girondin "men of statesmanship," with their pedantries, plausibilities, pusillanimities: "These two years," says he, "you have been whining about attacks, and plots, and danger from Paris; and you have not a scratch to show for yourselves."* —Danton gruffly rebukes him, from time to time: a Maximum of Patriotism whom one can neither own nor disown!

1492. But the second sore-place of the Mountain is this anomalous Monseigneur Equality Prince d'Orléans. Behold these men, says the Gironde; with a whilom Bourbon Prince among them: they are creatures of the D'Orléans Faction; they will have Phillippe made King; one King no sooner guillotined than another made in his stead! Girondins have moved, Buzot moved long ago, from principle and also from Jesuitism, that the whole race of Bourbons should be marched forth from the soil of France; this Prince Égalité to bring up the rear. Motions which might produce some effect on the public;—which the Mountain, ill at ease, knows not what to do with.

1493. And poor Orléans Égalité himself, for one begins to pity even him, what does he do with them? The disowned of all Parties, the rejected and foolishly bedrifted hither and thither, to what corner of Nature can he now drift with advantage! Feasible hope remains not for him: unfeasible hope, in pallid doubtful glimmers, there may still come, bewildering, not cheering or illuminating,—from the Dumouriez quarter; and how if not the time-wasted, Orléans Égalité, then perhaps the young unworn Chartres Égalité might rise to be a kind of King? Sheltered, if sheltered it be, in the clefts of the Mountain, poor Egalité will wait: one refuge in Jacobinism, one in Dumouriez and Counter-Revolution, are there not two chances? However the look of him, Dame Genlis says, is grown gloomy; sad to see. Sillery also, the Genlis's Husband, who hovers about the Mountain, not on it, is in a bad way. Dame Genlis is come to Raincy, out of England and Bury St. Edmunds, in these days; being summoned by Égalité with her young charge, Mademoiselle Égalité,—that so Mademoiselle might not be counted among Emigrants and hardly dealt with. But it proves a raveled business: Genlis and charge find that they must retire to the Netherlands; must wait on the Frontiers, for a week or two; till Monseigneur, by Jacobin help, get it wound up. "Next morning," says Dame Genlis, "Monseigneur, gloomier than ever, gave me his arm, to lead me to the carriage. I was greatly troubled; Mademoiselle burst into tears; her Father was pale and trembling. After I had got seated, he stood immovable at the carriage-door, with his eyes fixed on me; his mournful and painful look seemed to implore pity;—'Adieu, Madam!' said he.• The altered sound of his voice completely overcame me; unable to utter a word, I held out my hand; he grasped it close; then turning, and advancing sharply toward the postilions, he gave them a sign, and we rolled away."*

1494. Nor are Peace-makers wanting; of whom likewise we mention two; one fast on the crown of the Mountain, the other not yet alighted anywhere. Danton and Barrère. Ingenious Barrère, Old-Constituent and Editor, from the slopes of the Pyrenees, is one of the usefulest men of this Convention, in his way. Truth may lie on both sides, on either side, or on neither side; my friends, ye must give and take: for the rest, success to the winning side! This is the motto of Barrère. Ingenious, almost genial, quick-sighted, supple, graceful; a man that will prosper. Scarcely Belial in the assembled Pandemonium was plausibler to ear and eye. An indispensable man: in the great *Art of Varnish* he may be said to seek his fellow. Has there an explosion arisen, as many do arise, a confusion, unsightliness, which no tongue can speak of, nor eye look on; give it to Barrère; Barrère shall be Committee-Reporter of it; you shall see it transmute itself into a regularity, into the very beauty and improvement that was needed. Without one such man, we say, how were this Convention bested? Call him not, as exaggerative Mercier does, "the greatest liar in France:" nay it may be argued there is not truth enough in him to make a real lie of. Call him, with Burke, Anacreon of the Guillotine, and a man serviceable to this Convention.

1495. The other Peace-maker whom we name is Danton. Peace, O peace with one another! cries Danton often enough: Are we not alone against the world; a little band of brothers? Broad Danton is loved by all the Mountain; but they think him too easy-tempered, deficient in suspicion: he has stood between Dumouriez and much censure, anxious not to exasperate our only General: in the shrill tumult Danton's strong voice reverberates, for union and pacification. Meetings there are; dinings with the Girondins: it is so pressingly essential that there be union. But the Girondins are haughty and respectable: this Titan Danton is not a man of Formulas and there rests on him a shadow of September. "Your Girondins have no confidence in me:" this is the answer a conciliatory Meillan gets from him; to all the arguments and pleadings this conciliatory Meillan can bring, the repeated answer is, "Ils n'ont point de confiance."†—The tumult will get ever shriller; rage is growing pale.

* Genlis, "Mémoires" (London, 1825), iv. 118.
† "Mémoires de Meillan, Représentant du Peuple" (Paris, 1823), p. 51.

1496. In fact, what a pang is it to the heart of a Girondin, this first withering probability that the despicable unphilosophic anarchic Mountain, after all, may triumph! Brutal Septemberers, a fifth-floor Tallien "a Robespierre without an idea in his head," as Condorcet says, "or a feeling in his heart:" and yet we, the flower of France, cannot stand against them; behold the scepter departs from us; from us and goes to them! Éloquence, Philosophism, Respectability avail not: "against Stupidity the very gods fight to no purpose,

"Mit der Dummheit kampfen Gotter selbst vergebens!"

Shrill are the plaints of Louvet; his thin existence all acidified into rage and preternatural insight of suspicion. Wroth is young Barbaroux; wroth and scornful. Silent, like a Queen with the aspic on her bosom, sits the wife of Roland; Roland's Accounts never yet got audited, his name become a byword. Such is the fortune of war, especially of revolution. The great gulf of Tophet and 10th of August opened itself at the magic of your eloquent voice; and lo now, it will not close at your voice! It is a dangerous thing such magic. The Magician's Famulus got hold of the forbidden Book and summoned a goblin: Plait-il (What is your will) said the Goblin, The Famulus, somewhat struck, bade him fetch water: the swift goblin fetched it, pail in each hand; but lo, would not cease fetching it! Desperate, the Famulus shrieks at him, smites at him, cuts him in two; lo, two goblin water-carriers ply; and the house will be swum away in Deucalion Deluges.

CHAPTER IV.

FATHERLAND IN DANGER.

1497. Or rather we will say, this Senatorial war might have lasted long; and Party tugging and throttling with Party might have suppressed and smothered one another, in the ordinary bloodless Parliamentary way; on one condition; that France had been at least able to exist, all the while. But this Sovereign People has a digestive faculty, and cannot do without bread. Also we are at war, and must have victory; at war with Europe, with Fate and Famine: and behold, in the spring of the year, all victory deserts us.

1498. Dumouriez had his outposts stretched as far as Aix-la-Chapelle, and the beautifulest plan for pouncing on Holland, by stratagem, flat-bottomed boats and rapid intrepidity; wherein too he had prospered so far; and unhappily could prosper no farther. Aix-la-Chapelle is lost; Maestricht will not surrender to mere smoke and noise: the flat-bottomed boats have to launch themselves again, and return the way they came. Steady now, ye rapidly intrepid men; retreat with firmness, Pathian-like! Alas, were it General Miranda's fault; were it the War-minister's fault; or were it Dumouriez's own fault and that of Fortune: enough, there is nothing for it but retreat,—well if it be not even flight; for already terror-stricken cohorts and stragglers pour off, not waiting for order; flow disastrous, as many as 10,000 of them, without halt till they see France again.* Nay worse: Dumouriez himself is perhaps secretly turning traitor? Very sharp is the tone in which he writes to our Committees. Commissioners and Jacobin Pillagers have done such incalculable mischief; Hassenfratz sends neither cartridges nor clothing; shoes we have, deceptively "soled with wood and pasteboard." Nothing in short is right. Danton and Lacroix, when it was they that were Commissioners, would needs join Belgium to France;—of which Dumouriez might

have made the prettiest little Duchy for his own secret behoof! With all these things the General is wroth: and writes to us in a sharp tone. Who knows what this hot little General is meditating? Dumouriez Duke of Belgium or Brabant; and say, Égalité the younger King of France: there were an end for our Revolution!—Committee of Defense gazes, and shakes its head: who except Danton, defective in suspicion, could still struggle to be of hope?

1499. And General Custine is rolling back from the Rhine Country; conquered Mentz will be reconquered, the Prussians gathering round to bombard it with shot and shell. Mentz may resist, Commissioner Merlin, the Thionviller, "making sallies, at the head of the besieged;"—resist to the death; but not longer than that. How sad a reverse for Mentz! Brave Forster, brave Lux planted Liberty-trees, amid ça-iraing music, in the snow-slush of last winter, there; and made Jacobin Societies; and got the territory incorporated with France; they came hither to Paris, as Deputies or Delegates, and have their eighteen francs a-day; but see, before once the Liberty-tree is got rightly in leaf, Mentz is changing into an explosive crater; vomiting fire, bevomited with fire!

1500. Neither of these men shall again see Mentz; they have come hither only to die. Forster has been round the Globe; he saw Cook perish under Owhyhee clubs; but like this Paris he has yet seen or suffered nothing. Poverty escorts him: from home there can nothing come, except Job's news: the eighteen daily francs, which we here as Deputy or Delegate with difficulty "touch," are in paper assignats, and sink fast in value. Poverty, disappointment, inaction, obloquy; the brave heart slowly breaking! Such is Forster's lot. For the rest, Demoiselle Théroigne smiles on you in the Soirées; "a beautiful brown-locked face," of an exalted temper: and contrives to keep her carriage. Prussian Trenck, the poor subterranean Baron, jargons and jangles in an unmelodious manner. Thomas Paine's face is red-pustuled, "but the eyes uncommonly bright." Convention Deputies ask you to dinner: very courteous; "we all play at plump-sack."* "It is the Explosion and New-creation of a World," says Forster, "and the actors in it, such small mean objects, buzzing round one like a handful of flies."

1501. Likewise there is war with Spain. Spain will advance through the gorges of the Pyrenees; rustling with Bourbon banners, jingling with artillery and menace. And England has donned the red coat; and marches, with Royal Highness of York,—whom some once spake of inviting to be our King. Changed that humor now: and ever more changing; till no hatefuler thing walk this Earth than a denizen of that tyrannous Island; and Pitt be declared and decreed, with effervescence, "L'ennemi du genre humain (The enemy of mankind);" and, very singular to say, you make order that no Soldier of Liberty give quarter to an Englishman. Which order, however, the Soldier of Liberty does but partially obey. We will take no Prisoners then, say the Soldiers of Liberty; they shall all be "Deserters" that we take.† It is a frantic order; and attended with inconvenience. For surely, if you give no quarter, the plain issue is that you will get none; and so the business become as broad as it was long.—Our "recruitment of 300,000 men," which was the decreed force for this year, is like to have work enough laid to its hand.

1502. So many enemies come wending on; penetrating through throats of mountains, steering over the salt sea; toward all points of our territory; rattling chains at us. Nay, worst of all: there is an

* Dumouriez, iv. 16-73.

* Forster's "Briefwechsel," ii. 514, 460, 631.
† See Dampmartin, "Événemens," ii. 213-230.

enemy within our own territory itself. In the early days of March the Nantes Post-bags do not arrive; there arrive only instead of them Conjecture, Apprehension, bodeful wind of Rumor. The bodefulest proves true. Those fanatic peoples of La Vendée will no longer keep under: their fire of insurrection, heretofore dissipated with difficulty, blazes out anew, after the King's Death, as a wide conflagration; not riot, but civil war. Your Cathelineaus, your Stofflets, Charettes, are other men than was thought: behold how their Peasants, in mere russet and hodden, with their rude arms, rude array, with their fanatic Gaelic frenzy and wild-yelling battle-cry of *God and the King*, dash at us like a dark whirlwind; and blow the best-disciplined Nationals we can get into panic and sauve-qui-peut! Field after field is theirs; one sees not where it will end. Commandant Santerre may be sent there; but with non-effect; he might as well have returned and brewed beer.

1503. It has become peremptorily necessary that a National Convention cease arguing, and begin acting. Yield one party of you to the other, and do it swiftly. No theoretic outlook is here, but the close certainty of *ruin*; the very day that is passing over us must be provided for.

1504. It was Friday the Eighth of March when this Job's-post from Dumouriez, thickly preceded and escorted by so many other Job's-posts, reached the National Convention. Blank enough are most faces. Little will it avail whether our Septemberers be punished or go unpunished; if Pitt and Cobourg are coming in, with one punishment for us all; nothing now between Paris itself and the Tyrants but a doubtful Dumouriez and hosts in loose-flowing loud retreat!—Danton the Titan rises in this hour as always in the hour of need. Great is his voice, reverberating from the domes:—Citizen-Representatives, shall we not, in such crisis of Fate, lay aside discords? Reputation: O what is the reputation of this man or of that? "Que mon nom soit flétri; que la France soit libre (Let my name be blighted; let France be free)!" It is necessary now again that France rise, in swift vengeance, with her million right-hands, with her heart as of one man. Instantaneous recruitment in Paris; let every Section of Paris furnish its thousands; every Section of France! Ninety-six Commissioners of us, two for each Section of the Forty-eight, they must go forthwith, and tell Paris what the Country needs of her. Let Eighty more of us be sent, post-haste, over France; to spread the fire-cross, to call forth the might of men. Let the Eighty also be on the road, before this sitting rise. Let them go, and think what their errand is. Speedy Camp of 50,000 between Paris and the North Frontier; for Paris will pour forth her volunteers! Shoulder to shoulder, one strong universal death-defiant rising and rushing; we shall hurl back these Sons of Night yet again; and France, in spite of the world, be free!"—So sounds the Titan's voice: into all Section-houses; into all French hearts. Sections sit in Permanence, for recruitment, enrollment, that very night. Convention Commissioners, on swift wheels, are carrying the fire-cross from Town to Town, till all France blaze.

1505. And so there is Flag of *Fatherland in Danger* waving from the Town-hall, Black Flag from the top of Notre-Dame Cathedral; there is Proclamation, hot eloquence; Paris rushing out once again to strike its enemies down. That, in such circumstances, Paris was in no mild humor can be conjectured. Agitated streets; still more agitated round the Salle de Manège! Feuillans-Terrace crowds itself with angry Citizens, angrier Citizenesses; Varlet perambulates with portable chair; ejaculations of no measured

kind, as to perfidious fine-spoken Hommes d'état' friends of Dumouriez, secret-friends of Pitt and Cobourg, burst from the hearts and lips of men. To fight the enemy? Yes, and even to "freeze him with terror (glacer d'effroi)." but first to have domestic Traitors punished! Who are they that, carping and quarreling, in their jesuitic most *moderate* way, seek to shackle the Patriotic movement? That divide France against Paris, and poison public opinion in the Departments? That when we ask for bread, and a Maximum fixed price, treat us with lectures on Free-trade in grains? Can the human stomach satisfy itself with lectures on Free-trade; and are we to fight the Austrians in a moderate manner, or in an immoderate? This Convention must be *purged*.

1506. "Set up a swift Tribunal for Traitors, a Maximum for Grains:" thus speak with energy the Patriot Volunteers, as they defile through the Convention Hall, just on the wing to the Frontiers:— perorating in that heroical Cambyses's vein of theirs: beshouted by the Galleries and Mountain; bemurmured by the Right-side and Plain. Nor are prodigies wanting: lo, while a Captain of the Section Poissonnière perorates with vehemence about Dumouriez, Maximum and Crypto-Royalist Traitors, and his troop beat chorus with him, waving their Banner overhead, the eye of a Deputy discerns, in this same Banner, that the cravates or streamers of it have Royal fleur-de-lis! The Section-Captain shrieks; this goop shriek, horror-struck, and "trample the Banner under foot:" seemingly the work of some Crypto-Royalist Plotter? Most probable:*—or perhaps at bottom, only the *old* Banner of the Section, manufactured prior to the Tenth of August, when such streamers were according to rule!†

1507. History, looking over the Girondin Memoirs, anxious to disentangle the truth of them from the hysterics, finds these days of March, especially this Sunday the 10th of March, play a great part. Plots, plots; a plot for murdering the Girondin Deputies; Anarchists and Secret-Royalists plotting, in hellish concert, for that end! The far greater part of which is hysterics. What we do find indisputable is, that Louvet and certain Girondins were apprehensive they might be murdered on Saturday, and did not go to the evening sitting; but held council with one another, each inciting his fellow to do something resolute, and end these Anarchists; to which, however, Pétion, opening the window, and finding the night very wet, answered only, "Ils ne feront rien," and "composedly resumed his violin," says Louvet;‡ thereby, with soft Lydian tweedle-deeing, to wrap himself against eating cares. Also that Louvet felt especially liable to being killed; that several Girondins went abroad to seek beds: liable to being killed; but were not. Farther that, in very truth, Journalist Deputy Gorsas, prisoner of the Departments, be and his Printer had their houses broken into (by a tumult of Patriots, among whom red-capped Varlet, American Fournier loom forth, in the darkness of the rain and riot); had their wives put in fear; their presses, types and circumjacent equipments beaten to ruin; no Mayor interfering in time; Gorsas himself escaping, pistol in hand, "along the coping of the back wall." Farther that Sunday, the morrow, was not a work-day; and the streets were more agitated than ever: Is it a new September, then, that these Anarchists intend? Finally, that no September came; —and also that hysterics, not unnaturally, had reached almost their acme.§

1508. Vergniaud denounces and deplores; in

* Moniteur (in "Histoire Parlementaire," xxv 6).

* "Choix des Rapports," xi. 277.
† "Histoire Parlementaire," xxv. 72.
‡ Louvet, 'Mémoires," p. 72
§ Meillan, pp. 23, 24; Louvet, pp. 71-80.

sweetly turned periods. Section 'Bonconseil, *Good-counsel* so-named, not Mauconseil or *Ill-counsel* as it once was, does a far notabler thing: demands that Vergniaud, Brissot, Guadet, and other denunciatory, fine-spoken Girondins, to the number of Twenty-two, be put under arrest! Section Good-counsel, so named ever since the 10th of August, is sharply rebuked, like a Section of Ill-counsel:* but its word is spoken, and will not fall to the ground.

1509. In fact, one thing strikes us in these poor Girondins: their fatal shortness of vision; nay fatal poorness of character, for that is the root of it. They are as strangers to the People they would govern; to the thing they have come to work in. Formulas, Philosophies, Respectabilities, what has been written in Books, and admitted by the Cultivated Classes: *this* inadequate *Scheme* of Nature's working is all that Nature, let her work as she will, can reveal to these men. So they perorate and speculate; and call on the Friends of Law, when the question is not Law or No-Law, but Life or No-Life. Pedants of the Revolution, if not Jesuits of it! Their Formalism is great; great also is their Egoism. France rising to fight Austria has been raised only by plot of the 10th of March, to kill Twenty-two of *them!* This Revolution Prodigy, unfolding itself into terrific stature and articulation, by its own laws and Nature's, not by the laws of Formula, has become unintelligible, incredible as an impossibility, the "waste chaos of a Dream." A Republic founded on what they call the Virtues; on what we call the Decencies and Respectabilities: this they will have, and nothing but this. Whatsoever other Republic Nature and Reality send, shall be considered as not sent; as a kind of Nightmare Vision, and thing non-extant; disowned by the Laws of Nature and of Formula. Alas, dim for the best eyes is this Reality; and as for these men, they will not look at it with eyes at all, but only through "faceted spectacles" of Pedantry, wounded Vanity; which yield the most portentous fallacious spectrum. Carping and complaining forever of Plots and Anarchy, they will do one thing; prove, to demonstration, that the Reality will not translate into their Formula; that they and their Formula are incompatible with the Reality: and, in its dark wrath, the Reality will extinguish it and them! What a man *kens* he *can*. But the beginning of a man's doom is, that vision withdrawn from him; that he see not the reality, but a false spectrum of the reality; and following that, step darkly, with more or less velocity, downward to the utter Dark; which is the great Sea of Darkness, whither all falsehoods, winding or direct, continually flow!

1510. This 10th of March we may mark as an epoch in the Girondin destinies; the rage so exasperated itself, the misconception so darkened itself. Many desert the sittings; many come to them armed.† An honorable Deputy, setting out after breakfast, must now, besides taking his Notes, see whether his Priming is in order.

1511. Meanwhile with Dumouriez in Belgium it fares ever worse. Were it again General Miranda's fault, or some other's fault, there is no doubt whatever but the "Battle of Nerwinden," on the 18th of March, is lost; and our rapid retreat has become a far too rapid one. Victorious Cobourg, with his Austrian prickers, hangs like a dark cloud on the rear of us; Dumouriez never off horseback night or day; engagement every three hours; our whole discomfited Host rolling rapidly inward, full of rage, suspicion and sauve-qui-peut! And then Dumouriez himself, what his intents may be? Wicked seem-

ingly and not charitable! His dispatches to Committee openly denounce a factious Convention, for the woes it has brought on France and him. And his speeches—for the General has no reticence! The execution of the Tyrant this Dumouriez calls the Murder of the King. Danton and Lacroix, flying thither as Commissioners once more, return very doubtful; even Danton now doubts.

1512. Three Jacobin Missionaries, Proly, Dubuisson, Pereyra, have flown forth, sped by a wakeful Mother Society: they are struck dumb to hear the General speak. The Convention, according to this General, consists of 300 scoundrels and 400 imbeciles: France cannot do without a King   "But we have executed our King."   "And what is it to me," hastily cries Dumouriez, a General of no reticence, "whether the King's name be Ludovicus or Jacobus?"   "Or Philippus!" rejoins Proly;—and hastens to report progress. Over the Frontiers such hope is there.

CHAPTER V.
SANSCULOTTISM ACCOUTRED.

1513. Let us look, however, at the grand internal Sansculottism and Revolution Prodigy whether it stirs and waxes: there and not elsewhere may hope still be for France. The Revolution Prodigy, as Decree after Decree issues from the Mountain, like creative *fiats*, accordant with the nature of the Thing,—is shaping itself rapidly, in these days, into terrific stature and articulation, limb after limb. Last March, 1792, we saw all France flowing in blind terror; shutting town-barriers, boiling pitch for Brigands: happier, this March, that it is a seeing terror, that a creative Mountain exists, which can say *fiat!* Recruitment proceeds with fierce celerity, nevertheless our Volunteers hesitate to set out, till Treason be punished at home; they do not fly to the frontiers; but only fly hither and thither, demanding and denouncing. The Mountain must speak new *fiat* and new *fiats*.

1514. And does it not speak such? Take, as first example, those Comités Révolutionnaires for the arrestment of Persons Suspect. Revolutionary Committee, of Twelve chosen Patriots, sit in every Township of France; examining the Suspect, seeking arms, making domiciliary visits and arrestments;—caring, generally, that the Republic suffer no detriment. Chosen by universal suffrage, each in its Section, they are a kind of elixir of Jacobinism, some 44,000 of them awake and alive over France! In Paris and all Towns, every house-door must have the names of the inmates legibly printed on it, "at a height not exceeding five feet from the ground," every Citizen must produce his certificatory Carte de Civisme, signed by Section-President, every man be ready to give account of the faith that is in him. Persons Suspect had as well depart this soil of Liberty! And yet departure too is bad, all Emigrants are declared Traitors, their property become National, they are "dead in Law,"—save, indeed, that for *our* behoof they shall "live yet fifty years in Law," and what heritages may fall to them in that time become National too! A mad vitality of Jacobinism, with 44,000 centers of activity, circulates through all fibers of France.

1515. Very notable also is the Tribunal Extraordinaire:* decreed by the Mountain, some Girondins dissenting, for surely such a Court contradicts every formula;—other Girondins assenting, nay co-operating, for do not we all hate Traitors, O ye people of Paris?—Tribunal of the Seventeenth, in Autumn last was swift; but this shall be swifter. Five Judges; a standing Jury, which is named from Paris and the

---
* Moniteur (Séance du 12 Mars), 15 Mars.
† Meillan, "Mémoires," pp. 85, 24.

* Moniteur, No. 70 (du 11 Mars), No. 76, etc.

Neighborhood, that there be not delay in naming it: they are subject to no Appeal; to hardly any Law-forms, but must "get themselves convinced" in all readiest ways; and for security are bound "to vote audibly;" audibly, in the hearing of a Paris Public. This is the Tribunal Extraordinaire; which, in a few months, getting into most lively action, shall be entitled Tribunal Révolutionnaire; as indeed it from the very first has entitled itself: with a Herman or a Dumas for Judge-President, with a Fouquier-Tin-ville for Attorney-General, and a Jury of such as Citizen Leroi, who has surnamed himself Dix-Août "Leroi August-Tenth," it will become the wonder of the world. Herein has Sansculottism fashioned for itself a Sword of Sharpness: a weapon magical; tempered in the Stygian hell-waters; to the edge of it all armor, and defense of strength or of cunning shall be soft; it shall mow down Lives and Brazen-gates; and the waving of it shed terror through the souls of men.

1516. But speaking of an amorphous Sansculottism taking form, ought we not, above all things, to specify how the Amorphous gets itself a Head? Without metaphor, this Revolution Government continues hitherto in a very anarchic state. Executive Council of Ministers, Six in number, there is; but they, especially since Roland's retreat, have hardly known whether they were Ministers or not. Convention Committees sit supreme over them; but then each Committee as supreme as the others: Committee of Twenty-one, of Defense, or General Surety; simultaneous or successive, for specific pur-poses. The Convention alone is all-powerful,—espe-cially if the Commune go with it; but it is too numerous for an administrative body. Wherefore, in this perilous quick-whirling condition of the Re-public, before the end of March we obtain our small Comité de Salut Public;* as it were, for miscella-neous accidental purposes requiring dispatch;—as it proves, for a sort of universal supervision, and uni-versal subjection. They are to report weekly, these new Committee-men; but to deliberate in secret. Their number is Nine, firm Patriots all, Danton one of them; renewable every month:—yet why not re-elect them if they turn out well? The flower of the matter is, that they are but nine; that they sit in secret. An insignificant looking thing at first, this Committee; but with a principle of growth in it! Forwarded by fortune, by internal Jacobin en-ergy, it will reduce all Committees and the Conven-tion itself to mute obedience, the Six Ministers to Six assiduous Clerks; and work its will on the Earth and under Heaven, for a season. A "Commit-tee of Public Salvation" whereat the world still shrieks and shudders.

1517. If we call that Revolutionary Tribunal a Sword, which Sansculottism has provided for itself, then let us call the "Law of the Maximum" a Prov-ender-scrip, or Haversack, wherein, better or worse, some ration of bread may be found. It is true, Polit-ical Economy, Girondin free-trade, and all law of supply and demand, are hereby hurled topsy-turvy: but what help? Patriotism must live; the "cupid-ity of farmers" seem to have no bowels. Wherefore this Law of the Maximum, fixing the highest price of grains, is, with infinite effort, got passed;† and shall gradually extend itself into a Maximum for all manner of comestibles and commodities: with such scrambling and topsy-turvying as may be fancied! For now if, for example, the farmer will not sell? The farmer shall be forced to sell. An accurate Ac-count of what grain he has shall be delivered in to the Constituted Authorities: let him see that he say

* Moniteur, No. 83 (du 24 Mars 1793), Nos. 86, 98, 99, 100.
† Moniteur. (du 20 Avril, etc., to 20 Mai 1793).

not too much; for in that case, his rents, taxes and contributions will rise proportionally: let him see that he say not too little; for, on or before a set day, we shall suppose in April, *less* than one-third of this declared quantity must remain in his barns, more than two-thirds of it must have been thrashed and sold. One can denounce him, and raise penalties.

1518. By such inextricable overturning of all Com-mercial relations will Sansculottism keep life in; since not otherwise. On the whole, as Camille Des-moulins says once, "while the Sansculottes fight, the Monsieurs must pay." So there come Impots Pro-gressifs (Ascending Taxes); which consume, with last-increasing voracity, the "superfluous revenue" of men; beyond fifty-pounds a year, you are not ex-empt; rising into the hundreds, you bleed freely; into the thousands and tens of thousands, you bleed gushing. Also there come Requisitions; there comes "Forced-Loan of a Milliard," some 50,000,000 Sterl-ing; which of course they that *have* must lend. Unexampled enough; it has grown to be no country for the Rich, this; but a country for the Poor! And then if one fly, what stands it? Dead in Law; nay kept alive fifty years yet, for *their* accursed behoof! In this manner therefore it goes; topsy-turvying, ça-ira-ing:—and withal there is endless sale of Emi-grant National-Property, there is Cambon with end-less cornucopia of Assignats. The Trade and Finance of Sansculottism; and how, with Maximum and Bakers' queues, with Cupidity, Hunger, Denunciation and Paper-money, it led its galvanic-life, and began and ended,—remains the most interesting of all Chapters in Political Economy: still to be written.

1519. All which things, are they not clean against Formula? O Girondin Friends, it is not a Republic of the Virtues we are getting; but only a Republic of the Strengths, virtuous and other!

CHAPTER VI.

THE TRAITOR.

1520. But Dumouriez, with his fugitive Host, with his King Ludovicus or King Philippus? There lies the crisis; there hangs the question: Revolution Prodigy, or Counter-Revolution?—One wide shriek covers that North-east region. Soldiers, full of rage, suspicion and terror, flock hither and thither; Du-mouriez, the many-counseled, never off horseback, knows now no counsel that were not worse than none: the counsel, namely, of joining himself with Cobourg; marching to Paris, extinguishing Jacobin-ism, and, with some new King Ludovicus or King Philippus, restoring the Constitution of 1791!*

1521. Is wisdom quitting Dumouriez; the herald of Fortune quitting him? Principle, faith political or other beyond a certain faith of mess-rooms, and honor of an officer, had him not to quit. At any rate his quarters in the Burgh of Saint-Amand; his head-quarters in the Village of Saint-Amand des Boues, a short way off,—have become a Bedlam. National Representatives are riding and running; of the "three Towns," Lille, Valenciennes or ever Condé, which Dumouriez wanted to snatch for himself, not one can be snatched; your Captain is admitted, but the Town-gate is closed on him, and then alas the Prison-gate, and "his men wander about the ramparts." Couriers gallop breath-less; men wait, or seem waiting, to assassinate, to be assassinated; Battalions nigh frantic with such sus-picion and uncertainty, with Vive-la-République and Sauve-qui-peut, rush this way and that;—Ruin and Desperation in the shape of Cobourg lying entrenched close by.

1522. Dame Genlis and her fair Princess d'Orléans

* Dumouriez, "Mémoires," iv. c. 7-10.

find this Burgh of Saint-Amand no fit place for them; Dumouriez's protection is grown worse than none. Tough Genlis, one of the toughest women, a woman, as it were, with nine lives in her; whom nothing will beat: she packs her bandboxes; clear for flight in a private manner. Her beloved Princess she will—leave here, with the Prince Chartres Egalité her Brother. In the cold gray of the April morning, we find her accordingly established in her hired vehicle, on the street of Saint-Amand; postillions just cracking their whips to go,—when behold the young Princely Brother, struggling hitherward hastily calling: bearing the Princess in his arms! Hastily he has clutched the poor young lady up, in her very night-gown, nothing saved of her goods except the watch from the pillow; with brotherly despair he flings her in, among the bandboxes, into Genlis's chase, into Genlis's arms: Leave her not, in the name of Mercy and Heaven! A shrill scene, but a brief one:—the postillions crack and go. Ah, whither? Through by-roads and broken hill-passes; seeking their way with lanterns after nightfall; through perils, and Cobourg Austrians, and suspicious French Nationals: finally, into Switzerland; safe though nigh moneyless.* The brave young Égalité has a most wild Morrow to look for; but now only himself to carry through it.

1523. For indeed over at that Village named of the Mudbaths, Saint-Amand'des Boues, matters are still worse. About four o'clock on Tuesday after, noon, the 2d of April, 1793, two Couriers come galloping as if for life; Mon Général! Four National Representatives, War-Minister at their head, are posting hitherward from Valenciennes; are close at hand, with what intents one may guess! While the Couriers are yet speaking, War-Minister and National Representatives, old Camus the Archivist, for chief speaker of them, arrive. Hardly has Mon Général had time to order out the Hussar Regiment de Berchigny; that to take rank and wait near by, in case of accident. And so, enters War-Minister Beurnonville, with an embrace of friendship, for he is an old friend; enter Archivist Camus and the other three following him.

1524. They produce Papers, invite the General to the bar of the Convention; merely to give an explanation or two. The General finds it unsuitable, not to say impossible, and that "the service will suffer." Then comes reasoning; the voice of the old Archivist getting loud. Vain to reason loud with this Dumouriez, he answers mere angry irreverences. And so, amid planned staff-officers, very gloomy-looking, in jeopardy and uncertainty, these poor National messengers debate and consult, retire and re-enter, for the space of some two hours: without effect. Whereupon Archivist Camus, getting quite loud, proclaims in the name of the National Convention, for he has the power to do it, That General Dumouriez is arrested: "Will you obey the National mandate, General?"—"Pas dans ce moment-ci (Not at this particular moment)." answers the General also aloud; then glancing the other way, utters certain unknown vocables, in a mandatory manner; seemingly a German word-of-command.† Hussars clutch the Four National Representatives, and Beurnonville, the War-Minister; pack them out of the apartment; out of the Village, over the lines to Cobourg, in two chaises that very night,—as hostages, prisoners: to lie long in Maestricht and Austrian strongholds!‡ Facta est alea.

1525. This night Dumouriez prints his "Procla-

* Genlis, iv. 139.
† Dumouriez, iv. 159, etc.
‡ Their narrative, written by Camus (in Toulongeon, iii. app. 60-87).

mation;" this night and the morrow the Dumouriez Army, in such darkness visible, and rage of semi-desperation as there is, shall meditate what the General is doing, what they themselves will do in it. Judge whether this Wednesday was of halcyon nature, for any one! But on this Thursday morning, we discern Dumouriez with small escort, with Chartres Égalité and a few staff officers, ambling along the Condé Highway: perhaps they are for Condé, and trying to persuade the Garrison there; at all events, they are for an interview with Cobourg, who waits in the woods by appointment, in that quarter. Nigh the Village of Doumet, three National Battalions, a set of men always full of Jacobinism, sweep past us; marching rather swiftly,—seemingly in mistake by a way we had not ordered. The General dismounts, steps into a cottage, a little from the wayside; will give them right order in writing. Hark! what strange growling is heard; what barkings are heard, loud yells of "Traitors," of "Arrest!" the National Battalions have wheeled round, are emitting shot! Mount, Dumouriez, and spring for life! Dumouriez and Staff strike the spurs in, deep; vault over ditches, into the fields, which prove to be morasses; sprawl and plunge for life; bewhistled with curses and lead. Sunk to the middle, with or without horses, several servants killed, they escape out of shot-range, to General Mack the Austrian's quarters. Nay they return on the morrow, to Saint-Amand and faithful foreign Berchigny; but what boots it? The Artillery has all revolted, is jingling off to Valenciennes! all have revolted, are revolting except only foreign Berchigny, to the extent of some poor 1500, none will follow Dumouriez against France and Indivisible Republic: Dumouriez's occupation's gone.*

1526. Such an instinct of Frenchhood and Sans-culottism dwells in these men; they will follow no Dumouriez nor Lafayette, nor any mortal on such errand. Shriek may be of Sauve-qui-peut, but will also be of Vive-la-République. New National Representatives arrive; new General Dampierre, soon killed in battle; new General Custine; the agitated Hosts draw back to some camp of Famars; make head against Cobourg as they can.

1527. And so Dumouriez is in the Austrian quarters; his drama ended, in this rather sorry manner A most shifty, wiry man; one of Heaven's Swiss; that wanted only work. Fifty years of unnoticed toil and valor; one year of toil and valor, not unnoticed, but seen of all countries and centuries; then thirty other years again unnoticed, of Memoir-writing, English Pension, scheming and projecting to no purpose: Adieu, thou Swiss of Heaven, worthy to have been something else!

1528. His Staff go different ways. Brave young Égalité reaches Switzerland and the Genlis Cottage; with a strong crabstick in his hand, a strong heart in his body: his Princedom is now reduced to that. Égalité the Father sat playing whist, in his Palais Égalité, at Paris, on the 6th day of this same month of April, when a catch-pole entered. Citoyen Égalité is wanted at the Convention Committee!† Examination, requiring Arrestment; finally requiring Imprisonment, transference to Marseilles and the Castle of If! Orléansdom has sunk in the black waters; Palais Égalité, which was Palais Royal, is like to become Palais National.

CHAPTER VII.
IN FIGHT.

1529. Our Republic, by paper Decree, may be "One and Indivisible;" but what profits it while

* "Mémoires," iv. 162-180.
† See Montgaillard, iv. 144.

these things are? Federalists in the Senate, renegadoes in the Army, traitors everywhere! France, all in desperate recruitment since the 10th of March, does not fly to the frontier, but only flies hither and thither. This defection of contemptuous diplomatic Dumouriez falls heavy on the fine-spoken high-sniffing Hommes d'état whom he consorted with; forms a second epoch in their destiny.

1530. Or perhaps more strictly we might say, the second Girondin epoch, though little noticed then, began on the day when, in reference to this defection, the Girondins broke with Danton. It was the 1st day of April; Dumouriez had not yet plunged across the morasses to Cobourg, but was evidently meaning to do it, and our Commissioners were off to arrest him; when what does the Girondin Lasource see good to do, but rise, and jesuitically question and insinuate at great length, whether a main accomplice of Dumouriez had not probably been—Danton! Gironde grins sardonic assent; Mountain holds its breath. The figure of Danton, Levasseur says, while this speech went on, was noteworthy. He sat erect with a kind of internal convulsion struggling to keep itself motionless; his eye from time to time flashing wilder, his lip curling in Titanic scorn.* Lasource, in a fine-spoken attorney manner, proceeds: there is this probability to his mind, and there is that; probabilities which press painfully on him, which cast the Patriotism of Danton under a painful shade;—which painful shade, he, Lasource, will hope that Danton may find it not impossible to dispel.

1531. "Les Scélérats!" cries Danton, starting up, with clenched right-hand, Lasource having done; and descends from the Mountain, like a lava-flood: his answer not unready. Lasource's probabilities fly like idle dust; but leave a result behind them. "Ye were right, friends of the Mountain," begins Danton, "and I was wrong: there is no peace possible with these men. Let it be war, then! They will not save the Republic with us: it shall be saved without them; saved in spite of them." Really a burst of rude Parliamentary eloquence this; which is still worth reading in the old Moniteur. With fire-words the exasperated rude Titan rives and smites these Girondins; at every hit the glad Mountain utters chorus: Marat, like a musical bis, repeating the last phrase.† Lasource's probabilities are gone; but Danton's pledge of battle remains lying.

1532. A third epoch, or scene in the Girondin Drama, or rather it is but the completion of this second epoch, we reckon from the day when the patience of virtuous Pétion finally boiled over; and the Girondins, so to speak, took up this battle-pledge of Danton's, and decreed Marat accused. It was the 11th of the same month of April, on some effervescence rising, such as often rose; and President had covered himself, mere Bedlam now ruling; and Mountain and Gironde were rushing on one another with clenched right-hands, and even with pistols in them; when, behold, the Girondin Duperret drew a sword! Shriek of horror rose, instantly quenching all other effervescence, at sight of the clear murderous steel; whereupon Duperret returned it to the leather again;—confessing that he did indeed draw it, being instigated by a kind of sacred madness, "sainte fureur" and pistols held at him; but that if he parricidally had chanced to scratch the outmost skin of National Representation with it, he too carried pistols, and would have blown his brains out on the spot.‡

* "Mémoires de Réné Levasseur" (Bruxelles, 1830), i. 164.
† Séance du 1 Avril 1793 (in "Histoire Parlementaire," xxv 34-35).
‡ "Histoire Parlementaire." xv. 397.

1533. But now in such posture of affairs, virtuous Pétion rose, next morning, to lament these effervescences, this endless Anarchy invading the Legislative Sanctuary itself; and here, being growled at and howled at by the Mountain, his patience, long tried, did, as we say, boil over; and he spake vehemently, in high key, with foam on his lips; "whence," says Marat, "I concluded he had got la rage," the rabidity, or dog-madness. Rabidity smites others rabid: so there rises new foam-lipped demand to have Anarchists extinguished; and specially to have Marat put under Accusation. Send a representative to the Revolutionary Tribunal? Violate the inviolability of a Representative? Have a care, O Friends! This poor Marat has faults enough but against Liberty, or Equality, what fault? That he has loved and fought for it, not wisely but too well. In dungeons and cellars, in pinching poverty, under anathema of men; even so, in such fight, has he grown so dingy, -bleared; even so has his head become a Stylites one. Him you will fling to your Sword of Sharpness! while Cobourg and Pitt advance on us, fire spitting?

1534. The Mountain is loud, the Gironde is loud and deaf; all lips are foamy. With "Permanent-Session of twenty-four hours," with vote by roll-call and a dead-lift effort, the Gironde carries it: Marat is ordered to the Revolutionary Tribunal, to answer for that February Paragraph of Forestallers at the door, lintel, with other offenses; and, after a little hesitation, he obeys.*

1535. Thus is Danton's battle-pledge taken up; there is, as he said there would be, "war without truce or treaty (ni trève ni composition)." Wherefore, close now with one another, Formula and Reality, in death-grips, and wrestle it out; both of you cannot live, but only one!

CHAPTER VIII.

IN DEATH-GRIPS.

1536. It proves what strength, were it only of inertia, there is in established Formulas, what weakness in nascent Realities, and illustrates several things, that this death-wrestle should still have lasted some six weeks or more. National business, discussion of the Constitutional Act, for our Constitution should decidedly be got ready, proceeds along with it. We even change our Locality; we shift, on the 10th of May, from the old Salle de Manège into our new Hall, in the Palace, once a King's but now the Republic's, of the Tuileries. Hope and ruth flickering against despair and rage, still struggle in the minds of men.

1537. It is a most dark confused death-wrestle, this of the six weeks. Formalist frenzy against Realist frenzy; Patriotism, Egoism, Pride, Anger, Vanity, Hope and Despair, all raised to the frenetic pitch: Frenzy meets Frenzy, like dark clashing whirlwinds; neither understand the other; the weaker, one day, will understand that *it* is verily swept down! Girondism is strong as established Formula and Respectability: do not as many as Seventy-two of the Departments, or say respectable Heads of Departments, declare for us? Calvados, which loves its Buzot, will even rise in revolt, so hint the Addresses; Marseilles, cradle of Patriotism, will rise; Bourdeaux will rise, and the Gironde Department, as one man; in a word, who will *not* rise, were our Représentation Nationale to be insulted, or one hair of a Deputy's head harmed! The Mountain, again, is strong as Reality and Audacity. To the Reality of the Mountain are not all furthersome things possible? A new 10th of August, if needful; nay a new 2d of September!—

* Moniteur (du 16 Avril 1793, et seqq.).

1538. But, on Wednesday, afternoon, 24th day of April, year 1793, what tumult as of fierce jubilee is this ? It is Marat returning from the Revolutionary Tribunal! A week or more of death-peril; and now there is triumphant acquittal; Revolutionary Tribunal can find no accusation against this man. And so the eye of History beholds Patriotism, which had gloomed unutterable things all week, break into loud jubilee, embrace its Marat; lift him into a chair of triumph, bear him shoulder-high through the streets. Shoulder-high is the injured People's-friend, crowned with an oak-garland; amid the wavy sea of red night-cap, carmagnole jackets, grenadier bonnets and female mob-caps; far-sounding like a sea! The injured People's-friend has here reached his culminating point; he too strikes the stars with his sublime head.

1539. But the Reader can judge with what face President Lasource, he of the "painful probabilities," who presides in this Convention Hall, might welcome such jubilee-tide, when it got thither, and the Decreed of Accusation floating on the top of it! A National Sapper, spokesman on the occasion, says, the People know their Friend, and love his life as their own; "Whosoever wants Marat's head must get the Sapper's first."* Lasource answered with some vague painful mumblement,—which, says Levasseur, one could not help tittering at.† Patriot Sections, Volunteers not yet gone to the Frontiers, come demanding the "purgation of traitors from your own bosom ;" the expulsion, or even the trial and sentence, of a factious Twenty-two.

1540. Nevertheless the Gironde has got its Commission of Twelve; a Commission specially appointed for investigating these troubles of the Legislative Sanctuary: let Sansculottism say what it will, Law shall triumph. Old-Constituent Rabaut Saint-Etienne presides over this Commission : "It is the last plank whereon a wrecked Republic may perhaps still save herself." Rabaut and they therefore sit, intent; examining witnesses; launching arrestments; looking out into a waste dim sea of troubles,—the womb of Formula, or perhaps her grave! Enter not that sea, O Reader! There are dim desolation and confusion: raging women and raging men. Sections come demanding Twenty-two; for the *number* first given by Section Bonconseil still holds, though the names should even vary. Other sections, of the wealthier kind, come denouncing such demand; nay the same Section will demand to-day, and denounce the demand to-morrow, according as the wealthier sit, or the poorer. Wherefore, indeed, the Girondins decree that all Sections shall close "at ten in the evening ;" before the working people come: which Decree remains without effect. And nightly the Mother of Patriotism wails doleful; doleful, but her eye kindling! And Fournier l'Américain is busy, and the two banker Freys, and Varlet Apostle of Liberty; the bull-voice of Marquis St. Huruge is heard. And shrill women vociferate from all Galleries, the Convention ones and downward. Nay a "Central Committee" of all the Forty-eight Sections looms forth huge and dubious; sitting dim in the Archevéché, sending Resolutions, receiving them: a Center of the Sections; in dread deliberation as to a New 10th of August!

1541. One thing we will specify, to throw light on many: the aspect under which, seen through the eyes of these Girondin Twelve, or even seen through one's own eyes, the Patriotism of the softer sex presents itself. There are Female Patriots, whom the Girondins call Megæras, and count to the extent of 8,000; with serpent-hair, all out of curl; who have

changed the distaff for the dagger. They are of "the Society called Brotherly," Fraternelle, say *Sisterly*, which meets under the roof of the Jacobins. "Two thousand daggers," or *so*, have been ordered,—doubtless for them. They rush to Versailles, to raise more women ; but the Versailles women will not rise.*

1542. Nay behold, in National Garden of Tuileries —Demoiselle Théroigne herself is become as a brownlocked Diana (were that possible) attacked by her own dogs, or she-dogs! The Demoiselle, keeping her carriage, is for Liberty indeed, as she has full well shown ; but then for Liberty with Respectability : whereupon these serpent-haired Extreme She Patriots do now fasten upon her, tatter her, shamefully fustigate her, in their shameful way; almost fling her into the Garden ponds, had not help intervened. Help, alas, to small purpose. The poor Demoiselle's head and nervous-system, none of the soundest, is so tattered and fluttered that it will never recover; but flutter worse and worse, till it crack; and within year and day we hear of her in mad-house and straitwaistcoat, which proves permanent!—Such brownlocked Figure did flutter, and inarticulately jabber and gesticulate, little able to *speak* the obscure meaning it had, through some segment of the Eighteenth Century of Time. She disappears here from the Revolution and Public History forevermore.†

1543. Another thing we will not again specify, yet again beseech the Reader to imagine : the reign of Fraternity and Perfection. Imagine, we say, O Reader, that the Millennium were struggling on the threshold, and yet not so much as groceries could he had,—owing to traitors. With what impetus would a man strike traitors, in that case! Ah, thou canst not imagine it; thou hast thy groceries safe in the shops, and little or no hope of a Millennium ever coming !—But indeed, as to the temper there was in men and women, does not this one fact say enough : the height SUSPICION had risen to? Preternatural we often called it; seemingly in the language of exaggeration : but listen to the cold deposition of witnesses. Not a musical Patriot can blow himself a snatch of melody from the French Horn, sitting mildly pensive on the house-top, but Mercier will recognize it to be a signal which one Plotting Committee is making to another. Distraction has possessed Harmony herself; lurks in the sound of "Marseillaise" and "Ça-ira."‡ Louvet, who can see as deep into a mill-stone as the most, discerns that we shall be invited back to our old Hall of the Manége, by a Deputation ; and then the Anarchists will massacre Twenty-two of us, as we walk over. It is Pitt and Cobourg ; the gold of Pitt.—Poor Pitt! They little know what work he has with his own Friends of the People; getting them bespied, beheaded, their habeas-corpuses suspended, and his own Social Order and strong-boxes kept tight,—to fancy him raising mobs among his neighbors!

1544. But the strangest fact connected with French or indeed with human Suspicion. is perhaps this of Camille Desmoulins. Camille's head, one of the clearest in France, has got itself so saturated through every fiber with Preternaturalism of Suspicion, that looking back on that 12th of July, 1789, when the thousands rose round him, yelling responsive at his word in the Palais-Royal Garden, and took cockades, he finds it explicable only on this hypothesis, That they were all hired to do it, and set on by the For-

---

* Buzot, "Mémoires," pp. 69, ¼; Meillan, "Mémoires," pp. 192, 195, 196. See "Commission des Douze" in ("Choix des Rapports," xii. 69-131).

† "Deux Amis," vii. 77-80; Forster, i. 514; Moore, i. 70. She did not die till 1817; in the Salpétriére, in the most abject state of insanity; see Esquirol, "Des Maladies Mentales" (Paris, 1838), i. 445-450.

‡ Mercier, "Nouveau Paris," vi. 63.

---

* Séance du 26 Avril. An 1er in (Moniteur, No. 116).
† Levasseur, "Mémoires," i. c. 6.

cign and other Plotters. "It was not for nothing," says Camille with insight, "that this multitude burst up round me when I spoke!" No, not for nothing. Behind, around, before, it is one huge Preternatural Puppet-play of Plots; Pitt pulling the wires.* Almost I conjecture that I, Camille myself, am a Plot and wooden with wires.—The force of insight could no farther go.

1545. Be this as it will, History remarks that the Commission of Twelve, now clear enough as to the Plots; and luckily having "got the threads of them all by the end," as they say,—are launching Mandates of Arrest rapidly in these May days; and carrying matters with a high hand; resolute that the sea of troubles shall be restrained. What chief Patriot, Section-President even, is safe? They can arrest him; tear him from his warm bed, because he has made irregular Section Arrestments! They arrest Varlet Apostle of Liberty. They arrest Procureur-Substitute Hébert, Père Duchesne; a Magistrate of the People, sitting in Town-hall; who, with high solemnity of martyrdom, takes leave of his colleagues; prompt he, to obey the Law; and solemnly acquiescent, disappears into prison.

1546. The swifter fly the Sections, energetically demanding him back; demanding not arrestment of popular Magistrates, but of a traitorous Twenty-two. Section comes flying after Section;—defiling energetic, with their Cambyses-vein of oratory: nay the Commune itself comes, with Mayor Pache at its head; and with question not of Hébert and the Twenty-two alone, but with this ominous old question made new, "Can you save the Republic, or must we do it?" To whom President Max Isnard makes fiery answer: If by fatal chance, in any of those tumults which since the 10th of March are ever returning, Paris were to lift a sacrilegious finger against the National Representation, France would rise as one man, in never-imagined vengeance, and shortly "the traveler would ask, on which side of the Seine Paris had stood!"† Whereat the Mountain bellows only louder, and every Gallery; Patriot Paris boiling round.

1547. And Girondin Valazé has nightly conclaves at his house; sends billets, "Come punctually, and well armed, for there is to be business." And Megæra women perambulate the streets, with flags, with lamentable alleleu.‡ And the Convention-doors are obstructed by roaring multitudes: fine-spoken hommes d'état are hustled, maltreated, as they pass; Marat will apostrophize you, in such death-peril, and say, Thou too art of them. If Roland ask leave to quit Paris, there is order of the day. What help? Substitute Hébert, Apostle Varlet, must be given back; to be crowned with oak-garlands. The Commission of Twelve, in a Convention overwhelmed with roaring Sections, is broken; then on the morrow, in a Convention of rallied Girondins, is reinstated. Dim Chaos, or the sea of troubles, is struggling through all its elements; writing and chafing toward some Creation.

CHAPTER IX.
EXTINCT.

1548. Accordingly, on Friday the 31st of May, 1793, there comes forth into the summer sunlight one of the strangest scenes. Mayor Pache with Municipality arrives at the Tuileries Hall of Convention; sent for, Paris being in visible ferment; and gives the strangest news.

1549. How, in the gray of this morning, while we

* See "Histoire des Brissotins," par Camille Desmoulins (a pamphlet of Camille's Paris, 1793).
† Moniteur. Séance du 25 Mai 1793.
‡ Meillan, "Mémoires," p. 195; Buzot, pp. 60, 84.

sat Permanent in Town-hall, watchful for the commonweal, there entered, precisely as on a 10th of August, some Ninety-six extraneous persons; who declared themselves to be in a state of Insurrection; to be plenipotentiary Commissioners from the Forty-eight Sections, sections or members of the Sovereign People, all in a state of Insurrection; and farther that we, in the name of said Sovereign in Insurrection, were dismissed from office. How we thereupon laid off our sashes, and withdrew into the adjacent Saloon of Liberty. How, in a moment or two, we were called back; and reinstated: the Sovereign pleasing to think us still worthy of confidence. Whereby, having taken new oath of office, we on a sudden find ourselves Insurrectionary Magistrates, with extraneous Committee of Ninety-six sitting by us; and a Citoyen Henriot, one whom some accuse of Septemberism, is made Generalissimo of the National Guard; and since six o'clock, the tocsins ring, and the drums beat:—Under which peculiar circumstances, what would an august National Convention please to direct us to do?*

1550. Yes, there is the question! "Break the Insurrectionary Authorities," answer some with vehemence. Vergniaud at least will have "the National Representatives all die at their post;" this is sworn to, with ready loud acclaim. But as to breaking the Insurrectionary Authorities,—alas, while we yet debate, what sound is that? Sound of the Alarm-Cannon on the Pont Neuf; which it is death by the Law to fire without order from us!

1551. It does boom off there nevertheless; sending a stound through all hearts. And the tocsins discourse stern music; and Henriot with his Armed Force has enveloped us! And Section succeeds Section, the livelong day; demanding with Cambyses-oratory, with the rattle of muskets, That traitors, Twenty-two or more, be punished; that the Commission of Twelve be irrevocably broken. The heart of the Gironde dies within it; distant are the Seventy-two respectable Departments, this fiery Municipality is near! Barrère is for a middle course granting something. The Commissioner of Twelve declares that, not waiting to be broken, it hereby breaks itself, and is no more. Fain would Reporter Rabaut speak his and its last words; but he is hellowed off. Too happy that the Twenty-two are still left unviolated! Vergniaud, carrying the laws of refinement to a great length, moves, to the amazement of some, that "the Sections of Paris have deserved well of their country." Whereupon, at a late hour of the evening, the deserving Sections retire to their respective places of abode. Barrère shall report on it. With busy quill and brain he sits, secluded; for him no sleep to-night. Friday the last of May has ended in this manner.

1552. The Sections have deserved well: but ought they not to deserve better? Faction and Girondism is struck down for the moment, and consents to be a nullity; but will it not, at another favorable moment rise, still feller; and the Republic have to be saved in spite of it? So reasons Patriotism, still Permanent; so reasons the Figure of Marat, visible in the dim Section-world, on the morrow. To the conviction of men!—And so at eventide of Saturday, when Barrère had just got the thing all vanished by the labor of a night and day, and his Report was setting off in the evening mail-bags, tocsin peals out again. Générale is beating; armed men taking station in the Place Vendome and elsewhere, for the night; supplied with provisions and liquor. There under the summer stars, will they wait, this night what is to be seen and to be done, Henriot and Town-hall givin due signal.

* "Débats de la Convention" (Paris, 1828), iv. 187, 223; Moniteur, Nos. 152, 153, 154, An Ier.

1553. The Convention, at sound of générale, hastens back to its Hall; but to the number only of a Hundred; and does little business, puts off business till the morrow. The Girondins do not stir out thither, the Girondins are abroad seeking beds.—Poor Rabaut, on the morrow morning, returning to his post, with Louvet and some others, through streets all in ferment, wrings his hands, ejaculating, "Illa suprema dies!"* It has become Sunday the 2d day of June 1793, by the old style; by the new style, year One of Liberty, Equality, Fraternity. We have got to the last scene of all, that ends this history of the Girondin Senatorship.

1554. It seems doubtful whether any terrestrial Convention had ever met in such circumstances as this National one now does. Tocsin is pealing; Barriers shut; all Paris is on the gaze, or under arms. As many as 100,000 under arms they count: National Force; and the Armed Volunteers, who should have flown to the Frontiers and La Vendée; but would not. treason being unpunished; and only flew hither and thither! So many, steady under arms, environ the National Tuileries and Garden. There are horse, foot, artillery, sappers with beards: the artillery one can see with their camp-furnaces in this National Garden, heating bullets red, and their match is lighted. Henriot in plumes rides, amid a plumed Staff: all posts and issues are safe; reserves lie out, as far as the Wood of Boulogne, the choicest Patriots nearest the scene. One other circumstance we will note: that a careful Municipality, liberal of camp-furnaces, has not forgotten provision carts. No member of the Sovereign need now go home to dinner; but can keep rank—plentiful victual circulating unsought. Does not this People understand Insurrection? Ye *not* uninventive, Gnalches!

1555. Therefore let a National Representation, "mandatories of the Sovereign," take thought of it. Expulsion of your Twenty-two, and your Commission of Twelve: we stand here till it be done! Deputation after Deputation, in ever stronger language, comes with that message. Barrère proposes a middle course:—Will not perhaps the inculpated Deputies consent to withdraw voluntarily; to make a generous demission and self-sacrifice for the sake of one's country? Isnard, repentant of that search on which river-bank Paris stood, declares himself ready to demit. Ready also is Te-Deum Fauchet;· old Dusaulx of the Bastille, " vieux radoteur (old dotard)," as Marat calls him, is still readier. On the contrary, Lanjuinais the Breton declares that there is one man who never will demit voluntarily ; but will protest to the uttermost, while a voice is left him. And he accordingly goes on protesting; amid rage and clangor; Legendre crying at last: " Lanjuinais, come down from the Tribune, or I will fling thee down (ou je te jette en bas)!" For matters are come to extremity. Nay they do clutch hold of Lanjuinais, certain zealous Mountain-men; but cannot fling him down, for he "cramps himself on the railing;" and "his clothes get torn." Brave Senator, worthy of pity! Neither will Barbaroux demit; he "has sworn to die at his post, and will keep that oath." Whereupon the Galleries all rise with explosion ; brandishing weapons, some of them ; and rush out, saying: "Allons, then; we must save our country!" Such a Session is this of Sunday the 2d of June.

1556. Churches fill, over Christian Europe, and then empty themselves: but this Convention empties not, the while: a day of shrieking contention, of agony, humiliation and tearing of coat-skirts; villa suprema dies! Round stand Henriot and his Hundred Thousand copiously refreshed from tray and

basket: nay he is "distributing five francs a-piece," we Girondins saw it with our eyes; five francs to keep them in heart! And distraction of armed riot encumbers our borders, jangles at our Bar; we are prisoners in our own Hall: Bishop Grégoire could not get out for a besoin actuel without four gendarmes to wait on him! What is the character of a National Representative become? And now the sunlight falls yellower on western windows, and the chimney-tops are flinging longer shadows; the refreshed Hundred Thousand nor their shadows, stir not! What to resolve on? Motion rises, superfluous one would think, That the Convention go forth in a body; ascertain with its own eyes whether it is free or not. Lo, therefore, from the Eastern Gate of the Tuileries, a distressed Convention issuing; handsome Hérault Séchelles at their head; he with hat on, in sign of public calamity, the rest bareheaded,—toward the Gate of the Carrousel: wondrous to see: toward Henriot and his plumed Staff. "In the name of the National Convention, make way!" Not an inch of way does Henriot make: "I receive no orders, till the Sovereign, yours and mine, have been obeyed." The Convention presses on; Henriot prances back, with his Staff, some fifteen paces, "To arms! Cannoneers, to your guns!"—flashes out his puissant sword, as the Staff all do, and the Hussars all do. Cannoneers brandish the lit match; Infantry present arms,—alas, in the level way, as if for firing! Hatted Hérault leads his distressed flock, through their pinfold of a Tuileries again; across the Garden, to the Gate on the opposite side. Here is Feuillans-Terrace, alas, there is our old Salle de Manége; but neither at this Gate of the Pont Tournant is there egress. Try the other: and the other: no egress. We wander disconsolate through armed ranks; who indeed salute with *Live the Republic,* but also with *Die the Gironde.* Other such sight, in the year one of Liberty, the westering sun never saw.

1557. And now behold Marat meets us; for he lagged in this Suppliant Procession of ours: he has got some hundred elect Patriots at his heels; he orders us, in the Sovereign's name, to return to our place, and do as we are bidden and bound. The Convention returns. "Does not the Convention," says Couthon with a singular power of face, "see that it is free,"—none but friends round it? The Convention, overflowing with friends and armed Sectioners, proceeds to vote as bidden. Many will not vote, but remain silent; some one or two protests. in words, the Mountain has a clear unanimity. Commission of Twelve, and the denounced Twenty-two, to whom we add Ex-Ministers Clavière and Le Brun, these, with some slight extempore alterations (this or that orator proposing, but Marat disposing), are voted to be under "Arrestment in their own houses." Brissot, Buzot, Vergniaud, Gaudet, Louvet, Gensonné, Barbaroux, Lasource, Lanjuinais, Rabaut,—Thirty-two, by the tale; all that we have known as Girondins, and more than we have known as Girondins, and more than we have known. They, "under the safeguard of the French People;" by and by, under the safeguard of two Gendarmes each, shall dwell peaceably in their own houses; as Non-Senators; till farther order. Herewith ends Séance of Sunday the 2d of June, 1793.

1558. At ten o'clock, under mild stars, the Hundred Thousand, their work well finished, turn homeward. Already yesterday, Central Insurrection Committee had arrested Madame Roland; imprisoned her in the Abbaye. Roland has fled, no man knows whither.

1559. Thus fell the Girondins by Insurrection, and became extinct as a Party: not without a sigh from most Historians. The men were men of parts,

* Louvet. " Mémoires," p. 69.

of Philosophic culture, decent behavior ; not condemnable in that they were Pedants, and had not better parts; not condemnable but most unfortunate. They wanted a Republic of the Virtues, wherein themselves should be head ; and they could only get a Republic of the Strengths, wherein others than they were head.

For the rest, Barrère shall make Report of it. The night concludes with a "civic promenade by torch-light :"* surely the true reign of Fraternity is now not far !

BOOK FOURTH.

TERROR.

CHAPTER I.

CHARLOTTE CORDAY.

1560. In the leafy months of June and July, several French Departments germinate a set of rebellious *paper*-leaves named Proclamations, Resolutions, Journals, or Diurnals, "of the Union for Resistance to Oppression." In particular, the Town of Caen, in Calvados, sees its paper-leaf of Bulletin de Caen suddenly bud, suddenly establish itself as Newspaper there ; under the Editorship of Girondin National Representatives !

1561. For among the proscribed Girondins are certain of a more desperate humor. Some, as Vergniaud, Valazé, Gensonné, "arrested in their own houses," will await with stoical resignation what the issue may be. Some, as Brissot, Rabaut, will take to flight, to concealment; which, as the Paris Barriers are opened again in a day or two, is not yet difficult. But others there are who will rush with Buzot to Calvados; or far over France, to Lyons, Toulon, Nantes and elsewhither, and then rendezvous at Caen: to awaken as with war-trumpet the respectable Departments; and strike down an anarchic Mountain Faction; at least not yield without a stroke at it. Of this latter temper we count some score or more, of the Arrested, and of the Not-yet-arrested : a Buzot a Barbaroux, Louvet, Gundet, Pétion, who have escaped from Arrestment in their own homes: a Salles, a Phythagorean Valady, a Duchâtel, the Duchâtel that came in blanket and night-cap to vote for the life of Louis, who have escaped from danger and likelihood of Arrestment. These, to the number at one time of Twenty-seven, do accordingly lodge here, in the "Intendance, or Departmental Mansion," of the town of Caen in Calvados; welcomed by Persons in Authority; welcomed and defrayed, having no money of their own. And the Bulletin de Caen comes forth, with the most animating paragraphs: How the Bourdeaux Department, the Lyons Department, this Department after the other is declaring itself; sixty, or say sixty-nine, or seventy-two† respectable Departments either declaring. or ready to declare. Nay Marseilles, it seems. will march on Paris by itself, if need be. So has Marseilles Town said, That she will march. But on the other hand, that Montélimart Town has said, No thoroughfare; and means even to "bury herself" under her own stone and mortar first,—of this he no mention in Bulletin de Caen.

1562. Such animating paragraphs we read in this new Newspaper; and fervors and eloquent sarcasm ; tirades against the Mountain, from the pen of Deputy Salles ; which resemble, say friends, Pascal's

* Bouzot. "Mémoires," p. 310. See "Pièces Justificatives," of Narratives. Commentaries. etc., in Buzot, Louvet, Méillan: "Documents Complémentaires," in "Histoire Parlementaire," xxviii. 1–78.
† Meillan, pp. 72, 73; Louvet, p. 120.

"Provincials." What is more to the purpose, these Girondins have got a General in chief, one Wimpfen: formerly under Dumouriez; also a secondary questionable General Puisaye, and others: and are doing their best to raise a force for war. National Volunteers, whosoever is of right heart: gather in, ye National Volunteers, friends of Liberty; from our Calvados Townships, from the Eure, from Brittany, from far and near: forward to Paris and extinguish Anarchy ! Thus at Caen, in the early July days, there is a drumming and parading, a perorating and consulting ; Staff and Army; Council ; Club of Carabots, Anti-Jacobin friends of Freedom, to denounce atrocious Marat. With all which, and the editing of Bulletins, a National Representative has his hands full.

1563. At Caen it is most animated; and, as one hopes, more or less animated in the "Seventy-two Departments that adhere to us." And in a France begirt with Cimmerian invading Coalitions, and torn with an internal La Vendée, *this is*, the conclusion we have arrived at: To put down Anarchy by Civil War ! *Durum et durum*, the Proverb says, non faciunt murum. La Vendée burns; Santerre can do nothing there; he may return home and brew beer. Cimmerian bombshells fly all along the North. That Siege of Mentz is become famed :—lovers of the Picturesque (as Goethe will testify), washed country-people of both sexes, stroll thither on Sundays, to see the artillery work and counter-work ; "you only duck a little while the shot whizzes past." * Condé is capitulating to the Austrians; Royal Highness of York, these several weeks, fiercely batters Valenciennes. For, alas, our fortified Camp of Famars was stormed ; General Dampierre was killed ; General Custine was blamed,—and indeed is now come to Paris to give "explanations."

1564. Against all which the Mountain and atrocious Marat must even make head as they can. They, anarchic Convention as they are, publish Decrees, expostulatory, explanatory, yet not without severity ; they ray-forth Commissioners, singly or in pairs, the olive-branch in one hand, yet the sword in the other. Commissioners come even to Caen; but without effect. Mathematical Romme, and Prieur named of the Cote d'Or, venturing thither, with their olive and sword, are packed into prison : there may Romme lie, under lock and key, "for fifty days;" and meditate his New Calendar, if he please. Cimmeria, La Vendée, and Civil War ! Never was Republic One and Indivisible at a lower ebb.

1565. Amid which dim ferment of Caen and the World, History specially notices one thing: in the lobby of the Mansion de l'Intendance, where busy Deputies are coming and going, a young Lady with an aged valet, taking grave graceful leave of Deputy Barbaroux.† She is of stately Norman figure ; in her twenty-fifth year ; of beautiful still countenance; her name is Charlotte Corday, heretofore styled D'Armans, while Nobility still was. Barbaroux has given her a Note to Deputy Duperret,—him who once drew his sword in the effervescence. Apparently she will to Paris on some errand ? "She was a Republican before the Revolution, and never wanted energy." A completeness, a decision is in this fair female Figure: "By energy she means the spirit that will prompt one to sacrifice himself for his country." What if she, this fair young Charlotte, had emerged from her secluded stillness, suddenly like a Star; cruel-lovely, with half-angelic, half-demonic splendor ; to gleam for a moment, and in a

* "Belagerung von Mainz" (Goethe's "Werke," xxx. 278–334).
† Meillan. p. 75; Louvet, p. 114.

moment be extinguished : to be held in memory, so bright complete was she, through long centuries!—Quitting Cimmerian Coalitious without, and the dim-simmering 25,000,000 within, History will look fixedly at this one fair Apparition of a Charlotte Corday; will note whither Charlotte moves, how the little Life burns forth so radiant, then vanishes swallowed of the Night.

1566. With Barbaroux's Note of Introduction, and slight stock of luggage, we see Charlotte on Tuesday the 9th of July seated in the Caen Diligence, with a place for Paris. None takes farewell of her, wishes her Good-journey : her Father will find a line left, signifying that she is gone to England, that he must pardon her, and forget her. The drowsy Diligence lumbers along ; amid drowsy talk of Politics, and praise of the Mountain; in which she mingles not: all night, all day, and again all night. On Thursday, not long before noon, we are at the bridge of Neuilly ; here is Paris, with her thousand black domes, the goal and purpose of thy journey ! Arrived at the Inn de la Providence in the Rue des Vieux Augustins, Charlotte demands a room ; hastens to bed ; sleeps all afternoon and Night, till the morrow morning.

1567. On the morrow morning, she delivers her Note to Duperret. It relates to certain Family Papers which are in the Minister of the Interior's hands; which a Nun at Caen, an old Convent friend of Charlotte's, has need of; which Duperret shall assist her in getting : this then was Charlotte's errand to Paris? She has finished this in the course of Friday ;—yet says nothing of returning. She has seen and silently investigated several things. The Convention, in bodily reality, she has seen; what the Mountain is like. The living physiognomy of Marat she could not see; he is sick at present and confined to home.

1568. About eight on the Saturday morning, she purchases a large sheath-knife in the Palais Royal ; then straightway, in the Place des Victoires, takes a hackney-coach : " To the Rue de l'Ecole de Médecine, No. 44." It is the residence of the Citoyen Marat!—The Citoyen Marat is ill, and cannot be seen; which seems to disappoint her much. Her business is with Marat, then? Hapless beautiful Charlotte; hapless squalid Marat! From Caen in the utmost West, from Neuchâtel in the utmost East, they two are drawing nigh each other; they two have, very strangely, business together.—Charlotte, returning to her Inn, dispatches a short Note to Marat; signifying that she is from Caen, the seat of rebellion ; that she desires earnestly to see him, and " will put it in his power to do France a great service." No answer. Charlotte writes another Note still more pressing; sets out with it by coach, about seven in the evening, herself. Tired day-laborers have again finished their Week; huge Paris is circling and simmering, manifold according to its vague wont: this one fair Figure has decision in it; drives straight,—toward a purpose.

1569. It is yellow July evening, we say, the 13th of the month; eve of the Bastille day,—when " M. Marat," four years ago, in the crowd of the Pont-Neuf, shrewdly required of that Besenval Hussar-party, which had such friendly dispositions, " to dismount, and give up their arms, then ;" and become notable among Patriot men. Four years: what a road he has traveled ;—and sits now, about half-past seven of the clock, stewing in slipper-bath; sore afflicted; ill of Revolution Fever,—of what other malady this History had rather not name. Excessively sick and worn, poor man: with precisely eleven-pence-half-penny of ready-money, in paper; with slipper-bath; strong three-footed stool for writing on, the while; and a squalid—Washer-woman, one may call her: that is his civic establishment in Medical-School Street ; thither and not elsewhither has his road led him. Not to the reign of Brotherhood and Perfect Felicity: yet surely on the way toward that?—Hark, a rap again ! A musical woman's voice, refusing to be rejected : it is the Citoyenne who would do France a service. Marat, recognizing from within, cries, Admit her. Charlotte Corday is admitted.

1570. Citoyen Marat, I am from Caen the seat of rebellion, and wished to speak with you.—Be seated, mon enfant. Now what are the Traitors doing at Caen ? What Deputies are at Caen ? Charlotte names some Deputies. " Their heads shall fall within a fortnight," croaks the eager People's-friend, clutching his tablets to write: Barbaroux, Pétion, writes he with bare shrunk arm, turning aside in the bath: Pétion, and Louvet, and—Charlotte has drawn her knife from the sheath ; plunges it, with one sure stroke, into the writer's heart. " A moi, chère amie (Help, dear) ! " no more could the Death-choked say or shriek. The helpful Washer-woman running in, there is no Friend of the People, or Friend of the Washer-woman left ; but his life with a groan gushes out, indignant, to the shades below.*

1571. And so Marat People's-friend is ended ; the lone Stylites has got hurled down suddenly from his Pillar,—whitherward He that made him knows. Patriot Paris may sound triple and tenfold, in dole and wail ; re-echoed by Patriot France ; and the Convention, " Chabot pale with terror, declaring that they are to be all assassinated," may decree him Pantheon Honors, Public Funeral, Mirabeau's dust making way for him ; and Jacobin Societies, in lamentable oratory, summing up his character, parallel him to One, whom they think it honor to call " the good Sansculotte,"—whom we name not here ;† also a Chapel may be made, for the urn that holds his Heart, in the Place du Carrousel ; and newborn children be named Marat ; and Lago-di-Como Hawkers bake mountains of stucco into unbeautiful Busts and David paint his Picture, or Death.-Scene ; and such other Apotheosis take place as the human genius, in these circumstances, can devise : but Marat returns no more to the light of this Sun. One sole circumstance we have read with clear sympathy, in the Old Moniteur Newspapers: how Marat's Brother comes from Neuchâtel to ask of the Convention, " that the deceased Jean-Paul Marat's musket be given him."‡ For Marat too had a brother and natural affections ; and was wrapped once in swaddling-clothes, and slept safe in a cradle like the rest of us. Ye children of men !—A sister of his, they say, lives still to this day in Paris.

1572. As for Charlotte Corday, her work is accomplished ; the recompense of it is near and sure. The chère amie, and neighbors of the house, flying at her, she " overturns some movables," intrenches herself till the gendarmes arrive; then quietly surrenders; goes quietly to the Abbaye Prison: she alone quiet, all Paris sounding, in wonder, in rage or admiration, round her. Duperret is put in arrest, on account of her; his Papers sealed,—which may lead to consequences. Fauchet, in like manner; though Fauchet had not so much as heard of her. Charlotte, confronted with these two Deputies, praises the grave firmness of Duperret, censures the dejection of Fauchet.

1573. On Wednesday morning, the thronged Palais de Justice and Revolutionary Tribunal can see her

* Moniteur, Nos. 197, 198, 199 : " Histoire Parlementaire," xxviii. 301-305; " Deux Amis," x. 368-374.
† See " Éloge funèbre de Jean-Paul Marat," prononcé à Strasbourg (in Barbaroux, pp. 125-131); Mercier, etc.
‡ Séance du 16 Septembre 1793.

facc; beautiful and calm: she dates it "fourth day of the Preparation of Peace." A strange murmur ran through the Hall, at sight of her; you could not say of what character.* Tinville has his indictments and tape-papers: the cutler of the Palais Royal will testify that he sold her the sheath-knife; "All these details are needless," interrupted Charlotte; "it is 1 that killed Marat." By whose instigation?—"By no one's." What tempted you, then? His crimes. "I killed one man," added she, raising her voice extremely (extrêmement), as they went on with their questions, "I killed one man to save a hundred thousand; a villain to save innocents; a savage wild-beast to give repose to my country. I was a Republican before the Revolution; I never wanted energy." There is therefore nothing to be said. The public gazes astonished: the hasty limners sketch her features, Charlotte not disapproving: the men of law proceed with their formalities. The doom is Death as a murderess. To her Advocate she gives thanks; in gentle phrase, in high-flown classical spirit. To the Priest they send her she gives thanks; but needs not any shriving and ghostly or other aid from him.

1574. On this same evening therefore, about half-past seven o'clock, from the gate of the Conciergerie, to a City all on tip-toe, the fatal Cart issues; seated on it a fair young creature, sheeted in red smock of Murderess: so beautiful, serene, so full of life; journeying toward death,—alone amid the World. Many take off their hats, saluting reverently, for what heart but must be touched?† Others growl and howl. Adam Lux, of Mentz, declares that she is greater than Brutus; that it were beautiful to die with her: the head of this young man seems turned. At the Place de la Révolution, the countenance of Charlotte wears the same still smile. The executioners proceed to bind her feet; she resists, thinking it meant as an insult; on a word of explanation, she submits with cheerful apology. As the last act, all being now ready, they take the neckerchief from her neck, a blush of maidenly shame overspreads that fair face and neck; the cheeks were still tinged with it when the executioner lifted the severed head, to show it to the people. "It is most true," says Forster, "that he struck the cheek insultingly; for I saw it with my eyes: the Police imprisoned him for it."‡

1575. In this manner have the Beautifulest and the Squalidest come in collision, and extinguished one another. Jean-Paul Marat and Marie-Anne Charlotte Corday both, suddenly, are no more. "Day of the Preparation of Peace?" Alas, how were peace possible or preparable, while, for example, the hearts of lovely Maidens, in their convent-stillness, are dreaming not of Love-paradises and the light of Life, but of Codrus's-sacrifices and Death well-earned? That 25,000,000 hearts have got to such temper, this is the Anarchy; the soul of it lies in this; whereof not peace can be the embodiment! The death of Marat, whetting old animosities tenfold, will be worse than any life. O ye hapless Two, mutually extinctive, the Beautiful and the Sonalid, sleep ye well,—in the Mother's bosom that bore you both!

1576. This is the History of Charlotte Corday; most definite, most complete; angelic-demonic: like a Star! Adam Lux goes home, half-delirious; to pour forth his Apotheosis of her, in paper and print; to propose that she have a statue with this inscription, *Greater than Brutus.* Friends represent his danger; Lux is reckless; thinks it were beautiful to die with her.

* "Procès de Charlotte Corday," etc. ("Histoire Parlementaire," xxviii. 311–338).
† "Deux Amis," x. 374–384.
‡ "Briefwechsel," i. 506.

CHAPTER II.

IN CIVIL WAR.

1577. But during these same hours, another guillotine is at work, on another; Charlotte, for the Girondins, dies at Paris to-day; Chalier, by the Girondins, dies at Lyons to-morrow.

1798. From rumbling of cannon along the streets of that City, it has come to firing of them, to rabid fighting: Nièvre Chol and the Girondins triumph;—behind whom there is, as everywhere, a Royalist Faction waiting to strike in. Trouble enough at Lyons; and the dominant party carrying it with a high hand! For, indeed, the whole South is astir; incarcerating Jacobins; arming for Girondins: wherefore we have got a "Congress of Lyons;" also a "Revolutionary Tribunal of Lyons," and Anarchists shall tremble. So Chalier was soon found guilty, of Jacobinism, of murderous Plot, "address with drawn dagger on the 6th of February last; and, on the morrow, he also travels his final road, along the streets of Lyons, "by the side of an ecclesiastic, with whom he seems to speak earnestly,"—the axe now glittering nigh. He could weep, in old years, this man, and "fall on his knees on the pavement," blessing Heaven at sight of Federation Programmes or the like; then he pilgrimed to Paris, to worship Marat and the Mountain: now Marat and he are both gone; —we said he could not end well. Jacobinism groans inwardly, at Lyons; but dare not outwardly. Chalier, when the Tribunal sentenced him, made answer: "My death will cost this City dear."

1579. Montélimart Town is not buried under its ruins; yet Marseilles is actually marching, under order of a "Lyons Congress;" is incarcerating Patriots; the very Royalists now showing face. Against which a General Cartaux fights, though in small force; and with him an Artillery Major, of the name of—Napoleon Bonaparte. This Napoleon, to prove that the Marseillese have no chance ultimately, not only fights but writes; publishes his "Supper of Beaucaire," a Dialogue which has become curious.* Unfortunate Cities, with their actions and their reactions; Violence to be paid with violence in geometrical ratio; Royalism and Anarchism both striking in;—the final net-amount of which geometrical series, what man shall sum?

1580. The Bar of Iron has never yet floated in Marseilles Harbor; but the body of Rebecqui was found floating, self-drowned there. Hot Rebecqui, seeing how confusion deepened, and Respectability grew poisoned with Royalism, felt that there was no refuge for a Republican but death. Rebecqui disappeared: no one knew whither; till one morning, they found the empty case or body of him risen to the top, tumbling on the salt waves;† and perceived that Rebecqui had withdrawn forever.—Toulon likewise is incarcerating Patriots; sending delegates to Congress: intriguing, in case of necessity, with the Royalists and English. Montpellier, Bourdeaux, Nantes: all France, that is not under the swoop of Austria and Cimmeria, seems rushing into madness and suicidal ruin. The Mountain labors: like a volcano in a burning volcanic Land. Convention Committees, of Surety, of Salvation, are busy night and day: Convention Commissioners whirl on all highways: bearing olive-branch and sword, or now perhaps sword only. Chaumette and Municipals come daily to the Tuileries demanding a Constitution: it is some weeks now since he resolved, in Town-hall, that a Deputation "should go every day,‡ and demand a Constitution, till one were got;"

* See Hazlitt. H. 529–541.
† Barbaroux. p. 29.
‡ "Deux Amis," x. 345.

whereby suicidal France might rally and pacify itself; a thing inexpressibly desirable.

1581. This then is the fruit your Anti-anarchic Girondins have got from that Levying of War in Calvados? This fruit, we may say: and no other whatsoever. For indeed, before either Charlotte's or Chalier's head had fallen, the Calvados War itself had, as it were, vanished, dream-like, in a shriek! With "seventy-two Departments" on our side, one might have hoped better things. But it turns out that Respectabilities, though they will vote, will not fight. Possession always is nine points in Law; but in Law-suits of *this* kind, one may say, it is ninety-and-nine points. Men do what they were wont to do; and have immense irresolution and inertia: they obey him who has the symbols that claim obedience. Consider what, in modern society, this one fact means: the Metropolis is with our enemies! Metropolis, *Mother-city*; rightly so named: all the rest are but as her children, her nurselings. Why, there is not a leathern Diligence, with its post-bags and luggage-boots, that lumbers out from her, but is as a huge life-pulse; she is the heart of all. Cut short that one leathern Diligence, how much is cut short!—General Wimpfen, looking practically into the matter, can see nothing for it but that one should fall back on Royalism; get into communication with Pitt? Dark innuendos he flings out, to that effect: whereat we Girondins start, horror-struck. He produces as his Second in command a certain "Ci-devant," one Comte Puisaye; entirely unknown to Louvet; greatly suspected by him.

1582. Few wars, accordingly, were ever levied of a more insufficient character than this of Calvados. He that is curious in such things may read the details of it in the Memoirs of that same Ci-devant Puisaye, the much-enduring man and Royalist: How our Girondin National forces, marching off with plenty of wind-music, are drawn out about the old Château of Brécourt, in the wood-country near Vernon, to meet the Mountain National forces advancing from Paris. How on the fifteenth afternoon of July, they did meet;—and, as it were, shrieked mutually, and took mutually to flight, without loss: How Puisaye thereafter,—for the Mountain Nationals fled first, and we thought ourselves the victors,—was roused from his warm bed in the Castle of Brécourt; and had to gallop without boots; our Nationals, in the night-watches, having fallen unexpectedly into sauve-qui-peut:—and in brief the Calvados War had burnt priming; and the only question now was, Whitherward to vanish, in what hole to hide oneself!*

1583. The National Volunteers rush homeward faster than they came. The Seventy-two Respectable Departments, says Meillan, "all turned round and forsook us, in the space of four-and-twenty hours." Unhappy those who, as at Lyons for instance, have gone too far for turning! "One morning," we find placarded on our Intendance Mansion, the Decree of Convention which casts us Hors la loi, into Outlawry; placarded by our Caen Magistrates;—clear hint that we also are to vanish. Vanish indeed: but whitherward? Gorsas has friends in Rennes: he will hide thee,—unhappily will not lie hid. Gaudet, Lanjuinais are on cross-roads, making for Bourdeaux. To Bourdeaux! cries the general voice, of Valor alike and of Despair. Some flag of Respectability still floats there, or is thought to float.

1584. Thitherward therefore; each as he can? Eleven of these ill-fated Deputies, among whom we may count as twelfth, Friend Riouffe the Man of Letters, do an original thing: Take the uniform of National Volunteers, and retreat southward with the

Breton Battalion, as private soldiers of that corps These brave Bretons had stood truer by us than any other. Nevertheless, at the end of a day or two, they also do now get dubious, self-divided; we must part from them; and, with some half-dozen as convoy or guide, retreat by ourselves,—a solitary marching detachment, through waste regions of the West.*

CHAPTER III.

RETREAT OF THE ELEVEN.

1585. It is one of the notablest Retreats, this of the Eleven, that History presents: The handful of forlorn Legislators retreating there, continually, with shouldered firelock and well-filled cartridge-box, in the yellow autumn; long hundreds of miles between them and Bourdeaux; the country all getting hostile, suspicious of the truth; simmering and buzzing on all sides, more and more. Louvet has preserved the Itinerary of it; a piece worth all the rest he ever wrote.

1586. O virtuous Pétion, with thy early white head, O brave young Barbaroux, has it come to this? Weary ways, worn shoes, light purse;—encompassed with perils as with a sea! Revolutionary Committees are in every Township; of Jacobin temper; our friends all cowed, our cause the losing one. In the Borough of Moncontour, by ill chance, it is market-day: to the gaping public such transit of a solitary Marching Detachment is suspicious; we have need of energy, of promptitude and luck, to be allowed to march through. Hasten, ye weary pilgrims! The country is getting up; noise of you is bruited day after day, a solitary Twelve retreating in this mysterious manner; with every new day, a wider wave of inquisitive pursuing tumult is stirred up till the whole West will be in motion. "Cussy is tormented with gout, Buzot is too fat for marching." Riouffe, blistered, bleeding, marches only on tiptoe; Barbaroux limps with sprained ankle, yet ever cheery, full of hope and valor. Light Louvet glances hare-eyed, not hare-hearted: only virtuous Pétion's serenity "was but once seen ruffled."† They lie in straw lofts, in woody brakes; rudest paillasse on the floor of a secret friend is luxury. They are seized in the dead of night by Jacobin mayors and tap of drum; get off by firm countenance, rattle of muskets and ready wit.

1587. Of Bordeaux, through fiery La Vendée and the long geographical spaces that remain, it were madness to think: well if you can get to Quimper on the sea-coast, and take shipping there. Faster, ever faster! Before the end of the march, so hot has the country grown, it is found advisable to march all night. They do it; under the still night-canopy they plod along:—and yet behold, Rumor has out-plodded them. In the paltry Village of Carhaix (be its thatched huts and bottomless peat-bogs long notable to the Traveler), one is astonished to find light still glimmering; citizens are awake, with rush-lights burning, in that nook of the terrestrial Planet; as we traverse swiftly the one poor street, a voice is heard saying, "There they are (Les voilà qui passent)!"‡ Swifter, ye doomed lame Twelve: speed ere they can arm; gain the Woods of Quimper before day, and lie squatted there!

1588. The doomed Twelve do it; though with difficulty, with loss of road, with peril and the mistakes of a night. In Quimper are Girondin friends, who perhaps will harbor the homeless, till a Bourdeaux ship weigh. Wayworn, heart-worn, in agony of suspense, till Quimper friendship get warning, they lie there, squatted under the thick wet boscage;

* "Mémoires de Puisaye" (London, 1803), ii. 142-167.

* Louvet, pp. 101-137; Meillan, pp. 81, 241-270.
† Meillan, pp. 110-137.
‡ Louvet, pp. 138-164.

suspicious of the face of man. Some pity to the brave; to the unhappy! Unhappiest of all Legislators, O when ye packed your luggage, some score or two-score months ago, and mounted this or the other leathern vehicle, to be Conscript Fathers of a regenerated France, and reap deathless laurels,—did you think your journey was to lead *hither?* The Quimper Samaritans find them squatted; lift them up to help and comfort; will hide them in sure places. Thence let them dissipate gradually; or there they can lie quiet, and write Memoirs till a Bordeaux ship sail.

1589. And thus, in Calvados all is dissipated; Romme is out of prison, meditating his Calendar; ringleaders are locked in his room. At Caen the Corday family mourns in silence: Buzot's House is a heap of dust and demolition; and amid the rubbish sticks a Gallows, with this inscription, *Here dwelt the Traitor Buzot, who conspired against the Republic.* Buzot and the other vanished Deputies are hors la loi, as we saw; their lives free to take where they can be found. The worse fares it with the poor Arrested visible Deputies at Paris. "Arrestment at home" threatens to become "Confinement in the Luxembourg;" to end: *where?* For example, what pale-visaged thin man is this, journeying toward Switzerland as a Merchant of Neuchâtel, whom they arrest in the town of Moulins? To Revolutionary Committee he is suspect. To Revolutionary Committee, on probing the matter, he is evidently: Deputy Brissot! Back to the Arrestment, poor Brissot; or indeed to strait confinement,—whither others are fated to follow. Rabaut has built himself a false-partition, in a friend's house; lives, in invisible darkness, between two walls. It will end, this same Arrestment business, in Prison, and the Revolutionary Tribunal.

1590. Nor must we forget Duperret, and the seal put on his papers by means of Charlotte. One Paper is there, fit to breed woe enough: A secret solemn Protest against that suprema dies of the 2d of June! This Secret Protest our poor Duperret had drawn up, the same week, in all plainness of speech; waiting the time for publishing it: to which Secret Protest his signature, and that of other honorable Deputies not a few, stands legibly appended. And now, if the seals were once broken, the Mountain still victorious? Such Protestors, your Merciers, Bailleuls, Seventy-three by the tale, what yet remains of Respectable Girondism in the Convention, may tremble to think!—These are the fruits of levying civil war.

1591. Also we find, that in these last days of July, the famed Siege of Mentz is *finished:* the Garrison to march out with honors of war: not to serve against the Coalition for a year. Lovers of the picturesque, and Goethe standing on the Chaussée of Mentz, saw, with due interest, the Procession issuing forth, in all solemnity:

1592. "Escorted by Prussian horse came first the French Garrison. Nothing could look stranger than this latter; a column of Marseillese, slight, swarthy, parti-colored, in patched clothes, came tripping on; —as if King Edwin had opened the Dwarf Hill, and sent out his nimble Host of Dwarfs. Next followed regular troops; serious, sullen; not as if downcast or ashamed. But the remarkablest appearance, which struck every one, was that of the Chasers (Chasseurs) coming out mounted; they had advanced quite silent to where we stood, when their Band struck up the 'Marseillaise.' This revolutionary Te-Deum has in itself something mournful and bodeful, however briskly played; but at present they gave it in altogether slow time, proportionate to the creeping step they rode at. It was piercing and fearful, and a most

serious-looking thing, as these cavaliers, long, lean men, of a certain age, with mien suitable to the music, came pacing on: singly you might have likened them to Don Quixote; in mass, they were highly dignified.

1593. "But now a single troop became notable: that of the Commissioners or Représentans. Merlin of Thionville, in hussar uniform, distinguishing himself by wild beard and look, had another person in similar costume on his left; the crowd shouted out, with rage, at sight of this latter, the name of a Jacobin Townsman and Clubbist; and shook itself to seize him. Merlin drew bridle; referred to his dignity as French Representative, to the vengeance that should follow any injury done; he would advise every one to compose himself, for this was not the *last time* they would see him here."[*] Thus rode Merlin; threatening in defeat. But what now shall stem that tide of Prussians setting in through the opened North-east? Lucky if fortified Lines of Weissembourg, and impassabilities of Vosges Mountains confine it to French Alsace, keep it from submerging the very heart of the country!

Furthermore, precisely in the same days, Valenciennes Siege is finished, in the North-west:—fallen, under the red hail of York! Condé fell some fortnight since. Cimmerian Coalition presses on. What seems very notable too, on all these captured French Towns there flies not the Royalist fleur-de-lis, in the name of a new Louis the Pretender; but the Austrian flag flies; as if Austria meant to keep them for herself! Perhaps General Custine, still in Paris, can give some explanation of the fall of these strong-places? Mother Society, from tribune and gallery, growls loud that he ought to do it;—remarks, however, in a splenetic manner that "the Monsieurs of the Palais Royal" are calling Long-life to this General.

1594. The Mother Society, purged now, by successive "scrutinies or épurations," from all taint of Girondism, has become a great Authority; what we can call shield-bearer or bottle-holder, nay call it fugleman, to the purged National Convention itself. The Jacobins Debates are reported in the Moniteur, like Parliamentary ones.

CHAPTER IV.

O NATURE.

1595. But looking more especially into Paris City, what is this that History, on the 10th of August, Year One of Liberty, "by old-style, year 1793," discerns there? Praised be the Heavens, a new Feast of Pikes!

For Chaumette's "Deputation every day" has worked out its result: a Constitution. It was one of the rapidest Constitutions ever put together; made, some say in eight days, by Hérault Séchelles and others; probably a workmanlike, road-worthy Constitution enough;—on which point, however, we are, for some reasons, little called to form a judgment. Workmanlike or not, the 44.000 Communes of France, by overwhelming majorities, did hasten to accept it; glad of any Constitution whatsoever. Nay Departmental Deputies have come, the venerablest Republicans of each Department, with solemn message of acceptance: and now what remains but that our new Final Constitution he proclaimed, and sworn to, in Feast of Pikes? The Departmental Deputies, we say, are come some time ago; Chaumette very anxious about them, lest Girondin Monsieurs, Agio-jobbers, or were it even

* "Belagerung von Mainz" (Goethe's "Werke." xxx. 315).

Filles de joie of a Girondin temper, corrupt their morals.* Tenth of August, immortal Anniversary, greater almost than Bastille July, is the Day.

1596. Painter David has not been idle. Thanks to David and the French genius, there steps forth into the sunlight, this day, a Scenic Phantasmagory unexampled:—whereof History, so occupied with real Phantasmagories, will say but little.

1597. For one thing, History can notice with satisfaction, on the ruins of the Bastille, a *Statue of Nature*; gigantic, spouting water from her two mammelles. Not a Dream this; but a fact, palpable visible. There she spouts, great Nature; dim, before daybreak. But as the coming Sun ruddies the East, come countless Multitudes, regulated and unregulated; come Departmental Deputies, come Mother Society and Daughters; comes National Convention, led on by handsome Hérault, soft wind-music breathing note of expectation. Lo, as great Sol scatters his first fire-handful, tipping the hills and chimney-heads with gold, Hérault is at great Nature's feet (she is plaster-of-paris merely); Hérault lifts, in an iron saucer, water spouted from the sacred breasts; drinks of it, with an eloquent Pagan Prayer, beginning, "O Nature!" and all the Departmental Deputies drink, each with what best suitable ejaculation or prophetic-utterance is in him;—amid breathings, which become blasts, of wind-music; and the roar of artillery and human throats: finishing well the first act of this solemnity.

1598. Next are processionings along the Boulevards: Deputies or Officials bound together by long indivisible tricolor ribbon ; general "members of the Sovereign" walking pell-mell, with pikes, with hammers, with the tools and emblems of their crafts; among which we notice a Plow, and ancient Baucis and Philemon seated on it, drawn by their children. Many-voiced harmony and dissonance filling the air. Through Triumphal Arches enough : at the basis of the first of which, we descry—whom thinkest thou ? —the Heroines of the Insurrection of Women. Strong Dames of the Market, they sit there (Théroigne too ill to attend, one fears), with oak-branches, tricolor bedizenment ; firm seated on their Cannons. To whom handsome Hérault, making pause of admiration, addresses soothing eloquence; whereupon, they rise and fall into the march.

1599. And now mark, in the Place de la Révolution, what other august Statue may this be; veiled in canvas,—which swiftly we shear off, by pulley and cord? The *Statue of Liberty!* She too is of plaster, hoping to become of metal; stands where a Tyrant Louis Quinze once stood. "Three thousand birds" are let loose, into the whole world, with labels round their neck, *We are free; imitate us.* Holocaust of Royalist and ci-devant trumpery, such as one could still gather, is burnt; pontifical eloquence must be uttered, by handsome Hérault and Pagan orisons offered up.

1600. And then forward across the River; where is new enormous Statuary: enormous plaster Mountain ;—Hercules-People, with uplifted all-conquering club; "many-headed dragon of Girondin Federalism rising from fetid marsh :"—needing new eloquence from Hérault. To say nothing of Champ-de-Mars, and Fatherland's Altar there: with urn of slain Defenders, Carpenter's-level of the Law; and such exploding, gesticulating and perorating, that Hérault's lips must be growing white, and his tongue cleaving to the roof of his mouth.*

1601. Toward six o'clock let the wearied President, let Paris Patriotism generally sit down to what repast, and social repasts, can be had; and with flow-

ing tankard or light-mantling glass, usher in this New and Newest Era. In fact, is not Romme's New Calendar getting ready ? On all house-tops flicker little tricolor Flags, their flagstaff a Pike and Liberty-Cap. On all house-walls—for no Patriot not suspect will be behind another,—there stand printed these words: *Republic one and indivisible; Liberty, Equality, Fraternity, or Death.*

1602. As to the New Calendar, we may say here rather than elsewhere that speculative men have long been struck with the inequalities and incongruities of the Old Calendar; that a new one has long been as good as determined on. Maréchal the Atheist, almost ten years ago, proposed a new Calendar, free at least from superstition: this the Paris Municipality would now adopt, in defect of a better: at all events, let us have either this of Maréchal's or a better,—the New Era being come. Petitions, more than once, have been sent to that effect ; and indeed for a year past, all Public Bodies, Journalists and Patriots in general, have dated *First Year of the Republic.* It is a subject not without difficulties. But the Convention has taken it up: and Romme, as we say, has been meditating it : not Maréchal's New Calendar, but a better New one of Romme's and our own. Romme, aided by a Monge, a Lagrange and others, furnish mathematics ; Fabre d'Eglantine furnishes poetic nomenclature ; and so, on the 5th of October, 1793, after trouble enough, they bring forth this New Republican Calendar of theirs, in a complete state ; and by Law get it put in action.

1603. Four equal Seasons, Twelve equal months of Thirty days each; this makes 360 days; and five odd days remain to be disposed of. The five odd days we will make Festivals, and name the five Sansculottides, or Days without Breeches. Festival of Genius; Festivals of Labor; of Actions; of Rewards; of Opinion : these are the five Sansculottides. Whereby the great Circle, or Year, is made complete: solely every fourth year, whilom called Leap-year, we introduce a sixth Sansculottide; and name it Festival of the Revolution. Now as to the day of Commencement, which offers difficulties, is it not one of the luckiest coincidences that the Republic herself commenced on the 21st of September : close on the Autumnal Equinox ! Autumnal Equinox, at midnight for the meridian of Paris, in the year whilom Christian 1792, from that moment shall the New Era reckon itself to begin. Vendémiaire, Brumaire, Frimaire ; or as one might say, in mixed English, Vintagearious, Fogarious, Frostarious : these are our three Autumn months. Nivose, Pluviose, Ventose, or say, Snowous, Rainous, Windous, make our Winter season. Germinal, Floréal, Prairial, or Buddal, Floweral, Meadowal, are our Spring season. Messidor, Thermidor, Fructidor, that is to say (dor being Greek for *gift*), Reapidor, Heatidor, Fruitidor, are Republican Summer. These Twelve, in a singular manner, divide the Republican Year. Then as to minuter subdivisions; let us venture at once on a bold stroke: adopt your decimal subdivision: and instead of the World-old Week, or Se'ennight, make it a Tennight, or Décade :—not without results. There are three Decades, then, in each of the months, which is very regular, and the Décadi, or Tenth-day, shall always be the "Day of Rest." And the Christian Sabbath, in that case ? Shall shift for itself!

1604. This, in brief, is the New Calendar of Romme and the Convention ; calculated for the meridian of Paris, and Gospel of Jean Jacques: not one of the least afflicting occurrences for the actual British reader of French History :—confusing the soul with Messidors, Meadowals: till at last, in self-defense, one is forced to construct some ground-scheme, or rule of Commutation from New-style to Old-style,

* "Deux Amis," xi. 73.
* "Choix des Rapports," xii. 435-442.

and have it lying by him. Such ground-scheme, almost worn out in our service, but still legible and printable, we shall, now, in a Note, present to the reader. For the Romme Calendar, in so many News-papers, Memoirs, Public Acts, has stamped itself deep into that section of Time: a New Era that lasts some Twelve years and odd is not to be despised.* Let the Reader, therefore, with such ground-scheme, help himself, where needful, out of New-style into Old-style, called also "slave-style (stile-esclave);"— whereof we, in these pages, shall as much as possible use the latter only.

1605. Thus with new Feast of Pikes, and New Era or New Calendar, did France accept her New Consti-tution: the most Democratic Constitution ever com-mitted to paper. How it will work in practice? Patriot Deputations, from time to time, solicit frui-tion of it; that it be set-a-going. Always, however, this seems questionable; for the moment, unsuit-able. Till, in some weeks, Salut Public, through the organ of Saint-Just, makes report, that, in the present alarming circumstances, the state of France is Revolutionary; that her "Government must be Revolutionary till the Peace." Solely as Paper, then, and as a Hope, must this poor new Constitution ex-ist;—in which shape we may conceive it lying, even now, with an infinity of other things, in that Limbo near the Moon. Farther than paper it never got, nor ever will get.

CHAPTER V.

SWORD OF SHARPNESS.

1606. In fact, it is something quite other than paper theorems, it is iron and audacity that France now needs.

Is not La Vendée still blazing;—alas too literally; rogue Rossignol burning the very corn-mills? Gen-eral Santerre could do nothing there; General Ros-signol, in blind fury, often in liquor, can do less than nothing. Rebellion spreads, grows ever madder. Happily those lean Quixote-figures, whom we saw re-treating out of Mentz, "bound not to serve against the Coalition for a year," have got to Paris. National Convention packs them into post-vehicles and con-veyances; sends them swiftly, by post, into La Ven-dée. There valiantly struggling, in obscure battle and skirmish, under rogue Rossignol, let them, un-laureled, save the Republic, and "be cut down grad-ually to the last man."†

* September 22d of 1792 is Vendemiaire 1st of Year One, and the new months are all of 30 days each; therefore

	ADD			DAYS
Vendemiaire	21		September	30
Brumaire	21		October	31
Frimaire	20		November	30
Nivose	20		December	31
Pluviose	19		January	31
Ventose	18		February	28
Germinal	20		March	31
Floreal	19		April	30
Prairial	19		May	31
Messidor	18		June	30
Thermidor	18		July	31
Fructidor	17		August	31

There are 5 Sansculottides, and in leap-year a sixth, to be added at the end of Fructidor. Romme's first Leap-year is "An 4" (1795, not 1796), which is another troublesome circumstance, every fourth year, from "September 22d" round to "February 29" again.
The New Calendar ceased on the 1st of January, 1806. See "Choix des Rapports," xiii. 83-99; xix. 199.

† "Deux Amis," xi. 147; xiii. 160-192, etc.

1607. Does not the Coalition, like a fire-tide, pour in; Prussia through the opened North-east; Austria, England through the North-west? General Hou-chard prospers no better there than General Custine did: let him look to it! Through the Eastern and the Western Pyrenees Spain has deployed itself, spreads, rustling with Bourbon banners, over the face of the South. Ashes and embers of confused Giron-din civil war covered that region already. Marseilles is damped down, not quenched; to be quenched in blood. Toulon, terror-struck, too far gone for turn-ing, has flung itself, ye righteous Powers, into the hands of the English! On Toulon Arsenal there flies a flag,—nay not even the Fleur-de-lis of a Louis Pretender; there flies that accursed St. George's Cross of the English and Admiral Hood! What remnant of sea-craft, arsenals, roperies, war-navy France had, has given itself to these enemies of human nature, "ennemis du genre humain." Be-leaguer it, bombard it, ye Commissioners Barras, Fré-ron, Robespierre Junior; thou General Cartaux, Gen-eral Dugommier; above all, thou remarkable Artil-lery-Major, Napoleon Bonaparte! Hood is fortifying himself, victualing himself; means, apparently, to make a new Gibralter of it.

1608. But lo, in the Autumn night, late night, among the last of August, what sudden, red sun-blaze is this that has risen over Lyons City; with a noise to deafen the world? It is the Powder-tower of Lyons, nay the Arsenal with four Powder-towers, which has caught fire in the Bombardment; and sprung into the air, carrying "117 houses" after it. With a light, one fancies, as of the noon sun; with a roar second only to the Last Trumpet! All living sleepers far and wide it has awakened. What a sight was that, which the eye of History saw, in the sud-den nocturnal sun-blaze! The roofs of hapless Lyons, and all its domes and steeples made momen-tarily clear; Rhone and Saone streams flashing sud-denly visible; and height and hollow, hamlet and smooth stubble-field, and all the region round;— heights, alas, all scarped and counterscarped, into trenches, curtains, redoubts; blue Artillery-men, little Powder-devilkins, plying their hell-trade there through the not ambrosial night! Let the darkness cover it again; for it pains the eye. Of a truth, Chalier's death is costing the City dear. Con-vention Commissioners, Lyons Congresses have come and gone: and action there was and reaction; bad ever growing worse; till it has come this: Commis-sioner Dubois-Crancé, "with 70,000 men, and all the Artillery of several Provinces," bombarding Lyons day and night.

1609. Worse things still are in store. Famine is in Lyons, and ruin and fire. Desperate are the sallies of the besieged; brave Précy, their National Colonel and Commandant, doing what is in man: desperate but ineffectual. Provisions cut off: nothing enter-ing our city but shot and shells! The Arsenal has roared aloft: the very Hospital will be battered down and the sick buried alive. A black Flag hung on this latter noble Edifice, appealing to the pity of the besiegers; for though maddened, were they not still our brethren? In their blind wrath, they took it for a flag of defiance and aimed thitherward the more. Bad is growing ever worse here: and how will the worse stop, till it have grown worst of all? Commissioner Dubois will listen to no pleading, to no speech, save this only. We surrender at discretion. Lyons contains in it subdued Jacobins; dominant Girondins; secret Royalists. And now, mere deaf madness and cannon-shot enveloping them, will not the desperate Municipality fly at last, into the arms of Royalism itself? Majesty of Sardinia was to bring help, but it failed. Emigrant d'Autichamp, in name of the Two Pretender Royal Highnesses, is coming through Switzerland with help ; coming, not yet come : Précy hoists the Fleur-de-lis!

1610. At sight of which all true Girondins sorrowfully fling down their arms :—Let our Tricolor brethren storm us, then, and slay us in their wrath ; with you we conquer not. The famishing women and children are sent forth : denf Dubois sends them back ;—rains in mere fire and madness. Our "redoubts of cotton-bags" are taken, retaken ; Précy under his Fleur-de-lis is valiant as Despair. What will become of Lyons? It is a siege of seventy days.*

1612. Or see, in these same weeks, far in the Western waters : breasting through the Bay of Biscay, a greasy dingy little Merchant-ship, with Scotch skipper; under hatches whereof sit, disconsolate,—the last forlorn nucleus of Giroudism, the Deputies from Quimper! Several have dissipated themselves, whithersoever they could. Poor Riouffe fell into the talons of Revolutionary Committee and Paris Prison. The rest sit here under hatches ; Reverend Pétion with his gray hair, angry Buzot, suspicious Louvet, brave young Barbaroux, and others. They have escaped from Quimper, in this sad craft; are now tacking and struggling; in danger from the waves, in danger from the English, in still worse danger from the French :—banished by Heaven and Earth to the greasy belly of this Scotch skipper's Merchant-vessel, unfruitful Atlantic raving round. They are for Bourdeaux, if peradventure hope yet linger there. Enter not Bourdeaux, O Friends! Bloody Convention Representatives, Tallien and such like, with their edicts, with their Guillotine, have arrived there; Respectability is driven under ground ; Jacobinism lords it on high. From that Réole landing-place, or Beak of Ambès, as it were, pale Death, waving his Revolutionary Sword of Sharpness, waves you elsewhither!

1613. On one side or the other of that Bec d'Ambès, the Scotch Skipper with difficulty moors, a dexterous greasy man ; with difficulty lands his Girondins ;— who, after reconnoitering, must rapidly burrow in the Earth : and so, in subterranean ways, in friends' back-closets, in cellars, barn-lofts, in caves of Saint-Emilion and Libourne, stave-off cruel Death,† Unhappiest of all Senators!

CHAPTER VI.
RISEN AGAINST TYRANTS.

1614. Against all which incalculable impediments, horrors and disasters, what can a Jacobin Convention oppose? The uncalculating Spirit of Jacobinism, and Sansculottic sansformulistic Frenzy! Our Enemies press in on us, says Danton, but they shall not conquer us. "we will burn France to ashes rather (nous brûlerons la France)."

1615. Committees, of Sureté, of Salut, have raised themselves "à la hauteur, to the height of circumstances." Let all mortals raise themselves à la hauteur. Let the 44,000 Sections and their Revolutionary Committees stir every fiber of the Republic; and every Frenchman feel that he is to do or die. They are the life circulation of Jacobinism, these Sections and Committees: Danton, through the organ of Barrère and Salut Public, gets decreed, That there be in Paris, by law, two meetings of Section weekly; also that the Poorer Citizen be paid for attending, and have his day's wages of Forty Sous.‡ This is the celebrated "Law of the Forty Sous;" fiercely stimulant to Sansculottism, to the life-circulation of Jacobinism.

* "Deux Amis," xi. 80–143.
+ Louvet, pp. 180–199.
‡ Moniteur, Séance du 5 Septembre, 1793.

1616. On the 23d of August, Committee of Public Salvation, as usual through Barrère, had promulgated, in words not unworthy of remembering, their Report, which is soon made into a Law, of Levy in Mass. "All France, and whatsoever it contains of men or resources, is put under requisition," says Barrère; really in Tyrtæan words, the best we know of his. "The Republic is one vast besieged city." Two hundred and fifty Forges shall, in these days, be set up in the Luxembourg Garden, and round the outer wall of the Tuileries ; to make gun-barrels ; in sight of Earth and Heaven! From all hamlets, toward their Departmental Town ; from all Departmental Towns, toward the appointed Camp and seat of war, the Sons of Freedom shall march ; their banner is to hear · "Le Peuple Français debout contre les Tyrans (The French People risen against Tyrants). The young men shall go to the battle ; it is their task to conquer: the married men shall forge arms, transport baggage and artillery ; provide subsistence : the women shall work at soldiers' clothes, make tents, serve in the hospitals ; the children shall scrape old linen into surgeon's lint ; the aged men shall have themselves carried into public places ; and there, by their words, excite the courage of the young; preach hatred to Kings and unity to the Republic."* Tyrtæan words ; which tingle through all French hearts.

1617. In this humor, then, since no other serves, will France rush against its enemies. Headlong, reckoning no cost or consequence ; heeding no law or rule but that supreme law, Salvation of the People! The weapons are, all the iron that is in France; the strength is, that of all the men, women and children that are in France. There, in their 250 shed smithies, in Garden of Luxembourg or Tuileries, let them forge gun-barrels, in sight of Heaven and Earth.

1618. Nor with heroic daring against the Foreign foe, can black vengeance against the Domestic be wanting. Life-circulation of the Revolutionary Committees being quickened by that Law of the Forty Sous, Deputy Merlin,—not the Thionviller, whom we saw ride out of Mentz, but Merlin of Douai, named subsequently Merlin Suspect,—comes, about a week after, with his world-famous Law of the Suspect : ordering all Sections, by their Committees, instantly to arrest all Persons Suspect; and explaining withal who the Arrestable and Suspect especially are. "Are suspect," says he, "all who by their actions, by their connections, speakings, writings have "—in short become Suspect.† Nay Chaumette, illuminating the matter still farther, in his Municipal Placards and Proclamations, will bring it about that you may almost recognize a Suspect on the streets, and clutch him there,—off to Committee and Prison. Watch well your words, watch well your looks : if Suspect of nothing else, you may grow, as came to be a saying, "Suspect of being Suspect!" For are we not in a state of Revolution?

1619. No frightfuler Law ever ruled in a Nation of men. All Prisons and Houses of Arrest in French land are getting crowded to the ridge-tile : Forty-four thousand Committees, like as many companies of reapers or gleaners, gleaning France, are gathering their harvest, and storing it in these Houses. Harvest of Aristocrat tares! Nay, lest the 44,000, each on its own harvest-field, prove insufficient, we are to have an ambulant "Revolutionary Army!" 6,000 strong, under right captains, this shall perambulate the country at large, and strike in wherever it finds such harvest-work slack. So have Municipality and Mother Society petitioned; so has Convention decreed.‡ Let Aristocrats, Federalists, Monsieurs van-

* "Débats," Séance du 23 Aout, 1793.
† Moniteur, Séance du 17 Septembre, 1793.
‡ Moniteur, Séance du 5, 9, 11 Septembre.

ish, and all men tremble: "the Soil of Liberty shall be purged,"—with a vengeance.

1620. Neither hitherto has the Revolutionary Tribunal been keeping holiday. Blanchelande, for losing Saint-Domingo; "Conspirators of Orléans" for "assassinating," for assaulting the sacred Deputy Léonard-Bourbon: these with many Nameless, to whom life was sweet, have died. Daily the great Guillotine has its due. Like a black Specter, daily at eventide glides the Death-tumbril through the variegated throng of things. The variegated street shudders at it, for the moment; next moment forgets it: The Aristocrats! They were guilty against the Republic; their death, were it only that their goods are confiscated, will be useful to the Republic: Vive la République!

1621. In the last day of August fell a notabler head—General Custine's. Custine was accused of harshness, of unskillfulness, perfidiousness; accused of many things: found guilty, we may say, of one thing, unsuccessfulness. Hearing his unexpected Sentence, "Custine fell down before the Crucifix," silent for the space of two hours: he fared, with moist eyes and a look of prayer, toward the Place de la Révolution; glanced upward at the clear suspended axe; then mounted swiftly aloft,* swiftly was struck away from the lists of the Living. He had fought in America; he was a proud, brave man; and his fortune led him *hither*.

1622. On the 2d of this same month, at three in the morning, a vehicle rolled off, with closed blinds, from the Temple to the Conciergerie. Within it were two Municipals; and Marie-Antoinette, once Queen of France! There in that Conciergerie, in ignominious dreary cell, she, secluded from children, kindred, friend and hope, sits long weeks, expecting when the end will be.†

1623. The Guillotine we find, get always a quicker motion, as other things are quickening. The Guillotine, by its speed of going, will give index of the general velocity of the Republic. The clanking of its huge axe, rising and falling there, in horrid systole-diastole, is portion of the whole enormous life movement and pulsation of the Sansculottic System!—"Orléans Conspirators" and Assaulters had to die, in spite of much weeping and entreating: so sacred is the person of a Deputy. Yet the sacred can become desecrated: your very Deputy is not greater than the Guillotine. Poor Deputy Journalist Gorsas: we saw him hide at Rennes, when the Calvados War burnt priming. He stole, afterward, in August, to Paris; lurked several weeks about the Palais ci-devant Royal; was seen there, one day; was clutched, identified, and without ceremony, being already "out of the law," was sent to the Place de la Révolution. He died, recommending his wife and children to the pity of the Republic. It is the 9th day of October, 1793. Gorsas is the first Deputy that dies on the scaffold; he will not be the last.

1624. Ex-Mayor Bailly is in Prison; Ex-Procureur Manuel. Brissot and our poor Arrested Girondins have become Incarcerated Indicted Girondins; universal Jacobinism clamoring for their punishment. Duperret's Seals are *broken!* Those Seventy-three Secret Protesters, suddenly one day, are reported upon, are decreed accused; the Convention-doors being "previously shut," that none implicated might escape. They were marched, in a very rough manner, to Prison that evening. Happy those of them who chanced to be absent! Condorcet has vanished into darkness; perhaps, like Rabaut, sits between two walls, in the house of a friend.

* "Deux Amis," xi. 148-188.
† See "Mémoires particuliers de la Captivité à la Tour du Temple" (by the Duchesse d'Angoulême, Paris, 21 Janvier. 1817).

CHAPTER VII.
MARIE-ANTOINETTE.

1625. On Monday the 14th of October, 1793, a Cause is pending in the Palais de Justice, in the new Revolutionary Court, such as those old stone-walls never witnessed: the trial of Marie-Antoinette. The once brightest of Queens, now tarnished, defaced, forsaken, stands here at Fouquier-Tinville's Judgment-bar; answering for her life. The Indictment was delivered her last night.* To such changes of human fortune what words are adequate? Silence alone is adequate.

1626. There are few Printed things one meets with of such tragic, almost ghastly, significance as those bald Pages of the Bulletin du Tribunal Révolutionnaire, which bear title, *Trial of the Widow Capet.* Dim, dim, as if in disastrous eclipse; like the pale kingdoms of Dis! Plutonic Judges, Plutonic Tinville; encircled, nine times, with Styx and Lethe, with Fire-Phlegethon and Cocytus named of Lamentation! The very witnesses summoned are like Ghosts; exculpatory, inculpatory, they themselves are all hovering over death and doom; they are known, in our imagination, as the prey of the Guillotine. Tall ci-devant Count d'Estaing, anxious to show himself Patriot, cannot escape; nor Bailly, who when asked if he knows the Accused, answers with a reverent inclination toward her, "Ah, yes, I know Madame." Ex-Patriots are here, sharply dealt with, as Procureur Manuel; Ex-Ministers, shorn of their splendor. We have cold Aristocratic impassivity, faithful to itself even in Tartarus; rabid stupidity, of Patriot Corporals, Patriot Washer-women, who have much to say of Plots, Treasons, August 10th, old Insurrection of Women. For all now has become a crime in her who has *lost*.

1627. Marie-Antoinette, in this her utter abandonment, and hour of extreme need, is not wanting to herself, the imperial woman. Her look, they say, as that hideous Indictment was reading, continued calm; "she was sometimes observed moving her fingers, as one plays on the piano." You discern, not without interest, across that dim Revolutionary Bulletin itself, how she bears herself queenlike. Her answers are prompt, clear, often of Laconic brevity; resolution, which has grown contemptuous without ceasing to be dignified, veils itself in calm words. "You persist, then, in denial?"—"My plan is not denial: it is the truth I have said, and I persist in that." Scandalous Hébert has borne his testimony as to many things: as to one thing, concerning Marie-Antoinette and her little Son.—wherewith Human Speech had better not farther be soiled. She has answered Hébert; a Juryman begs to observe that she has not answered as to *this.* "I have not answered," she exclaims with noble emotion, "because Nature refuses to answer to such a charge brought against a Mother. I appeal to all the Mothers that are here." Robespierre, when he heard of it, broke out into something almost like swearing at the brutish blockheadism of this Hébert:† on whose foul head his foul lie has recoiled. At four o'clock on Wednesday morning, after two days and two nights of interrogating, jury charging, and other darkening of counsel, the result comes out: sentence of Death. "Have you anything to-say?" The Accused shook her head, without speech. Night's candles are burning out; and with her too Time is finishing, and it will be Eternity and Day. This Hall of Tinville's is dark, ill-lighted except where she stands. Silently she withdraws from it, to die.

* "Procès de la Reine" (" Deux Amis," xi. 251-381).
† Villate, "Causes secrètes de la Révolution de Thermidor" (Paris, 1825, p. 179.)

1628. Two Processions, or Royal progresses, three-and-twenty years apart, have often struck us with a strange feeling of contrast. The first is of a beautiful Archduchess and Dauphiness, quitting her Mother's City, at the age of fifteen; toward hopes such as no other Daughter of Eve then had: "On the morrow," says Weber an eye-witness, "the Dauphiness left Vienna. The whole city crowded out; at first with a sorrow which was silent. She appeared: you saw her sunk back into her carriage: her face bathed in tears hiding her eyes now with her handkerchief, now with her hands; several times putting out her head to see yet again this Palace of her Fathers, whither she was to return no more. She motioned her regret, her gratitude to the good Nation,which was crowding here to bid her farewell. Then arose not only tears; but piercing cries, on all sides. Men and Women alike abandoned themselves to such expression of their sorrow. It was an audible sound of wail, in the streets and avenues of Vienna. The last Courier that followed her disappeared, and the crowd melted away."*

1629. The young imperial Maiden of Fifteen has now become a worn discrowned Widow of Thirty-eight; gray before her time: this is the last Procession: "Few minutes after the trial ended, the drums were beating to arms in all Sections; at sunrise the armed force was on foot, cannons getting placed at the extremities of the Bridges, in the Squares, Crossways, all along from the Palais de Justice to the Place de la Révolution. By ten o'clock, numerous patrols were circulating in the Streets; 30,000 foot and horse drawn up under arms. At eleven, Marie-Antoinette was brought out. She had on an undress of piqué blanc: she was led to the place of execution, in the same manner as an ordinary criminal; bound, on a Cart; accompanied by a Constitutional Priest in Lay dress: escorted by numerous detachments of infantry and cavalry. These, and the double row of troops, all along her road, she appeared to regard with indifference. On her countenance there was visible neither abashment nor pride. To the cries of Vive la République and *Down with Tyranny*, which attended her all the way, she seemed to pay no heed. She spoke little to her Confessor. The tricolor Streamers on the house-tops occupied her attention, in the Streets du Roule and Saint-Honoré; she also noticed the Inscriptions on the house-fronts. On reaching the Place de la Révolution, her looks turned toward the Jardin National, whilom Tuileries; her face at that moment gave signs of lively emotion. She mounted the Scaffold with courage enough; at a quarter past Twelve, her head fell; the Executioner showed it to the people, amid universal long continued cries of Vive la République."†

CHAPTER VIII.

THE TWENTY-TWO.

1630. Whom next, O Tinville! The next are of a different color: our poor Arrested Girondin Deputies. What of them could still be laid hold of; our Vergniaud, Brissot, Fauchet, Valazé, Gensonné; the once flower of French Patriotism, Twenty-two by the tale: hither, at Tinville's Bar onward from the "safeguard of the French People," from confinement in the Luxembourg, imprisonment in the Conciergerie have they now, by the course of things, arrived. Fouquier-Tinville must give what account of them he can.

1631. Undoubtedly this trial of the Girondins is the greatest that Fouquier has yet had to do. Twen-

ty-two, all chief Republicans, ranged in a line there; the most eloquent in France; Lawyers too: not without friends in the auditory. How will Tinville prove these men guilty of Royalism, Federalism, Conspiracy against the Republic? Vergniaud's eloquence awakes once more; "draws tears," they say. And Journalists report, and the Trial lengthens itself out day after day, "threatens to become eternal," murmur many. Jacobinism and Municipality rise to the aid of Fouquier. On the 28th of the month, Hébert and others come in deputation to inform a Patriot Convention that the Revolutionary Tribunal is quite "shackled by Forms of Law;" that a Patriot Jury ought to have "the power of cutting short, of terminer les débats, when they feel themselves convinced." Which pregnant suggestion, of cutting short, passes itself, with all dispatch, into a Decree.

1632. Accordingly, at ten o'clock on the night of the 30th of October, the twenty-two, summoned back once more, receive this information, That the Jury feeling themselves convinced have cut short, have brought in their verdict; that the Accused are found guilty, and the Sentence on one and all of them is, Death with confiscation of goods.

1633. Loud natural clamor rises among the poor Girondins; tumult; which can only be repressed by the gendarmes. Valazé stabs himself, falls down dead on the spot. The rest, amid loud clamor and confusion, are driven back to their Conciergerie; Lesource exclaiming "I die on the day when the People have lost their reason, ye will d e when they recover it."* No help! Yielding to violence, the Doomed uplift the Hymn of the Marseillese; return singing to their dungeon.

1634. Riouffe, who was their Prison mate in these last days, has lovingly recorded what death they made. To our notions, it is not an edifying death. Gay satirical Pot-pourri by Ducos; rhymed Scenes of Tragedy, wherein Barrère and Robespierre discourse with Satan: death's eve spent in "singing" and "sallies of gayety," with "discourses on the happiness of peoples" these things, and the like of these, we have to accept for what they are worth. It is the manner in which the Girondins make *their* Last Supper. Valazé, with bloody breast, sleeps cold in death; hears not the singing. Vergniaud has his dose of poison; but it is not enough for his friends, it is enough only for himself; wherefore he flings it from him; presides at this Last Supper of the Girondins, with wild coruscations of eloquence, with song and mirth. Poor human Will struggles to assert itself; if not in way then in that.†

1635. But on the morrow morning all Paris is out; such a crowd as no man had seen. The Death-carts, Valazé's cold corpse stretched among the yet living Twenty-one, roll along. Bare-headed, hands bound, in their shirt sleeves, coat flung loosely round the neck: so fare the eloquent of France; benumbered, beshouted. To the shouts of Vive la République, some of them keep answering with countershouts of Vive la République. Others, as Brissot, sit sunk in silence. At the foot of the scaffold they again strike up, with appropriate variations, the Hymn of the Marseillese. Such an act of music; conceive it well! The yet Living chant there; the chorus so rapidly wearing weak! Samson's axe is rapid; one head per minute, or little less. The chorus is wearing weak; the chorus is worn *out*;—farewell forevermore, ye Girondins. Te-Deum Fauchet has become silent; Valazé's dead head is lopped: the sickle of the Guillotine has reaped the Girondins all away.

"The eloquent, the young, the beautiful, the brave!" exclaims Riouffe. O Death, what feast is toward in thy ghastly Halls!

1636. Nor, alas, in the far Bourdeaux region will Girondism fare better. In caves of Saint-Emilion, in loft and cellar; the weariest months roll on; apparel worn, purse empty; wintry November come; under Tallien and his Guillotine, all hope now gone. Danger drawing ever nigher, difficulty pressing ever straiter, they determine to separate. Not unpathetic the farewell; tall Barbaroux, cheeriest of brave men, stoops to clasp his Louvet: "In what place soever thou findest my Mother," cries he, "try to be instead of a son to her; no resource of mine but I will share with thy Wife, should chance ever lead me where she is "*

1637. Louvet went with Gaudet, with Salles and Valadi; Barbaroux with Buzot and Pétion. Valadi soon went southward, on a way of his own. The two friends and Louvet had a miserable day and night; the 14th of the November month, 1793. Sunk in wet, weariness and hunger, they knock, on the morrow, for help, at a friend's country-house. The faint-hearted friend refuses to admit them. They stood therefore under trees, in the pouring rain. Flying desperate, Louvet thereupon will to Paris. He sets forth, there and then, splashing the mud on each side of him, with a fresh strength gathered from fury or frenzy. He passes villages, finding "the sentry asleep in his box in the thick rain;" he is gone, before the man can call after him. He hilks Revolutionary Committees, rides in carriers' carts, covered carts and open; lies hidden in one, under knapsacks and cloaks of soldiers' wives on the Street of Orléans, while men search for him; has hair-breadth escapes that would fill three romances; finally he gets to Paris, to his fair Helpmate; gets to Switzerland, and waits better days.

1639. Poor Guadet and Salles were both taken, ere long; they died by the Guillotine in Bourdeaux; drums beating to drown their voice. Valadi also is caught, and guillotined. Barbaroux and his two comrades weathered it longer, into the summer of 1794; but not long enough. One July morning, changing their hiding-place, as they have often to do, "about a league from Saint-Emilion, they observe a great crowd of country-people;" doubtless, Jacobins come to take them? Barbaroux draws a pistol, shoots himself dead. Alas, and it was not Jacobins: it was harmless villagers going to a village wake. Two days afterward, Buzot and Pétion were found in a Corn-field, their bodies half-eaten by dogs.†

1640. Such was the end of Girondism. They arose to regenerate France, these men, and have accomplished *this!* Alas, whatever quarrel we had with them, has not their cruel fate abolished it? Pity only survives. So many excellent souls of heroes sent down to Hades; they themselves given as a prey to dogs and all manner of birds! But, here too, the will of the Supreme Power was accomplished. As Vergniaud said: "the Revolution, like Saturn, is devouring its own children."

BOOK FIFTH.

TERROR THE ORDER OF THE DAY.

CHAPTER I.

RUSHING DOWN.

1641. We are now, therefore, got to that black precipitous Abyss; whither all things have long been tending; where, having now arrived on the giddy

verge, they hurl down, in confused ruin; headlong, pell-mell, down, down;—till Sansculottism have consummated itself; and in this wondrous French Revolution, as in a Doomsday, a World have been rapidly, if not born again, yet destroyed and engulfed. Terror has long been terrible: but to the actors themselves it has now become manifest that their appointed course is one of Terror; and they say: Be it so. "Que la Terreur soit à l'ordre du jour."

1642. So many centuries, say only from Hugh Capet downward, had been adding together, century transmitting it with increase to century, the sum of Wickness, of Falsehood, Oppression of man by man. Kings were sinners, and Priests were, and People. Open scoundrels rode triumphant, bediademed, becoroneted, bemitered; or the still fataler species of Secret-Scoundrels, in their fair-sounding formulas, sueciosities, respectabilities, hollow within; the race of Quacks was grown many as the sands of the sea. Till at length such a sum of Quackery had accumulated itself as, in brief, the Earth and the Heavens were weary of. Slow seemed the Day of Settlement; coming on all imperceptible, across the bluster and fanfaronade of Courtierisms, Conquering-Heroisms, Most Christian Grand Monarqueisms, Well-beloved Pompadourisms: yet behold it was always coming; behold it has come, suddenly, unlooked for by any man! The harvest of long centuries was ripening and whitening so rapidly of late; and now it has grown *white*, and is reaped rapidly, as it were, in one day. Reaped, in this Reign of Terror; and carried home, to Hades and the Pit!—Unhappy Sons of Adam: it is ever so; and never do they know it, nor will they know it. With cheerfully smoothed countenances, day after day, and generation after generation, they, calling cheerfully to one another, Well-speed-ye, are at work, *sowing the wind.* And yet, as God lives, they *shall reap the whirlwind:* no other thing, we say, is possible,—since God is a Truth, and His World is a Truth.

1643. History, however, in dealing with this Reign of Terror, has had her own difficulties. While the Phenomenon continued in its primary state, as mere "Horrors of the French Revolution," there was abundance to be said and shrieked. With and also without profit. Heaven knows, there were terrors and horrors enough: yet that was not all the Phenomenon; nay, more properly, that was not the Phenomenon at all, but rather was the *shadow* of it, the negative part of it. And now, in a new stage of the business, when History, ceasing to shriek, would try rather to include under her old Forms of speech or speculation this new amazing Thing; that so some accredited scientific Law of Nature might suffice for the unexpected Product of Nature, and History might get to speak of it articulately, and draw inferences and profit from it: in this new stage, History we must say, babbles and flounders perhaps in a still painfuler manner. Take, for example, the latest Form of speech we have seen propounded on the subject as adequate to it, almost in these months, by our worthy M. Roux, in his "Histoire Parlementaire." The latest and the strangest: that the French Revolution was a dead-lift effort, after 1800 years of preparation, to realize—the Christian Religion!* *Unity, Indivisibility, Brotherhood or Death,* did indeed stand printed on all Houses of the Living; also on Cemeteries, or Houses of the Dead, stood printed, by order of Procureur Chaumette, *Here is Eternal Sleep:*† but a Christian Religion realized by the Guillotine and Death Eternal "is suspect to me," as Robespierre was wont to say, "m'est suspecte."

1644. Alas, no, M. Roux! A Gospel of Brother-

---

* Louvet, p. 213.
† "Recherches Historiques sur les Girondins" (in "Mémoires de Buzot." p. 107.

* "Histoire Parlementaire," (Introd.), i. 1 et seqq.
† "Deux Amis," xii. 78.

hood, not according to any of the Four old Evangelists, and calling on men to repent, and amend *each his own* wicked existence, that they might be saved; but a Gospel rather, as we often hint, according to a new Fifth Evangelist Jean-Jacques, calling on men to amend *each the whole world's* wicked existence, and be saved by making the Constitution. A thing different and distant toto cœlo, as they say: the whole breadth of the sky, and farther if possible!—It is thus, however, that History, and indeed all human Speech and Reason does yet, what Father Adam began life by doing: strive to *name* the new Things it sees of Nature's producing,—often helplessly enough.

1645. But what if History were to admit, for once, that all the Names and Theorems yet known to her fall short? That this grand Product of Nature was even grand, and new, in that it came not to range itself under old recorded Laws of Nature at all, but to disclose new ones? In that case, History, renouncing the pretension to *name* it at present, will *look* honestly at it, and name what she can of it! Any approximation to the right Name has value: were the right Name itself once here, the Thing is known henceforth; the Thing is then ours, and can be dealt with.

1646. Now surely not realization, of Christianity or of aught earthly, do we discern in this Reign of Terror in this French Revolution of which it is the consummating. Destruction rather we discern,—of all that was destructible. It is as if 25,000,000, risen at length into the Pythian mood, had stood up simultaneously to say, with a sound which goes through far lands and times, that this Untruth of an Existence had become insupportable. O ye Hypocrisies and Speciosities, Royal mantles, Cardinal plush-cloaks, ye Credos, Formulas, Respectabilities, fair-painted Sepulchres full of dead men's bones—behold, ye appear to us to be altogether a Lie. Yet our Life is not a Lie; yet our Hunger and Misery is not a Lie! Behold we lift 'up, one and all, our 25,000,000 right-hands; and take the Heavens, and the Earth, and also the Pit of Tophet to witness, that either ye shall be abolished, or else we shall be abolished!

1647. No inconsiderable Oath, truly: forming, as has often been said, the most remarkable transaction in these last thousand years. Wherefrom likewise there follow, and will follow, results. The fulfillment of this Oath; that is to say, the black desperate battle of Men against their whole Condition and Environment,—a battle, alas, withal, against the Sin and Darkness that was in themselves as in others: this is the Reign of Terror. Transcendental despair was the purport of it, though not consciously so. False hopes, of fraternity, Political Millennium, and .what not, we have always seen: but the unseen heart of the whole, transcendental despair, was not false; neither has it been of no effect. Despair pushed far enough, completes the circle, so to speak; and becomes a kind of genuine productive hope again.

1648. Doctrine of Fraternity, out of old Catholicism, does, it is true, very strangely in the vehicle of a Jean-Jacques Evangel, suddenly plump down out of its cloud-firmament; and from a theorem determined to make itself a practice. But just so do all creeds, intentions, customs, knowledges, thoughtsand things, which the French have, suddenly plump down; Catholicism, Classicism, Sentimentalism, Cannibalism: all *isms* that make up Man in France are rushing and roaring in that gulf; and the theorem has become a practice, and whatsoever cannot swim sinks. Not Evangelist Jean-Jacques alone; there is not a Village Schoolmaster but has contributed his quota: do we not *thou* one another, according to the Free Peoples of Antiquity? The French Patriot, in red Phrygian night-cap of Liberty, christens his poor little red infant Cato,—Censor, or else of Utica. Gracchus has become Babœuf, and edits Newspapers; Mutius Scævola, Cordwainer of that ilk, presides in the Section Mutius-Scævola: and in brief, there is a world wholly jumbling itself, to try what will swim.

1649. Wherefore we will, at all events, call this Reign of Terror a very strange one. Dominant Sansculottism makes, as it were, free arena; one of the strangest temporary states Humanity was ever seen in. A nation of men, full of wants and void of habits! The old habits are gone to wreck because they were old: men, driven forward by Necessity and fierce Pythian Madness, have, on the spur of the instant, to devise for the want the *way* of satisfying it. The Wonted tumbles down; by imitation, by invention, the Unwonted hastily builds itself up. What the French National head has in it comes out: if not a great result, surely one of strangest.

1650. Neither shall the Reader fancy that it was all black, this Reign of Terror: far from it. How many hammer-men and square-men, bakers and brewers, washers and wringers, over this France, must ply their old daily work, let the Government be one of Terror or one of Joy! In this Paris there are Twenty-three theaters nightly; some count as many as Sixty Places of Dancing.* The Playwright manufactures,—pieces of a strictly Republican character. Ever fresh Novel-garbage, as of old, fodders the Circulating Libraries.† The "Cesspool of Agio," now in a time of Paper Money, works with a vivacity unexampled, unimagined; exhales from itself "sudden fortunes," like Aladdin-Palaces: really a kind of miraculous Fata-Morganas, since you *can* live in them, for a time. Terror is as a sable ground, on which the most variegated of scenes paints itself. In startling transitions, in colors all intensated, the sublime, the ludicrous, the horrible succeed one another; or rather, in crowding tumult, accompany one another.

1651. Here, accordingly, if anywhere, the "hundred tongues," which the old Poets often clamor for, were of supreme service! In defect of any such organ on our part, let the Reader stir up his own imaginative organ: let us snatch for him this or the other significant glimpse of things, in the fittest sequence we can.

CHAPTER II.

DEATH.

1652. In the early days of November there is one transient glimpse of things that is to be noted: the last transit to his long home of Philippe d'Orléans Égalité. Philippe was "decreed accused," along with the Girondins, much to his and their surprise; but not tried along with them. They are doomed and dead, some three days, when Philippe, after his long 'half-year of durance at Marseilles, arrives in Paris. It is, as we calculate, the third of November, 1793.

1653. On which same day, two notable Female Prisoners are also put inward there: Dame Dubarry and Josephine Beauharnais. Dame whilom Countess Dubarry, Unfortunate-female, had returned from London; they snatched her, not only as Ex-harlot of a whilom Majesty, and therefore suspect; but as having "furnished the Emigrants with money." Contemporaneously with whom there comes the wife Beauharnais, soon to be the widow: she that is Josephine Tascher Beauharnais; thatshall be Josephine Empress Bonaparte,—for a black Divineress of the Tropics prophesied long since that she should be

* Mercier. ii. 124.
† Moniteur of these months. dassim.

a Queen and more. Likewise, in the same hours, poor Adam Lux, nigh turned in the head, who, according to Forster, "has taken no food these three weeks," marches to the Guillotine for his Pamphlet on Charlotte Corday: he "sprang to the scaffold;" said "he died for her with great joy." Amid such fellow-travelers does Philippe arrive. For, be the month named Brumaire, year 2 of Liberty, or November, year 1793 of Slavery, the Guillotine goes always (Guillotine va toujours).

1634. Enough, Philippe's indictment is soon drawn, his jury soon convinced. He finds himself made guilty of Royalism, Conspiracy and much else; nay, it is a guilt in him that he voted Louis's Death, though he answers, "I voted in my soul and conscience." The doom he finds is death forthwith; this present 7th dim day of November is the last day that Philippe is to see. Philippe, says Montgaillard, thereupon called for breakfast: sufficiency of "oysters, two cutlets, best part of an excellent bottle of claret;" and consumed the same with apparent relish. A Revolutionary Judge, or some official Convention Emissary, then arrived, to signify that he might still do the State some service by revealing the truth about a plot or two. Philippe answered that, on him, in the pass things had come to, the State had, he thought, small claim; that nevertheless, in the interest of Liberty, he, having still some leisure on his hands, was willing, were a reasonable question asked him, to give a reasonable answer. And so, says Montgaillard, he leant his elbow on the mantel-piece, and conversed in an undertone, with great seeming composure; till the leisure was done, or the Emissary went his way.

1655. At the door of the Conciergerie, Philippe's attitude was erect and easy, almost commanding. It is five years, all but a few days, since Philippe, within these same stone walls, stood up with an air of graciosity, and asked King Louis, "Whether it was a Royal Session, then, or a Bed of Justice?" O Heaven!—Three poor blackguards were to ride and die with him : some say, they objected to such company, and had to be flung in, neck and heels;* but it seems not true. Objecting or not objecting, the gallows-vehicle gets under way. Philippe's dress is remarked for its elegance; green frock, waistcoat of white piqué, yellow buckskins, boots clear as Warren: his air, as before, entirely composed, impassive, not to say easy and Brummellean-polite. Through street after street; slowly, amid execrations;—past the Palais Égalité, whilom Palais Royal ! The cruel Populace stopped him there, some minutes. Dame de Buffon, it is said, looked out on him in Jezebel head-tire; along the ashlar 'Wall there ran these words in huge tricolor print, REPUBLIC ONE AND INDIVISIBLE: LIBERTY, EQUALITY, FRATERNITY OR DEATH : *National Property.* Philippe's eyes flashed hell-fire, one instant; but the next instant it was gone, and he sat impassive. Brummellean-polite. On the scaffold, Samson was for drawing off his boots: "Tush," said Philippe, "they will come better off *after*; let us have done (dépêchons-nous) !"

1656. So Philippe was not without virtue, then ? God forbid that there should be any living man without it ! He had the virtue to keep living for five-and-forty years;—other virtues perhaps more than we know of. But probably no mortal ever had such things recorded of him; such facts, and also such lies. For he was a *Jacobin Prince of the blood ;* consider what a combination ! Also, unlike any Nero, any Borgia, he lived in the Age of Pamphlets. Enough for us : Chaos *has* re-absorbed him ; may it late or never hear his like again!—Brave young Orléans Égalité, deprived of all, only not deprived of

* Forster, ii. 629; Montgaillard, iv. 141-157.

himself, is gone to Coire in the Grisons, under the name of Corby, to teach Mathematics. The Égalité Family is at the darkest depths of the Nadir.

1657. A far nobler Victim follows; one who will claim remembrance from several centuries : Jeanne-Marie Philipon, the Wife of Roland. Queenly, sublime in her uncomplaining sorrow, seemed she to Riouffe in her Prison. "Something more than is usually found in the looks of women painted itself," says Riouffe,* " in those large black eyes of hers, full of expression and sweetness. She spoke to me often, at the Grate; we were all attentive round her in a sort of admiration and astonishment; she expressed herself with a purity, with a harmony and prosody that made her language like music, of which the ear could never have enough. Her conversation was serious, not cold ; coming from the mouth of a beautiful woman, it was frank and courageous as that of a great man." " And yet her maid said : ' Before you, she collects her strength ; but in her own room, she will sit three hours sometimes leaning on the window and weeping.' " She has been in Prison, liberated once, but recaptured the same hour, ever since the 1st of June: in agitation and uncertainty; which has gradually settled down into the last stern certainty, that of death. In the Abbaye Prison, she occupied Charlotte Corday's apartment. Here in the Conciergerie, she speaks with Riouffe, with Ex-Minister Clavière; calls the beheaded Twenty-two "Nos amis" (our Friends),—whom we are soon to follow. During these five months, those *Memoirs* of hers were written, which all the world still reads.

1658. But now, on the 8th of November, "clad in white," says Riouffe, "with her long black hair hanging down to her girdle," she is gone to the Judgment-bar. She returned with a quick step; lifted her finger, to signify to us that she was doomed· her eyes seemed to have been wet. Fouquier-Tinville's questions had been "brutal;" offended female honor flung them back on him, with scorn, not without tears. And now, short preparations soon done, she too shall go her last road. There went with her a certain Lamarche. "Director of Assignat-printing;" whose dejection she endeavored to cheer. Arrived at the foot of the scaffold, she asked for pen and paper, " to write the strange thoughts that were rising in her ;"† a remarkable request; which was refused. Looking at the Statue of Liberty which stands there, she says bitterly : " O Liberty, what things are done in thy name !" For Lamarche's sake, she will die first ; show him how easy it is to die: " Contrary to the order," said Samson.—" Pshaw, you cannot refuse the last request of a Lady ;" and Samson yielded.

1659. Noble white Vision, with its high queenly face, its soft proud eyes, long black hair flowing down to the girdle; and as brave a heart as ever beat in woman's bosom ! Like a white Grecian Statue, serenely complete, she shines in that black wreck of things ;—long memorable. Honor to great Nature who, in Paris City, in the Era of Noble Sentiment and Pompadourism, can make a Jeanne Philipon and nourish her to clear perennial Womanhood, though but on Logics, Encyclopédies, and the Gospel according to Jean-Jacques ! Biography will long remember that trait of asking for a pen " to write the strange thoughts that were rising in her." It is as a little light-beam, shedding softness, and a kind of sacredness, over all that preceded: so in her too there was an Unnamable; she too was a Daughter of the Infinite; there were mysteries which Philosophism had not dreamt of !—She left long written counsels

* "Mémoires" ("Sur les Prisons." i.). pp. 55-57.
† "Mémoires de Madame Roland" (Introd.) i. 68.

to her little Girl; she said her Husband would not survive her.

1660. Still crueler was the fate of poor Bailly, First National President, First Mayor of Paris: doomed now for Royalism, Fayettism; for that Red-Flag Business of the Champ-de-Mars;—one may say in general, for leaving his Astronomy to meddle with Revolution. It is the 10th of November, 1793, a cold bitter drizzling rain, as poor Bailly is led through the streets; howling Populace covering him with curses, with mud; waving over his face a burning or smoking mockery of a Red Flag. Silent, unpitied, sits the innocent old man. Slow faring through the sleety drizzle, they have got to the Champ-de-Mars; Not there! vociferates the cursing Populace; such Blood ought not to stain an Altar of the Fatherland; not there; but on that dung-heap by the River-side! So vociferates the cursing Populace; Officiality gives ear to them. The Guillotine is taken down, though with hands numbed by the sleety drizzle; is carried to the River-side; is there set up again, with slow numbness; pulse after pulse still counting itself out in the old man's weary heart. For hours long; amid curses and bitter frost-rain! "Bailly, thou tremblest," said one. "Mon ami, it is for cold," said Bailly, "c'est de froid." Crueler end had no mortal.[*]

1661. Some days afterward, Roland, hearing the news of what happened on the 8th, embraces his kind Friends at Rouen, leaves their kind house which had given him refuge; goes forth, with farewell too sad for tears. On the morrow morning, 16th of the month, "some four leagues from Rouen, Paris-ward, near Bourg-Baudoin, in M. Normand's Avenue," there is seen sitting leant against a tree the figure of a rigorous wrinkled man; stiff now in the rigor of death; a cane-sword run through his heart; and at his feet this writing: "Whoever thou art that findest me lying, respect my remains: they are those of a man who consecrated all his life to being useful; and who has died as he lived, virtuous and honest." "Not fear, but indignation, made me quit my retreat, on learning that my Wife had been murdered. I wished not to remain longer on an Earth polluted with crimes."[†]

1662. Barnave's appearance at the Revolutionar Tribunal was of the bravest; but it could not stead him. They have sent for him from Grenoble; to pay the common smart. Vain is eloquence, forensic or other, against the dumb Clotho-shears of Tinville. He is still but two-and-thirty, this Barnave, and has known such changes. Short while ago, we saw him at the top of Fortune's wheel, his word a law to all Patriots: and now surely he is at the *bottom* of the wheel; in stormful altercation with a Tinville Tribunal, which is dooming him to die!‡ And Pétion, once also of the Extreme Left, and named Pétion Virtue, where is he? Civilly dead; in the Caves of Saint-Émilion: to be devoured of dogs. And Robespierre, who rode along with him on the shoulders of the people, is in Committee of Salut; civilly alive; not to live always. So giddy-swift whirls and spins this immeasurable tormentum of a Revolution; wild-booming; not to be followed by the eye. Barnave, on the Scaffold, stamped with his foot; and looking upward was heard to ejaculate, "This, then, is my reward!"

1663. Deputy Ex-Procureur Manuel is already gone; and Deputy Osselin, famed also in August and September, is about to go: and Rabaut, discovered treacherously between his two walls, and the Brother of Rabaut. National Deputies not a few! And Generals: the memory of General Custine cannot be

defended by his Son; his Son is already guillotined. Custine the Ex-Noble was replaced by Houchard the Plebeian: he too could not prosper in the North; for him too there was no mercy; he has perished in the Place de la Révolution, after attempting suicide in Prison. And Generals Biron, Beauharnais, Brunet whatsoever General prospers not; tough old Lückner, with his eyes grown rheumy; Alsatian Westermann, valiant and diligent in La Vendée: *none of them can*, as the Psalmist sings, *his soul from death deliver.*

1664. How busy are the Revolutionary Committees; Sections with their Forty Halt-pence a day! Arrestment on arrestment falls quick, continual; followed by death. Ex-Minister Clavière has killed himself in Prison. Ex-Minister Lebrun, seized in a hay-loft, under the disguise of a working man, is instantly conducted to death."[*] Nay, withal, is it not what Barrère calls "coining money on the Place de la Révolution"? For always the "property of the guilty, if property he have," is confiscated. To avoid accidents, we even make a Law that suicide shall not defraud us: that a criminal who kills himself does not the less incur forfeiture of goods. Let the guilty tremble, therefore, and the suspect, and the rich, and in a word all manner of Culottic men! Luxembourg Palace, once Monsieur's, has become a huge loathsome Prison; Chantilly Palace too, once Condé's:—And their landlords are at Blankenburg, on the wrong side of the Rhine. In Paris are now some Twelve Prisons; in France some 44,000: thitherward, thick as brown leaves in Autumn, rustle and travel the suspect; shaken down by Revolutionary Committees, they are swept thitherward, as into their store-house,—to be consumed by Samson and Tinville. "The Guillotine goes not ill (La Guillotine ne va pas mal)."

CHAPTER III.

DESTRUCTION.

1665. The suspect may well tremble; but how much more the open rebels;—the Girondin Cities of the South! Revolutionary Army is gone forth, under Ronsin the Playwright; 6,000 strong; "in red night-cap, in tricolor waistcoat, in black-shag trousers, black-shag spencer, with enormous mustachioes, enormous saber,—in carmagnole complete;"† and has portable guillotines. Representative Carrier has got to Nantes, by the edge of blazing La Vendée, which Rossignol has literally set on fire: Carrier will try what captives you make; what accomplices they have, Royalist or Girondin: his guillotine goes always (va toujours); and his wool-capped "Company of Marat." Little children are guillotined, and aged men. Swift as the machine is, it will not serve; the Headsman and all his valets sink, worn down with work; declare that the human muscles can no more.‡ Whereupon you must try fusillading; to which perhaps still frightfuler methods may succeed.

1666. In Brest, to like purpose, rules Jean-Bon Saint-André: with an Army of Red Night-caps. In Bourdeaux rules Tallien, with his Isabeau and henchmen; Guadets, Cussys, Salleses, many fall; the bloody Pike and Night-cap bearing supreme sway; the Guillotine coining money. Bristly fox-haired Tallien, once Able Editor, still young in years, is now become most gloomy, potent; a Pluto on Earth, and has the keys of Tartarus. One remarks, however, that a certain Senhorina Cabarus, or call her rather Senhora and wedded not yet widowed Dame de Fontenai, brown beautiful woman, daughter of Cabarus the Spanish Merchant,—has softened the red bristly

---

* "Vie de Bailly" (in "Mémoires." i.), p. 29.
† "Mémoires de Madame Roland" (Introd.),ii. 88.
‡ Forster, ii. 629.

* Moniteur, 11. 30 Decembre 1793; Louvet, p. 287.
† See Louvet, p. 301.
‡ "Deux Amis," xii. 249-251.

countenance; pleading for herself and friends; and prevailing. The keys of Tartarus, or any kind of power, are something to a woman; gloomy Pluto himself is not insensible to love. Like a new Proserpine, she, by this red gloomy Dis, is gathered; and, they say, softens his stone heart a little.

1667. Maignet, at Orange in the South; Lebon, at Arras in the North, become world's wonders. Jacobin Popular Tribunal, with its National Representative, perhaps where Girondin Popular Tribunal had lately been, rises here and rises there; wheresoever needed. Fouchés, Maignets, Barrasses, Frérons scour the Southern Departments; like reapers, with their guillotine-sickle. Many are the laborers, great is the harvest. By the hundred and the thousand, men's lives are cropt; cast like brands into the burning.

1668. Marseilles is taken, and put under martial law; lo, at Marseilles, what one besmutted red-bearded corn-ear is this which they cut;—one gross Man, we mean, with copper-studded face; plenteous beard, or beard stubble, of a tile color? By Nemesis and the Fatal Sisters, it is Jourdan Coupe tête! Him they have clutched, in these martial-law districts; him too, with their "national razor" their rasoir national, they sternly shave away. Low now is Jourdan the Headsman's own head;—low as Deshuttes's and Varigny's, which he sent on pikes, in the Insurrection of Women! No more shall he, as a copper Portent, be seen gyrating through the Cities of the South; no more sit judging, with pipes and brandy, in the Ice-tower of Avignon. The all-hiding Earth has received him, the bloated Tile-beard; may we never look upon his like again!—Jourdan one names; the other Hundreds are not named. Alas, they, like confused fagots, lie massed together for us; counted by the cart-load: and yet not an individual fagot-twig of them but had a Life and [History; and was cut, not without pangs as when a Kaiser dies!

1669. Least of all cities can Lyons escape. Lyons, which we saw in dread sun-blaze, that Autumn night when the Powder-tower sprang aloft, was clearly verging toward a sad end. Inevitable: what could desperate valor and Préey do; Dubois-Crancé, deaf as Destiny, stern as Doom, capturing their "redoubts of cotton-bags;" hemming them in, ever closer, with his Artillery-lava? Never would that ci-'evant D'Antichamp arrive; never any help from Blankenburg. The Lyons Jacobins were hidden in cellars: the Girondin Municipality waxed pale, in famine, treason and red fire. Préey drew his sword, and some Fifteen Hundred with him; sprang to saddle, to cut their way to Switzerland. They cut fiercely; and were fiercely cut, and cut down; not hundreds: hardly units of them ever saw Switzerland.* Lyons, on the 9th of October, surrenders at discretion; it is become a devoted Town. Abbé Lamourette, now Bishop Lamourette, whilom Legislator, he of the old Baiser-l'Amourette or Delilah-Kiss, is seized here; is sent to Paris to be guillotined: " he made the sign of the cross," they say, when Tinville intimated his death-sentence to him; and died as an eloquent Constitutional Bishop. But woe now to all Bishops, Priests, Aristocrats and Federalists that are in Lyons! The manes of Chalier are to be appeased; the Republic, maddened to the Sibylline pitch, has bared her right arm. Behold! Representative Fouché, it is Fouché of Nantes, a name to become well-known; he with a Patriot company goes duly, in wondrous Procession, to raise the corpse of Chalier. An Ass housed in Priest's cloak, with a miter on his head, and trailing the Mass-Books, some say the very Bible, at its tail, passes through Lyons streets: escorted by

multitudinous Patriotism, by clangor as of the Pit; toward the grave of Martyr Chalier. The body is dug up, and burnt: the ashes are collected in an Urn; to be worshiped of Paris Patriotism. The Holy Books were part of the funeral pile.; their ashes are scattered to the wind. Amid cries of "Vengeance! Vengeance!"—which, writes Fouché, shall be satisfied.*

1670. Lyons in fact is a Town to be abolished: not Lyons henceforth, but "Commune Affranchie (Township Freed):" the very name of it shall perish. It is to be razed, this once great City, if Jacobinism prophesy right; and a Pillar to be erected on the ruins, with this Inscription, *Lyons rebelled against the Republic; Lyons is no more.* Fouché, Couthon, Collot, Convention Representatives succeed one another : there is work for the hangman; work for the hammer-man, *not* in building. The very houses of Aristocrats, we say, are doomed. Paralytic Couthon borne in a chair, taps on the wall, with emblematic mallet, saying , "La Loi te frappe (the Law strikes thee;)" masons, with wedge and crow-bar, begin demolition. Crash of downfall, dim ruin and dust-clouds fly in the winter wind. Had Lyons been of soft stuff, it had all vanished in those weeks, and the Jacobin prophecy had been fulfilled. But Towns are not built of soap-froth; Lyons Town is built of stone. Lyons, though it rebelled against the Republic, *is* to this day.

1671. Neither have the Lyons Girondins all one neck, that you could dispatch it at one swoop. Revolutionary Tribunal here, and Military commission, guillotining, fusillading, do what they can: the kennels of the Place des Terreaux run red; mangled corpses roll down the Rhone. Collot d'Herbois, they say, was once hissed on the Lyons stage: but with what sibilation, of world cat-call or hoarse Tartarean Trumpet, will ye hiss him now, in this his new character of Convention Representative,—not to be repeated! Two hundred and nine men are marched forth over the River, to be shot in mass, by musket and cannon, in the Promenade of the Brotteaux. It is the second of such scenes; the first was of some Seventy. The corpses of the first were flung into the Rhone, but the Rhone stranded some ; so these now, of the second lot, are to be buried on land. Their one long grave is dug ; they stand ranked, by the loose mold ridge ; the younger of them singing the "Marseillaise." Jacobin National Guards give fire; but have again to give fire, and again; and to take the bayonet and the spade, for though the doomed all fall, they do not all die ;—and it becomes a butchery too horrible for speech. So that the very Nationals, as they fire, turn away their faces. Collot snatching the musket from one such National, and leveling it with unmoved countenance, says, "It is thus a Republican ought to fire."

1672. This is the second Fusillade, and happily the last : it is found too hideous, even inconvenient. There were 209 marched out; one escaped at the end of the Bridge: yet behold, when you count the corpses they are 210. Rede us this riddle, O Collot ? After long guessing, it is called to mind that two individuals, here in the Brotteaux ground, did attempt to leave the rank, protesting with agony that they were not condemned men, that they were Police Commissaries: which two we repulsed, and disbelieved, and shot with the rest !† Such is the vengeance of an enraged Republic. Surely this, according to Barrère's phrase, is Justice, "under rough forms (sous des formes acerbes)." But the Republic, as Fouché says, must "march to Liberty over corpses." Or again, as Barrère has it: "None but the dead do

---

* "Deux Amis," xi. 145.

* Moniteur (du 17 Novembre 1793), etc

† "Deux Amis," xii. 251-256.

not come back (Il n'y a que les morts qui ne reviennent pas)." Terror hovers far and wide: "the guillotine goes not ill."

1673. But before quitting those Southern regions, over which History can cast only glances from aloft, she will alight for a moment, and look fixedly at one point: the Siege of Toulon. Much battering and bombarding, heating of balls in furnaces or farmhouses, serving of artillery well and ill, attacking of Ollionles Passes, Forts Malbosquet there has been: as yet to small purpose. We have had General Cartaux here, a whilom Painter elevated in the troubles of Marseilles. General Doppet, a whilom Medical man elevated in the troubles of Piemont, who under Crancé, took Lyons but cannot take Toulon. Finally we have General Dugommier, a pupil of Washington. Convention Représentans also we have had; Barrases, Salicettis, Robespierres the Younger:—also an Artillery Chef de brigade, of extreme diligence, who often takes his nap of sleep among the guns; a short, taciturn, olive-complexioned young man, not unknown to us. by name Bonaparte; one of the best Artillery-officers yet met with. And still Toulon is not taken. It is the fourth month now; December, in slave style; Frostarious or Frimaire, in new-style: and still their cursed Red-Blue Flag flies there. They are provisioned from the Sea; they have seized all heights, felling wood, and fortifying themselves; like the cony, they have built their nest in the rocks.

1674. Meanwhile Frostarious is not yet become Snowous or Nivose, when a Council of War is called. Instructions have just arrived from Government and Salut Public. Carnot, in Salut Public, has sent us a plan of siege; on which plan General Dugommier has this criticism to make, Commissioner Salicetti has that; and criticisms and plans are very various; when that young Artillery-Officer ventures to speak; the same whom we saw snatching sleep among the guns, who has emerged several times in this History, —the name of him Napoleon Bonaparte. It is his humble opinion, for he has been gliding about with spy-glasses, with thoughts, That a certain Fort l'Eguillette can be clutched, as with lion-spring, on the sudden; wherefrom, were it once ours, the very heart of Toulon might be battered ; the English Lines, were, so to speak, turned inside out, and Hood and our Natural Enemies must next day either put to sea, or be burnt to ashes. Commissioners arch their eyebrows, with negatory sniff: who is this young gentleman with more wit than we all ? Brave veteran Dugommier, however, thinks the idea worth a word; questions the young gentleman; becomes convinced; and there is for issue, Try it.

1675. On the taciturn bronze countenance, therefore, things being now all ready, there sits a grimmer gravity than ever, compressing a hotter central-fire than ever. Yonder, thou seest, is Fort l'Eguillette; a desperate lion-spring, yet a possible one; this day to be tried!—Tried it is; and found good. By stratagem and valor, stealing through ravines, plunging fiery through the fire-tempest, Fort l'Eguilette is clutched at, is carried the smoke having, cleared, we see the Tricolor fly on it; the bronze-complexioned young man was right. Next morning, Hood, finding the interior of his lines exposed, his defenses turned inside out, makes for his shipping. Taking such Royalists as wished it on board with him, he weighs anchor; on this 19th of December, 1793. Toulon is once more the Republic's !

1676. Cannonading has ceased at Toulon; and now the guillotining and fusillading may begin. Civil horrors, truly: but at least that infamy of an English domination is purged away. Let there be Civic Feast universally over France so reports Barrère,

or Painter David; and the Convention assist in a body.* Nay, it is said, these infamous English (with an attention rather to their own interest than to ours) set fire to our store-houses, arsenals, warships in Toulon Harbor, before weighing; some score of brave war-ships, the only ones we now had ! However, it did not prosper, though the flames spread far and high; some two ships were burned, not more; the very galley-slaves ran with buckets to quench. These same proud Ships, Ship l'Orient and the rest, have to carry this same young Man to Egypt first: not yet can they be changed to ashes, or to Sea-Nymphs; not yet to sky-rockets, O ship l'Orient; nor become the prey of England,—before their time !

1677. And so over France universally, there is Civic Feast and high-tide, and Toulon sees fusillading, grape-shotting in mass, as Lyons saw; and "death is poured out in great floods (vomie à grands flots) ;" and 12,000 Masons are requisitioned from the neighboring country, to raze Toulon from the face of the Earth. For it is to be razed, so reports Barrère; all but the National Shipping Establishments; and to be called henceforth not Toulon, but Port of the Mountain. There in black death-cloud we must leave it:— hoping only that Toulon too is built of stone; that perhaps even 12,000 Masons cannot pull it down, till the fit pass.

1678. One begins to be sick of "death vomited in great floods." Nevertheless, hearest thou not, O Reader (for the sound reaches through centuries), in the dead December and January nights, over Nantes Town,—confused noises, as of musketry and tumult, just of rage and lamentation; mingling with the everlasting moan of the Loire waters there! Nantes Town is sunk in sleep; but Représentant Carrier is not sleeping, the wool-capped Company of Marat is not sleeping. Why unmoors that flat-bottomed craft, that gabarre; about eleven at night; with Ninety Priests under hatches? They are going to Belle Isle? In the middle of the Loire stream, on signal given, the gabarre is scuttled; she sinks with all her cargo. "Sentence of Deportation," writes Carrier, "was executed vertically." The Ninety Priests, with their gabarre coffin, lie deep ! It is the first of the Noyades, what we may call Drownages, of Currier, which have become famous forever.

1679. Guillotining there was at Nantes, till the Headsman sank worn out; then fusillading "in the Plain of St. Mauve;" little children fusilladed, and women with children at the breast: children and women by the hundred and twenty; and by the 500, so hot is La Vendée; till the very Jacobins grew sick, and all but the Company of Marat cried, Hold ! Wherefore now we have got Noyading; and on the 24th night of Frostarious, year 2, which is 14th of December, 1793, we have a second Noyade; consisting of "138 persons."†

1680. Or why waste a gabarre, sinking it with them ? Fling them out; fling them out, with their hands tied; pour a continual hail of lead over all the space, till the last struggles of them be sunk ! Unsound sleepers of Nantes, and the Sea-villages thereabout, hear the musketry amid the night-winds; wonder what the meaning of it is. And women were in that gabarre; whom the Red Night-caps were stripping naked; who begged, in their agony, that their smocks might not be stripped from them. And young children were thrown in, their mothers vainly pleading: "Wolflings," answered the Company of Marat, "who would grow to be wolves."

1681. By degrees, daylight itself witnesses Noyades: women and men are tied together, feet and

* Moniteur, 1793. Nos. 101 (31 Decembre), 95, 96, 98, etc.

† "Deux Amis," xii. 266-272; Moniteur, du 2 Janvier 1794.

feet, hands and hands; and flung in: this they call Marriage Républicain (Republican Marriage.) Cruel is the panther of the woods, the she-bear bereaved of her whelps; but there is in man a hatred crueler than that. Dumb, out of suffering now, as pale swoln corpses, the victims tumble confusedly seaward along the Loire stream; the tide rolling them back: clouds of ravens darken the River; wolves prowl on the shoal-places: Carrier writes, "Quel torrent révolutionnaire(What a torrent of Revolution)!" For the man is rabid; and the Time is rabid. These are the Noyades of Carrier; twenty-five by the tale, for what is done in darkness comes to be investigated in sunlight:* not to be forgotten for centuries.—We will turn to another aspect of the Consummation of Sansculottism; leaving this as the blackest.

1682. But indeed men are all rabid: as the Time is. Representative Lebon, at Arras, dashes his sword into the blood flowing from the Guillotine; exclaims, "How I like it!" Mothers, they say, by his orders, have to stand by while the Guillotine devours their children; a band of music is stationed near; and, at the fall of every head, strikes up its "Ca-ira."† In the Burgh of Bedouin, in the Orange region, the Liberty-tree has been cut down overnight. Representative Maiguet, at Orange, hears of it: burns Bedouin Burgh to the last dog-hutch; guillotines the inhabitants, or drives them into the caves and hills.‡ Republic One and Indivisible! She is the newest Birth of Nature's waste inorganic Deep, which men name Orcus, Chaos, primeval Night; and knows one law, that of self-preservation. Tigresse Nationale: meddle not with a whisker of her! Swift-rending is her stroke; look what a paw she spreads;—pity has not entered into her heart.

1683. Prudhomme, the dull-blustering Printer and Able Editor, as yet a Jacobin Editor, will become a renegade one, and publish large volumes, on these matters, "Crimes of the Revolution;" adding innumerable lies withal, as if the truth were not sufficient. We, for our part, find it more edifying to know, one good time, that this Republic and National Tigress *is* a New-Birth; a Fact of Nature among Formulas, in an Age of Formulas; and to look, oftenest in silence, how the so genuine Nature-Fact will demean itself among these. For the Formulas are partly genuine, partly delusive, suppositious: we call them, in the language of metaphor, regulated modeled *shapes;* some of which have bodies and life still in them; most of which, according to a German Writer, have only emptiness, "glass-eyes glaring on you with a ghastly affectation of life, and in their interior unclean accumulation of beetles and spiders!" But the Fact, let all men observe, is a genuine and sincere one; the sincerest of Facts; terrible in its sincerity, as very Death. Whatsoever is equally sincere may front it, and beard it; but whatsoever is *not?*—

CHAPTER IV.

CARMAGNOLE COMPLETE.

1684. Simultaneously with this Tophet-black aspect, there unfolds itself another aspect; which one may call a Tophet-red aspect, the Destruction of the Catholic Religion; and indeed, for the time being, of Religion itself. We saw Romme's New Calendar establish its *Tenth* Day of Rest; and asked, what would become of the Christian Sabbath? The Calendar is hardly a month old, till all this is set at

rest. Very singular, as Mercier observes: last Corpus-Christi Day, 1792, the whole world, and Sovereign Authority itself, walked in religious gala, with a quite devout air;—Butcher Legendre, supposed to be irreverent, was like to be massacred in his Gig, as the thing went by. A Gallican Hierarchy, and Church, and Church Formulas seemed to flourish, a little brown-leaved or so, but not browner than of late years or decades; to flourish far and wide, in the sympathies of an unsophisticated People: defying Philosophism, Legislature and the Encyclopédie. Far and wide, alas, like a brown-leaved Vallombrosa: which waits but one whirl-blast of the November wind, and in an hour stands bare! Since that Corpus-Christi Day, Brunswick has come, and the Emigrants, and La Vendée, and eighteen months of Time; to all flourishing, especially to brown-leaved flourishing, there comes, were it never so slowly, an end.

1685. On the 7th of November, a certain Citoyen Parens, Curate of Boissise-le-Bertrand, writes to the Convention that he has all his life been preaching a lie, and is grown weary of doing it; wherefore he will now lay down his Curacy and stipend, and begs that an august Convention would give him something else to live upon. "Mention honorable," shall we give him? Or "reference to Committee of Finances?" Hardly is this got decided, when goose Gobel, Constitutional Bishop of Paris, with his Chapter, with Municipal and Departmental escort in red night-caps, makes his appearance, to do as Parens has done. Goose Gobel will now acknowledge "no Religion but Liberty;" therefore he doffs his Priest-gear, and receives the Fraternal embrace. To the joy of Departmental Momoro, of Municipal Chaumette and Héberts, of Vincent and the Revolutionary Army! Chaumette asks, Ought there not, in these circumstances, to be among our intercalary Days Sans-breeches, a Feast of Reason?* Proper surely! Let Atheist Maréchal, Lalande, and little Atheist Naigeon rejoice; let Clootz, Speaker of Mankind, present to the Convention his "Evidences of the Mohammedan Religion," "a work evincing the nullity of all Religions,"—with thanks. There shall be Universal Republic now, thinks Clootz; and "one God only, Le Peuple."

1686. The French nation is of gregarious imitative nature; it needed but a fugle-motion in this matter; and goose Gobel, driven by Municipality and force of circumstances, has given one. What Curé will be behind him of Boissise: what Bishop behind him of Paris? Bishop Grégoire, indeed, courageously declines; to the sound of "We force no one; let Grégoire consult his conscience;" but Protestant and Romish by the hundred volunteer and assent. From far and near, all through November into December, till the work is accomplished, come Letters of renegation, come Curates who "are learning to be Carpenters," Curates with their new-wedded Nuns: has not the day of Reason dawned, very swiftly, and become noon? From sequestered Townships come Addresses, stating plainly, though in Patois dialect, That "they will have no more to do with the black animal called Curay (animal noir appelé Curay)."†

1687. Above all things, there come Patriotic Gifts, of Church-Furniture. The remnant of bells, except for tocsin, descend from their belfries, into the National melting-pot to make cannon. Censers and all sacred vessels are beaten broad; of silver, they are fit for the poverty-stricken Mint; of pewter, let them become bullets, to shoot the "enemies du genre humain." Dalmatics of plush made breeches for him

---

* "Procès de Carrier" (4 tomes, Paris, 1795).
† "Les Horreurs des Prisons d'Arras" (Paris, 1823).
‡ Montgaillard. iv. 200.

* Moniteur, Séance du 17 Brumaire (7th November), 1793.
† "Analyse du Moniteur" (Paris, 1801), ii. 280.

who had none; linen albs will clip into shirts for the Defenders of the Country; old-clothesmen, Jews or Heathen, drive the briskest trade. Chalier's Ass-Procession, at Lyons, was but a type of what went on, in those same days, in all Towns. In all Towns and Townships as quick as the guillotine may go, so quick goes the axe, and the wrench: sacristies, lutrins, altar-rails are pulled down; the Mass-Books torn into cartridge-papers: men dance the Carmagnole all night about the bonfire. All highways jingle with metallic Priest-tackle, beaten broad; sent to the Convention, to the poverty-stricken Mint. Good Sainte-Geneviève's Chasse is let down: alas, to be burst open, this time, and burnt on the Place de Grève. Saint Louis's Shirt is burnt; —might not a Defender of the Country have had it? At Saint-Denis Town, no longer Saint-Denis but Franciade, Patriotism has been down among the Tombs, rummaging: the Revolutionary army has taken spoil. This, accordingly, is what the streets of Paris saw:

1688. "Most of these persons were still drunk, with the brandy they had swallowed out of chalices; —eating mackerel on the patenas! Mounted on Asses, which were housed with Priests' cloaks, they reined them with Priests' stoles: they held clutched with the same hand communion-cup and sacred wafer. They stopped at the doors of Dram-shops; held out ciboriums and the landlord, stoup in hand, had to fill them thrice. Next came Mules high-laden with crosses, chandeliers, censers, holy-water vessels, hyssops;—recalling to mind the Priests of Cybele, whose panniers, filled with the instruments of their worship, served at once as store-house, sacristy and temple. In such equipage did these profaners advance toward the Convention. They enter there, in an immense train, ranged in two rows; all masked like mummers in fantastic sacerdotal vestments: bearing on hand-barrows their heaped plunder,—ciboriums, suns, candelabras, plates of gold and silver."*

1689. The Address we do not give; for indeed it was in strophes, sung vivâ voce, with all the parts —Danton glooming considerably, in his place, and demanding that there be prose and decency in future.† Nevertheless the captors of such spolia opima crave, not untouched with liquor, permission to dance the Carmagnole also on the spot: whereto an exhilarated Convention cannot but accede. Nay "several Members," continues the exaggerative Mercier, who was not there to witness, being in Limbo now, as one of Duperret's *Seventy-three*. "several Members, quitting their curule chairs, took the hand of girls flaunting in Priests' .vestures, and danced the Carmagnole along with them." Such Old-Hallowtide have they, in this year, once named of Grace 1793.

1690. Out of which strange fall of Formulas, tumbling there in confused welter, betrampled by the Patriotic dance, is it not passing strange to see a *new* Formula arise? For the human tongue is not adequate to speak what "triviality run distracted" there is in human nature. Black Mumbo-Jumbo of the woods, and most Indian Wau-waus, one can understand: but this of Procureur Anaxagoras. whilom John-Peter, Chaumette? We will say only: Man is a born idol-worshiper, *sight*-worshiper, so sensuous-imaginative is he; and also partakes much of the nature of the ape.

1691. For the same day. while this brave Carmagnole-dance has hardly jigged itself out, there arrive Procureur Chaumette and Municipals and Departmentals, and with them the strangest freightage: a New-Religion! Demoiselle Candeille, of the Opera;

* Mercier, iv. 134. See Moniteur, Séance du 10 Novembre.
† See also Moniteur, Séance du 26 Novembre.

a woman fair to look upon, when well rouged; she, borne on palanquin shoulder-high; with red woolen nightcap; in azure mantle; garlanded with oak; holding in her hand the Pike of the Jupiter-People, sails in: heralded by white young women girt in tricolor. Let the world consider it! This, O National Convention wonder of the universe, is our New Divinity; *Goddess of Reason.* worthy, and alone worthy of revering. Her henceforth we adore. Nay were it too much to ask of an august National Representation that it also went with us to the ci-devant Cathedral called of Notre-Dame, and executed a few strophes in worship of her?

1692. President and Secretaries give Goddess Candeille, borne at due height round their platform, successively the Fraternal kiss; whereupon she, by decree, sails to the right-hand of the President and there alights. And now, after due pause and flourishes of oratory, the Convention, gathering its limbs, does get under way in the required procession toward Notre-Dame;—Reason, again in her litter, sitting in the van of them, borne, one judges, by men in the Roman costume; escorted by wind-music, red-night-caps, and the madness of the world. And so, straightway, Reason taking seat on the high-altar of Notre-Dame, the requisite worship or quasi-worship is, say the Newspapers, *executed*; National Convention chanting the 'Hymn to Liberty,' words by Chénier, music by Grossic." It is the first of the *Feasts of Reason;* first communion-service, of the New Religion of Chaumette.

1693. "The corresponding Festival in the Church of Saint-Eustache," says Mercier, "offered the spectacle of a great tavern. The interior of the choir represented a landscape decorated with cottages and boskets of trees. Round the choir stood tables overloaded with bottles, with sausages, pork-puddings, pastries and other meats. The guests flowed in and out through all doors: whosoever presented himself took part of the good things: children of eight, girls as well as boys, put hand to plate, in sign of Liberty; they drank also of the bottles, and their prompt intoxication created laughter. Reason sat in azure mantle aloft, in a serene manner; Cannoneers, pipe in mouth, serving her as acolytes. And out of doors," continues the exaggerative man, "were mad multitudes dancing round the bonfire of Chapel-balus, trades, of Priests' and Canons' stalls; and the dancers-—I exaggerate nothing,—the dancers nigh bare of breeches, neck and breast naked, stockings down, went whirling and spinning, like those Dust-vortexes, forerunners of Tempest and Destruction."* At Saint-Gervais Church, again, there was a terrible "smell of herrings;" Section or Municipality having provided no food, no condiment, but left it to chance. Other mysteries, seemingly of a Cabiric or even Paphian character, we leave under the Veil, which appropriately stretches itself "along the pillars of the aisles,"—not to be lifted aside by the hand of History.

1694. But there is one thing we should like almost better to understand than any other; what Reason herself thought of it, all the while. . What articulate words poor Mrs. Momoro, for example, uttered; when she had become ungoddessed again, and the Bibliopolist and she sat quiet at home, at supper? For he was an earnest man, Bookseller Momoro; and had notions of Agrarian Law. Mrs. Momoro, it is admitted, made one of the best Goddesses of Reason; though her teeth were a little defective.—And now if the Reader will represent to himself that such visible Adoration of Reason went on "all over the Republic." through these November and December weeks, till the Church wood-work was burnt out, and

* Mercier, iv. 127-146.

the business otherwise completed, he will perhaps feel sufficiently what an adoring Republic it was, and without reluctance quit this part of the subject.

1695. Such gifts of Church-spoil are chiefly the work of the Armée Révolutionnaire; raised, as we said, some time ago. It is an army with portable guillotine; commanded by Playwright Ronsin in terrible mustachioes; and even by some uncertain shadow of Usher Maillard, the old Bastille Hero, Leader of the Menads, September Man in Gray! Clerk Vincent of the War-Office, one of Pache's old Clerks, "with a head heated by the ancient orators," had a main hand in the appointments at least in the staff-appointments.

1696. But of the marchings and retreatings of these 6,000 no Xenophon exists. Nothing, but an inarticulate hum, of cursing and sooty frenzy, surviving dubious in the memory of ages! They scour the country round Paris; seeking Prisoners; raising Requisitions; seeing that Edicts are executed, that the Farmers have thrashed sufficiently; lowering Churchbells or metallic Virgins. Detachments shoot forth dim, toward remote parts of France; nay new Provincial Revolutionary Armies rise dim, here and there, as Carrier's Company of Marat, as Tallien's Bourdeaux Troop; like sympathetic clouds in an atmosphere all electric. Ronsin, they say, admitted in candid moments, that his troops were the elixir of the Rascality of the Earth. One sees them drawn up in market-places; travel-splashed, rough-bearded, in carmagnole complete; the first exploit is to prostrate what Royal or Ecclesiastical monument, crucifix or the like, there may be: to plant a cannon at the steeple; fetch down the bell without climbing for it, bell and belfry together. This, however, it is said, depends somewhat on the size of the town; if the town contains much population, and these perhaps of a dubious choleric aspect, the Revolutionary Army will do its work gently, by ladder and wrench; nay perhaps will take its billet without work at all; and, refreshing itself with a little liquor and sleep, pass on to the next stage.* Pipe in check, saber on thigh; in Carmagnole complete!

1697. Such things have been; and may again be. Charles Second sent out his Highland Host over the Western Scotch Whigs: Jamaica Planters got Dogs from the Spanish Main to hunt their Maroons with: France too is bescoured with a Devil's Pack, the baying of which, at this distance of half a century, still sounds in the mind's ear.

CHAPTER V.

LIKE A THUNDER-CLOUD.

1698. But the grand and indeed substantially primary and generic aspect of the Consummation of Terror remains still to be looked at; nay blinkard History has for most part all but *overlooked* this aspect, the soul of the whole; that which makes it terrible to the Enemies of France. Let Despotism and Cimmerian Coalitions consider. All French men and French things are in a State of Requisition; Fourteen Armies are got on foot; Patriotism, with all that it has of faculty in heart or in head, in soul or body or breeches-pocket, is rushing to the Frontiers, to prevail or die! Busy sits Carnot, in Salut Public; busy, for his share, in "organizing victory." Not swifter pulses that Guillotine, in dread systole-diastole in the Place de la Révolution, than smites the Sword of Patriotism, smiting Cimmeria back to its own borders, from the sacred soil.

1699. In fact, the Government is what we can call Revolutionary: and some men are "à la hauteur," on

* "Deux Amis." xii. 62–65.

a level with the circumstances; and others are not à la hauteur,—so much the worse for them. But the Anarchy, we may say, has *organized* itself: Society is literally overset; its old forces working with mad activity, but in the inverse order; destructive and self-destructive.

1700. Curious to see how all still refers itself to some head and fountain; not even an Anarchy but must have a center to revolve round. It is now some six months since the Committee of Salut Public came into existence; some three months since Danton proposed that all power should be given it, and "a sum of 50,000,000," and the "Government be declared Revolutionary." He himself, since that day, would take no hand in it, though again and again solicited; but sits private in his place on the Mountain. Since that day, the Nine, or if they should even rise to Twelve, have become permanent, always re-elected when their term runs out; Salut Public, Sûreté Générale have assumed their ulterior form and mode of operating.

1701. Committee of Public Salvation, as supreme; of General Surety, as subaltern: these, like a Lesser and Greater Council, most harmonious hitherto, have become the center of all things. They ride this Whirlwind; they, raised by force of circumstances, insensibly, very strangely, thither to that dread height:—and guide it, and seem to guide it. Stranger set of Cloud-Compellers the Earth never saw. A Robespierre, a Billaud, a Collot, Couthon, Saint-Just; not to mention still meaner Amars, Vadiers, in Sûreté Générale: these are your Cloud-Compellers. Small intellectual talent is necessary: indeed where among them, except in the head of Carnot, busied organizing victory, would you find any? The talent is one of instinct rather. It is that of divining aright what this great dumb Whirlwind wishes and wills; that of willing, with more frenzy than any one, what all the world wills. To stand at no obstacles: to heed no considerations, human or divine; to know well that, of divine or human, there is one thing needful, Triumph of the Republic, Destruction of the Enemies of the Republic! With this one spiritual endowment, and so few others, it is strange to see how a dumb inarticulately storming Whirlwind of things puts, as it were, its reins into your hand, and invites and compels you to be leader of it.

1702. Hard by sits a Municipality of Paris: all in red night-caps since the 4th of November last; a set of men fully "on a level with circumstances," or even beyond it. Sleek Mayor Pache, studious to be safe in the middle; Chaumettes, Héberts, Varlets, and Henriot their great Commandant; not to speak of Vincent the War-clerk, of Momoros, Dobsents and such-like: all intent to have Churches plundered, to have Reason adored, Suspects cut down, and the Revolution triumph. Perhaps carrying the matter *too far*? Danton was heard to grumble at the civic strophes; and to recommend prose and decency. Robespierre also grumbles that, in overturning Superstition, we did not mean to make a religion of Atheism. In fact, your Chaumette and Company constitute a kind of Hyper-Jacobinism, or rabid "Faction des Enragés;" which has given orthodox Patriotism some umbrage, of late months. To "know a Suspect on the streets;" what is this but bringing the *Law of the Suspect* itself into ill odor? Men half-frantic, men zealous over-much,—they toil there, in their red night-caps, restlessly, rapidly, accomplishing what of Life is allotted them.

1703. And the 44,000 other Townships, each with Revolutionary Committee, based on Jacobin Daughter Society; enlightened by the spirit of Jacobinism; quickened by the Forty Sous a day!—The

French Constitution spurned always at anything like Two Chambers; and yet, behold. has it not verily got Two Chambers? National Convention, elected, for one; Mother of Patriotism, self-elected, for another! Mother of Patriotism has her Debates reported in the Moniteur, as important state-procedures; which indisputably they are. A Second Chamber of Legislature we call this Mother Society;—if perhaps it were not rather comparable to that old Scotch Body named Lords of the Articles, without whose origination, and signal given, the so-called Parliament could introduce no bill, could do no work? Robespierre himself, whose words are a law, opens his incorruptible lips copiously in the Jacobins Hall. Smaller Council of Salut Public, Greater Council of Sûreté Générale, all active Parties, come here to plead; to shape beforehand what decision they must arrive at, what destiny they have to expect. Now if a question arose, Which of those Two Chambers, Convention, or Lords of the Articles, was the *stronger* ? Happily they as yet go hand in hand.

1704. As for the National Convention, truly it has become a most composed Body. Quenched now the old effervescence ; the Seventy-three locked in ward ; once noisy Friends of the Girondins sunk all into silent men of the Plain, called even " Frogs of the Marsh (Crapauds du Marais)!" Addresses come ; Revolutionary Church-plunder comes ; Deputations, with prose or strophes : these the Convention receives. But beyond this, the Convention has one thing mainly to do : to listen what Salut Public proposes, and say, Yea.

1705. Bazire followed by Chabot, with some impetuosity, declared, one morning, that this was not the way of a Free Assembly. "There ought to be an Opposition side, a Coté Droit," cried Chabot; "if none else will form it, I will. People say to me, You will all get guillotined in your turn, first you and Bazire, then Danton, then Robespierre himself."[*] So spake the Disfrocked, with a loud voice: next week, Bazire and he lie in the Abbaye; wending, one may fear, toward Tinville and the Axe; and "people say to me "—what seems to be proving true! Bazire's blood was all inflamed with Revolution Fever ; with coffee and spasmodic dreams.[†] Chabot, again, how happy with his rich Jew-Austrian wife, late Fräulein Frey! But he lies in Prison; and his two Jew-Austrian Brothers-in-Law, the Bankers Frey, lie with him; waiting the urn of doom. Let a National Convention, therefore, take warning, and know its function. Let the Convention, all as one man, set its shoulder to the work; not with bursts of Parliamentary eloquence, but in quite other and serviceabler ways!

1706. Convention Commissioners, what we ought to call Representatives, "Représentans on mission," fly, like the Herald Mercury, to all points of the Territory ; carrying your behests far and wide. In their "round hat, plumed with tricolor feathers, girt with flowing tricolor taffeta ; in close frock, tricolor sash, sword and jack-boots,' these men are powerfuler than King or Kaiser. They say to whomso they meet, Do ; and he must do it: all men's goods are at their disposal ; for France is as one huge City in Siege. They smite with Requisitions and Forced-loan; they have the power of life and death. Saint-Just and Lebas order the rich classes of Strasburg to "strip off their shoes" and send them to the Armies, where as many as "10.000 pairs" are needed. Also, that within four-and-twenty hours "a thousand beds" be got ready ;[‡] wrapped in matting, and sent under way. For the time presses!—Like swift bolts, issu-

* Débats. du 10 Novembre. 1793
† "Dictionnaire des Hommes Marquans," i. 115.
‡ Moniteur du 27 Novembre. 1793.

ing from the fuliginous Olympus of Salut Public, rush these men, oftenest in pairs; scatter your thunder-orders over France ; make France one enormous Revolutionary thunder-cloud.

CHAPTER VI.
DO THY DUTY.

1707. Accordingly, alongside of these bonfires of Church-balustrades, and sounds of fusillading and noyading, there rise quite another sort of fires and sounds : Smithy-fires and Proof-volleys for the manufacture of arms.

1708. Cut off from Sweden and the world, the Republic must learn to make steel for itself; and, by aid of Chemists, she has learnt it. Towns that knew only iron, now know steel: from their new dungeons at Chantilly, Aristocrats may hear the rustle of our new steel furnace there. Do not bells transmute themselves into cannon; iron stancheons into the white-weapon (arme blanche), by sword-cutlery? The wheels of Langres scream, amid their sputtering fire-halo: grinding mere swords. The stithies of Charleville ring with gun-making. What say we, Charleville? Two hundred and fifty-eight Forges stand in the open spaces of Paris itself; a hundred and forty of them in the Esplanade of the Invalides, fifty-four in the Luxembourg Garden : so many Forges stand ; grim Smiths beating and forging at lock and barrel there. The Clock-makers have come, requisitioned, to do the touch-holes, the hard-solder and file-work. Five great Barges swing at anchor on the Seine Stream, loud with boring ; the great press-drills grating harsh thunder to the general ear and heart. And deft Stock-makers do gouge and rasp; and all men bestir themselves, according to their cunning:—in the language of hope, it is reckoned that "a thousand finished muskets can be delivered daily."[*] Chemists of the Republic have taught us miracles of swift tanning :[†] the cordwainer bores and stitches;—not of "wood and pasteboard," or he shall answer it to Tinville! The women sew tents and coats, the children scrape surgeon's-lint, the old men sit in the market-places; able men are on march ; all men in requisition: from town to town flutters, on the Heaven's winds, this Banner, THE FRENCH PEOPLE RISEN AGAINST TYRANTS.

1709. All which is well. But now arises the question: What is to be done for saltpeter? Interrupted Commerce and the English Navy shut us out from saltpeter; and without saltpeter there is no gunpowder, Republican Science again sits meditative ; discovers that saltpeter exists here and there, though in attenuated quantity ; that old plaster of walls holds a sprinkling of it;—that the earth of the Paris Cellars holds a sprinkling of it, diffused through' the common rubbish ; that were these dug up and washed saltpeter might be had. Whereupon, swiftly, see! the Citoyens, with up-shoved bonnet rouge, or with doffed bonnet, and hair toil-wetted; digging fiercely, each in his own cellar, for saltpeter. The Earth-heap rises at every door ; the Citoyennes with hod and bucket carrying it up; the Citoyens, pith in every muscle, shoveling and digging: for life and saltpeter. Dig, my *braves*; and right well speed ye! What of saltpeter is essential the Republic shall not want.

1710. Consummation of Sansculottism has many aspects and tints : but the brightest tint, really of a solar or stellar brightness, is this which the Armies give it. That same fervor of Jacobinism. which internally fills France with hatreds, suspicions, scaffolds and Reason worship, does, on the Frontiers, show ti-

* "Choix des Rapports." xiii. 189.
† Ibid., xv. 360.

self as a glorious Pro patria mori. Ever since Dumouriez's defection, three Convention Representatives attend every General. Committee of Salut has sent them: often with this Laconic order only: "Do thy duty (Fais ton devoir)." It is strange, under what impediments the fire of Jacobinism, like other such fires, will burn. These Soldiers have shoes of wood and pasteboard, òr go booted in hay-ropes in dead of winter; they skewer a bast mat round their shoulders, and are destitute of most things. What then? It is for Rights of Frenchhood, of Manhood, that they fight; the unquenchable spirit, here as elsewhere, works miracles. "With steel and bread," says the Convention Representative, "one may get to China." The Generals go fast to the guillotine; justly and unjustly. From which what inference? This, among others: That ill success is death; that in victory alone is life! To conquer or die is no theatrical palabra, in these circumstances, but a practical truth and necessity. All Girondinism, Halfness, Compromise is swept away. Forward ye Soldiers of the Republic, captain and man! Dash, with your Gaelic impetuosity, on Austria, England, Prussia, Spain, Sardinia; Pitt, Cobourg, York, and the Devil, and the world! Behind us is but the Guillotine; before us is Victory, Apotheosis and Millennium without end!

1711. See, accordingly, on all Frontiers, how the Sons of Night, astonished after short triumph, do recoil;—the Sons of the Republic flying at them, with wild Ça-ira or Marsellese Aux armes, with the temper of cat-o'-mountain, or demon incarnate; which no Son of Night can stand! Spain, which came bursting through the Pyrenees, rustling with Bourbon banners, and went conquering here and there for a season, falters at such cat-o'-mountain welcome; draws itself in again; too happy now were the Pyrenees impassable. Not only does Dugommier, conqueror of Toulon, drive Spain back; he invades Spain. General Dugommier invades it by the Eastern Pyrenees; General Müller shall invade it by the Western. *Shall*, that is the word: Committee of Salut Public has said it; Representative Cavaignac, on mission there, must see it done. Impossible! cries Müller.—Infallible! answers Cavaignac. Difficulty, impossibility, is to no purpose. "The Committee is deaf on that side of its head," answers Cavaignac, "n'entend pas de cette oreille là. How many wantest thou of men, of horses, cannons? Thou shalt have them. Conquerors, conquered, or hanged, forward we must."* Which things also, even as the Representative spake them, were *done*. The Spring of the new Year sees Spain invaded: and redoubts are carried, and Passes and Heights of the most scarped description; Spanish field-officerism struck mute at such cat-o'-mountain spirit, the cannon forgetting to fire.† Swept are the Pyrenees; Town after Town flies open, burst by terror or the petard. In the course of another year, Spain will crave Peace; acknowledge its sins and the Republic; nay, in Madrid, there will be joy as for a victory, that even Peace is got.

1712. Few things, we repeat, can be notabler than these Convention Representatives, with their power more than kingly. Nay at bottom are they not Kings, *Able-men*, of a sort: chosen from the 749 French Kings; with this order, Do thy duty? Representative Levasseur, of small stature, by trade a

mere pacific Surgeon-Accoucheur, has mutinies to quell; mad hosts (mad at the Doom of Custine) bellowing far and wide; he alone amid them, the one small Representative,—small, but as hard as flint, which also carries *fire* in it! So too, at Hondschooten, far in the afternoon, he declares that the Battle is not lost; that it must be gained; and fights, himself, with his own obstetric hand;—horse shot under him, or say on foot, "up to the haunches in tidewater;" cutting stoccado and passado there, in defiance of Water, Earth, Air and Fire, the choleric little Representative that he was! Whereby, as natural, Royal Highness of York had to withdraw,—occasionally at full gallop; like to be swallowed by the tide; and his Siege of Dunkirk became a dream, realizing only much loss of beautiful siege-artillery and of brave lives.*

1713. General Houchard, it would appear, stood behind a hedge on this Hondschooten occasion; wherefore they have since guillotined him. A new General Jourdan, late Sergeant Jourdan, commands in his stead; he, in long-winded battles of Watigny, "murderous artillery-fire mingling itself with sound of Revolutionary battle-hymns," forces Austria behind the Sambre again; has hopes of purging the soil of Liberty. With hard wrestling, with artillery-ing and ça-ira-ing, it shall be done. In the course of a new Summer, Valenciennes will see itself beleaguered; Condé beleaguered; whatsoever is yet in the hands of Austria beleaguered and bombarded: nay, by Convention Decree, we even summon them *all* "either to surrender in twenty-four hours, or else be put to the sword;"—a high saying, which, though it remains unfulfilled, may show what spirit one is of.

1714. Representative Drouet, as an Old-dragoon, could fight by a kind of second nature; but he was unlucky. Him, in a night-foray at Maubeuge, the Austrians took alive, in October last. They stripped him almost naked, he says; making a show of him as King-taker of Varennes. They flung him into carts; sent him far into the interior of Cimmeria, to "a Fortress called Spitzberg" on the Danube River; and left him there at an elevation of perhaps 150 feet, to his own bitter reflections. Reflections; and also devices! For the indomitable Old-dragoon constructs wing-machinery, of Paper kite; saws window-bars; determines to fly down. He will seize a boat, will follow the River's course; land somewhere in Crim Tartary, in the Black Sea or Constantinople region: à la Sindbad! Authentic History, accordingly, looking far into Cimmeria, discerns dimly a phenomenon. In the dead night-watches, the Spitzberg sentry is near fainting with terror: Is it a huge vague Portent descending through the night-air? It is a huge National Representative Old-dragoon, descending by Paper-kite: too rapidly, alas! For Drouet had taken with him "a small provision-store, twenty pounds weight or thereby;" which proved accelerative; so he fell, fracturing his leg; and lay there, moaning, till day dawned, till you could discern clearly that he was not a Portent but a Representative.†

1715. Or see Saint-Just, in the Lines of Weissembourg, though physically of a timid apprehensive nature, how he charges with his "Alsatian Peasants armed hastily" for the nonce; the solemn face of him blazing into flame; his black hair and tricolor hat-taffeta flowing on the breeze! These our Lines of Weissembourg were indeed forced, and Prussia and the Emigrants rolled through: but we re-force the Lines of Weissembourg; and Prussia and the Emi-

---

* There is, in "Prudhomme," an atrocity à la Captain Kirk reported of this Cavaignac, which has been copied into Dictionaries of "Hommes Marquans," of "Biographie Universelle," etc.: which not only has no truth in it, but, much more singular, is still capable of being proved to have none.

† "Deux Amis," xiii. 205-260; Toulongeon, etc.

* Levasseur, "Mémoires," ii. c. 2-7.

† His narrative (in "Deux Amis," xiv. 177-186).

grants roll back again still faster,—hurled with bayonets-charge and fiery ça-ira-ing.

1716. Ci-devant Sergeant Pichegru, ci-devant Sergeant Hoche, risen now to be Generals, have done wonders here. Tall Pichegru was meant for the Church; was Teacher of Mathematics once, in Brienne School,—his remarkablest Pupil there was the Boy Napoleon Bonaparte. He then, not in the sweetest humor, enlisted, exchanging ferula for musket; and had got the length of the halberd, beyond which nothing could be hoped; when the Bastille barriers falling made passage for him, and he is here. Hoche bore a hand at the literal overturn of the Bastille; he was, as we saw, a Sergeant of the Gardes Françaises, spending his pay in rush-lights and cheap editions of books. How the Mountains are burst, and many an Enceladus is disimprisoned; and Captains founding on Four parchments of Nobility are blown with their parchments across the Rhine, into Lunar Limbo!

1717. What high feats of arms, therefore, were done in these Fourteen Armies; and how, for love of Liberty and hope of Promotion, low-born valor cuts its desperate way to Generalship; and, from the central Carnot in Salut Public to the outmost drummer on the Frontiers, men strove for their Republic, let Readers fancy. The snows of Winter, the flowers of Summer continue to be stained with warlike blood. Gaelic impetuosity mounts ever higher with victory; spirit of Jacobinism weds itself to national vanity: the Soldiers of the Republic are become, as we prophesied, very Sons of Fire. Barefooted, barebacked: but with bread and iron you can get to China! It is one Nation against the whole world; but the Nation has that within her which the whole world will not conquer. Cimmeria, astonished, recoils faster or slower: all round the Republic there rises fiery, as it were, a magic ring of musket-volleying and ça-ira-ing. Majesty of Prussia, as Majesty of Spain, will by and by acknowledge his sins and the Republic; and makes a Peace of Bâle.

1718. Foreign Commerce, Colonies, Factories in the East and in the West, are fallen or falling into the hands of sea-ruling Pitt, enemy of human nature. Nevertheless what sound is this that we hear, on the first of June, 1794; sound as of war-thunder borne from the Ocean too, of tone most piercing? War-thunder from off the Brest waters; Villaret-Joyeuse and English Howe, after long manœuvring, have ranked themselves there; and are belching fire. The enemies of human nature are on their own element; cannot be conquered; cannot be kept from conquering. Twelve hours of raging cannonade; sun now sinking westward through the battle-smoke: six French Ships taken, the Battle lost; what Ship soever can still sail. making off! But how is it, then, with that *Vengeur* Ship, she neither strikes nor makes off? She is lamed, she cannot make off; strike she will not. Fire rakes her fore and aft from victorious enemies; the *Vengeur* is sinking. Strong are yet Tyrants of the sea; yet we also, are we weak? Lo! all flags, streamers, jacks, every rag of tricolor that will yet run on rope, fly rustling aloft: the whole crew crowds to the upper deck; and with universal, soul-maddening yell, shouts Vive la République,—sinking, sinking. She staggers, she lurches, her last drunk whirl; Ocean yawns abysmal; down rushes the *Vengeur*, carrying Vive la République along with her, unconquerable, into Eternity.* Let foreign Despots think of that. There is an Unconquerable in man, when he stands on his Rights of Man: let Despots and Slaves and all people know this, and only them that stand on the Wrongs of Man tremble to know it.—So has History written, nothing doubting, of the sunk *Vengeur*.

1719. —— Reader! Mendez Pinto, Münchausen, Cagliostro, Psalmanazar have been great; but they are not the greatest. O Barrère, Barrère, Anacreon of the Guillotine! must inquisitive pictorial History, in a new edition, ask again, "How is it with the *Vengeur*," in this its glorious suicidal sinking: and, with resentful brush, dash a bend-sinister of contumelious lamp-black through thee and it? Alas, alas! The *Vengeur*, after fighting bravely, did sink altogether as other ships do, her captain and above 200 of her crew escaping gladly in British boats; and this same enormous inspiring Feat, and rumor "of sound most piercing," turns out to be an enormous inspiring Nonentity, extant nowhere save, as falsehood, in the brain of Barrère! Actually so.* Founded, like the World itself, on *Nothing;* proved by Convention Report, by solemn Convention Decree and Decrees, and wooden "*Model of the Vengeur;*" believed, bewept, besung by the whole French People to this hour, it may be regarded as Barrère's masterpiece; the largest, most inspiring piece of blague manufactured, for some centuries, by any man or nation. As such, and not otherwise, be it henceforth memorable.

<hr>

CHAPTER VII.

FLAME-PICTURE.

1720. In this manner, mad-blazing with flame of all imaginable tints, from the red of Tophet to the stellar-bright, blazes off this Consummation of Sansculottism.

But the hundredth part of the things that were done, and the thousandth part of the things that were projected and decreed to be done, would tire the tongue of History. Statue of the Peuple Souverain, high as Strasburg Steeple; which shall fling its shadow from the Pont Neuf over Jardin National and Convention Hall;—enormous, in Painter David's Head! With other the like enormous Statues not a few: realized in paper Decree. For, indeed, the Statue of Liberty herself is still but Plaster, in the Place de la Révolution. Then Equalization of Weights and Measures, with decimal division; Institutions, of Music and much else; Institute in general; School of Arts, School of Mars. Elèves de la Patrie, Normal Schools: amid such Gun-boring, Altar-burning, Saltpeter-digging, and miraculous improvements in Tannery!

1721. What, for example, is this that Engineer Chappe is doing, in the Park of Vincennes? In the Park of Vincennes; and onward, they say, in the Park of Lepelletier Saint-Fargeau the assassinated Deputy; and still onward to the Heights of Econen and farther, he has scaffolding set up, has post-driven in; wooden arms with elbow-joints are jerking and fugling in the air, in the most rapid mysterious manner! Citoyens ran up, suspicious. Yes, O Citoyens, we are signaling: it is a device this, worthy of the Republic; a thing for what we will call Far-writing without the aid of post-bags; in Greek it shall be named Telegraph.—Télégraphe sacré! answers Citoyenism: For writing to Traitors, to Austria?—and tears it down. Chappe had to escape, and get a new Legislative Decree. Nevertheless he has accomplished it, the indefatigable Chappe, this his Far-writer, with its wooden arms and elbow-

* Compare Barrère ("Choix des Rapports," xvi. 416-421); Lord Howe (" Annual Register " of 1794, p. 86), etc.

* Carlyle's " Miscellanies," § Sinking of the *Vengeur*.

joints, can intelligibly signal; and lines of them are set up, to the North Frontiers and elsewhither. On an Autumn evening of the Year Two, Far-writer having just written that Condé Town has surrendered to us, we send from the Tuileries Convention-Hall this response in the shape of Decree; "The name of Condé is changed to Nord-Libre (North-Free). The Army of the North ceases not to merit well of the country:"—To the admiration of men! For lo, in some half hour, while the Convention yet debates, there arrives this new answer: "I inform thee (Je t'annonce), Citizen President, that the Decree of Convention, ordering change of the name Condé into North-Free; and the other, declaring that the Army of the North ceases not to merit well of the country; are transmitted and acknowledged by Telegraph. I have instructed my Officer at Lille to forward them to North-Free by express. *Signed*, CHAPPE."*

1722. Or see, over Fleurus in the Netherlands, where General Jourdan, having now swept the soil of Liberty, and advanced thus far, is just about to fight, and sweep or be swept, hangs there not in the Heaven's Vault some Prodigy, seen by Austrian eyes and spy-glasses: in the similitude of an enormous Wind-bag, with netting and enormous Saucer depending from it? A Jove's Balance, O ye Austrian spy-glasses? One saucer-scale of a Jove's Balance; *your* poor Austrian scale having kicked itself quite aloft, out of sight? By Heaven, answer the spy-glasses, it is a Montgolfier, a Balloon, and they are making signals! Austrian cannon-battery barks at this Montgolfier; harmless as dog at the Moon: the Montgolfier makes its signals; detects what Austrian ambuscade there may be, and descends at its ease.†—What will not these devils incarnate contrive?

1723. On the whole, is it not, O Reader, one of the strangest Flame-Pictures that ever painted itself; flaming off there, on its ground of Guillotine-black? And the nightly Theatres are Twenty-three; and the Salons de danse are Sixty; full of mere Égalité, Fraternité and Carmagnole. And Section Committee-rooms are Forty-eight; redolent of tobacco and brandy: vigorous with twenty-pence a-day, coercing the Suspect. And the Houses of Arrest are Twelve, for Paris alone; crowded and even crammed. And at all turns, you need your "Certificate of Civism;" be it for going out, or for coming in; nay without it you cannot, for money, get your daily ounces of bread. Dusky red-capped Bakers'-queues; wagging themselves; not in silence! For we still live by Maximum, in all things; waited on by these two, Scarcity and Confusion. The faces of men are darkened with suspicion; with suspecting, or being suspect. The streets lie unswept; the ways unmended. Law has shut her Books; speaks little, save impromptu, through the throat of Tinville. Crimes go unpunished; not crimes against the Revolution.‡ "The number of foundling children," as some compute, "is doubled."

1724. How silent now sits Royalism; sits all Aristocratism; Respectability that kept its Gig! The honor now, and the safety, is to Poverty. not to Wealth. Your Citizen, who would be fashionable, walks abroad, with his Wife on his arm, in red-wool night-cap, black-shag spencer, and carmagnole complete. Aristocratism crouches low, in what shelter is still left; submitting to all requisitions, vexations; too happy to escape with life. Ghastly châteaus stare on you by the wayside; disroofed, diswindowed;

which the National House-broker is peeling for the lead and ashlar. The old tenants hover disconsolate, over the Rhine with Condé; a spectacle to men. Ci-devant Seigneur, exquisite in palate, will become an exquisite Restaurateur Cook in Hamburg; Ci-devant Madame, exquisite in dress, a successful Marchande des Modes in London. In Newgate-Street, you meet M. le Marquis, with a rough deal on his shoulder, adze and jack-plane under arm; he has taken to the joiner trade; it being necessary to live (faut vivre).*—Higher than all Frenchmen the domestic Stock-jobber flourishes,—in a day of Paper-money. The Farmer also flourishes: "Farmers' houses," says Mercier, "have become like Pawnbrokers' shops;" all manner of furniture, apparel, vessels of gold and silver accumulate themselves there: bread is precious. The Farmers' rent is Paper-money, and he alone of men has bread: Farmer is better than Landlord, and will himself become Landlord.

1725. And daily, we say, like a black Specter, silently through that Life-tumult passes the Revolution Cart; writing on the walls its MENE, MENE, *Thou art weighed, and found wanting!* A Specter with which one has grown familiar. Men have adjusted themselves: complaint issues not from that Death-tumbril. Weak women and ci-devants, their plumage and finery all tarnished, sit there; with a silent gaze, as if looking into the Infinite Black. The once light lip wears a curl of irony, uttering no word; and the Tumbril fares along. They may be guilty before Heaven, or not; they are guilty, we suppose, before the Revolution. Then does not the Republic "coin money" of them, with its great axe? Red Night-caps howl dire approval: the rest of Paris looks on; if with a sigh, that is much: Fellow creatures whom sighing cannot help; whom black Necessity and Tinville have clutched.

1726. One other thing, or rather two other things, we will still mention; and no more: The Blond Perukes; the Tannery at Meudon. Great talk is of these Perruques blondes: O Reader, they are made from the Heads of Guillotined women! The locks of a Duchess, in this way, may come to cover the scalp of a Cordwainer; her blonde German Frankism his black Gaelic poll, if it be bald. Or they may be worn affectionately as relics; rendering one suspect?† Citizens use them, not without mockery; of a rather cannibal sort.

1727. Still deeper into one's heart goes that Tannery at Meudon; not mentioned among the other miracles of tanning! "At Meudon," says Montgaillard with considerable calmness, "there was a Tannery of Human Skins; such of the Guillotined as seemed worth flaying; of which perfectly good washleather was made;" for breeches, and other uses. The skin of the men, he remarks, was superior in toughness (*consistance*) and quality to chamois; that of the women was good for almost nothing, being so soft in texture!‡—History looking back over Cannibalism, through "Purchas's Pilgrims," and all early and late Records, will perhaps find no terrestrial Cannibalism of a sort, on the whole, so detestable. It is a manufactured, soft-feeling, quietly elegant sort; a sort perfide! Alas, then, is man's civilization only a wrappage, through which the savage nature of him can still burst, infernal as ever? Nature still makes him; and has an Infernal in her as well as a Celestial.

---

f * "Choix des Rapports, xv. 378-384.
† 26th June, 1794 (see " Rapport de Guyton-Morveau sur les Aérostats." in Moniteur du 6 Vendémiaire, An. 2).
‡ Mercier, v. 25; "Deux Amis," xii. 142-169.

* See " Deux Amis," xv. 189-192; "Mémoires de Genlis," "Founders of the French Republic," etc., etc.
† Mercier, ii. 134.
‡ Montgaillard, iv. 290.

BOOK SIXTH.

THERMIDOR.

CHAPTER I.

THE GODS ARE ATHIRST.

1728. What, then, is this Thing called La Révolution, which, like an Angel of Death, hangs over France, noyading, fusillading, fighting, gun-boring, tanning human skins? La Révolution is but so many Alphabetic Letters; a thing nowhere to be laid hands on, to be clapt under lock and key: where is it? what is it? It is the Madness that dwells in the hearts of men. In this man it is, and in that man; as a rage or as a terror, it is in all men. Invisible, impalpable; and yet no black Azrael, with wings spread over half a continent, with sword sweeping from sea to sea, could be a truer Reality.

1729. To explain, what is called explaining, the march of this Revolutionary Government, be no task of ours. Man cannot explain it. A paralytic Couthon, asking in the Jacobins, "What hast thou done to be hanged if Counter-Revolution should arrive?" a somber Saint-Just, not yet six-and-twenty, declaring that "for Revolutionists there is no rest but in the tomb:" a sea-green Robespierre converted into vinegar and gall; much more an Amar and Vadier a Collot and Billaud: to inquire what thoughts, predetermination or prevision, might be in the head of these men? Record of their thought remains not; Death and Darkness have swept it out utterly. Nay, if we even had their thought, all that they could have articulately spoken to us, how insignificant a fraction were that of the Thing which realized itself, which decreed itself, on signal given by them! As has been said more than once, this Revolutionary Government is not a self-conscious but a blind fatal one. Each man, enveloped in his ambient-atmosphere of revolutionary fanatic Madness, rushes on, impelled and impelling; and has become a blind brute Force; no rest for him but in the grave! Darkness and the mystery of horrid cruelty cover it for us, in History; as they did in Nature. The chaotic Thunder-cloud, with its pitchy black and its tumult of dazzling jagged fire, in a world all electric: thou wilt not undertake to show how that comported itself,—what the secrets of the dark womb were; from what sources, with what specialties, the lightning it held did, in confused brightness of terror, strike forth, destructive and self-destructive, till it ended? Like a Blackness naturally of Erebus, which by will of Providence had for once mounted itself into dominion and the Azure: is not this properly the nature of Sansculottism consummating itself? Of which Erebus Blackness be it enough to discern that this and the other dazzling fire-bolt, dazzling fire-torrent, does by small Volition and great Necessity, verily issue,—in such and such succession; destructive so and so; self-destructive so and so: till it end.

1730. Royalism is extinct; "sunk," as they say, "in the mud of the Loire;" Republicanism dominates without and within: what, therefore, on the 15th day of March, 1794, is this? Arrestment, sudden really as a bolt out of the Blue, has hit strange victims; Hébert Père Duchesne, Bibliopolist Momoro, Clerk Vincent, General Ronsin: high Cordelier Patriots, red-capped Magistrates of Paris, Worshipers of Reason, Commanders of Revolutionary Army! Eight short days ago, their Cordelier Club was loud, and louder than ever, with Patriot denunciations. Hébert Père Duchesne had "held his tongue and his heart these two months at sight of Moderates, Crypto-Aristocrats, Camilles, Scélérats in the Convention itself: but could not do it any longer; would, if other remedy, were not, invoke the sacred right of Insurrection." So spake Hébert in Cordelier Session; with vivats, till the roofs rang again.* Eight short days ago; and now already! They rub their eyes: it is no dream; they find themselves in the Luxembourg. Goose Gobel too; and they that burnt Churches! Chaumette himself, potent Procureur, *Agent National*, as they now call it, who could "recognize the Suspect by the very face of them," he lingers but three days; on the third day be too is hurled in. Most chop-fallen, blue, enters the National Agent this Limbo whither he has sent so many. Prisoners crowd round, jibing and jeering; "Sublime National Agent," says one, "in virtue of thy immortal Proclamation, lo there! I am suspect, thou art suspect, he is suspect, we are suspect, ye are suspect, they are suspect!"

1731. The meaning of these things? Meaning! It is a Plot; Plot of the most extensive ramifications; which, however, Barrère holds the threads of. Such Church-burning and scandalous masquerades of Atheism, fit to make the Revolution odious: where indeed could they originate but in the gold of Pitt! Pitt indubitably, as Preternatural Insight will teach one, did hire this Faction of Enragés, to play their fantastic tricks: to roar in their Cordeliers Club about Moderatism; to print their Père Duchesne: worship sky-blue Reason in red night-cap; rob Altars,—and bring the spoil to *us!*

1732. Still more indubitable, visible to the mere bodily sight, is this: that the Cordeliers Club sits pale with anger and terror; and has "veiled the Rights of Man,"—without effect. Likewise that the Jacobins are in considerable confusion; busy "purging themselves (s'épurant)," as in times of Plot and public Calamity they have repeatedly had to do. Not even Camille Desmoulins but has given offense: nay there have risen murmurs against Danton himself; though he bellowed them down, and Robespierre finished the matter by "embracing him in the Tribune."

1733. Whom shall the Republic and a jealous Mother Society trust? In these times of temptation, of Preternatural Insight! For there are Factions of the Stranger, "de l'étranger," Factions of Moderates, of Enragés; all manner of Factions: we walk in a world of Plots; strings universally spread, of deadly gins and fall-traps, baited by the gold of Pitt! Clootz, Speaker of Mankind so-called, with his "Evidences of Mohammedan Religion," and babble of Universal Republic, him an incorruptible Robespierre has purged away. Baron Clootz, and Paine rebellious Needleman lie, these two months, in the Luxembourg; limbs of the Faction de l'étranger. Representative Phélippeaux is purged out: he came back from La Vendée with an ill report in his month against rogue Rossignol, and our method of warfare there. Recant it, O Phélippeaux, we entreat thee! Phélippeaux will not recant; and is purged out. Representative Fabre d'Églantine, famed nomenclator of Romme's Calendar, is purged out; nay, is cast into the Luxembourg: accused of Legislative Swindling "in regard to moneys of the India Company." There with his Chabots, Bazires, guilty of the like, let Fabre wait his destiny. And Westermann friend of Danton, he who led the Marseillese on the 10th of August, and fought well in La Vendée, but spoke not well of rogue Rossignol, is purged out. Lucky, if he too go not to the Luxembourg. And your Prolys, Guzmans, of the Faction of the Stranger, they have gone; Pereyra, though he fled, is gone, "taken in the disguise of a Tavern

* Moniteur, du 17 Ventose (7th March), 1794.

Cook." I am suspect, thou art suspect, he is suspect!—

1734. The great heart of Danton is weary of it. Danton is gone to native Arcis, for a little breathing-time of peace: Away, black Arachne-webs, thou world of Fury, Terror and Suspicion; welcome, thou everlasting Mother, with thy spring greenness, thy kind household loves and memories; true art thou, were all else untrue! The great Titan walks silent, by the banks of the murmuring Aube, in young native haunts that knew him when a boy; wonders what the end of these things may be.

1735. But strangest of all, Camille Desmoulins is purged out. Couthon gave as a test in regard to Jacobin purgation the question, "What hast thou done to be hanged if Counter-Revolution should arrive?" Yet Camille, who could so well answer this question, is purged out! The truth is, Camille, early in December last, began publishing a new Journal, or Series of Pamphlets, entitled the Vieux Cordelier (Old Cordelier). Camille, not afraid at one time to "embrace Liberty on a heap of dead bodies," begins to ask now, Whether among so many arresting and punishing Committees, there ought not to be a "Committee of Mercy?" Saint-Just, he observes, is an extremely solemn young Republican, who "carries his head as if it were a Saint-Sacrement," adorable Hostie, or divine Real-Presence! Sharply enough, this old Cordelier,—Danton and he were of the earliest primary Cordeliers, shoots his glittering war-shafts into your new Cordeliers;—your Héberts, Momoros, with their brawling brutalities and despicabilities; say, as the Sun-god (for poor Camille is a Poet) shot into that Python Serpent sprung of mud.

1736. Whereat, as was natural, the Hébertist Python did hiss and writhe amazingly; and threaten "sacred right of Insurrection;"—and, as we saw, get cast into Prison. Nay, with all the old wit, dexterity and light graceful poignancy, Camille, translating "out of Tacitus, from the Reign of Tiberius," pricks into the Law of the Suspect itself; making it odious! Twice, in the Decade, his wild Leaves issue; full of wit, nay, of humor, of harmonious ingenuity and insight,—one of the strangest phenomena of that dark time; and smite, in their wild-sparkling way, at various monstrosities, Saint-Sacrament heads, and Juggernaut idols, in a rather reckless manner. To the great joy of Josephine Beauharnais, and the other 5,000 and odd Suspect, who fill the Twelve Houses of Arrest; on whom a ray of hope dawns! Robespierre, at first approbatory, knew not at last what to think; then thought, with his Jacobins that Camille must be expelled. A man of true Revolutionary spirit, this Camille; but with the unwisest sallies; whom Aristocrats and Moderates have the art to corrupt! Jacobinism is in uttermost crisis and struggle; enmeshed wholly in plots, corruptibilities; neck-gins and baited fall-traps of Pitt enuemi du genre humain. Camille's First Number begins with " O Pitt!"—his last is dated 15 Pluviose, Year 2, 3d February, 1794; and ends with these words of Montezuma's, "Les dieux ont soif (The gods are athirst)."

1737. Be this as it may, the Hébertists lie in Prison only some nine days. On the 24th of March, therefore, the Revolution Tumbrils carry through that Life-tumult a new cargo: Hébert, Vincent, Momoro, Ronsin, Nineteen of them in all, with whom, curious enough, sits Clootz Speaker of Mankind. They have been massed swiftly into a lump, this miscellany of Nondescripts; and travel now their last road. No help. They too must "look through the little window;" they too "must sneeze into the sack," éternuer dans le sac: as they have done to others, so is it done to them. Sainte-Guillotine, meseems, is worse than the old Saints of Superstition; a man-devouring Saint? Clootz, still with an air of polished sarcasm, endeavors to jest, to offer cheering "arguments of Materialism :" he requested to be executed last, " in order to establish certain principles,"—which hitherto, I think, Philosoplfy has got no good of. General Ronsin too, he still looks forth with some air of defiance, eye of command: the rest are sunk in a stony paleness of despair. Momoro, poor Bibliopolist, no Agrarian Law yet realized, they might as well have hanged thee at Evreux, twenty months ago, when Girondin Buzot hindered them. Hébert Père Duchesne shall never in this world rise in sacred right of insurrection; he sits there low enough, head sunk on breast; Red Night-caps shouting round him, in frighttul parody of his Newspaper Articles, "Grand choler of the Père Duchesne!" Thus perish they : the sack receives all their heads. Through some section of History, Nineteen specter-chimeras shall flit, squeaking and gibbering; till Oblivion swallow them.

1738. In the course of a week, the Revolutionary Army itself is disbanded ; the General having become spectral. This Faction of Rabids, therefore, is also purged from the Republican soil; here also the baited fall-traps of that Pitt have been wrenched up harmless; and anew there is joy over a Plot Discovered. The Revolution, then, is verily devouring its own children ? All Anarchy, by the nature of it, is not only destructive but self-destructive.

CHAPTER II.
DANTON, NO WEAKNESS.

1739. Danton meanwhile has been pressingly sent for from Arcis : he must return instantly, cried Camille, cried Phélippeaux and Friends, who scented danger in the wind. Danger enough! A Danton, a Robespierre, chief products of a victorious Revolution, are now arrived in immediate front of one another; must ascertain how they will live together, rule together. One conceives easily the deep mutual incompatibility that divided these two: with what terror of feminine hatred the poor sea-green Formula looked at the monstrous colossal Reality, and grew greener to behold him ;—the Reality, again struggling to think no ill of a chief-product of the Revolution; yet feeling at bottom that such chief-product was little other than a chief wind-bag, blown large by Popular air ; not a man, with the heart of a man, but a poor spasmodic incorruptible pedant, with a logic-formula instead of heart; of Jesuit or Methodist-Parson nature; full of sincere-cant, incorruptibility, of virulence, poltroonery ; barren as the east-wind! Two such chief-products are too much for one Revolution.

1740. Friends, trembling at the results of a quarrel on their part, brought them to meet. " It is right," said Danton, swallowing much indignation, " to repress the Royalists: but we should not strike except where it is useful to the Republic; we should not confound the innocent and the guilty."—"And who told you," replied Robespierre with a poisonous look, " that one innocent person had perished ?"— " Quoi," said Danton, turning round to Friend Pâris self-named Fabricius, juryman in the Revolutionary Tribunal: "Quoi, not one innocent? What sayest thou of it, Fabricius?"*—Friends, Westermann, this Pâris and others urged him to show himself, to ascend the Tribune and act. The man Danton was not prone to show himself; to act, or uproar for his own safety. A man of careless, large, hoping nature ; a large nature that could rest: he would sit whole hours, they say, hearing Camille talk, and liked

* "Biographie des Ministres," § Danton.

nothing so well. Friends urged him to fly; his Wife urged him: "Whither fly?" answered he: "If freed France cast me out, there are only dungeons for me elsewhere. One carries not his country with him at the sole of his shoe!" The man Danton sat still. Not even the arrestment of Friend Hérault, a member of Salut, yet arrested by Salut, can rouse Danton.—On the night of the 30th of March Juryman Pâris came rushing in; haste looking through his eyes: A clerk of the Salut Committee had told him Danton's warrant was made out, he is to be arrested this very night! Entreaties there are and trepidation, of poor Wife, of Pâris and Friends: Danton sat silent for a while; then answered, 'Ils n'oseraient (They dare not);" and would take no measures. Murmuring "They dare not," he goes to sleep as usual.

1741. And yet, on the morrow morning, strange rumor spreads over Paris City: Danton, Camille, Phélippeaux, Lacroix have been arrested over-night! It is verily so: the corridors of the Luxembourg were all crowded, Prisoners crowding forth to see this giant of the Revolution enter among them. "Messieurs," said Danton politely, "I hoped soon to have got you all out of this: but here I am myself; and one sees not where it will end."—Rumor may spread over Paris: the Convention clusters itself into groups: wide-eyed, whispering "Danton arrested!" Who, then, is safe? Legendre, mounting the Tribune, utters at his own peril, a feeble word for him; moving that he be heard at that Bar before indictment; but Robespierre frowns him down: "Did you hear Chabot or Bazire? Would you have two weights and measures?" Legendre cowers low: Danton, like the others, must take his doom.

1742. Danton's Prison-thoughts were curious to have; but are not given in any quantity: indeed few such remarkable men have been left so obscure to us as this Titan of the Revolution. He was heard to ejaculate: "This time twelvemonth, I was moving the creation of that same Revolutionary Tribunal. I crave pardon for it of God and man They are all Brothers Cain: Brissot would have had me guillotined as Robespierre now will. I leave the whole business in a frightful welter (gâchis épouvantable); not one of them understands anything of government. Robespierre will follow me; I drag down Robespierre. O, it were better to be a poor fisherman than to meddle with governing of men."—Camille's young beautiful Wife, who had made him rich not in money alone, hovers round the Luxembourg, like a disembodied spirit, day and night. Camille's stolen letters to her still exist; stained with the mark of his tears.' " I carry my head like a Saint-Sacrament?" so Saint-Just was heard to mutter: "perhaps he will carry his like a Saint-Denis."

1743. Unhappy Danton, thou still unhappier light Camille, once light Procureur de la Lanterne, ye also have arrived, then, at the Bourn of Creation, where, like Ulysses Polytlas at the limit and utmost Gades of his voyage, gazing into that dim Waste beyond Creation, a man does see the Shade of his Mother, pale, ineffectual:—and days when his Mother nursed and wrapped him are all-too sternly contrasted with this day! Danton, Camille, Hérault, Westermann, and the others, very strangely massed up with Bazires, Swindler Chabots, Fabre d'Eglantines, Bankers Freys, a most motley Batch, "Fournée" as such things will be called, stand ranked at the Bar of Tinville. It is the 2d of April, 1794. Danton has had but three days to lie in Prison; for the time presses.

1744. What is your name? place of abode? and the like, Fouquier asks; according to formality.

* "Aperçu sur Camille Desmoulins" (in "Vieux Cordelier," Paris, 1825), pp. 1-29.

"My name is Danton," answers he; "a name tolerably known in the Revolution; my abode will soon be Annihilation (dans le Neant); but I shall live in the Pantheon of History." A man will endeavor to say something forcible, be it by nature or not! Herault mentions epigrammatically that he "sat in this Hall, and was detested of Parlementeers." Camille makes answer, "My age is that of the bon Sansculotte Jesus; an age fatal to Revolutionists." O Camille, Camille! And yet in that Divine Transaction, let us say, there did lie, among other things, the fatalest Reproof ever uttered here below to Worldy Right-honorableness; "the highest fact," so devout Novalis calls it, "in the Rights of Man." Camille's real age, it would seem, is thirty-four. Danton is one year older.

1745. Some five months ago, the Trial of the Twenty-two Girondins was the greatest that Fouquier had then done. But here is a still greater to do; a thing which tasks the whole faculty of Fouquier; which makes the very heart of him waver. For it is the voice of Danton that reverberates now from these domes; in passionate words, piercing with their wild sincerity, winged with wrath. Your best Witnesses he shivers into ruin at one stroke. He demands that the Committee-men themselves come as Witnesses, as Accusers; he "will cover them with ignominy." He raises his huge stature, he shakes his huge black head, fire flashes from the eyes of him,—piercing to all Republican hearts: so that the very Galleries, though we filled them by ticket, murmur sympathy; and are like to burst down and raise the People, and deliver him! He complains loudly that he is classed with Chabots, with swindling Stock-jobbers; that his Indictment is a list of platitudes and horrors. "Danton hidden on the 10th of August?" reverberates he, with the roar of a lion in the toils: "where are the men that had to press Danton to show himself, that day? Where are these high-gifted souls of whom he borrowed energy? Let them appear, these Accusers of mine: I have all the clearness of my self-possession when I demand them. I will unmask the three shallow scoundrels " (les trois plats coquins), Saint-Just, Couthon, Lebas, "who fawn on Robespierre, and lead him toward his destruction. Let them produce themselves here; I will plunge them into Nothingness, out of which they ought never to have risen." The agitated President agitates his bell; enjoins calmness, in a vehement manner: "What is it to thee how I defend myself?" cries the other: " the right of dooming me is thine always. The voice of a man speaking for his honor and his life may well drown the jingling of thy bell!" Thus Danton, higher and higher; till the lion-voice of him "dies away in his throat:" speech will not utter what is in that man. The Galleries murmur ominously; the first day's Session is over.

1746. O Tinville, President Herman, what will ye do? They have two days more of it, by strictest Revolutionary Law. The Galleries already murmur. If this Danton were to burst your mesh-work!— Very curious indeed to consider. It turns on a hair: and what a hoity-toity were there, Justice and Culprit changing places; and the whole History of France running changed! For in France there is this Danton only that could still try to govern France. He only, the wild amorphous Titan:—and perhaps that other olive-complexioned individual, the Artillery-Officer at Toulon, whom we left pushing his fortune in the South!

1747. On the evening of the second day, matters looking not better but worse and worse, Fouquier and Herman, distraction in their aspect, rush over to Salut Public. What is to be done? Salut Public rapidly concocts a new Decree; whereby if men "insult Justice," they may be "thrown out of the Debates." For indeed, withal, is there not "a Plot in the Luxembourg Prison?" Ci-devant General Dillon, and others of the Suspect, plotting with Camille's Wife to distribute assignats: to force the Prisons, overset the Republic? Citizen Laflotte himself Suspect but desiring enfranchisement, has reported said Plot for us:—a report that may bear fruit! Enough, on the morrow morning, an obedient Convention passes this Decree. Salut rushes off with it to the aid of Tinville, reduced now almost to extremities. And so, Hors de Débats (Out of the Debates), ye insolents! Policemen, do your duty! In such manner, with a dead-lift effort, Salut, Tinville, Herman, Leroi Dix-Août, and all staunch jurymen setting heart and shoulder to it, the Jury becomes "sufficiently instructed;" Sentence is passed, is sent by an Official, and torn and trampled on; *Death this day.* It is the 5th of April, 1794. Camille's poor Wife may cease hovering about this Prison. Nay let her kiss her poor children; and prepare to enter it, and to follow!—

1748. Danton carried a high look in the Death-cart. Not so Camille: it is but one week, and all is so topsy-turvied; angel Wife left weeping; love, riches, revolutionary fame, left all at the Prison-gate; carnivorous Rabble now howling round. Palpable, and yet incredible; like a madman's dream! Camille struggles and writhes; his shoulders shuffle the loose coat off them, which hangs knotted, the hands tied: "Calm, my friend," said Danton: "heed not that vile canaille (laissez là cette vile canaille)." At the foot of the Scaffold, Danton was heard to ejaculate: "O my Wife, my well-beloved, I shall never see thee more, then!"—but, interrupting himself: "Danton, no weakness!" He said to Hérault-Séchelles stepping forward to embrace him : "Our heads will meet *there*," in the Headsman's sack. His last words were to Samson the Headsman himself: "Thou wilt show my head to the people; it is worth showing."

1849. So passes, like a gigantic mass of valor, ostentation, fury, affection and wild revolutionary force and manhood, this Danton, to his unknown home. He was of Arcis-sur-Aube; born of "good farmer-people" there. He had many sins; but one worst sin he had not, that of Cant. No hollow Formalist, deceptive and self-deceptive, *ghastly* to the natural sense, was this; but a very Man: with all his dross he was a Man; fiery-real, from the great fire-bosom of Nature herself. He saved France from Brunswick; he walked straight his own wild road, whither it led him. He may live for some generations in the memory of men.

CHAPTER III.
THE TUMBRILS.

1750. Next week, it is still but the 10th of April, there comes a new Nineteen; Chaumette, Gobel, Hébert's Widow, the Widow of Camille; these also roll their fated journey; black Death devours them. Mean Hébert's Widow was weeping, Camille's Widow tried to speak comfort to her. O ye kind Heavens, azure, beautiful, eternal behind your tempests and Time-clouds, is there not pity in store for all! Gobel, it seems, was repentant; he begged absolution of a Priest; died as a Gobel best could. For Anaxagoras Chaumette, the sleek head now stripped of its bonnet rouge, what hope is there? Unless Death *were* "an eternal sleep?" Wretched Anaxagoras, God shall judge thee, not I.

1751. Hébert, therefore, is gone, and the Hébertists; they that robbed Churches, and adored blue Reason in red night-cap. Great Danton, and the Dantonists; they also are gone. Down to the catacombs: they are become silent men! Let no Paris Municipality, no Sect or Party of this hue or that, resist the will of Robespierre and Salut. Mayor Puche, not prompt enough in denouncing these Pitt Plots, may congratulate about them now. Never so heartily; it skills not! His course likewise is to the Luxembourg. We appoint one Fleuriot-Lescot Interim-Mayor in his stead: an "architect from Belgium," they say, this Fleuriot; he is a man one can depend on. Our new Agent-National is Payan, lately Juryman; whose cynosure also is Robespierre.

1752. Thus then, we perceive, this confusedly electric Erebus-cloud of Revolutionary Government has altered its shape somewhat. Two masses, or wings, belonging to it; an over-electric mass of Cordelier Rabids, and an under-electric of Dantonist Moderates and Clemency-men,—these two masses, shooting bolts at one another, so to speak, have annihilated one another. For the Erebus-cloud, as we often remark, is of suicidal nature; and in jagged irregularity, darts its lightning withal into itself. But now these two discrepant masses being mutually annihilated, it is as if the Erebus-cloud had got to internal composure; and did only pour its hell-fire lightning on the World that lay under it. In plain words, Terror of the Guillotine was never terrible till now. Systole, diastole, swift and ever swifter goes the Axe of Samson. Indictments cease by degrees to have so much as plausibility: Fouquier chooses from the Twelve Houses of Arrest what he calls Batches, "Fournées," a score or more at a time; his Jurymen are charged to make feu de file, file-firing till the ground be clear. Citizen Laflotte's report of Plot in the Luxembourg is verily bearing fruit! If no speakable charge exist against a man, or Batch of men, Fouquier has always this: a Plot in the Prison. Swift and ever swifter goes Samson; up, finally, to three-score and more at a Batch. It is the high-day of Death: none but the Dead return not.

1753. O dusky D'Espréménil, what a day is this the 22d of April, thy last day! The Palais Hall here is the same stone Hall, where thou, five years ago, stoodest perorating, amid endless pathos of rebellious Parlement, in the gray of the morning: bound to march with D'Agoust to the Isles of Hières. The stones are the same stones: but the rest, Men, Rebellion, Pathos, Peroration, see, it has all fled, like a gibbering troop of ghosts, like the phantasms of a dying brain. With D'Espréménil, in the same line of Tumbrils, goes the unformulest medley. Chapelier goes, ci-devant popular President of the Constituent; whom the Menads and Maillard met in his carriage on the Versailles Road. Thouret likewise, ci-devant President, father of Constitutional Law-acts; he whom we heard saying long since, with a loud voice, "The Constituent Assembly has fulfilled its mission!" And the noble old Malesherbes, who defended Louis and could not speak, like a gray old rock dissolving into sodden water: he journeys here now, with his kindred, daughters, sons, and grandsons, his Lamoignons, Châteaubriands; silent, toward Death.—One young Châteaubriand alone is wandering amid the Natchez, by the roar of Niagara Falls, the moan of endless forests: Welcome thou great Nature, savage, but not false, not unkind, unmotherly; no Formula thou, or rabid jangle of Hypothesis. Parliamentary Eloquence, Constitution-building and the Guillotine; speak thou to me, O Mother, and sing my sick heart thy mystic everlasting lullaby-song, and let all the rest be far!—

1754. Another row of Tumbrils we must notice: that which holds Elizabeth, the Sister of Louis. Her Trial was like the rest; for Plots, for Plots. She was among the kindliest, most innocent of women. There sat with her, amid four-and-twenty others, a once timorous Marchioness de Crussol; courageous now; expressing toward her the liveliest loyalty. At the foot of the Scaffold, Elizabeth with tears in her eyes thanked this Marchioness; said she was grieved she could not reward her. "Ah, Madame, would your Royal Highness deign to embrace me, my wishes were complete "—"Right willingly, Marquise de Crussol, and with my whole heart."* Thus they : at the foot of the Scaffold. The Royal Family is now reduced to two a girl and a little boy. The boy, once named Dauphin, was taken from his Mother while she yet lived; and given to one Simon, by trade a Cordwainer on service then about the Temple-prison, to bring him up in principles of Sansculottism. Simon taught him to drink, to swear, to sing the carmagnole. Simon is now gone to the Municipality : and the poor boy, hidden in a tower of the Temple from which in his fright and bewilderment and early decrepitude he wishes not to stir out, lies perishing, "his shirt not changed for six months ;" amid squalor and darkness, lamentably,† —so as none but poor Factory Children and the like are wont to be lamented, and *not* be lamented !

1755. The Spring sends its green leaves and bright weather, bright May, brighter than ever: Death pauses not. Lavoisier, famed Chemist, shall die and not live ; Chemist Lavoisier was Farmer-General Lavoisier too, and now " all the Farmers-General are arrested ;" all, and shall give an account of their moneys and incomings; and die for " putting water in the tobacco " they sold. Lavoisier begged a fortnight more of life, to finish some experiments: but " the Republic does not need such ;" the axe must do its work. Cynic Chamfort, reading these inscriptions of *Brotherhood or Death*, says, " It is a Brotherhood of Cain ;" arrested, then liberated ; then about to be arrested again, this Chamfort cuts and slashes himself with frantic uncertain hand ; gains, not without difficulty, the refuge of death. Condorcet has lurked deep, these many months ; Argus-eyes watching and searching for him. His concealment is become dangerous to others and himself ;· he has to fly again, to skulk, round Paris, in thickets and stone-quarries. And so at the* Village of Clamars, one bleared May morning, there enters a Figure, ragged, rough-bearded, hunger-stricken ; asks breakfast in the tavern there. Suspect by the look of him ! "Servant out of place, savest thou ? " Committee-President of Forty-Sous finds a Latin Horace on him : " Art not thou one of those Ci-devants that were wont to keep servants? *Suspect !*" He is haled forthwith, breakfast unfinished, toward Bourg-la-Reine, on foot he faints with exhaustion : is set on a peasant's horse ; is flung into his damp prison-cell : on the morrow, recollecting him, you enter ; Condorcet lies dead on the floor. They die fast, and disappear : the Notabilities of France disappear, one after one, like lights in a Theater, which you are snuffing out.

1756. Under which circumstances, is it not singular, and almost touching, to see ParisCity drawn out, in the meek May nights, in civic ceremony, which they call " Souper Fraternel," Brotherly Supper? Spontaneous, or partially spontaneous, in the twelfth, thirteenth fourteenth nights of this May month, it is seen. Along the Rue Saint-Honoré, and main Streets and Spaces, each Citoyen brings forth what of supper the stingy *Maximum* has yielded him, to the open air; joins it to his neighbor's supper; and with common table, cheerful light burning fre-

quent, and what due modicum of cut-glass and other garnish and relish is convenient, they eat frugally together, under the kind stars.* See it, O Night! With cheerfully pledged wine-cup, hob-nobbing to the Reign of Liberty, Equality, Brotherhood, with their wives in best ribbons, with their little ones romping round, the Citoyens, in frugal Love-feast, sit there. Night in her wide empire sees nothing similar. O my brothers, why is the reign of Brotherhood *not* come ! It is come, it shall have come, say the Citoyens frugally hob-nobbing.—Ah me ! these everlasting stars, do they not look down " like glistening eyes, bright with immortal pity, over the lot of man ! "—

1757. One lamentable thing, however, is, that individuals will attempt assassination—of Representatives of the People. Representative Collot. Member even of Salut, returning home, "about one in the morning," probably touched with liquor, as he is apt to be, meets on the stairs the cry "Scélérat !" and also the snap of a pistol : which latter flashes in the pan ; disclosing to him, momentarily, a pair of truculent saucer-eyes, swart grim-clenched countenance; recognizable as that of our little fellow-lodger, Cityoyen Amiral, formerly "a clerk in the Lotteries." Collot shouts *Murder*, with lungs fit to awaken all the Rue Favart. Amiral snaps a second time ; a second time flashes in the pan ; then darts up into his apartment and, after there firing, still with inadequate effect, one musket at himself and another at his captor, is clutched and locked in Prison.† An indignant little man this Amiral, of Southern temper and complexion, of " considerable muscular force." He denies not that he meant to " purge France of a Tyrant ; " nay avows that he had an eye to the Incorruptible himself, but took Collot as more convenient !

1758. Rumor enough hereupon : heaven-high congratulation of Collot, fraternal embracing, at the Jacobins and elsewhere. And yet, it would seem, the assassin mood proves catching. Two days more, it is still but the 23d of May, and toward nine in the evening, Cécile Rénault, Paper-dealer's daughter, a young woman of soft blooming look, presents herself at the Cabinet-maker's in the Rue Saint-Honoré, desires to see Robespierre. Robespierre cannot be seen : she grumbles irreverently. They lay hold of her. She has left a basket in a shop hard by ; in the basket are female change of raiment and two knives! Poor Cécile : examined by Committee, declares she " wanted to see what a tyrant was like:" the change of raiment was " for my own use in the place I am surely going to."—" What place ?"—" Prison ; and then the Guillotine, " answered she.—Such things come of Charlotte Corday ; in a people prone to imitation, and monomania ! Swart choleric men try Charlotte's feat, and their pistols miss fire ; soft blooming young women try it, and only half-resolute. leave their knives in a shop.

1759. O Pitt, and ye Faction of the Stranger, shall the Republic never have rest ; but he torn continually by baited springes, by wires of explosive spring-guns ? Swart Amiral, fair young Cécile, and all that knew them, and, many that did not know them, lie locked, waiting the scrutiny of Tinville.

CHAPTER IV.
MUMBO-JUMBO.

1760. But on the day they call Décadi. New-Sabbath, 20th Prairial, 8th June by old style, what thing is this going forward in the Jardin National, whilom Tuileries Garden?

* Montgaillard. iv. 200.
† Duchesse d'Angoulême. Captivité à la Tour du Tempre." pp· 37-71.
‡ "Tribunal Révolutionnaire" du 8 Mal, 1794 (Moniteur. No. 231).

* "Tableaux de la Révolution," § Soupers Fraternels; Mercier ii. 150.
† Riouffe, p. 73; "Deux Amis," xii. 298-302.

1761. All the world is there, in holiday clothes:* foul linen went out with the Hébertists; nay Robespierre, for one, would never countenance that; but went always elegant and frizzled, not without vanity even,—and had his room hung round with sea-green Portraits and Busts. In holiday clothes, we say, are the innumerable Citoyens and Citoyennes: the weather is of the brightest; cheerful expectation lights all countenances. Juryman Vilate gives breakfast to many a Deputy, in his official Apartment, in the Pavillon ci-devant of Flora; rejoices in the bright-looking multitudes, in the brightness of leafy June, in the auspicious Décadi or New-Sabbath. This day, if it please Heaven, we are to have, on improved Anti-Chaumette principles: a New Religion.

1762. Catholicism being burned out, and Reason-worship guillotined, was there not need of one? Incorruptible Robespierre, not unlike the Ancients, as Legislator of a free people, will now also be Priest and Prophet. He has donned his sky-blue coat, made for the occasion; white silk waistcoat broidered with silver, black silk breeches, white stockings, shoe-buckles of gold. He is President of the Convention; he has made the Convention *decree*, so they name it, décréter the "Existence of the Supreme Being," and likewise "ce principe consolateur of the Immortality of the Soul." These consolatory principles, the basis of rational Republican Religion, are getting decreed; and here, on the blessed Décadi, by help of Heaven and Painter David, is to be our first act of worship.

1763. See, accordingly, how after Decree passed, and what has been called "the scraggiest Prophetic Discourse ever uttered by man"—Mohammed Robespierre, in sky-blue coat and black breeches, frizzled and powdered to perfection, bearing in his hand a bouquet of flowers and wheat-ears, issues proudly from the Convention Hall; Convention following him, yet, as is remarked, with an interval. Amphitheater has been raised, or at least Monticule or Elevation; hideous Statues of Atheism, Anarchy and such like, thanks to Heaven and Painter David, strike abhorrence into the heart. Unluckily, however, our Monticule is too small. On the top of it not half of us can stand; wherefore there arises indecent shoving, nay treasonous irreverent growling. Peace, thou Bourdon de l'Oise; peace, or it may be worse for thee!

1764. The sea-green Pontiff takes a torch, Painter David handing it; mouths some other froth-rant of vocables which happily one cannot hear; strides resolutely forward, in sight of expectant France; sets his torch to Atheism and Company, which are but made of pasteboard steeped in turpentine. They burn up rapidly; and, from within, there rises "by machinery," an incombustible Statue of Wisdom, which, by ill hap, gets besmoked a little; but does stand there visible in as serene attitude as it can.

1765. And then? Why, then, there is other Processioning, scraggy Discoursing, and—this *is* our Feast of the Etre Suprême; our new Religion, better or worse, is come!—Look at it one moment, O Reader, not two. The shabbiest page of Human Annals: or is there, that thou wottest of, one shabbier? Mumbo-Jumbo of the African woods to me seems venerable beside this new Deity of Robespierre; for this is a *conscious* Mumbo-Jumbo, and *knows* that he is machinery. O sea-green Prophet, unhappiest of wind-bags blown nigh to bursting, what distracted Chimera among realities art thou growing to! This then, this common pitch link for artificial fireworks of turpentine and paste-board; *this* is the miraculous Aaron's Rod thou wilt stretch over a bag-ridden hell-ridden France, and bid her plagues

cease? Vanish, thou and it!—"Avec ton Etre Suprême," said Billaud, "tu commences membéter (With thy Etre Suprême thou beginnest to be a bore to me)."*

1766. Catherine Théot, on the other hand, "an ancient serving-maid seventy-nine years of age," inured to Prophecy and the Bastille from of old, sits in an upper room in the Rue de Contrescarpe, poring over the Book of Revelations, with an eye to Robespierre; finds that this astonishing thrice-potent Maximilien really is the Man spoken of by Prophets, who is to make the Earth young again. With her senile old Marchionesses, ci-devant honorable women among whom Old-Constituent Dom Gerle, with his addle head, cannot be wanting. They sit there, in the Rue de Contrescarpe; in mysterious adoration. Mumbo is Mumbo, and Robespierre is his prophet. A conspicuous man this Robespierre. He has his volunteer Body-guard of Tappe-durs, let us say Strike-sharps, fierce Patriots with feruled sticks; and Jacobins kissing the hem of his garment. He enjoys the admiration of many, the worship of some; and is well worth the wonder of one and all.

1767. The grand question and hope, however, is: Will not this Feast of the Tuileries Mumbo-Jumbo be a sign perhaps that the Guillotine is to abate? Far enough from that! Precisely on the second day after it, Couthon, one of the "three shallow scoundrels," gets himself lifted into the Tribune, produces a bundle of papers. Couthon proposes that, as Plots still abound, the Law of the Suspect shall have extension; and Arrestment new vigor and facility. Farther, that as in such case business is like to be heavy, our Revolutionary Tribunal too shall have extension; be divided, say, into Four Tribunals, each with its President, each with its Fouquier or Substitute of Fouquier, all laboring at once, and any remnant of shackle or dilatory formality be struck off; in this way it may perhaps still overtake the work. Such is Couthon's Decree of the 22d Prairial, famed in those times. At hearing of which Decree, the very Mountain gasped, awe-struck; and one Ruamps ventured to say that if it passed without adjournment and discussion, he, as one Representative, "would blow his brains out." Vain saying! The Incorruptible knit his brows; spoke a prophetic fateful word or two; the Law of Prairial is Law; Ruamps glad to leave his rash brains where they are. Death then, and always Death! Even so. Fouquier is enlarging his borders; making room for Batches of a Hundred and fifty at once;—getting a Guillotine set up of improved velocity, and to work under cover, in the apartment close by. So that Salut itself has to intervene, and forbid him. "Wilt thou demoralize the Guillotine," asks Collot, reproachfully, "démoraliser le supplice!"

1768. There is indeed danger of that; were not the Republican faith great, it were already done. See, for example, on the 17th of June, what a *Batch*, Fifty-four at once! Swart Amiral is here, he of the pistol that missed fire: young Cécile Rénault, with her father, family, entire kith and kin; the Widow of D'Espréménil; old M. de Sombreuil of the Invalides, with his Son,—poor old Sombreuil, seventy-three years old, his Daughter saved him in September, and it was but for *this*. Faction of the Stranger, fifty-four of them! In red shirts and smocks, as Assassins and Faction of the Stranger, they flit along there; red baleful Phantasmagoria, toward the land of Phantoms.

---

* Vilate. "Causes Secrétes de la Révolution du 9 Thermidor."

* See Vilate, "Causes Secrétes." (Vilate's Narrative is very curious; but is not to be taken as true without sifting; being at bottom, in spite of its title, not a *Narrative*, but a *Pleading*.)

1769. Meanwhile, will not the people of the Place de la Révolution, the inhabitants along the Rue Saint-Honoré, as these continual Tumbrils pass, begin to look gloomy? Republicans too have bowels. The Guillotine is shifted, then again shifted; finally set up at the remote extremity of the South-east:[*] Suburbs Saint-Antoine and Saint-Marceau, it is to be hoped, if they have bowels, have very tough ones.

CHAPTER V.

THE PRISONS.

1770. It is time now, however, to cast a glance into the Prisons. When Desmoulins moved for his Committee of Mercy, these Twelve Houses of Arrest held 5,000 persons. Continually arriving since then, there have now accumulated 12,000. They are Ci-devants, Royalists; in far greater part, they are Republicans, of various Girondin, Fayettish, Un-Jacobin color. Perhaps no human habitation or Prison ever equaled in squalor, in noisome horror, these Twelve Houses of Arrest. There exist records of personal experience in them, "Mémoires sur les Prisons;" one of the strangest Chapters in the Biography of Man.

1771. Very singular to look into it: how a kind of order rises up in all conditions of human existence; and wherever two or three are gathered together, there are formed modes of existing together, habitudes, observances, nay gracefulnesses, joys! Citoyen Coittant will explain fully, how our lean dinner, of herbs and carrion, was consumed not without politeness and place-aux-dames: how Seigneur and Shoe-black, Duchess and Doll-Tearsheet, flung pellmell into a heap, ranked themselves according to method: at what hour "the Citoyennes took to their needlework;" and we, yielding the chairs to them, endeavored to talk gallantly in a standing posture, or even to sing and harp more or less. Jealousies, enmities are not wanting; nor flirtations of an effective character.

1772. Alas, by degrees, even needlework must cease: Plot in the Prison rises, by Citoyen Laflotte and Preternatural Suspicion. Suspicious Municipality snatches from us all implements: all money and possession, of means or metal, is ruthlessly searched for, in pocket, in pillow and paillasse, and snatched away; red-capped Commissaries entering every cell. Indignation, temporary desperation, at robbery of its very thimble, fills the gentle heart. Old Nuns shriek shrill discord; demand to be killed forthwith. No help from shrieking! Better was that of the two shifty male Citizens, who, eager to preserve an implement or two, were it but a pipe-picker, or needle to darn hose with, determined to defend themselves: by tobacco. Swift then, as your fell Red Caps are heard in the Corridor rummaging and slamming, the two Citoyens light their pipes, and begin smoking. Thick darkness envelops them. The Red Night-caps, opening the cell, breathe but one mouthful; burst forth into chorus of barking and coughing, "Quoi, Messieurs," cry the two Citoyens, "you don't smoke? Is the pipe disagreeable? Est-ce que vous ne fumez pas?" But the Red Night-caps have fled with slight search: "Vous n'aimez pas la pipe?" cry the Citoyens, as their door slams-to again.[†] My poor brother Citoyens, O surely, in a reign of Brotherhood, you are not the two I would guillotine!

1773. Rigor grows, stiffens into horrid tyranny; Plot in the Prison getting ever rifer. This Plot in the Prison, as we said, is now the stereotype formula of Tinville: against whomsoever he knows no crime,

this is a ready-made crime. His Judgment-bar has become unspeakable; a recognized mockery; known only as the wicket one passes through, toward Death. His Indictments are drawn out in blank; you insert the Names after. He has his moutons, detestable traitor jackals, who report and bear witness; that they themselves may be allowed to live, —for a time. His Fournées, says the reproachful Collot, "shall in no case exceed three-score;" that is his maximum. Nightly come his Tumbrils to the Luxembourg, with the fatal Roll-call; list of the Fournée of to-morrow. Men rush toward the Grate; listen, if their name be in it? One deep-drawn breath, when the name is not in: we live still one day! And yet some score or scores of names were in. Quick these, they clasp their loved ones to their heart, one last time; with brief adieu, wet-eyed, or dry-eyed, they mount, and are away. This night to the Conciergerie; through the Palais misnamed of Justice, to the Guillotine to-morrow.

1774. Recklessness, defiant levity, the Stoicism if not of strength yet of weakness, has possessed all hearts. Weak women and Ci-devants, their locks not yet made into blond perukes, their skins not yet tanned into breeches, are accustomed to "act the Guillotine" by way of pastime. In fantastic mummery, with towel-turbans, blanket-ermine, a mock Sanhedrim of Judges sits, a mock Tinville pleads; a culprit is doomed, is guillotined by the oversetting of two chairs. Sometimes we carry it farther: Tinville himself, in his turn, is doomed, and not to the Guillotine alone. With blackened face, hirsute, horned, a shaggy Satan snatches him not unshrieking; shows him, with outstretched arm and voice, the fire that is not quenched, the worm that dies not; the monotony of Hell-pain, and the What hour? answered by, It is Eternity.[*]

1775. And still the Prisons fill fuller, and still the Guillotine goes faster. On all high-roads march flights of Prisoners, wending toward Paris. Not Cidevants now; they, the noisy of them, are mown down; it is Republicans now. Chained two and two they march; in exasperated moments singing their "Marseillaise." A hundred and thirty-two men of Nantes, for instance, march toward Paris, in these same days: Republicans, or say even Jacobins to the marrow of the bone; but Jacobins who had not approved Noyading.[†] Vive la République rises from them in all streets of towns: they rest by night in unutterable noisome dens, crowded to choking; one or two dead on the morrow. They are wayworn, weary of heart; can only shout: Live the Republic; we, as under horrid enchantment, dying in this way for it!

1776. Some 400 Priests, of whom also there is record, ride at anchor "in the roads of the Isle of Aix," long months; looking out on misery, vacuity, waste Sands of Oleron and the ever-moaning brine. Ragged, sordid, hungry; wasted to shadows: eating their unclean ration on deck, circularly, in parties of a dozen, with finger and thumb; beating their scandalous clothes between two stones; closed in horrible miasmata, closed under hatches, seventy of them in a berth, through night; so that the "aged Priest is found lying dead in the morning, in the attitude of prayer!"[‡] How long, O Lord!

Not forever; no. All Anarchy, all Evil, Injustice, is, by the nature of it, dragon's-teeth; suicidal, and cannot endure.

---

* Montgaillard, iv. 237.
† "Maison d'Arrêt de Port-Libre," par Coittant, etc. ("Mémoires sur les Prisons," ii.).

* Montgaillard, iv 218; Riouffe, p. 273.
† "Voyage de Cent Trente-deux Nantais" ("Prisons," ii. 288–335).
‡ Relation de ce qu'ont souffert pour la Religion les Prêtres déportés en 1794, dans la rade de l'Île d'Aix.' (Ib., ii. 387–485).

CHAPTER VI.

TO FINISH THE TERROR.

1777. It is very remarkable, indeed, that since the Etre-Suprême Feast, and the sublime continued harangues on it, which Billaud feared would become a bore to him, Robespierre has gone little to Committee; but held himself apart, as if in a kind of pet. Nay they have made a Report on that old Catherine Théot, and her Regenerative Man spoken of by the Prophets; not in the best spirit. This Théot mystery they affect to regard as a Plot; but have evidently introduced a vein of satire, of irreverent banter, not against the Spinster alone, but obliquely against her Regenerative Man! Barrère's light pen was perhaps at the bottom of it: read through the solemn snuffling organs of old Vadier of the Sûreté Générale, the Théot Report had its effect; wrinkling the general Republican visage into an iron grin. Ought these things to be?

1778. We note farther, that among the Prisoners in the Twelve Houses of Arrest, there is one whom we have seen before Senhora Fontenai, born Cabarus, the fair Proserpine whom Representative Tallien Pluto-like did gather at Bourdeaux, not without effect on himself! Tallien is home, by recall, long since, from Bourdeaux; and in the most alarming position. Vain that he sounded, louder even than ever, the note of Jacobinism, to hide past shortcomings: the Jacobins purged him out; two times has Robespierre growled at him words of omen from the Convention Tribune. And now his fair Cabarus, hit by denunciation, lies Arrested, Suspect, in spite of all he could do!—Shut in horrid pinfold of death, the Senhora smuggles out to her red-gloomy Tallien the most pressing entreaties and conjurings: Save me; save thyself. Scest thou not thy own head is doomed; thou with a too fiery audacity: a Dantonist withal; against whom lie grudges? Are ye not all doomed, as in the Polyphemus Cavern: the fawningest slave of you will be but eaten last!—Tallien feels with a shudder that it is true. Tallien has had words of omen, Bourdon has had words, Fréron is hated and Barras: each man "feels his head if it yet stick on his shoulders."

1779. Meanwhile Robespierre, we still observe, goes little to Convention, not at all to Committee; speaks nothing except to his Jacobin House of Lords, amid his body-guard of Tappe-durs. These "forty-days," for we are now far in July, he has not showed face in Committee: could only work there by his three shallow scoundrels, and the terror there was of him. The Incorruptible himself sits apart; or if seen stalking in solitary places in the fields, with an intensely meditative air; some say, "with eyes red-spotted,"[*] fruit of extreme bile: the lamentablest sea-green Chimera that walks the Earth that July! O hapless Chimera,—for thou too hadst a life, and heart of flesh,—what is this that the stern gods, seeming to smile all the way, have led and let thee to! Art not thou he, who, few years ago, was a young Advocate of promise; and gave up the Arras Judgeship rather than sentence one man to die?—

1780 What his thoughts might be? His plans for finishing the Terror? One knows not. Dim vestiges there flit of Agrarian Law; a victorious Sansculottism become Landed Proprietor; old Soldiers sitting in National Mansions, in Hospital Palaces of Chambord and Chantilly; peace bought by victory; breaches healed by Feast of Etre Suprême;—and so, through seas of blood, to Equality, Frugality, worksome Blessedness, Fraternity, and Republic of the virtues. Blessed shore, of such a sea of Aristocrat blood: but how to land on it? Through one last

[* "Deux Amis." 347-373.]

wave: blood of corrupt Sansculottists; traitorous or semi-traitorous Conventionals, rebellious Talliens, Billauds, to whom with my Etre Suprême I have become a bore, with my Apocalyptic Old Woman a laughing-stock!—So stalks he, this poor Robespierre, like a sea-green ghost, through the blooming July. Vestiges of schemes flit dim. But *what* his schemes or his thoughts were will never be known to man.

1781. New Catacombs, some say, are digging for a huge simultaneous butchery. Convention to be butchered, down to the right pitch, by General Henriot and Company: Jacobin House of Lords made dominant; and Robespierre Dictator.[*] There is actually, or else there is not actually, a List made out; which the Hair-dresser has got eye on, as he frizzled the Incorruptible locks. Each man asks himself, Is it I?

1782. Nay, as Tradition and rumor of Anecdote still convey it, there was a remarkable bachelor's dinner, one hot day, at Barrère's. For doubt not, O Reader, this Barrère and others of them gave dinners; had "country-house at Clichy," with elegant enough sumptuosities, and pleasures high-rouged.[†] But at this dinner we speak of, the day being so hot, it is said. the guests all stript their coats, and left them in the drawing-room, from oh udinner-table Carnot glided out, driven by a necessity: needing of all things paper; groped in Robespierre's pocket; found a list of Forty, his own name among them;—and tarried not at the wine-cup that day!—Ye must bestir yourselves, O Friends: ye dull Frogs of the Marsh, mute ever since Girondism sank under, even you now must croak or die! Councils are held, with word and beck; nocturnal, mysterious as death. Does not a feline Maximilien stalk there; voiceless as yet; his green eyes red-spotted; back bent, and hair up? Rash Tallien, with his rash temper and audacity of tongue; he shall *bell the cat.* Fix a day; and be it soon, lest never!

1783. Lo, before the fixed day, on the day which they call 8th of Thermidor, 26th July, 1794, Robespierre himself reappears in Convention; mounts to the Tribune! The biliary face seems clouded with new gloom: judge whether your Talliens, Bourdons, listened with interest. It is a voice bodeful of death or of life. Long-winded, unmelodious as the screech-owl's sounds that prophetic voice: Degenerate condition of Republican spirit; corrupt Moderatism; Sûreté, Salut Committees themselves infected; backsliding on this hand and on that; I, Maximilien, alone left incorruptible, ready to die at a moment's warning. For all which what remedy is there? The Guillotine; new vigor to the all-healing Guillotine; death to traitors of every hue! So sings the prophetic voice; into its Convention sounding-board. The old song this: but to-day, O Heavens, has the sounding-board ceased to act? There is not resonance in this Convention: there is, so to speak, a gasp of silence; nay a certain grating of one knows not what!—Lecointre, our old Draper of Versailles, in these questionable circumstances, sees nothing he can do so safe as rise, "insidiously" or not insidiously, and move, according to established wont, that the Robespierre Speech be "Printed and sent to the Departments." Hark: gratings, even of dissonance! Honorable Members hint dissonance; Committee-Members, inculpated in the Speech, utter dissonance, demand "delay in printing." Ever higher rises the note of dissonance; inquiry is even made by Editor Fréron: "What has become of the Liberty of Opinions in this Convention?" The Order to print and transmit, which had got passed, is rescinded. Robespierre, greener than ever before, has to retire, foiled; discerning that it is mutiny, that evil is nigh!

[* "Deux Amis." xii. 350-358.]
[† See Vilate.]

1784. Mutiny is a thing of the fatalest nature in all enterprises whatsoever: a thing so incalculable, swift-frightful: not to be dealt with in *fright*. But mutiny in a Robespierre Convention, above all,—it is like fire seen sputtering in the ship's powder-room! One death-defiant plunge at it, this moment, and you may still tread it out: hesitate till next moment, —ship and ship's captain, crew and cargo are shivered far; the ship's voyage has suddenly ended between sea and sky. If Robespierre can, to-night, produce his Heuriot and Company, and get his work done by them, be and Sansculottism may still subsist some time; if not, probably not. Oliver Cromwell, when that Agitator Sergeant stept forth from the ranks, with plea of grievances, and began gesticulating and demonstrating, as the mouth-piece of Thousands expectant there,—discerned, with those truculent eyes of his, how the matter lay; plucked a pistol from his holsters; blew Agitator and Agitation instantly out. Noll was a man fit for such things.

1785. Robespierre, for his part, glides over at evening to his Jacobin House of Lords; unfolds there, instead of some adequate resolution, his woes, his uncommon virtues, incorruptibilities; then, secondly, his rejected screech-owl Oration;—reads this latter over again; and declares that he is ready to die at a moment's warning. Thou shalt not die! shouts Jacobinism from its thousand throats. "Robespierre, I will drink the hemlock with thee," cries Painter David, "Je boirai la ciguë avec toi;"—a thing not essential to *do*, but which, in the fire of the moment, can be said.

1786. Our Jacobin sounding-board, therefore, does act! Applauses heaven-high cover the rejected Oration; fire-eyed fury lights all Jacobin features: Insurrection a sacred duty; the Convention to be purged; Sovereign People under Henriot and Municipality; we will make a new June-Second of it: To your tents, O Israel! In this key pipes Jacobinism; in sheer tumult of revolt. Let Tallien and all Opposition men make off. Collot d'Herbois, though of the supreme Salut, and so lately near shot, is elbowed, bullied; is glad to escape alive. Entering Committee-room of Salut, all dishevelled, he finds sleek somber Saint-Just there among the rest; who in his sleek way asks, "What is passing at the Jacobins?"—"What is passing?" repeats Collot, in the unhistrionic Cambyses vein: "What is passing? Nothing but revolt and horrors are passing. Ye want our lives; ye shall not have them." Saint-Just stutters at such Cambyses oratory; takes his hat to withdraw. That *Report* he had been speaking of, Report on Republican Things in General we may say, which is to be read in Convention on the morrow, he cannot show it them, at this moment: a friend has it; he, Saint-Just, will get it, and send it, were he once home. Once home, he sends not it, but an answer that he will not send it; that they will hear it from the Tribune to-morrow.

1787. Let every man, therefore, according to a well-known good-advice, "pray to Heaven, and keep his powder dry!" Paris, on the morrow, will see a thing. Swift scouts fly dim or invisible, all night, from Sûreté and Salut; from conclave to conclave; from Mother Society to Town-hall. Sleep, can it fall on the eyes of Talliens, Frérons, Collots? Puissant Henriot, Mayor Fleuriot, Judge Coffinhal, Procureur Payan, Robespierre and all the Jacobins are getting ready.

CHAPTER VII.
GO DOWN TO.

1788. Tallien's eyes beamed bright, on the morrow, 9th of Thermidor, "about nine o'clock," to see that the Convention had actually met. Paris is in rumor: but at least we are met, in Legal Convention here; we have not been snatched seriatim; treated with a *Pride's Purge* at the door. "Allons, brave men of the Plain," late Frogs of the Marsh! cried Tallien with a squeeze of the hand, as he passed in; Saint-Just's sonorous voice being now audible from the Tribune, and the game of games begun.

1789. Saint-Just is verily reading that Report of his green Vengeance, in the shape of Robespierre, watching nigh. Behold, however, Saint-Just has read but few sentences, when interruption rises rapid crescendo; when Tallien starts to his feet, and Billaud, and this man starts and that,—and Tallien, a second time, with his: "Citoyens, at the Jacobins last night, I trembled for the Republic. I said to myself, if the Convention dare not strike the Tyrant then I myself dare, and with this I will do it, if need be," said he, whisking out a clear-gleaming Dagger, and brandishing it there; the Steel of Brutus, as we call it. Whereat we all bellow, and brandish, impetuous acclaim. "Tyranny! Dictatorship! Triumvirate!" And the Salut Committee-men accuse, and all men accuse, and uproar, and impetuously acclaim. And Saint-Just is standing motionless, pale of face; Couthon ejaculating, "Triumvir?" with a look at his paralytic legs. And Robespierre is struggling to speak, but President Thuriot is jingling the bell against him, the Hall is sounding against him like an Æolus-Hall; and Robespierre is mounting the Tribune-steps and descending again; going and coming, like to choke with rage, terror, desperation: —and mutiny is the order of the day![*]

1790. O President Thuriot, thou that wert Elector Thuriot, and from the Bastille battlements sawest Saint-Antoine rising like the Ocean-tide, and hast seen much since, sawest thou ever the like of this? Jingle of bell, which thou jinglest against Robespierre, is hardly audible amid the Bedlam storm; and men rage for life. "President of Assassins," shrieks Robespierre, "I demand speech of thee for the last time!" It cannot be had. "To you, O virtuous men of the Plain," cries he, finding audience one moment, "I appeal to you!" The virtuous men of the Plain sit silent as stones. And Thuriot's bell jingles, and the Hall sounds like Æolus's Hall. Robespierre's frothing lips are grown "blue;" his tongue dry, cleaving to the roof of his mouth. "The blood of Danton chokes him," cry they. "Accusation! Decree of Accusation!" Thuriot swiftly puts that question. Accusation passes; the incorruptible Maximilien is decreed Accused.

1791. "I demand to share my Brother's fate, as I have striven to share his virtues," cries Augustin, the Younger Robespierre: Augustin also is decreed. And Couthon, and Saint-Just, and Lebas, they are all decreed; and packed forth,—not without difficulty, the Ushers almost trembling to obey. Triumvirate and Company are packed forth, into Salut Committee-room; their tongue cleaving to the roof of their mouth. You have but to summon the Municipality; to cashier Commandant Henriot, and launch Arrest at him; to regulate formalities; hand Tinville his victims. It is noon: the Æolus-Hall has delivered itself; blows now victorious, harmonious, as one irresistible wind.

1792. And so the work is finished? One thinks so: and yet it is not so. Alas, there is yet but the first act finished; three or four other acts still to come; and an uncertain catastrophe! A huge City holds in it so many confusions: 700,000 human heads; not one of which knows what its neighbor is doing, nay not what itself is doing.—See, accordingly, about three in the afternoon, Commandant Henriot, how instead of sitting cashiered, arrested, he gallops along the Quais, followed by Municipal Gendarmes, "trampling down several persons!" For the Town-hall sits deliberating, openly insurgent: Barriers to be shut; no Jailor to admit any prisoner this day;—and Henriot is galloping toward the Tuileries, to deliver Robespierre. On the Quai de la Ferraillerie, a young Citoyen, walking with his wife, says aloud: "Gendarmes, that man is not your Commandant; he is under arrest." The Gendarmes strike down the young Citoyen with the flat of their swords.*

1793. Representatives themselves (as Merlin the Thionviller), who accost him, this puissant Henriot flings into guard-houses. He bursts toward the Tuileries Committee-room, "to speak with Robespierre:" with difficulty, the Ushers and Tuileries Gendarmes, earnestly pleading and drawing saber, seize this Henriot; get the Henriot Gendarmes persuaded not to fight; get Robespierre and Company packed into hackney-coaches, sent off under escort, to the Luxembourg and other Prisons. This, then, is the end? May not an exhausted Convention adjourn now, for a little repose and sustenance, "at five o'clock?"

1794. An exhausted Convention did it; and repented it. The end was not come; only the end of the second-act. Hark, while exhausted Representatives sit at victuals,—tocsin bursting from all steeples, drums rolling in the summer evening: Judge Coffinhal is galloping with new Gendarmes, to deliver Henriot from Tuileries Committee-room; and does deliver him! Puissant Henriot vaults on horseback; sets to haranguing the Tuileries Gendarmes; corrupts the Tuileries Gendarmes too; trots off with them to Town-hall. Alas, and Robespierre is not in Prison: the Jailor showed his Municipal order, durst not, on pain of his life, admit any Prisoner; the Robespierre Hackney-coaches, in this confused jangle and whirl of uncertain Gendarmes, have floated safe, —into the Town-hall! There sit Robespierre and Company, embraced by Municipals and Jacobins in sacred right of Insurrection; redacting Proclamations; sounding tocsins; corresponding with Sections and Mother Society. Is not here a pretty enough third-act of a natural Greek Drama; catastrophe more uncertain than ever?

1795. The hasty Convention rushes together again, in the ominous nightfall: President Collot, for the chair is his, enters with long strides, paleness on his face; claps on his hat; says with solemn tone: "Citoyens, armed Villains have beset the Committee rooms, and got possession of them. The hour is come, to die at our post!" "Oui," answer one and all: "We swear it!" It is no rodomontade, this time, but a sad fact and necessity; unless we do at our posts, we must verily die. Swift therefore, Robespierre, Henriot, the Municipality, are declared Rebels; put Hors la Loi, (Out of Law.) Better still, we appoint Barras Commandant of what Armed-force is to be had; sent Missionary Representatives to all Sections and quarters, to preach, and raise force; will die at least with harness on our back.

1796. What a distracted City; men riding and running, reporting and hearsaying; the Hour clearly in travail,—child not to be named till born! The poor Prisoners in the Luxembourg hear the rumor; tremble for a new September. They see men making signals to them, on skylights and roofs, apparently signals of hope: cannot in the least make out what it is.† We observe, however, in the eventide, as usual, the Death-tumbrils faring South-eastward, through Saint-Antoine, toward their Barrier du

Trone. Saint-Antoine's tough bowels melt; Saint-Antoine surrounds the Tumbrils; says, It shall not be. O Heavens, why should it! Henriot and Gendarmes, scouring the streets that way, bellow, with waved sabers, that it must. Quit hope, ye poor Doomed! The Tumbrils move on.

1797. But in this set of Tumbrils there are two other things notable: one notable person; and one want of a notable person. The notable person is Lieutenant-General Loiserolles, a nobleman by birth and by nature; laying down his life here for his son. In the Prison of Saint-Lazare, the night before last, hurrying to the Grate to hear the Death-list read, he caught the name of his son. The son was asleep at the moment. "I am Loiserolles," cried the old man: at Tinville's bar, an error in the Christian name is little; small objection was made.—The want of the notable person, again, is that of Deputy Paine! Paine has sat in the Luxembourg since January; and seemed forgotten; but Fouquier had pricked him at last. The Turnkey, List in hand, is marking with chalk the outer doors of to-morrow's Fournée. Paine's outer door happened to be open, turned back on the wall; the Turnkey marked it on the side next him, and hurried on; another Turnkey came and shut it; no chalk-mark now visible, the Fournée went without Paine. Paine's life lay not there.—

1798. Our fifth-act, of this natural Greek Drama, with its natural unities, can only be painted in gross; somewhat as that antique Painter, driven desperate, did the foam. For through this blessed July night, there is clangor, confusion very great, of marching troops; of Sections going this way, Sections going that· of Missionary Representatives reading Proclamations by torch-light; Missionary Legendre, who has raised force somewhere, emptying out the Jacobins, and flinging their key on the Convention table: "I have locked their door: it shall be Virtue that reopens it." Paris, we say, is set against itself, rushing confused, as Ocean-currents do, a huge Mahlstrom, sounding there, under cloud of night. Convention sits permanent on this hand; Municipality most permanent on that. The poor prisoners hear tocsin and rumor; strive to bethink them of the signals apparently of hope. Meek continual Twilight streaming up, which will be Dawn and a To-morrow, silvers the Northern hem of Night; it wends and wends there, that meek brightness, like a silent prophecy, along the great ring-dial of the Heaven. So still, eternal! and on Earth all is confused shadow and conflict; dissidence, tumultuous gloom and glare; and "Destiny as yet sits wavering, and shakes her doubtful urn."

1799. About three in the morning the dissident Armed-forces have met. Henriot's armed-force stood ranked in the Place de Grève; and now Barras's. which he has recruited, arrives there; and they front each other, cannon bristling against cannon. Citoyens! cries the voice of Discretion loudly enough, Before coming to bloodshed, to endless civil-war, hear the Convention Decree read. "Robespierre and all rebels Out of Law?"—Out of Law? There is terror in the sound. Unarmed Citoyens disperse rapidly home. Municipal Cannoneers, in sudden whirl, anxiously unanimous, range themselves on the Convention side. with shouting. At which shout, Henriot descends from his upper room, far gone in drink, as some say; finds his Place de Grève empty; the cannons' mouth turned toward him; and on the whole,—that it is now the catastrophe!

1800. Stumbling in again, the wretched drunksobered Henriot announces: "All is lost!" "Miserable, it is thou that hast lost it!" cry they; and fling him, or else he flings himself, out of window: far enough down; into mason-work and

* "Précis des Evénemens du Neuf Thermidor," par C. A. Meda, ancien Gendarme (Paris, 1825).
† "Mémoires sur les Prisons," ii. 277.

horror of cess pool; not into death but worse. Augustin Robespierre follows him: with the like fate. Saint-Just, they say, called on Lebas to kill him; who would not. Couthon crept under a table; attempting to kill himself; not doing it.—On entering that Sanhedrim of Insurrection, we find all as good as extinct; undone, ready for seizure. Robespierre was sitting on a chair, with pistol-shot blown through not his head but his under-jaw; the suicidal hand had failed.* With prompt zeal, not without trouble, fish up even Henriot and Augustin, bleeding and foul; pack them all, rudely enough, into carts; and shall, before sunrise, have them safe under lock and key. Amid shoutings and embracings.

1801. Robespierre lay in an anteroom of the Convention Hall, while his Prison-escort was getting ready; the mangled jaw bound up rudely with bloody linen: a spectacle to men. He lies stretched on a table, a deal-box his pillow; the sheath of the pistol is still clutched convulsively in his hand. Men bully him, insult him: his eyes still indicate intelligence; he speaks no word. "He had on the sky-blue coat he had got made for the Feast of the Etre Suprême"—O Reader, can thy hard heart hold out against that? His trousers were nankeen; the stockings had fallen down over the ankles. He spake no word more in this world.

1802. And so, at six in the morning, a victorious Convention adjourns. Report flies over Paris as on golden wings; penetrates the Prisons: irradiates the faces of those that were ready to perish: turnkeys and moutons, fallen from their high estate, look mute and blue. It is the 28th day of July, called 10th of Thermidor, year 1794.

1803. Fouquier had but to identify; his Prisoners being already Out of Law. At four in the afternoon, never before were the streets of Paris seen so crowded. From the Palais de Justice to the Place de la Révolution, for *thither* again go the Tumbrils this time, it is one dense stirring mass: all windows crammed; the very roofs and ridge-tiles budding forth human Curiosity, in strange gladness. The Death-tumbrils, with their motley Batch of Outlaws, some Twenty-three or so, from Maximilien to Mayor Fleuriot and Simon the Cordwainer, roll on. All eyes are on Robespierre's Tumbril, where he, his jaw bound in dirty linen, with his half-dead Brother and half dead Henriot, lie shattered; their "seventeen hours" of agony about to end. The Gendarmes point their swords at him to show the people which is he. A woman springs on the Tumbril; clutching the side of it with one hand, waving the other, Sibyl-like, and exclaims: "The death of thee gladdens my very heart, m'enivre de joie;" Robespierre opened his eyes; "Scélérat, go down to Hell, with the curses of all wives and mothers!" At the foot of the scaffold, they stretched him on the ground till his turn came. Lifted aloft, his eyes again opened; caught the bloody axe. Samson wrenched the coat off him; wrenched the dirty linen from his jaw: the jaw fell powerless, there burst from him a cry; hideous to hear and see. Samson, thou canst not be too quick!

1804. Samson's work done, there bursts forth shout on shout of applause. Shout, which prolongs itself not only over Paris, but over France, but over Europe, and down to this generation. Deservedly, and also undeservedly. O unhappiest Advocate of Arras, wert thou worse than other Advocates? Stricter man, according to his Formula, to his Credo, and his

* Meda, p. 384. (Meda asserts that it was he who, with infinite courage though in a left-handed manner, shot Robespierre. Meda got promoted for his services of this night, and died general and baron. Few credited Meda in what was otherwise incredible.)

Cant, of probities, benevolences, pleasures-of-virtue and such like, lived not in that age. A man fitted in some luckier settled age, to have become one of those incorruptible barren Pattern-Figures, and have had marble-tablets and funeral-sermons. His poor landlord, the Cabinet-maker in the Rue Saint-Honoré, loved him; his Brother died for him. May God be merciful to him and to us!

1805. This is the end of the Reign of Terror; new glorious *Revolution* named *of Thermidor;* of Thermidor 9th, year 2; which, being interpreted into old slave-style means 27th of July, 1794. Terror is ended; and death in the Place de la Révolution, were the "*Tail* of Robespierre" once executed; which service Fouquier, in large Batches, is swiftly managing.

BOOK SEVENTH.

VENDÉMIAIRE.

CHAPTER I.

DECADENT.

1806. How little did anyone suppose that here was the end not of Robespierre only, but of the Revolution System itself! Least of all did the mutinying Committee-men suppose it; who had mutinied with no view whatever except to continue the National Regeneration with their own heads on their shoulders. And yet so it verily was. The insignificant stone they had struck out, so insignificant anywhere else, proved to be the Keystone; the whole archwork and edifice of Sansculottism began to loosen, to crack, to yawn; and tumbled piecemeal, with considerable rapidity, plunge after plunge; till the Abyss had swallowed it all, and in this upper world Sansculottism was no more.

1807. For despicable as Robespierre himself might be, the death of Robespierre was a signal at which great multitudes of men, struck dumb with terror heretofore, rose out of their hiding-places; and, as it were, saw one another, how multitudinous they were; and began speaking and complaining. They are countable by the thousand and the million; who have suffered cruel wrong. Ever louder rises the plaint of such a multitude; into a universal continuous peal, of what they call Public Opinion. Camille had demanded a "Committee of Mercy," and could not get it; but now the whole nation resolves itself into a Committee of Mercy; the Nation has tried Sansculottism, and is weary of it. Force of Public Opinion! What King or Convention can withstand it? You in vain struggle; the thing that is rejected as "calumnious" to-day must pass as veracious with triumph another day: gods and men have declared that Sansculottism cannot be. Sansculottism, on that 9th night of Thermidor suicidally "fractured its under-jaw;" and lies writhing, never to rise more.

1808. Through the next fifteen months, it is what we may call the death agony of Sansculottism. Sansculottism, Anarchy of the Jean-Jacques Evangel, having now got deep enough, is to perish in a new singular system of Culottism and Arrangement. For Arrangement is indispensable to man: Arrangement, were it grounded only on that old primary Evangel of Force, with Scepter in the shape of Hammer! Be there method, be there order, cry all men; were it that of the Drill-sergeant! More tolerable is the drilled Bayonet-rank, than that undrilled Guillotine, incalculable as the wind.—How Sansculottism, writhing in death-throes, strove some twice, or even three times, to get on its feet again; but fell always, and was flung resupine the next instant;

and finally breathed out the life of it, and stirred no more: this we are now, from a due distance, with due brevity, to glance at; and then—O Reader!—Courage, I see land!

1809. Two of the first acts of the Convention, very natural for it after this Thermidor, are to be specified here: the first is, renewal of the Governing Committees. Both Sûreté Générale and Salut Public, thinned by the Guillotine, need filling up: we naturally fill them up with Talliens, Frérous, victorious Thermidorian men. Still more to the purpose, we appoint that they shall, as Law directs, not in name only but in deed, be renewed and changed from period to period; a fourth part of them going out monthly. The Convention will no more lie under bondage of Committees, under terror of death; but be a free Convention; free to follow its own judgment, and the Force of Public Opinion. Not less natural is it to enact that Prisoners and Persons under Accusation shall have right to demand some " Writ of Accusation," and see clearly what they are accused of. Very natural acts; the harbingers of hundreds not less so.

1810. For now Fouquier's trade, shackled by Writ of Accusation, and legal proof, is as good as gone; effectual only against Robespierre's Tail. The Prisons give up their Suspect; emit them faster and faster. The Committees see themselves besieged with Prisoners' friends; complain that they are hindered in their work: it is as with men rushing out of a crowded place; and obstructing one another. Turned are the tables: Prisoners pouring out in floods; Jailors, Moutons and the Tail of Robespierre going now whither they were wont to send!—The Hundred and thirty-two Nantese Republicans, whom we saw marching in irons, have arrived; shrunk to Ninety-four, the fifth man of them choked by the road. They arrive: and suddenly find themselves not plenders for life, but denouncers to death. Their Trial is for acquittal, and more. As the voice of a trumpet, their testimony sounds far and wide, mere atrocities of a Reign of Terror. For a space of nineteen days; with all solemnity and publicity. Representative Carrier, Company of Marat; Noyadings, Loire Marriages, things done in darkness, come forth into light: clear is the voice of these poor resuscitated Nantese; and Journals, and Speech, and universal Committee of Mercy reverberate it loud enough, into all ears and hearts. Deputation arrives from Arras; denouncing the atrocities of Representative Lebon. A tamed Convention loves its own life: yet what help? Representative Lebon, Representative Carrier must wend toward the Revolutionary Tribunal; struggle and delay as we will, the cry of a Nation pursues them louder and louder. Them also Tinville must abolish;—if indeed Tinville himself be not abolished.

1811. We must note, moreover, the decrepit condition into which a once omnipotent Mother Society has fallen. Legendre flung her keys on the Convention table, that Thermidor night; her President was guillotined with Robespierre. The once mighty Mother came, some time after, with a subdued countenance, begging back her keys: the keys were restored her; but the strength could not be restored her; the strength had departed forever. Alas, one's day is done. Vain that the Tribune in mid-air sounds as of old: to the general ear it has become a horror, and even a weariness. By and by, Affiliation is prohibited: the mighty Mother sees herself suddenly childless; mourns as so hoarse a Rachel may.

1812. The Revolutionary Committees, without Suspects to prey upon, perish fast; as it were, of famine. In Paris the old Forty-eight of them are reduced to twelve; their *Forty sous* are abolished: yet a little

while, and Revolutionary Committees are no more. Maximum will be abolished; let Sansculottism find food where it can.* Neither is there now any Municipality; any center at the Town-hall. Mayor Fleuriot and Company perished; whom we shall not be in haste to replace. The Town-hall remains in a broken submissive state; knows not well what it is growing to; knows only that it is grown weak, and must obey. What if we should split Paris into, say, a Dozen separate Municipalities; incapable of concert! The Sections were thus rendered safe to act with :—or indeed might not the Sections themselves be abolished? You had then merely your Twelve manageable pacific Townships, without center or subdivision;† and sacred right of Insurrection fell into abeyance!

1813. So much is getting abolished; fleeting swiftly into the Inane. For the Press speaks, and the human tongue; Journals, heavy and light, in Philippic and Burlesque: a renegade Fréron, a renegade Prudhomme, loud they as ever, only the contrary way. And Ci-devants show themselves, almost parade themselves; resuscitated as from death-sleep; publish what death-pains they have had. The very Frogs of the Marsh croak with emphasis. Your protesting Seventy-three shall with a struggle, be emitted out of Prison, back to their seats; your Louvets, Isnards, Lanjuinais, and wrecks of Girondism recalled from their hay-lofts, and caves in Switzerland, will resume their place in the Convention :‡ natural foes of Terror!

1814. Thermidorian Talliens, and mere foes of Terror, rule in this Convention, and out of it. The compressed Mountain shrinks silent more and more. Moderatism rises louder and louder: not as a tempest, with threatenings; say rather, as the rushing of a mighty organ-blast, and melodious deafening Force of Public Opinion, from the 25,000,000 windpipes of a Nation all in Committee of Mercy: which how shall any detached body of individuals withstand ?

CHAPTER II.

LA CABARUS.

1815. How, above all, shall a poor National Convention withstand it ? In this poor National Convention, broken, bewildered by long terror, perturbations and guillotinement, there is no Pilot, there is not now even a Danton, who could undertake to steer you anywhither, in such press of weather. The utmost a bewildered Convention can do, is to veer, and trim, and try to keep itself steady; and rush, undrowned, before the wind. Needless to struggle, to fling helm a-lee, and make *'bout ship !* A bewildered Convention sails not in the teeth of the wind; but is rapidly blown round again. So strong is the wind, we say; and so changed; blowing fresher and fresher as from the sweet South-west; your devastating North-easters, wild Tornado-gusts of Terror, blown utterly out! All Sansculottic things are passing away; all things are becoming Culottic.

1816. Do but look at the cut of clothes; that light

---

* 24th Decembre, 1794 (Moniteur, No. 97).
† October. 1795 (Dulaure, viii. 454-456).
‡ "Deux Amis," xiii. 5-39.

visible Result, significant of a thousand things which are not so visible. In winter, 1793, men went in red night-cap; Municipals themselves in sabots; the very Citoyenues had to petition against such head-gear. But now in this winter, 1794, where is the red night-cap? With the things beyond the Flood. Your moneyed Citoyen ponders in what most elegant style he shall dress himself; whether he shall not even dress himself as the Free Peoples of Antiquity. The more adventurous Citoyenne has already done it. Behold her, that beautiful adventurous Citoyenne: in costume of the Ancient Greeks, such Greek as Painter David could teach; her sweeping tresses snooded by glittering antique fillet; bright-dyed tunic of the Greek women; her little feet naked, as in Antique Statues, with mere sandals, and winding-strings of ribbon,—defying the frost!

1817. There is such an effervescence of Luxury. For your Emigrant Ci-devants carried not their mansions and furnitures out of the country with them; but left them standing here: and in the swift changes of property, what with money coined on the Place de la Révolution, what with Army furnishings, sales of Emigrant Domains and Church Lands and King's Lands, and then with the Aladdin's-lamp of Agio in a time of Paper-money, such mansions have found new occupants. Old wine, drawn from Ci-devant bottles, descends new throats. Paris has swept herself, relighted herself; Salons, Soupers not Fraternal, beam once more with suitable effulgence, very singular in color. The fair Cabarus is come out of Prison; wedded to her red-gloomy Dis, whom they say she treats too loftily : fair Cabarus gives the most brilliant soirées. Round her is gathered a new Republican Army, of Citoyennes in sandals; Ci-devant or other : what remnants soever of the old grace survive are rallied there. At her right-hand, in this cause, labors fair Josephine the Widow Beauharnais, though in straitened circumstances; intent, both of them, to blandish down the grimness of Republican austerity, and recivilize mankind.

1818. Recivilize, even as of old they were civilized : by witchery of the Orphic fiddle-bow, and Euterpean rhythm; by the Graces, by the Smiles! Thermidorian Deputies are there in those soirées; Editor Fréron, Orateur du Peuple; Barras. who has known other dances than the Carmagnole. Grim Generals of the Republic are there; in enormous horse-collar neck-cloth, good against saber-cuts : the hair gathered all into one knot, "flowing down behind, fixed with a comb." Among which latter do we not recognize. once more, that little bronze-complexioned Artillery-Officer of Toulon, home from the Italian Wars! Grim enough; of lean, almost cruel aspect: for he has been in trouble, in ill-health; also in ill-favor, as a man promoted, deservingly or not, by the Terrorists and Robespierre Junior. But does not Barras know him? Will not Barras speak a word for him? Yes.—if at any time it will serve Barras so to do. Somewhat forlorn of fortune, for the present, stands that Artillery-Officer; looks, with those deep earnest eyes of his, into a future as waste as the most. Taciturn; yet with the strangest utterances in him, if you awaken him, which smite home, like light or lightning;—on the whole, rather dangerous? A "dissocial" man? Dissocial enough; a natural terror and horror to all Phantasms, being himself of the genus Reality! He stands here, without work or outlook, in this forsaken manner;—glances, nevertheless, it would seem, at the kind glance of Josephine Beauharnais; and, for the rest, with severe countenance, with open eyes, and closed lips, waits what will betide.

1819. That the Balls, therefore, have a new figure this winter, we can see. Not Carmagnoles, rude

"whirl-blasts of rags," as Mercier called them, "precursors of storm and destruction:" no, soft Ionic motions, fit for the light sandal and antique Grecian tunic! Efflorescence of Luxury has come out : for men have wealth; nay new-got wealth; and under the Terror you durst not dance, except in rags. Among the innumerable kinds of Balls, let the hasty reader mark only this single one : the kind they call Victim Balls (Bals à Victime). The dancers, in choice costume, have all crape round the left arm : to be admitted, it needs that you be a Victime; that you have lost a relative under the Terror. Peace to the Dead; let us *dance* to their memory! For in all ways one must dance.

1820. It is very remarkable, according to Mercier, under what varieties of figure this great business of dancing goes on. "The women," says he, are "Nymphs, Sultanas; sometimes Minervas, Junos, and even Dianas. In lightly-unerring gyrations they swim there; with such earnestness of purpose; with perfect silence, so absorbed are they. What is singular," continues he, "the onlookers are as it were mingled with the dancers; form, as it were, a circumambient element round the different contra-dances, yet without deranging them. It is rare, in fact, that a Sultana in such circumstances experiences the smallest collision. Her pretty foot darts down, an inch from mine; she is off again; she is as a flash of light: but soon the measure recalls her to the point she set out from. Like a glittering comet she travels her ellipse; revolving on herself, as by a double effect of gravitation and attraction."[*] Looking forward a little way, into Time, the same Mercier discerns Merveilleuses in "flesh-colored drawers" with gold circlets; mere dancing Houris of an artificial Mohammed's-Paradise: much too Mohammedan. Montgaillard, with his splenetic eye, notes a no less strange thing; that every fashionable Citoyenne you meet is in an interesting situation. Good Heavens, *every?* Mere pillows and stuffing! adds the acrid man;—such in a time of depopulation by war and guillotine, being the fashion.[†] No farther seek its merits to disclose.

1821. Behold also, instead of the old grim Tappedurs of Robespierre, what new' street-groups are these? Young men habited not in black-shag Carmagnole spencer. but in superfine habit carré, or spencer with rectangular tail appended to it; "square-tailed coat," with elegant anti-guillotinish specialty of collar; "the hair plaited at the temples," and knotted back, long-flowing, in military wise; young men of what they call the Muscadin or Dandy species! Fréron, in his fondness, names them Jeunesse Dorée, Golden or Gilt Youth. They have come out, these Gilt Youths, in a kind of resuscitated state; they wear crape round the left arm, such of them as were *Victims*. More, they carry clubs loaded with lead; in an angry manner: any Tappe-dur, or remnant of Jacobinism they may fall in with, shall fare the worse. They have suffered much: their friends guillotined : their pleasures, frolics, superfine collars ruthlessly repressed: 'ware now the base Red Night-caps who did it! Fair Cabarus and the Army of Greek sandals smile approval. In the Théâtre Feydeau, young Valor in square-tailed coat eyes Beauty in Greek sandals, and kindles by her glances: Down with Jacobinism! No Jacobin hymn or demonstration, only Thermidorian ones, shall be permitted here: we beat down Jacobinism with clubs loaded with lead.

1822. But let any one who has examined the Dandy nature, how petulant it is, especially in the gregarious state, think what an element, in sacred right

<hr>

* Mercier. "Nouveau Paris," iii. 138, 153.
† Montgaillard, iv. 436-442.

of insurrection, this Gilt Youth was! Broils and battery; war without truce or measure! Hateful is Sansculottism, as Death and Night. For indeed is not the Dandy *culottic*, liabilatory, by law of existence; "a cloth-animal; one that lives, moves and has his being in cloth?"

1823. So goes it, waltzing, bickering; fair Cabarus, by Orphic witchery, struggling to recivilize mankind. Not uusuccessfully, we hear. What utmost Republican grimness can resist Greek sandals, in Ionic motion, the very toes covered with gold rings?* By degrees the indisputablest new-politeness rises; grows, with vigor. And yet, whether, even to this day, that inexpressible tone of society known under the old Kings, when Sin had "lost all its deformity" (with or without advantage to us), and airy Nothing had obtained such a local habitation and establishment as she never had,—be recovered? Or even, whether it be not lost beyond recovery!†—Either way, the world must contrive to struggle on.

CHAPTER III.
QUIBERON.

1824. But, indeed, do not these long-flowing hair-queues of a Jeunesse Dorée in semi-military costume betoken, unconsciously, another still more important tendency? The Republic, abhorrent of her Guillotine, loves her Army.

1825. And with cause. For, surely, if good fighting be a kind of honor, as it is in its season; and be with the vulgar of men, even the chief kind of honor; then here is good fighting, in good season, if there ever was. These Sons of the Republic, they rose, in mad wrath, to deliver her from Slavery and Cimmeria. And have they not done it? Through Maritime Alps, through gorges of Pyrenees, through Low Countries, Northward along the Rhine-valley, far is Cimmeria hurled back from the sacred Motherland. Fierce as fire, they have carried her Tricolor over the faces of all her enemies;—over scarped heights, over cannon-batteries, it has flown victorious, winged with rage. She has "1,100,000 fighters on foot," this Republic: "at one particular moment she had," or supposed she had, "1,700,000."‡ Like a ring of lightning, they, volleying and ça-ira-ing, begirdle her from shore to shore. Cimmerian Coalition of Despots recoils, smitten with astonishment and strange pangs.

1826. Such a fire is in these Gaelic Republican men; high-blazing; which no Coalition can withstand! Not scutcheons, with four degrees of nobility; but ci-devant Sergeants, who have had to clutch Generalship out of the cannon's throat, a Pichegru, a Jourdan, a Hoche lead them on. They have bread, they have iron: "with bread and iron you can get to China."§—See Pichegru's soldiers, this hard winter, in their looped and windowed destitution, in their "straw-rope shoes and cloaks of bast-mat," how they overrun Holland, like a demon host, the ice having bridged all waters; and rush shouting from victory to victory! Ships in the Texel are taken by hussars on horseback: fled is York; fled is the Stadtholder, glad to escape to England, and leave Holland to fraternize.‖ Such a Gaelic fire, we say, blazes in this People, like the conflagration of grass and dry-jungle; which no mortal can withstand,—for the moment.

1827. And even so it will blaze and run, scorching all things; and, from Cadiz to Archangel, mad Sansculottism, drilled now into Soldiership, led on by some "armed Soldier of Democracy" (say, that

monosyllabic Artillery-Officer), will set its foot cruelly on the necks of its enemies; and its shouting and their shrieking shall fill the world!—Rash Coalesced Kings, such a fire have ye kindled; yourselves fireless, *your* fighters animated only by drill-sergeants, mess-room moralities and the drummer's cat! However, it is begun, and will not end: not for a matter of twenty years. So long, this Gaelic fire, through its successive changes of color and character, will blaze over the face of Europe, and afflict and scorch all men:—till it provoke all men; till it kindle another kind of fire, the Teutonic kind, namely; and be swallowed up, so to speak, in a day! For there is a fire comparable to the burning of dry-jungle and grass; most sudden, high-blazing: and another fire which we liken to the burning of coal, or even of anthracite coal; difficult to kindle, but then which no known thing will put out. The ready Gaelic fire, we can remark farther,—and remark not in Pichegrus only, but in innumerable Voltaires, Racines, Laplaces, no less; for a man, whether he fight or sing, or think, will remain the same unity of a man,—is admirable for roasting eggs, in every conceivable sense. The Teutonic anthracite again, as we see in Luthers, Leibnitzes, Shakespeares, is preferable for smelting metals. How happy is our Europe that has both kinds!—

1828. But be this as it may, the Republic is clearly triumphing. In the spring of the year, Mentz Town again sees itself besieged; will again change master: did not Merlin the Thionviller, "with wild beard and look," say it was not for the last time they saw him there? The Elector of Mentz circulates among his brother Potentates this pertinent query, Were it not advisable to treat of Peace? Yes! answers many an Elector from the bottom of his heart. But, on the other hand, Austria hesitates; finally refuses, being subsidied by Pitt. As to Pitt, whoever hesitate, he, suspending his Habeas-corpus, suspending his Cash-payments, stands inflexible,—spite of foreign reverses: spite of domestic obstacles, of Scotch National Conventions and English Friends of the People, whom he is obliged to arraign, to hang, or even to see acquitted with jubilee: a lean inflexible man. The Majesty of Spain, as we predicted, makes Peace; also the Majesty of Prussia: and there is a Treaty of Bâle.* Treaty with black Anarchists and Regicides! Alas, what help? You cannot hang this Anarchy; it is like to hang you: you must needs treat with it.

1829. Likewise, General Hoche has even succeeded in pacificating La Vendée. Rogue Rossignol and his "Infernal Columns" have vanished: by firmness and justice, by sagacity and industry, General Hoche has done it. Taking "Movable Columns," not infernal; girdling-in the Country; pardoning the submissive, cutting down the resistive, limb after limb of the Revolt is brought under. La Rochejacquelin, last of our Nobles, fell in battle; Stofflet himself makes terms; Georges-Cadoudal is back to Brittany, among his Chouans: the frightful gangrene of La Vendée seems veritably extirpated. It has cost, as they reckon in round numbers, the lives of 100,000 fellow-mortals; with noyadings, conflagratings by infernal column, which defy arithmetic. This is the La Vendée War.†

1830. Nay in few months, it does burst-up once more, but once only;—blown upon by Pitt, by our Ci-devant Puisaye of Calvados, and others. In the month of July, 1795, English Ships will ride in Quiberon roads. There will be debarkation of chiv-

---

* Montgaillard. Mercier (ubi supra).
† De Staël. "Considérations," iii. c. 10, etc.
‡ Toulongeon, iii. c. 7: v. c. 10, (p. 194).
‖ 19th January, 1795 (Montgaillard, iv. 287-311).

* 5th April. 1795 (Montgaillard, iv. 319).
† "Histoire de la Guerre de la Vendée," par M. le Comte de Vauban: "Mémoires de Madame de la Rochejacuelin," etc.

alrous Ci-devants, of volunteer Prisoners-of-war—
eager to desert ; of fire-arms, Proclamations, clothes-
chests, Royalists and specie. Whereupon also, ou
the Republican side, there will be rapid stand-to-
arms; with ambuscade marchings by Quiberon
beach, at midnight; storming of Fort Penthièvre;
war-thunder mingling with the roar of the nightly
main ; and such a morning light as has seldom
dawned : debarkation hurled back into its boats, or
into the devouring billows, with wreck and wail;—
in one word, a Ci-devant Puisaye as totally ineffectual here as he was in Calvados, when he rode from
Vernon Castle without boots.*

1831. Again, therefore, it has cost the lives of
many a brave man. Among whom the whole world
laments the brave Son of Sombreuil. Ill-fated
family! The father and younger son went to the
guillotine; the heroic daughter languishes, reduced
to want, hides her woes from History : the elder son
perishes here; shot by military tribunal as an Emigrant; Hoche himself cannot save him. If all wars,
civil and other, are misunderstandings, what a thing
must right-understanding be!

CHAPTER IV.

LION NOT DEAD.

1832. The Convention, borne on the tide of Fortune toward foreign Victory, and driven by the
strong wind of Public Opinion toward Clemency and
Luxury, is rushing fast ; all skill of pilotage is needed, and more than all, in such a velocity.

1833. Curious to see, how we veer and whirl, yet
must ever whirl round again, and scud before the
wind. If, on the one hand, we re-admit the Protesting Seventy-three, we, on the other hand, agree to
consummate the Apotheosis of Marat; lift his body
from the Cordeliers Church, and transport it to the
Pantheon of Great Men—flinging out Mirabeau to
make room for him. To no purpose: so strong
blows Public Opinion! A Gilt Youthhood, in plaited hair-tresses, tears down his Busts from the
Théâtre Feydeau; tramples them under foot ; scatters them, with vociferation, into the Cess-pool of
Montmartre.† Swept is his Chapel from the Place
du Carrousel; the Cess-pool of Montmartre will receive his very dust. Shorter godhood had no divine
man. Some four months in this Pantheon, Temple
of All the Immortals ; then to the Cess-pool, grand
Cloaca of Paris and the World! "His Busts at one
time amounted to 4,000." Between Temple of All
the Immortals and Cloaca of the World, how are
poor human creatures Whirled!

1834. Furthermore the question arises, When will
the Constitution of Ninety-Three, of 1793, come into
action? Considerate heads surmise, in all privacy
that the Constitution of Ninety-three will never
come into action. Let them busy themselves to get
ready a better.

1835. Or, again, where now are the Jacobins?
Childless, most decrepit, as we saw, sat the mighty
Mother; gnashing not teeth, but empty gums, against
a traitorous Thermidorian Convention and the current of things. Twice were Billaud, Collot and Company accused in Convention, by a Lecointre, by a
Legendre; and the second time, it was not voted
calumnious. Billaud from the Jacobin tribune says,
"The lion is not dead; he is only sleeping." They
ask him in Convention, What he means by the
awakening of the lion? And bickerings, of an extensive sort, arose in the Palais-Egalité between Tappe-

* "Deux Amis," xiv. 94-106; Pulsaye, "Mémoires," iii.-
vii.

† Mon Iteur, du 25 Septembre, 1794 du 4 Février, 1795.

durs and the Gilt Youthhood; cries of "Down with
the Jacobins, Jacoquins," coquin meaning scoundrel!
The Tribune in mid-air gave battle-sound; answered only by silence and uncertain gasps. Talk
was in Government Committees, of "suspending" the
Jacobin Sessions. Hark, there!—it is in All-hallow-
tine, or on the Hallow-eve itself, month ci-devant
November, year once named of Grace 1794, sad eve
for Jacobinism,—volley of stones dashing through
our windows, with jingle and execration! The female Jacobins, famed Tricoteuses with knitting-
needles, take flight; are met at the doors by a Gilt
Youthhood and "mob of 4,000 persons;" are hooted,
flouted, hustled ; fustigated in a scandalous manner,
cotillons retroussés;—and vanish in mere hysterics.
Sally out, ye male Jacobins! The male Jacobins
sally out; but only to battle, disaster and confusion.
So that armed Authority has to intervene; and
again on the morrow to intervene; and suspend the
Jacobin Sessions forever and a day.*—Gone are the
Jacobins; into invisibility; in a storm of laughter
and howls. Their Place is made a Normal School.
the first of the kind seen; it then vanishes into a
"Market of Thermidor Ninth;" into a Market of
Saint-Honoré, where is now peaceable chaffering for
poultry and greens. The solemn temples, the great
globe itself; the baseless fabric! Are not we such
stuff, we and this world of ours, as Dreams are made
of?

1836. Maximum being abrogated, Trade was to
take its own free course. Alas, Trade, shackled,
topsy-turvied in the way we saw, and now suddenly
let-go again, can for the present take no course at all ;
but only reel and stagger. There is, so to speak, no
Trade whatever for the time being. Assignats, long
sinking, emitted in such quantities, sink now with
an alacrity beyond parallel. "Combien?" said one
to a Hackney-coachman, "What fare? Six thousand livres," answered he: some 300 pounds sterling,
in Paper-money.† Pressure of Maximum withdrawn
the things it compressed likewise withdraw. "Two
ounces of bread per day" is the modicum allotted :
wide waving, doleful are the Bakers' Queues : Farmers' houses are become pawnbrokers' shops.

1837. One can imagine, in these circumstances,
with what humor Sansculottism growled in its
throat "La Cabarus;" beheld Ci-devants return dancing, the Thermidor effulgence of re-civilization, and
Balls in flesh-colored drawers. Greek tunics and
sandals; hosts of Muscadins parading, with their
clubs loaded with lead ;—and we here, cast out, abhorred, "picking offals from the street ;"‡ agitating
in Bakers' Queue for our two ounces of bread !
Will the Jacobin lion, which they say is meeting
secretly "at the Archevêché, in bonnet rouge with
loaded pistols," not awaken? Seemingly, not. Our
Collot, our Billaud, Barrère, Vadier, in these last
days of March, 1795, are found worthy of Déportation,
of Banishment beyond seas; and shall, for the
present, be trundled off to the Castle of Ham. The
lion is dead ;—or writhing in death-throes!

1838. Behold, accordingly, on the day they call
12th of Germinal (which is also called 1st of April,
not a lucky day), how lively are these streets of
Paris once more! Floods of hungry women, of
squalid hungry men; ejaculating, "Bread, bread,
and the Constitution of Ninety-three!" Paris has
risen, once again like the Ocean-tide; is flowing

* Moniteur, Séances du 10-12 Novembre, 1794; "Deux
Amis," xiii. 43-49.

† Mercier, ii. 94. ("1st February, 1796, at the Bourse of
Paris, the gold louis," of 20 francs in silver, "costs 5,300
francs in assignats." Montgaillard, iv. 419.)

‡ Fantin Desodoards, "Histoire de la Révolution," vii.
c. 4.

toward the Tuileries, for Bread and a Constitution.
Tuileries Sentries do their best; but it serves not:
the Ocean-tide sweeps them away; inundates the
Convention Hall itself; howling, Bread and the Constitution.

1839. Unhappy Senators, unhappy People, there is
yet, after all toils and broils, no Bread, no Constitution. " Du pain, pas tant de longs discours (Bread,
not bursts of Parliamentary eloquence)!" so wailed
the Menads of Maillard five years ago and more: so
wail ye to this hour. The Convention, with unalterable countenance, with what thought one knows
not, keeps its seat in this waste howling chaos; rings
its storm-bell from the Pavilion of Unity. Section
Lepelletier, old Filles Saint-Thomas, who are of the
money-changing species; these and Gilt Youthhood
fly to the rescue: sweep chaos forth again, with leveled bayonets. Paris is declared "in a state of siege."
Pichegru, Conqueror of Holland, who happens to be
here, is named Commandant, till the disturbance
end. He, in one day, so to speak, ends it. He accomplishes the transfer of Billaud, Collot and Company, dissipating all opposition "by two cannon-
shots," blank cannon-shots, and terror of his name;
and thereupon, announcing, with a Laconicism which
should be imitated, "Representatives, your decrees
are executed," * lays down his Commandantship.

1840. This Revolt of Germinal, therefore, has
passed, like a vain cry. The Prisoners rest safe in
Ham, waiting for ships; some 900 "chief Terrorists
of Paris" are disarmed. Sansculottism, swept forth
with bayonets, has vanished, with its misery, to the
bottom of Saint-Antoine and Saint-Marceau.—Time
was when Usher Maillard with Menads could alter
the course of Legislation; but that time is not.
Legislation seems to have got bayonets; Section Lepelletier takes its firelock, not for us! We retire to
our dark dens; our cry of hunger is called a plot of
Pitt; the Saloons glitter, the flesh-colored Drawers
gyrate as before. It was for "The Cabarus," then,
and her Muscadins and Money-changers that we
fought! It was for Balls in flesh-colored drawers
that we took Feudalism by the beard, and did and
dared, shedding our blood like water? Expressive
Silence, muse thou their praise!—

CHAPTER V.

LION SPRAWLING ITS LAST.

1841. Representative Carrier went to the Guillotine, in December last; protesting that he acted by
orders. The Revolutionary Tribunal, after all it has
devoured, has now only, as Anarchic things do, to
devour itself. In the early days of May, men see a
remarkable thing: Fouquier-Tinville pleading at the
Bar once his own. He and his chief Jurymen, Leroi
August-Tenth, Juryman Vilate, a Batch of Sixteen;
pleading hard, protesting that they acted by orders:
but pleading in vain. Thus men break the axe
with which they have done hateful things; the axe
itself having grown hateful. For the rest, Fouquier
died hard enough. "Where are thy Batches?"
howled the people.—"Hungry canaille," asked Fouquier, "is thy Bread cheaper, wanting them?"

1842. Remarkable Fouquier; once but as other
Attorneys and Law-beagles, which hunt ravenous on
this Earth, a well known phasis of human nature;
and now thou art and remainest the most remarkable Attorney that ever lived and hunted in the Upper Air! For, in this terrestrial Course of Time,
there was to be an Avatar of Attorneyism; the
Heavens had said, Let there be an Incarnation, not
divine, of the venatory Attorney-spirit which keeps
its eye on the bond only;—and lo, this was it; and

* Moniteur, Séance du 13 Germinal (2d April), 1795.

they have attorneyed it in its turn. Vanish, then,
thou rat-eyed Incarnation of Attorneyism; who at
bottom wert but as other Attorneys, and too hungry
sons of Adam! Juryman Vilate had striven hard for
life. and published, from his Prison, an ingenious
Book, not unknown to us; but it would not stand:
he also had to vanish; and this his Book of the
"Secret Causes of Thermidor" full of lies, with par-
ticles of truth in it undiscoverable otherwise, is all
that remains of him.

1843. Revolutionary Tribunal has done; but vengeance has not done. Representative Lebon, after
long struggling, is handed over to the ordinary Law
Courts,'and by them guillotined. Nay at Lyons and
elsewhere, resuscitated Moderatism, in its vengeance, will not wait the slow process of Law; but
bursts into the Prisons, sets fire to the Prisons;
burns some three-score imprisoned Jacobins to dire
death, or chokes them "with the smoke of straw."
There go vengeful truculent "Companies of Jesus,"
"Companies of the Sun;" slaying Jacobinism wherever they meet with it; flinging it into the Rhone-
stream;' which once more bears seaward a horrid
cargo.* Whereupon, at Toulon, Jacobinism rises in
revolt; and is like to hang the National Representatives.—With such action and reaction, is not a poor
National Convention hard bested? It is like the
settlement of winds and waters, of seas long tornado-
beaten; and goes on with jumble and with jangle.
Now flung aloft, now sunk in trough of the sea, your
Vessel of the Republic has need of all pilotage and
more.

1844. What Parliament that ever sat under the
Moon had such a series of destinies as this National
Convention of France? It came together to make the
Constitution, and instead of that, it has had to
make nothing but destruction and confusion; to
burn-up Catholicisms, Aristocratisms; to worship
Reason and dig Saltpeter; to fight Titanically with
itself and with the whole world. A Convention
decimated by the Guillotine; above the tenth man
has bowed his neck to the axe. Which has seen
Carmagnoles danced before it, and patriotic strophes
sung amid Church-spoils; the wounded of the 10th
of August defile in hand-barrows; and, in the Pandemonial Midnight, *Égalité's* dames in tricolor
drink lemonade, and spectrum of Sieyes mount, saying, Death sans phrase. A Convention which has
effervesced, and which has congealed; which has
been red with rage, and also pale with rage; sitting
with pistols in its pocket, drawing sword (in a moment of effervescence): now storming to the four
winds, through a Danton-voice, Awake, O France,
and smite the tyrants; now frozen mute under its
Robespierre, and answering his dirge-voice by a dubious gasp. Assassinated, decimated; stabbed at,
shot at, in baths, on streets and staircases; which
has been the nucleus of Chaos. Has it not heard the
chimes at midnight? It has deliberated, beset by
100,000 armed men with artillery furnaces and pro-
vision-carts. It has been betocسined, bestormed;
overflooded by black deluges of Sansculottism; and
has heard the shrill cry, *Bread and Soap*. For, as we
say, it was the nucleus of Chaos; it sat as the center
of Sansculottism; and had spread its pavilion on the
waste Deep, where is neither path nor landmark,
neither bottom nor shore. In intrinsic valor, ingenuity, fidelity, and general force and manhood, it
has perhaps not far surpassed the average of Parliaments; but in frankness of purpose. in singularity
of position, it seeks its fellow. One other Sansculottic submersion, or at most two, and this wearied vessel of a Convention reaches land.

* Moniteur du 27 Juin, du 31 Aout, 1795; "Deux Amis,"
xiii. 121-129.

1845. Revolt of Germinal 12th ended as a vain cry; moribund Sansculottism was swept back into invisibility. There it has lain moaning these six weeks: moaning, and also scheming. Jacobins disarmed, flung forth from their Tribune in mid-air, must needs try to help themselves, in secret conclave under ground. Lo therefore, on the First day of the month Prairial, 20th of May, 1795, sound of the générale once more; beating sharp ran-tan, To arms, to arms!

1846. Sansculottism has risen, yet again, from its death-lair; waste, wild-flowing, as the unfruitful Sea. Saint-Antoine is afoot: 'Bread and Constitution of Ninety-three," so sounds it; so stands it written with chalk on the hats of men. They have their pikes, their firelocks; Paper of Grievances; standards; printed Proclamation, drawn-up in quite official manner,—considering this, and also considering that, a much-enduring Sovereign People, are in Insurrection; will have Bread and the Constitution of Ninety-three. And so the Barrière are seized, and the générale beats, and tocsins discourse discord. Black deluges overflow the Tuileries; spite of sentries, the Sanctuary itself is invaded: enter, to our Order of the Day, a torrent of disheveled women, wailing, "Bread! Bread!" President may well cover himself; and have his own tocsin rung in "the Pavilion of Unity;" the ship of the State again labors and leaks; overwashed, near to swamping, with unfruitful brine.

1847. What a day, once more! Women are driven out: men storm irresistibly in; choke all corridors, thunder at all gates. Deputies, putting forth head, obtest, conjure; Saint-Antoine rages, "Bread and Constitution." Report has risen that the "Convention is assassinating the women:" crushing and rushing, clangor and furor! The oak doors have become as oak tambourines, sounding under the axe of Saint-Antoine; plaster-work crackles, wood-work booms and jingles; door starts up;—bursts-in Saint-Antoine with frenzy and vociferation, with Rag-standards, printed Proclamation, drum-music: astonishment to eye and ear. Gendarmes, loyal Sectioners charge through the other door; they are recharged: musketry exploding: Saint-Antoine cannot be expelled. Obtesting Deputies obtest vainly: Respect the President; approach not the President! Deputy Féraud, stretching out his hands, baring his bosom scarred in the Spanish wars, obtests vainly; threatens and, resists vainly. Rebellious Deputy of the Sovereign, if thou have fought, have not we too? We have no Bread, no Constitution! They wrench poor Féraud; they tumble him, trample him, wrath waxing to see itself work: they drag him into the corridor, dead or near it; sever his head, and fix it on a pike. Ah, did an unexampled Convention want this variety of destiny, too, then? Féraud's bloody head goes on a pike. Such a game has begun; Paris and the Earth may wait how it will end.

1848. And so it billows free through all Corridors: within and without, far as the eye reaches, nothing but Bedlam, and the great Deep broken loose! President Boissy d'Anglas sits like a rock: the rest of the Convention is floated "to the upper benches;" Sectioners and Gendarmes still ranking there to form a kind of wall for them. And Insurrection rages; rolls its drums; will rend its Paper of Grievances, will have this decreed, will have that. Covered sits President Boissy; unyielding; like a rock in the heating of seas. They menace him, level muskets at him, he yields not; they hold up Féraud's bloody head to him, with grave stern air he bows to it, and yields not.

1849. And the Paper of Grievances cannot get itself read for uproar and the drums roll, and the

throats bawl; and Insurrection, like sphere-music, is inaudible for very noise: Decree us this, Decree us that. One man we discern bawling "for the space of an hour at all intervals." "Je demande l'arrestation des coquins et des lâches." Really one of the most comprehensive Petitions ever put up; which indeed, to this hour, includes all that you can reasonably ask Constitution of the Year One, Rotten-Borough, Ballot-Box, or other miraculous Political Ark of the Covenant to do for you to the end of the world! I also demand arrestment of the Knaves and Dastards, and nothing more whatever.—National Representation, deluged with black Sansculottism, glides out, for help elsewhere, for safety elsewhere; here is no help.

1850. About four in the afternoon, there remain hardly more than some Sixty Members: mere friends, or even secret leaders; a remnant of the Mountain-crest, held in silence by Thermidorian thralldom. Now is the time for them; now or never let them descend, and speak! They descend, these Sixty, invited by Sansculottism: Romme of the New Calendar, Ruhl of the Sacred Phial, Goujon, Duquesnoy, Soubrany, and the rest. Glad Sansculottism forms a ring for them; Romme takes the President's chair; they begin resolving and decreeing. Fast enough now comes Decree after Decree, in alternate brief strains, or strophe and antistrophe,—what will cheapen bread, what will awaken the dormant lion. And at every new decree, Sansculottism shouts "Decreed, decreed!" and rolls its drums.

1851. Fast enough; the work of months in hours, —when see, a Figure enters, whom in the lamplight we recognize to be Legendre: and utters words: fit to be hissed out! And then see, Section Lepelletier or other Muscadin Section enters, and Gilt Youth, with leveled bayonets, countenances screwed to the sticking place! Tramp, tramp, with bayonets gleaming in the lamp-light: what can one do, worn down with long riot, grown heartless, dark, hungry, but roll back, but rush back, and escape who can? The very windows need to be thrown up, that Sansculottism may escape fast enough. Money-changer Sections and Gilt Youth sweep them forth, with steel besom, far into the depths of Saint-Antoine. Triumph once more! The Decrees of that Sixty are not so much as rescinded; they are declared null and non-extant. Romme, Ruhl, Goujon and the ringleaders, some thirteen in all, are decreed Accused. Permanent-session ends at three in the morning.* Sansculottism, once more flung resupine, lies sprawling; sprawling its last.

1852. Such was the 1st of Prairial, 20th of May, 1795. Second and 3d of Prairial, during which Sansculottism still sprawled, and unexpectedly rang its tocsin, and assembled in arms, availed Sansculottism nothing. What though with our Rommes and Ruhls, accused but not yet arrested, we make a new "True National Convention" of our own, over in the East; and put the others Out of Law? What though we rank in arms and march? Armed Force and Muscadin Sections, some 30,000 men, environ that old False Convention: we can but bully one another; bandying nicknames, "Muscadins," against "Blood-drinkers (Buveurs de Sang)." Féraud's Assassin, taken with the red hand, and sentenced, and now near to Guillotine and Place de Grève, is retaken; is carried back into Saint-Antoine:—to no purpose. Convention Sectionaries and Gilt Youth come, according to Decree, to seek him; nay to disarm Saint-Antoine! And they do disarm it: by rolling of cannon, by springing upon enemy's can non; by military audacity, and terror of the Law. Saint-Antoine surrenders its arms; Santerre even

* "Deux Amis." xiii. 129-146.

advising it, anxious for life and brew-house. Féraud's Assassin flings himself from a high roof: and all is lost.*

1853. Discerning which things, old Ruhl shot a pistol through his old white head; dashed his life in pieces, as he had done the Sacred Phial of Rheims. Romme, Goujon and the others stand ranked before a swiftly-appointed, swift Military Tribunal. Hearing the sentence, Goujon drew a knife, struck it into his breast, passed it to his neighbor Romme; and fell dead. Romme did the like; and another all but did it; Roman-death rushing on there, as in electric-chain, before your Bailiffs could intervene! The Guillotine had the rest.

They were the *Ultimi Romanorum.* Billaud, Collot and Company are now ordered to be tried for life; but are found to be already off, shipped for Sinn-marri, and the hot mud of Surinam. There let Billaud surround himself with flocks of tame parrots: Collot take the yellow fever, and drinking a whole bottle of brandy, burn up his entrails.† Sansculottism sprawls no more. The dormant lion has become a dead one; and now, as we see, any hoof may smite him.

CHAPTER VI.

GRILLED-HERRINGS.

1854. So dies Sansculottism, the *body* of Sansculottism; or is changed. Its ragged Pythian Carmagnole-dance has transformed itself into a Pyrrhic, into a dance of Cabarus Balls. Sansculottism is dead; extinguished by new *isms* of that kind, which were its own natural progeny; and is buried, we may say, with such deafening jubilation and disharmony of funeral-knell on their part, that only after some half-century or so does one begin to learn clearly why it ever was alive.

1855. And yet a meaning lay in it: Sansculottism verily was alive, a New-Birth of TIME; nay it still lives, and is not dead but changed. The *soul* of it still lives; still works far and wide, through one bodily shape into another less amorphous, as is the way of cunning Time with his New-Births:—till, in some perfected shape, it embrace the whole circuit of the world! For the wise man may now everywhere discern that he must found on his manhood, not on the garnitures of his manhood. He who, in these Epochs of our Europe, founds on garnitures, formulas, culottisms of what sort soever, is founding on old cloth and sheepskin, and cannot endure. But as for the body of Sansculottism, that is dead and buried,—and, one hopes, need not reappear, in primary amorphous shape, for another thousand years.

1856. It was the frightfulest thing ever born of Time? One of the frightfulest. This Convention, now grown Anti-jacobin, did, with an eye to justify and fortify itself, publish Lists of what the Reign of Terror had perpetrated: Lists of Persons guillotined. The Lists, cries splenetic Abbé Montgaillard, were not complete. They contain the names of, How many persons thinks the Reader?—Two thousand all but a few. There were above 4,000, cries Montgaillard: so many were guillotined, fusilladed, noyaded, done to dire death; of whom 900 were women.‡ It is a horrible sum of human lives, M. l'Abbé:—some ten times as many shot rightly on a field of battle, and one might have had his Glorious-Victory with Te-Deum. It is not far from the two-hundredth part of what perished in the entire Seven-

Years War. By which Seven-Years War, did not the great Fritz wrench Silesia from the great Theresa; and a Pompadour, stung by epigrams, satisfy herself that she could not be an Agnès Sorel? The head of man is a strange vacant sounding-shell, M. l'Abbé; and studies Crocker to small purpose.

1857. But what if History somewhere on this Planet were to hear of a Nation, the third soul of whom had not, for thirty weeks each year, as many third-rate potatoes as would sustain him?* History, in that case, feels bound to consider that starvation is starvation; that starvation from age to age presupposes much; History ventures to assert that the French Sansculotte of Ninety-three, who, roused from long death-sleep, could rush at once to the frontiers, and die fighting for an immortal Hope and Faith of Deliverance for him and his, was but the *second*-miserablest of men! The Irish Sans-potato, had he not senses, then, nay a soul? In his frozen darkness, it was bitter for him to die famishing; bitter to see his children famish. It was bitter for him to be a beggar, a liar, and a knave. Nay, if that dreary Greenland-wind of benighted Want, perennial from sire to son, had frozen him into a kind of torpor and numb callosity, so that he saw not, felt not, —was this, for a creature with a soul in it, some assuagement; or the cruelest wretchedness of all?

1858. Such things were; such things are; and they go on in silence peaceably;—and Sansculottisms follow them. History, looking back over this France through long times, back to Turgot's time for instance, when dumb Drudgery staggered up to its King's Palace, and in wide expanse of sallow faces, squalor and winged raggedness, presented hieroglyphically its Petition of Grievances; and for answer got hanged on "a new gallows forty feet high,"—confesses mournfully that there is no period to be met with, in which the general 25,000,000 of France suffered *less* than in this period which they name Reign of Terror! But it was not the Dumb Millions that suffered here; it was the Speaking Thousands, and Hundreds, and Units; who shrieked and published, and made the world ring with their wail, as they could and should: that is the grand peculiarity. The frightfulest Births of Time are never the loud-speaking ones, for these soon die, they are the silent ones, which can live from century to century! Anarchy, hateful as Death, is abhorrent to the whole nature of man; and so must itself soon die.

1859. Wherefore let all men know what of depth and of height is still revealed in man; and with fear and wonder, with just sympathy and just antipathy, with clear eye and open heart, contemplate it and appropriate it; and draw innumerable inferences from it. This inference, for example, among the first: That "if the gods of this lower world will sit on their glittering thrones, indolent as Epicurus's gods, with the living Chaos of Ignorance and Hunger weltering uncared-for at their feet, and smooth Parasites preaching, Peace, peace, when there is no peace," then the dark Chaos, it would seem, will rise;—has risen, and, O Heavens, has it not tanned their skins into breeches for itself? That there be no second Sansculottism in our Earth for a thousand years, let us understand well what the first was; and let Rich and Poor of us go and do *otherwise.*—But to our tale.

1860. The Muscadin Sections greatly rejoice; Cabarus Balls gyrate; the well-nigh insoluble problem, *Republic without Anarchy*, have not we solved it?—Law of Fraternity or Death is gone: chimerical *Obtain-who-need* has become practical *Hold-who-have.* To anarchic Republic of the Poverties there has succeeded orderly Republic of the Luxuries; which will continue as long as it can.

* Toulongeon, v. 297; Moniteur, Nos. 244, 245, 246.
† "Dictionnaire des Hommes Marquans," §§ Billaud, Collot.
‡ Montgaillard, iv. 241.

* "Report of the Irish Poor-Law Commission," 1836.

1861. On the Pont au Change, on the Place de Grève, in long sheds, Mercier, in these summer evenings, saw working-men at their repast. One's allotment of daily bread has sunk to an ounce and a half "Plates containing each three grilled herrings, sprinkled with shorn onions, wetted with a little vinegar; to this add some morsel of boiled prunes, and lentils swimming in a clear sauce: at these frugal tables, the cook's gridiron hissing near by, and the pot simmering on a fire between two stones, I have seen them ranged by the hundred; consuming without bread, their scant messes, far too moderate for the keenness of their appetite and the extent of their stomach."* Seine water, rushing plenteous by, will supply the deficiency.

1862. O Man of Toil, thy struggling and thy daring these six long years of insurrection and tribulation, thou hast profited nothing by it, then? Thou consumest thy herring and water, in the blessed gold-red evening. O why was the Earth so beautiful, becrimsoned with dawn and twilight, if man's dealings with man were to make it a vale of scarcity, of tears, not even soft tears? Destroying of Bastilles, discomfiting of Brunswicks, fronting of Principalities and Powers, of Earth and Tophet, all that thou hast dared and endured,—it was for a republic of the Cabarus Saloons? Patience; thou must have patience: the end is not yet.

CHAPTER VII.

THE WHIFF OF GRAPE-SHOT.

1863. In fact, what can be more natural, one may say inevitable, as a Post-Sansculottic transitionary state, than even this? Confused wreck of a Republic of the Poverties, which ended in Reign of Terror, is arranging itself into such composure as it can. Evangel of Jean-Jacques, and most other Evangels, becoming incredible, what is there for it but return to the old Evangel of Mammon? Contrat-Social is true or untrue, Brotherhood is Brotherhood or Death: but money always will buy money's worth: in the wreck of human dubitations, this remains indubitable, that Pleasure is pleasant. Aristocracy of Feudal Parchment has passed away with a mighty rushing; and now, by a natural course, we arrive at Aristocracy of the Money-bag. It is the course through which all European Societies are, at this hour, traveling. Apparently a still baser sort of Aristocracy? An infinitely baser; the basest yet known.

1864. In which, however, there is this advantage, that, like Anarchy itself, it cannot continue. Hast thou considered how Thought is stronger than Artillery-parks, and (were it fifty years after death and martyrdom, or were it 2,000 years) writes and unwrites Acts of Parliament, removes mountains; models the World like soft clay? Also how the beginning of all Thought, worth the name, is Love; and the wise head never yet was without first the generous heart? The Heavens cease not their bounty; they send us generous hearts into every generation. And now what generous heart can pretend to itself, or be hoodwinked into believing, that Loyalty to the Money-bag is a noble Loyalty? Mammon, cries the generous heart out of all ages and countries, is the basest of known Gods, even of known Devils. In him what glory is there, that ye should worship him? No glory discernible; not even terror: at best, detestability, ill-matched with despicability!—Generous hearts, discerning, on this hand, widespread Wretchedness, dark without and within, moistening its ounce-and-half of bread with tears; and, on that hand, mere Balls in flesh-colored

*"Nouveau Paris," iv. 116.

drawers, and inane or foul glitter of such sort,—cannot but ejaculate, cannot but announce: Too much, O divine Mammon; somewhat too much!—The voice of these, once announcing itself, carries *fiat* and pereat in it, for all things here below.

1865. Meanwhile we will hate Anarchy as Death, which it is; and the things worse than Anarchy shall be hated *more*. Surely Peace alone is fruitful. Anarchy is destruction; a burning up, say, of Shams and Insupportabilities; but which leaves Vacancy behind. Know this also, that out of a world of Unwise nothing but an Unwisdom can be made. Arrange it, constitution-build it, sift it through ballot-boxes as thou wilt, it is and remains an Unwisdom, —the new prey of new quacks and unclean things, the latter end of it slightly better than the beginning. Who can bring a wise thing out of men unwise? Not one. And so Vacancy and general Abolition having come for this France, what can Anarchy do more? Let there be Order, were it under the Soldier's Sword; let there be Peace, that the bounty of the Heavens be not spilt; that what of Wisdom they do send us bring fruit in its season!—It remains to be seen how the quellers of Sansculottism were themselves quelled, and sacred right of Insurrection was blown away by gunpowder; wherewith this singular eventful History called "French Revolution" ends.

1866. The Convention, driven such a course by wild wind, wild tide, and steerage and non-steerage, these three years, has become weary of its own existence, sees all men weary of it; and wishes heartily to finish. To the last it has to strive with contradictions; it is now getting fast ready with a Constitution, yet knows no peace. Sieyes, we say, is making the Constitution once more; has as good as made it. Warned by experience, the great Architect alters much, admits much. Distinction of Active and Passive Citizen, that is, Money-qualification for Electors: nay Two Chambers, "Council of Ancients," as well as "Council of Five-hundred:" to that conclusion have we come! In a like spirit, eschewing that fatal self-denying ordinance of your Old Constituents, we enact not only that actual Convention Members are re-eligible, but that Two-thirds of them must be re-elected. The Active Citizen Electors shall for this time have free choice of only One-third of their National Assembly. Such enactment, of Two-thirds to be re-elected, we append to our Constitution; we submit our Constitution to the Townships of France, and say, Accept *both*, or reject both. Unsavory as this appendix may be, the Townships, by overwhelming majority, accept and ratify. With Directory of Five; with Two good Chambers, double-majority of them nominated by ourselves, one hopes this Constitution may prove final. *March* it will; for the legs of it, the re-elected Two-thirds, are already here, able to march. Sieyes looks at his paper-fabric with just pride.

1867. But now see how the contumacious Sections, Lepelletier foremost, kick against the pricks. Is it not manifest infraction of one's Elective Franchise, Rights of Man, and Sovereignty of the People, this appendix ,of re-electing *your* Two-thirds? Greedy tyrants, who would perpetuate yourselves!—For the truth is, victory over Saint-Antoine, and long right of Insurrection, has spoiled these men. Nay spoiled all men. Consider, too, how each man was free to hope what he liked; and now there is to be no hope, there is to be fruition, fruition of *this*.

1868. In men spoiled by long right of Insurrection, what confused ferments will rise, tongues once begun wagging! Journalists declaim, your Lacretelles, Laharpes; Orators spout. There is Royalism traceable in it, and Jacobinism. On the West Frontier, in deep secrecy, Pichegru, durst he trust his Army, is treating with Condé: in these Sections, there spout wolves in sheep's clothing, masked Emigrants and Royalists.* All men, as we say, had hoped, each that the Election would do something for his own side: and now there is no Election, or only the third of one. Black is united with white against this clause of the Two-thirds; all the Unruly of France, who see their trade thereby near ending.

1869. Section Lepelletier, after Addresses enough, finds that such clause is a manifest infraction; that it, Lepelletier for one, will simply not conform thereto; and invites all other free Sections to join it, "in central Committee," in resistance to oppression.† The Sections join it, nearly all; strong with their 40,000 fighting men. The Convention therefore may look to itself! Lepelletier, on this 12th day of Vendémiaire, 4th of October, 1795, is sitting in open contravention, in its Convent of Filles Saint-Thomas, Rue Vivienne, with guns primed. The Convention has some 5,000 regular troops at hand, Generals in abundance; and a Fifteen-hundred of miscellaneous persecuted Ultra-Jacobins, whom in this crisis it has hastily got together and armed, under the title of *Patriots of Eighty-nine*. Strong in Law, it sends its General Menou to disarm Lepelletier.

1870. General Menou marches accordingly, with due summons and demonstration: with no result. General Menou, about eight in the evening, finds that he is standing ranked in the Rue Vivienne emitting vain summonses; with primed guns pointed out of every window at him; and that he cannot disarm Lepelletier. He has to return, with whole skin, but without success; and be thrown into arrest as "a traitor." Whereupon the whole 40,000 join this Lepelletier which cannot be vanquished: to what hand shall a quaking Convention now turn? Our poor Convention, after such voyaging, just entering harbor, so to speak, has *struck on the bar*;—and labors there frightfully, with breakers roaring round it, 40,000 of them, like to wash it, and its Sieyes Cargo, and the whole future of France into the deep! Yet one last time, it struggles, ready to perish.

1871. Some call for Barras to be made Commandant; he conquered in Thermidor. Some, what is more to the purpose, bethink them of the Citizen Bonaparte, unemployed Artillery-Officer, who took Toulon. A man of head, a man of action: Barras is named Commandant's-Cloak; this young Artillery-Officer is named Commandant. He was in the Gallery at the moment, and heard it; he withdrew, some half-hour, to consider with himself; after a half-hour of grim compressed considering, to be or not to be, he answers *Yea*.

1872. And now, a man of head being at the center of it, the whole matter gets vital. Swift, to Camp of Sablons; to secure the Artillery, there are not twenty men guarding it! A swift Adjutant, Murat is the name of him, gallops; gets thither some minutes within time, for Lepelletier was also on march that way: the Cannon are ours. And now beset this post, and beset that; rapid and firm: at Wicket of the Louvre, in Cul-de-sac Dauphin, in Rue Saint-Honoré, from Pont-Neuf all along the north Quays, southward to Pont-ci-devant Royal.—rank round the Sanctuary of the Tuileries, a ring of steel discipline; let every gunner have his match burning, and all men stand to their arms!

1873. Thus there is Permanent-session through the night; and thus at sunrise of the morrow there is seen sacred Insurrection once again: vessel of

State laboring on the bar; and tumultuous sea all round her, beating *générale*, arming and sounding,— not ringing tocsin, for we have left no tocsin but our own in the Pavilion of Unity. It is an imminence of shipwreck, for the whole world to gaze at. Frightfully she labors, that poor ship, within cable length of port; huge peril for her. However, she has a man at the helm: Insurgent messages, received and not received; messenger admitted blindfolded; counsel and counter-counsel: the poor ship labors!—Vendémiaire 13th, year 4: curious enough, of all days, it is the 5th day of October, anniversary of that Menadmarch six years ago; by sacred right of Insurrection we are got thus far.

1874. Lepelletier has seized the Church of Saint-Roch; has seized the Pont-Neuf, our picket there retreating without fire. Stray shots fall from Lepelletier; rattle down on the very Tuileries Staircase. On the other hand, women advance disheveled, shrieking, Peace; Lepelletier behind them waving his hat in sign that we shall fraternize. Steady! The Artillery-Officer is steady as bronze; can, if need were, be quick as lightning. He sends 800 muskets with ball-cartridges to the Convention itself; honorable Members shall act with these in case of extremity: whereat they look grave enough. Four of the afternoon is struck.* Lepelletier, making nothing by messengers, by fraternity or hat-waving, bursts out, along the Southern Quai Voltaire along streets and passages. treble-quick, in huge veritable onslaught! Whereupon, thou bronze Artillery-Officer—? "Fire!" say the bronze lips. And roar and thunder, roar and again roar, continual, volcano-like, goes his great gun, in the Cul-de-sac Dauphin against the Church of Saint-Roch; go his great guns on the Pont-Royal; go all his great guns;—blow to air some 200 men, mainly about the Church of Saint-Roch! Lepelletier cannot stand such horseplay; no Sectioner can stand it; the 40,000 yield on all sides, scour toward covert. "Some hundred or so of them gathered about the *Théâtre de la République*; but," says he, "a few shells dislodged them. It was all finished at six."

1875. The Ship is *over* the bar, then: free she bounds shoreward,—amid shouting and vivats! Citoyen Bonaparte is "named General of the Interior, by acclamation;" quelled Sections have to disarm in such humor as they may; sacred right of Insurrection is gone forever! The Sieyes Constitution can disembark itself, and begin marching. The miraculous Convention Ship has got to land;—and is there, shall we figuratively say, changed, as Epic Ships are wont, into a kind of *Sea Nymph*, never to sail more; to roam the waste Azure, a Miracle in History!

1876. "It is false," says Napoleon, "that we fired first with blank charge; it had been a waste of life to do that." Most false: the firing was with sharp and sharpest shot, to all men it was plain that here was no sport; the rabbets and plinths of Saint-Roch Church show splintered by it to this hour.—Singular: in old Broglie's time, six years ago, this Whiff of Grape-shot was promised; but it could not be given then; could not have profited then. Now, however, the time is come for it, and the man; and behold, you have it; and the thing we specifically call *French Revolution* is blown into space by it, and become a thing that was!—

CHAPTER VIII.

FINIS.

1877. Homer's Epos, it is remarked, is like a Bas-Relief sculpture: it does not conclude, but merely ceases. Such, indeed, is the Epos of Universal His-

---

* Napoleon, *Las Cases* ("Choix des Rapports," xvii. 808-411).

† "Deux Amis," xiii. 375-406.

* Moniteur, Séance du 5 Octobre, 1795.

tory itself. Directorates, Consulates, Emperorships, Restorations, Citizen-Kingships succeed this Business in due series, in due genesis one out of the other. Nevertheless the First-parent of all these may be said to have gone to air in the way we see. A Baboeuf Insurrection, next year, will die in the birth; stifled by the Soldiery. A Senate, if tinged with Royalism, can be purged by the Soldiery; and an 18th of Fructidor transacted by the mere show of bayonets.* Nay Soldiers' bayonets can be used à posteriori on a Senate, and make it leap out of window,—still bloodless; and produce an 18th of Brumaire.† Such changes must happen: but they are managed by intriguings, caballings, and then by orderly word of command; almost like mere changes of Ministry. Not in general by sacred right of Insurrection, but by milder methods growing ever milder, shall the events of French History be henceforth brought to pass.

1878. It is admitted that this Directorate, which owned, at its starting, these three things, an "old table, a sheet of paper, and an ink-bottle," and no visible money or arrangement whatever,‡ did wonders: that France, since the Reign of Terror hushed itself, has been a new France, awakened like a giant out of torpor; and has gone on, in the Internal Life of it, with continual progress. As for the External form and forms of Life, what can we say, except that out of the Eater there comes Strength; out of the Unwise there comes *not* Wisdom!—Shams are burnt up; nay, what as yet is the peculiarity of France, the very Cant of them is burned up. The new Realities are not yet come: ah no, only Phantasms. Paper models, tentative Prefigurements of such! In France there are now 4,000,000 Landed Properties; that black portent of an Agrarian Law is, as it were, *realized.* What is still stranger, we understand all Frenchmen have "the right of duel:" the Hackney-coachman with the Peer, if insult be given: such is the law of Public Opinion. Equality at least in death! The Form of Government is by Citizen King, frequently shot at, not yet shot.

1879. On the whole, therefore, has it not been fulfilled what was prophesied, ex post facto indeed, by the Arch-quack Cagliostro, or another? He, as he looked in rapt vision and amazement into these things, thus spake :§ "Ha! What is *this?* Angels, Uriel, Anachiel, and ye other Five: Pentagon of Rejuvenescence; Power that destroyedst Original Sin: Earth, Heaven, and thou Outer Limbo, which

* Moniteur. du 4 Septembre, 1797.
† 9th November. 1799 ("Choix des Rapports," xvii. 1-96).
‡ Bailleul, "Examen critique des Considerations de Mad. de Staël." 215.
§ "Diamond Necklace" (Carlyle's Miscellanies).

men name Hell! Does the EMPIRE OF IMPOSTURE waver? Burst there, in starry sheen, updarting, Light-rays from out of *its* dark foundations; as it rocks and heaves, not in travail-throes but in death-throes? Yea, Light-rays, piercing, clear, that salute the Heavens,—lo, they *kindle* it; their starry clearness becomes as red Hell-fire!

1880. "IMPOSTURE is in flames, Imposture is burnt up: one red sea of Fire, wild-billowing, enwraps the World; with its fire-tongue licks at the very Stars. Thrones are hurled into it, and Dubois Miters, and Prebendal Stalls that drop fatness, and—ha! what see I?—all the *Gigs* of Creation: all, all! Woe is me! Never since Pharaoh's Chariots, in the Red Sea of water, was there wreck of Wheel-vehicles like this in the Sea of Fire. Desolate, as ashes, as gases, shall they wander in the wind.

1881. "Higher, higher yet flames the Fire-Sea; crackling with new dislocated timber: hissing with leather and prunella. The metal Images are molten; the marble Images become mortar-lime; the stone Mountains sulkily explode. RESPECTABILITY, with all her collected Gigs inflamed for funeral pyre, wailing, leaves the Earth: not to return save under new Avatar. Imposture how it burns, through generations: how it is burnt up; for a time. The World is black ashes;—which, ah, when will they grow green? The Images all run into amorphous Corinthian brass: all Dwellings of men destroyed; the very mountains peeled and riven, the valleys black and dead; it is an empty World! Woe to them that shall be born then!——A King, a Queen (ah me!) were hurled in; did rustle once; flew aloft, crackling; like paper-scroll. Iscariot Égalité was hurled in; thou grim De Launay, with thy grim Bastile; whole kindreds and peoples; five millions of mutually destroying Men. For it is the End of the dominion of IMPOSTURE (which is darkness and opaque Fire-damp); and the burning up, with unquenchable fire, of all the Gigs that are in the Earth." This prophecy, we say, has it not been fulfilled, is it not fulfilling?

1882. And so here, O Reader, has the time come for us two to part. Toilsome was our journeying together; not without offence; but it is done. To me thou wert as a beloved shade, the disembodied or not yet embodied spirit of a Brother. To thee I was but as a Voice. Yet was our relation a kind of sacred one; doubt not that! For whatsoever once sacred things become hollow jargons, yet while the Voice of Man speaks with Man, hast thou not there the living fountain out of which all sacrednesses sprang, and will yet spring? Man, by the nature of him, is definable as "an incarnated Word." Ill stands it with me if I have spoken falsely; thine also it was to hear truly. Farewell.

CHRONOLOGICAL SUMMARY OF THE FRENCH REVOLUTION.

[DRAWN UP BY "PHILO," FOR EDITION 1857.]

THE BASTILLE.

(May 10, 1774—October 5, 1789.)

1774.

Louis XV. dies, at Versailles, May 10, 1774; of small-pox, after a short illness; Great-grandson of Louis XIV.; are then 64; in the 59th year of his nominal " reign." Retrospect to 1774; sad decay of " Realized Ideals," secular and sacred. Scenes about Louis XV.'s death-bed. Scene of the Noblesse entering, " with a noise like thunder," to do homage to the New King and Queen. New King, Louis XVI., was his Predecessor's Grandson; age then near 20, —born August 23, 1754. New Queen was Marie-Antoinette, Daughter (8th daughter, 12th child) of the great Empress Maria Theresa and her Emperor Francis (originally " Duke of Lorraine," but with no territory there; her great this time was under 19 (born November 2, 1755). Louis and she were wedded four years ago (May 16, 1770); but had as yet no children—none till 1778, when their first was born; A Daughter known long afterward as Duchess d'Angoulême. Two Sons followed, who were successively called " Dauphin;" but died both, the second in very miserable circumstances, while still in boyhood. Their fourth and last child, a Daughter (1786), lived only 11 months. These two were now King and Queen, piously reckoning themselves " too young to reign."

December 16, 1773, Tea, a celebrated cargo of it, had been flung out in the harbor of Boston, Massachusetts: June 7, 1775, Battle of Bunker's Hill, first of the American War, is fought in the same neighborhood,—far over seas.

1744—1783.

Change of Administration. Maurepas, a man now 73 years old and of great levity, is appointed Primo-Minister: Vergennes favorably known for his correct habits, for his embassies in Turkey, in Sweden, gets the Department of Foreign Affairs. Old Parlement is reinstated; "Parlement Maupeou," which had been invented for getting edicts, particularly tax-edicts, " registered," and made available in law, is dismissed. Turgot, made Controller-General of Finances ("Chancellor of the Exchequer" and something more), August 24, 1774, gives rise to high hopes, being already known as a man of much intelligence speculative and practical, of noble patriotic intentions, and of a probity beyond question.

There are many changes; but one steady fact of supreme significance, continued Deficit of Revenue.—that is the only History of the Period. Noblesse and Clergy are exempt from direct imposts; no tax that can be devised, on such principle, will yield due ways and means. Meanings of that fact: little surmised by the then populations of France. Turgot aiming at juster principles, cannot: " Corn-trade" (domestic) " made free," and many improvements and high intentions:—much discontent at Court in consequence; famine-riots withal, and " gallows forty feet high." Turgot will tax Noblesse and Clergy like the other ranks; tempest of astonishment and indignation in consequence: Turgot dismissed, May, 1776. Flat snuff-boxes come out, this summer, under the name of Turgotines, as being "*platitudes*" (in the notion of a fashionable snuffing public), like the Plans of this Controller. Necker, a Genevese become rich by Banking in Paris, and well seen by the Philosophe party, is appointed Controller in his stead (1776);—and there is continued Deficit of Revenue.

For the rest, Benevolence, Tolerance, Doctrine of universal Love and Charity to good and bad. Skepticism, Philosophism, Sensualism: portentous " Electuary," of sweet taste, into which " Good and Evil," the distinctions of them lost, have been mashed up. Jean-Jacques, Contrat-Social; universal Millennium, of Liberty, Brotherhood, and whatever is desirable, expected to be rapidly approaching on those terms. Balloons, Horse-races, Anglomania. Continued Deficit of Revenue. Necker's plans for " filling up the Deficit " are not approved of, and are only partially gone into: Frugality is of slow operation; curtailment of expenses occasions numerous dismissals, numerous discontents at Court: from Noblesse and Clergy, if their privilege of exemption be touched, what is to be hoped?

American-English War (since April, 1755); Franklin, and Agents of the Revolted Colonies, at Paris (1776 and afterward), where their Cause is in high favor. French Treaty with Revolted Colonies, February 6, 1778; extensive Official smugglings of supplies to them (in which Beaumarchais is much concerned) for some time before. Departure of French " volunteer" Auxiliaries, under Lafayette, 1778. " Volunteers" these, not sanctioned, only countenanced and furthered, the public clamor being strong that way. War from England, in consequence; Rochambeau to America, with public Auxiliaries, in 1780: —War not notable, except by the Siege of Gibraltar, and by the general result arrived at shortly after.

Continued Deficit of Revenue: Necker's ulterior plans still less approved of; by Noblesse and Clergy, least of all. January, 1781, he publishes a Compte Rendu (" Account Rendered," of himself and them), " Two hundred thousand copies of it sold;—and is dismissed in the May following. Returns to Switzerland; and there writes New Books, on the same interesting subject or pair of subjects. Maurepas dies, November 21, 1781: the essential " Prime Minister " is henceforth the Controller-General, if any such could be found; there being an ever-increasing Deficit of Revenue,—a Millennium thought to be just coming on, and evidently no money in the pocket. Siege of Gibraltar (September 13, to middle of November, 1782): Siege futile on the part of France and Spain; hopeless since that day (September 13) of the red-hot balls. General result arrived at is important: American Independence recognized (Peace of Versailles, January 20, 1783). Lafayette returns in illustrious condition; named Scipio Americanus by some able-editors of the time.

1783—1787.

Ever-increasing Deficit of Revenue. Worse, not better, since Necker's dismissal. After one or two transient Controllers, who can do nothing, Calonne, a memorable one, is nominated, November, 1783. Who continues, with lavish expenditure raised by loans, contenting all the world by his liberality, " quenching fire by oil thrown on it;" for three years and more. " All the world was holding out its hand, I held out my hat." Ominous scandalous Affair called of the Diamond Necklace (Cardinal de Rohan, Dame de Lamotte, Arch-Quack Cagliostro the principal actors), tragically compromising the Queen's name who had no vestige of concern with it, becomes public as Criminal-Trial, 1785: penal sentence on the above active parties and others, May 31, 1786: with immense rumor and conjecture from all mankind. Calonne, his borrowing resources being out, convokes the Notables (First Convocation of the Notables) February 22, 1787, to sanction his new Plans of Taxing; who will not hear of them or of him: so that he is dismissed, and " exiled," April 8, 1787. First Convocation of Notables,—who treat not of this thing only, but of all manner of public things, and mention States-General among others,—sat from February 22 to May 25, 1787.

1787.

Cardinal Loménie de Brienne, who had long been ambitious of the post, succeeds Calonne. A man now of sixty; dissolute, worthless;—devises Tax-Edicts, Stamp-tax (Edit du Timbre, July 6, 1787) and others, with " successive loans," and the like: which the Parlement, greatly to the joy of the Public, all virtually in opposition; Parlements, at Paris and elsewhere, have a cheap method of becoming glorious. Contests of Loménie and Parlement. Beds-of-Justice (first of them, August 6, 1787); Lettres-de-Cachet, and the like methods; general " Exile" of Parlement (August 15, 1787), who return upon conditions, September 20. Increasing ferment of the Public. Loménie helps himself by temporary shifts till he can, privately, get ready for wrestling down the rebellious Parlement.

1788. JANUARY—SEPTEMBER.

Spring of 1788, grand scheme of dismissing the Parlement altogether, and nominating instead a "Plenary

Court (Cour Plénière)," which shall be obedient in "registering" and in other points. Scheme detected before quite ripe: Parlement in permanent session thereupon; haranguing all night (May 3); applausive idle crowds inundating the Outer Courts; D'Espréménil and Goeslard de Monsabert seized by military in the gray of the morning (May 4), and whirled off to distant places of imprisonment: Parlement itself dismissed to exile. Attempt to govern (that is, to raise supplies) by Royal Edict simply,—"Plenary Court" having expired in the birth. Rebellion of all the Provincial Parlements; idle Public more and more noisily approving and applauding. Destructive Hail-storm, July 13, which was remembered next year. Royal Edict (August 8), That States-General, often vaguely promised before, shall actually assemble in May next. Proclamation (August 16), That "Treasury Payments be henceforth three-fifths in cash, two-fifths in paper,"—in other words, that the Treasury is fallen insolvent. Loménie thereupon immediately dismissed: with immense explosion of popular rejoicing, more riotous than usual. Neckor, favorite of all the world, is immediately (August 24) recalled from Switzerland to succeed him, and be "Saviour of France."

1788. NOVEMBER—DECEMBER.

Second Convocation of the Notables (November 5—December 12), by Necker, for the purpose of settling *how*, in various essential particulars, the States-General shall be held. For instance, Are the Three Estates to meet as one Deliberative Body? Or as Three, or Two? Above all, what is to be the relative force, in deciding, of the Third Estate or Commonalty? Notables, as other less formal Assemblages had done and do, depart without settling any of the points in question; most points remain unsettled.—especially that of the Third Estate and its relative force. Elections begin everywhere, January, 1789. Troubles of France seem now to be about becoming Revolution in France. Commencement of the "French Revolution,"—henceforth a phenomenon absorbing all others for mankind,—is commonly dated here.

1789. MAY—JUNE.

Assembling of States-General at Versailles; Procession to the Church of St. Louis there, May 4. Third Estate has the Nation behind it; wishes to be a main element in the business. Hopes, and (led by Mirabeau and other able heads) decides, that it must be the main element of all,—and will continue "inert," and do nothing, till that come about; namely, till the other Two Estates, Noblesse and Clergy, be joined with it; in which conjunct state it can outvote them, and may become what it wishes. "Inertia," or the scheme of doing only harangues and adroit formalities, is adopted by it; adroitly persevered in, for seven weeks: much to the hope of France; to the alarm of Necker and the Court.

Court decides to intervene. Hall of Assembly is found shut (Saturday June 20); Third-Estate Deputies take Oath, celebrated "Oath of the Tennis-Court," in that emergency. Emotion of French mankind. Monday June 22, Court does intervene, but with reverse effect: Séance Royale, Royal Speech, giving open intimation of much significance. "If you Three Estates cannot agree, I the King will myself achieve the happiness of my People." Noblesse and Clergy leave the Hall along with King; Third Estate remains pondering this intimation. Enter Supreme-Usher de Brézé, to command departure; Mirabeau's fulminant words to him: exit De Brézé, fruitless and worse,' amid seas of angry people." All France on the edge of blazing out: Court recoils; Third Estate, other two now joining it on order, triumphs, successful in every particular. The States-General are henceforth "National Assembly;" called in Books distinctively "Constituent Assembly;" that is, Assembly meant "to make the Constitution,"—perfect Constitution, under which the French People might realize their Millennium.

1789. JUNE—JULY.

Great hope, great excitement, great suspicion. Court terrors and plans: old Maréchal Broglie,—this is the Broglie who was young in the Seven-Years War; son of a Marshal Broglie, and grandson of another, who much filled the Newspapers in their time. Gardes Françaises at Paris need to be confined to their quarters; and cannot (June 26). Sunday, July 12, News that Necker is dismissed, and gone homeward overnight: panic terror of Paris, kindling into hot frenzy:—ends in besieging the Bastille; and in taking it, chiefly by infinite noise, the Gardes Françaises at length mutely assisting in the rear. Bastille falls, "like the City of Jericho, by sound," Tuesday, July 14, 1789. Kind of "fire-baptism" to the Revolution; which continues insuppressible thenceforth, and beyond hope of suppression. All France, "as National Guards, to suppress Brigands and enemies to the making of the Constitution," takes arms.

1789. AUGUST—OCTOBER.

Scipio Americanus, Mayor Bailly and "Patrollotism versus Patriotism" (August, September). Hope, terror,

suspicion. excitement, rising ever more, toward the transcendental pitch:—continued scarcity of grain. Progress toward 5th of October, called here "insurrection of Women." Regiment de Flandre has come to Versailles (September 23); Officers have had a dinner (October 3), with much demonstration and gesticulative foolery, of an anti-constitutional and monarchic character. Paris, semi-delirious, hears of it (Sunday, October 4), with endless emotion;—next day, some "10,000 women" (men being under awe of "Patrollotism") march upon Versailles; followed by endless miscellaneous multitudes, and finally by Lafayette and National Guards. Phenomena and procedure there. Result is, they bring the Royal Family and National Assembly home with them to Paris; Paris thereafter Center of the Revolution, and October 5 a memorable day.

1789. OCTOBER—DECEMBER.

"First Emigration," of certain higher Noblesse and Princes of the Blood; which more or less continues through the ensuing years, and at length on an altogether profuse scale. Much legal inquiring and procedure as to Philippe d'Orléans and his (imaginary) concern in this 5th of October; who retires to England for a while, and is ill seen by the polite classes there.

THE CONSTITUTION.

(January, 1790—August 12, 1792.)

1790.

Constitution-building, and its difficulties and accompaniments. Clubs, Journalisms; advent of anarchic souls from every quarter of the world. February 4, King's visit to Constituent Assembly; emotion thereupon and National Oath, which flies over France. Progress of swearing it, detailed. General "Federation," or mutual Oath of all Frenchmen, otherwise called "Feast of Pikes" (July 14, Anniversary of Bastille-day), which also is a memorable Day. Its effects on the Military, in Lieutenant Napoleon Bonaparte's experience.

General disorganization of the Army, and attempts to mend it. Affair of Nanci (catastrophe is August 31); called "Massacre of Nanci;" irritation thereupon. Mutineer Swiss sent to the Galleys; solemn Funeral-service for the Slain at Nanci (September 20), and riotous menaces and mobs in consequence. Steady progress of disorganization, of anarchy spiritual and practical. Mirabeau, desperate of Constitution-building under such accompaniments, has interviews with the Queen, and contemplates great things.

1791. APRIL—JULY.

Death of Mirabeau (April 2): last chance of guiding or controlling this Revolution gone thereby. Royal Family, still hopeful to control it, means to get away from Paris as the first step. Suspected of such intention; visit to St. Cloud violently prevented by the Populace (April 19). Actual Flight to Varennes (June 20); and misadventures there: return captive to Paris, in a frightfully worsened position, the fifth evening after (June 25). "Republic" mentioned in Placards, during King's Flight; generally reprobated. Queen and Darnave. A Throne held up; as if "set on its vertex," to be held there by hand. Should not this runaway King be deposed? Immense assemblage petitioning at Altar of Fatherland to that effect (Sunday, July 17), is dispersed by musketry, from Lafayette and Mayor Bailly, with extensive shrieks following, and leaving remembrances of a very bitter kind.

1791. AUGUST.

Foreign Governments, who had long looked with disapproval on the French Revolution, now set about preparing for actual interference. Convention of Pilnitz (August 25—27); Emperor Leopold II., Friedrich Wilhelm, II. King of Prussia, with certain less important Potentates, and Emigrant Princes of the Blood, assembling at this Pilnitz (Electoral Country-house near Dresden), express their sorrow and concern at the impossible posture of his now French Majesty, which they think calls upon regular Governments to interfere and mend it: they themselves, prepared at present to to "resist French aggression" on their own territories, will co-operate with said Governments in "interfering by effectual methods." This Document, of date August 27, 1791, rouses violent indignations in France; which blaze up higher and higher, and are not quenched for twenty-five years after. Constitution finished; accepted by the King (September 14). Constituent Assembly proclaims " in a sonorous voice " (September 30), that its Sessions are all ended;—and goes its ways amid "illuminations."

1791. OCTOBER—DECEMBER.

Legislative Assembly, elected according to the Constitution, the first and also the last Assembly of that character, meets October 1, 1791: sat till September 21, 1792; a Twelvemonth all but nine days. More republican than its predecessor: inferior in talent; destitute, like it, of parliamentary experience. Its debates, futilities, staggering parliamentary procedure (Book V. cc. 1–3) Court "pretending to be dead,"—not "aiding the Constitution to march." Sunday, October 16, L'Escuyer, at Avignon, murdered in a Church; Massacres in the Ice-Tower follow. Suspicions of their King, and of each other; anxieties about foreign attack, and whether they are in a right condition to meet it; painful questionings of Ministers, continual changes of Ministry,—occupy France and its Legislative with sad debates, growing ever more desperate and stormy in the coming months. Narbonne (Madame de Staël's friend) made War-Minister, December 7; continues for nearly half a year; then Servan, who lasts three months; then Dumouriez, who, in that capacity, lasts only five days (had, with Roland as Home-Minister, been otherwise in place for a year or more); mere "Ghosts of Ministries."

1792. FEBRUARY—APRIL.

Terror of rural France (February, March); Camp of Jalès; copious Emigration. February 7, Emperor Leopold and the King of Prussia, mending their Pilnitz offer, mak. public Treaty, That they specially will endeavor to keep down disturbance, and if attacked will assist one another. Sardinia, Naples, Spain, and even Russia and the Pope, understood to be in the rear of these two. April 20, French Assembly, after violent debates, decrees war against Emperor Leopold. This is the first Declaration of War; which the others followed, pro and contra, all round, like pieces of a great Firework blazing out now here now there. The Prussian Declaration which followed first, some months after, is the immediately important one.

1792. JUNE.

In presence of these alarming phenomena, Government cannot act; will not, say the People. Clubs, Journalists, Sections (organized population of Paris) growing ever more violent and desperate. Issue forth (June 20) in vast Procession, the combined Sections and leaders, with banners, with demonstrations; marching through the streets of Paris, "to quicken the Executive," and give it a fillip as to the time of day. Called "Procession of the Black Breeches" in this Book. Immense Procession, peaceable but dangerous; finds the Tuileries gates closed, and no access to his Majesty; squeezes, crushes, and is squeezed, crushed against the Tuileries gates and doors till they give way; and the admission to his Majesty, and the dialogue with him, and behaviour in his House, are of an utterly chaotic kind, dangerous and scandalous, though not otherwise than peaceable. Giving rise to much angry commentary in France and over Europe. June 20 henceforth is a memorable Day. General Lafayette sudden-ly appears in the Assembly; without leave, as is splenetically observed; makes fruitless attempt to reinstate authority in Paris (June 28); withdraws as an extinct popularity.

1792. JULY.

July 6, Reconciliatory Scene in the Assembly, derisively called Baiser l'amourette. "Third Federation," July 14, being at hand, could not the assembling "Federates" be united into some Nucleus of Force near Paris? Court answers, No; not without reason of its own. Barbaroux writes to Marseilles for "500 men that know how to die;" who accordingly get under way, though like to be too late for the Federation. Sunday, July 22, Solemn Proclamation that the "Country is in Danger."

July 24, Prussian Declaration of War; and Duke of Brunswick's celebrated Manifesto, threatening France "with military execution" if Royalty were meddled with: the latter bears date, Coblentz, July 27, 1792, in the name of both Emperor and King of Prussia. Duke of Brunswick commands in chief: Nephew (sister's son) of Frederick the Great; and Father of our unlucky "Queen Caroline;" had served, very young, in the Seven-Years War, under his Father's Brother, Prince Ferdinand; often in command of detachments bigger or smaller; and had gained distinction by his swift marches, audacity and battle-spirit: never hitherto commanded any wide system of operations: nor ever again till 1806, when he suddenly encountered ruin and death at the very starting (Battle of Jena, October 14 of that year). This Proclamation, which awoke endless indignation in France and much criticism in the world elsewhere, is understood to have been prepared by other hands (French-Emigrant chiefly, who were along with him in force), and to have been signed by the Duke much against his will. "Insigne vengeance,'" "military execution," and other terms of overbearing menace; Prussian Army, and Austrians from Netherlands, are advancing in that humor. Marseillese, "who know how to die," arrive in Paris (July 29); dinner-scene in the Champs Elysées.

1792. AUGUST.

Indignation waxing desperate at Paris: France, boiling with ability and will, tied up from defending itself by "an inactive Government" (fatally unable to act). Secret con-

claves, consultations of Municipality and Clubs; Danton understood to be the presiding genius there. Legislative Assembly is itself plotting and participant; no other course for it. August 10, Universal Insurrection of the Armed Population of Paris; Tuileries forced, Swiss Guards cut to pieces. King, when once violence was imminent, and before any act of violence, had with Queen and Dauphin sought shelter in the Legislative-Assembly Hall. They continue there till August 13 (Friday-Monday), listening to the debates, in a reporter's box. Are conducted thence to the Temple "as Hostages,"—do not get out again except to die. Legislative Assembly has its Decree ready, That in terms of the Constitution in such alarming crisis a National Convention (Parliament with absolute powers) shall be elected; Decree issued that same day, August 10, 1792. After which the Legislative only waits in existence till it be fulfilled.

THE GUILLOTINE.

(August 10, 1792—October 4, 1795.)

1792. AUGUST—SEPTEMBER.

Legislative continues its sittings till Election be completed. Enemy advancing, with farmed Emigrants, enter France. Luxembourg region; take Longwy, almost without resistance (August 23); prepare to take Verdun. Austrians besieging Thionville; cannot take it. Dumouriez seizes the Passes of Argonne, August 29. Great agitation in Paris. Sunday, September 2 and onward till Thursday 6, September Massacres: described Book I. cc. 4–6. Prussians have taken Verdun, September 2 (Sunday, while the Massacres are beginning): except on the score of provisions and of weather, little or no hindrance. Dumouriez waiting in the Passes of Argonne. Prussians detained three weeks forcing these. Famine, and torrents of rain. Battle or Cannonade of Valmy (September 20): French do not fly, as expected. Convention meets, September 22, 1792; Legislative had sat till the day before, and now gives place to it: Republic decreed, same day. Austrians, renouncing Thionville, besiege Lille (September 28—October 8); cannot: "fashionable shaving-dish," the splinter of a Lille bombshell. Prussians, drenched deep in mud, in dysentery and famine, are obliged to retreat: Goethe's account of it. Total failure of that Brunswick Enterprise.

1792. DECEMBER—1793. JANUARY.

Revolutionary activities in Paris and over France; King shall be brought to "trial." Trial of the King (Tuesday, December 11—Sunday, 16). Three Votes (January 15–17, 1793): Sentence, Death without respite. Executed, Monday, January 21, 1793, morning about 10 o'clock. English Ambassador quits Paris; French Ambassador ordered to quit England (January 24). War between the two countries imminent.

1793. FEBRUARY.

Dumouriez, in rear of the retreating Austrians, has seized the whole Austrian Netherlands, in a month or less (November 4—2d of December last); and now holds that territory. February 1, France declares War against England and Holland; England declares in return, February 11: Dumouriez immediately invades Holland; English, under Duke of York, go to the rescue: rather successful at first. Committee of Salut Public (instituted January 21, day of the King's Execution) the supreme Administrative Body at Paris.

1793. MARCH—JULY.

Mutual quarrel of Parties once the King was struck down: Girondins or Limited "legal" Republicans versus Mountain or Unlimited: their strifes detailed, Book III. cc. 3, 7–9. War to Spain, March 7. Three Epochs in the wrestle of Girondins and Mountain: first, March 10, when the Girondins fancy they are to be "Septembered" by the anarchic population: anarchic population does demand "Arrestment of Twenty-two" by name, in return. Revolutionary Tribunal instituted, Danton's contrivance, that same day (March 10). Battle of Neerwinden in Holland (March 18): Dumouriez, quite beaten, obliged to withdraw homeward faster and faster. Second Girondin Epoch, April 1, when they broke with Danton. General Dumouriez, a kind of Girondin in his way, goes over to the Enemy (April 3). Famine, or scarcity in all kinds; Law of Maximum (fixing a price on commodities), May 20. Third Girondin Epoch, "illa suprema dies," Convention beset by Armed Sections under Henriot (Sunday June 2); Girondins, the Twenty-two and some more, put "under arrest in their own houses;"—never got out again, but the reverse, as it proved.

1793. JULY.

Revolt of the Departments in consequence, who are of Girondin temper; their attempt at civil war. Comes to nothing; ends in "a mutual shriek" (at Vernon in Normandy, July 13). Charlotte Corday has assassinated Marat at Paris two days before (Saturday, July 13). Great Republican vengeances in consequence: Girondin Deputies, Barbaroux, Pétion, Louvet, Gaudet, etc., wander ruined, disguised over France: the Twenty-two, Brissot, Vergniaud, etc., now imprisoned, await trial; Lyons and other Girondin Cities to be signally punished. Valenciennes, besieged by Duke of York since May, surrenders July 26.

1793. AUGUST—OCTOBER.

Mountain, victorious, resting on the "Forty-four thousand Jacobin Clubs and Municipalities;"—its severe summary procedure rapidly developing itself into a "Reign of Terror." Law of the Forty Sous (Sectioners to be paid for attending meetings), Danton's Contrivance, August 5. Austrians force the Lines of Weissembourg, penetrate into France on the East side: Dunkirk besieged by Duke of York (August 22): Lyons bombarded by Dubois-Crancé of the Mountain, Powder-Magazine explodes; Barrère's Proclamation of Levy in Mass, "France risen against Tyrants" (August 23). "Revolutionary Army" (anarchic Police-force of the Mountain), September 5-11. Law of the Suspect, September 17. Lyons, after frightful sufferings, surrenders to Dubois-Crancé (October 9): "To be razed from the Earth." Same day Gorsas at Paris, a Girondin Deputy, captured in a state of outlawry, is "immediately guillotined" (October 9): first Deputy who died in that manner. Execution of Queen Marie-Antoinette, Wednesday, October 16. Execution of the Twenty-two, after trial of some length, "'Marseillaise' sung in chorus" at the scaffold (October 31).—General Jourdan has driven Cobourg and the Austrians over the Sambre again, October 16 (Day of the Queen's death); Duke of York repulsed from Dunkirk, "like to be swallowed by the tide," a month before.

1793. NOVEMBER—DECEMBER.

Reign of Terror, and Terror the Order of the Day. Execution of D'Orléans Égalité, November 6; of Madame Roland, November 8; of Mayor Bailly, November 10. Goddess of Reason (First of them, at Paris) sails into the Convention, same day (November 10): Plunder of Church's; "Carmagnole complete." Convention "*Representatives* on Mission:" St. Just and Lebon, at Strasburg, "Strip off your shoes; 10,000 pairs wanted; likewise 1000 beds,—under way in twenty-four hours" (November 27). Spanish War, neglected hitherto, and not successful; may become important? Toulon, dangerously Girondin in dangerous vicinity, Hood and the English and even "Louis XVIII." there; is besieged, Napoleon serving in the Artillery; is captured, December 19; "To be razed from the Earth." Carrier at Nantes: Noyadings by night, second of them December 14; become "Marriages of the Loire," and other horrors. Lebon at Arras. Maignet at Orange. "Death poured out in great floods (vomie à grands flots)." Lines of Weissembourg "retaken by St. Just charging with Peasants" (*ends* the Year).

1794.

"Revolution eating its own children:" the Hébertists guillotined, Anacharsis Clootz among them, March 24;

Danton himself and the Dantonists (April 3), which is the acme of the process. Armies successful: Pichegru in the Netherlands; defeat of Austrians at Moncron, April 29; of Austrian Emperor at Turcoing, May 18: successes of Dugommier against Spain (May 23), which continue in brilliant series, till the business ends, and he ends "killed by a cannon-shot," six months hence. June 1, Howe's Sea-victory; and Fable of the *Vengeur.* General Jourdan: Battle of Fleurus, sore stroke against the Austrian Netherlands (June 26).

Conspiracy of Mountain against Robespierre: Tallien and others desirous not to be "eaten." Last scenes of Robespierre: July 28 (to Thermidor, Year 2), guillotined with his Consorts;—which, unexpectedly, ends the Reign of Terror. Victorious French Armies: enter Cologne, October 6; masters of Spanish bulwarks (Dugommier shot), October 17: Duke of York and Dutch Stadtholder in a ruinous condition. Reaction against Robespierre: "whole Nation a Committee of Mercy." Jacobins Club assaulted by mob; shut up, November 10-12. Law of Maximum abolished, December 24. Duke of York gone home; Pichegru and 70,000 overrun Holland; frost so hard, "hussars can take ships."

1795.

Stadtholder quits Holland, January 19; glad to get across to England; Spanish Cities "opening to the petard" (Itosas first, January 5, and rapidly thereafter, till almost Madrid come in view). Continued downfall of Sansculottism. Effervescence of luxury; La Cabarus; Greek Costumes; Jeunesse Dorée; balls in flesh-colored drawers. Sansculottism rises twice in Insurrection; both times in vain. Insurrection of Germinal ("12 Germinal," Year 3, April 1, 1795); ends by "two blank cannon-shot" from Pichegru.

1795. APRIL—OCTOBER.

Prussia makes Peace of Bâle (Basel), April 5; Spain, Peace of Bâle a three-months later. Armies everywhere successful: Catalogue of Victories and Conquests hung up in the Convention Hall. Famine of the lower classes. Fouquier Tinville guillotined (May 8). Insurrection of Prairial, the Second attempt of Sansculottism to recover power ("1 Prairial," May 20); Deputy Féraud massacred: issues in the Disarming and Finishing of Sansculottism. Emigrant Invasion, in English ships, lands at Quiberon, and is blown to pieces (July 15-20): La Vendée, which had before been three years in Revolt, is hereby kindled into a "Second" less important "Revolt of La Vendée," which lasts some eight months. Reactionary "Companies of Jesus," "Companies of the Sun," assassinating Jacobins in the Rhone Countries (July, August). New Constitution: Directory and Consuls,—Two-thirds of the Convention to be re-elected. Objections to that clause. Section Lepelletier, and miscellaneous Discontented, revolt against it: Insurrection of Vendémiaire, Last of the Insurrections ("13 Vendémiaire, Year 4," October 5, 1795); quelled by Napoleon. On which "The Revolution," as defined here, ends.—Anarchic Government, if still anarchic, proceeding by softer methods than that of continued Insurrection.